THE SOCIOLOGY OF ISLAM

The Sociology of Islam

Secularism, Economy and Politics

Tugrul Keskin

ITHACA
PRESS

THE SOCIOLOGY OF ISLAM
Secularism, Economy and Politics

Published by
Ithaca Press
8 Southern Court
South Street
Reading
RG1 4QS
UK

www.ithacapress.co.uk
www.twitter.com/Garnetpub
www.facebook.com/Garnetpub
thelevant.wordpress.com

Ithaca Press is an imprint of Garnet Publishing Limited.

First Paperback Edition

ISBN-13: 978-0-86372-425-1

British Library Cataloguing-in-Publication Data
A catalogue record for this book is available from the British Library

Typeset by Samantha Barden
Jacket design by Garnet Publishing

Printed and bound in Lebanon by International Press:
interpress@int-press.com

I dedicate this book to the children of the Stolen Generation in Australia who have been oppressed, colonized and killed in the name of the civilization project. Removing children from their Aboriginal families in Australia between the years 1909 and 1969 was an official government policy. As a result of this inhumane act, one out of every ten Aboriginal children was taken forcefully from their families and placed in missionary schools. I therefore dedicate this book to those who have suffered at the hands of 'civilization' and the empire, to the children of the Stolen Generation and to David Gulpilil Ridjimiraril Dalaithngu, who reminds us of this stolen past and future …

Contents

ISLAM AND MUSLIM SOCIETIES

Contributors

Dr Tugrul Keskin is an Assistant Professor of International and Middle Eastern Studies, an affiliated faculty of Black Studies, Sociology and the Center for Turkish Studies, and the Middle East Studies Coordinator for International Studies at Portland State University. His research and teaching interests include Sociology of Islam and the Middle East, Social and Political Theory, Post-Colonial Theory, Islamic Movements, Development and Urbanization in the Middle East, Sociology of Africa, and Modern Kurdish, Uyghur and Turkish Nationalism. Previously, Dr Keskin taught as an instructor of Sociology and Africana Studies at Virginia Tech University and has also taught as a Visiting Assistant Professor of Sociology at James Madison and Radford Universities. He received his PhD in Sociology from Virginia Tech, with certificate degrees in Africana Studies, Social and Political Thought, and International Research and Development. He is the founder of the Sociology of Islam Listserv, and the editor of the Sociology of Islam and Muslim Societies Newsletter. He is a board member and book review editor of Sociologists Without Border.

http://tugrulkeskin.blogspot.com
Email: tugrulkeskin@pdx.edu

Basak Ozoral is a PhD candidate at the McGill University, the Institute of Islamic Studies. Her dissertation is: 'Economic Engagement of Religious Ethics in a Global Economy: The Rising of Islamic Capital in Central Anatolia as a New Economic Power'. Her research claims that the challenge of capitalism in different religious and cultural contexts has resulted in cultural pluralism but economic homogeneity in the global world system. Thus, the integration process of Muslim societies into the global economy resulted in the possibility of discussion concerning alternative ways of modernization.

Email: bozoral@yahoo.ca
basak.ozoral@mail.mcgill.ca

Ovamir Anjum is Imam Khattab Endowed Chair of Islamic Studies at the University of Toledo in the Department of Philosophy. He obtained his PhD in Islamic intellectual history at the University of Wisconsin-Madison. He also holds a Masters degree in Social Sciences from the University of Chicago and a Masters in Computer Science from the University of Wisconsin-Madison. His dissertation, entitled 'Reason and Politics in Medieval Islamic Thought: The Taymiyyan Moment', is an account of Islamic political and constitutional thought from the formation of the Sunni Caliphate discourse until the critical intervention of Ibn Taymiyya (d. 728/1328). His areas of interest include Islamic political and constitutional thought, theology (usul al-din), and spirituality (Sufism). He also has a strong interest in contemporary discourse on Islam, democracy, and secularism. During 2007–2009, he served as the Senior Fellow at the Lubar Institute for the Study of the Abrahamic Religions (LISAR), UW-Madison, and taught at the Religious Studies Program at the same. He is currently working on a monograph on the history of Islamic political thought with a focus on Ibn Taymiyya.

Email: ovamir.anjum@utoledo.edu

Joshua D. Hendrick currently teaches in international studies at the University of Oregon. He received his PhD in sociology from the University of California, Santa Cruz and his MA in socio-cultural anthropology from Northern Arizona University in Flagstaff, AZ. His dissertation is titled *Globalization & Marketized Islam in Turkey: The Case of Fethullah Gülen*. Researched as a political ethnography, Dr Hendrick's work addresses the cultural dynamics of Turkey's ongoing tensions between secularism and Islam by explaining the discursive and organizational strategies of the education and business community known to the world as 'the Gülen Movement' (GM). M. Fethullah Gülen is Turkey's most famous and controversial religious personality and his followers now attract a great deal of international attention due to the extent of their 100-country-wide education network. Rather than posing a threat to Turkish secularism, Dr Hendrick presents the GM as a fascinating case by which to observe the moderation of Muslim politics in the global era. Joshua Hendrick is a member of the editorial board for the Sociology of Islam and Muslim Societies, and a member of the Sociology of the Middle East Joint Association Working Group at the American Sociological Association (ASA) and the Middle Eastern Studies Association (MESA).

Email: hendrick@uoregon.edu

Husnul Amin is an assistant professor at the International Islamic University, Islamabad. The Hague. He received his degree from the Institute of Social Studies in the Netherlands. His dissertation is on 'From Islamism to Post-Islamism: A Study of New Intellectual Discourse on Islam and Modernity in Pakistan'. The study examines the articulation, refinement, nurture and proliferation of a new discursive circle in Pakistan that seceded from Mawdudi's political Islam at different points of time. The research argues that the post-9/11 debates, introduction of new electronic media and General Musharraf's Enlightened Moderation project inaugurated the expansionary phase of this intellectual movement in Pakistan. Husnul Amin also writes for an Urdu daily newspaper *Daily Mashriq*, publishing from Peshawar, Pakistan.

http://www.iss.nl/News/ISS-PhD-student-Husnul-Amin
Email: husnulamin@yahoo.com

Corri B. Zoli is a research fellow at the Institute of National Security and Counterterrorism (INSCT), a multidisciplinary research center at Syracuse University's College of Law and the Maxwell School of Citizenship and Public Affairs. At INSCT, Zoli co-directs the Islam and International Humanitarian Law and the Postconflict Justice and Islam programs, and she helps to manage the New Battlefields/Old Laws: From the Hague Convention to Asymmetric Warfare project, as well as a National Science Foundation national study for developing educational pathways for servicepersons. Zoli received her PhD in cultural studies from Syracuse University, where she used an international political economic genealogy to trace the beginnings of a modern social science architecture in European colonialism and the early routes of historical globalization. Zoli's present research focuses on the role of culture (identity, religion, norms) in contemporary international security challenges. Zoli is also an affiliated scholar at the Syracuse University Humanities Center.

Email: cbzoli@syr.edu

Melanie Reddig is lecturer at the Heinrich-Heine University of Düsseldorf. She studied sociology, history and science of media and received her PhD from the Institute of Social Science at the Heinrich-Heine University of Düsseldorf. Her research focuses on sociological explanations for the rise of religious fundamentalism and terrorism. In 2007 she edited together with Thomas Kron a volume on transnational terrorism from a sociological viewpoint (*Analysen des transnationalen Terrorismus. Soziologische Perspektiven*, Wiesbaden: VS Verlag). In this volume she argues that an increasing feeling of a global relative deprivation in the Islamic world contributes decisively to the current strength of the global jihad.

Email: reddig@phil-fak.uni-duesseldorf.de

David L. Johnston is a Visiting Scholar at the University of Pennsylvania and teaches as an adjunct at St. Joseph's University. He served for sixteen years as a pastor and teacher in Algeria, Egypt and the West Bank. After completing a PhD in Islamic Studies at Fuller Theological Seminary, he became a research affiliate and part-time lecturer at Yale University. His research focuses on the intersection of Islamic law and theology and on Muslim–Christian dialogue. His articles and essays have appeared in *Islamochristiana, Islamic Law and Society, Die Welt des Islams, The Maghreb Review* and *Comparative Islamic Studies*. He is the author of two books, *Evolving Muslim Theologies of Justice: Jamal al-Banna, Mohammad Hashim Kamali and Khaled Abou El Fadl* (Penang, Malaysia: Universiti Sains Malaysia, 2010), and *Earth, Empire and Sacred Text: Muslims and Christians as Trustees of Creation* (London: Equinox, 2010).

Email: jodavid@sas.upenn.edu

Jeremy F. Walton is an assistant professor/Faculty Fellow in New York University's Religious Studies Program. He received his PhD in Anthropology from the University of Chicago (2009); he is currently in the process of editing his dissertation manuscript, 'Horizons and Histories of Liberal Piety: Civil Islam and Secularism in Contemporary Turkey', for publication. Dr Walton has co-edited, with John Kelly, Beatrice Jaregui and Sean T. Mitchell, the collection *Anthropology and Counterinsurgency* and has book chapters in *Anthropology and Counterinsurgency, Orienting Istanbul: Cultural Capital of Europe?* and

Survey of the Sociology of Islam & Muslim Societies: Secularism, Economy and Politics. He has delivered numerous academic presentations and papers, including 'The Pious Aesthetics of Publicness: Making Space Virtuous in Istanbul', 'Unveiling Secularism', 'What Does the Headscarf "Mean" Anyway?' and 'Good Muslim World, Bad Muslim World'. Dr Walton is a member of the American Anthropological Association and has served on the Editorial Board for *Sociology of Islam and Muslim Societies.* His teaching and research broadly interrogate the complex relationships among Islamic practice, the politics of contemporary secularism, and global regimes of publicness.

Email: jeremy.walton@nyu.edu

Katarzyna Górak-Sosnowska is an assistant professor at the Department of Sociology, Warsaw School of Economics and lecturer at the Faculty of Oriental Studies, Warsaw University. Her research interests include socio-economic problems of MENA countries and Islam in Poland and wider Europe. She published (in Polish): *The Arab World Towards Globalization* (2007) and *The Prospects of the Arab World through the Lens of the Millennium Development Goals* (2007). As a trainer in intercultural education she co-developed teaching manuals *In the World of Islam* (2007, English translation: 2009) and *Language Encounters: Key to Dialogue* (2008).

http://www.sgh.waw.pl/prywatne/kgorak/
Email: katarzyna.gorak@gmail.com

Leon Moosavi is a PhD student at Lancaster University, UK. His thesis is concerned with a sociological examination of the experiences of Muslim converts in Britain. He is focusing on their experiences in relation to Islamophobia, white privilege, belonging and performance. He is due to complete his doctoral research in 2011. He can be reached for further discussion on: reza_moosavi@hotmail.co.uk.

Cristina Maria de Castro is a Sociology Professor at the Faculty of Philosophy and Human Sciences, linked to the Universidade Federal de Minas Gerais, Brazil. She obtained her PhD degree in Social Sciences from the Universidade Federal de São Carlos, UFSCar, in 2007. She also acted as a visiting researcher at the International Institute for the Study of Islam in the Modern World, ISIM, based in Leiden, the Netherlands, in 2005 and 2007. In the same week of her thesis defense, she was approved for a very competitive program for new PhDs in one of the most renowned research institutions in Brazil, the Brazilian Centre for Analysis and Planning, CEBRAP. From 2008 to 2010, she worked as a Postdoctoral Fellow and Collaborator Professor at the Graduate Program in Sociology, in UFSCar. Her research focuses on the production of Islamic knowledge and its practice in Brazil and counted on the cooperation of ISIM, from 2007 to 2008. Her PhD thesis on the construction of Muslim identities in Brazil is soon to be published in the USA, by Lexington Publishers.

Email: cristinamcastro@ig.com.br

Enzo Pace is Professor of Sociology of Religion at the University of Padova, where he is head of the Department of Sociology; he served as President of the International Society for the Sociology of Religion (ISSR) and was Directeur d'Etudes invité at EHESS (Paris). He conducted the first survey on Muslims in Italy (1999) and is presently managing a new research on religious diversity in Italy (Islam, Sikh Panth and African Pentecostal Churches). Recent publications include: *Sociologia dell'islam*, Roma, Carocci, 2004 (transl. in Portuguese, Vozes, 2005); 'Religion as Communication', in N. Ammerman (ed.), *Everyday Religion*, Oxford University Press, 2007; 'A Peculiar Pluralism', in *Journal of Modern Italian Studies* 12 (1), 2007; *Raccontare Dio. La religione come comunicazione*, Il Mulino, 2008; 'The Inner-World Mysticism and a Successful Social Integration of the Sikh Panth', in E. Barker (ed.), *The Centrality of Religion in the Social Life*, Ashgate, 2008; 'The Socio-cultural and Socio-religious Origins of Human Rights', in P. Clarke (ed.), *The Oxford Handbook of the Sociology of Religion*, Oxford University Press, 2009; *Le religioni pentecostali*, Carocci, 2010 (with A. Butticci).

Email: vincenzo.pace@unipd.it

Annalisa Frisina, PhD in Sociology, is Researcher and Lecturer at the University of Padua, where she teaches Qualitative Social Research Methods. She wrote one monography on *Young Muslims of Italy and their Strategies of Citizenship* (Bologna: Carocci, 2007) and many articles on cultural and religious diversity in the everyday lives of children of migrants in Italy. Her most recent works are: 'Young Muslims' Everyday Tactics and Strategies: Resisting Islamophobia, Negotiating Italianness, Becoming Citizens', in *Journal of Intercultural Studies* (in press), and 'Discussing Religious Pluralism in Italy: An Exploratory Study with Young People of Foreign Origin', in *Social Compass* (forthcoming, January 2011).

Email: annalisa.frisina@unipd.it

David O. Ogungbile is a senior lecturer in the Department of Religious Studies, Obafemi Awolowo University, Ile-Ife, Nigeria. He received a Master of Theological Studies (World Religions) from Harvard University, and PhD (Religious Studies) from Obafemi Awolowo University, Nigeria. He was a Fellow at the Harvard University W.E.B. Du Bois Institute for African and African American Research (2007–2009). He specializes in Comparative Religion and Sociology of Religion. His researches cover African Religions and Religions in Africa. He is co-editor with Sola Akinrinade *et al.* of *Rethinking the Humanities in Africa* and *The Humanities, Nationalism and Democracy*. David has published extensively in international journals including the *Journal of Interdisciplinary Gender Studies, Nordic Journal of African Studies, Journal of Religious Thought, Africana Marburgensia*, and *Asia Journal of Theology*. He is a contributor to *Encyclopedia of African Religion*, Vols 1 & 2 (2009), *Encyclopedia of Sex and Gender* (2007), *Encyclopedia of Religion, Communication and Media* (2006), *Encyclopedia of Religion* (2005), and *Encyclopaedia of Religious Rites, Rituals and Festivals* (2004). His article 'Religious Experience and Women Leadership in Nigerian Islam', which appeared in the *Journal of Interdisciplinary Gender Studies* (2004) has republished in *Gender and Behaviour* (2004), and *Jenda: A Journal of Culture and African Women Studies* (2004); and it is being republished in *Anthology of Gender*, being edited by Oyeronke Oyewumi. He is currently working on the manuscript 'Cultural Memories, Performance, and Meanings in Indigenous Festivals and Celebrations among the Yoruba of Southwestern Nigeria'.

http://www.ogungbile.net/
Email: dogungb@fas.harvard.edu

Joseph B. Tamney is Professor Emeritus of Sociology at Ball State University. He received his BS and MA from Fordham University, and his PhD from Cornell University. He has been a member of the editorial Board for the Encyclopedia of Religion and Society, an editor of Sociology of Religion (1994–2000) and of the ASA religion section Newsletter, and president of the Association for the Sociology of Religion. His published works include *The Resilience of Christianity in the Modern World*, *American Society in the Buddhist Mirror*, *The Struggle Over Singapore's Soul: Western Modernization and Asian Culture*, *The Resilience of Conservative Religion*, and, with Linda Hsueh-Ling Chiang, *Modernization, Globalization, and Confucianism in Chinese Societies*. With Fenggang Yang, he co-edited *State, Market, and Religions in Chinese Societies*. His most recent publications include: 'Buddhism under Study' in *American Sociology of Religion: Histories*, Anthony J. Blasi ed., and 'Malaysia's Islamist Landscape', in Jane's *Islamic Affairs Analyst*.

Radwan Ziadeh is a Prins Global Fellow at Hagop Kevorkian Center for Near Eastern Studies at New York University and a Visiting Scholar at The Center for Contemporary Arab Studies (CCAS) at Georgetown University. He was most recently a Reagan–Fascell Fellow at the National Endowment for Democracy (NED) at Washington, DC and Visiting Scholar at the Center for the Study of Human Rights at Columbia University in New York City he was also a Visiting Fellow at Chatham House (The Royal Institute of International Affairs) in London and a Visiting Scholar at Carr Center for Human Rights at Harvard University (2008–2009). In 2007–2008 he was a Senior Fellow at the United States Institute of Peace (USIP) in Washington, DC. He is the founder and director of the Damascus Center for Human Rights Studies in Syria, and co-founder and executive director of the Syrian Center for Political and Strategic Studies in Washington, DC. He is the managing editor of the Transitional Justice in the Arab World project. His most recent book is *Power and Policy in Syria: Intelligence Services, Foreign Relations and Democracy in the Modern Middle East* (to be published by I.B. Tauris in 2010). He has written ten books, including *The Clash of Values Between Islam and the West*, with Kevin James O'Toole (2010).

Email: radwan.ziadeh@gmail.com

Rachel Woodlock, M.Islam.Std. (Melb), is a researcher and lecturer at the School of Political and Social Inquiry, Monash University. She is currently working on a major social attitudes survey of religious Muslim Australians. This project compares attitudes and experiences of Muslims with a critical analysis of the discourse around Muslim settlement and integration in the West. Her other research interests include conversion, religious pluralism, Muslim feminism, and heterodox Islamic religious movements. She recently contributed 'Islamic Beliefs and Practices' to the *Encyclopedia of Religion in Australia* (Port Melbourne, Vic: Cambridge University Press, 2009) edited by James Jupp.

http://www.rachelwoodlock.com/
Email: rachel.woodlock@monash.edu

Siti Kusujiarti is Professor of Sociology at Warren Wilson College, North Carolina, US. She is also an adjunct professor of Southeast Asian Studies at Ohio University. She received her master and PhD degrees from the University of Kentucky, specializing in rural sociology, gender and Southeast Asian Studies. Originally from Indonesia, her dissertation is entitled 'Hidden Power in Gender Relations among Indonesians: A Case Study in a Javanese Village, Indonesia'. This dissertation addresses gender relations in Javanese rural areas, looking at power relations in the households, community and state levels. The research argues that power is conceptualized differently in Javanese society because of the influence of local cultures and various religions, including Islam. This different conception of power calls for different analyses of gender relations. More recently, her research focuses on disaster, gender relations and religious relations, especially looking at the increasing roles of Islam in various facets of Indonesian society. She has been conducting research in Aceh post-tsunami and after the implementation of Shari'ah law to analyse the impact of these two historic events on gender relations.

Email: skusujia@warren-wilson.edu

Kathryn Schellenberg is Associate Professor of Sociology and chair of the Department of Sociology, Anthropology and Criminal Justice at the University of Michigan-Flint. Originally from Canada, she received a PhD from the University of Utah. Before turning her research focus to the United Arab Emirates, she studied aspects of work and the workplace in the US and Canada including: impacts of turbulence on high-tech firms and workers and implications of information technologies on policing. Her current project examines whether UAE nationals are a 'minority' within their own country.

Email: kathsch@umflint.edu

Mohamed Daassa is a lecturer in history and foreign languages at the University of Michigan-Flint. He received his PhD from the University of Paris-Sorbonne. Originally from Tunisia, he has studied the situation of Muslims in France and the relationships between French political institutions and Islam, North African immigrants in France, and the integration of European Muslims in European societies.

The chief characteristic of the Islamic Concept of Life is that it does not admit a conflict, nay, not even a significant separation between life–spiritual and life–mundane. It does not confine itself merely in purifying the spiritual and the moral life of man in the limited sense of the word. Its domain extends to the entire gamut of life. It wants to mould individual life as well as the social order in healthy patterns, so that the Kingdom of God may really be established on the earth and so that peace, contentment and well-being may fill the world as waters fill the oceans. The Islamic Way of Life is based on this unique approach to life and a peculiar concept of man's place in the Universe.

Mawdudi, *The Islamic Way of Life*

The need of a constantly expanding market for its products chases the bourgeoisie over the whole surface of the globe. It must nestle everywhere, settle everywhere, establish connections everywhere.

Karl Marx, *The Communist Manifesto*

Preface

Tugrul Keskin

The idea for this book flourished in my mind a couple of years ago, when I was planning to attend the Southern Sociological Society (SSS) meeting. The Sociology Department at Virginia Tech was the organizing institution for the annual meeting, and we had planned to organize panels and paper submissions, and were tasked with arranging the entire conference. Michael Hughes, who was president of the SSS at the time, and my mentor Dale Wimberley recommended that I organize a panel on Islam and Muslim societies. At first I hesitated at the idea of organizing a panel on Islam in the American South. I thought it may not be a good idea, and wondered who would participate and how many sociologists study or focus on Islam and Muslim societies in the South. But my concerns were unfounded. As a result of this very successful, positive experience, I continued to organize panels on Islam and Muslim societies at the SSS annual meetings over the next three years. I met with some of the contributors in these meetings, including some wonderful sociologists who influenced my academic path.

It is always difficult to list and thank all the people who help or contribute to a project or research effort, because a large undertaking such as this is a multidimensional effort, and is produced by not just the researcher alone, but there is an important role played by those within his or her social environment, including friends, family, colleagues and teachers. I would like to first thank all the contributors.

Thanks to all my friends for their critical insights and support, and to those colleagues and fellow sociologists without whom this work would not have been possible. In particular I would like to recognize Dale Wimberley, Ted Fuller, Ellsworth Fuhrman, Tim Luke, Michael Hughes, Terry Kershaw, Wolfgang Natter, Ananda Abeysekara, Judith

Blau, Kemal Silay and Birol Yesilada for their valuable theories and perspectives, which I have explored further within my research. Thanks also to William Robinson, William Domhoff, David Harvey, Bryan Turner, Charles Kurzman, Amy Goodman, and thinkers, authors and political figures who are not with us today but contributed to and shaped my academic views, such as Mawlana Mawdudi, Sayyid Qutb, Ernest Gellner, Maxime Rodinson, Malcolm X, Franz Fanon, Edward Said and Karl Marx, whose work has influenced me in many ways. More generally, for their encouragement and support, I owe a debt of the deepest gratitude to my loyal friends and colleagues, Kaeyoung Shin, Husnul Amin, Ismail Secer, Dogu Aytun, Hamdi Palamut, Mustafa Yildirim, and Basak Gokcora to name just a few.

Last but not least, to my wife Sharon, without whose help and patience during my studies this book would not have been possible. I appreciate her guidance and understanding in difficult times. They must all surely know that this project was undertaken as much at their expense as it was at my own, I only hope I have not disappointed them. Responsibility for all remaining shortcomings and mistakes are exclusively my own and my thanks also go to so many others whose names I could not list.

1

The Sociology of Islam

Tugrul Keskin

Those who do not rule in accordance with God's revelations are the disbelievers.
Al-Maeda (44) *The Qur'an*

The theological understanding of Islam has been studied for the last 1,400 years. But this understanding cannot fully explain current social, political and economic transformations in the world today. In the modern world, we have a global financial system, a nation state, an oil-based economy, neo-liberal capitalism, popular culture, urbanization and social movements. In order to understand these phenomena in relation to Islam and Muslim societies, we must apply a sociological understanding of Islam as Ibn Khaldun did in the Muqaddimah in the fourteenth century.

In this context, the study of Islam as a religion is a very specific subject, but according to sociologist Anthony Giddens, every structure (such as Islam) has human agency. In the context of Islam, the agents are Muslims, and as sociologists, we systematically study Muslim behaviour within the structure of the religion. We also look carefully at the current and historic socio-economic and political context and the impact it has on human agency and behaviour. In this way, sociology is uniquely positioned to provide a multidimensional perspective and approach to the study of Islam and Muslim societies. Therefore, the sociology of Islam can be described as a systematic study of the social, political and economic aspects and transformation of Muslim societies in the context of an increasingly globalized world.

Today, we witness rapid changes in society, politics and the economy as a result of technological innovations, urbanization and the increased growth in access to education, as well as to media, as an overall trend.

However, all of these changes have occurred within a different framework than those that took place a century ago in the era of industrialization. This is because the scale of change now taking place is global; therefore, there is no escape from it, as described by Weber (1996). However, it is not most accurately described as an iron cage either. These changes are best characterized as a revolution in human history, because they intend to create a new individual who is very different from those that lived in the pre-capitalist period. Today's new individual is more work oriented, consumes more, produces more, is more educated, reads more and lives in the city. I refer to this as a new stage in the development of capitalism, based on mass production and mass consumption and driven by the dehumanization of a global economic system.

In this new era, we observe the emergence of some social and political concepts that have swept the globe, such as modernity, secularism, democracy, human rights and freedom. According to pro-capitalist scholars such as Milton Friedman, Friedrich von Hayek and Karl Popper, all of these concepts are at least related to or are products of the capitalist system. I tend to agree with their observations; however, the system of capitalism also leads to unintended negative consequences for society, such as inequality, growth of the military machine, the atomic bomb, standardization of our daily life and the destruction of diversity, increased disciplinization, and rules and regulations that predominate in the name of the common good.

Today, while we have more bureaucratic political structures, we at least tend to be more rational, and society is more modern and secular than ever. We have departed from the social space, or a more mechanical form of solidarity where religion used to be a dominant institution, and are moving more towards an emphasis on an economically driven society. In this new society, mass production and mass consumption dominate every aspect of human life, including relations between people. Unlike Peter Berger's argument (1999), I believe that we are now less religious and more driven by rational economics. In this context, Islam is the last world religion that has not been disciplined and secularized; therefore, in this chapter I examine the domestication of Islam from the neo-liberal economic process, and this analysis is undertaken within the theoretical framework of the sociology of Islam.

Sociology of Islam and Muslim Societies

The historical transformation of modernity in Muslim societies reminds me of the very complex story of the Hagia Sophia, a church that was built between the years 532 and 537 in Istanbul in Turkey. For almost a thousand years, the Hagia Sophia had the largest church dome in the world. Until the Ottoman Sultan Mehmet conquered Istanbul in 1453 in the name of Allah and Islam, Hagia Sophia stood as a sacred place of worship for the Christian community. After Sultan Mehmet conquered Istanbul, he was named the Fatih, a title that was specifically given to describe a conqueror by the religious *ulama* in the Ottoman Empire. Fatih Sultan Mehmet transformed the Hagia Sophia from a church into a mosque, and Muslims used the Hagia Sophia as a place of worship for almost 500 years. However, following the collapse of the Ottoman Empire and the emergence of the Turkish republic, the first president, Mustafa Kemal Atatürk, transformed the building into a museum.

In the modern world, what does this museum represent? Are museums related to an archaic and mythical past, or are they more a product of modernity and an attempt by the modern world to capture and examine the past? What was the purpose of transforming the building into a museum, which has since become a tourist attraction in modern society these last seventy years or more? Does religion relate or belong in some way to a museum, and can it be expected to become obsolete one day like other museum relics? These questions are pertinent to the sociology of Islam and the role of religion; more specifically, its relationship to the capitalist economic system in a modern society.

In order to understand the true role of religion in modern society, one must look at the impact of the economic system in the nineteenth and twentieth centuries. In the modern world, the forces of the capitalist economic system have restructured the collective identity of religion and confined it to a place that exists as a direct link between the individual and God. This is referred to as the privatization of religion (Casanova 1994; Berger 1999). However, Islam, Christianity and Judaism should each be viewed as structures that enable individuals to regulate every aspect of their daily lives, in the same way that capitalism does. This dynamic demonstrates a clash between two powerful actors: religion and the economic system.

In this clash or competition, capitalism operates, extends and reproduces itself within powerful forces such as the division of labour, market conditions, bureaucracy, rationality, the media, education and urbanization. Each of these is either an output or condition of modernity. Capitalism is able to gradually domesticate Islam and become the more powerful force, through the increased interaction of individuals with the marketplace. Karl Polanyi describes the move towards a market society as 'the great transformation' (Polanyi 2001).

In this neo-liberal era, capitalism shapes and encroaches on the daily lives of individuals, and this extends from their eating habits to their prayers. Consequently, God is no longer in the church or mosque, but exists instead in the public and social space. Religion, or 'God', has stepped into and claimed its place in the market and is now regulated according to the norms of the marketplace. This has marked the beginning of the commodification of religion. In this context, the new interpretation of religion is a result of the clash between capitalism and religion. The original meaning and message of religion has been lost in the hands of the neo-liberal individual, who now attempts to interpret it and fit it neatly within his or her daily life.

Modern forces of capitalism have created an individual who works at least eight to ten hours a day, lives in a secular city (Cox 1965), has a nuclear family and operates within a consumer society that – because of the Industrial Revolution – encourages excessive consumption that extends beyond the basic needs of its citizens. This is what it means to live according to a modern way of life. The modern individual has little time for praying or attending church or mosque; therefore, his new religion is capitalism, which can be understood as a form of religion without a God.

Secularism and modernity should be treated as concepts that inevitably interact with each other and cannot be separated from the major characteristics of societal development and the capitalist economic context in which they arise. If modernity is defined within the context of urbanization, individualization, education, rationalization and industrialization, then one must understand its role in the minimization of traditional ways of life. In this sense, modernity is a product of the economic conditions that characterize nineteenth-century capitalism and global capitalism in the late twentieth century.

The sociology of Islam has greatly benefited from Ernest Gellner's work on Muslim society. Gellner questions the collective Muslim identity, which is understood to be embedded within the framework of Islam (Gellner 1981). According to his work, there is no clear definition of a collective Muslim identity. Therefore, a single Muslim society does not actually exist; instead there are multiple identities among Muslims based on their interaction with and understanding of Islam (Zubaida 1995).

According to many Islamists in the twentieth century, however, the Muslim collective identity and Islamic political tradition are being threatened by economic globalization. Adherents to this view believe that the Muslim collective identity, or the *ummah*, must be re-established in the mind of the Muslims. Many political Islamists also view Islam as an alternative to Western capitalism and modernity. However, in his well-known works on Islam and capitalism, and Islam and Marxism, Rodinson explores the compatibility between Islam, and both the capitalist and Marxist economic systems, and disagrees with this perspective (Rodinson 2007). According to Rodinson, Islam is inherently compatible with capitalism. David Harvey's book *A Brief History of Neo-liberalism* (Harvey 2005) is also relevant to this research, regarding his ability to understand how Islamist movements have reacted to market conditions. Islam has been used as the sword of Allah, which means that Islam is understood to bring social justice for all to a society, whereas neo-liberalism or new market conditions should be viewed as a mechanism of the domestication of religion within the global age.

Harvey's historical explanation of neo-liberalism shows us that this disciplinization is taking place globally and is not limited to one specific geographic location. Neo-liberal capitalism does not leave space for other economic, social and political systems (including religious systems) to coexist. This phenomenon demonstrates the invisible and powerful hand of global market conditions.

The Market: The Engine of Transformation

The expansion of globalization and global capitalism has shaped and restructured the position of Islam in contemporary Muslim societies, similar to what happened in eighteenth-, nineteenth- and twentieth-century Europe. In these societies, what has taken place is an Islamization and desecularization of society in response to new economic conditions.

This has not always been the trajectory of events. For example, in nineteenth-century Europe industrialization and the emergence of capitalism triggered a process of secularization that led to the formation of the 'secular urban individual', whereas the reverse is true in the case of a number of Muslim societies. While global capitalism may ultimately promote secularism in these societies, their adaptation of neo-liberal economic policies tends to result initially in the formation of more intense Islamic devotion. This is a result of a resurgence of collective identity, which tends to become stronger in these societies in response to Western neo-liberal intrusion. An example of this phenomenon may be found in the case of new urban migrants to Turkey and Pakistan.

After the 1950s, the capitalist economy began to shift towards a more globalized economic structure, which established its own social and political hegemony. This stage of capitalism was significantly more complex and multifaceted than the Weberian, Marxist and Durkheimian understanding of early capitalism. This new stage was neo-liberalism and had its own social and political dynamics. Neo-liberalism is not just an economic-based hegemonic system; it is also a social and political order, and its policies are carried out and imposed on the developing world by states that act in the interests of the capitalist class. This is what I will refer to as a new form of capitalist globalization. This form of globalization causes deregulation, privatization and the withdrawal of the state from many areas of social provision. These are the central themes of the neo-liberal period.

According to David Harvey, the revolutionary turning point in the world's social and economic history took place in the years 1978–1980 (Harvey 2005). This economic transformation was called neo-liberal capitalist globalization and resulted in the current international division of labour because of the globalization of commodity chains. This has led to the emergence of industrial capitalism and rapid urbanization, increased levels of education and the establishment of market-oriented democracies in developing nations and countries.

The concept of a 'market oriented democracy' has a different meaning today and involves different characteristics from the original idea of democracy. The original meaning of democracy referred to the ability of a state to provide social and economic equality among classes and citizens. Therefore, some of the democratic nature of the state has been lost in the process of neo-liberal capitalist globalization.

The secularization thesis, first proposed by theorists such as Peter Berger, suggests that secularism is the inevitable end result of a society's process of modernization. It is the idea that modernization, bureaucracy, rationalization and urbanization are expected to contribute to directly diminishing the role of religion in the social and political spheres. However, contrary to this expectation, over the last thirty years religion has returned to a prominent position in social and public life, particularly within Muslim societies. According to classical theorists such as Marx, Weber and Durkheim, as societies and neo-liberal economics advance, religion was expected to be confined to the private lives of individuals, or what Jose Casanova has referred to as the 'privatization of religion' (Casanova 1994). The theory of secularization suggests that the secular would inevitably replace the sacred society. According to Norris and Inglehart, 'during the last decade, however, this thesis of the slow and steady death of religion has come under growing criticism; indeed, secularization theory is currently experiencing the most sustained challenge in its long history' (Inglehart, R., and Norris, P., *Sacred and Secular: Religion and Politics Worldwide* (Cambridge: Cambridge University Press, 2004)). The present study examines some of the factors that have led to a temporal resurgence of religious observance, in contrast to the secularization theory that proposed that religion would inevitably decline.

Modernity and Its Challenges

Modernity has brought with it a chain reaction of events in many socio-political settings worldwide. In Europe, it led to the secularization of society. The response within Muslim societies, however, has been different and therefore unexpected. Modernity in these societies has instead led to a widespread trend of religious revivalism. This has occurred as a direct reaction to modernity, which has been imposed on traditional societies by external actors and influences, and in reaction to Western capitalism and its destructive impacts as experienced by local and traditional communities. Today, as a result of this trend of religious revivalism, particularly in Muslim societies, secularization theory needs to be updated to respond to evidence that suggests that there is no one direct path to secularism. Along this line of inquiry, this research explores the root causes of religious revivalism and how this trend fits or does not fit existing theories of secularization.

If the theory of secularization is accurate, then why are we faced with religious revivalism today? In the nineteenth century, it is undisputed that economic transformation had the effect of readjusting the role of religion in social and political spaces in Europe. We also know that neo-liberal economic globalization today is the main proponent of political and social change, and the role of religion is now shaped by this process in Muslim societies. It is equally important to understand both the patterns and the distinct characteristics of this trend, as well as some of the potential ramifications for Muslim countries. The ultimate condition of a society that has been modernized may still be secularism; however, the path to reach the secular society may not be direct or immediate and includes many mediating factors and influences.

When the economic transformation brought about by the emergence of capitalism took place in the nineteenth century, the relationship of society and politics was readjusted by this new mode of production, and the sacred and the secular became involved in a struggle. According to Peter Berger (1999), modern societies in general are more religious today than in the past, implying that secularization is not taking place. His idea therefore does not support the premise that the secularization of modern societies is inevitable.

In order to understand whether secularism is inevitable or not, it is necessary to know that religious revivalism or the return to God has indeed been influenced by new market conditions. However, this in itself is only one side of the equation. Religious thought also shapes economic activities, for example in the case of the emergence of the Islamic financial system and non-interest banking. The system of non-interest banking shows that Islam, and by extension social movements more broadly, is also adapting to and reshaping economic structures according to their own terms as an ongoing and mutual process.

To answer the question of how religious revivalism or the return to God has been influenced by new market conditions, in my view secularism is in fact an important component of modernity and it is best understood as a by-product of capitalism and neo-liberalism, the newest stage of modern capitalism. The concepts religious revivalism, secularism and modernity are therefore inextricably connected to one another. Modernity is facilitated by new modes of production, and this has resulted in new lifestyles in cities, mass consumption and production, the emergence of selfish individualism above social solidarity, routinization and discipline, and these sets of changes have transformed political power structures from religion-based empires into secular states in which God does not play any true role.

Today, these new modern forms of social life and organization have created an unexpected by-product in Muslim societies; a process of desecularization, with Islam playing a growing role in the political and social arena. In part, this can be understood as a result of the phenomenon described by Samuel Huntington that, 'while Asians became increasingly assertive as a result of economic development, Muslims in massive numbers were simultaneously turning toward Islam as a source of identity, meaning, stability, legitimacy, development, power, and hope, hope epitomized in the slogan "Islam is the solution"' (Huntington 1993). It appears that the more Muslim countries have adopted neo-liberal economic policies, the more they have experienced a parallel trend of Islamic revivalism and a pattern of desecularization.

As we are beginning to understand, unlike the case of European modernization and the trend towards the secularized and modern man, the neo-liberal economy in Muslim countries has instead led to the rise of more religious social structures. These conditions specifically characterize the period marking the beginning of neo-liberal capitalist globalization.

Emergence of Class Structure in Muslim Societies

Neo-liberal economic processes shape, influence and restructure the opportunities and motivations of Islamic movements and parties. Through these relationships we see the increased polarization of Islam, resulting from the mutually constitutive process that is taking place between new economic conditions and religious groups. Under these new conditions, Islamic movements' understanding of modernity has undergone a shift, from more traditional views to a set of market-based perspectives on Islam. In this process, Islam has also restructured and acted upon the market, as in the system of non-interest banking. In order to take this analysis to a level of greater depth, two divergent conceptions of Islam must be explored.

The first describes Muhammad as a 'merchant', represented within the Fethullah Gülen movement. From the beginning of neo-liberalism, the Gülen movement has been a beneficiary of this process through its ability to adapt to and find its place within changing economic conditions, and has therefore played the role of the pro-globalist movement. The 'Merchant Muhammad' concept is modern and market friendly, and has arisen in response to neo-liberalism. By contrast, the second conception of Muhammad is that of the 'Meccan Muhammad' or the idea that

Muhammad can be described as a proponent of the social welfare state and is by definition opposed to neo-liberalism. The Jama'at movement in Pakistan more closely resembles the Meccan Muhammad understanding of Islam. The Jama'at has opposed neo-liberalism and represents an expression of anti-globalist solidarity in the Islamic context; therefore, the movement symbolizes Islam as a social welfare state. Followers of the Gülen movement are involved in and are able to benefit from the economic spoils of neo-liberalist globalization, whereas the Jama'at represents the interests of more traditional elements of society and classical Islam within Pakistan. In both cases, religion is a manifestation of either opposition to or collaborative benefit from neo-liberalist globalization.

Islam is now undergoing a process of transformation in response to its interaction with neo-liberalism, sometimes giving way to secularization, like Christianity did in Europe, but not in any predictable trajectory. In addition, although the Enlightenment and the French Revolution both played an important role in the transformation of Christianity, one of the most critical components or agents of this transformation emerged from the Industrial Revolution and the development of capitalism in the nineteenth century. However, we must understand why it is that neo-liberalism in Muslim countries has often resulted in an increase rather than a decrease in religious social and political activity and organization in Turkey and Pakistan, while the trajectory in Europe has been the opposite.

The difference between Europe and Turkey or Pakistan, as just two examples, is that Europe experienced a significantly different path to economic development than many of the Muslim societies. The European path to economic development was an organic process, which was based on technology and mechanical inventions such as the steam engine and the use of colonialism to obtain scarce resources. In addition, while both the Gülen movement in Turkey and the Jama'at in Pakistan are proponents of desecularization, they approach globalism and neo-liberal economics very differently. The Gülen movement benefits from neo-liberal economics and works within the system to promote its interests, while the Jama'at in Pakistan works in opposition to forces of globalization. The crux then is to understand the historical elements that have caused either a pro- or anti-globalist orientation of a society or a social movement in the modern era, over roughly the last thirty years.

Secularism and Islam

This study applies a historical-comparative research approach to the examination of pro-globalist and anti-globalist responses to modernity. This approach is used in order to compare forms of secularism within social and political movements in Turkey and Pakistan from the early 1980s to the present. This period marks the beginning of market neo-liberalism in the two countries. The historical-comparative perspective is used as a means to compare two distinct social systems and to examine the elements that are common across them and those that are unique. The approach also facilitates an in-depth examination of long-term societal change; specifically, the rise of desecularization and pro- versus anti-globalist attitudes across different historical and cultural contexts.

Beyond a purely theological understanding, religion is also a form of tradition, which is embedded in social, political and economic structures. It challenges modernity and represents a more traditional way of life and a pre-modern and pre-capitalist period. According to Max Weber, religion, and more specifically Protestant Christianity, played an important role in shaping the spirit of capitalism and the work ethic (Weber 1996); however, the powerful economic structure of capitalism has cultivated and crystallized Protestantism and confined religion to the sphere of private life in Europe. In his book *Public Religions in the Modern World*, secularization scholar and sociologist Jose Casanova refers to this process of the decline of religion in public life as the domestication or 'privatization of religion' (Casanova 1994).

According to scholars of the secularization thesis, as a result of capitalist economic development, the inevitable trajectory was that, 'with the diffusion of modern life forms, including urbanization, industrialization, rationalization, and pluralization, the social relevance of religion and the Church would decrease, and religious worldviews would gradually be replaced by a scientific, rationalized, and secular interpretation of the world' (Pollack and Olson 2008). For the last two decades, the assumption that secularization was inevitable went under the scrutiny and critique of pro-religious and conservative scholars.

A prominent scholar and proponent of secularization theory, sociologist Peter Berger, changed his perspective regarding his original belief in the decline of religious belief and the privatization of religion in the modern world (Berger 1967). In his more recent book *The*

Desecularization of the World, he confesses that 'my point is that the assumption that we live in a secularized world is false' (Berger 1999). Pollack and Olson also claim that 'religion is back on the political agenda of Western societies' (Pollack and Olson 2008). As such, Berger proposes that there may be a more complex path to secularism or desecularism than the more simplistic secularization thesis, and this path may include more factors that are able to shift an outcome in either direction.

Today, the Weberian understanding of the relationship between religion and the economy, and the belief that religious ideas shape economic structures and vice versa, has come into question. Similar to secularization theorists, Weber believed that the neo-liberal economy would inevitably lead to an increasingly religious society. The neo-liberal economy has instead fuelled a trend of religious revivalism, specifically in Muslim societies. Especially from the early 1980s, there has been a trend of desecularization in the Islamic world.

Capitalism is an economic concept and ideology that first developed in the era of industrialization (Tucker 1978) and in the context of the expansion of colonialism. It was developed and conceived not just as a hegemonic ideology but as a part of human development, in opposition to religious hegemony in the late eighteenth- and early nineteenth-century Europe. New forms of economic transformation have become powerful, not just in the sense of restructuring the economic environment, but also in their ability to influence social and political ideals of the society and the state. This transformation of economic, social and political aspects of Europe led to the separation of church and state. Religious structures had previously controlled the society and state, but not in the modern sense, because the modern state is a product of capitalism in the context of complex bureaucracies (Gorski 2003).

Religion and the European Context

As a brief overview to the economic, political and social transformation of European societies, the changes that took place between the sixteenth and eighteenth centuries began with mercantilism, a system based on the state's control of trade and the economy. This took place in the embryonic stages of modern capitalism or neo-liberal capitalist globalization that we see today (which facilitates privatization, deregulation of the market and promotion of polyarchy in the political sense), and the emergence of a global bourgeoisie. The economic revolution of mercantilism also led to social and political ramifications in Europe, which paved the way to modernization, industrialization and finally the system of modern capitalism based on mass production and mass consumption. One of the most complex aspects of this emerging trend was the modernization of European societies and the economy as the main driver of change from traditional to modern social structures.

The year 1789, at the start of the French Revolution, was an important turning point. Critical thinking emerged in opposition to the ruling class and the predominant religious structure, and this came partly as a result of mercantilism. The French Revolution was a political transformation that produced change in these societies. A modern state was born in the European political arena as a result of the French Revolution, and the Church began to lose its power over society and the newly emerging nation state. This transformation reshaped the social and political order within Europe, and led to the emergence of the separation between church and state and modern capitalist democracy. In this context, secularism was born as an opponent of the new state order against the Church-dominated society. The state was separated from religious institutions, because the foundation of this new and emerging political entity was the economy and class structure.

Another important stage in the development of capitalism in this era was the invention of the Watt steam engine in England, at the same time as the French Revolution. However, this invention did not actually result in significant economic change until the early nineteenth century. It revolutionized the economy, established factories in urban centres and led to the creation of the modern, secular, urban individual.

The division of labour also materialized as part of this economic transformation. New actors such as bureaucracy and rationalization (Gorski 2003) and secularism (Chadwick 2000) appeared on the political scene in Europe and represented the beginning stages of the modern nation state. These actors played a crucial role in the development of the modern capitalist market. Traditional actors such as the Church, clergy, peasants, serfs, lords and kings had been replaced by emerging actors of capitalist development (Kumar 1995). The rapid accumulation of wealth had eliminated or weakened many of the old structures of power, because the engine of this change was this economic transformation, which was the emergent system of capitalism (Tucker 1978). The departure from traditional societies and the move towards assembly-based capitalist societies occurred in the late nineteenth and early twentieth centuries, and the traditional religious dogma regarding the 'absolute truth' of God no longer existed. According to author Barrington Moore, this transformation was the revolutionary origin of capitalist democracy (Moore 1993).

The economic-based Industrial Revolution led European societies in a different direction. Rapid urbanization (Cox 1965; Simmel 1971), the emergence of the modern capitalist class structure, the increased disciplinization of labour (the idea that capitalism tightly structures and disciplines the worker), individualization and education, were all at the centre of these new changes. Contrary to Weber's argument regarding the Protestant ethic and the spirit of capitalism, in reality, the economy reshaped the role of the Church and clergy in Europe; not the reverse. In this way, religion was effectively removed from public life and this can be understood as the privatization of religion, and as a specific phase of modernity. This process can also be described as the 'domestication of religion' by capitalism.

In the pre-capitalist period, the clergy were the representatives of religion, and due to the status ascribed to religion at the time, they were one of the most powerful actors. By contrast, in the capitalist period, the bourgeoisie were the most powerful actors and were the new representatives of the capitalist class. In Muslim societies, with the emergence of neo-liberalism and privatization we have seen the emergence of a new class structure, which is more religious and conservative. Generally, this includes representatives of the lower class strata of society in addition to the upwardly mobile lower class, and the middle classes. This stratum of society uses religion in order to create and maintain social solidarity and networks. These networks, in turn, are used to obtain a greater share in the marketplace. However, once those in this social strata gain a foothold in the marketplace through the use of religion and traditional networks, they begin to lose the religious foundation that brought them there. This is what I refer to as the 'domestication of religion' by the market, and, as I will describe, this process is inevitable in the context of every interaction between the market and religion.

Without a doubt, the nineteenth century saw the creation of rapid and chaotic transformation in Europe as a result of the capitalist revolution. Old-style agrarian societies, multi-ethnic empires, and Church-dominated social structures were transformed at this time into the more industrialized and secular nation states that we see today (Goody 2004). The eighteenth and nineteenth centuries also witnessed the emergence of early capitalism mostly based on industrialization. In his well-known book *Social Origins of Dictatorships and Democracy*, Barrington Moore argues that the process of industrialization in England culminated in the establishment of a relatively free society. The Church was eliminated from public and political life because the economy had become the main controlling mechanism of state transformation (Moore 1993). Economic life had taken the place of religious life in Europe, and religion was confined to the private sphere of individuals. Privatization, in the modern sense, began with the privatization of religion, or what is now called secularism.

With the establishment of the international financial organizations and the United Nations after the Second World War, another stage of capitalism began to emerge. This new phase appeared to be more global than ever, and it was then that the seeds of global capitalism of the early 1980s neo-liberalism were sown.

Transformation of Islam in a Globalized World

To my understanding, globalization has helped to create two different forms of Islamic movements. In the context of the global marketplace, the reaction by Islamic groups to global market forces differs depending on the state structure and the prevailing economic and political context in which they emerged. Different environments produce different types of Islamic movements with different objectives. First, there are the Shari'a-based movements that attempt to create an Islamic state; these demonstrate the Islamization of everyday life or a metaphorical return to the golden age of Islam and the re-establishment of the Islamic order. This type of Islam exists and flourishes in cases where the nation state is very weak and the political process is relatively open. The Jama'at-e-Islami of Pakistan represents this type of Islam and directly attacks and opposes the authoritarian state structure and tries to delegitimize the state. A strong and independent bourgeoisie or financial structure does not exist fully, and the state is still weak or at least dependent on outside sources.

The second case is the market-oriented form of Islam, or Weberian Islam, or Jihad in the market, found in Turkey, Malaysia and Indonesia.

I will refer to this type of Islam as the 'modernity-friendly' version of Islam. In these cases, an emerging Islamic bourgeoisie shapes the Islamic identity in specific Muslim societies. This is an Islamic power structure that is driven and reinforced by market forces. The Fethullah Gülen movement is one of the best examples of this case.

Merchant Muhammad versus Meccan Muhammad

Another way of describing these two perceptions of Islam can be found in Dale Eickelman's analogy of 'Merchant Muhammad' versus 'Meccan Muhammad' (Eickelman 1994). These two perspectives of Islam are based on divergent social, political and economic underpinnings. Merchant Muhammad is best represented by the Gülen movement; whereas Meccan Muhammad is represented by the Jama'at.

Why do we have different forms of Islam?

Islam is not a static religion, and, like water, it takes the shape of a cup when it enters it. At the same time, however, it never loses its origin or meaning. In Islam, there is no central authority like the Vatican. The Qur'an is the only central authority that binds together Muslims.

In this context, globalization is based on three dimensions today: the first dimension is the economic structure of capitalism, especially financial capitalism, which is based on consumerism. Consumerism creates and shapes identities. In Muslim-populated societies we see the emergence of a new Islamic-oriented bourgeoisie, which is the source of societal transformations that have taken place in Malaysia, Indonesia and Turkey. In this example, the Islamic-oriented bourgeoisie controls the media and has a large share in the market. For example, the Independent Industrialists and Businessmen's Association, or MUSIAD, represents the powerful interests of specifically Muslim businessmen in Turkey. This is a new kind of bourgeoisie, which uses Islam in order to benefit from the current economic structure.

The second important dimension of globalization is the technology, especially digital technology, and technological changes that we see causing a fragmentation of authority. This fragmentation entails a polycentric power structure that may breed autonomy or create independent political, social and economic interests groups. In this case, the fragmentation of authority is also related to the decentralization of power in market-oriented Muslim societies.

The third dimension of globalization demonstrates non-material market forces that include democracy, human rights and the public sphere. These aspects of globalization are also linked to technology, which plays an important role in political participation. More technological usage leads to more democratic politics, greater respect for human rights and greater political participation in the public sphere.

The Domestication and Secularization of Religion

Neo-liberal capitalism and market conditions are powerful forces that shape and influence the daily life of individuals and have far-reaching impacts, both in our work lives and our belief systems. Market-oriented Islamic movements are forging ahead with their objectives by working within prevailing market conditions. In this process, their perspective towards modernity has undergone a rapid transformation. By contrast, in response to similar economic conditions, Shari'a-based Islamic movements are becoming more radicalized. If these movements are not able to adapt more effectively to prevailing economic forces and conditions that are beyond their control, they will lose their relevance within a few decades as the response cycle reaches its inevitable conclusion of domestication of the religion. In this process, religion is gradually controlled by capitalism. Significantly, capitalism's growing dominance over religion has in a number of cases followed a pattern best characterized by the initial increase in religious observance as a reaction to modernization, succeeded by domestication of the religion by the market, finally ending with decreased levels of religious observance. The eventual result, however, is a resecularization of society after the domestication process has ended. This does not mean that religion will disappear, but that religion will be modified and redefined.

This is a predictable dynamic in certain contexts, particularly when the forces of modernity directly challenge long-held traditional social structures and arise externally to a society. Thus, it is important that we examine the trajectory from the domestication of religion, when religion will still exist in the public space but in a less powerful form, to full secularization, when the role of religion in society is redefined according to the interaction between religion and economic conditions. Domestication of religion is therefore understood to be a step towards the secularization of society. As such, material conditions will determine the role of religion in the public sphere.

BIBLIOGRAPHY

Berger, P., *The Desecularization of the World: Resurgent Religion and World Politics* (Washington, DC: The Ethics and Public Policy Center, 1999).

Berger, P. L., *The Sacred Canopy: Elements of a Sociological Theory of Religion* (Garden City, NY: Doubleday, 1967).

Casanova, J., *Public Religions in the Modern World* (Chicago, IL: The University of Chicago Press, 1994).

Chadwick, O., *The Secularization of the European Mind in the Tenth Century* (Cambridge: Cambridge University Press, 2000).

Cox, H., *The Secular City* (New York: The Macmillan Company, 1965).

Gellner, E., *Muslim Society* (Cambridge: Cambridge University Press, 1981).

Goody, J., *Capitalism and Modernity: The Great Debate* (Malen, MA: Polity Press, 2004).

Gorski, P. S., *The Disciplinary Revolution: Calvinism and the Rise of the State in Early Modern Europe* (Chicago: The University of Chicago Press, 2003).

Harvey, D., *A Brief History of Neo-liberalism* (Oxford: Oxford University Press, 2005).

Huntington, S. P., 'The Clash of Civilizations?' (Foreign Affairs, summer 1993).

Inglehart, R., and Norris, P., *Sacred and Secular: Religion and Politics Worldwide* (Cambridge: Cambridge University Press, 2004)

Kumar, K., *From Post-Industrial to Post-Modern Society: New Theories of Contemporary World* (Oxford: Blackwell, 1995).

Moore, B., *Social Origins of Dictatorships and Democracy* (Boston, MA: Beacon Press, 1993).

Polanyi, K., *The Great Transformation: The Political and Economic Origins of Our Time* (Boston: Beacon Press, 2001).

Pollack, D., and Olson, D. V. A., *The Role of Religion in Modern Societies* (New York: Routledge, 2008).

Rodinson, M., *Islam and Capitalism* (London: Saqi Books, 2007).

Simmel, G., *Georg Simmel on Individuality and Social Forms: Selected Writings* (Chicago: The University of Chicago Press, 1971).

Tucker, R. C., (ed.), *The Marx–Engels Reader* (New York: Norton, 1978).

Weber, M., *The Protestant Ethic and The Spirit of Capitalism* (Los Angeles, CA: Roxbury Publishing Company, 1996).

Zubaida, S., 'Is there a Muslim Society? Ernest Gellner's Sociology of Islam', in *Economy and Society* 24(2) 1995, pp. 151–188.

ISLAM, ECONOMY AND POLITICS

2

Islam and Moral Economy

Basak Ozaral

Introduction

Over the last few decades the world has witnessed an unprecedented acceleration in the pace of globalization and the consequent infiltration of 'Western' capitalism and its associated value systems into every aspect of global structure. These include, but are not limited to, the economic, cultural and political systems, as well as education, technology, language and media. Economic rationality and globalization are the motors powering this phenomenal expansion. The powerful impact of modernity, which is becoming ever more dominant, has created its own antithesis in reactionary movements that have responded to Western capitalism with political and economic resistance worldwide, but especially so in Muslim countries. Modern capitalism as a process has become enmeshed in the other systems and cultures, and has appeared as the dominant paradigm of our age. However, not only the traditional Left, but also increasing numbers of Islamic writers, have criticized the imbalances of power inherent in forms of capitalist domination. As a result, in many Muslim countries the compatibility of Islam with modern capitalism has become a hotly debated topic over the past few decades. This subject has mainly been studied under the rubric of Islamic economics, and stems from the broader question of how a Muslim should act in the modern world.[1] Thus, Islamic economics, with its emphasis on morality governing economic transactions, has developed a substantial response to the challenges posed by a global economy shaped by modern rational capitalism.

This chapter seeks to examine the rise of this new field and its origins. Although many studies have been done on modern Islamic economic thought – criticizing it for its alleged incoherence, incompleteness, impracticality and irrelevance[2] – relatively little has been published that strives to contextualize specifically Islamic responses to the hegemony of Western capitalism in the social and economic conditions prevalent in the Muslim lands. This chapter seeks to partially address this lacuna in the hope that it will invite further research on this topic.

It may well be asserted that detachment from moral values, so characteristic of modern capitalist economics, is directly relevant to the aforementioned Muslim response to capitalism. Indeed, Muslims react most strongly to those aspects of Westernization that seek to create a new economic and social order devoid of a governing morality. In order to understand the evolution of morality in the modern system I will address some of the questions concerning the function of morality in global capitalism. I will then deal with the critiques of capitalism by Western thinkers. This is important, as many of these have been appropriated by Muslim scholars in their own deconstruction of modern capitalism. This study will then focus on the historical evolution of the Islamic moral economy, as well as on its salient institutions, before concluding with the origin and the state of the field of Islamic economics today.

The Function of Morality in Social and Economic Life

Contemporary literature in social sciences is of the view that economic commodities and processes cannot be theorized without embedding them in the larger socio-cultural context. Alasdair MacIntyre, for instance, points out that it is impossible to conceive of and analyse social life independent of morality. MacIntyre's emphasis on the concept of ethics comes to life in social living forms, and he argues that the recognition of a specific social life as being distinct from others necessitates recognition of its unique moral code.[3] In every age some form of morality conducive to social harmony has been preached, but explaining the rationale underlying this morality has always been fraught with difficulties. Morality seems to set out a code for ideal relations between human beings.[4] In fact, a lot of people who discuss ethics think that the core debate in ethics is over the meaning of the word 'morality'. However, there is no universally valid, objective definition of morality, and it is regarded here as a set of customs and habits that shape how we think about the way we should live and relate to each other. The fundamental 'anti-moral' instinct of man is generally accepted as 'egoism' and, carried to its extreme, can develop to enormous proportions.[5] It is an instinctive source of satisfaction to certain human natures to witness the suffering of others because a reduction of the latter's capacity for action is regarded by an ego of this kind as an increase of its own power and as an enhancement of its own glorification.[6] The key questions here are: what would it mean for a society to exist without a moral code or ethical practices? And how would people without a morality think and behave?

Numerous philosophers have discussed the role and importance of moral values in society. The general assumption is that human behaviour in isolation from societal concepts of morality does not have standard checks and limits constraining it. However, without limits on the behaviour of individuals, societies cannot survive for long, and, in the long term, all societies do tend to destroy themselves in fighting over resources, prestige and power; the 'brakes' on this unchecked human behaviour take the form of social constructs known as morality. Moral values and culture play an important role in restraining selfishness and bringing order to society. Moral values are defined by many philosophers as codes of conduct put forward by a society and culture, and as informal aspects of institutions which constrain human behaviours. Deepak Lal makes the general but important point that in comparison to other animals, man is unique because of his intelligence and ability to change his circumstances through learning. He does not have to mutate into a new species to adapt to a changed environment. He learns new ways of surviving in unfamiliar environments and then passes them on through social customs. According to Lal, these social customs form the culture of the relevant group, which is then transmitted to new members of the group who do not then have to reinvent these 'new' ways for themselves.[7] As a result, the majority of the people in a given society tend to be happy with the order and mechanisms of the system. However, the result of a change or the loss of 'brakes' results in an increase in revolutionary pressure on the mechanism. In short, it appears that changes in social and economic life are very closely linked to changes in cultural and moral codes within that society.

Detachment of Morality from Economy and the Nature of Capitalism

Indeed, the evolving nature of moral codes closely corresponds with social and historical transformation of societies. Thus, historical analyses and investigation of the moral codes of societies go hand in hand.[8] It can be argued that morality is one of the major factors in determining relations within the economic systems, so modern capitalism needs a specific moral code to bring about the highest form of actualization of the concept of private property. Capitalism is the only example of a system which dominates by limitless economic effectiveness. It is generally accepted by liberal economists that all the economic behaviours of man are rational and aim to achieve maximum economic satisfaction. However, as explained in the previous section, checks, such as moral, religious, political and cultural considerations, prevent the domination of limitless economic effectiveness in society. The fundamental conditions for establishing a system with maximum economic effectiveness may be set out as follows:

1 Producers have to aim for maximum profit. Money and the search for profit become the measure of all things, completing the circle of disembodied economic transactions in which ethical constraints are no longer considered part of the process.
2 Intellectual activity in a society should primarily be geared only towards scientific and technical research that maximizes profit and lowers production costs. Studies which aim only at understanding the universe are of secondary importance at best. According to W. Montogomery Watt, the classical view of knowledge was primarily what may be called 'knowledge for living', whereas since enlightenment in the West, knowledge has mainly been seen as an instrument for attaining and maintaining power.[9]
3 Workers (everybody has to work, and people who are unable to work, such as the elderly or others who cannot produce must conform to a dependent status) must devote more and more of their time to work and be economically flexible in their choice of work.
4 The production should be consumed by the society. Individual and collective needs have to be supplied. This also requires that people's 'needs' constantly increase to consume the extra produce.
5 These conditions must be limitless. Cultural and moral constraints should be minimal and there should be little or no political interference, because economic effectiveness depends on a free market. This means that the market has to grow continually and that the entire world must become a single market.

In the West over the past few decades, society has managed to abolish most of these brakes on economic development by separating societal morality from the realm of economy, even from that of law, and this transformation from religiously inspired morality to rationalism has been made possible by secularization. This is R. Swedberg's take on the process:

> The concept of 'economic sphere' essentially denotes that economic activities, as history evolves, tend to become separate from other human activities and also to a certain extent governed by their own rules of laws ('limited autonomy' or 'Eigengesetzlichkeit', in Weber's terminology) ... The economic sphere clashes, for example, with the religious sphere in capitalist society because it is very difficult to regulate rational economic actions through religious rules.[10]

As Werner Sombart and Karl Polanyi claim, before the rise of market economy, the logic and principles of economic life were in accordance with the needs of a subsistence economy and were under the control of non-economic factors such as religious and political forces.[11] Since socio-cultural factors and moral codes were decisive in affecting the characteristic features of an economic system, transformation into a new culture necessitated a change in the moral codes of society. In fact, the emergence of economic theory as an independent science was a significant phase in the transformation of moral codes of a medieval Christian society into a modern secular one.

Pre-modern economies may be considered 'moral' because they were an integral part of society, and the integration of non-economic institutions into the larger societal structures is the characteristic feature of a moral economy.[12] Naturally, how economic and social relations work together may differ depending on various contexts, but the common thread running through an understanding of a pre-modern moral economy is that aims, objectives and processes are informed and directed by non-economic institutions.[13] Indeed, economic matters have been considered throughout human history, but the notion of an independent science of economics only arose relatively recently, around the mid-1800s. Until that time, economics was generally considered as an inferior part of a broader study of political, moral and theological matters. Part of the explanation for these changes lies in the claim that specialization would produce major gains in social thought. But, at the same time, the view emerged that economics was not just specializing, it was adopting the new methods of the natural sciences. The use of mathematics was seen as central to this endeavour. The current view of the detachment of economics from moral science and morals in particular is alien to much of the history of the discipline. E. Kenneth Boulding, who asserted that economics 'only became a science by escaping from the casuistry and moralizing of medieval thought',[14] summarizes this conventional view.

The idea that institutionalized capitalist countries today are experiencing a deep legitimating – essentially a moral – crisis seems widespread,[15] and as Daniel Bell maintains, the loss of a common moral ground is the most important problem of the modern capitalism of the twentieth century.[16] Brigitte Berger described this problem as the transformation of the moral question 'from the crises of religion to the crises of secularity'.[17] The change in emphasis entailed a turning point in the behaviour of individuals and society, as the market broke away from normative influences embedded in the non-economic structures.[18] The market became disembedded, autonomous, self-regulating and entirely self-serving in nature, purpose and outcome. One could say that in modernity the market takes on a life of its own, which is represented by the commodification of the entire spectrum of social life.

In this context, Michel Foucault argues that the notion of an independent science of economics playing a role as a disciplinary power to control society is evidenced by the constant pressure to subject all decisions to a maximization of profit; and by promoting the desire to be as efficient as possible in the service of capital.[19] As a result of this process, it is hard to say that 'immoral' decisions being taken by an individual within this structure are ever 'wrong'. This is because the structure of capitalist society essentially dictates that decisions be made in a world where the sole absolute goal is the maximization of profit. Motives and actions under this system are only immoral if they inhibit this overriding principle. In other words, the process of embeddedness is reversed, with modern society becoming embedded in the market and 'refashioning its ethos and relations after its own image'.[20] The tentacles of market society extend to such an extent that the economic theory becomes the sole vehicle of analysis and all aspects of social life are objectified, quantified and couched in terms of maximizing profit and efficiency, and human beings are turned into 'Homo economicus'. Thus, capitalist economy has been associated with a view of human rationality which is founded on individual egoism, ends–means calculations and a largely utilitarian calculus of benefits. Capitalism is represented by commodities, without moral ties, capable of being owned as private property and valued insofar as they contribute to a productive process measured by the margin of profit.[21]

In fact, Adam Smith, whose 1776 work *The Wealth of Nations* is the foundational document of modern capitalism, did not distinguish between economic and cultural factors in his analysis, and claimed that capitalism had its own morality and that an 'invisible hand'[22] of self-interest guided the free market towards greater prosperity for all. But self-interest, in Smith's view, is not the same as selfishness. Modern capitalism's father believed that it is in everyone's economic self-interest to behave morally – which entails being trustworthy. However, Polanyi claims that Smith's idea of a self-adjusting market implied a stark utopia. Such an institution could not exist for any length of time without annihilating the human and natural substance of society; it would have physically destroyed man and transformed his surroundings into a wilderness.[23] Polanyi argues that labour is the activity of human beings, land is no more than subdivided nature, and the supply of money and credit in modern societies is necessarily shaped by governmental policies. Modern economic theory pretends that these fictitious commodities will behave in the same way as real commodities, but Polanyi insists that this sleight of hand has fatal consequences. It means that economic theorizing is based on a lie, and this lie places human society at risk. According to Polanyi, it is simply wrong to treat nature and human beings as objects whose price can be determined entirely by the market. This is part of what Polanyi means by his claim that 'laissez-faire was planned'; it requires statecraft and repression to impose the logic of the market and its attendant risks on ordinary people. Polanyi insists that free market capitalism is not a real choice; it is only a utopian vision.[24]

With the full development of capitalism, principles of profit and economic rationalism have attained complete control over, and fashion, all economic relationships. The utilization of science and technology by the emerging economic institutions has changed the characteristics of the economic system. Emergence of factories where the labour discipline is coupled with technical specialization and coordination is an indication of this phenomenon. The progress of industrialization and the advance of modern capitalism are very closely related in this aspect. Sombart explains that in the industrialization process, dissolution of the intimate relationship between the worker and his work created a new class in European society: those who 'own the means of production' and exploit the proletariat. The emergence of the working class or proletariat was the result of the organization of industry. Sombart highlights that the worker was also separated from his own work by the capitalistic organization, as he had no economic interest in the results of his work.[25] As Marx mentioned, this class separation was a crucial moment in economic history: from that point on, the process of isolation and alienation of man accelerated. According to Karl Marx, the legally 'free' labourer has only a business relationship with his employer, and monetary value has replaced all kinds of traditional social human bonds. In reality, free man has become unfree, he cannot exist freely without working or without money, because he has lost the moral support and protection of his society.

In addition, the overproduction of capital as a result of 'over-saving'; which could no longer find productive investment within national borders, led to the emergence of imperialism. Imperialism had the effect of supplanting the traditional subsistence-based economic systems and turning the colonies into producers of raw materials for the mother countries, thereby creating a very substantial power imbalance.[26] Simultaneously, Western rationality was accepted as a universal rationality, inherently superior to any competing worldviews.[27] Rather than the non-economic institutions such as family, religion and community forming the bonds of society, the market became the integrative mechanism pervading all aspects of the non-economic structures.[28] Modern capitalism has become entangled in other systems and cultures and it has forced all cultures to accept its rationality.[29] Those who were subjected to these forces were driven to respond to the challenges posed by the new system in creative ways.[30]

A Historical Background on Economic Ethic of Islam

The economic structures that existed in the pre-modern Islamic world were subject to market forces but were governed by a moral system which every religion is expected to offer its believers. The economic structure of Muslim societies was shaped according to their economic and historical needs, allowing for regional variations. In Maxime Rodinson's view, the

Qur'an, aside from its primary and central authority for the believing Muslims, is not a book of political economy, nor does it present judgements that blame or approve of capitalism. In addition, in Islamic religion there is no separation between 'this-worldly' and 'otherworldly' activities, rather, both are interwoven.[31] Furthermore, contrary to the general perception, Islamic societies had fairly advanced economic institutions and, from the beginning, Islam seems to have encouraged commerce and trade. Before he became a prophet, Muhammad was a merchant in Mecca, an important caravan centre, and there are many sayings attributed to him which praise and encourage commerce. His successors, too, sought to promote commercial activities. Indeed, Rodinson claims that in Islamic traditions, the search for profit, trade and production for the market, gained as much favour as was indicated in the verses of the Qur'an.[32] Early Islamic society was aware of many advanced business techniques, and they used 'checks' and other kinds of business contracts for trade.[33] However, Islam encouraged not only private accumulation of capital but also its redistribution. Muslims are expected to both earn and employ their accumulated capital for the service of mankind. Thus, while private accumulation of wealth is acknowledged, encouraged and legitimized, its circulation within society is given great importance. This circulation is supposed to be carried out through charity, which is constantly recommended in the Qur'an and prophetic traditions (*Hadith*) and is a signal characteristic of Islamic societies. Besides this, public benefit (*maslaha*) was emphasized by Islamic tradition and became an important criterion for judging the trustworthiness of social institutions, including the character of particular forms of property. The essential social services in Muslim society, such as health and education, have traditionally been provided by private charitable institutions.[34] Care for the poor in society was certainly included in the broad definition of charity. Charitable practices were an important force of social cohesion, making individuals, communities, institutions and states all operate as benefactors and thus binding communities together in the process.[35]

The Institution of *Waqf*

Although *waqfs* (endowments) have a history considerably older than Islam,[36] they quickly became a characteristic Islamic institution as Muslims were urged strongly to endow their assets in the service of the community.[37] More precisely, although the concept of these endowments did not originate in the Islamic world,[38] they were highly encouraged by Islamic law and governments, and so became very common institutions in the early and medieval Muslim worlds. For instance, by the end of the eighteenth century it is estimated that there were roughly 20,000 Ottoman *waqfs* in operation.[39] The specific meaning of *waqf* is to 'freeze' the right of ownership over a property and to use its benefits for charity and public welfare, such as schools, law colleges, public works, soup kitchens and aid for orphans. Essentially, a person commits a pious deed, declaring part of his or her property to be henceforth inalienable, and designates persons or public utilities as beneficiaries of its yields.[40] In short, property is withdrawn from individual or government ownership and its rent is used for public necessities, as chosen by the donor. In the sixteenth- and seventeenth-century Ottoman era, a significant portion of the land in the Islamic world, up to 40–50 per cent, was endowed in this way and thus lay outside private ownership. Health, education and other social services were the principal beneficiaries of these endowments.[41] It can be argued that by thus catering to the needs of the society, *waqfs* played an important role in maintaining social stability and provided the basis for civil society. Thus, an understanding of the socio-economic role of *waqfs* is crucial to our analysis of the economic life of Muslim societies. However, some economic historians have criticized the institution of *waqf* in Muslim societies; for instance, according to Bryan S. Turner, capital locked in *waqf* institutions prevented the accumulation of large private savings necessary to establish complex economic institutions, such as large factories, banks and holdings.[42] He argues that in Muslim societies, a ruler could only seize *waqf* property by disregarding the Shari'a law. Because of this 'freezing' of capital, accumulated wealth was a source of rent, not capital, and consequently, a rational bourgeois class could not develop in Muslim societies. Weber also claims that *waqfs* impeded the development of capital accumulation in the Muslim world, since urban merchants, because of the absence of security in property holding, never transformed their accumulations into industry and capitalist production. Rather, they invested their accumulations in non-economic areas, particularly *waqfs*, and, as in the ancient economy, these accumulations served only as a source of rent and not as a source of acquisitive capital.[43]

Abolition of *Waqfs* and the Beginning of Economic Intervention of the West in Muslim Markets

Waqf remained central to the economic life of Muslim societies for over a millennium. However, the situation began to change with the spread of industrialization in Europe and the consequent search for new markets and sources of raw materials. This brought European powers and their economic interests into contact and conflict with those of the Muslim lands; and *waqfs* were a causality of the power imbalance inherent in these contacts. By the middle of the eighteenth century, for example, the Ottoman Empire began to lose lands in the wars for the first time in its history, and because of political and economic weaknesses it was forced to borrow a significant amount from European countries. This pressure, strongly felt during the treaties of Paris, London and Berlin, was expressed bluntly in 1860 in response to the Ottoman government's request for a loan after the Crimean War. Among the conditions imposed by the British government were that foreign citizens should be granted the right to possess state-owned lands under the same conditions as Ottoman subjects, and that the *waqf* system be abolished.[44]

This demand was renewed as a combined Anglo–French position in 1867. The pressure of the 'financial protectorate' reached new heights when, in 1881, the Ottoman government declared bankruptcy, which led to the establishment of the Public Debt Administration, *Duyûn-u Umumiye*.[45] To the Ottoman state, which was being crushed under financial pressure from the Western powers, the huge revenue potential that the *waqfs* represented must have seemed irresistible.[46]

Both the British and French colonial powers were hostile to the *waqfs*,[47] which tied down real property and prevented it from circulating in the free market. The state, by definition, was an accomplice in the project of capitalism, so in order to enrich itself it had to modernize (i.e., create a free market economy). Thus, the *waqfs* had to lose their important role in socio-economic life in Muslim communities. Under pressure from the European powers to establish the primacy of legal structures within which contracts could be enforced, the Porte was pressurized to declare the right of foreign nationals to own property by a new land and tax law reform. The process of destruction of *waqfs* followed different paths in different parts of the Islamic world. Indeed, the most important reason for the decline of *waqfs* was 'centralization' in the nineteenth century. Together with other institutions; *waqfs* were totally subjugated to the will of the central state under pressure from Western powers. With this modern system of administration and taxation, the *waqfs* lost their use for government.[48] In the Ottoman state, the centralization of the institution of *waqf*, which had increased in the *tanzimat* era, was solidified by the creation of Departments of *Waqf* in central government. The crucial step was the abolition of the financial autonomy of *waqfs* through the declaration that the collection of *waqf* revenues would be realized by the Ministry of Finance. By the 1830s, *waqfs* were left completely under the remit of the Ministry of Finance.[49] The central authority began to usurp increasing proportions of this revenue, and the payment of the collected revenue to the *waqfs* was delayed as well as curtailed. The outstanding debt of the state to the *waqf* administration was constantly on the rise. While, on the one hand, its revenues were thus usurped, on the other, the Central Waqf Administration (CWA) was made responsible for some of the loss-making state economic enterprises. It was forced to invest in and manage these enterprises, which were totally unrelated to the *waqf* system. Furthermore, the CWA was forced to purchase the shares of some of these enterprises and then resell these at a drastic discount to the municipalities. Thus, *waqf* funds originally endowed by private persons were channelled to state enterprises. The revenues and assets of all the education-related *waqfs* were transferred to the Ministry of Education. Indeed, former tenants were made co-owners of the *waqf* property and were induced by the state to purchase the rest of the *waqfs*' assets, so the assets would simply be sold off to the highest bidder.[50] Thus, the *waqf* system was first brought under state control and then marginalized.[51]

With the gradual weakening of the Ottoman state, the gates of the 'capitulations'[52] were opened, and European capital entered the markets. When the level of trade with the West began to increase, Europeans attempted to secure the institutional conditions for the domination of their products and uniformity of laws in business matters to their advantage. This was, after all, the era of colonization and the great powers were determined to impose their own systems on the vast regions that they colonized.[53] Small- and medium-sized local economic institutions, craftsmen and guilds could not compete with these mass-produced European products, and were decimated.[54] Thus, Muslim lands came under the economic domination of the West and the delicate socio-economic structure in Muslim societies was destroyed by colonialism and the accompanying capitalism that was quick to supplant the local economic institutions with its own structural components.

Islamic Responses to Modern Capitalism

Because of colonization during the nineteenth century, Muslim societies lost much of their power on a global scale, both in the political and economic spheres. The cultural impact of Western countries was also direct and often overwhelming. These powerful forces shook the very foundations of the Islamic moral economy. Increasing contact with Western economies resulted in unpredictable and apparently uncontrollable economic and social change, which in turn led to a variety of reactions. Many Muslim intellectuals, concerned about the loss of social solidarity, tried to prevent Muslims from assimilating into the damaging effects of materialism.[55] This Muslim response has grown ever stronger since then. For many Muslim intellectuals and entrepreneurs now the key question is how a Muslim should act in a world shaped by the capitalist system, and how can one best capture the energy, dynamism and wealth of the new economic forms without compromising one's moral principles and social identity.

The major disagreement was over whether capitalism could be harnessed to the benefit of the Islamic society without radically transforming and ethically compromising the latter. For a number of Muslim writers, this concern was one way of engaging with the new world order through a continuous adherence to these moral values, and without losing possible economic benefits. Jamal al-Din Afghani (1838–1897), who gave some thought to the dangers of capitalism and industrialization, argued that the Islamic moral core was best expressed in the notions of cooperation and social solidarity. He insisted that the materialistic dimension of the capitalist system tended to dissolve the social bonds which gave Islamic society meaning as well as order. So, according to al-Afghani, Muslims had to re-establish a moral order in order to ensure cooperation within Muslim *ummah*.[56] Muhammad Iqbal, the poet-philosopher from Pakistan, saw a moral decline at the heart of capitalism. He was increasingly concerned by the effects of European capitalism's driving forces on the Islamic moral order.[57] In these responses to the penetration of the Muslim lands by capitalist culture, Islam played a major role in view of the cohesion it lent to the social order.

Muslim writers focused on the need to restore a moral economy governed by the norms of Islam.

Rodinson has argued that modern Muslim apologists organize the precepts of Islam in a way that shows Islam to be a religion of justice in social matters. For him, it is always possible to justify any such claims, as every society seems to have its own overall conception of social justice, but this total conception can be reflective of the opinion of a particular social strata, group or individual.[58] Therefore, he argues, the Qur'an does not represent the social ideal of all Muslims; rather, it was the social ideal of the Prophet and restricted groups at both Mecca and Medina. Nevertheless, despite the presence of the ideal of social justice in Islam, the right to own property, whether this be consumer goods or in the form of productive means, has never been questioned.[59] S. D. Goitein argues that, although during the earlier centuries of Islam many Muslim merchants were in the first and second echelon of the state, they never became an organized body or an independent class, failing to obtain political power.[60] Goitein states that despite the existence of a Muslim bourgeoisie which strove for both power and honour during the Middle Ages, their struggles were not against the political power and did not aim to take over the state.[61] When Muslim societies met with the issue of class divisions and unequal opportunities, the question of property became the central point of contention. Muslim intellectuals acknowledged that absolute economic equality was neither possible nor desirable, but they did not believe that this should be the basis for class formation and social division. That is how Islam, in theory, strikes a balance between individualism and collectivism.

According to the fundamental rules of this moral economy, the ethical regulation of human transactions was seen as part of God's purpose. Thus, the Muslim critics of capitalism contended that the restoration of an Islamic order would provide the material basis for the spiritual revival that would create social solidarity. Consequently, the question of ownership of property became one of the most serious discussions in Islamic *fiqh*. Its reinvention in a distinctively Islamic sense for the modern era (surrounded by the regulations devised by Islamic jurisprudence to ensure the proper handling of property – its nature, its obligations, its limits, the question of *riba*, *zakat*, etc. – would supply the material beneath its ethical re-establishment. Muslim intellectuals contended that Islam allows man the freedom to earn wealth only by those means through which a person renders some real and useful service to the community and thereby entitles him or herself to fair and just compensation for it. Mandatory charity in Islam engages directly with the key issues of the moral economy – treating it not merely as an economic enterprise, but also as an ethical one.

Moreover, many Muslim writers, aware of the power and success of capitalism, argued that all economic transactions be tied to an Islamic moral system while retaining their capacity for productive and material efficiency. They argued that any economic operation under the *fiqh* rules on trade, finance, taxation, property, *riba* (interest), etc., would ensure both material and moral prosperity.

Today, however, economic reasoning is the primary criterion for explaining human behaviour, and the study of economy has become an independent science. The problematic contradiction here is that many Muslim intellectuals seem to accept that they are engaging with a discourse not of their own making, by merely acknowledging the existence of the economy as a realm of human activity independent from its societal context.

Economics has created its own make-believe world in which all participants, as economic agents, are assumed to behave in much the same way to maximize profit and accumulate material goods. All other systems of analysis have been dismissed as being based on non-rational economic behaviours.[62] This was in part aimed at predicting and prescribing how an individual would and should conduct his or her economic relationships. However, it is also an analytical model that claims to explain human nature and thus it is ideologically charged and expressive of a particular system of values.[63] Muslim writers argue that it is necessary to imagine an alternative economic order which is determined by particular Islamic principles to perform a socially integrative function: that of incorporating Islamic values and ethics into the practices of everyday life, including economic transactions. It is to be expected that Muslim scholars should differ on the degree of autonomy allowed to reasoned interpretation through *ijtihad*, as well as on the selection of jurists to be cited as authoritative sources for understanding the fundamental rules of an Islamic economy.[64] Writings of such Muslim intellectuals as Muhammad Baqir al-Sadr, Sayyid Qutb and Sayyid Abul al-Ala Mawdudi helped define the heuristics of the field, though these are generally devoid of interest in, or appreciation of, the economic concepts or tools developed in Western societies.[65] These intellectuals argue that Islamic economics come about as the natural conclusion of Islamic ideology and therefore are justified entirely independently of other systems of economics. However, paradoxically, they also wish to engage successfully with modern capitalism though strongly insisting on ethical distinctiveness and moral codes of 'Islamic economics'.

The Main Characteristics of Islamic Moral Economy

Until the 1970s Islamic economics remained a largely theoretical discussion, but the sudden rise in oil prices and resulting prosperity provided an opportunity for these ideas to be turned into reality. The aim was for Islamic economics to develop an effective and workable system of economic life that would not simply be morally preferable, but would also improve the material lives of Muslims. Muslim scholars agreed that economic development is only desirable when economic transactions are in harmony with the values and culture of the *ummah* – the Islamic community. However, they are aware that Islamic institutions have to use the same economic tools to compete in the global capitalist market. Baqir al-Sadr and others argue that it would in fact be demonstrably more efficient to apply the Islamic precepts of social justice to the capitalistic economic system.[66] By the 1990s, this had developed into the justification of an Islamic economy in terms that were unmistakably neo-liberal in their underlying rationale, as can be seen in the argument that free competition and prohibition of monopoly are central to any truly Islamic economy.[67]

However, the question that arises then is how can an Islamic economy restore the moral values of the Islamic world by using the effective economic principles that at once preserve these moral values and yet successfully compete in the system of modern secular capitalism. According to Muslim intellectuals, an economic system could be judged on the basis of two further categories associated with economic discourse: the concept of 'society' and the concept of the individual. In both of these areas they tried to imagine distinctively Islamic equivalents – the *ummah* and the Homo Islamicus – abstracting these concepts from their function in secular economic discourse.

From this point of view, individuals who behave according to the ethical commands of Islam would form the foundation of the Islamic economy. Here, the charity payment (*zakat*) and the prohibition on *riba* would be the main instruments of Islamic moral economy. *Zakat*, a mandatory charity, is one of the pillars of the Islamic moral economy, and it has an important role to play in the fields of social welfare and fair distribution of wealth. One of Islam's most forceful medieval theologians, Ibn Qayyim, explains the aim of *zakat* as being the promotion of socio-economic justice and the development of compassion and care for others.[68] *Zakat* does not refer to charitable gifts given out of kindness or generosity, but rather to the compulsory systematic donation of 2.5 per cent of one's total wealth each year to benefit the poor. *Zakat* represents a key component of the moral economy since it epitomizes a number of essential ideas: the notion that the individual holds property as a trust from God; therefore, that property must be used for a higher good, thus forming the basis of a truly Islamic society.[69]

The other major feature of Islamic economic thought is the prohibition of *riba*, a prohibition that enjoys a central place in the imagination of the Islamic economy and, it can possibly be argued, lies at the very heart of Islamic views of a moral economy – just as it looms large in the ideas of many Muslim intellectuals concerning the fundamental injustice of capitalism.[70] Islam, scholars argue, is opposed to exploitation in every form, and stands for fair and equitable dealings among all men; demanding interest from someone who is constrained to borrow to meet his essential consumption requirement is economic exploitation. Charging of interest on loans taken for productive purposes is also prohibited because, it is argued, this is not an equitable form of transaction.[71] *Riba* is considered a form of oppression because, it is claimed, it transfers wealth from the poor to the rich and contributes to the imbalance in the distribution of wealth in society. Muslim thinkers argue that this is against social interest, contrary to the will of God, and encourages love of money and the desire to accumulate wealth for its own sake, besides making men selfish and miserly.[72] The dilemma such thinkers face here is that the modern banking system is organized on the basis of a fixed payment called interest which falls under one of the categories of *riba*. This is why the practices of the modern banking system are seen by many proponents of Islamic economics as the chief obstacle in the compatibility of their ethical systems with modern capitalism, which has come to the fore over the last few decades, and they seek to offer an alternative framework to allow for rising capital uncontaminated by *riba*.

While a basic tenet of Islamic banking – the outlawing of *riba*, a term that encompasses not only the concept of usury, but also that of interest – has seldom been recognized as applicable beyond the Islamic world, many of its guiding principles have. The majority of these principles are based on simple morality and common sense, which form the bases of many religions, including Islam.[73]

Disenchantment with the value-neutral capitalist financial systems has led many to look for ethical values in their financial dealings. Thus, the advocates of Islamic banking conceive of it as an instrument for the development of an Islamic economic order. The Islamic financial system employs the concept of participation in the enterprise by utilizing the funds at risk on a profit-and-loss-sharing basis. This, it is claimed, by no means implies that investments with Islamic financial institutions are necessarily speculative, as the speculative risk can be curbed by careful investment policies, diversification of risk and prudent management.

Insofar as these institutions provide some Muslims with financial security and with a sense that their investments accord with their Islamic ethical obligations, they perform an important service. Obviously, they operate very differently from what may have been conceived of by early Muslim scholars, but they have nevertheless contributed to the transformation of Muslim identities and to new ways of thinking about being a Muslim in the modern world.

Conclusion

Because of the colonization of Muslim countries and the imposition on them of a capitalist economic system, the traditional moral economy was weakened and eventually supplanted by a new system that could not shoulder the social responsibilities of its predecessor. This drastic change produced a number of strong reactions, one of the major ones being the development of an Islamic economic system. The ideological basis of the need for this new system rests on two claims. First, that the modern systems cannot fill the gap that Westernization has created to the disadvantage of Muslim societies. And second, those Islamic societies need an economic system capable of providing social justice along with economic prosperity. It was in an attempt to add Islamic moral and ethical values, without ignoring economic benefits, that many Muslims found new possibilities through these institutions, engaging with the world while also manifesting their Islamic identity. Although modern economic institutions are the product of Western modernization, Muslim societies are trying to make them compatible with their ancient traditions and moral values.

NOTES

1 The theory of Islamic economics was developed by a number of Muslim intellectuals. See Baqir Al Sadr's *Iqtisaduna: Our Economics* (Tehran: World Organization of Islamic Services, 1982–1984); Muhammad Nejatullah Siddiq's *Muslim Economic Thinking* (Jeddah: International Center for Research in Islamic Economics, 1981); Sayyed Mahmood Taleqani's *Islam and Ownership*, tr. A. Jabbari and F. Rajaee (Lexington, KY: Mazda Publishers, 1983); and Abul al-Ala Mawdudi's *Let Us Be Muslims*, a translation of *Shahadat Haq* (Leicester: Islamic Foundation, 1986), which can be counted among the most significant works in helping to formulate Islamic economics.

2 Timur Kuran argues that the connection between Islamic religion and Islamic banking is 'imaginary'. Timur Kuran, 'Islam and Underdevelopment: An Old Puzzle Revisited', *Journal of Institutional and Theoritical Economics*, Vol. 153, 1997, p. 73.

3 Alasdair MacIntyre, *A Short History of Ethics* (London: Routledge, 1991), p. 3.

4 Jacques Thiroux, *Ethics: Theory and Practice* (New Jersey: Prentice-Hall, 1995), p. 3.

5 Arthur Schopenhauer, *The Basis of Morality* (New York: Dover Publications, 2005), p. 19.

6 Ibid.

7 Deepak Lal, 'Morality and Capitalism: Learning from the Past', John Dunning (ed.), *The Moral Imperatives of Global Capitalism* (Oxford: OUP, 2002).

8 MacIntyre, p. 3.

9 W. Montgomery Watt, *Islamic Fundamentalism and Modernity* (London; New York: Routledge, 1988), p. 13.

10 R. Swedberg, *Max Weber and the Idea of Economic Sociology* (New Jersey: Princeton University Press, 1998), p. 133.

11 Karl Polanyi, *The Great Transformation* (Boston: Beacon Press, 1957), p. 57.

12 Swedberg, p. 133.

13 George Dalton (ed.), *Primitive, Archaic and Modern Economies: Essays of Karl Polanyi* (New York: Doubleday, 1968), p. 65.

14 E. Kenneth Boulding, *Economics as a Science* (New York: McGraw-Hill, 1970), p. 117.

15 See, for example, D. Bell, *The Cultural Contradictions of Capitalism* (New York: Basic Books, 1996); B. Berger (ed.), *The Culture of Modern Entrepreneurship* (San Francisco: ICS Press, 1990).

16 The term 'revitalization' and/or 'revival' has also been largely used in literature covering Islamic movements. Yet Robert Wuthnow defined a movement as a

'revitalization movement' only if there was an attempt to restore or reconstruct patterns of moral order that had been radically disrupted or threatened. Robert Wuthnow, *Meaning and Moral Order: Explorations in Cultural Analysis* (Berkeley: University of California Press, 1987), p. 233.

17 Berger, p. 248.

18 E. P. Thompson, 'The Moral Economy of the English Crowd', *Past and Present, The Unknown Mayhew: Selections from the Morning Chronicle,* 1849–1850 (London: Merlin Press, 1971), pp. 50, 76–136.

19 Foucault places the forms of control over society into two categories: sovereign and disciplinary. Sovereign power is exerted in the postwar world by governments and international organizations. It seeks to make the world safe for the free flow of capital by removing any major obstacles. Disciplinary power is explained above. See Michel Foucault, *Discipline and Punish: The Birth of the Prison* (New York: Vintage, 1977), pp. 75–81.

20 W. J. Booth, 'On the Idea of the Moral Economy', *The American Political Science Review*, Vol. 88, No. 3: 653667, 1994, p. 656.

21 Charles Tripp, *Islam and the Moral Economy* (Cambridge: UK, 2006), p. 3.

22 R. Swedberg also underlines that his 'invisible hand' is completed with an 'individual soul', arguing against the popular image of Smith as a one-dimensional advocate of the virtues of the market. Smith does indeed speak of how the individual, by pursuing his or her own interests, may also further those of society in general. See pp. 13–14.

23 Polanyi, p. 3.

24 Polanyi, pp. 3–4.

25 Peter Koslowski (ed.), *Methodology of the Social Sciences, Ethics and Economics in the Newer Historical School: From Max Weber and Rickert to Sombart and Rothacker* (Berlin; New York: Springer, 1997), p. 57.

26 Caglar Keyder, *State and Class in Turkey: A Study in Capitalist Development* (London and New York: Verso, 1987), p. 62.

27 Roy Dilley (ed.), *Contesting Markets: Analyses of Ideology, Discourse and Practice* (Edinburgh: Edinburgh University Press, 1992), pp. 18–23; Georg Simmel, *The Philosophy of Money* (New York: Routledge, 1990), pp. 429–31.

28 Dilley, pp. 10–12, 25–26.

29 Kathryn Dean, *Capitalism and Citizenship: The Impossible Partnership* (London; New York: Routledge, 2003), pp. 131–137.

30 Tripp, p. 13.

31 Maxime Rodinson, *Islam and Capitalism* (New York: Pantheon Books, 1973), pp. 17–19.

32 Ibid., pp. 17–19.

33 Janet Abu-Lughod, *Before the European Hegemony* (New York and Oxford: OUP, 1989), p. 216.

34 See: William L. Cleveland, *Islam against the West: Shakib Arslan and the Campaign for Islamic Nationalism* (Austin: University of Texas Press, 1985), pp. 115–118.

35 Michael Bonner, Mine Ener and Amy Singer (eds), *Poverty and Charity in Middle Eastern Contexts* (New York: State University of New York Press, 2003), p. 2.

36 Ancient Mesopotamia, Greece and Rome, as well as the pre-Islamic Arabs, certainly knew of such endowments. Murat Çizakça, *A History of Philanthropic Foundations: The Islamic World from the Seventh Century to the Present* (Istanbul:

Boğaziçi University Press, 2000), p. 5. In the legal discussion of the second and early third century AH (After Hijra) we find several legal institutions that in the later legal doctrine were subsumed under the heading of *waqf* and left their trace in that doctrine (see J. Schacht, 'Early Doctrines') *Encyclopedia of Islam*, Vol. XI (Leiden: Brill, 2002), p. 59.

37 Daniel Crecelius, 'Introduction', *Journal of the Economic and Social History of the Orient* (JESHO), Vol. 38, 1995, No. 3.

38 Ibid. p. 5.

39 Timur Kuran, 'The Provision of Public Goods Under Islamic Law: Origins, Impact and Limitations of the Waqf System', *Law and Society Review* 35 (4) (December 2001), pp. 841–897.

40 *Encyclopedia of Islam*, Vol. XI (Leiden: Brill, 2002), p. 59.

41 Ibid., p. 6.

42 B. Turner, *Weber and Islam: A Critical Study* (London and Boston: Routledge, 1974), p. 124.

43 M. Weber, *Economy and Society* (New York, NY: Bedminster Press, 1968), p. 197.

44 Nazif Öztürk, *Elmalili M. Hamdi Yazir Gozuyle Wakiflar* (Ankara: TDV, 1995), p. 52; Caglar Keyder, *State and Class in Turkey* (New York: Verso, 1987), p. 21.

45 Sevket Pamuk, *Osmanli Ekonomisi ve Dunya Kapitalizmi (1820–1913)* (Ankara: Yurt Yayincilik, 1984), pp. 28–29.

46 The revenue potential was, indeed, huge: it represented 25–50 per cent of the state budget during the eighteenth century. Cizakca, p. 81.

47 David S. Powers, 'The Islamic Family Endowment', *Vanderbilt Journal of Transnational Law*, 32 (4), 1989, pp. 535–571.

48 Keyder, p. 21. The Ministry of Awqaf, *Nezaret*, was founded by Abdulhamid I, and played a crucial role in the centralization of the *waqf* system. See Cizakca, p. 82.

49 Cizakca, p. 89.

50 Cizakca, pp. 89–90.

51 Cizakca, p. 232.

52 All of the commercial privileges included, either explicitly or implicitly, the following provisions with respect to the status of non-Muslims and merchants in Dar al-Islam: 1. General security of person and property such as testamentary rights, freedom of worship, burial and dress. Repairs to ships, emergency relations, aid against attack by corsairs. Permission to address complaints to the head of the Muslim community. 2. Exterioriality, including consular jurisdiction. Consul's salary. 3. Abolition of collective responsibility. *The Encyclopedia of Islam*, Vol. 3, (Leiden: Brill, 1971), pp. 1178–1179.

53 Cizakca, p. 76.

54 First, higher transportation costs raise the prices of imported manufactured goods. Second, by limiting the commercialization and export orientation of agriculture, they also delay the destruction of the more or less self-sufficient nature of rural economies, specialization in agriculture and the rise of demand for manufactured goods. Sevket Pamuk, *The Ottoman Empire and European Capitalism (1820–1913)* (Cambridge: CUP, 1987), p. 119.

55 Tripp, p. 35.

56 Nikki Keddie, *Islamic Response to Imperialism: Political and Religious Writings of Sayyid Jamāl ad-Dīn 'al-Afghānī* (Berkeley: University of California Press, 1983), pp. 65–70.

57 Muhammad Iqbal, *The Reconstruction of Religious Thought in Islam* (Lahore, 1968), p. 156.
58 Rodinson, p. 19.
59 Ibid., p. 21.
60 S. D. Goitein, *Studies in Islamic History and Institutions* (Leiden: Brill, 1968), p. 218.
61 Ibid., p. 254.
62 Robert Heilbroner, *The Nature and Logic of Capitalism* (New York: Norton, 1986), pp. 53–69.
63 Alan Macfarlane, *The Culture of Capitalism* (Oxford and New York: Blackwell Publishers, 1987), pp. 223–224.
64 Tripp, p. 111.
65 Timur Kuran, 'On the Notion of Economic Justice in the Contemporary Islamic World', *International Journal of Middle East Studies* (Cambridge: CUP, 1989), pp. 171–191.
66 Baqir al-Sadr, *Iqtisaduna: Our Economics* (Tehran: World Organization of Islamic Services, 1982–1984), p. 293.
67 Tripp, p. 115.
68 S. M. Ghazanfar and A. Amin Islahi, 'Some Aspects of Ibn Qayyim's Economics', in S. M. Ghazafar (ed.), *Medieval Islamic Economic Thought* (London and New York: Routledge, 2003), p. 134.
69 Tripp, p. 124.
70 Taqiuddin al-Nabahani, *The Economic System in Islam* (New Delhi: Milli Publications, 2002), pp. 172–176.
71 Z. Ahmed, 'Prohibition of Interest in Islam', in *Journal of Islamic Banking and Finance* (Karachi, Vol. 1, No. 1, 1984), p. 20.
72 Muhammad Nejatullah Siddiqi, *Muslim Economic Thinking* (Jeddah: International Center for Research in Islamic Economics, 1981), p. 63.
73 *Islamic Finance: Euro Money* (1997).

BIBLIOGRAPHY

Abu-Lughod, Janet, *Before the European Hegemony* (Oxford and New York: OUP, 1989).

Ahmed, Z., 'Prohibition of Interest in Islam', *Journal of Islamic Banking and Finance* (Karachi, Vol. 1, No. 1, 1984).

Al-Nabahani, Taqiuddin, *The Economic System in Islam* (New Delhi: Milli Publications, 2002).

Al Sadr, Baqir, *Iqtisaduna: Our Economics* (Tehran: World Organization of Islamic Services, 1982–1984).

Bell, D., *The Cultural Contradictions of Capitalism* (Basic Books, 1996).

Berger, B. (ed.), *The Culture of Modern Entrepreneurship* (San Francisco: ICS Press, 1990).

Bonner, Michael Mine, and Ener, Amy Singer (eds), *Poverty and Charity Middle Eastern Contexts* (New York: State University of New York Press, 2003).

Booth, W. J., 'On the Idea of the Moral Economy', *The American Political Science Review*, Vol. 88, No. 3, 1994.

Boulding, Kenneth E., *Economics as a Science* (New York: McGraw Hill, 1970).

Çizakça, Murat, *A History of Philanthropic Foundations: The Islamic World from the Seventh Century to the Present* (Istanbul: Boğaziçi University Press, 2000).

Cleveland, William L., *Islam Against the West: Shakib Arslan and the Campaign for Islamic Nationalism* (Austin: University of Texas Press, 1985).

Crecelius, Daniel, 'Introduction', JESHO, Vol. 38, 1995, No. 3.

Dalton, George (ed.), *Primitive, Archaic and Modern Economies: Essays of Karl Polanyi* (New York: Doubleday, 1968).

Dean, Katryn, *Capitalism and Citizenship: The Impossible Partnership* (London and New York: Routledge, 2003).

Dilley, Roy (ed.), *Contesting Markets: Analyses of Ideology, Discourse and Practice* (Edinburgh: Edinburgh University Press, 1992).

Foucault, Michael, *Discipline and Punish: The Birth of the Prison* (New York: Vintage, 1977).

Ghazanfr S. M., and Islahi, A. Amin, 'Some Aspects of Ibn Qayyim's Economics', in Ghazafar, S. M. (ed.), *Medieval Islamic Economic Thought* (London and New York: Routledge, 2003).

Goitein, S. D., *Studies in Islamic History and Institutions* (Leiden: Brill, 1968).

Heilbroner, Robert, *The Nature and Logic of Capitalism* (New York: Norton, 1986).

Iqbal, Muhammad, *The Reconstruction of Religious Thought in Islam* (Lahore, 1968).

Keddie, Nikki, *Islamic Response to Imperialism: Political and Religious Writings of Sayyid Jamāl ad-Dīn 'al-Afghānī* (Berkeley: University of California Press, 1983).

Keyder, Caglar, *State and Class in Turkey: A Study in Capitalist Development* (London and New York: Verso, 1987).

Koslowski, Peter (ed.), *Methodology of the Social Sciences, Ethics and Economics in the Newer Historical School: From Max Weber and Rickert to Sombart and Rothacker* (Berlin and New York: Springer, 1997).

Kuran, Timur, 'On the Nation of Economic Justice in the Contemporary Islamic World', *International Journal of Middle East Studies* (Cambridge: CUP, 1989).
—'Islam and Underdevelopment: An Old Puzzle Revisited', *Journal of Institutional and Theoretical Economics*, Vol. 153, 1997.
—'The Provision of Public Goods under Islamic Law: Origins, Impact and Limitations of the Waqf System', *Law and Society Review* 35 (4), December 2001.
Lal, Deepak, 'Morality and Capitalism: Learning from the Past', in Dunning, John (ed.), *The Moral Imperatives of Global Capitalism* (Oxford: OUP, 2002).
Macfarlane, Alan, *The Culture of Capitalism* (Oxford: Blackwell Publishers, 1989).
MacIntyre, Alasdair, *A Short History of Ethics* (London: Routledge, 1991).
Öztürk, Nazif, *Elmalili M. Hamdi Yazir Gozuyle Wakiflar* (Ankara: TDV, 1995).
Pamuk, Sevket, *Osmanli Ekonomisi ve Dunya Kapitalizmi (1820–1913)* (Ankara: Yurt Yayincilik, 1984).
—*The Ottoman Empire and European Capitalism (1820–1913)* (Cambridge: CUP, 1987).
Polanyi, Karl, *The Great Transformation* (Boston: Beacon Press, 1957).
Rodinson, Maxime, *Islam and Capitalism* (New York: Pantheon Books, 1974).
Rothschild, Kurt W., *Ethics and Economic Theory* (Aldershot: Edward Elgar Publishing Company, 1993).
Thompson, E. P., 'The Moral Economy of the English Crowd', *Past and Present,* Vol. 50, 1970.
Thiroux, Jacques, *Ethics: Theory and Practice* (New Jersey: Prentice-Hall, 1995).
Tripp, Charles, *Islam and the Moral Economy* (Cambridge: CUP, 2006).
Turner, B., *Weber and Islam: A Critical Study* (London and Boston: Routledge, 1974).
Schopenhauer, Arthur, *The Basis of Morality* (New York: Dover Publications, 2005).
Simmel, Georg, The *Philosophy of Money* (New York: Routledge, 1990).
Siddiq, Muhammad Nejatullah, *Muslim Economic Thinking* (Jeddah: International Center for Research in Islamic Economics, 1981).
Swedberg, R., *Marx Weber and the Idea of Economic Sociology* (Princeton: Princeton University Press, 1998).
Watt, W. Montgomery, *Islamic Fundamentalism and Modernity* (London and New York: Routledge, 1988).
Wuthnow, Robert, *Meaning and Moral Order: Explorations in Cultural Analysis* (Berkeley: University of California Press,1987).

3

Has Modernity Ruptured Islamic Political Tradition?

Ovamir Anjum

I discuss here the interaction of Islam and politics in the contemporary Middle East, in particular in relation to understanding the trajectories of Islamism and modernity in the region. Studies of contemporary Islam frequently identify phenomena in the twentieth-century Muslim world, which are then given distinctive labels such as Islamism, Islamic fundamentalism, or political Islam, etc., to distinguish them from what is identified as traditional Islam. These new fangled movements, it is said, were a breakaway from the tradition, and, more significantly, they were a reaction to modernity – they were instances of 'Third Worldisms' under an Islamic guise. Finally, it is often argued that the rise in the late twentieth century of pious puritans on the one hand and militant vigilantes on the other is evidence of the failure of these initial movements. I critique these accounts on theoretical grounds, and advocate an alternative way to study Islam and politics. On a disciplinary level, I argue that satisfactory accounts of contemporary Islamic movements require not only attention to the sociology of Muslim societies alongside Islamic tradition, but indeed a framework which overcomes that dichotomy.

Two questions are immediately germane to my *problématique*: how modern Western secular ideas have interacted with the Islamic tradition that existed prior to the colonial encounter that produced contemporary Muslim societies, and how lived conditions (socio-political and economic) relate to traditions of ideas and practices. The philosopher Alasdair MacIntyre has reflected on the nature and lives of intellectual traditions in his study of Western thought, and the anthropologist and critic Talal Asad has developed the idea of discursive tradition with concern for lived complex traditions like Islam and Christianity in mind.[1] These two thinkers inform my treatment of questions about the encounter of Islamic political tradition with Western modernity. MacIntyre reflects on the issues of maturity and transformation of traditions as a result of encounter with other rival traditions, in particular examining the problem of the epistemological crisis that such encounters might produce, and the possibility of rupture: for a tradition to continue, he argues, '[s]ome core of shared belief, constitutive of allegiance to the tradition, has to survive every rupture'.[2]

I argue that a proper understanding of what is called Islamism, and more generally the interaction of Islam and politics in the contemporary Islamic world, is not possible without a serious engagement with the classical tradition of Islamic political thought and history. Far from suggesting we bring back the essentialist understanding of Islam and politics that the orientalists have been criticized for espousing and using that to explain contemporary Islam, I argue we must take seriously the discourse of lived Islam. However, taking that discourse seriously forces us to consider the tradition which these groups claim to adhere to and reform to, as well as the history which shapes their memories and desires. Recent socio-political studies of Islamism, seeking to go past the old generalist accounts of Islam, have emphasized socio-political factors, but have not successfully rid themselves of reductive and essentialist explanations.[3] More specifically, since contemporary Islamic groups persistently draw on various classical Islamic visions of a normative political order, and since the very memories and desires of the people in the Islamic world are shaped by and recorded in that tradition, continued examination of that tradition remains indispensable. In arguing this, I argue for an epistemic continuity between the pre-colonial and contemporary periods in the Islamic world at a level untenable in the West, where modernity has been a most profound and historically unique rupture. In the Islamic world, of course, modernity has been imposed or embraced in limited quarters, but can be best seen still as a powerful intrusion rather than a basic reordering of life.

I begin with a critical engagement with one of the most highly regarded sociological studies of these issues, namely the French scholar Olivier Roy's study of the involvement of Islamic groups in the political sphere, boldly titled *The Failure of Political Islam*.[4] In articulating my critique, I employ Talal Asad's seminal work on the anthropology of Islam and secularism, and in particular on secularization in Egypt during the twentieth century.

Despite its seeming boldness, Roy's study is superior in many ways to many others on the subject in its vision, sensitivity and methodological rigour; as a sociologist, he pays special attention to issues such as groups, identity, culture and ideology, and explicitly parts from the generalist accounts, suggesting that Islam's political attitude cannot be essentialized, taking both the orientalists and Muslim reformist intellectuals to task for such simplistic explanations. 'Concrete political practices during [Islam's history] have been numerous and complex, and Muslim societies have been sociologically diverse.' He contends one must go past such broad statements as, 'In Islam, there is no separation between religion and politics.' Refusing to fall into what he calls the orientalist error of either lumping all Islamic currents together or accepting one view within Islam to the exclusion of all others, he explicitly focuses only on what he calls 'the Islamist current' or Islamism.

Roy defines it as the ideology of 'the activist groups who see in Islam as much a political ideology as a religion' and who, in so doing, are breaking from the main Islamic tradition. These movements, in particular the Muslim Brotherhood in Egypt and Jama'at-e-Islami in South Asia,[5] starting in the 1930s and 1940s, 'mounted challenges against both the West and the regimes in place in the Middle East'. The poignant question Roy asks is: 'Does contemporary political Islam offer an alternative to Muslim societies?' (p. vii) His answer is a loud and clear no.

Roy insists that Islam is not the reason for the failure of states in the Middle East; states in much of the Third World suffer from similar crises of corruption, instability and failure to modernize: in his words, 'Islam is not a "cause". Could it have been a cure? I believe that the Islamist moment closed a door: that of revolution and the Islamic state. Only the rhetoric remains' (pp. x–xi).

However, despite its resounding and indubitable failure, Islamism has not disappeared from the scene, but indeed it is spreading and 'being integrated into politics, leaving its mark on mores and conflicts'. Nonetheless, starting with the last two to three decades of the twentieth century, it has 'lost its original impetus'; it has 'social-democratized' itself. 'It no longer offers a model for a different society or a brighter future.' More specifically, Roy writes,

> Islamism has been transformed into a type of neo-fundamentalism, concerned solely with reestablishing Muslim law, the Shari'a, without inventing new political forms, which means that it is condemned

> to serving as a mere cover for a political logic that eludes it – a logic in which we ultimately find the traditional ethic, tribal, or communal divisions, ever ready to change their discourse of legitimization, hidden beneath the new social categories and regimes.

We should note here that Roy's decisive judgement on the performance of Islamism is based on specific criteria: it has failed because it did not furnish new, redemptive, political forms, nor did it succeed on the whole in bringing about revolutions that it promised. Later, he offers intellectual reasons for why this project did not simply fail historically, but was structurally doomed to fail because it was fundamentally flawed. It is this second type of critique that I single out for investigation here.

Roy's conclusion is that Islamism, especially in its obsession with the state, was a break from the long-standing Islamic tradition of the *ulama*, which has been by and large not only apolitical and legalistic, but also, due to its decentralized authority, anti-totalitarian.

> The Shari'a has two characteristics, its autonomy and its incompletion. The Shari'a does not depend on any state, on any actual positive law, on any political decision; it thereby creates a space that is parallel to the political space, to power, which, it is true, can circumvent the Shari'a or manipulate it (hence the strong theme of the corruption of the judge), but which cannot make it into something other than what it is: an autonomous, infinite commentary.[6]

What stands out in Roy's account is the resistance of the Shari'a to institutionalization, its lack of 'institutional closure' as well as 'conceptual closure' (p. 10); perhaps what Roy means by this is that the Shari'a is actualized through the opinion of a judge (*qadi*), which is always just that, and can be objected to on the basis of Shari'a. These features of the Shari'a make totalitarianism unlikely, except in complete violation of it; such as Atatürk or Saddam Hussein's secular totalitarianisms. Roy calls it 'a weakness in the political space' – which means that a government's aggression can never incontestably claim the Shari'a as its basis, that it can be (and historically has been) condemned on 'ethical' grounds as tyranny and un-Islamic.

However, there has also been activist reformist tradition in Islamic history in the margins of this main tradition, which in Roy's view has been idealistic, *utopian*, fixated on the golden-age ideal of early Islam, and perpetually *unfulfilled*. Islamism was no exception: it was a reaction to modernity built on this utopian reformist tradition in Islamic history, which was unique in that it adopted Marxist ideology and vocabulary and built on anti-colonialism and anti-Westernism that had brewed in the Third World.

Roy's key analytical contention is that the Islamist movements' attempts to return to true Islam are deceptive, they are merely Third Worldisms, a product of modernity, for 'modernity itself produces its own forms of protest' (p. 1). 'As much from a sociological as from an intellectual point of view, these movements are products of the modern world' (p. 3), for their recruits are rarely traditionally educated mullahs; rather they are products of secular education, from recently urbanized or impoverished middle classes, who received their political education from the Marxists on college campuses and injected it with Qur'anic terminology. They have left behind traditional values of chivalry and respect for authority and they are fascinated by consumerist values, willing recipients of Western cultural imperialism. Roy, of course, is far from alone in this judgement.[7]

If not traditional, is Islamism properly modern? According to Roy, not really. It is anti-modern, because Islamists fail, like traditional Islam, to theoretically separate virtue and piety from what they imagine public political institutions to be. Islamism failed because it reproduced a flaw in the Shari'a. The significance of this particular critique will become clear shortly.

A Critique

I have presented Roy's views at length, partly because of their formidable theoretical as well as empirical insights, and partly because these virtues allow my own critique to be more fruitful. I will critique the two fundamental premises of Roy's analysis: that Islamism is best seen as a reaction to modernity, and that its project failed because the commitment to the Shari'a is inherently contradictory to political institutions.

Is Islamism Islamic?

I contend that even though Roy explicitly decries reducing the interaction between Islam and politics to any one form as essentialism, his judgement on the Shari'a as being monolithically apolitical (lacking certain closures), and any attempt to engage in the Shari'a-based politics as necessarily breaking away from that tradition cannot be but seen as his own residual essentialism. Islamism may well be an instance of Third Worldism and a mere reaction to modernity, but that judgement, I argue, cannot be made based merely on sociological factors (such as dress code, vocabulary of resistance, class status or use of modern technology). Any such judgement will have to presume a definition of proper Islam, and some criteria for belonging to the proper Islamic tradition. How else could one understand Roy's charge that '[t]he Islamists engage in a political and social reading of the Qur'an, made possible precisely by the distortion of Muslim tradition'?[8] This charge is perhaps even self-contradictory, since Roy began with the disclaimer that he takes 'at its word what Islamism says about Islam ... without taking up the other visions of Islam and without studying the texts of the Qur'an or the Sunna' (p. viii).

Roy's own vivid presumptions of what proper religion consists of makes more than a subtle contribution to his view of Islamists; they are worst of all guilty of 'disenchantment of the world ... For they borrow from this modernity the refusal to return to the real tradition in the name of an imaginary Tradition: they reject popular religious practice, the village, Sufism, philosophy' (p. 22). Judgments like this, indeed, tell us more about what secularism takes to be the proper role of religion than about Islamism's relationship to Islam.

The lack of a satisfactory way to resolve this conundrum, I conclude, is a key deficiency that Roy's work shares with many others on contemporary Islam.

Building on the work of Talal Asad, I have argued elsewhere that Islam is best understood as a discursive tradition, which, for our purpose, means that it is a set of commitments, both intellectual and practical, related to belief and reason.[9] And while not independent of sociological reality, what is traditionally Islamic is not determined by such factors as Roy has enumerated: one may wear jeans and use Marxist or liberal democratic vocabulary, while also arguing persuasively that one is traditionally Islamic. Put differently, we must pay attention to the *conceptual grammar* and not merely the *vocabulary* of the concepts to determine their merit in the coin of tradition.[10]

This lack of attention to the structure and history of Islamic discursive tradition further disables questions about the use that various Islamists and modernist reformers might have authentically made of that tradition. All calls for authenticity, to Roy, become merely guises for anti-Westernism. This characterization of Muslim activist movements as doubly pathological is a result of the perspective which desires a clear distinction between modernity and tradition, both of which it seeks to define through a set of dichotomies, in which true tradition is unchanging, non-rational and backward-looking, in direct contrast with modernity.[11]

Any simple attempt to define Islamism in familiar terms – diverse, evolving and contested as it is – should meet with some scepticism. While an Islamist might identify readily with some of Roy's characterizations (most likely those that are general and applicable to almost any engaged Muslim), others are quite contested among the Islamists (those that are of analytical interest). For instance, the positions of Islamists with respect to such issues as the right to individual interpretation of the Qur'an are almost as varied as they are within the entire Muslim community, which includes staunch traditionalists as well as liberal modernists, although the Islamists admittedly have more often than not argued for the traditionally accepted interpretations in Islamic history that favoured individual exercise of reason. They have also been chastised by more radical modernists for not having gone far enough in rejecting the Islamic tradition.[12]

Similarly, the emphasis of the early Islamists on 'reform from the top' has been contested from the very outset,[13] and particularly diluted by new generations of Islamists who – at times as a result of political frustrations and at others as a result of internal discursive development – have formulated different opinions on the matter.[14]

The wide reception and reproduction of Islamism makes it naturally more difficult to justify marginalizing Islamism as merely fortuitous or as a product of local social or political conditions. An account of Islamism must lie at the centre of any attempt to understand the workings of the modern Muslim world. Of course, the variance from one version of Islamist politics to another is significant enough that any general account without proper attention to local circumstances would be incomplete.

Modernity and Its Pathologies

Roy's reliance on Third Worldism and response-to-modernity explanation presumes a *ubiquitous and unified modernity*, which itself needs no further examination, rather than prompting us to examine the exact ways in which the secular modernity may have been exported–imported, and specific ways in which secularism works in specific circumstances.

On the flip side, the explanation, or rather explaining away, of what has been called Islamism as a reaction to modernity allows 'Islamism' to be seen as a passing fad, which is over and can be judged and evaluated. Since political Islam is episodic and disconnected, one does not need the investigation of Islamic tradition in order to understand it, nor does one have to engage seriously with Islamist discourse itself in a give-and-take form: one can observe 'them', their appearance and vocabulary, rather than examine and engage with their writings and arguments. The Islamist critique can, in this view, pose no challenge to the liberal, secular theory, which is presumed to be lucid, unified and unproblematic.[15]

Is the Shari'a Apolitical?

The other aspect of Roy's critique that I wish to question is his judgement that Shari'a is essentially apolitical, and Islamism's attempt to politicize it was futile for that reason. Roy is right that the paradigmatic and essentialist inseparability of Islam and politics, as held by some orientalists, cannot be maintained. He is also right in suggesting that the legal (*fiqh*) tradition that is identified within many cases tended to be apolitical, and in any case not conducive to providing the legal foundation of a modern nation state.

Many contemporary scholars have advanced our understanding of how this different structuring of law and politics in the Shari'a might relate, positively and negatively, to the projects of liberalism, democracy and nation-building. Sherman Jackson, for instance, has pointed out that the mainstream medieval jurists like al-Qarafi explicitly deliberated on limiting the legal tradition that Roy calls 'autonomous, infinite commentary' for political purposes, without compromising the autonomy of law. Indeed, these scholars emphasize the ways in which this legal pluralism may be more conducive to the autonomy of moral communities in a democracy than standard models of liberal secularism.

In my own work on Islamic political tradition, I have argued that one major and far-reaching critique of the apolitical tendencies of mainstream Islamic legal tradition was undertaken from within, by Ibn Taymiyya – a formidable fourteenth-century jurist–theologian whose work is important not least because of the key role his thought plays in the majority of contemporary Islamists and modernists. Ibn Taymiyya is popular among contemporary Islamists of various inclinations precisely because he sought to recover the Shari'a-based politics by limiting, though by no means eliminating, the fluid authority of the legists, and sharing it with the rulers – so long as they committed themselves to the ideal of the Shari'a.[16]

Roy summarily dismisses the activist–reformist tradition of Islam as recurrent fundamentalism of Islamic history, which remained perpetually unfulfilled, because it was *utopian*. Incidentally, as I have argued elsewhere, Ibn Taymiyya's distinctive contribution was precisely his *political pragmatism*, which loosened the utopian and ahistorical demands that the dominant juristic tradition made on the ruler. The readings of Islamic tradition by contemporary groups are many, some profound and refreshing, some mediocre and self-serving; no single judgement on all will do.[17] The apolitical nature of Islamic tradition cannot be taken for granted, nor can the various Islamists' claims be dismissed simply on these grounds.

To sum up my critique of studies of contemporary Islam, of which Roy's is only one particularly fine example, I contend that to see all engagements of Islam with the political sphere as merely a reaction to modernity and Western domination, inauthentic both to Islamist tradition and modernity, allows a casual dismissal that is not only theoretically flawed, but especially alarming if juxtaposed with the frequent observation by scholars that an overwhelming number of people in some Muslim societies identify with it. In the words of John Voll regarding Egypt, 'If one looks at those who are actively involved in some way in the Islamic resurgence then the number of people is in the millions and, in some respects, represents the majority of the society.'[18] The resilience and popularity of Islamism raises another interesting problem. Some studies treat Islamist movements as though they were shaped entirely by a single core group of ideologues with a singular vision. This is far from the case. Emerging in a milieu of resistance against colonialism or its legacy, and necessarily lacking any institutional authority to impose an ideology, an important criterion of their success must have been their persuasiveness to the literate portion of the Muslim populace. On the level playing field, where religious approaches to modern challenges were all equally bereaved of institutional support, the only discriminating factor was their aptness to the public eye. This relatively free market of ideas, bound, of course, by traditional limitations on Islamic discourses as well as local conditions, is one way to account for the authenticity and acceptability of Islamic programmes by the masses, and may explain the resilience and popularity of Islamic movements. Whatever their failures, it may be fair to suggest that they have been an effective, perhaps the most effective, means of political empowerment of the masses and democratization in the contemporary Islamic world.

Contemporary Islamic discourse is a living tradition, and the only way to understand it, and to understand how a variety of Muslim groups and individuals relate to it, is to engage with it. This is not to say that an outside observer is not in a position to critique Islam or Islamism, but that that engagement cannot be like studying an object, objectively, from outside, but rather an entry into a discourse, in which one may point out incoherence within the claims of a certain tradition, or even flaws in the tradition itself on grounds of one's own commitments and history.[19]

Critiquing Islamism: the Problem of Situatedness

Roy's work is not devoid of this kind of substantive critique of Islamism, and it is to one such contention of Roy that I now turn. Roy contends that the Islamist political project is flawed inherently because it followed the Islamic tradition in its fatal error of conflating political institutions and personal virtue. Roy writes:

> In my view, [Islamism] has failed because Islamist thought, at the end of an intellectual trajectory that tries to integrate modernity, ultimately meets up with the 'Islamic political imagination' of the tradition and its essential premise: politics can be founded only on individual virtue.[20]

The desire to mix up virtue with politics explains to Roy why the Shari'a has failed, politically speaking, in history, and why Islamism met the same fate. But we may ask: why require separation of law and ethics with such decisiveness? To require putting an end to injustice, tyranny, oppression, domination, cruelty – practices that violate nearly universally held, if variously understood and prioritized, values of justice, freedom and happiness – makes immediate sense. That the Islamist groups have failed in accomplishing a just and stable society may be a valid critique; but how is a conceptual separation between law (public) and ethics (private) necessary to attain these ends? I will ignore here the question of whether the Shari'a indeed relies only on personal virtue of the ruler, or whether it conceptually separates law (public) and ethics (private) – or even if there is one unified view on these issues that can be spoken of as Shari'a's view; it is sufficient to note that Western scholars have traditionally noted that Islamic law is different in origin and nature from Western conceptions of positive law.[21]

It is exactly this issue, namely a particular type of separation of public and private, and law and ethics, that Talal Asad has identified as a historical precondition for secular modernity in the West. In his study of secularization attempts in Egypt, Asad points out how this aspect of the Shari'a, of 'mixing' law and ethics, was explicitly targeted by the modernizing Egyptian intellectuals and elite. In other words, what scholars like Roy take to be self-evident is, according to Asad, a product of Western history. Indeed, Roy himself recognizes at a general level this problem of imposing the accidents of Western history onto non-Western traditions, but fails to see that his own premise is precisely such an exercise.

Roy, accordingly, chastises much of Western analyses of the Islamic political world for their erroneous comparativism. He complains that Western scholars often either deem Islamic political thought irrelevant to the real political situation or explain the problem of Muslim states' failure to conform to the modern nation state model in terms of absences in the Islamic intellectual tradition (such as lack of territorial boundaries). In perhaps the most sophisticated parts of his analysis, Roy writes:

> But far from being inherently and originally marked by a lack, Islamic political thought is inscribed within a different configuration of the relationship between power and law. That this configuration is in turn a source of difficulties is not in doubt, but one must measure it in relation to its original meaning, not in relation to the Western state. What is original is the place of the Shari'a, Muslim law, with respect to power.

Modern Western democratic liberalism, Roy says, emerges in reaction to totalitarian possibilities that the early modern nation state acquired by monopolizing religion (religion of the king is the religion of the people?); thus, the ideals that embody the solutions are conceptually solutions to these problems. In Islamic history, totalitarianism never posed a serious threat due to these structural features of the Shari'a (or the Shari'a as historically, though not incontestably, existed); hence, the ideals that inform the solution, even while borrowing Western vocabulary, were concerned with a different set of threats: these, according to Roy, are the autonomy of the family space, the home, the honour and justice in the political domain (pp. 10–11). In other words, according to Roy, liberty is valued in the Islamic world in the private sphere, while the value demanded in the political sphere is justice.

This analysis is insightful, and while I find compelling the idea that the Muslim political resistance demands reflect the shape of structural vacancies specific to Islamic history as much as Western demands reflect Western history, Roy's specific catalogue of concepts that motivate Muslim politics (liberty in the private sphere and justice in the political) is contestable, if only because he does not spend much effort trying to understand the history that might have shaped Islamic politics and its vacancies and tensions, and because the wide variety of Muslim societies and discourses cannot be lumped together.

While Roy does not further reflect on the implications of this insight and arguably goes on to contradict it himself, it leads us to the more general question of how Muslim political resistance and its ideals are to be understood. Recent data such as Gallup's recent poll show that nearly 80 per cent of Muslims desire both democracy and the Shari'a at a political level.[22] They see the Shari'a as not only compatible with democracy but indeed desirous of it. This can be seen as the triumph of a key Western construct which has developed in its specific form only in the modern West. Since the Muslim world is clearly not impervious to the lessons of Western history, what are we to make of the Muslim desire to reject secularism in favour of the Shari'a? Is this to be seen as simply political naiveté, ignorance of the necessary interdependence of liberal-secular political ideals, economic capitalism and individualistic ethics – as it has been in the West? Or are we to understand it as forms of political ideals amenable to the historical experience and structural conditions of the Islamic world?

Roy emphasizes that in the modern world there are many 'secularisms': French *laïcité* is not British secularism, where the Anglican Church is formally the state church, or American secularism, where 'no president can be elected who does not speak of God'.[23] Regardless, however, what unites them all, in Roy's view, is the necessity of hypocrisy every religion must embrace when dealing with 'earthly political realities'.[24] Islam, he forcefully contends, is following suit.

How can these different expectations or predictions be understood and analysed? Without paying attention simultaneously to sociology as well as discursive tradition, we run the risk of knitting our premises into the conclusions, as I suggest Roy has done. The only way we can know whether the various societies in the Islamic world are bound to secularize in some way (French, British, American, some other way?), or to find alternative ways to arrange its political life effectively and prosperously without effecting a rupture from their past, is to pay attention both to their socio-political arrangements as well as their evolving perceptions of their past.

NOTES

1 Talal Asad, *Genealogies of Religion: Discipline and Reasons of Power in Christianity and Islam* (Baltimore: Johns Hopkins University Press, 1993) and idem., *Formations of the Secular* (Stanford University Press, 2003).

2 Alasdair MacIntyre, *Whose Justice? Which Rationality?* (Notre Dame: University of Notre Dame Press, 1988), p. 356.

3 Put differently, modern studies are often caught between the essentialist presumption, 'Islam is the problem', and the social scientists' impulse, 'Islam is naught', in studying a movement that claims 'Islam is the solution'. For examples of the account that favours essentialist explanations with little regard for the particularities of Muslim societies and claims, see Bernard Lewis's *What Went Wrong? The Clash Between Islam and Modernity in the Middle East* (New York: Harper Perennial, 2003) and *The Crisis of Islam: Holy War and Unholy Terror* (New York: Modern Library, 2003). For an emphasis on social, political and economic factors, to the exclusion of Islam's history or tradition, see Shireen Hunter, in *Politics of Islamic Revivalism* (Bloomington: Indiana University Press, 1988), p. ix.

4 Olivier Roy, *Failure of Political Islam*, tr. Carol Volk (New York: Harvard University Press, 1994). The following remark, directed at Norwegian policy-makers, relies on Roy's account, thus giving us a recap of his account as well as evidence of its influence: 'The Islamists wants to purify Islam and reform the state with a particular emphasis on the introduction of Shari'a – the holy law of Islam. Although implementation of the Shari'a is a goal, society needs to be Islamized. The Islamists approve of schooling for women and their participation in social and economic life. Islamists maintain their right to individual interpretation of the Qur'an and the Sunna (Traditions of the Prophet's life) and they can therefore be considered anticlerical. The importance the Islamists place in society means that their political philosophy centres on the leader (*amir*) and the advisory council (*shura*). Islamists believe in the reform of the state through social and political action. To accomplish this it is necessary to "leave the mosque", so to speak. The Islamists hence advocate a reform of society from "the top".' 'Political Islam in South Asia', *Are Knudsen* (a study prepared for the Norwegian Department of Foreign Affairs, September 2002), <http://www.cmi.no/publications/file/?796=political-islam-in-south-asia> (accessed 29 March 2009).

5 The most detailed accounts of the two movements are Richard Mitchell, *The Society of the Muslim Brothers* (Oxford: OUP, 1993), originally published in 1969; and Seyyed Vali Reza Nasr, *The Vanguard of the Islamic Revolution: The Jama'at-e Islami of Pakistan* (Berkeley: University of California Press, 1994).

6 Roy, *Failure*, pp. 9–10.
7 For example, A. Ayalon, 'From Fitna to Thawra', *Studia Islamica*, Vol. 66 (1987); and N. Keddie, 'Islamic Revival as Third Worldism', in J. P. Digard (ed.), *Le Cuisinier et le Philosophe: Hommage a Maxime Rodinson* (Paris: Maisonneuve et Larose, 1982). Philip Khoury similarly writes that Islam is used as only 'the most convenient, readily available instrument' of domination and manipulation by certain urban classes, who see Islam as 'a vehicle of political and economic demands, rather than being itself the "impulse" behind these demands'. See his 'Islamic Revivalism and Crisis of the Secular State in the Arab World, an Historical Appraisal', in Ibrahim Ibrahim (ed.), *Arab Resources: The Transformation of a Society* (London: Croom Helm, 1983), p. 215.
8 Roy, *Failure*, p. 49.
9 Ovamir Anjum, 'Islam as a Discursive Tradition: Talal Asad and His Interlocutors', *Comparative Studies of South Asia, Africa and the Middle East* 27 (3) (2007).
10 With respect to living traditions like Islamism, an outsider's judgement without examining arguments is particularly unjustified. Khurram Murad, a follower of Mawdudi and a leading thinker in his own right, speaks explicitly of the problem of using Western vocabulary, '[C]an we convey Islam in our time, talk about it meaningfully, without recourse to some contemporary vocabulary? Do we use contemporary vocabulary only because we are caught in the web of Western discourse or because we have succumbed to the success of Western ideas? ... I think we can only make contemporary men hear and understand the message of God through the words that he knows ... Only when we meet him on common territory, however small, can we hold him by the hand and take him along to a new territory.' Khurran Murad, ed. and trans., *The Islamic Movement: The Dynamics of Power and Change* (The Islamic Foundation, 1984), p. 18. One may, of course, find this argument unconvincing, but ignoring it is hardly responsible scholarship.
11 Talal Asad suggests precisely this: '[M]any writers describe the movements in Iran and Egypt as only partly modern and suggest that it's their mixing of tradition and modernity that accounts for their "pathological" character. This kind of description paints Islamic movements as being somehow inauthentically traditional on the assumption that "real tradition" is unchanging, repetitive and non-rational. In this way, these movements cannot be understood on their own terms as being at once modern and traditional, both authentic and creative at the same time. The development of politico-religious movements ought to force people to rethink the uniquely Western model of secular modernity. One may want to challenge aspects of these movements, but this ought to be done on specific grounds. It won't do to measure everything by grand conceptions of authentic modernity.' Talal Asad, 'Modern Power and the Reconfiguration of Religious Traditions', an interview with Saba Mahmood, *Stanford Electronic Humanities Review*, <http://www.stanford.edu/group/SHR/5-1/text/asad.html> (accessed 29 March 2009).
12 One instance of what we might consider 'engaged criticism' is provided by Fazlur Rahman, in particular in his *Islam and Modernity* (University of Chicago Press, 1984). Rahman, who ended his career as a professor at the University of Chicago, was a modern Muslim reformist, and a particularly able, sophisticated, intimate but clearly ideologically motivated critic of Islamism and Islamic tradition

generally. He was personally familiar with one influential instance of Islamism, Abul al-Ala Mawdudi's Jama'at-e-Islami in mid-twentieth-century Pakistan. He chastises this group for failing to take modern reform of the Islamic intellectual tradition seriously, for aligning in their politics with the more traditional *ulama* movements, and generally for failing to give sufficient weight to establishing institutions of higher learning that would respond to the challenges of the modern world (p. 117). Rahman is also critical, on the other hand, of those who have earned degrees in Islam from Western universities but have in the process become 'orientalists' – their work 'is not Islamically purposeful or creative' (p. 124). While Rahman's concerns are serious, his own ambivalence towards Western modernity shows the difficulty of determining how and what to reform while staying true to Islam – staying connected, that is, to the Islamic tradition in some authentic way. Rahman's passionate and at times radical critiques of Islamic tradition, including his untraditional view of such fundamental sources as *Hadith* and the Qur'an, amounted to a total rupture with the history of Islam – a position that was belied by his own adherence to some aspects of the tradition itself. (See, for instance, his posthumously published *Revival and Reform in Islam*). To press the issue of engaged critique further, no account of Jama'at-e-Islami's shortcomings based on Rahman's critique would be sufficient or fair without taking into account the Jama'at's direct or indirect response to Rahman's concerns, *and* without forming a subjective view on the matter. This instance simply demonstrates the messy and involved nature of dealing with questions of discursive continuity, rupture and transformation in complex traditions.

13 For an early critique of Abul al-Ala Mawdudi by a co-founder of Jama'at-e-Islami, a highly regarded and 'traditionally' trained scholar, Abul Hasan Ali Nadwi (or Nadvi; d. 1999), see S. Vali Reza Nasr, *Mawdudi and the Making of Islamic Revivalism* (Oxford: OUP, 1996), p. 62. Nasr, writing in the same vein as Roy, repeats the expected thesis that Mawdudi's interpretation was new and untraditional, as shown by Nadwi. The particular point of dispute was how to interpret the main purpose of the Qur'an, as addressed to human success or primarily the exposition of other-worldly realities. The dispute is better understood, however, as internal polemics, and a matter of degree rather than nature: Nadwi did not deny the Qur'an's this-worldly dimension – as the entire edifice of Islamic jurisprudence relies on it; nor did Mawdudi, as is clear from his exegesis, deny the spiritual and allegorical aspect of the Qur'an. Although I cannot demonstrate this in this brief space, in my view Mawdudi's mastery of the traditions of jurisprudence or theology, while not outstanding – he seems not to have appreciated the full complexity and subtlety of either tradition – was far from mediocre. The traditional *ulama*'s attacks against his qualifications, which Nasr highlights, need to be seen in the proper polemical context. Regardless, this is best seen as an internal Islamist debate: both authors influenced, albeit to different degrees, the tradition of Islamism.

14 See, for instance, Azzam Tamimi, *Rachid Ghannouchi: A Democrat Within Islamism* (Oxford: OUP, 2001); Brian Glancy, *Liberalism Without Secularism? Rachid Ghannouchi and the Theory and Politics of Islamic Democracy* (Dublin, 2007); John Esposito and John Voll, *Islam and Democracy* (Oxford: OUP, 1996).

15 This presumption is beginning to be challenged, although in a rudimentary way and often unheeded, by studies pointing out the similarities between the Islamist

critiques of secular liberalism and the 'internal' Western philosophical critiques of the same; one such study being the political scientist Roxanne Euben's *Enemy in the Mirror* (1999).

16 Ovamir Anjum, 'Reason and Politics in Medieval Islamic Thought: The Taymiyyan Moment', PhD Dissertation, University of Wisconsin-Madison, 2008.

17 As Yahya Michot's recent work, *Muslims Under Non-Muslim Rule* (Interface Publications, 2007) has argued that some of the more radical Islamist groups have often misunderstood Ibn Taymiyya's work in this regard – as they have the classical juristic tradition. But that may be a result of lack of prolonged engagement with the tradition rather than an attempt to intentionally break from it.

18 Quoted in Saba Mahmood, 'Islamism and Fundamentalism', *Middle East Report*, Nov.–Dec. 1994, p. 29.

19 Talal Asad writes, 'To write about a tradition is to be in a certain narrative relation to it, a relation that will vary according to whether one supports or opposes the tradition, or regards it as morally neutral. The coherence that each party finds, or fails to find, in that tradition will depend on their particular historical position. In other words, there clearly is not, nor can there be, such a thing as a universally acceptable account of a living tradition. Any representation of tradition is contestable. What shape that contestation takes, if it occurs, will be determined not only by the powers and knowledges each side deploys, but by the collective life they aspire to – or to whose survival they are quite indifferent.' Talal Asad, 'The Idea of an Anthropology of Islam', *Occasional Paper* (Georgetown University Center for Contemporary Arab Studies, 1986), p. 17.

20 Roy, *Failure*, p. 21.

21 *Baber Johansen, Contingency in a Sacred Law: Legal and Ethical Norms in the Muslim Fiqh* (Brill, 1999), in particular see the first chapter, 'Introduction: The Muslim Fiqh as Sacred Law: Religion, Law and Ethics in a Normative System', in particular pp. 47–72. Also see Talal Asad, *Formations*, p. 242.

22 John Esposito and Dalia Mogahed, *Who Speaks for Islam?* (Gallup Press, 2008); see also, <http://www.gallup.com/poll/104731/Muslims-Want-Democracy-Theocracy.aspx> (accessed 30 March 2009), for data that indicates that a vast majority of Muslims in most countries want the Shari'a as well as democracy as their political system.

23 Olivier Roy, *Secularism Confronts Islam* (Columbia University Press, 2007), p. 13.

24 Roy, *Secularism*, p. 25.

4

Neo-liberalism and 'Third Way' Islamic Activism: Fethullah Gülen and Turkey's New Elite

Joshua D. Hendrick

The World's Most Influential Public Intellectual

The May–June 2008 editions of *Foreign Policy* (*FP*) and *Prospect* magazines published a list of the '100 most influential public intellectuals in the world'. The editors of these two influential publications asked their readers to vote for the top twenty. Among the top 100 were two Turkish citizens: the renowned author and social commentator, Orhan Pamuk, and the retired imam and religious leader, M. Fethullah Gülen. Pamuk's inclusion on the list came as no surprise. He was an internationally bestselling author, and in 2006 he was awarded the Nobel Prize for Literature. By contrast, Fethullah Gülen's books have never sold well internationally, and up until recently, his influence has been restricted to the Turkish context. For the past twenty-five years in Turkey, however, no one individual has aroused more praise or more controversy than Fethullah Gülen.

Known as Hocaefendi ('esteemed teacher') to those who admire him, Fethullah Gülen is the figurehead atop the so-called 'Gülen Movement' (GM), a transnational Islamic advocacy community that has attracted international media attention in recent years because of the extent of its education network, which now spans over 100 countries.[1] If Gülen's inclusion in the *FP*/*Prospect* poll surprised many, his victory was nothing short of dumbfounding. About a week after announcing the list of 100, tens of thousands of votes were registered in Gülen's favour. When he surged past his competitors, *FP* and *Prospect* thought they had a problem with a computer hacker infiltrating their online voting system. After a week of checking and re-checking, however, *FP* and *Prospect* named Mr Fethullah Gülen 'The World's Most Influential Public Intellectual' (Nuttal 2008).

Scepticism

Despite his recognition as an influential public intellectual, Fethullah Gülen is also known for allegations of pretence. Fears about *Fethullahcılar* ('Fethullahists') infiltrating the Turkish bureaucracy and patiently 'Islamicizing' the secular nature of the Turkish Republic are common. In 1999, Gülen faced charges that he was the leader of a clandestine organization that directly threatened the integrity of the Turkish state. In a video excerpt that GM followers insist was edited and taken out of context, Fethullah Gülen instructed his community as follows:

> You must move in the arteries of the system, without anyone noticing your existence, until you reach all the power centres ... You must wait until such time as you have gotten all the state power, until you have brought to your side all the power of the constitutional institutions in Turkey ... Until that time, any step taken would be too early ... Now, I have expressed my feelings and thoughts to you all – in confidence ... trusting your loyalty and sensitivity to secrecy. I know that when you leave here – [just] as you discard your empty juice boxes, you must discard the thoughts and feelings expressed here.[2]

By the time this clip aired on Turkish television, Fethullah Gülen had moved to the United States for 'health reasons'. In May 2006, a lower Ankara court acquitted Gülen on all charges against him, a summary judgement that was upheld by Turkey's 11th Court and again in the 9th branch of the Supreme Court of Appeals. Despite his vindication, however, Gülen remained in the US.

Does Fethullah Gülen's legal vindication and his growing recognition as an influential public intellectual indicate that the perceived 'clash' between Islam and secularism in Turkey has given way to pluralism, moderation and cooperation?[3] If so, how are observers of Turkish politics expected to understand the revival of tension between secularism and Islam? What role does the GM play in promoting or ameliorating revived tensions, and what are the implications of the GM's continued success? This chapter addresses these questions by situating the GM in the context of Turkey's political and economic transformation in the twenty-first century. Unlike much of the literature on the GM, which is either unnecessarily alarmist[4] or uncritically hagiographic,[5] this chapter offers an alternative analysis. Because the GM is organized in fluid, self-replicating and self-adjusting social and economic networks, this chapter begins by outlining the features of network advocacy and the opportunities that expand in the context of Turkey's integration into the global economy. After highlighting the salience of social networks in the field of collective mobilization, it introduces the reader to Anthony Giddens' notion of 'third way' politics in the contemporary era of post-Cold War globalization. In so doing, the GM is posited as exemplifying a Turkish–Islamic variant 'third way' theory as it is expressed in Islamic terms. This is followed by a brief overview of Turkey's twentieth-century development model and an introduction to the significance of the 1980 military coup and the 1982 constitution that followed. The second half of this chapter provides the reader with a brief overview of GM's transnational advocacy network and argues that its aims are neither as conniving as alarmists maintain, nor as benign as loyal followers insist. Rather, the GM is assessed as an advocacy network that exemplifies a specifically Muslim variant of global neo-liberalism, and is thus representative of Turkish integration.

I. Globalization, Transnational Advocacy Networks, and 'A-Political Politics'

Margaret Keck and Katheryn Sikkink (1998) define networks as 'forms of organization characterized by voluntary, reciprocal, and horizontal patterns of communication and exchange' (p. 8). Networks constitute themselves both as 'structures', organizationally bounded institutions linked by a common identity and shared purpose, *and* as 'agents', actors in their own right that affect society in such a way that is greater than the sum of the actors who constitute their parts.[6] Relationships cultivated between network actors serve as start-up investments for the generation of social capital.[7] Nan Lin defines social capital in this regard as 'resources embedded in a social structure, which are accessed and/or mobilized in purposive actions'.[8] Social capital is measured by the relative surplus available to individual actors in a network, the level of access to those resources, and the strategic use of those resources once accessed.

The case of the GM exemplifies the fact that the underlying effect of an advocacy network is 'persuasion or socialization ... since they are not powerful in the traditional sense of the word, they must use the power of their information, ideas, and strategies to alter the information and value contexts within which states make policies' (p. 16). Having capitalized on Turkey's integration, the GM built influence by investing in the global economy, by recruiting international sympathizers, and by reframing democracy, market competition, human rights and religious freedom as specifically 'Islamic' social codes. In so doing, the GM plays an active role in the current effort to wrestle domestic hegemony from Turkey's twentieth-century oligarchy, which has recently illustrated that it can no longer stop 'the emergence of a new Turkey'.[9]

'Third Way' Political Islam and Its Discontents

In career history interviews with senior members in the GM enterprise (i.e., first- and second-generation students of Fethullah Gülen who now work as editors, writers, journalists and/or executives at a GM-affiliated media, publishing or financial–trade institution) a recurring theme emerged. According to these individuals, the GM's strategy is best understood as a 'non-political' engagement with Turkish and world society.[10] Based on this data, I conclude that GM loyalists frame their political engagement as 'non-political' in line with Anthony Giddens' notion of 'third way', 'dialogic' politics, or, better still, with the politics of 'reflexive modernization'.[11] 'The third way' is Giddens' prescription for Europe's social democratic parties (specifically Britain's New Labour Party) to acknowledge that the old Left–Right dichotomies have given way to the transformative processes of neo-liberal restructuring. 'Politics' has since penetrated the private sphere and individuals have subsequently shifted their political agendas away from 'emancipation' and 'ideology' towards what he calls 'life politics' – personal gratification and self-protection:

> Life politics is a politics of a reflexively mobilized order … which, on an individual and collective level, has radically altered the existential parameters of social activity … life politics concerns political issues which flow from processes of self-actualization in post-traditional contexts, where globalizing influences intrude deeply into the reflexive project of the self, and conversely where processes of self-realization influence global strategies.[12]

Taking the place of old political institutions (i.e., parties and unions) are trust networks rooted in lifestyle–identity groups that now function as the primary mechanisms for collective representation. Rather than ideological contestation, 'third way politics' promotes 'dialogue' between opposing groups, and aims for 'tolerance' instead of universal acceptance:

> Dialogic democracy presumes only that dialogue in a public space provides a means of living along with the other in a relation of mutual tolerance – whether that 'other' be an individual or a global community of religious believers.[13]

Giddens' 'third way' is reminiscent of what GM loyalists and sympathizers refer to as Gülen's 'middle way' (in this case, between militant secularism and radical Islam). According to Ahmet Kuru:

> Gülen's understanding of the middle way opposes both fatalism and the denial of destiny. For him, a Muslim can possess self-confidence about his or her own individual efficacy and productive power, while still believing in destiny and preserving his or her humility toward God.[14]

Jenny White cites the GM's middle way as exemplary of a general trend towards 'Muslimhood' in Turkey, a sociological state of being, whereby an Islamist confrontation with the state is deemed impossible:

> This evolution toward a moderate, non-confrontational Islamic participation project was the harbinger of a further receding of Islam into a cultural, ethical stance … [Turkish Muslimhood] projects a pluralist vision of an Islamic public sphere that reflects more closely the diverse nature of Islam in Turkey.[15]

The problem with the 'third way' (i.e., the 'middle way,' 'Muslimhood') is that 'dialogue' between individuals who are consumed with the constant necessity to make 'life choices' in an open and free public sphere (i.e., life-politics) presupposes the illusion of middle-class equality:

> [In third way theory] society is viewed as basically composed of middle classes; the only exceptions are a small elite of very rich on one side, and those who are 'excluded' on the other … By redefining the structural inequalities systematically produced by the market in terms of 'exclusion', one can dispense with the structural analysis of their causes, thereby avoiding the fundamental question of which changes in power relations are needed to tackle them … [The notion of a dialogic 'third way' democracy] makes clear the refusal to acknowledge that a society is always hegemonically

> constituted through a certain structure of power relations, [which] leads to accepting the existing hegemony and remaining trapped within the configuration of forces.[16]

The GM's collective effort to distance itself from politics needs to be understood within the context of global neo-liberalism, a hegemonic narrative that presupposes the inevitable collapse of political antagonism under 'third way' democratic institutions. Consciously or unconsciously, the GM's claim to offer a 'middle way' between militant secularism and radical Islamism is a local variant of Giddens' notion of dialogic politics, and is illustrative of little more than the localization of neo-liberal normativity. A central argument of this study, therefore, is that neo-liberal restructuring in post-1980 Turkey has led to a crisis of social hegemony, whereby former 'out groups' have taken advantage of newfound opportunities in the market to make a claim for social power. The GM is a product of this restructuring, and should thus be viewed as a primary collective actor in the localization (i.e., nationalization) of globalizing processes in Turkey.

Exclusivity and the Politics of Development

Turkey's twentieth-century founder and first president, Mustafa Kemal Atatürk ('Father of the Turks'), reframed the country's development project in accordance with a European sense of national self-determination, industrialization and secularization. The philosophy of nationalist Turkey was thus ultimately termed Kemalism, and was promoted to encapsulate 'six arrows' (populism, nationalism, republicanism, secularism, reformism and statism).[17] Over the course of the twentieth century, a 'Kemalist alliance' emerged, which connected Atatürk's Cumhuriyet Halk Partisi (People's Republican Party, CHP) with the civilian and military bureaucracies, state-sanctioned media holdings and industrial, family-based capital. With periods of turbulence and transition, the Kemalist alliance dominated Turkey's development project until its breakdown in the 1970s.

Twentieth-century industrialization was the responsibility of vertically integrated family-based capital, whose initial priority was to wrestle control of the Turkish economy from foreign holdings. To protect young domestic industries, state agencies heavily subsidized a number of family-based companies to allow for the emergence of a

'Turkish-owned' industrial sector (Buğra 1995). This initial effort to protect young domestic ventures from foreign competition, however, ultimately morphed into an oligarchy based on state favouritism, which excluded both foreign capital *and* small domestic capital from competing.[18] According to Buğra, state favouritism from the 1930s to the 1970s was 'more subtle than one that could be described in terms of sheer nepotism' because it was not merely a situation whereby handouts and favours were extended through patronage networks, 'it was a relationship in which the businessman, to be successful, had to convince political authorities of his desire and ability to serve the state throughout entrepreneurial activity' (p. 50). While there were only a handful of holdings selected to manage the Turkish economy before the Second World War (e.g., Koc Holding in the 1920s and Sabancı Holding in the 1930s), after the war a dozen new holdings joined the ranks of Turkey's oligarchy. By the 1970s, approximately 150 of Turkey's nearly 400 large private enterprises were represented by 30 holding companies.[19] State regulation and political favouritism led to the formation of an economy managed by a powerful state bureaucracy and a vassal group of loyal businessmen.

Exclusivity and the Politics of Social Engineering

Turkey's project of national self-determination was dictated by an oligarchic alliance whose actors promoted universalism (i.e., nationalism) on the one hand, and exclusivity (i.e., restricted access to business, industry, politics and education) on the other. Just as it was for all nationalist sentiments in the modern era, however, Kemalists had to contend for legitimacy and authority in Turkey's public sphere. Unlike their Ottoman predecessors, who governed over a multi-racial, multi-ethnic, multi-religious society that spanned three continents, Kemalists governed over a relatively small 'national' territory that was imagined as being rightfully dominated (culturally, linguistically and demographically) by one group.[20] Islam amounted to a formidable opponent, rather than to a unifying aspect of Turkish culture. For this reason, the most controversial 'arrow' in the Kemalist vision was the inclusion of 'secularism', as it was modelled after French *laïcité* (*laiklik*). In its Turkish form, secularism connoted less of a 'separation' between church and state than it did the 'monopolization' of faith and knowledge by the state. By controlling Anatolia's primary cultural unifier, Kemalists assumed that they could disconnect Turkey's citizenry from its Ottoman past. To accomplish this goal, the early regime abolished the institution of the Islamic Caliphate (1923), outlawed polygamy (1925), dissolved Sufi orders (1925), outlawed shrine veneration (1925), replaced Islamic law (*şeriat*) with the Swiss civil code (1926), outlawed the fez and the turban (1927), and reformed the written Turkish language from Arabic to Roman script (1927) (Zürcher 2004).

Via a new universal education system, Turkish students were inculcated with an *ethnicized* variation of national identity. State-produced textbooks presented Islam as an alien import adopted by Turks who lived under foreign rule, 'an Arab, not a universal, religion that corrupted and stifled the secular genius of the Turkish people' (Kaplan, p. 80). The best thing ever to happen to Islam was the Turkish people, not the other way around. Consolidating Islam was the responsibility of the Diyanet Işleri Başkanlığı, or 'Diyanet' (The Turkish Presidency of Religious Affairs, established in 1924). Brotherhoods (*cemaat*) and Sufi orders (*tarikat*) not validated by the Diyanet were outlawed. In response, many met in secret to discuss the identity and teachings of their respective leaders (Yavuz 2003a). The most widespread of such communities formed to distribute and read the *Risale-i Nur Kulliyeti* (RNK, Epistles of Light),[21] a commentary on the Qur'an authored by Said Nursi (d. 1960), an influential member of the Ottoman *ulema*. Atatürk and the CHP viewed Nursi's charismatic influence and aversion to state-administered secularism as a threat to the Kemalist project.[22] Nursi lived most of his life after 1923 under house arrest. His teachings were banned and upon his death he was buried in secret to prevent pilgrimage to his tomb. Immediately following his death, a number of groups emerged to claim rights to Nursi's teachings.[23] While never meeting Said Nursi in person, the young Fethullah Gülen was influenced by the RNK, and later came to agree that its Qur'anic commentary had no equal in the world. Adapting Nursi's plight against 'Western materialism' and 'positivism', Fethullah Gülen framed his community's teleology as a project to cultivate 'real civilization':

> When ignorance and unfed hearts and souls increase, materialism and carnality gradually subvert the desire for truth and annul any nobility of purpose … Wholly addicted to triviality and self-indulgence, they will deny any achievement to our ancestors and remain willfully ignorant of what real culture and civilization can make possible. (Gülen 2000: 194)

The rise of the 'Nur Movement' and its most influential offshoot under the guidance of Fethullah Gülen was forced to wait until the 1980s.

The 1980 Coup and the 'Turkish–Islamic Synthesis'

In the 1970s, financial turbulence led to political turmoil. The country started and ended the decade with a military coup. When the military seized control in September 1980, the economy was in ruins, unemployment was well into double digits, the education system was broken, inflation was rampant and the national debt was still growing. After seven failed governments in as many years, the end of the 1970s was marred by low-level urban warfare between Turkey's hard-line leftist and rightist political camps (Zürcher 2004). When the military seized control, a long-term overhaul of Turkey's development project was viewed as necessary for the prosperity of the country.

For this reason, the military regime authored a new constitution in 1982, which sought a middle ground between Turkey's Left and Right by extending rights to labour in regard to suitable working conditions and access to unemployment benefits. With regard to civil organizing, the constitution's amended bill of rights implemented a series of social, economic and political liberties, and stipulated that all individuals were equal before the law. Article XXVIII stipulated that individuals had a right to privacy and to freedom of thought, and that the news media was free and not liable to censorship without a court order, which could only be obtained 'when national security or the "indivisible integrity of the state" was threatened'. While many restrictions on free speech and free organizing remained,[24] the 1982 constitution created opportunities for previously marginalized groups to express themselves in the public sphere, and to mobilize their resources to compete in the Turkish economy.

In early 1983, the military ceded power back to the civilian sector. The architect of the stabilization and transition regime was Turgut Özal, a conservative technocrat brought in to restore the governing autonomy of the Turkish elite. Over the course of the next decade, Özal led Turkey's Anavatan Partesi ('Motherland Party', ANAP) in overseeing the implementation of a staggered and uneven liberalization programme. He also facilitated the expansion of a social policy that began under military rule. In an effort to stymie Turkey's Left–Right divide and to counteract any potential influence from Khomeini's Iran, the state sought to revive Islam as a glorified component of Turkey's national identity. A conservative return to Turkey's 'Islamic roots' was viewed as something to be exploited in the interests of stability. The result was 'a new constitution based on a "*Turkish-Islamic synthesis*", a combination of nationalism and Islam [that] was intended to constrain the causes of political chaos' (Baskan 2004: 220).

As soon as the 1982 constitution lifted discursive and organizational barriers associated with religion, Islamic activists flooded Turkey's religious marketplace (Inrovigne 2006; Yavuz 2003a). The GM was a primary player from the very beginning. In the 1960s, an initial group of followers converged around Gülen, and in the 1970s they led a fundraising campaign that sought religiously motivated donations from a growing constituency of conservative Anatolian entrepreneurs. Early followers used collected funds to build student dormitories, to buy apartments and to organize 'summer camps' to recruit conservative Turkish youth. During the 1980 junta, Gülen consolidated his dormitories into private corporations, which set the stage for the GM's emergence in private education in the post-1983 period. Within a short period of time, so-called 'Gülen schools' distinguished themselves in Turkey's competitive education system. In the 1990s, the GM expanded to Central Asia, Russia and the Balkans. In the late 1990s and early 2000s, the model was globalized to Southeast Asia, Africa, Latin America, Western Europe, Australia and the US. The GM has since emerged as Turkey's most influential religious community, and as one of the country's most powerful political interest groups.

II. A Success Story in Turkish Integration: The Gülen Movement

The Opportunity of Education

When discussing the GM's initial move into the education sector, Mustafa Bey, a first-generation student of Fethullah Gülen, explained that the vision for the schools emerged as a market rationalization of religious persecution:

> During the coup [1980–1983], the military government took over the properties of all [religious] foundations (*vakfi*). Hocaefendi [Fethullah Gülen] felt that this might happen as he was inspired by a verse in the Qur'an … [He] stopped his ongoing constructions before the military took over … he thought that the military would take them. This shows that Hocaefendi acted in accordance with

> the primary sources of religion … In order to prevent its takeover, he changed the legal condition of the dorm and turned it into a school and registered it as private property. He gathered a board of directors consisting of businessmen. So that school wasn't taken by the military government because it was the property of a corporation. This school became a model for future schools. Anybody who wanted to open a [Gülen] school started a company and owned a school in the name of that company [emphasis added]. (Field interview, 1 March 2007)

The first dormitory-turned-school was called Yamanlar ('the very good ones'). Before the incorporation of Yamanlar, 'official' GM institutions included the Türkiye Öğretmenler Vakfı (Turkish Teachers Foundation, established in 1976) and the Akyazılı Orta ve Yüksek Eğitim Vakfı (Foundation of Middle and Higher Education in Akyazılı, established in 1976) (Yavuz 2003a: 183). In 1979, followers published the first edition of *Sızıntı* ('source of a leak; trickle of water'), the oldest and most widely distributed of the GM's many periodicals. Despite these earlier developments, however, it was not until the incorporation of Yamanlar that Gülen 'acted with the primary sources of religion' to privatize his mission.[25] Throughout the 1980s, GM loyalists opened hundreds of organizationally autonomous Yamanlar-modelled institutions throughout Turkey. In addition to grade schools and high schools, in 1996, followers opened the community's first domestic university (Fatih Üniversitesi). In 1991, the GM took advantage of a state-led project to establish Turkish influence in the newly independent countries of Central Asia by expanding the community's activities to their Turkic-speaking brethren. Later in the decade, followers opened schools in East and Southeast Asia, and ultimately in Australia, Africa, Europe, Latin America and the US.

Students attend GM schools for a variety of reasons – a high-quality competitive education, an English-language medium, training in information and communication technologies, and opportunities for international travel and social–professional networking. In every country where they operate, GM schools adhere to the requirements of national curriculums and quickly earn reputations for academic excellence. A sample of recent successes is as follows. In 2007, students from the GM's Yamanlar (Izmir), Fatih (Istanbul) and Samanyolu (Ankara) high schools in Turkey won an overwhelming majority of the medals presented at the Turkish Scientific and Technological Research Council's (TÜBIAK) annual science competition (*Zaman Gazetesi*, 12 December 2007). In Kazakhstan over 90 per cent of students educated at GM schools since 1992 have gone to university. In Nigeria, the Ministry of Education allocated $340 million for scholarships to the 'Turkish schools' in that country (*Daily Champion*, 17 September 2008). In the US, students at the GM's Amity School in Brooklyn won a NASA-sponsored physics competition (*Today's Zaman*, 9 March 2007).

The market success of GM schools around the world has led to a growing reputation of elitism, as they attract only those students who can afford the high price of an imported education. In Central Asia, where GM schools are now among the region's primary elite institutions, tuition, board and fees can run as high as (US) $12,000 per student per annum. In Kyrgyzstan, at Bishkek's Silk Road International School, it is now the policy of the school 'to enhance educational opportunities for the children of foreigners and diplomats living and working in the Kyrgyz Republic'.[26] Yusef, a student from Baku who graduated from a GM high school before moving to Istanbul to attend Turkey's prestigious Boğaziçi Üniversitesi, spoke of the GM's reputation in Azerbaijan as follows:

> Before I started in this school, there were the advertisements for it. And it was very popular. It was prestigious to be a student of that school. It's like a comparison between Harvard, Princeton and an ordinary university in the USA. We can call those schools 'our Harvard'. Their quality of education was much better than the others. Unbelievable quality. Our teachers were very intelligent. So, my family wanted me to apply for that school. (Field interview, 9 February 2007)

The GM's mobilization in Turkey was a direct result of the country's failure to meet the needs of its growing urban youth population. The GM's trans-nationalization was the result of a calculated campaign to take advantage of Turkey's liberalization by seizing upon opportunities in the global marketplace. But if in 2005, private education in Turkey accounted for only 3 per cent of the country's total education system, how does the GM manage to develop and sustain such a large and loyal community of followers? Answer: competition.

Teaching to the Test

In 1997, compulsory education in Turkey was raised from five to eight years. Lack of capacity in secondary and tertiary education led to the development of a centralized, highly competitive testing system.[27] In 1973, Turkey's Ministry of Education developed the Öğrenci Seçme Sınavı (ÖSS, 'Student Selection Exam') to regulate enrolment at Turkish universities (Güvenç 1998). In 2003, 1.5 million students took the ÖSS and less than 11 per cent passed (Simsek and Yildirm 2004). In 2005, 1.6 million made the attempt, and again, less than 400,000 attended (Aksit 2006).

Similar to other industrialized states in the region (e.g., Egypt), the result of intense competition led to the development of a highly competitive tutoring market. Supplemental education has since become a billion-dollar industry, and hundreds of companies now compete for teenage clientele by advertising the successes of past students. In 2004, the average cost for an examination preparatory course in Turkey, known as a *dershane* (pl. *dershaneler*), was (US) $4,711. In 2002, the total out-of-pocket expenditure for *dershane* instruction was (US) $650 million, 18 per cent of Turkey's total private expenditure (World Bank 2005a: 21). Since the mid-1980s, GM *dershaneler* (and private high schools) have consistently produced the top performers on the annual nationwide entrance exam.[28] Why are students at GM schools so successful? Answer: the success of individual students equates to the legitimacy of the GM in general.

In what began as a system of dormitory living in the early 1970s, GM activists recruit Turkish youth via a system of '*ışık evleri*' (lighthouses) and *sohbet* (reading groups). The former refers to privately owned apartments occupied by four to six university students who live together as potential future activists in the broader GM network.[29] According to Fethullah Gülen, *ışık evleri* are at once student apartments, recruitment tools, social conditioning facilities and training barracks for what he calls 'the army of light':

> The lighthouses are places where deficiencies of people that may have been caused by their human characteristics are closed up. They are sacred places where plans and projects are produced, the continuality of the metaphysical tension is provided and courageous and faithful persons are raised ... Here these soldiers of spirituality and truth raised in lighthouses will pour the light God has given

> them for inspiration onto empty minds and help them flourish on the way to the conquest of the world in spirit and reality. These houses are one workbench, one school where *saboluncu* [emulators of alien culture] generations who shape themselves without a way, without a method and according to different charm centers, are flourished and [where] the return back to the roots of spirit and meaning are provided. (Gülen 1998b: 12)

According to Gülen, lighthouses remove potential participants in 'the happy future' from the evils of the present, the carnality of materialism, 'greed, infatuations, needs, and fantasies' (Gülen 1998a: 29). Only in the lighthouse can a young mind learn to filter out the corrupt influences of modern life, while continuing to focus his energies on worldly and spiritual studies. Younger students learn these teachings after participating in *sohbet*, which are reading groups organized regularly to recite and discuss the writings of Said Nursi and Fethullah Gülen. Middle and high school-aged students first learn of *ışık evleri* and *sohbet* while studying for high school and university placement exams. This is because one of the responsibilities of the university students living at an *ışık ev* is to offer free tutoring to middle and high school students who are preparing for exams. After becoming familiar with the lighthouses and comfortable with *sohbet*, older college students inform those being tutored that if they wish, they can receive a discount at a particular *dershane* company by mentioning their affiliation with the house or with a specific person. Regardless of one's desire to become a recruit in Gülen's 'army of light', discounts and access to capable and expensive *dershane* institutions prove beneficial when resources are scarce and when budgets are tight. The point to emphasize is that many, if not most, of the students living in the hundreds of *ışık ev* in Turkey are not alumni of GM private high schools; they are, rather, alumni of GM *dershaneler*.

GM-owned *dershane* companies are now definitive players in the education of Turkey's urban youth, constituting 12 per cent of the sector in Istanbul alone.[30] And just as connections are essential before attending the *dershane*, when a student scores well on the ÖSS, teachers from GM *dershane* companies contact their former students to inquire about their living arrangements upon entering university.[31] Freshmen students are offered a subsidized room at an *ışık ev*, and after moving in, the recruitment cycle continues. If a student actively participates, if he tutors high school visitors, attends *sohbet* regularly, and performs well in his own exams, then as he progresses through school he will likely be asked if he is interested in becoming an *abi–abla* ('older brother'– 'older sister'). An *abi* is given the responsibility of managing the needs of the house, of organizing *sohbet*, supervising other students and serving as the primary liaison between the house and the larger GM network. While unpaid, if a student performs well he creates opportunities for himself to find a professional position in the GM business network after university. Since the mid-1990s, that network has expanded to over 100 countries. In addition to the schools, there are hundreds of affiliated companies, a far-reaching publication sector, Turkey's largest business-related NGO, Turkey's largest 'participation bank' (i.e., interest-free 'Islamic bank'), a globally expansive public relations initiative, a first-response catastrophe relief organization, and a very successful media corporation. While space inhibits an analysis of each sector, in the following sections I provide a brief introduction to the GM's collective mobilization in trade, banking and public relations.

Trade

Outside Turkey, GM schools are incorporated into umbrella Turkish trade and business associations. These smaller associations receive little or no subsidies from Ankara and organize their production primarily for export (Özbüdün and Keymen 2002: 311). Initial capital for GM schools is generated in the form of *himmet* (religiously-motivated donation), which is collected from benefactors in an organized fundraising system. Potential donors are told that *himmet* is a religious rite, and that trust networks in the GM would assure it going to a 'faithful' cause (i.e., growth of the movement). In this way, schools provide these businessmen with 'the service' (*hizmet*) of satisfying their obligatory rites according to the Islamic tenet of giving while they simultaneously create opportunities to expand their business.

In 2005, 124 separate business and cultural associations that represented nearly 10,000 Turkish businessmen came together to form Turkey's newest and largest NGO, Türkiye Işadamları Sanayiciler Konfederasyonu (The Confederation of Businessmen and Industrialists in Turkey, TUSKON). Since its inception, TUSKON has organized a series of 'trade bridge' summits with Central Asia (September 2006), Pacific Asia (April 2007, June 2008), Africa (May 2006, 2007, 2008), and most recently the US (May 2009). These conferences are showcases for Anatolian exporters who underwrite the GM's transnational education initiative. At the summits, students from GM schools work as interpreters and general volunteers. In May 2006, 400 such volunteers worked at a two-day summit in Istanbul that led to (US) $200 million in trade deals with African businesses (TUSKON Africa Report 2006). At the outset of the Turkey–Africa follow-up conference in May 2007, participants sought to double the previous year and sign (US) $500 million in contracts. After two days, (US) $2 billion was the final tally (TUSKON Africa Report 2007). The April 2007 summit with businesses and dignitaries from Pacific Asian nations resulted in (US) $750 million, three times its initial target. TUSKON's president, Rizanur Meral, highlighted the significance of GM schools in Southeast Asia, explaining, 'schools started by Turkish entrepreneurs play a crucial role in creating connections with businessmen of the region' (*Today's Zaman*, 9 April 2007). The immediate successes of the TUSKON trade summits are indicative of a new sphere of influence in Turkey's political economy. This new powerbase draws from a globally networked religious community to expand its potential and to galvanize its resources.

Banking

Consolidating these resources is the job of the GM's Bank Asya (BA) (formerly Asya Finans), an interest-free institution that began with (US) $26 million of start-up capital from sixteen businessmen loyal to Fethullah Gülen. In July 2007, BA's assets totalled (US) $4 billion. In May 2006, BA went public with 20 per cent of its assets offered in its initial public offering, despite a demand that was 50 per cent higher. When I enquired about BA's rapid success, a senior BA executive and board member gleefully explained, 'It was a record in Turkey. It was mentioned in the *Financial Times* based in London' (Field interview, 24 July 2007). Although the newest of Turkey's four 'interest-free' lending institutions, since 2001 BA has been the market leader, and the fastest growing with 149 branches (as of June 2009). To add to the source of pride, in 2008 BA became the only participating bank that was majority Turkish-owned.[32]

BA's rapid rise in the banking sector was due in part to increased liberalization, and in part to new market opportunities created after the 2001 economic collapse: 'This foundation's active growth has averaged 60 per cent a year since then [2001]. This continued to 2006. 2007 looks like it will follow suit again … Each year, it grows 60 per cent; you can calculate how huge a growth this is' (Field interview 24 July 2007).

Since 2001, BA has invested in projects throughout the Middle East, the Arab Gulf, North Africa, Russia and the Ukraine. Domestically, it has increased its capacity and is now involved in several major public works projects in Istanbul, including a new transcontinental bridge in Istanbul and a new metro system that will connect European and Asian Istanbul via an underwater transit. While BA's public stance is to claim only a loose affiliation with the GM, it is a key player in the expansion of the GM as a whole and functions as the primary sponsor for the GM's most public and most wide-reaching national and international media and public relations events.

Public Relations

The most public GM organization in Turkey is the Gazeteciler ve Yazılar Vakfı (Journalists and Writers Foundation, GYV, established in 1994). Part think-tank, part publishing house, the GYV solicits donations from the GM network to produce a series of journals and books that are either written or inspired by Fethullah Gülen. Operating as the GM's central marketing and public relations outlet, the GYV also hosts domestic and international conferences that address national and international issues ranging from the relationship between state policy and secularism to the so-called 'Kurdish Question', to EU–Turkish relations. Over the past several years, GM loyalists in Europe and the US have adapted the GYV model, and similar institutes now operate all over the United States, Western Europe and Australia.

Among the activities of these organizations is lobbying for influence from connected and influential people in American and European politics, academia and business. Strategies include the growing frequency of 'award dinners', such as those sponsored by The Rumi Forum in Washington, DC and The Niagara Foundation in Chicago. In early March 2007, the former held a dinner event where they offered the Turkish and Spanish prime ministers 'Dialogue of Civilizations' awards in recognition of their 2006 agreement to lead European nations in dialogue. The Rumi Forum also gave awards to high-profile Islamic studies academics, John Esposito and John Voll, as well as to the director of the 'Religion and Peace Initiative' at the US Institute of Peace, David Smock. In a similar event, the Niagara Foundation gave an award to

Exelon Corporation CEO, John Rowe, for his environmental perspective on big industry. At that dinner, the importance of trade between the US and Turkey, as well as continued political friendship, took precedent. At each award ceremony, Fethullah Gülen sent a letter of support and congratulations to the recipients (Field notes, 17 June 2007). In February 2007, efforts by both organizations reached Washington, DC, when their directors met with Democratic US representative, Janet Schakowsky (D-IL), to lobby against Congress passing 'the Armenian Genocide Resolution'. For two years running, the New York-based Turkish Cultural Center hosted Democratic presidential candidate and then New York Senator, Hillary Rodham Clinton, at its annual Ramadan Friendship Dinner. After attending the 2007 dinner, which was also attended by Turkey's prime minister, Recep Tayyip Erdoğan, and both New York State senators, a senior columnist for the GM-affiliated *Zaman* newspaper explained to his readers that these activities were not coincidental: 'All these activities show that a very powerful Turkish lobby is being established in the US. This new dialogue, which will open a new page in Turkish–US relations, is as important as Turkey's EU bid' (*Today's Zaman*, 5 October 2007).

In addition to political lobbying, GYV-model institutions in Europe and the US also engage in a project of *controlled intellectualization*, whereby they strive to monopolize the intellectual treatment of Fethullah Gülen by organizing and sponsoring conferences dedicated to the 'contributions of the Gülen Movement'. Participants at these conferences include both GM-affiliated public intellectuals (journalists from *Zaman* and scholars from varying theology and social sciences departments in Turkey, Europe and the US) as well as sympathetic 'outside' academics who focus on the GM as a topic of humanities or social science research. These events are typically co-sponsored by host universities, and typically result in a book publication.[33] Tied to these conferences are 'interfaith trips', whereby GM benefactors sponsor a two-week tour of Turkey for influential people in American and European academic and faith communities, as well as for journalists and political attachés.[34] Such strategies indicate a calculated effort to recruit sympathizers among community and business leaders, academics, politicians and policy makers. By cultivating foreign sympathy, the GM gains credibility and establishes legitimacy as a global actor.[35] Considering the level of support the GM now receives from an eager Western audience, these efforts have proven to bear fruit.

Conclusion

In secular Turkey religious communities are often accused of mounting 'secret plans' to overthrow the Republic and to implement Islamic law. Since the 1970s, the GM has remained at the top of the list of usual suspects. By taking advantage of newfound economic and organizational capacity, however, the GM is no longer outflanked by its oligarchic rivals. When alarmists assert that the GM is 'hiding a secret agenda' to secretly infiltrate the state and to initiate a passive Islamic revolution in Turkey, GM-affiliated journalists and outreach coordinators can respond by presenting the movement and its interests as embodying the social mores of modernity (i.e., democracy, free markets, individual liberty, human rights, etc.) *to a greater extent* than Turkey's secularist elite. This message has not gone unnoticed by European and American observers desperate for alternatives to al-Qa'ida and the Muslim Brotherhood (*Ikwan*).

In 2006, the US RAND Corporation produced a policy initiative entitled 'Building Moderate Muslim Networks'. The report's aim was to locate and publicize the efforts of Muslim identity organizations around the world that have internalized the neo-liberal worldview of American-led globalization. RAND specifically cited the Turkish movement of Fethullah Gülen as a model from which American interests can learn, and a group that American interests should try to promote on a global scale (106). Echoing RAND's stamp of approval, the *Economist* magazine suggested that the GM was 'one of the most powerful and best-connected of the networks that are competing to influence Muslims around the globe ... On the face of things, the Gülen movement seems more benign – from a Western point of view – than either the [Muslim] Brotherhood or any of the other networks that compete for a similar role' (6 March 2008). The *New York Times* praised the GM in Pakistan, where its journalists acknowledged that the GM's PakTurk Education Consortium (seven schools) offered Pakistani youth a 'mild alternative' to Saudi-inspired Wahhabism prevalent in that country's madrassa system of education (Tavernise 2008).

How did the GM manage to subvert the iron fist of Turkish secularism to become the world's archetype for 'moderate Islam'? It did so by pooling economic resources through trust networks independent of Turkey's development alliance, and by taking advantage of the organizational and discursive framing opportunities provided by Turkey's experience with neo-liberal restructuring. The irony of the GM's 'middle way', however, is that instead of 'representing the people' (i.e., the subaltern, poor, working majority of the Turkish nation) it is representative of a neo-conservative elite cadre of religious nationalists. In GM media, Kurdish separatists who attack military installations continue to be labelled 'terrorists'. Alevis who insist on their rights as religious minorities continue to be labelled 'Muslims'. The claims of the Armenian diaspora continue to be designated as self-serving and/or outlandish. Indeed, rather than the 'movement for world peace' that its followers claim it to be, or the 'Islamist organization hiding a secret agenda' that its critics maintain, the GM is more correctly viewed as a piously identified, neo-conservative advocacy network that markets its brand of 'civil–cosmopolitan Islam' in the interests of accumulation, legitimacy and collective influence (Hendrick 2008). Contradicting the efforts of twentieth-century Islamic activism in general, the GM's goals are not to undermine the Turkish state in an effort to implement Islamic law. Its goal is to passively claim its share of social power among Turkey's ruling elite, and to subsequently redefine the status quo in the image of 'the new Turkey'.

NOTES

1 *The Economist* 2008a, 2008b; Göle 2008, Hudson 2008, Tavernise 2008.
2 Krespin, R., 'The Upcoming Elections in Turkey (2): The AK Party's Power Base', MEMRI.org, *Inquiry and Analysis No. 375*, 19 July 2007. The full text and translation is widely published online, and the video is available for viewing at youtube.com: <http://www.youtube.com/watch?v=oNi3Z3qZ7Z4&mode=related&search>.
3 This argument is presented by Burna Turam in *Between Islam and the Secular State* (2006), pp. 6–13.
4 Çetinkaya (2007); Krespin (2009, 2007); Rubin (2008); Yanardağ (2006).
5 Aras and Caha (2000); Can (1996); Carroll (2007); Ernege (2008, 2005); Hunt and Aslandogan (eds) (2006); Kuru (2005); Sarıtoprak (ed.) (2005); Schwartz (2008); Ünal and Williams (eds) (2000); Ünal (2005); White (2003); Yavuz and Esposito (eds) (2003); Yürtsever (ed.) (2008).
6 Keck and Sikkink (1998), p. 5.
7 Broadbent (2003); Keck and Sikkink (1998); Lin (1999); Lubeck (2000); Melucci (1996); Passy (2003).
8 Nan Lin, p. 35.
9 Yavuz (2006).
10 This chapter is based on findings derived from research conducted in Turkey and in the US from November 2005 to September 2008. Primary fieldwork was

conducted from November 2006–July 2007 at Akademi (the Academy) in Istanbul, an all-in-one publishing house, think-tank, library, theological training centre, meeting place, school and mosque that functions as the GM's central ideational node. In addition to fieldwork and interviews at Akademi, I conducted career history interviews with individuals at the GM's Bank Asya, PASIAD (Pacific Asia Businessmen and Industrialists Association), *Zaman Gazetesi* (newspaper), FEM Dershanesi (supplemental educational institution), Fatih University, the Gazeteciler ve Yazılar Vakfı (Journalists and Writers Foundation), and TUSKON (Confederation of Businessmen and Industrialists in Turkey). I also spent time with four college-age students from Central Asia who were studying university in Istanbul, and who were living at GM-owned student apartments. To supplement, I conducted additional research with seven former students at GM schools, one member of Turkey's AKP government, an operative in the centre-Left Democratic Left Party (DSP), and a senior editor at a major non-GM Turkish newspaper. In the US, I conducted supplemental research at two GM cultural institutes and at four GM-sponsored and GM-promoted conferences. Also in the US, I corresponded with ten 'recruited sympathizers' in American academia who were either courted by the GM to participate in one of their promotional conferences, and/or who worked for the GM at one of their institutions in Turkey or around the world. In total I conducted forty formal interviews, took part in over a hundred informal conversations and conducted approximately 1,000 hours of participant observation.

11 Giddens (1991, 1994, 1998); Giddens, Beck, and Lash (1994).

12 Giddens, p. 214.

13 Ibid., p. 115.

14 Ahmet Kuru, p. 129.

15 Jenny White (2004) p. 88.

16 Chantal Mouffe (2005) pp. 62–63.

17 Metin Heper (ed.) (1991, 1985); Bernard Lewis (1961); Taha Parla and Andrew Davidson (2003), Erik J. Zürcher (2004).

18 Biannchi (1984); Demir, Açar, and Toprak (2004); Heper (ed.) (1991, 1985); Ütkülü (2001); Yavuz (2003a).

19 Buğra, p. 56.

20 Kaplan (2006); Parla and Davidson (2004).

21 For the purposes of this chapter, Said Nursi is introduced only to provide the reader with an overview of the 'Nur' tradition, to which Fethullah Gülen and the GM are affiliated. The RNK is published by a number of publishing houses in Turkey, most of which are affiliated with one of the seven 'Nur communities'. The RNK is divided into multiple volumes: *The Words*, *The Letters*, *The Rays* and *The Flashes*, each of which are often found subdivided or abridged for easier access and publication. A complete e-copy of the RNK is available at <http://www.nursistudies.com/>. See Sükran Vahide, *Islam in Modern Turkey: An Intellectual Biography of Bediüzzaman Said Nursi* (2005) for a biography from a sympathetic perspective. For a detailed account of his sociological impact on the formation and mobilization of Islamic political identity in Turkey, see Serif Mardin, *Religion and Social Change in Modern Turkey: The Case of Bediüzzaman Said Nursi* (1989); and Hakan Yavuz, *Islamic Political Identity in Turkey* (2003), pp. 151–178; Hakan Yavuz, 'Being Modern in the Nurcu Way', in *ISIM Review* October 2003, pp. 7, 14; Hakan Yavuz, 'Islam in the Public Sphere: The Case of

the Nur Movement', in *Turkish Islam and the Secular State: The Gülen Movement* (2003b), pp. 1–18.

22 Mardin (1989); Turam (2006); Yavuz (2000, 2003a); Zürcher (2004).

23 The first split occurred when a group of Nursi's immediate followers sought to mass-produce and mass-distribute the RNK (and thus to reform the text in accordance with the Turkish language reform). A smaller group, the Yazıcılar (scribes), refused, and contended that the 'truth' of the RNK lay in the purity of the text itself, which was handwritten in Ottoman Turkish. The former group believed that Nursi's teachings required a broad audience. In 1971 this group published the first edition of *Yeni Asya* (New Asia), and has since come to be known as such. Following the 1980 coup, and the subsequent passage of the 1982 constitution, another major division occurred, pitting supporters and opponents of the post-coup political landscape against one another. Soon after, the group splintered to focus on Nursi's Kurdish origins and to advocate the glorification of Nursi' efforts for Kurdish rights in the southeast. Despite their differences, however, the Nur unite in the belief that Said Nursi authored a blueprint for a specifically Muslim engagement with the modern world.

24 Specifically, Section IV, Article 15 stipulated that in the event of 'war, mobilization, or state of emergency, the exercise of fundamental rights and freedoms could be partially or entirely suspended'. Article 301 of the Turkish Penal Code stipulated, 'A person who denigrates "Turkishness", the Republic, or the Grand National Assembly shall be punishable by imprisonment of between six months and three years.' Restrictions such as these are priority concerns for European officials negotiating Turkey's integration into the EU. Today, the European Parliament insists on their reform before they continue to consider Turkey's membership (Rein 2007).

25 Yamalar Koleji now runs ten campuses and is among Turkey's elite private educational companies, <http://www.yamanlar.k12.tr/>.

26 SRIS Mission Statement: available at <http://www.sris.com.kg/>.

27 Aksit (2006); Güvenç (1998); Simsek and Yildirm (2004); Tansel and Bircan (2002).

28 GM-affiliated *dershane* companies control approximately 12 per cent of the supplemental education market in Turkey (Turkish Ministry of Education 2007). Established in 1984, FEM Dersanesi is now the most highly acclaimed supplemental education company in Istanbul, with forty-three branches, and with the most successful students in twenty-two of the last twenty-three years on Turkey's university placement exam (ÖSS). Anafen, which prepares younger students for the high school entrance exam (ÖKS) is also based in Istanbul, and operates nationwide. Other successful GM-affiliated supplemental education companies include Yesilirmak Dersanesi in Bursa, Maltepe Dersanesi in Ankara, Nil Dersanesi in Erzurum, and Korfez Dersanesi in Izmir. In the 2007 ÖSS exam, many students in the top 1 per cent in each of the above cities attended these respective preparation schools and/or attended GM-affiliated private high schools (see 'The Highest Scores on the OSS are Published', *Zaman Gazetesi* 13 July 2007, <http://www.fem.com.tr/>).

29 Funds for board come from a combination of modest fees collected from students themselves, and from sympathetic neighbourhood businesses solicited to contribute to the GM network as a matter of religious donation (*himmet*).

The money colleted from students varies from lighthouse to lighthouse; some students pay nothing, others pay as much as (US) $200 a month. In all cases, however, rent and board is heavily or totally subsidized by donations (*himmet*) collected from sympathetic or affiliated benefactors.

30 Turkish Ministry of Education, 'Private Education General Directorate', 2007 'List of Schools', <http://ookgm.meb.gov.tr/OkulListe.aspx. Accessed 10 April 2007>.

31 Field Interviews, 19 January 2007, 9 February 2007, 1 March 2007, 8 March 2007, 13 June 2007, 3 July 2007, 16 July 2007.

32 There are four interest-free banks in Turkey. In addition to Bank Asya are Kuveyt Turk, Turkiye Finans, and Albaraka Turk. All are members of Turkey's Association of Participation Banks (Turkiye Katlim Bankalari Birligi); however, only Bank Asya is majority-owned by Turkish shareholders (80 per cent). In April 2008, Turkiye Finans sold 60 per cent of its shares to Saudi Arabia's NCB. Kuveyt Turk originates from Kuwait, and Albaraka Bank is a member of Pakistan's Albaraka Banking Group. A fifth, Ilhas Bank, was a financial victim of the 2001 banking crisis.

33 The largest of such conferences to date was held in London and was co-sponsored by the GM's London-based Dialogue Society in conjunction with the House of Lords, The English Parliament, The London School of Economics, SOAS, The University of Sussex and The Middle East Institute. The first was held in Washington, DC in 2002 and was sponsored by the Rumi Forum in conjunction with The Center for Muslim–Christian Understanding at Georgetown University. This was followed in April 2005 by a conference in Madison, Wisconsin sponsored by the GM's Dialogue International, and then in 2005 in Houston sponsored by the GM's Institute for Interfaith Dialogue (IID). Following Houston, the IID sponsored successive conferences dedicated to the GM in March 2006 in Dallas, TX (with SMU University); and two in November 2006 in San Antonio, TX and Norman, Oklahoma (in conjunction with the University of Texas, San Antonio and the University of Oklahoma, respectively). Following the Dialogue Society's October 2007 London conference there was one in Rotterdam, Holland, and another in the US sponsored by the Turkish Cultural Center in New York City. The latter was co-sponsored by The Institute for Turkish Studies and the Middle East Institute at Columbia University. Both were held in November 2007. In November 2008, the Rumi Forum in Washington, DC hosted its second GM conference at Georgetown University (www.gulenconference.us), and in March 2009, the Atlas Foundation in Louisiana sponsored a follow-up at Louisiana State University in Baton Rouge. The most recent was held at Potsdam University in Berlin and was sponsored by the GM's Forum for Intercultural Dialogue Berlin (FID BERLIN e.V.).

34 A non-exhaustive list of GYV-modelled organizations around the world is as follows: The Dialogue Society in London, The Affinity Cultural Foundation in Auburn, NSW (Australia), The Australian Intercultural Society in Monee Ponds, VIC, Indialogue in New Delhi, The Canadian Institute for Interfaith Dialogue in Ontario, The Institute for Interfaith Dialogue (IID), the Raindrop Foundation, the Institute for International Commerce and Partnership (IICP) and Gülen Institute in Houston, Texas. Together these institutions have nearly two-dozen branches across Texas and Oklahoma: the Niagara Foundation and Niagara Educational Services in Chicago, the Science Academy of Chicago, The Rumi

Forum in Washington, DC, The Atlas Interfaith Foundation in New Orleans, The Lehigh Dialogue Center in Bethlehem, PA, The Center for Cultural Connections in Irvine (CA), Dialogue International in Madison, the Holy Dove Foundation in Indianapolis, the Iowa Dialogue Center in Des Moines, The Istanbul Center for Culture and Dialogue in Atlanta, the Dialogue Institute in Athens (GA), The Boston Dialogue Foundation, the Scioto Educational Foundation in Columbus (OH), The Bloomington Muslim Dialogue Group, The Northern Lights Society in St Paul, The Intercultural Friendship Group at UI – Urbana, The Rose Garden Foundation in Portland (OR), Ebru TV and the Light Publishing in Somerset (NJ), the Interfaith Dialogue Center in Newark (NJ) and The Turkish Cultural Center in New York City.

35 In 2003, the Institute for Interfaith Dialogue in Houston sponsored one such trip that included a humanities and comparative religion professor at Rice University. Explaining that she was immediately captivated by the GM and with Fethullah Gülen's writings, this professor wrote a book comparing Gülen's thought with that of European and Chinese philosophy as observed in the work of Plato, John Stuart Mill, Immanuel Kant, John Paul Sartre and Confucius. In the first month of its publication by *The Light Publishing* (a subsidiary of the GM-owned Kaynak Holding) in 2007, *Dialogue of Civilizations* was a bestseller under the category 'Islam' on Amazon.com. The book tour consisted of a city-by-city schedule of visits to GM-cultural foundations throughout the US.

BIBLIOGRAPHY

Print–Electronic Media

Daily Champion (Lagos) 'Yobe Sends 595 Students to Turkish Schools' (17 September 2008).

Economist 2008a, 'Beyond the Veil' (12 June 2008).

—2008b, 'How Far They Have Traveled' (12 March 2008).

Fagan, Gerladine, 'Said Nursi Ban Brands Moderate Muslims as Extremists', *Forum 18* (27 June 2007).

Göle, Nilüfer, '"Turkish Schools World's Most Global Movement," says Sociologist', *Today's Zaman* (10 June 2008).

Gülerce, Hüseyin, 'An Iftar Dinner in New York', *Today's Zaman* (5 October 2007).

Hudson, Alexandra, *Turkish Islamic Preacher: Threat or Benefactor* (Reuters UK, 14 May 2008).

Hürriyet Gazetesi, '*ABD, Fethullah Gülen Yesil Kartı vermedi*' ('The US Not to Issue Fethullah Gülen a Green Card'), accessed online 25 July 2008.

Nuttall, Tom, 'How Gülen Triumphed', *Prospect*, Issue 148 (July 2008).

Sabah, 'Arinc Opens School in Sudan' (1 July 2007).

Schwartz, Stephen, 'The Real Fethullah Gülen', *Prospect*, Issue 148 (July 2008).

Tavernise, Sabrina, 'Turkish Schools Offer Pakistan a Gentler Vision of Islam', *New York Times* (Pacific Northwest Print Edition, 4 May 2008).

Today's Zaman, 'Turkish School Wins NASA-Sponsored Science Olympics' (9 March 2007).

—'Winner at Turkish Olympics are Champions of Peace' (4 June 2007).

—'President Gül Inaugurates Turkish School in Kenya' (23 February 2009).

—'PM Erdoğan Call on Doğan to Shake Off "Bad Habit"' (25 February 2009).

—'Babacan Visits Turkish School in Mexico' (10 December 2008).

—'Babacan Visits High School in Tajikistan' (28 November 2008).

—'Small Enterprises Star in TUSKON's Trade Bridge with Pacific' (9 April 2007).

—'Bank Asya Sees Increase in 2008 Profits Despite Crisis' (25 February 2009).

Turkish Daily News, 'Gülen: The Law Judges Deeds Not Intentions' (24 June 1999), accessed online 8 July 2008.

Turkish Ministry of Education, 'Private Education General Directorate', 2007 'List of Schools', http://ookgm.meb.gov.tr/OkulListe.aspx.

TUSKON 2007, *Turkey–Africa Trade Bridge Report*, available at http://www.tuskon.org.tr/gnl/dok_arsiv_en.php.

Zaman Gazetesi, '*ÖSS'de basarı arttı, dereceler Türkiye'ye yayıldi*' ('The Results of the Most Successful Students on the ÖSS are Published') (13 July 2007).

—'Sudanese Students in Turkish Schools "An Honor"' (16 March 2006).

—'Yamanlar, Fatih and Samanyolu Make Their Mark in Science Olympics' (13 December 2007).

Scholarly Sources

Aksit, Necmi, 'Educational Reform in Turkey', *International Journal of Educational Development* (March 2006), pp. 129–137.

Aras, Bulent, and Omer, Caha, 'Fethullah Gülen and his Liberal "Turkish Islam Movement"', *MERIA*, Vol. 4 (4) (2000), pp. 30–42.

Baskan, Filiz, 'The Political Economy of Islamic Finance in Turkey: The Role of Fethullah Gülen and Asya Finans', in Henry and Wilson (eds), *The Politics of Islamic Finance* (Edinburgh University Press, 2004), pp. 216–239.

Berkes, Niyazi, *The Development of Secularism in Turkey* (New York: Routledge Press, 1998).

Biancchi, Robert, *Interest Groups and Political Development in Turkey* (Princeton: Princeton University Press, 1984).

Broadbent, Jeremy, 'Movement in Context: Thick Networks and Japanese Environmental Protest', in Diani and McAdam (eds), *Social Movements and Networks* (New York: OUP, 2003), pp. 204–232.

Buğra, Ayse, *State and Business in Modern Turkey* (Binghampton: SUNY Press, 1994).

Can, Eyüp, *Fethullah Gülen Hocaefendi ile Ufuk Turu* (A Tour of New Horizons with Fethullah Gülen) (Istanbul: AD Yayincilik, 1996).

Carrol, Jill, *A Dialogue of Civilizations: Gülen's Islamic Ideals and Humanistic Discourse* (Somerset: The Light Publishing, 2007).

Castells, Manuel, *The Rise of the Network Society: The Information Age: Economy, Society and Culture Volume 1* (Malden: Blackwell Publishers, 1996).

Çetinkaya, Hikmet, *Fethullah Gülen, ABD, ve AKP* (Fethullah Gülen, the USA, and the AKP) (Istanbul: Gunizi Yayincilik, 2007).

Demir, Omer, Açar, Mustafa, and Toprak, Metin, '"Anatolian Tigers of Islamic Capital" Prospects and Challenges', *Middle Eastern Studies* 40 (6) (2004), pp. 166–188.

Ergene, Enes, *Tradition Witnessing the Modern Age* (Somerset: Tughra Books, 2008).

—*Gülen Hareketinin Analizi Geleceğin Modern Çağa Tanıklıgı* (*Tradition Witnessing the Modern Age: An Analysis of the Gülen Movement*) (Istanbul: Kaynak Kültür Yayınları, 2005).

Giddens, Anthony, *The Third Way: The Renewal of Social Democracy* (Cambridge: Polity Press, 1999).

—'Living in a Post-Traditional Society', in Beck, Giddens, and Lash, *Reflexive Modernization* (Palo Alto: Stanford University Press, 1994), pp. 56–109.

—*Modernity and Self-Identity: Self and Society in the Late Modern Age* (Stanford University Press, 1991).

Gülen, Fethullah M., *Towards a Lost Paradise* (Izmir: Kaynak Publishing, 1998a).

—*Prizma II* (Istanbul: Nil Yayınları, 1998b).

—*Criteria or Lights of the Way* (Izmir: Kaynak Publishing, 1998c).

Güvenç, B., *History of Turkish Education* (Ankara: Turkish Education Association, 1998).

Heper, Metin (ed.), *Strong State and Economic Interest Groups: The Post 1980 Turkish Experience* (New York: Walter De Grutyer Publishing, 1991).

—*The State Tradition in Turkey* (Northgate: The Eothen Press, 1985).

Hendrick, Joshua D., 'Islamic Activism in the "Secular" Modern World System: Turkish Integration and the Civil/Cosmopolitan Movement of Fethullah Gülen', in Samman and al-Zoby (eds), *Islam and the Orientalist World System* (Boulder, CO: Paradigm Publishers, 2008).

Hunt, Robert and Alp, Aslandoğan (eds), *Muslim Citizens of the Globalized World* (Somerset, NJ: The Light Publishing, 2007).

Introvigne, Massimo, 'Turkish Religious Markets: A View Based on the Religious Economy Theory', in Yavuz (ed.), *The Emergence of a New Turkey* (University of Utah Press, 2006), pp. 23–48.

Kaplan, Sam, *The Pedagogical State: Education and the Politics of National Culture in Post-1980 Turkey* (Palo Alto, CA: Stanford University Press, 2006).

Keck, Margaret, and Sikkink, Katheryn, *Activists Beyond Borders* (Ithaca, NY: Cornell University Press, 1998).

Krespin, R., 'Fethullah Gülen's Grand Ambition: Turkey's Islamist Danger', *Middle East Quarterly*, Vol. XVI (1) (199), pp. 55–66.

—'The Upcoming Elections in Turkey (2): The AKP's Political Power Base', *MEMRI* Inquiry and Analysis Series No. 375 (July 2007). Accessed online 30 July 2007.

Kuru, Ahmet T., 'Globalization and Diversification of Islamist Movements: Three Turkish Cases', *Political Science Quarterly*, Vol. 120 (2) (2005).

—'Search for a Middle Way', in Esposito and Yavuz (eds), *Turkish Islam and the Secular State: The Gülen Movement* (Syracuse: Syracuse University Press, 2003), pp. 115–130.

Lewis, Bernard, *The Emergence of Modern Turkey* (New York: OUP, 1961).

Lin, Nan, 'Building a Network Theory of Social Capital', *Connections* 22 (1) (1991), pp. 28–51.

Lubeck, Paul, 'The Islamic Revival', in Cohen and Rai (eds), *Global Social Movements* (London: Athlone Press, 2000), pp. 146–164.

Mardin, Şerif, *Religion and Social Change in Modern Turkey: The Case of Bediüzzaman Said Nursi* (Albany: SUNY Press, 1989).

Melucci, Alberto, *Challenging Codes: Collective Action in the Information Age* (New York: Cambridge University Press, 1996).

Mouffe, Chantal, *On the Political* (New York: Routledge, 2005).

Özbüdün, Ergun, and Keymen, Fuat, 'Cultural Globalization in Turkey: Actors, Discourses, and Challenges', in Berger and Huntington (eds), *Many Globalizations* (New York: OUP, 2002).

Parla, Taha, and Davidson, Andrew, *Corporatist Ideology in Kemalist Turkey* (Syracuse University Press, 2004).

Passey, Florence, 'Social Networks Matter. But How?', in Diani and McAdam (eds), *Social Movements and Networks* (New York: OUP, 2003), pp. 21–48.

Rabasa, Angel, Bernard, Cheryl, Schwartz, Lowell, and Sickle, Peter, *Building Moderate Muslim Networks* (Washington, DC: RAND Corporation, 2006).

Rubin, Michael, 'Turkey Turning Point: Could There be an Islamic Revolution in Turkey?', *The National Review* (14 April 2008).

Sarıtoprak, Zeki (ed.), *The Muslim World Special Issue: Islam in Contemporary Turkey: The Contributions of Fethullah Gülen* 95 (3) (Blackwell Publishing, 2005).
—'An Islamic Approach to Peace and Nonviolence: A Turkish Experience', in *The Muslim World Special Issue: Islam in Contemporary Turkey: The Contributions of Fethullah Gülen* 95 (3) (2005), pp. 413–428.
Sarıtoprak, Zeki, and Griffith, Sydney, 'Fethullah Gülen and the '"People of the Book": A Voice from Turkey for Interfaith Dialogue', in *The Muslim World Special Issue: Islam in Contemporary Turkey: The Contributions of Fethullah Gülen* 95 (3) (2005), pp. 325–471.
Simsek, Hasan, and Yildirim, Ali, 'Turkey: Innovation and Tradition', in Rotberg (ed.), *Balancing Change and Tradition in Global Education Reform* (Oxford: Scarecrow Education, 2004), pp. 153–185.
Sukran, Vahide, *Islam in Modern Turkey: An Intellectual Biography of Bediuzzaman Said Nursi* (Albany: SUNY Press, 2005).
Tansel, Aysit, and Bircan, Fatma, 'Demand for Education in Turkey: A Tobit Analysis of Private Tutoring Expenditures', in *Economics of Education Review* 25 (2) (2006), p. 306.
—'Private Tutoring Expenditures in Turkey', ERF Working Paper Series 0333 (Ankara: Middle Eastern Technical University, 2002).
Turam, Berna, *Between Islam and the State* (Palo Alto, CA: Stanford University Press, 2006).
Ünal, Ali, *Geçmişten Geleceğe Köprü: Fethullah Gülen* (A Bridge from the Past to the Future: Fethullah Gülen) (Istanbul: Kaynak Kültür Yayınları, 2005).
Ünal, Ali, and Williams, Alphonse, *Advocate of Dialogue: Fethullah Gülen* (Fairfax, VA: The Fountain Press, 2000).
Ütkülü, Ütkü, '"The Turkish Economy" Past and Present', in Lovatt *et al.*, *Turkey Since 1970* (New York: Palgrave, 2001), pp. 1–40.
White, Jenny, 'The End of Islamism: Turkey's Muslimhood Model', in Hefner (ed.), *Remaking Muslim Politics: Pluralism, Contestation, and Democratization* (Princeton University Press, 2003), pp. 87–111.
The World Bank, 'How Much Does Turkey Spend on Education? Development of National Education Accounts to Measure and Evaluate Education Expenditures', Working Paper, Report Number 41058.Washington, DC, 2005a.
—*Turkey-Education Sector Study*, Report No. 32450-TU, Washington, DC, 2005b.
Yanardağ, Merdan, *Fethullah Gülen Hareketinin Perde Arkası: Turkiye Nasıl Kusatıldı?* (The Fethullah Gülen Movement's Hidden Plan: How has Turkey been Sieged?) (Siyah/Beyaz Yayincilik, 2006).
Yavuz, Hakan, 'Being Modern the Nurcu Way', in ISIM Newsletter (6) (2000), pp. 7 and 14.
—*Islamic Political Identity in Turkey* (New York: OUP, 2003a).
—'Islam in the Public Sphere', in Yavuz and Esposito (eds), *Turkish Islam and the Secular State* (Syracuse University Press, 2003b).
—'The Role of the New Bourgeoisie in the Transformation of the Turkish Islamic Movement', in Yavuz (ed.), *The Emergence of a New Turkey* (University of Utah Press, 2006), pp. 1–19.

Yavuz, Hakan, and Esposito, John (eds), *Turkish Islam and the Secular State* (Syracuse University Press, 2003).
Yilmaz, Ihsan, 'Beyond Post Islamism: A Critical Analysis of the Turkish Islamism's Transformation Toward Fethullah Gülen's Stateless Cosmopolitan Islam', in *Islam in the Age of Global Challenges: Alternative Perspectives of the Gülen Movement* [published conference proceedings] (Washington, DC: Rumi Forum, 2008), pp. 859–925.
—'State, Law, Civil Society and Islam in Contemporary Turkey', in *The Muslim World Special Issue. Islam in Contemporary Turkey: The Contributions of Fethullah Gülen*, Zeki Sarıtoprak (ed.), Vol. 95, No. 3 (Blackwell Publishing, 2005), pp. 385–412.
Yurtsever, Ali (ed.), *Islam in the Age of Global Challenges: Alternative Perspective of the Gülen Movement* (Washington, DC: Rumi Forum/Tuğhra Books, 2008).
Zürcher, Erik J., *Turkey: A Modern History* (New York: I.B. Tauris, 2004).

5

From Islamism to Post-Islamism: The Coming of a New Intellectual Trajectory in Pakistan

Husnul Amin

Like any other major world cultures, Islam contains within itself an astonishing variety of currents and counter-currents.

Edward Said

Introduction

Post-Islamism is a new intellectual response and social trend in Muslim societies that has emerged due to multifaceted crises of the idea and practice of creating an ideal Islamic state. Initially in Iran in the 1990s, this changing social and political trend was observed as a phenomenon that had resulted from the crisis of Islamists' experimentation to create an Islamic state. Later, not only was the term post-Islamism refined, but the number of such empirical examples also increased in Muslim societies. This dual process gave birth to a grand notion of post-Islamism that is deployable to various specific cases. This chapter concerns the articulation, refinement, nurture and proliferation of one such specific strand of post-Islamism in Pakistan.

For its proponents and those who applied it to empirical examples, post-Islamism is a project constituted of these features: 1) social and political conditions where the appeal of Islamism has dwindled due to multifaceted crises from within and without (Bayat 2005; Roy 2004); 2) exclusive, monopolist, puritan, statist and revolutionary accounts of political Islam are changing in favour of more inclusive, society-centric, vigilant accounts of individual liberties and concerns of women, youth and non-Muslims, and hermeneutically, a movement away from fixed scripture towards historicity (Bayat 2007); 3) a category of analysis that is not distinct but a 'variant of Islamism' (ibid.); 4) post-Islamism is not anti-Islamic or secular but 'secularization of state and prevalence of religious ethic in society' (ibid.); 5) it can become a pervasive argument only if an Islamist organization retreats from establishing an Islamic state (Tibi 2008).

This chapter traces the genesis and expansionary phase of post-Islamist intellectual discourse in Pakistan. This intellectual trajectory was inaugurated by a number of ex-Islamist public intellectuals through the newly liberated electronic media in the recent past. Articulators of this discourse were once ardent believers in Mawdudi's (twentieth-century revivalist and ideologue of Islamism) ideology and were activists in his Islamist party – the Jama'at-e-Islami Pakistan (founded in 1941 by Mawdudi). As a result of fractures and fissures within the Jama'at, Amin Ahsan Islahi (hereafter Islahi, exegete, scholar and co-founder of the Jama'at with Mawdudi) and Javed Ahmad Ghamidi (hereafter Ghamidi, exegete, intellectual and ex-member of the Jama'at) quit Mawdudi's party in the 1950s and 1970s respectively. After parting ways with Mawdudi's Jama'at, Ghamidi came under the intellectual influence of Islahi and laid the foundations of a post-Islamist intellectual discourse and social trend in Pakistan.

This chapter begins with an overview of the history of fractures in Mawdudi's Jama'at in the 1950s, the vantage point of Islahi's resignation, and finally Ghamidi's gradual transformation from Islamism to post-Islamism in the 1970s. To understand the gradual transformation of Ghamidi's ideas and his recommended strategy for social change, one must recognize the distinction between 'old Ghamidi' and the 'new Ghamidi'. The former is an embodiment of an Islamist activist in the mould of Mawdudi's ideology, while the latter seems to be a changed post-Islamist intellectual seeking transformation of society with a bottom-up approach. The post-Islamist Ghamidi and his intellectual discourse are comprehended through his biography, writings and audio–video discussions. Ghamidi, his disciples and followers subscribe to the lineage of the School of Shibli – a self-described category. Ghamidi inspired a number of writers, scholars, public speakers, teachers and TV anchors, who inaugurated the expansionary phase of post-Islamism. The central argument in this chapter is that through a rereading of the prophetic epoch, Ghamidi (the post-Islamist ideologue) had arrived at quite different conclusions. These conclusions provided the post-Islamists with the necessary weapons for not only attacking and/or discarding the

Islamist thesis on political Islam, but also adopting a different approach for social change in the Muslim polities. In the same way, this chapter vies for a location of post-Islamism in modernity. I argue that despite being embedded in tradition and the past, the post-Islamist discourse is modern. A discussion on four aspects of post-Islamism and modernity: 1) biography of Ghamidi – shows that he is 'modern' (not Modernist) in his lifestyle, attire, consumption, acquiring knowledge and receptive attitude towards modern scholarship; 2) unlike Mawdudi and traditionalists, Ghamidi's unique interpretative approach and line of *ijtihad* is a radical departure from the traditional and Islamists' frameworks; 3) post-Islamist reading and rereading of history (i.e., prophetic career) is original, critical and might have far-reaching consequences for individuals, states and societies; and 4) Ghamidi's intellectual-cum-social trajectory or discourse within the community has made extensive use of modern technologies and products.

The period of 1956–1958 was a turning point in the history of the Jama'at, as this was when a number of leading figures and intellectuals left the organization. Among such leading scholars, I focus on one grand scholar, Amin Ahsan Islahi, whose resignation from the Jama'at is treated here as the embryonic stage of post-Islamism in Pakistan. The shockwaves set in motion by Islahi's resignation on the issue of defining contours of the authority of the emir, left an everlasting effect. A discussion of this episode in this section is a gateway to the succeeding section, which dwells at length on the biography, context, discourse, emergence and flow of post-Islamist intellectual trajectory in Pakistan. I will illuminate how Ghamidi's interpretation of the prophetic career is different from Mawdudi's. The significance of this difference is twofold: 1) almost all trajectories of Islamic activism in the field of education, preaching, jihad and politics are guided and inspired by the very life and strategy of the prophet; and 2) a specific understanding of the prophetic career shapes the Islamic social forces' strategy for change and defines their attitude towards issues like gender equality, fine arts, waging jihad, relations with non-Muslims, etc.

Islamism Between Ideology and Pragmatic Politics

In 1947, the end of the colonial era in the sub-continent gave birth to two independent states – Pakistan and India – which resulted in the Jama'at splitting into Jama'at-e-Islami Hind and Jama'at-e-Islami

Pakistan. Mawdudi opted for migration to Pakistan in the hope that this country (Pakistan) created in the name of Islam would readily embrace his revivalist vision of an Islamic state (Nasr 1996: 41). This shows that the Jama'at accepted the new national boundaries as a legitimate reality and adjusted its politics accordingly. In the nascent state of Pakistan, the Jama'at initiated activism through well-knit workers, propagating political ideas of Mawdudi in society and the organization of its workers, which assumed an 'anti-state' gesture in politics. Inevitably, the Jama'at and the Pakistani state soon came into conflict over the question of the relationship between religion and the state–politics (Abadshahpuri 1989b: 141–146; Binder 1961; Nasr 1994). In the first decade of its existence, the Jama'at pursued its Islamic agenda through moral persuasion and societal reform more than political means. The issue of participation in the general elections in the province of Punjab (1951) was decided by the *shura* and the application of a unique method for the nomination of candidates. This unique method involved formation of voters' councils (*panchaiyyat*), which determined the most pious (*saleh*) candidates for the elections (Nasr 1994: 30). The goal was to avoid candidates canvassing for self-projection. Despite a crushing defeat in these elections, the Jama'at leadership considered participation a vehicle for broadening the party's social base. However, participation also brought out the pent-up grievances and accusations of misconduct by Jama'at candidates. A number of grievances were aired against some ardent members allegedly violating the ethical standards set by Mawdudi for Jama'at workers (ibid.: 33). Confusion, ambiguity, frustration and crisis followed. Disenchanted with the transformation of the Jama'at from an educational–religious movement to a political one, a number of Jama'at leaders left. According to Nasr, Mawdudi assumed the role of politician rather than scholar (1996: 43).

In response, Mawdudi formed an eight-member review committee (later reduced to four) to consult all Jama'at members in Pakistan and investigate the causes of their discontent with the Jama'at programme and strategy. The review committee submitted its report in November 1956 (Ahmad 2005: 12–13). The findings of the committee stunned the highest ranks of the Jama'at, including Mawdudi. They were confronted with accusations of transgressions, financial mismanagement by its own ardent members and deviation from original goals. The committee's report was submitted to *shura* in November 1956, unequivocally stating that the Jama'at had deviated from its own goals set by its founding members and Mawdudi himself (Nasr 1996: 34). The report suggested that the Jama'at should stay away from future general elections and instead concentrate on educational and *dawah*–preaching activities (Ahmad 1991: 7–11). For discussion on the review committee's findings, the *shura* convened on 25 November 1956. After fifteen days of consultation, the *shura* meeting ended with the adoption of a four-point resolution. According to Israr Ahmad, from the *shura* meeting (November 1956) to the Machichi Goth members' session (February 1957), the Jama'at suffered severe crises (*shadeed buhran*) which finally 'caused a death blow to the Jama'at of 1941' and gave birth to a '"new" Jamaat-e-Islami' (1991: 9). Significantly, this crisis precipitated the desertion of fifty to sixty ardent Jama'at members, including Amin Ahsan Islahi, and all members of the review committee (2005: 13).[1]

Choosing an Appropriate Strategy: Top-Down or Bottom-Up

The Jama'at's central *shura* meeting on the review committee's findings, which continued for fifteen days, saw a heated debate splitting the *shura* in half with contrasting approaches to the goals of societal and state transformation. One half insisted on the Jama'at's early return to its original bottom-up approach of 1951, while the other was adamant it continue with the recently adopted top-down strategy (Ahmad 1991: 24–26). In Israr Ahmad's opinion, Amin Ahsan Islahi belonged to the former group and not the latter (1991: 26; Islahi 1991: 53–78). The four-point resolution was to bridge this gap between the two camps, offering a temporary solution. To oversee and monitor the progress of the four-point resolution, another committee, with Islahi as a member, convened (Ahmad 1991: 27–28). The substance of the resolution, if adopted in letter and spirit, could have brought the Jama'at back to its four-point agenda set in 1951, thus stifling every effort at dragging it into the realm of active politics.[2] The mere anticipation of this end pitched the young and zealous leaders, desirous of an active political role even at the cost of compromising the Jama'at's ethical standards, against the *ulama*. Mawdudi, overwhelmed by the former's force of conviction, chose their company and parted ways with the opposing *ulama* group (Nasr 1994: 34). Israr Ahmad proclaimed that the Jama'at had deviated from its earlier chosen path. Dissatisfied with the review committee's findings and its fall-out, Mawdudi issued a charge sheet against members of the committee, calling into question its composition, terms of reference, jurisdiction and intentions (1991: 31–35). He accused members of the committee of conspiring against the Jama'at and demanded their resignations. The four members approached Islahi for justice. Islahi came to the defence of the committee's rights and findings and instead accused Mawdudi of being under the spell of some insiders' propaganda (Islahi 1991). He termed this campaign 'undemocratic' and against the Jama'at's constitution. Islahi vociferously 'defended the constitutional powers of the *shura* against what he regarded as encroachments upon them by the emir' (Nasr 1994: 36). Islahi's resentment over Mawdudi's autocratic attitude as emir appeared in the strongest terms: 'if this is democracy and *shura*cracy, then Mussolini, Hitler and Stalin were its better teachers ... In this regard, the nation does not require our services' (Islahi 1991: 77). This debate, between Mawdudi and Islahi, on violation or otherwise of democratic principle within the Jama'at, was held through correspondence in the late 1950s.

Islahi insisted on upholding balance and moderation (*tawazun*) between the four points outlined in 1951. As corollary, it implied that the Jama'at should pay more attention to the first three points (reform, training and organizing individuals and society) over the last one (reforming the government and state structures). Reform of the state and political structure, as understood from Islahi's view, would accompany the quantum of efforts gone into the first three tasks (reformation of individuals and society and its training and organization) (Ahmad 1991: 119; Islahi 1991; Nasr 1994: 38). Islahi also warned against the disruptive implications of following a 'reverse order' of the same process. That is, a reverse order was sure to fail (Ahmad 1991: 119). Here I want to add that Islahi's mutation from Islamism to post-Islamism remained incomplete; that is, he withdrew from a top-down to bottom-up approach but remained committed to the very idea and building blocks of an Islamic state. However, his hermeneutic approach shaped Ghamidi and the later post-Islamist discourse in Pakistan.

The Machichi Goth session ended with Mawdudi's celebration of a new strategy outlined in his long speech (Sayed Abul Aala Mawdudi 1997). At the cost of a split with the founding members and ardent supporters from the *ulama*, he consolidated his position within the Jama'at as sole 'spokesman' and leader of his own brainchild – the

Jama'at-e-Islami. With other choices dwindling, a number of ardent intellectuals, *ulama* and activists, including Islahi, quit the Jama'at in the following years. To Nasr, the Machichi Goth affair marked the 'end of ideology' and the beginning of pragmatic politics and decision-making in the party' (1994: 41). Although Islahi's and others' resignations did not result in a 'mass exodus' from the Jama'at, they did push the Jama'at into an ever-growing intellectual deficit. In my own analysis, Islahi and his intellectual input in the Jama'at was unparalleled by any other person except Mawdudi. He contributed to the development of vocabulary and jargon of Islamism through his works which remain popular among Jama'at activists. His presence in the Jama'at also served as a 'critical bridge' between an Islamist Mawdudi and his own intellectual lineage of Farahi and Shibli (both eminent theologians and scholars in the late nineteenth and early twentieth centuries). The loss of 'intellectual momentum' in the Jama'at is also reflected by the fact that 'most of Mawdudi's own seminal works, outlining his views on Islam, society and politics, had been written between 1932 and 1948' (Nasr 1994: 40).

The Jama'at's turbulent history has witnessed expulsions and resignations of a multitude of activists, including intellectuals and scholars. Mawlana Manzoor Naumani's resignation in 1941 was followed by more than fifty scholars or writers or *ulama* from the Jama'at in the 1950s. Likewise, Mawlana Abdul Rahim left the Jama'at in Bangladesh and developed his own intellectual trajectory. In the 1990s, a number of activists and *ulama* opposed the reforms inaugurated by Qazi Husain Ahmad – the then emir of the Jama'at – and formed their own 'Islamic movement' (*Tehreek-e-Islami*). Dr Israr Ahmad and Javed Ahmad Ghamidi also seceded from the Jama'at in late 1950s and late 1970s respectively. Ghamidi and Israr Ahmad are closely linked to Islahi, as both remained under the tutelage of the latter. Another scholar of the Farahi School, Wahiduddin Khan, developed a critique of Mawdudi's Islamist ideology in his classic *Error in Interpretation* (*t'abeer ki ghalati*) in the early 1960s. He left the Jama'at in 1962. Khan, who was an activist in Indian Jama'at and a member of central executive, attacked the very basis of Mawdudi's revivalist thought. The statement 'political reading of religion' (*din ki siyasi tashreeh*) was first used by Khan in his methodical critique of Mawdudi (Khan 1995).

Whereas the Jama'at and its ideology, organization and political struggle has received considerable academic attention, the seceding voices and their respective intellectual–social trajectories are often neglected. In what follows, I trace the historical roots of one intellectual trajectory – Ghamidi and his post-Islamist thought. I begin with two prominent scholars whose influence on Ghamidi is substantial and defining.

Before I discuss the genesis of post-Islamism, a brief introductory note is necessary regarding Ghamidi's teacher – Amin Ahsan Islahi – and Islahi's mentor, Hamid-ud-Din Farahi (hereafter Farahi). The latter was a great theologian–scholar and explorer of the theory of thematic coherence–Nazm-e-Qur'an in the Qur'an. Intellectually, post-Islamist scholarship subscribes to academic works of Farahi and Islahi (Ghamidi 2008; Nadeem 2008).

Intellectual Biography of Farahi and Islahi

Farahi (1862–1930) was a cousin and a student of the eminent theologian–historian Shibli Naumani. After acquiring skills in Arabic and Persian from tutors in a traditional manner, Farahi gained admission to MAO College. Commenting on Farahi's skills in Arabic and Persian, Sir Sayyid Ahmad Khan (Islamic modernist of the nineteenth century) lauded them as far better than the college's professors. After graduation from Allahabad University, Farahi taught at various places. During his teaching stint at Aligarh, Farahi learned Hebrew from German orientalist Joseph Horovitz (1874–1931) in return teaching him Arabic. Farahi conceived of an institution that would teach traditional and modern sciences in the Urdu language, which led to the formation of Uthmania University in Hyderabad (1919). Farahi returned to his village in 1925 and resumed the charge of his Madrassa al-Islah (The Reform School). Farahi's extraordinary finding in intellectual terms was the thesis of internal coherence in the Qur'an.

Mawlana Amin Ahsan Islahi was born in 1904 to a small landowning family of Bhamhur, a village in Azamgarh, U.P., India (Islahi 2004). In 1922, Islahi graduated from Farahi's Madrassa-al-Islah and began his career as a journalist; first editing a newspaper called *Medina* at Bijnawr, and then working at *Sach*, a newspaper edited by Mawlana Daryabadi. Like his contemporary, Mawdudi, Islahi too joined this modern profession instead of becoming a traditional theological functionary. The Indian freedom movement also influenced Islahi, and he worked as the president of a local chapter of the Congress Party.[3] In 1925, Farahi invited his former student, Islahi, to study the Qur'an under his tutorship. Farahi called on Islahi to help him complete his deliberation on the Qur'an based on his thematic coherence approach (Ghamidi 2008: 99–131). Islahi abandoned his career as a journalist and joined his teacher for thorough deliberations and understanding of the Qur'an from 1925 to 1930. After Farahi passed away in 1930, Islahi continued the dissemination of his approach and ideas. He founded The Hamidiyya Circle (Daiyerah-e-Hammidiyyah) in 1936, and started publishing a periodical called *The Reform* (*al-Islah*) which continued until 1939. Islahi and Mawdudi co-founded the Jama'at-e-Islami in 1941. He remained with the Jama'at for seventeen years. In 1958, Islahi parted ways with the Jama'at after differences between him and Mawdudi emerged over the authority of the emir and the nature of the constitution of the Jama'at.

According to Islahi, electioneering was a useless way of bringing about social change in society (Islahi 1991). For Islahi, the foremost objective of politicians was consolidation of power, not establishing Islam. Therefore, *dawah* and not 'political propaganda' was the right methodology. Islahi shifted his emphasis to the inner dimensions of individuals and society perpetually under attack from the most dreadful malaise – hypocrisy. In connection with Pakistan's leadership and their tactics to transform it into an Islamic state, Islahi wrote:

> Hypocrisy is a deadly disease, and there have been in every age and society some people who were afflicted with it, but we do not find in history a single nation whose leaders have chosen it as a 'national policy', taking it to be the 'key' to the 'resolution of all their problems'. In history there seems to be only one such nation and that is unfortunately our nation (Pakistani).[4]

The above description not only reflects Islahi's shifting emphasis in his post-Islamist intellectual and societal career but also the embryonic phase of a counter-discourse to the state-centred approach of the Islamists. Islahi's counter-discourse was based on his new vision of flooding society with a new reflective consciousness. This was not the job of politicians, and the realm was not the domain of political activism. Islahi's social analysis of bringing about a genuine change in society was premised on the belief that an intellectual transformation in light of the Qur'an was required. These initial premises transformed into a developed argument by Ghamidi and his circle in favour of the need for a society-centred social movement.

Following from his revivalist thought, Mawdudi aptly extended the application of duress (to situations of compulsion in which a person is left with no other options but to choose a lesser sin or evil) (Islahi 1991: 97). Mawdudi depicted Islam under siege or under duress from internal and external hegemonic forces. According to Islahi, Islam was not under such duress. The similarity between individuals and Islam will lead to a condition where Islam will 'require its followers to violate its principles for its political growth' (Iftikhar 2005: 77). Islahi accused Mawdudi of employing 'strategy' and 'practical wisdom' as the basis for determining permissible and impermissible. Whereas, argues Islahi, this principle in religion was associated with duress and not strategy (Islahi 1991: 99).

During the period of the Machichi Goth affair, Jama'at's future in electoral politics and the authority of the emir all attracted the interest of scholars. Almost all renowned scholarship on the Jama'at has deliberated on this episode (Bahadur 1977; Moten 2002; Nasr 1994). However, for the present researcher, Islahi's resignation from the Jama'at in 1958 transcends all bounds of mere internal dissent and schisms in Mawdudi's community. After his resignation (in 1958), Islahi lived a long life (d. 1997) with uncompromising attention towards completion of his monumental exegetical project – *Tadabbur-e-*Qur'an (*Reflecting on the* Qur'an: his nine-volume commentary on the Holy Book). This project started in 1958 and was completed in 1980. According to Islahi, the masterpiece – *Tadabbur-e-*Qur'an – is the outcome of almost a century of deliberations on the Qur'an; his teacher Farahi spent thirty to thirty-five years, while he devoted fifty-five years of his life to the task. The post-Islamists emphatically assert that Islahi's Tafseer has had no parallel in all of Islamic history (Nadeem 2008).

As opposed to the traditional methodology of exegesis (*tafseer bil riwayat*), Islahi followed a direct approach to the interpretation of the Qur'an. This approach seeks to comprehend meanings in the Qur'an in light of its language and context, while taking cues from dominant Arabic literature at the time of revelation. In addition, this approach strives towards understanding the context of every chapter, following the principle of internal coherence (*nazm*). The *nazm* principle states that each chapter is a complete, self-contained and well-knit unit of analysis, with common features of an introduction, a central theme and a suitable epilogue summarizing the entire content of the chapter (Masud 2007). In addition to intra-*surah* coherence, the Qur'an exhibits inter-*surah* coherence as well. Following this principle of internal order in the Qur'an, Islahi divided the book into seven well-defined groups of chapters, with each group eloquently exploring a central theme.[5]

Islahi considers his interpretative method 'scientific, rational, and based on common sense, without which the true message and beauty of the Qur'an cannot be understood or appreciated'.[6] About academic freedom and critical deliberation, Islahi expounds confidently that people should not expect blind submission from him, and that critical deliberation or reflection (*ghawar wa taddabur*) is the most exalted virtue of all human possessions (Nadeem 2008: 170–171).

Thus, the troika of Farahi–Islahi–Ghamidi founded a new school in the field of exegesis (*tafseer*), where the latter two adding to the exegetical principles laid down by Farahi. One of the main claims stemming from the Farahi–Islahi–Ghamidi *nazm* approach is the possibility of only one interpretation of the Qur'an, that is, monovocality of the text. This, if achieved, argues Ghamidi, can bridge the sectarian divide that feeds on the competing interpretations of the Qur'an without adhering to the principles of *nazm*. Further, this approach enhances the possibility of appropriating new space *within* the vocabulary and verses of the Qur'an compatible with efforts to socially reform and modernize Muslim societies. By using this approach, these scholars internalize the context of the Qur'an and thus differ with Islamic modernists, who historicize it. However, the claim to monovocality of the text may itself end up developing an exclusivist reading of the doctrinal sources. Some of his ex-fellows have examined empirical examples which reveal that post-Islamists' reliance on this approach might create inconsistency and incoherence (Ansari 2009).

Islahi's abandonment of Jama'at political activism and his determination to avoid practical politics did not mean that his ideas went unnoticed by the state and society. It also does not imply his detachment from issues and debates around him. He persistently printed his research findings in his own initiated journals: *Mithaq* (started in the 1960s), and then *Tadabbur* (started in 1981). As an intellectual, he used Qur'anic study circles and print activism to remain engaged with society and state. In 1961, Islahi established 'The Circle for Reflecting on the Qur'an'

(*Halqa-e-Tadabbur-e-*Qur'an), reinvented under the name of 'The Circle for Reflecting on the Qur'an and Hadith' in 1981 (Ghamidi 2008). In the latter, which continued until 1993, Islahi gave lectures on the Qur'an and *Hadith*. These circles were a kind of 'solidarity network' where the Qur'an became the central point of intellectual deliberations, and Islahi the teacher–mentor in a teacher–disciple relationship. This was the complete opposite of the sheikh–disciple relationship as envisaged in Sufism, where the disciple is obliged to follow the sheikh blindly without raising questions regarding his ideas or approach. The Qur'an being the centre of his *indhar* or activism, Islahi posed a considerable challenge to the dominant approaches of traditional *ulama*, and even the Islamists in some instances. Once an ardent member of the Jama'at, and now founder of his own Islamist organization – Tanzeem-e-Islami – Dr Israr Ahmad broke away from Islahi because of his non-traditional views concerning the punishment of stoning to death (*rajam*). The same view also invoked harsh criticism and protests from the traditional *ulama* and Islamists after a court of law decided on an adultery case in light of Islahi's views (Ghamidi 2008). After this controversy, the Zia regime reconstituted the court. In the aftermath of the turmoil in the early 1980s, Ghamidi broke his silence and defended his teachers' stance on the issue. In 1965, when Ayub Khan was running for the presidential elections against Fatima Jinnah, Islahi wrote an article in his journal. The article favoured Ayub Khan's candidacy in the election, and so the government had it circulated widely. It is worth recalling that in the same elections, Mawdudi and his Jama'at were supporting Fatima Jinnah against General Ayub Khan. Mawdudi's stance was in contrast to his own position about women's candidature for head of state. After winning the election, Ayub Khan contacted Islahi for a meeting, which was conditionally agreed upon.[7] According to Rauf, Islahi declined to accept Ayub's offer of appointing him as Vice Chancellor of Islamia University, Bahawalpur (Rauf 2006: 15). Furthermore, as an Islamist and member of the Jama'at, Islahi also spent weeks behind bars during the Anti-Qadiyani Movement in 1951. Furthermore, the government formed an Islamic Law Commission in 1956, where Islahi worked as a member. The commission was abolished in 1958 when Ayub Khan came to power.

Apart from his most important work, *Tadabbur-e-*Qur'an, Islahi wrote around eighteen books covering various religious, legal, social and political issues. Some of his books still form an important part of Jama'at training literature.

Ghamidi and Islahi met in 1973, and the former came under Islahi's influence. Islahi influenced Ghamidi's approach and method of understanding the Qur'an and *Hadith*.

From Islamism to Post-Islamism: Arrival of Ghamidi

This biographical account of Ghamidi derives primarily from his own autobiographical essays published in *Maqamaat* (Signposts). This book, written in a Persianized and Arabicized Urdu idiom, is a collection of Ghamidi's emotive and intellectual reflections on his own historical and socio-political development (2008: 13–44). Ghamidi explained the reasons for writing these autobiographical essays, as researchers' and writers' interest in his life, ideas and works grew. 'They wanted to know about us. In this quest, they made grave mistakes due to lack of authentic biographical information. So I decided to explain my intellectual development in these essays.'[8] Ghamidi's statement and the considerable Internet traffic on the subject is a good indicator, showing increasing trends in the size of his audience and expanding constituency – mostly urban, middle and upper-middle classes, modern educated youth. Ghamidi's narrative of his ceaseless struggle and, for that matter, of Mawdudi's, Farahi's and Islahi's, 'tell about a humble beginning, migration, and lonely struggle' (Masud 2009b). The drawback of autobiographies is that they are not critical.

Ghamidi was born on 18 April 1951 to a peasant family in the Sahiwal district of Punjab, Pakistan; exactly a decade after Mawdudi founded his Jama'at. His father wholeheartedly subscribed to a Sufi order of the sub-continent. Sufism was thus the first religio-intellectual school he was exposed to; a school he would later criticize harshly for its theology, method and Sheikh–Murid relationship (Ghamidi 2006: 159–188). After receiving his early education from local schools, Ghamidi did his matriculation in 1967 at Islamia High School in Pakpattan. In class seven, he was introduced to Mawdudi's literature by one of his teachers who was a member of the Jama'at at Pakpattan. This was the first major shift in his intellectual life. According to Ghamidi, he read all the major works by Mawdudi and this 'opened a new realm of knowledge and activism (*'ilm wa 'amal*)' (2008: 19–20).

Under the tutelage of a local religious functionary, Ghamidi acquired initial skills in Arabic and Persian. Ghamidi had finished all books taught on the traditional religious course, Dars-e-Nizami, alongside his Grade 10 studies (2008: 19). Like Mawdudi, Ghamidi's strength lies in his extraordinary reading skills. He relates that in Class 10 he requested an exemption from class attendance from his head teacher, so that he could concentrate on reading (ibid.: 21). After doing his matriculation, Ghamidi moved to the city of Lahore, the main cultural and intellectual centre of Punjab, Pakistan. In the elitist Government College (GC) Lahore, he opted for the subjects of English literature and philosophy. The GC and Lahore city presented, says Ghamidi, a galaxy of diverse scholars, poets and writers. He specifically mentions one private tutor who taught him Arabic, and whose lineage traces back to tutors of the late nineteenth-century intellectual tradition – Shibli and Farahi (ibid.: 22). Ghamidi recalls his five-year-long stay at GC and his scholarly appropriations:

> [in these years] my routine was such that I would leave my residence early in the morning and after attending lectures [at GC] would sit in the library till evening. I would also visit scholars and attend their discussions … I would spend hours reading books for free at certain bookshops where certain publishers had provided this facility. (2008: 23)

In 1973, one year after finishing his studies in English literature at GC Lahore, Ghamidi learned of Farahi, and through his works about Islahi (ibid.: 23). He approached Islahi in person and in this encounter realized:

> Religion is not just uncritical submission, rather something intelligible and transferrable to others. The truth dawned on me [Ghamidi] that the Qur'an is the ultimate arbiter (*qawl-e-faisal*); a scale for the entire religious content and a conclusive proof (*hujjat*) for the whole world. In the light of the Qur'an, we can judge the validity of Fiqh, *Hadith*, Philosophy, Mysticism, History and International Relations. For me, this was the starting point of exploring a 'new Qur'an' … the Mawlana [Islahi] told me that if I was interested in reading the Qur'an in this fashion then I should discard all desires of becoming a political leader in the Islamic mould. This entailed making a retreat for deliberation and

> intellectual contemplation. 'Be determined that if, in the way of truth, you stand alone and your own shadow (*saaya*) deserts you, never sacrifice your true convictions.' (Ibid.: 24)

Islahi's message was a call to abandon political Islam in favour of intellectual contemplation. This message echoed the call to Islahi by his teacher Farahi in 1922. Just as Islahi abandoned journalism to concentrate on the Qur'an and the Nazm-e-Qur'an principles; the call to Ghamidi inspired him in the same way. In essence, both calls culminated in the inauguration of profound intellectualism rather than populist genres of activism. In response, Ghamidi abandoned his graduation studies and joined Islahi as a disciple. This phase lasted for ten years in which Ghamidi acquired skills in reflection on the Qur'an, *Hadith* and some current issues in modern philosophy. The long teacher–disciple relationship ended in 1983 and had a profound impact on him:

> In 1983, when this phase of education [as a private student with Islahi] ended, it had shaken up my entire belief system. Everything seemed to be leaving its place: fiqh, jurisprudence, mysticism and theology were now looking for its basis in the Qur'an. All existing explanations of the right interpretation of religion had come under criticism. My castle of ideas had been demolished and its new construction demanded fresh arrangements. So this [intellectual arrangement] claimed the next seven years of my life. (2008: 26)

During this period, he confronted the reality of diminishing faith in the prevailing traditional approaches to understanding Islam. He had lost what he achieved ideologically as Islamist, and was ready to reconstruct his ideas on the new lines of Farahi–Islahi thought. During this long period, Ghamidi concentrated on the entire contents of religion and specifically determined the principles for reflection on the Qur'an, *Hadith* and extracting of Islamic injunction from these two sources. In the same period, he accessed the first critical work by Wahiduddin Khan (an ardent member of the Jama'at at the time) and was thus persuaded by Khan's critical assessment of Mawdudi's thought. In his work 'Error in Interpretation', Khan critically evaluated Mawdudi's assertion of Islam as a system of life and a movement. He asserted that Mawdudi had inverted the fundamental notion of religion, which is self-purification (*tazkiyya*) and not the establishment of a political empire (Khan 1995).

Ghamidi recalls those moments when his fast-established intellectual constructs crashed under the weight of serious academic scrutiny (Ghamidi 2008).

On Sufism, his criticism surpassed that of Mawdudi and others. While he was a believer in the utility and revival of the Sufi institution of Khanqah (Sufi lodge), as regards purification of the soul and solutions to psychological problems based on modern consumer culture and uprooted individuals in the metropolitan environments, he was extremely critical of the theology of Sufism. He considered it a parallel religion *vis-à-vis* the doctrine of *tazkiyya*, which is the goal of religion. His criticism of Sufism appears in his book *Burhan*. It seems that for Ghamidi, criticism of Sufism is more an issue of theological concern than sociological, as with Islamic modernists (see chapter 3).

Ghamidi had never been a student in the religious madrassa. On this very point, the traditional *ulama* question his position as a religious scholar. In response, he constructs an eclectic genealogy of scholars discussed later in this chapter.

After expulsion from the Jama'at, Ghamidi gradually felt increasingly distanced from Mawdudi's ideology and drifted under the influence of Islahi's intellectual currents. This period represents the most important phase in his intellectual transformation from 'Old Ghamidi' to 'New Ghamidi' (from Islamist Ghamidi to post-Islamist Ghamidi). The post-Islamist Ghamidi, like his teacher Islahi, after dissociating from Islamism, no longer believed in social transformation through power politics and state apparatuses. In his imagination, a corpus of *ulama*, intellectuals, writers and preachers should be produced to create a counter-discourse and then invade the habits and thoughts of entrenched social forces like feudalism, clergy, military dictatorships and socio-economic injustices. In my own analysis, as is also evident from his various activisms in the 1980s and 1990s, it was a conceptual and not a practical transformation.

As a religious scholar, the first change in his intellectual perspective came when he encountered unsatisfactory results from application of the Islamic law of inheritance. It was the first time Ghamidi faced the breakdown of a traditional interpretative framework. With a problem-based approach, Ghamidi tried to correct the results but it did not satisfy him. However, religion as a composite whole, its epistemological principles and interpretation, had not yet become the focus of his attention. The second transformative event occurred in 1982, after which he devoted himself to academic understanding of various Islamic sciences. However, instead of contemplation on philosophical and moral content prior to issues of Islamic law (Shari'a), Ghamidi's intellectual journey took the reverse order due to unfolding events in Zia's state-sponsored drive for Islamization. One of the remarkable events in the context of the same Islamization move changed the course of Ghamidi's intellectual career and social life. The judge of the Federal Shariat Court (FSC) judged a *rajam* case in light of the opinion of Islahi, Ghamidi's teacher. There were demonstrations and protests by the religious forces which resulted in FSC being entirely dissolved and reconstituted with *ulama* as its judges. Ghamidi, as a student of Islahi, came forward to address this situation (ibid.). After a critical review of Islahi's opinion and arguments surrounding the matter (the *rajam* punishment), he found it almost satisfactory. Ghamidi spent three years reading and comprehending works on that issue. It was the first time that religious content as a whole appeared as an issue before abrogating his previous problem-based approach (ibid.). He realized that the issue at hand was not confined to partial (*juzyee*) Islamic penalties; rather it involved general principles (*kuliyyat*). The latter involved a complex web of issues nested in more complicated debates. In 1985, continuing for ten consistent long years, he immersed himself in the content of religion as a whole and in the quest for the 'true religion' (*din-e-haq*). It was during this process in 1990–1991 that he felt the need to write a comprehensive single textbook on religion, explaining religious content from beginning to its ultimate end. In 1985, Ghamidi started publishing his own journal in Urdu, *Ishraq* (Renaissance), which became the medium for Ghamidi's ideas in Pakistan. The English journal *Renaissance* was launched in 1991. The scope of both the journals, however, was targeting a limited readership as it appealed mostly to the well-read and learned community. Later, a *dawah* edition was published in order to reach a wider audience. The Ishraq–*dawah* edition is regularly published from Karachi now. Leafing through Ghamidi's intellectual biography, Ghamidi explains:

> my own [intellectual] condition reflected a pantheon of ideas (*butkada-e-tasaweraat*) where I sculpted ideas and I worshiped them and then I smashed them down … in 1990, ultimately the ground was ready for laying the foundations of a new building/construct … I was turning 40, and had acquired clarity of thought to a greater

> extent ... I am working on my authorial project for the last 17 years now. (2008: 27)

In short, Ghamidi's graduation to his current intellectual standing is rooted in constant ruptures and transformations. His dissatisfaction with the existing revivalist approaches and the breakdown of the traditional framework was instrumental in shaping his intellectual development.

Interaction with a number of post-Islamist scholars revealed that their change from Islamist ideology and activism to the current worldview was a function of multiple internal and external crises. These issues caused their discontent, dissent and ultimate defection from Islamist thought and socio-political activism. For some, Jama'at's ideological vacuum became the ultimate cause; a popular post-Islamist scholar and ex-member of the Jama'at revealed the story of his defection as follows:

> I was an activist in the Jama'at and a member of its provincial *shura*. In 1991, I wrote a book raising a number of issues concerning music, family planning, and women's visibility in public places. After the book was out, the Jama'at senior members contacted and accused me of 'deviation' from the 'consensus position' (*ijmaai' masayel*). By God, I didn't know what the Ijmaai' position was; and what was the opinion of Mawdudi and other Islamists like Qutb on Ijmaa' ... I had many questions but no answers in Mawdudi's framework. I came to know about Ghamidi and his thoughts, which satisfactorily addressed my discontent.[9]

Other activists experienced a parallel–simultaneous process between Islamist activism and their turn to a post-Islamist worldview:

> My dissent, with the Jama'at ideology and activism, was a function of simultaneous processes: on the one hand, I listened to Ghamidi's audio lectures and his deep analysis enhanced my critical ability, and on the other hand, the Jama'at internal tensions were reinforcing my discontent. I must say that essentially, my switching to Ghamidi's ideas was the result of the logical appeal of it and not primarily my intellectual discontent within the Jama'at ... but these new ideas made me critical about the ideology and practices of the Jama'at activists.[10]

Yet, for others, the crisis was so deeply entrenched that it led them into a condition of near-disbelief and suspicion over the very existence of any creator:

> I subscribed to Barelvi [Sufi] ideology. In the 1980s, the Afghan jihad and then Mawdudi's ideology changed my views in favour of armed jihad. However, reading habit and critical thinking created some questions ... at a certain stage, I was left with only two options: either to live like a 'hypocrite', having a Muslim name and following materialism, where the primary aim is seeking worldly pursuits but religion accompanies you as a cultural identity; or deliberate on the whole issue from its foundations. I opted for the second one ... in this journey, I studied Arabic, comparative religions etc., ... as an activist, [I] closely observed Islamic movements ... but two scholars, Wahiduddin Khan [Indian scholar and ex-member of the Jama'at] and Ghamidi, and their approach was appealing to me in the light of my own knowledge and reason.[11]

The above discussion is self-evident in manifesting the dwindling strength and energies of the Islamist project to hold some of its most internal critics together. For the post-Islamists in question, their diminishing belief in Islamism was a result of numerous forces. Their dissent began with the ambiguity and fissures in mainstream Islamism (the Jama'at) and it further grew as a result of many Islamist experimentations – the state-led drive of Zia's Islamization in the 1980s, the Islamists' consistent defeats in the elections in the 1990s and the drop-scene of the Afghan jihad project. Despite inaugurating a reconstructionist phase in the 1980s, Ghamidi was attracted to various modes of activism. In the 1980s and 90s, he tried to revive one or other forms of activism to reach a larger public (2008: 18–44). However, this seems to have failed badly. Inspired by the Islamic Salvation Front's electoral success in Algeria, the then emir of the Jama'at established a political party called the Pakistan Islamic Front (PIF, established in 1993). Ghamidi and some of his fellows joined the PIF. However, they were soon disillusioned by the very idea of creating an Islamic state through elections. In response to the Jama'at defeat in the 1993 elections, Ghamidi wrote an essay, 'Islami Inqilab', where he seems to have totally discarded the possibility of an Islamic revolution through the electoral politics of the current Islamist parties (2006: 274–287). Analysis of their various social activisms in the 1980s and 90s shows that realization of their current worldview (strategy for social change) was greatly shaped by their increasing disillusionment with the Islamist project, both at state and society levels.

What follows exposes the major theoretical postulates of the post-Islamist intellectual movement. In the first place, Ghamidi's rereading of the prophetic career will be delineated. The critical rereading of the prophetic mission inaugurates new meaning and a post-Islamist discourse, which is not only in sharp contrast to the Islamist reading but also calls for defining key issues and debates anew.

Rereading of the Prophetic Career

Ghamidi's revisiting the prophetic era suggests that the Islamists' formulation of strategy by imitating the divinely guided life of the Prophet was a grave mistake and a clear deviation from divine rules. This scheme is divinely monitored and regulated, allowing no deviation. Before discussing the implications of the post-Islamists' revisiting the prophetic era, it is imperative to understand the concept of messengerhood (*risalat*) presented by Ghamidi and his school. The inauguration of this new framework (special status of the Messenger, his transcendental mission that ends in conclusive argument and administration of punishment and reward by him) enables them to engage critically with Islamists and traditionalists on a number of issues. This framework will be referred to as the IHF (Itmam-e-Hujjat Framework) throughout the rest of this chapter.

The IHF stems from distinguishing the concept of prophet (*nabi*) from that of messenger (*rasul*). A faulty notion of the prophetic career is said to be the cause of a number of modern misunderstandings in the Muslim world, which has set the wrong precedence/exemplary practices before us. The following will outline briefly Ghamidi's approach to the prophetic mission – the IHF.

For Ghamidi, the central theme of the Qur'an is a biographical account and the narrative of the prophetic admonition. According to this approach, the *nabi* admonishes his people and those he admonishes may sometimes harm him. All messengers enjoy the status of a *nabi* but not the other way around. The Messenger is sent with an additional responsibility to administer His scheme of reward and punishment (*dainoonat*) is assumed to be held on the Day of Judgement (Iftikhar 2005). In this capacity, the status of the Messenger is an elevated position with extraordinary responsibility. Out of many prophets, only about 313 were assigned this divine task to establish a divine scheme of reward and punishment on earth. This administration thus becomes a 'historical testimony to the truth of the Final Day of Judgment' (ibid.

2005: 83). The established divine practice in this connection is that the Messenger and his fellows will necessarily triumph over his nation in the Messenger's lifetime. He propagates a divine message until it becomes conclusive evidence and the addressees can be left in no doubt. In Qur'anic terms, this is a demonstration of 'testifying to the truth of God and religion before people' (*shahadah al-alnas*). After coming forth from the IHF, if the primary addressees of the Messenger still deny the truth out of sheer arrogance, then the divine punishment of them is administered either in the form of 1) the Messenger and his followers seeking a safe abode in which to establish a proper government and then punishing the opponents of the message with their own hands, or 2) in the shape of natural calamities and disasters (as with the people of Noah). In order to fulfil this onerous task, the Messenger's career is strictly and thoroughly guided and monitored by divine authority, and he has no liberty to take key decisions at his own discretion. All the stages of his career (preaching, migration, waging war, etc.) are divinely ordained and he is to administer only this whole scheme. It implies that the Messenger and his fellowmen are employed as divine instruments in this project. This divine scheme is not to be imitated in the contemporary world as is mistakenly done by the revivalists. The Islamists have failed to appreciate this divine scheme (Ghamidi 2006, 2008).

Following this scheme, the prophetic career necessarily divides into a number of stages. These are admonition (*inzaar*), general and augmented admonition (*inzaar-e-aam*), culmination of the conclusive evidence (*itmam-e-hujjat*), and finally, conclusion of the message and acquittal (*hijrat wa bar'at*).

In the final stage, the primary addressees are issued a last warning about the arrival of that dreadful day of worldly punishment, which has always been a theme in the message. Then comes the last ultimatum to choose between belief in the Messenger and his message or death.

Upon persistent denial, Muhammad was ordered to migrate to the nearest town of Medina to establish a state, and so to administer divine punishment on the deniers. The war at Badr represents the first phase of this coming of punishment in which most of the summit leadership was killed. The divine promised to assist in this war with the ratio of 1:10 (one Muslim fighter will triumph over ten pagans). The prophetic career passing through various stages culminated in the fall of Mecca to

Muhammad and his companions. The polytheists of Mecca were offered a categorical option (to embrace Islam or be killed), while the Nazarites and Israelites, similarly, had to choose between Islam and political subjugation (through *jizya*) or death (Iftikhar 2005: 85). Upon consolidating his position at Mecca and Medina, and after meting out punishment to the deniers, the Prophet sent messages to the rulers of a number of states. This episode ended with the life of Muhammad. The next question that arises is whether this divine scheme (as post-Islamists believe) is replicable in modern times (as Mawdudi described).

Compared to Mawdudi's understanding of the prophetic mission, which was to establish a divine kingdom on earth and which accordingly split the prophetic career along organizational stages, Ghamidi categorizes the mission into thematic–conceptual stages. The common notions that encompass these conceptual constructs are *dawah* and *naseeha*. Put simply, the revivalist vision that is derived from these interconnected points in the prophetic struggle is *dawah*. The *dawah* model integrates individuals, social groups, political parties, state structures and 'others'. *Dawah* is an interactive model where multiple voices and actors interact in a dialogic way.

The Question of Replication: An Internal Critique of Islamism

The above rereading falls in sharp contrast to Mawdudi's political reading of the prophetic mission. Using Ghamidi's IHF, a young post-Islamist scholar invalidates Mawdudi's Islamist interpretation of the prophetic career in the following words:

> Muhammad at Mecca was reminded time and again that his responsibilities do not exceed admonition ... in this whole period, Muhammad was not ordained to enforce religion nor enforcement of religion was declared the central aim of the Messengerhood ... As a result of 'preaching' and only preaching, without any 'revolutionary struggle', the Islamic state of Medina came into existence ... for this 'revolution', Muhammad never erected an 'organizational structure'; he never established a system of pledging; and never handed over his followers a 'strategy' for the enforcement of religion ... The revolution that emerged fourteen hundred years ago cannot be an 'exemplary strategy' for future revolutions. (Amjad 2000: 36)

This assertion has far-reaching consequences for revivalist thought and strategy. It clearly challenges the validity of the Islamist claim that the Prophet's mission was the establishment of an Islamic system, the enforcement of justice and the eradication of injustices. Ghamidi argues that this explanation of prophetic mission was dictated by 'a desire to forcefully inject pure politics into religion'. If the latter's explanation is followed, then by implication the prophetic efforts shall not be imitable for the Islamists' political struggle (Mawdudi 1996), which is devoid of appreciation for physical laws, as Mawdudi's assertion was:

> The life of the Prophet Muhammad and his fellows is not to be used as an example in this case [struggle for Islamic revival] because he was obliged to fulfill the prophetic mission as a first order. For this purpose he never established a political organization. And understandably so, as the Messenger is never meant to struggle for political change, rather, he concentrates on purification of hearts and souls of individuals. His mission is not to become an actor in the 'power struggle' but to preach and imbibe the moral principles in politics and economy. In the same vein, if one expects the Prophet to be a successful 'banker' and 'politician', then he is mistaken. He is an inviter ... He doesn't come up with an 'economic programme'. He doesn't bring any revolutionary programme ... the 'Caliphs' were not essentially *ulama* but 'political leaders' who were also well-acquainted with religion ... if the *ulama* and religious groups were to redirect their energies towards raising collective consciousness through preaching, education and exhortation then none of the current 'structures' could stand up to them: neither these status quo intuitions nor the US hegemony in the current form.[12]

How do post-Islamists make sense of the failure of Jama'at to transform Pakistan into its envisioned Islamic state? My analysis in this section is mainly based, but not restricted to, one of Ghamidi's essays, 'Islamic Revolution' (*Islami Inqilab*) written in the context of the Jama'at defeat in the 1993 general elections (2006: 274–287). The idea of this critique, I argue, is directed at the very ideological core of the Jama'at as expounded by Mawdudi. In discussions on alternative strategies for political change, in the given context of Pakistan, Ghamidi eliminates the first two of the following options: 1) seizing power through armed struggle; 2) popular uprising forcing the existing government to withdraw; 3) using elected representation to attain power; and 4) influencing the authors into accepting the ideology of Islamists (Ghamidi 1995). The legitimating of the first two options, entailing rebellion against the state (*khurooj*), is further subjected to numerous Shari'a conditions. These include the government's explicit denial of Shari'a (*kufr-e-bawwa*), the despotic nature of the government and the leader enjoying the support of the majority (Ghamidi 2006: 276–277).

For post-Islamists, the reasons for the Jama'at's political failure relate to strategy (*hikmat-e-amali*) and not eternal Shari'a per se. In his critical analysis of Jama'at electoral politics, Ghamidi mentions three prerequisites for its participation in active politics: 1) it should necessarily be led by a politician like Jinnah or Bhutto and not scholars, *ulama* and intellectuals like Mawdudi or Iqbal; 2) only political parties like the Muslim League or the People's Party and not religious organizations like the Jama'at should carry on this project; and 3) electoral strategy should be chalked out on the basis of existing realities with a clear focus to win the elections and not to propagate the ideology (*tawsee' dawat*) (1995: 11–13). Commenting on the Jama'at's fifty-year-long political struggle, Ghamidi points out that its failed strategy has:

> almost totally deprived it of its ideological identity, its goal of reforming the Muslims and its zeal of disseminating the truth ... transferred the leadership within the various levels of the party from scholars and intellectuals to people who are not only devoid of these abilities but are also politically ineffective. Consequently, an atmosphere of gloom prevails at its various frontiers. (1995: 13)

Post-Islamists' Theory of Social Change

In relation to their theory of social change, 'individual', 'state' and 'society' are widely used concepts in post-Islamist discourse. More generally, these terms are elusive and difficult to define. In contrast to the individual, an immediate difficulty one confronts is in distinguishing between state and society. To get to a working definition of the two, I tend to follow Hefner's approach of 'arenas' in which 'boundaries, rights, jurisdictions, and power distribution between state and societal agencies are debated, contested, and resolved (at least temporarily)'. According to Hefner, these arenas can be *structures* in physical terms, belonging to the state (such as ministries); they can be *institutions* (like universities and the parliaments); and they can be any other entity, however ambiguous, in the given state structure. Likewise, arenas can be *groups* and *organizations* enjoying a greater degree of autonomy from the state rules and regulations such as 'families, villages, and religious groups' (Hefner 2005: 113). In post-Islamist discourse, the basic unit in all these arenas is the individual. Individuals interact in various ways, dictate and are dictated to and shape and are shaped by these arenas. Only the individual possesses the ultimate capacity to change. Religion too, according to post-Islamists, addresses and inspires the individual in the broader context of these arenas (Nadeem 2008: 17–24).

In the larger context of the post-Islamists' model of social change, the transformative values, forces, actors and institutions of religion operate essentially and fundamentally on the individual, and through the individual on family, society and the state. The perplexing problem is the post-Islamists' treatment of the individual as a homogeneous category in the realm of *dawah*. This conceptualization fuses various social categorizations among individuals based on status, class, authority, position, ethnicity, creed, faith and sex into a uniform category of invitees–addressees. This runs the danger of another social stratification inherent in it; that is, the division of society among 'inviters' (*daag'ee*) and 'invitees–addressees' (*madg'oyeen*) such that the former occupies a more learned and pious position than the latter. However, this deduction is drawn out by post-Islamists' further explanation of their *dawah* model. They explain that *dawah* is not univocal (a proselytization of one class of individuals to other classes). Rather, it constitutes an interactive model of a mutually influencing, mutually shaping process:

> Cognizant societal transformation necessitates emergence of an inviter–invitee relationship in the society among individuals. The practice of *dawah* in Islam does not mean disconnecting from society under the shadow of [*dawah*] organizations. Rather it [*dawah*] constitutes a cultural/social value (*samajee qadr*) wherein a person simultaneously occupies the position of an inviter as well as an invitee. When we form organizations for *dawah* work, its logical outcome is dividing society along the lines of inviter and invitee … this stratification is against the Islamic conception of *dawah* … [our] model precludes nurture of those feelings, as self-righteousness and arrogance over one's piety, after which the inviter considers himself different from the rest, and thinks of others as sinful beings. (Nadeem 2008: 22)

Such a depiction of the individual–society–state relationship and the assumed dynamic role of religion in it scales up post-Islamists' focus on the individual in relation to society. In the competing Islamic discourses of social change, post-Islamism inaugurates, at least in discourse if not in a social movement, a society-centred model. This is an 'inside-out' approach as compared to the Islamists' 'outside-in' approach.

Society-oriented movements refer to those forms of intellectual and social activism seeking to 'transform society from within by utilizing new opportunity spaces in the market and media to change individual habits and social relations' (Yavuz 2003: 30). Unlike Sufi orders that invite individuals to an 'inward retreat', to withdraw from active life into the realm of private contemplation and personal piety, and contra-political Islamists who believe in political activism and mobilization for change of the 'unjust/un-Godly' system, Islamic movements with a society-centric approach recommend influencing social processes and individual behaviours as *foci* of intervention.

The agency and potential for change of individuals, in post-Islamist discourse, overrides the transformative capacity of the structure and the state. This is more in line with the 'phase one' of the prophetic career undertaken at Mecca. In this connection, post-Islamists insist on introducing a third condition between the House of Islam and the House of War. That is *dar-al-i'dad* (the House of Groundwork). This is an intellectual construct referring to a temporal–spatial space wherein Muslims should concentrate on moral rehabilitation and increasing economic strength. One can observe that even in the articulation of this new phase (the House of Groundwork) by post-Islamists, pursuance of the lost Muslim's political power reappears as a mediating variable. According to Tibi, 'power is a historical fact in conquests that were pursued in addition to trade and commerce as a means for the expansion of Islam' (Tibi 2009: 71). For Tibi, prior to the Western project of globalization, the Islamic venture of globalization mapped out the world into the House of War and the House of Islam, which lasted from the seventh to the seventeenth centuries (ibid.).

From the above description, it seems that post-Islamists consider an 'Islamic system' an empty aggregation until its content is filled with socio-politically aware individuals. The state is the aggregation of individual pieties and profanities of society. Society as a collective category is constituted not only of individuals but also of their mutual interactions, which the religion is purported to reform. These individuals (and various social groups) create their own social reality filled with the content of change or perpetuation of the status quo.[13] When political regimes change in a society, the ascension to power is the direct manifestation of the existing social realities.[14] The political process (elections) does not create new social realities but only transfers power from one political elite to another. Hence, society must first contain numerous such creative processes capable of instilling new social reality and productive energy:

> As against the intellectuals and religious leadership, the political leadership does not directly participate in the reconstruction of collective behaviour. Their job is to meet the demands of the masses based on the available opportunities ... The real job of a politician is to mobilize the nation. (Yusufi 2004: 49)

Such social transformation will precede the transformation of the state and governmental system. This is how post-Islamists have inaugurated a counter-discourse to Mawdudi's state-centric model of social change.

To Ghamidi, the concept 'reform' (*islah*) as opposed to 'revolution' fits well in the overall framework of Islam. Religious scholars and intelligentsia graduate into the fold of a new relationship with the state and society. That relationship is premised on the principles of exhortation (*naseeha*), preaching (*dawah*) and admonition (*indhar*). The principles invalidate those historic forces of regression and backwardness: a community consisting of spiritually blind followers, politically subjugated and intellectually uncritical believers. Intellectually, a more enlightened community, defined by a teacher–disciple relationship, and politically more freedom-based, emanating from brotherhood rather than blind devotion is recommended (Ghamidi 2006; Khan 2008; Yusufi 2004).

Religious ideas guide religious practices in society (Yusufi 2004). Therefore, any refocus of the prevailing religious practice in society, post-Islamists argue, is conditional upon a serious academic revision of the existing interpretations of religion (Nadeem 1995). Within competing worldviews and the multifaceted challenges of modern times, post-Islamist scholarship considers the superiority of new ideas, fresh thinking and creative knowledge in a dialectical way:

> Darwin's 'survival of the fittest' theory is still valid in the empire of ideas. Theories and ideologies unable to stand up to the stumbling blow of time and incapable of proving their superiority in the realm of reason are deemed to fade away. Aligarh's (modernism) and Deoband's (traditionalism) days are counted now. (Nadeem 2008: 171)

From a number of dispersed texts produced by the post-Islamists, I tend to conclude that they admire and acknowledge the spirit of the Reformation movement in Europe. In their analysis, the problem arises when the religious leadership begins 'worshipping the old (*qadeem*) and demonizing the new (*jadeed*)'. Their victory over new ideas results in an underdeveloped society (Ghamidi 2008: 165; Nadeem 1995; Yusufi 2004: 45–46).

In the post-Islamists' model of social change, man is primarily driven and shaped by ideas and not material conditions. Ideas are produced by intellectuals, *ulama* and institutions. The transformative leadership include intellectuals, religious leaders and political leaders. These leaders, where political leaders appear last, have a cardinal role to play in raising awareness, changing people's worldviews and shaping their behavioural and cultural norms (Yusufi 2004: 39–54). A young post-Islamist scholar, Yusufi, argues that it should not be assumed that an ideologue is restricted to the formulation of ideas only; rather:

> He fights against the old and deeply entrenched ideas in society and nurtures new ideas in it. He educates the society and introduces new avenues of thinking. He inculcates a different perspective of looking at the issues. He reconstructs the national behaviour. (2004: 42–43)

In post-Islamist discourse, the *ulama* and intellectuals should raise the discussion beyond modesty, adultery and vulgarity. Moral conduct is more about human conduct in society as global citizens. It also deals with honesty, dutifulness, patience, industriousness, rationality, material progress, work ethic, saving and investment, rule of law and fulfilling responsibilities.[15]

The New Media and Constituency of Post-Islamism

The new media landscape has revolutionized communications. From newspapers to traditional television operators, they are all feeling the heat of the shift of the locus of control into the users' domain. Pakistan is no exception to this proliferation of the new media landscape. Within the country, currently over sixty private television channels operate. However, artificial barriers, such as a failure to grant terrestrial transmission rights, have been erected which bar most of rural Pakistan from acquiring access to them. In the urban areas, however, the effect is visible on the middle and upper classes – normally those who can pay for cable with comfort. But these two segments of the population have a different religious–spiritual need set when it comes to watching programmes of a religious nature. Primarily, three facets concern them: identity, the rational man and leisure–lifestyle. This audience wishes to define its identity within the Islamic spectrum without having to adopt an ascetic lifestyle, seeking instead one which will allow them to make rational decisions in contrast to decisions based on divine guidance.

With notable exceptions, the post-Islamist circle can hardly be said to have found any considerable support and defenders among the traditional *ulama*. Its constituency is mainly located in the modern educated stratum with access to the new mass media. The new media (Internet and private TV channels) has introduced Ghamidi's work and ideas among the middle, upper-middle and elite classes. Yet it is far from becoming a popular social movement.[16] A number of factors are responsible for the appeal of Ghamidi and other post-Islamists' ideas to these classes.

One reason is the lack of erudite modern scholars who can debate with modern youth in their language. Ghamidi's own background as a graduate of the elite Government College Lahore, his command over English and modern vocabulary, and his logical (if and then) style is appreciated among the modern educated youth – male and female both. He develops his argument simultaneously from doctrinal and modern sources, and synthesizes divergent views in a way that makes everyone feel included in his discussion. Content analysis of various episodes of a popular talk show between Ghamidi and modern youth (both male and female as participants) aired on a private TV channel called Geo, reveals that he listens to their questions … Within the print media, an English daily, the *Daily Times*, which is considered to represent liberal views, has been more sympathetic towards Ghamidi and his fellows in its news reporting, editorials and columns.[17] The administrator of the Ghamidi group, created by a civil servant on Facebook, informed me that the majority of its membership is made up of young men and women. In addition, the majority of the membership supports Musharraf and his Enlightened Moderation project.[18] I also analysed gestures and impressions of other participants towards Ghamidi (as opposed to traditional *ulama* and Islamists) in a number of debates on private channels where Ghamidi or one of his interlocutors were panelists. I found that in almost 95 per cent of cases, the secular politicians, scholars, journalists, civil society and human rights activists supported Ghamidi and his views on various social issues. The most obvious example of this observation came from the famous 2006 debate on Geo on *hudud* laws (named *Zara Sochiay*). Despite insisting on moral and ethical dimensions through *naseeha* emanating from an elder, Ghamidi approves of minimal religious intervention in spaces of leisure, festivals, sports, music, drama and dance. Modern youths that come into conflict with the religious classes on these issues, often cite Ghamidi's views in their defence. The case of women's visibility in public spaces, their right to drive, love, marriage and leisure also resonate with the youth. The more educated and affluent sectors of society are particularly attracted to a liberal brand of Islam. This could be viewed from many different paradigms. In my interviews I found that there is an identity crisis which plagues these sectors. Islamic liberalism allows them to reconcile their modern lifestyle with religious sanction. This also seems to be a factor that provides solace to such sectors. Alternatively, this limited access to liberal Islam is also furthering the ideological rift between those who have access to such content and those who do not. Hence, the digital divide is noticeable in the attitudes towards religion of the upper, middle and lower segments of society.

In popular debate on the *hudud* laws in 2006, Ghamidi emerged as a reformist scholar who could be a point of 'overlapping consensus' between the *ulama* and the civil society and human rights activists. One columnist at a liberal newspaper expressed his views on Ghamidi as follows:

> The reformist approach appears to be making some headway but is limited by the short supply of liberal scholars of Islamic law compared to the literalist hordes produced by the seminaries. There is only one Ghamidi; there are a thousand Qazi Hussain Ahmeds [then emir of the Islamist Jama'at]. (Naqvi 2006)

One might argue that this discursive circle has earned privileged access on private media channels. These channels are constantly looking for sellable talk shows and ideas on religion in the contemporary situation. This circle has become known among Islamists as well as the traditional *ulama* in Pakistan for its unique position on many issues. The reaction to its members' thoughts surfaces not only in the private discussions of *ulama* and Islamists, in their Friday sermons, but also in the growing number of publications against them.[19] In 2006, the editor of *Ishraq* survived a murder attempt. Ghamidi and his family have received death threats for years, and he is now in exile in Malaysia. Still, the intellectuals who are the public face of the Ghamidi movement now produce even more publications, Internet sites, articles, pamphlets and other media for general consumption.

The terminologies used by Ghamidi in his books are extremely difficult, and addressed mainly to researchers and scholars. However, in talk shows and lectures, he articulates his ideas in a language intelligible to a wider public. The foundation of Ghamidi's thought movement is made up of three loosely related threads – the *ulama* (intellectuals), the business elite and public intellectuals.

Ghamidi personally trained the *ulama* during his formative phase. Nearly all of the scholars in this circle come from a modern education background such as engineering, law, business administration or political science (Ghamidi 2008). They remained disciples of Ghamidi for a number of years, receiving knowledge in classical Arabic, the Qur'an, *Hadith*, history, literature and hermeneutics.[20]

The second tier consists of businesspeople and industrialists within urban centres like Lahore and Karachi. They support and finance various projects of this discursive circle. The third tier consists of public intellectuals (writers, public speakers, social activists, university teachers, independent researchers, TV anchors, columnists and preachers). Individuals with loose ties rather than formal organizations share through the bond of a common framework–ideology for social change. For this category, I will borrow Khosrokhavar's term 'intermediary intellectuals' who 'borrow some intellectual ideas from the grand intellectuals but with considerable independence' (Khosrokhavar 2004: 8). Emerging events on the local, national and global scene are interpreted and analysed by these public intellectuals in light of that common framework and shared outlook. The shared outlook and the new religiously informed rational worldview become the basis of all analysis and critique.

Conclusion

The internal crisis of the Jama'at, which was the outcome of multiple causes, resulted in its own ardent activists' discontent. The incessant crises produced an ever-growing ideological vacuum, which kept the Jama'at intellectual class at loggerheads with Mawdudi's ideology. Over time, the Jama'at had to confront a critique from within by its own elite intellectual class and also its rank and file. Islahi's disagreement with Mawdudi in the 1950s on the authority of the emir and the non-democratic way of running Jama'at affairs, Khan's attack on the very foundations of Mawdudi's ideology and its conceptual basis in the early 1960s, and, finally, Ghamidi's reconstruction of the entire argument and its synthesis, groomed into a counter-worldview to Mawdudi – named here as post-Islamism. I refer to this discourse as post-Islamist because of some shared traits with other such discourses in Iran, Turkey and Saudi Arabia. It is a strand of the grand post-Islamist project.

This chapter has shown that the emergence and development of post-Islamism in Pakistan followed a unique path. The building blocks of this project were constructed over a period of 130 years in which Farahi, Islahi, Khan and Ghamidi intellectually contributed. In the case of Islahi and Ghamidi, this counter-worldview to Mawdudi emerged as an intellectual issue in the religious sphere. They followed its entire content over a long period of time, essentially and originally in the doctrinal sources. In this way, post-Islamism in Pakistan has a generational dimension. Farahi (d. 1930), Islahi (d. 1997), Khan (b. 1951) and Ghamidi (b. 1951) contributed to an entire body of theory. Farahi prevailed prior to Mawdudi, and he is important because he outlined the theory of *nazm*, which is the basis of contemporary post-Islamists' hermeneutics and their engagement with competing Islamic discourses.

In the 1980s and 90s, Ghamidi inaugurated the reconstructionist phase of post-Islamism. Although, as his biography reveals, this issue emerged as a result of his own discontent with the prevailing explanations and interpretative methods of Islamic discourses, it is evident from the contours of his own intellectual journey that a number of socio-political factors pushed him towards the reconstructionist phase of post-Islamism. One main determining cause came from his dwindling trust in Mawdudi's ideology and the state-led drive of Islamization in Pakistan in the Zia-ul-Haq regime. Most of Ghamidi's current ideas on democracy, jihad and gender relations appeared by the mid-1990s, but they were known to and influenced only a limited learned elite. However, their overall influence was limited to these circles.

The eruption of new electronic media in Pakistan in the post-2000 era inaugurated the expansionary phase of post-Islamism in Pakistan. The emergence of this modern media of communication became a counter-public space for post-Islamists *vis-à-vis* the traditional institutions of mosque and madrassa occupied by *ulama*. This opportunity was further augmented by Musharraf's Enlightened Moderation and the post-9/11 debates in Pakistan and across the globe. Post-Islamist scholars emerged as 'Islamo-liberal' intellectuals and expanded their influence in the middle and upper-middle classes, mostly in the urban areas (Ahmad 2010; Lacroix 2004). Here I conclude that while the expansionary phase of post-Islamism depends on the opportunistic spaces that appeared in the recent past and that gave these intellectuals unprecedented momentum, the historical data suggests that this discourse is not reducible to the opening of these spaces. The analysis suggests that for a better understanding of the development of post-Islamist discourse over time, one can break it down into its various phases. Concentration on the last phase (the expansionary phase) without knowing the historical trajectory of the discourse may be misleading.

Ghamidi's own Persianized Urdu expression about his intellectual journey explains the condition and trajectory of constantly changing discourse and practice. In his term 'pantheon of ideas', Ghamidi explains his own intellectual evolution of formulating ideas, following them and then smashing them down. The ideologues of both movements have responded to the challenge of modernity in a critical and creative way. Neither of them can be labelled an irrational or medieval response. Both have undergone a lifelong experience of engagement and passed through various phases: traditional–uncritical belief, engagement with Sufism, phases of scepticism and uncertainty, self-exploration and identity construction, and mobilization of middle-class, modern, educated individuals for reform and revival.

NOTES

1 The names of the committee members are Hakeem Abdul Rahim Ashraf, Mawlana Abdul Jabar Ghazi, Mawlana Abdul Ghafar Hasan and Sheikh Sultan Ahmad.
2 These points were: 1) reformation of individual Muslims, 2) training and organization of pious individuals, 3) societal reform, and 4) reforming the government and political structure. See Nasr's *Vanguard*, p. 31.
3 Accessed at <http://www.amin-ahsan-islahi.com/?=5>.
4 Ibid.
5 Seven groups was Islahi's modification of Farahi's nine groups. Similarly, Islahi viewed each two chapters or *surahs* within a group as forming a pair (*tawwam*).
6 See <http://www.amin-ahsan-islahi.com/?=5>.
7 Dr Rauf has mentioned the conditions put forward by Islahi as follows: no guard will stop Islahi, and the meeting will not be reported in the press (Rauf 2006: 10).
8 Telephone interviews with Ghamidi and Shehzad Saleem, November 2009.
9 Telephone interview with Dr Farooq Khan, February 2010. Dr Khan was expelled from the Jama'at in the early 1990s on the basis of his controversial views on gender and jihad.
10 Telephone interview with Saleem Safi, January 2010.
11 Telephone interview with Rehan Yusufi, 3 Feb 2010; also see his article 'Ishraq: Aik Dawat aik Mission', last accessed on 2 March 2010.
12 Ghamidi's interview with Saleem Safi. Accessed at <http://www/tv-almawrid.org>.
13 Ghamidi's panel interview with Saleem Safi. Accessed at <http://www/tv-almawrid.org>.
14 Face-to-face interview with Ghamidi in August 2007.
15 Ghamidi's interview at Dunya TV. See <http://www.youtube.com/watch?v=Fu1aVaFiZ4A>.
16 Telephone interviews with Khurshid Nadeem and Dr Farooq Khan, December 2009.
17 Browsing for Ghamidi's name within the English press in Pakistan returns more mentions by the *Daily Times* than any other paper.
18 Telephone interview with Sayyid Aamer Abdullah, 21 March 2010.
19 Field observations; also books and booklets attacking Ghamidi's worldview.
20 Field notes.

BIBLIOGRAPHY

Abadshahpuri, *Tareekhe-e-Jamaat-e-Islami* (The History of Jamaat-e-Islami), Vol. 2. (Lahore: Idara-e Maaref-e Islami, 1989).

Ahmad, D. I., *Tehreek-e-Jamaat-e-Islami: Aik Tehqiqi Mutalea* (Lahore: Maktaba Khuddam al-Qur'an, 2005).

Ahmad, I., *Tarikh-i Jamaat-i Islami: Ik Gumshudah Bab* (History of Jamaat-i Islami: A Lost Chapter) (Lahore: Maktabah-i Jadid Press, 1991).

Amjad, M., *Manhaj-e-Inqilab-e-Nabawi: Aik Khudawandee Qanoon say Ghalat Fahmee.* (Lahore: Danish Sara, 2000).

Ansari, N. A., *Apparatus of Oppression and Social Unconscious*, 2009.

Bahadur, K. *The Jama at-i-Islami of Pakistan: Political Thought and Political Action* (India: Chetana Publications, 1977).

Bayat, A., 'What is Post-islamism?', *ISIM Review* 16: 5 (2005).

Bayat, A., *Making Islam Democratic: Social Movements and the Post-Islamist Turn* (Stanford University Press, 2007).

Binder, L., *Religion and Politics in Pakistan* (Berkeley: University of California Press, 1961).

Ghamidi, J. A., *Islam: From Revolution to Implementation* (Lahore: Al-Mawrid, 1995).

Ghamidi, J. A., *Burhan* (Lahore: Al-Mawrid, 2006).

—*Maqamat* (Lahore: Al-Mawrid, 2008).

Hefner, R. W. (ed.), *Remaking Muslim Politics: Pluralism, Contestation, Democratization* (New Jersey: Princeton University Press, 2005).

Iftikhar, A., 'Jihad and the Establishment of Islamic Global Order: A Comparative Study of the Interpretative Approaches and Worldviews of Abu al-A'la Mawdudi and Javed Ahmad Ghamidi' (PhD thesis, Montreal: McGill University, 2005).

Islahi, A. A., *Maqalat-e-Islahi* (Islahi's Articles), Vol. 1, compiled and edited by Khalid Masud (Lahore: Faran Foundation, 1991).

Islahi, A. A., *Selections from the Tadabbur-i-Qur'an*, tr. Shehzad Saleem (Lahore: Al-Mawrid, 2004).

Khan, W., *Ta'beer ki Ghalati* (Error in Interpretation) (New Delhi: Maktaba al-Risala, 1995).

Khosrokhavar, F., 'The New Intellectuals in Iran', *Social Compass* 51 (2): 191 (2004).

Masud, M. K., 'Rethinking Shari'a: Javed Ahmad Ghamidi on Hudud', *Die Welt des Islams* 47 numbers 3 (4): 356–375 (2007).

Mawdudi, S. A. A., 'Islami Hukoomat kes Tarah Qayem Hoti Hay' (The Process of Islamic Revolution), in *Tehreek-e-Azadi-e-Hind awr Musalman*, Vol. 2, pp. 161–200 (Lahore: Islamic Publications Pvt. Ltd, 1996).

—*Tehreek-e-Islami ka Aayinda Layeha Amal* (Lahore: Islamic Publications Pvt. Ltd, 1997).

Moten, A. R., *Revolution to Revolution: Jamaat-e-Islami in the Politics of Pakistan* (Kuala Lampur: Islamic Book Trust, 2002).

Nadeem, K. A., *Islam awr Pakistan* (Lahore: Al-Mawrid, 1995).

—*Junoobi Asia kay Tanazur main Beeswi Sadi ka Fahm-e-Islam* (Lahore: Almawrid, 2008).

Naqvi, F., 'VIEW: Amendment: The Radical Option', in the *Daily Times* (2006).

Nasr, S. V. R., *The Vanguard of the Islamic Revolution: The Jama at-i Islami of Pakistan*: (University of California Press, 1994).

—*Mawdudi and the Making of Islamic Revivalism* (New York: OUP, 1996).

Rauf, A., 'Mawlana Amin Ahsan Islahi: A Study of Sociopolitical Thought' (PhD thesis, NIPS, Quaid-e-Azam University Islamabad, 2006).

Roy, O., *Globalized Islam: The Search for a New Ummah* (New York: Columbia University Press, 2004).

Tibi, B., 'Why They Can't Be Democratic?', in *Journal of Democracy* 19 (3): 43–48 (2008).

—*Islam's Predicament with Modernity* (New York: Routledge, 2009).

Yavuz, M. H., *Islamic Political Identity in Turkey* (New York: OUP, 2003).

Yusufi, R. A., *Urooj wa Zawal ka Qanoon awr Pakistan* (The Law of Rise and Fall and Pakistan) (Lahore: Dar al-Tazkeer, 2004).

Globalization and Islam

6

The Multicultural *Ummah*

Corri Zoli

> The vast world of Islam is actually like a Persian medallion carpet; it has incredible diversity and complexity, yet it is dominated by a unity into which all the complex geometric and arabesque patterns are integrated. One can gain a better grasp of the whole by separating the patterns and seeing how each is related to Islam as well as to cultural, ethnic, and linguistic factors. Then, reuniting the patterns yields a vision of the total spectrum of Islam, in which unity leads to diversity and diversity is integrated into unity.[1]

Introduction

It bears repeating that the Muslim community (or, better, communities) is an enormous, variegated entity – with a worldwide population of adherents of between 1.2–1.8 billion. Generally speaking, one-fifth of the world's population identifies with this affiliation, and nearly fifty countries have a majority Muslim population.[2] National culture is, however, only one axis inflecting the diversity of the *ummah*, though its influence in an international community still defined by a system of states cannot be underestimated. Moreover, the referent of the nation itself is a defining source of tension for the *ummah* for many reasons, many of which are bound up with histories of European colonialism. Dissatisfaction with the integration of Islamic states into the modern nation state system as a tacit form of Europeanization under which the Islamic *ummah* was recognizable, for instance, not on its own terms, but only as distinct nation state units is an exemplary instance in this record of grievances.[3] As we will see, in its expansive notion of community – a referent for both local and transnational belonging – the *ummah* provides important checks and balances for the modern nation state in and beyond the Muslim world.

To concretize this sense of the *ummah* and offer a bit more granularity to Seyyed Hossein Nasr's elegant description of Islam as a unity in diversity, I briefly contrast five different Muslim-majority nations in their range of religious practices: Indonesia, Iran, Saudi Arabia, Uzbekistan and Oman. For this comparison, I have drawn from a consistent, updated source, the US State Department's yearly International Religious Freedom Reports (begun in 2001), and focused on states' support for religious minorities – a flashpoint in tensions between religious freedom and containing extremisms in the current revivalist moment and as Islamist groups use religious practice for political mobilizing.[4] I have also selected states that, though they may be well known for other things, have received little attention with regard to this key matter of importance: their populations' diversity, understood in ethnic, religious, national and cultural terms. In this context, I make a tripartite argument: that the critical role of multiculturalism drives to the heart of the contemporary *ummah*; that multiculturalism is part and parcel of the *ummah*'s *raison d'être*, though it represents an interesting point of tension for Muslim-majority states; and that this transnational community's ability to offer a counter-narrative to the nation state (colonialism, authoritarianism) and to extremism depends upon a conscious embracing of its intrinsic multiculturalism.

Diversity of the Worldwide *Ummah*: Ongoing Challenge to the Nation State

As a point of reference, it is worth revisiting the contract, known as the Constitution of Medina, drafted by the Prophet Muhammad after the *hijra* (622) in 622 AD, that defined the *ummah* as a plural society at its inception. Though scholars treat this document as the world's first constitution, and while Muhammad himself was chosen by a delegation from the various warring clans for his skill and fidelity as a neutral arbiter of conflict, his role, the nature of his authority, and the emblematic document itself which defines and embodies the first *ummah* is rarely discussed in ways that few have ventured to explain. This formal agreement between all clans in Yathrib–Medina, including Jews and pagans, with the express goal of ending inter-tribal strife, formalized several inalienable rights and responsibilities for Muslims, Jews and pagans and, critically, brought them into one fold or community – known as the *ummah*. It is some indication of how far we have travelled from this initial idea and act, based in conflict resolution, generosity and pluralism, that the idea of an *ummah* comprised of Jews and pagans would appear anathema today. The social contract of Medina also formed the first Islamic state, principles of security based on an inclusive community, religious and cultural freedoms, individual and women's rights, and a judicial system; in short, it constituted Medina as a *haram*, that forgotten concept in the Islamic lexicon, so important to theorizing conflict today: a sacred locus free from violence and weapons.[5]

Let us fast forward to the present. It is perhaps no surprise that the world's largest Muslim population belongs to one of the most diverse and disparate nations: the Indonesian archipelago of over 17,000 islands, where Muslims total 88.2 per cent of the population, 90 per cent of whom are Sunni.[6] A bastion of diversity at every level, Indonesia comprises 300 distinct ethnic–cultural groups (speaking over 700 languages), many from the largest Javanese group, but also from Indian, European, Chinese, Arabic, Malay, indigenous and other legacies. Despite 4.6 million missed persons in the most recent census, The International Religious Freedom (IRF) Report 2006 notes six state-recognized religions: Islam, Protestantism, Catholicism, Buddhism, Confucianism, and Hinduism, and many minority groups: Jewish and Baha'i communities, and Muslim sects such as the Ahmadiyya, al-Qiyadah al-Islamiya, Darul Arqam, Jamaah Salamulla, and the Indonesian Islamic Propagation Institute.[7] Indonesia struggles with a common test for Muslim-majority states: balancing 'official' and minority faiths, especially Islamic minorities. In this challenge, the messianic Ahmadiyya movement, which traces its roots to Victorian British India, has raised Sunni ire especially for its belief in the prophet Ghulam Ahmad, a perceived threat to the singularity of the Prophet Muhammad. In response to this unwitting provocation, Ahmadis respond to Sunni's contesting their claim to Islam by reasserting their Muslim identity, wearing badges declaring the Muslim faith (*shahādah*), for instance – a move seen as inviting prosecution, often by appeal (since the late 1980s) to 'blasphemy laws', which may include life imprisonment, a fine or capital punishment.[8] Importantly, the Indonesian Constitution accords 'all persons the right to worship according to their own religion or belief', though it also states that 'the nation is based upon belief in one supreme God' and it supports laws restricting 'deviant' religious groups (i.e., forcing them to register). On 9 June 2008, a joint ministerial decree froze Ahmadiyya activities but prohibited increasing vigilantism against them – though banning them outright was preferred by the government-appointed Coordinating Board for Monitoring Mystical Beliefs in Society.[9]

What is clear in Indonesia is that official Sunnis not only predominate, they dominate government and civil society, especially with respect to minority and revivalist Islam, and exhibit deep suspicion about non-Indonesian Sunni imports (i.e., Wahhabi and other orthodoxies).[10] While the IRF 2008 Report notes progress in reduced violence from interreligious strife, including fewer major incidents – significant milestones – the IRF 2006 Report assessment still holds a key truth: the country's religious composition 'remained a politically charged issue', with minority faiths arguing that the census purposely 'undercounted non-Muslims'.[11] One lesson learned from Indonesia for contemplating the diversity of the global *ummah* is that the existence of diversity does not automatically guarantee its respect or social value – it may, in fact, as easily necessitate strict regulation or disavowal.

In contrast to Indonesia's constitutional provision for freedom of religion (though state and civil practice is more complicated), Shi'a-dominated Iran represents a more common norm among Muslim states in the region: Iran legally restricts religious freedom to the official religion, Ja'fari (Twelver) Shi'ism (Ithna Ashariyah), the largest branch of Shi'ism that views the twelve imams as the rightful successors to the Prophet Muhammad. While estimates are hard to come by, the IRF 2008 Report notes 89 per cent of Muslims are Shi'a and 9 per cent Sunni (mostly Turkmen, Arabs, Baluchs and Kurds living in specific regions), with Sufi Muslim at between two and five million people. The country's most recent data estimates that along with 71.6 million Muslims, there are 30,000 Zoroastrians (ethnic Persians from the official religion of the pre-Islamic Sassanid Empire), 79,000 Christians, 13,000 Jews, 28,000 'others' with 47,000 'not stated'.[12] Yet, unofficial statements place combined numbers of Baha'is (the largest of the non-Muslim population),[13] Jews, Christians (many, ethnic Armenians), Mandaeans and Zoroastrians at closer to 5 per cent of the total population. One can, thus, see another manifestation of the 'numbers game' when it comes to religious and often ethnic diversity: undercounting some groups and overcounting others to maintain a premeditated or politically useful religious composition. But this strategy has gained additional teeth in Iran, as other indicators reveal that minorities are emigrating at high rates due to deteriorating conditions, especially for Baha'is and Sufis, amid reports of 'government actions and rhetoric creat[ing] a threatening atmosphere for nearly all religious minorities'.[14] It is also worth noting that every year since 1999, Iran has been designated by the US State Department a Country of Particular Concern (CPC) for egregious violations of religious freedoms under the International Religious Freedom Act.

While there is no dearth of commentary about the intensity of Iran's projection of religious fervour and homogeneity, or the polemical purpose of these statements for regional and international audiences, this increasingly restrictive state (in word and deed) lies in marked contrast to its synthetic history, perhaps one of the best examples of a vibrant integrative (not assimilationist) Islam.[15] Scholars have long noted the role of Iran in shaping Islam without forgoing native, in this case, Persian traditions; that after the fall of its native dynasties Iran may have been historically Islamicized but could never be Arabized. As G. V. von Grunebaum writes, 'the Persian components of Islamic civilization are more difficult to separate out ... precisely because they are more fully integrated', so that 'the Muslim world itself' has 'long since come to accept Islamic civilization as a "Perso-Islamic synthesis"' (*Islam-i Ajam* or Persian Islam).[16] Such recent restrictive trends in Iran not only narrow the field of what constitutes 'Muslim' identity and thereby impoverishes the 'diversity in unity' of the worldwide *ummah*, but also repress powerful cultural tools and resources from the past that offer ways forward for blending traditions (whether native and modern or multiple cultural traditions) – without losing the saliency of prior generations' contributions.[17] Surely, for a world community as diverse as the *ummah* these are significant skills.

Third, like Iran, though its restrictive culture is far more entrenched and influential, Saudi Arabia's Qur'an-based legal framework requires all citizens to be Muslim, provides no legal recognition or protection for religious freedom, and prohibits the public (not private) practice of non-Muslim faiths.[18] Much has been made of the nation's conservative slant on Sunni Islam, with some abiding by the example set by first-generation Muslims, the 'sacred ancestors', or Salaf (i.e., Salafis or the textualist school).[19] But the Kingdom is also comprised of a Shi'a minority (at least 10 per cent) and 700,000 Sulaimani Ismailis, a subgroup of Shi'as located largely in Najran, and its nearly 28 million people include 8 million foreigners (nearly a million or more Indians, Bangladeshis, Pakistanis, Filipinos, Egyptians, as well as 250,000 Palestinians, 150,000 Lebanese, 130,000 Sri Lankans, 40,000 Eritreans and 25,000 Americans), all of whom practise various branches of Islam, Christianity (90 per cent of the Filipino community), Hinduism and Buddhism, among other faiths.[20] In its Wahhabi orientation towards Hanbali *fiqh*, the government legally discriminates against other religions and branches of Islam (though judges have recently been using all four Sunni schools of *fiqh*).[21] Non-citizens are required to carry *iqamas*, a legal resident identity card with a religious designation for 'Muslim' or 'non-Muslim'.[22]

Given this legal baseline, the IRF 2008 Report importantly detects a softening of government policies in the Kingdom: better protection of the right to possess personal religious materials; efforts to curb harassment by the *mutawwa'in* (religious police); more room for official human rights groups to operate in the country; some educational text reform; and larger public and private celebrations allowed for Shi'a. Most interesting is the government's recent devotion to combating intolerance and extremism within Islam and towards non-Muslims abroad. These efforts, led by King Abdullah bin Abdul Aziz Al Saud, are occurring, in part, through interfaith dialogue between Sunnis and Shi'as, as in the 'World Conference on Dialogue' (Madrid, Spain, 16–18 July 2008), sponsored by the Saudi-backed Muslim World League (MWL), and a follow-up conference planned to join Christians, Jews, Muslims and other faiths. The role of the Kingdom, as 'custodian of Islam's two sacred sites'; is not incidental, but drives to the point often made by seasoned analysts with experience in the region: to be effective, 'an initiative in the Muslim world 'must be respected not in London and Washington but in Jakarta and Karachi', as Vali Nasr notes.[23] Equally influential is the leadership that King Abdullah projects: 'free of the playboy image that besets some other Saudi royals', his credibility stems from the fact that he is known 'widely' as 'a pious person' who does not 'feel the need to appease conservatives' and is 'better-placed to stand up to reactionary clerics'.[24] Similar initiatives, including King Abdullah II of Jordan's Amman Message (2005), are important, if slightly less effective, given the perception of their leadership: the modernized Jordanian king has attempted to build consensus and wrest religious authority back from controversies exploited by militants (i.e., the valid schools of Islamic opinion, apostasy and issuing fatwas).[25]

The impressive audience for these initiatives speaks not only of a fresh beginning for regional leaders now willing to claim influence over the use and abuse of certain Islamic traditions, the implicit wedge extremists drive between rulers and the public in highly stratified societies, but also the utility and flexibility of the concept of the *ummah*. Active among ordinary Muslims is the transnational aspiration for a community of understanding where certain concepts – justice, rightly reasoned religious authority, thoughtful consensus – hold sway and cut both ways (i.e., against kings and the unrighteous). In many respects the *ummah* provides a powerful template for Muslims above and beyond the claim of belonging attributed to nation states – though state-based leaders can play a role in disseminating the message and building support for it, if representatives are deemed respectable leaders.

Fourth, religiously and ethnically dynamic Uzbekistan, Central Asia's most populous state (27.7 million in 2007), accounts for nearly half of the population of the region, a third of whom is 14 years old or younger. The country's religious composition is 88 per cent Muslim (predominantly Sunni, with 5 per cent Shi'a), nearly 10 per cent Eastern Orthodox, with significant Buddhist and Jewish minorities. Uzbeks make up the majority (80 per cent) ethnicity, with others including Russians, Tajiks, Kazakhs, Karakalpaks, Tatars, Koreans and Armenians.[26] While its constitution ensures religious freedom and separation of church and state, like Indonesia, Uzbekistan faces pressures from its manifestly diverse population. More pointedly, Uzbekistan exemplifies a signal challenge across the Muslim world today: government attempts to deal effectively with designated extremist organizations such as Hizb ut-Tahrir (HT), Tabligh Jamoat, Akromiya and others labelled Wahhabi.[27] Drawing from the 1998 Law on Freedom of Conscience and Religious Organizations and its amendments, which authorize liberal control over religion,[28] authorities have attempted to ban and prosecute HT membership, for instance, as matters, not of religious freedom, but of restricting political activity and preventing armed resistance against the state. Critics claim that such laws restrict legal avenues for spiritual expression, thereby inciting membership in Islamist groups; that due process, torture, and human rights violations occur in prosecuting members; and that other groups are tarnished with the overbroad brush of these policies (i.e.,

Jehovah's Witnesses are listed by police as security threats, along with HT and IMU).

There is no doubt that balancing religious liberties with ensuring domestic security in the post-9/11 period is a universal problem made all the more difficult by transnational movements that rival some states' resources and organizational sophistication. Still, Uzbekistan embodies a pattern that we have seen across many states: among Muslim-majority states, Islamic minorities (and not, for instance, Christian groups) prompt the most trenchant response by government and society. As Calfano and Sahliyeh (2008) have found in their comparative study, non-Islamic religious groups within the Organization of Islamic Conference (OIC) states 'have an increase in political rights, whereas Islamic groups practising a non-official version of the faith experienced reduced political rights and civil liberties'.[29] But while the Uzbek government remains suspicious of Muslims who worship outside state-approved institutions, it is coming to recognize that such suspicions invite abuse, especially in prosecuting militants. The government has reduced torture in arrests by transferring authority to issue arrest warrants from prosecutors to the courts (*habeas corpus*), for instance; the International Committee of the Red Cross monitors have been allowed to return to conduct prison visits (suspended in 2006); and officials have eased their campaigns against extremists, as their numbers decline. Still, hypersensitivity to homegrown Muslim minorities has neither abated nor been acknowledged, though it is likely to continue exerting pressure on states, as well as influencing the meaning of the idea of the *ummah*.

What is unique about the fifth state, the small Arab Sultanate of Oman (2.3 million people in 2006), is that it is home to the historic minority Ibadi movement (follower of Jabir ibn Zaid al-Azdi), distinct from Shi'a and Sunni denominations – though Ibadis also live in Zanzibar, North Africa and elsewhere.[30] This group traces its history to the eight-century dissenting Khariji, who famously reversed their support for the fourth and final 'Rightly Guided' caliph Ali ibn Abi Talib because, unlike Shi'as who believed that the imamate (leadership) belonged to the house of Ali, they claimed that any pious Muslim could lead the community. Ibadis make up the majority population in Oman, approximately 75 per cent of the population. But only 1.8 million of Oman's total population are citizens, according to the 2003 national census, and while the state does not track religious affiliation, Oman is comprised of Sunni Muslims with a small but significant population of Shi'a, as well as several Christian denominations (the majority of non-Muslims are non-citizen immigrant workers from South Asia), and small communities of naturalized Indian Hindus and Christian citizens originally from India and the Levant.

One key feature of Ibadhism is the deliberate choice of ruler (imam) by communal consensus. Most interesting is the role that Ibadis played historically in 'br[eaking] away from the body of Islam over the issue of proper government and the legitimate election of the head of state'.[31] The basis for their choice, as Valerie Hoffman notes, is 'the desire to found a righteous Muslim society and the belief that true Muslims are only to be found in their own sect'. Not only do Ibadis 'refer to themselves as "the Muslims" or "the people of straightness" (*ahl al-istiqama*)', but they define their faith by a critically reflective mechanism: they reserve the right to revolt against a ruler who deviates from the Prophet Muhammad's example. In their approach to leader selection the Ibadis demonstrate what some scholars call an inherent egalitarian impulse within Islam,[32] while others describe it as a homegrown democratic tradition.[33] A rarely explored potential implication of this approach to religious leadership and authority may also be a distinguishing feature of daily life in Oman: there is little religious or inter-ethnic-based strife. In fact, no reports of religious discrimination were documented from the inception of the International Religious Freedom Reports (2001).

Such snippets are designed only as entry points into the complex material community of Islam – one still structured at this time largely in terms of the nation state. Taken together, they invite contemplation of five prescient realizations for the worldwide *ummah*: the existence of diversity alone does not guarantee its vitality or value; indigenous approaches to maximizing diversity have often been lost, not to posterity, but to politics; a leader's public power projection is predicated upon ethical leadership defined as those who 'walk the walk' in the Prophet Muhammad's footsteps; contemporary national security matters, especially combating extremisms, are universal, though particularly challenging in the Muslim world; and collective human goods such as egalitarian and consensus-based models of social and political authority are part and parcel of Islam and, importantly, raised by dissenting or minority traditions.

Summarizing in this way also reveals key tensions between the often-critiqued nation state form in the Muslim world in relation to the often idealized *ummah*. Tensions include the limits of states in grappling with various orders of diversity, in balancing religious freedom with cultural dictates and national aims, and in retaining authority in light of internal and external influences and perceived threats.[34] The resulting challenges from these tensions are particularly evident in states' missteps: the use of religion to marginalize and exclude, shore up unaccountable authority, authorize social rules that do not serve an entire nation and, most damning, official use of religious practice to exert political and social control. On this last issue, when governments opportunistically leverage religious instruments for political ends, this not only sows the seeds of a future legitimacy crisis, but, as we will see, places the *ummah* in a critical role of counterbalancing the political regime, even functioning as a higher, idealized court of appeal that may garner greater loyalty than any national community. With the rise of multiple international actors, the *ummah* no longer plays this critical role with states alone.

To put this point another way, less visible at the state level of analysis is how ordinary Muslims are actively contemplating Islamic identity and practice today in ways that delimit the contemporary *ummah* and, at the same time, define the limits of the nation state as a vehicle to capture this dynamic Muslim identity. In fact, governments that exhibit the highest degrees of public censure ensure that such a self-reflective conversation does not include them (or states) at all. It is for this reason that the well-described tensions between authoritarian nation states and public opinion from the Arab or Muslim 'street' may not only feed departures from state-ordained rules (civil disobedience to extremisms) but may inspire transnational modes of discourse and belonging. I turn to these next.

Transnational or Virtual Islam: 'What Muslims Really Think'

I want to begin with two examples that go to the heart of this transnational *ummah*, its critical role with respect to nation states and other institutions that claim to speak for this multifaceted community, and the role of flexible Internet technologies and user-created content in providing direct representation for ordinary Muslims' perspectives. Less often considered in this context, but equally important, is the recent spate of public opinion polls that have begun to document, perhaps more than in any time before, what ordinary Muslims are thinking from different parts of the world, including diasporic populations.

The first example stems from the *We the Women* campaign on social networking sites like Facebook, Flikr and YouTube, begun by twenty-four-year-old Areej Khan, studying design at the School of Visual Arts in New York. Khan has said she attempted to open discussion over the ban on women drivers in Saudi Arabia because she felt 'her retired father was forced to spend much of his time "chauffeuring her, her mother and three sisters"'.[35] In Arabic and English, Khan's website notes:

> Women in Saudi Arabia are not allowed to drive. *We the Women* aims to start a conversation about it. This is a place where you can express yourself freely on the issue. Let's hit the wall and the discussion boards. Let's talk about it. If you're feeling a bit more adventurous, please visit the *Flickr* page to download a declaration bubble or a bumper sticker or two.

The campaign uses speech bubble stickers for download and public display, which are also uploaded as images to the Flickr *Declarations* webpage of the project. Underneath the logo is the phrase: 'To drive or not to drive, that is the question.'

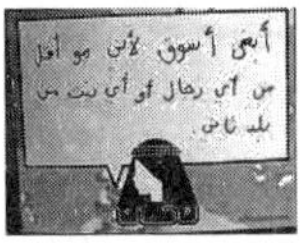

While a matter of long-standing debate, it is unclear whether this campaign has shifted the discourse on Saudi women driving or not, though signs are pointing to softening official positions. Saudi scholars Abdel-Mohsin al-Obaikan and Mohsin Awaji have said that there is nothing in Shari'a that bans women from driving, and the former judge and scholar Abdullah Al-Mutlaq has explicitly claimed that women should be allowed to drive, and that 'customs and traditions in our society must not rule us absolutely'.[36] The important observation for this argument is the recourse to and resourcefulness of Muslims using web technologies to promote and engage transnational public debate, to persuade and to garner support in the public sphere.

The second example involves savvy Internet users maximizing online networks to subvert recent government censure of protests against Iran's disputed national election results on 12 June 2009. As foreign journalists' visas were terminated, domestic journalists detained and websites and text-messaging platforms blocked, a coalition of high-tech Iranian users and supporters from around the world worked together through new media to get information out. A former Microsoft project manager and avowed digital activist noted that 'the filters and the restrictions have been going on for so long in Iran that experienced people are already prepared for this', though traffic and volume of messages have slowed.[37] Twitter, Facebook and iReport, among others, are providing news and images for outlets like CNN, *The New York Times* and others. Supporters in the US, Britain and elsewhere are publishing their computers' IP addresses to public forums like Twitter, so that Iranian users can access 'proxy servers' to visit blocked websites to organize rallies and protests. Likewise, YouTube has relaxed 'its usual restrictions on violent videos to allow images from Iran to reach the rest of the world', given the 'limitations being placed on mainstream media reporting from within Iran', making sure that 'citizens in Iran [are] able to use YouTube to capture their experiences for the world to see'.[38]

According to one report, US State Department officials are even using these same social network sources, as coverage has been banned, going so far as to advise and aid these websites to 'stay up and running' and even helping 'them stay ahead of anyone who would try to shut them down'.[39] One State Department senior official said that Twitter was asked to 'refrain from going down for periodic scheduled maintenance at this crucial time', adding that this advice was meant to 'highlight' to Twitter 'that this was an important means of communication, not with us but horizontally in Iran'.[40] Another user-generated Twitter solidarity strategy has included asking worldwide users to change personal identifying and time zone settings to make it appear as if they are located in Iran, to scuttle Iranian security forces 'hunting for bloggers using location and time zone searches'. As a webguide put it: 'if we all become "Iranians" it becomes much harder to find them'.[41] A developer of free software designed to refresh pages on sports and auction websites 'appear[ed] to have been used to attack Iranian President Mahmoud Ahmadinejad's website', he noted, when he discovered that traffic for his site had risen from a typical 700 visits per day to 41,000 on Monday. 'I suppose I am taking sides because I've put the site back up,' he noted, and 'I have no problems with it being used in this way.'[42] Yet other blogs and message boards are sharing information inside Iran by using Tor, a website that allows users to communicate anonymously by bouncing users' information through 'a distributed network of relays run by volunteers all around the world' thus preventing monitors from seeing which websites are being visited.[43] Much like the *We the Women* campaign, multifaceted social network strategies are informing an organized effort to engage and debate publically, defy censure, draw on international communities of supporters to do so, and, all the while, conduct this discourse within the broad framework of Islam. Some have gone further, arguing that these efforts, as well as the media technologies and social networks that enable them, are changing the world's Muslim population.

The role of globalization and new communication technologies in framing transnational public spaces and communities, as well as the rapid dissemination of ideas and images, has received much attention, if only recently by scholars studying transnational social and political movements and virtual Islam.[44] It is also here, where the concept of the multicultural *ummah* meets a critical driver of transnationalism, that analysis falls prey to pervasive idealism. Thus, a prerequisite in shifting from state to transnational frames for understanding today's multicultural *ummah* is realizing that similar and unhelpful conventions persist into the transnational sphere – most notably, reductive definitions of the *ummah* in dualistic terms, as a religious or political community (or as a religious community used by political tribes for political ends). Much energy has been spent on the majority–minority schism between Sunnis and Shi'a, especially orthodox variants, for instance, while little attention has been devoted to the internal diversity of these denominations, how their differences intensify in conflict zones, or the role of schools of Islamic jurisprudence in constituting different Sunni or Shi'a identities.[45]

More promising transnational framings of the *ummah* are to be found in approaches to the *ummah* as a transnational public sphere of normative reference and debate (Bowen 2004), as a mobile or travelling identity that transcends national belonging and state structures, and as a set of discourses and practices embedded in new communication habits and technologies, often referred to as virtual Islam, e-Muslims or dar-al Cyber Islam.[46] Though 'transnational Islam' refers to many phenomena,

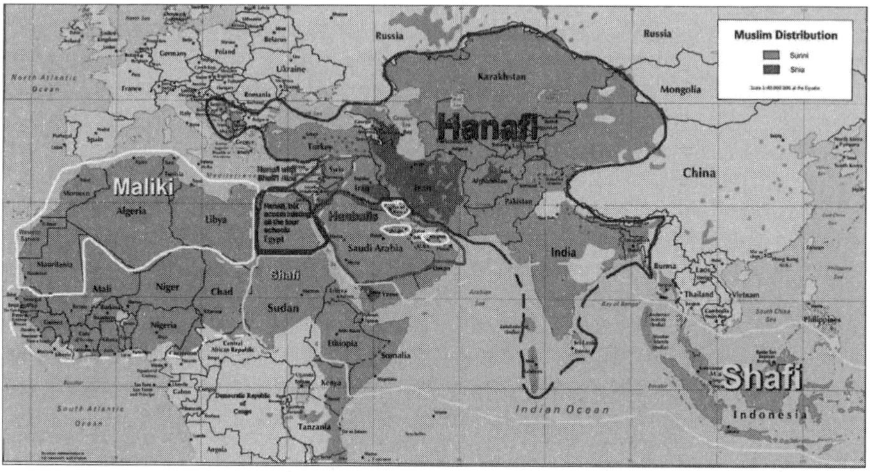

the three aspects which stand out in Bowen's analysis are 'demographic movements, transnational religious institutions, and the field of Islamic reference and debate', though the first two phenomena have 'obscured the importance of the third'. Keeping in mind that Bowen tends to focus on the critical consciousness of Muslims in France and Europe, he explores how transnational Islam 'creates and implies the existence and legitimacy of a global public space of normative reference and debate, and that even as this public space develops references to Europe it implies neither a "Euro-Islam" nor a "post-national" sense of European membership and citizenship'.[47] Bowen, thus, helpfully theorizes Islam as a transnational public space in a ways that does not reduce it to cross-state movement: migration, transnational religious movements or diasporic trends. While these are important, he notes, they 'do not exhaust transnationality', and they 'insufficiently' account for 'the possibility of quite distinct self understandings about boundaries and legitimacy on the part of both "host" countries and "immigrant" populations'. Bowen goes on to suggest that Islam in particular 'complicates current lines of transnational analysis by emphasizing its own universal norms and its practices of deliberating about religious issues across national boundaries'.[48]

This treatment of the *ummah* achieves something thus far missing: an ability to supersede primordial concepts of religion and politics configured within Western modern secular presuppositions. Islam's own 'history of movement, communication and institutional innovation', its style of 'intrinsic universality', its transnational dimensions, beginning with the core 'message' of the Qur'an, is one that 'turns away from localized deities and worships the transcendent God'. While many of the monotheistic faiths can make this claim, scholars have noted the key historical milestones of a deterritorialized Islam: shifting city capitals of the caliphate (Baghdad, Damascus, Cairo, Istanbul); the origin of Islam from migration (*hijra*) from Mecca to Medina (Eickelman and Piscatori 1990); Arabic as a cross-border language of international communication for scholars and jurists; the cross-cultural appeal of the annual pilgrimage, etc.[49] Even orthodox authorities would 'deny that Islam is or should be defined or bounded by local or national borders', and implicitly affirm 'Islam's transnational character' that may be 'diffuse' but remains 'powerful' insofar as it is derived 'from the ways in which rituals reproduce, and histories remind Muslims of, the shared duties and practices of Muslims across political boundaries', as well as in its 'impulse to refuse particularistic loyalties to ethnic groups or to a nation state'.

This is organizationally so. A deterritorialized Islam as a 'consciousness' that 'first and foremost creates an imagination of an Islamic community transcending specific boundaries and borders', one that supports the 'legitimacy' and 'imperative' of 'searching anywhere in the world for the highest authority on Islamic matters', creates networks of authority, learning and communication which 'are more historically and sociologically specific' than any generalized 'global *ummah*ood'. Of course different populations attend to different sources of authority (and scholars do so more than ordinary people) but a general feature of Islam is that 'it is to the most learned, wherever they may reside, [to which] the Muslim ought to listen'. This suggests that the 'worldwide communication of ideas' has far more to do with the contemporary *ummah* than movements of populations, and, further, it 'does not depend on it', and the transnational Islamic space of reference and debate extends across non-traditional spaces, i.e., Europe and the European Council for Fatwa and Research. In this sense, the contemporary multicultural *ummah* is transnational without being 'post-national'; it does 'not succeed an earlier space bounded by state boundaries', nor is it strictly diasporic, since Muslim public intellectuals engaged in serious discussions about how to adapt and adopt Islam to Europe, for instance, are unwilling to cut themselves off from the transnational space that has, since the beginning of Islamic history, been the appropriate sphere for reference and debate.

For Armando Salvatore (2007), the transnational Islamic public is 'probably the most powerful instantiation of an exit strategy from the Westphalian frame' into a subnational and transnational 'sphere' that both echoes Habermasian precepts of communicative action without becoming 'a national citizenry'. He goes on to explain its development in three ways: a long-standing notion in Islam of the public sphere as 'the common good to be made public'; a 'post-postcolonial' departure from a Third World emancipator agenda defined by Western modern national development schemes and a return to anti-imperialist priorities of justice and dignity; and the tensions of economic globalization that both relegates Western modernity to yet another cultural frame but requires new authentic Islamic responses. His theory of 'public Islam' is based on the important jurisprudential concept *maslaha*, the public interest or common good (Hoexter *et al.* 2002; Masud 1995 [1977]; Salvatore 2007) that helps support critiques of both delegitimized postcolonial regimes and their international agency support systems. The problem is one of exclusion at a subtle level, namely, the diversity of intellectual traditions within the contemporary *ummah*. *Maslaha* belongs to a reform-oriented lexicon, evident in an interesting example at the intersection of public and virtual Islam in the aptly titled Maslaha Foundation. It is difficult to suggest that *maslaha* is universally embraced, and some have pushed the concept too far to provide a Left–liberal political purpose that resides in the imagination of Western intellectuals rather than the Islamic public. We might more fruitfully consider this critical concept of the public good as defining an 'alternative cosmopolitanism' not yet in existence (van der Veer 2001) among Muslims.[50]

If idealism enters through the back door of an Islamic public, the more significant critique stems from Nancy Fraser's (2007) sense that the concept of the public sphere was developed 'not simply to understand communication flows' under globalization but 'to contribute a normative political theory of democracy'.[51] In that account the public sphere is 'a space for the communicative generation of public opinion', an 'inclusive and fair process' in which 'publicity discredits views that cannot withstand critical scrutiny and assures the legitimacy' of those that do. It thus matters 'who participates and on what terms', i.e., democratic precept (demos, people). The public sphere is, thus, a vehicle for marshalling public opinion as a political force, as civil society, where publicity holds officials accountable and assures state actions express the will of the citizenry, all of which means that 'a public sphere should correlate with a sovereign power' (2007: 7). As Fraser concludes, together these two ideas – the normative legitimacy and the political efficacy of public opinion – are essential to the public sphere in democratic theory. Obviously, in areas where public expression, including freedom of religion, is not a practised right or value. It is difficult to associate as 'legitimate public opinion with communicative arenas' where 'interlocutors are not fellow members of a political community with equal rights to participate in political life'. Further, it is hard to associate 'efficacious communicative power with discursive spaces that do not correlate with sovereign states' (Fraser 2007: 8). In short, public sphere theory since Jürgen Habermas has been informed by a Westphalian political imaginary – the tacit assumption of the state and territorial frame as bounding the political community. Indeed, Fraser notes, this same assumption pervades 'nearly every subsequent egalitarian critique of public sphere theory, including feminists, multiculturalists and antiracists' (Fraser 2007: 8). It is in this sense that speaking of 'transnational public spheres' – especially when one is making normative claims for them – becomes fraught.[52]

NOTES

1 For purposes of the epigraph I have condensed Seyyed Hossein Nasr's passage from *The Heart of Islam: Enduring Values for Humanity* (HarperCollins, 2004), p. 57.

2 See 'Islam's Global Reach', International Population Center, Department of Geography, San Diego State University. It is important to note that Muslims in India number approximately 129.6 million, third in population size behind Indonesia (213 million) and Pakistan (157.5 million), the countries with the largest populations of Muslims – but in India Muslims are not a majority. See <http://geography.sdsu.edu/Research/Projects/IPC/publication/US_NEWS_ISLAM_MAP.pdf>; Bruce Vaughn, 'Islam in South and Southeast Asia', *CRS Report for Congress*, RS21903, 8 February 2005; Vartan Gregorian, *Islam: A Mosaic Not a Monolith*, (Washington: Brookings Institute, 2003).

3 Following the Islamic Revolution in Iran, the Iran–Iraq War of 1980–1988 and the gender controversy in negotiating the Rome Statute of the International Criminal Court, key Islamic states abandoned IHL in favour of a radical form of Islam in shaping their approaches to armed conflict. Instead of weakening the

military forces of the enemy, the key humanitarian parameter defined by the St Petersburg Declaration, the objective in war became to manifest one's faith through the spilling of one's own, or an infidel's, blood. As the growth of radical Muslim terrorism directed at states and their citizens came to dominate discourse in the 1990s and especially since September the 11th, discussion about Islam as a source of IHL principles virtually disappeared, until now. For instance, in the case of adopting international law among Muslim states, historians note that by the 1970s, the Arab–Israeli conflict and the various armed conflicts in colonial states had brought signs of shifting attitudes among some Islamic states and Muslim groups towards international law, especially as some began to consider Islamic law as an alternative.

4 The International Religious Freedom Reports submitted annually to Congress by the Department of State in compliance with Section 102(b) of the International Religious Freedom Act (IRFA) of 1998 are an annual supplement to the Human Rights Reports.

5 'Reflections on the "Constitution of Medina": An Essay on Methodology and Ideology in Islamic Legal History', in *UCLA Journal of Islamic and Near Eastern Law* 1, No. 1 (Fall/Winter 2001–2002), pp. 103–133; Jonathan Berkey, *The Formation of Islam: Religion and Society in the Near East, 600–1800* (Cambridge University Press), p. 64; Montogemery Watt, *Muhammad at Medina* (Oxford University Press, 1956); R. B. Serjeant, 'The Constitution of Medina', in *Islamic Quarterly* 8 (1964), pp. 3–16; R. B. Serjeant, 'Haram and Hawtah: The Sacred Enclave in Arabia', in A. R. Badawi (ed.), *Mélanges Taha Husai* (Cairo: al-Maaref, 1962), pp. 41–58; R. B. Serjeant, 'The Sunnah Jâmi'ah, Pacts with the Yathrib Jews, and the Tahrîm of Yathrib: Analysis and Translation of the Documents Comprised in the So Called "Constitution of Medina"', in *BSOAS* 41 (1978), pp. 1–42; Moshe Gil, 'The Constitution of Medina: A Reconsideration', in *Israel Oriental Studies* 4 (1974), p. 45.

6 US Department of State, Bureau of Democracy, Human Rights and Labor, International Religious Freedom Report (US–IRFR) 2006, 'East Asia and Pacific: Indonesia'. See <http://www.state.gov/g/drl/rls/irf/2006/71281.htm>. The Indonesian Central Statistic Bureau (BPS) 2000 census (conducted every ten years) determined 5.9 per cent Protestant, 3.1 per cent Catholic, 1.8 per cent Hindu, 0.8 per cent Buddhist and 0.2 per cent 'other' (i.e., indigenous religions, other Christian groups and Jewish).

7 'East Asia and Pacific: Indonesia' US–IRFR 2008. See <http://www.state.gov/g/drl/rls/irf/2008/108407.htm>.

8 Ibid. See Noorhaid Hasan, 'Saudi Expansion, the Salafi Campaign, and Arabized Islam in Indonesia', in Madawi Al-Rasheed, *Kingdom Without Borders: Saudi Arabia's Political, Religious, and Media Frontiers* (North Mankato: Coughlan Publishing, 2009), pp. 263–282.

9 The Council of Ulemas (MUI) reissued a 1980 fatwa that banned the Ahmadiyyas, given their 'deviant' practices from fundamental Islamic tenets, in an effort, according to civil society activists, to restrict minorities. Telly Nathalia and Olivia Rondonuwu, 'Indonesia's Religious Tolerance under Threat' (Reuters, 10 Jun 2008). See <http://www.reuters.com/article/latestCrisis/idUSJAK90261>.

10 This messianic movement emerged in British India, but is now active in many areas of the Western world, Asia and Africa, as well as the Indian sub-continent.

'Ahmadis' in John L. Esposito (ed.), *The Oxford Dictionary of Islam* (*Oxford Islamic Studies Online*). See <http://www.oxfordislamicstudies.com/article/opr/t125/e85>.

11 Some examples include: 1 June 2008 ambush of 1,000 people rallying at the National Monument in Jakarta (Monas) to defend the rights of Ahmadiyya to practise their faith by Hizb ut-Tahrir members, Islamic Community Forum (FUI), and Islamic Defenders Front (FPI), who attacked participants with bamboo sticks and stones, leaving more than seventy seriously injured. Police made no arrests and did not intervene in the attacks; 13 January 2008 attack against a house in Ampenan Village, West Nusa Tenggara, demanding Shi'a followers stop celebrating in the name of the Prophet Muhammad's grandson, Hussein.

12 US Department of State, Bureau of Democracy, Human Rights and Labor, International Religious Freedom Report 2008, 'Near East and North Africa: Iran'. See <http://www.state.gov/g/drl/rls/irf/2008/108482.htm>.

13 US-IRFR 2006 notes 5 per cent, whereas US-IRFR 2008 reports 2 per cent – suggesting that the discrepancy may have to do with emigration, especially of Jewish communities that were significant in numbers prior to the 1979 Islamic Revolution.

14 US Department of State, Bureau of Democracy, Human Rights and Labor, International Religious Freedom Report 2008, 'Near East and North Africa: Iran'. See <http://www.state.gov/g/drl/rls/irf/2008/108482.htm>.

15 Sufism, with its historic influence in the region, its belief in a direct and personal experience with the divine, is an important example of a different past: often considered a wellspring for Islamic devotion in the evolution of the faith, Sufis face increasing repression in Iran, including defamatory attacks in newspapers and sermons by Shi'a clerics. A November 2007 Islamic Revolutionary Guards Corps Report, *Looming Damages and Threats*, lists them (with Baha'is, feminists, and others) as threats to the regime. US-IFRR 2008, 'Near East & North Africa: Iran'. See <http://www.state.gov/g/drl/rls/irf/2008/108482.htm>.

16 See Ibn Khaldūn's *The Muqaddimah*, tr. Franz Rosenthal (Princeton University Press, 1969); G. V. von Grunebaum, 'The Sources of Islamic Civilization', in P. M. Holt, A. Lambton, and B. Lewis (eds), *Islamic Society and Civilization* (Cambridge University Press, 1970), p. 501; Mehdi Amin Razavi (ed.), Seyyed Hossein Nasr, *The Islamic Intellectual Tradition in Persia* (Richmond, Surrey: Curzon Press, 1996), p. 157: 'The appearance of the school of *ishraq* … meant the propagation of Islamic philosophy in a form that was dearer to the heart of Islam than the earlier schools of thought … and close to the ethos of Persian Islam and spread wherever Persian Islamic culture was dominant'; Bernard Lewis, 'Iran in History', lecture, Mortimer and Raymond Sackler Institute of Advanced Studies, Tel Aviv University, 18 January 1999. See <http://www.dayan.org/mel/lewis.pdf>; Ehsan Yarshater, 'The Persian Presence in the Islamic World', in R. G. Hovannisian and G. Sabagh (eds), *The Persian Presence in the Islamic World* (Cambridge University Press, 1998), pp. 6–7. Steven Blackburn in his review in *The Muslim World* 93 (January 2003), pp. 145–148, notes that while Yarshater may not go so far as to say that 'Islam was subsequently Persianized', he sees 'the Arab irruptions as catalysts for further cultural advances, not only among Persians, but all the peoples which Islam touched', and that while the 'primary contributions of the Arabs in language, scholarship, and religion' are

'undeniable ... those of the Persians, who in turn influenced the Turks and the peoples of the sub-continent in terms of literature, mysticism, and various aspects of the fine arts, allowed the Islamic civilization to attain new cultural heights once the initial élan of the Arabs was spent' (p. 146).

17 US-IRFR 2006, 'Near East and North Africa: Iran'. See <http://www.state.gov/g/drl/rls/irf/2006/71281.htm>.

18 US Department of State, Bureau of Democracy, Human Rights and Labor, International Religious Freedom Report 2006, 'Near East and North Africa: Saudi Arabia'. See <http://www.state.gov/g/drl/rls/irf/2006/71281.htm>.

19 John L. Esposito, *What Everyone Needs to Know About Islam*, p. 50.

20 'Saudi Arabia', in Eleanor Abdella Doumato and Joseph A. Kéchichian, *The Oxford Encyclopedia of the Islamic World*. See <http://www.oxfordislamicstudies.com/article/opr/t236/e0709?_hi=0&_pos=1>.

21 Once fault is determined by a court, for instance, a Muslim male receives 100 per cent of the compensation determined, a male Jew or Christian receives 50 per cent, and all others (i.e., Hindus, Buddhists and Sikhs) receive one-sixteenth of what a male Muslim would receive. Women's testimony is likewise worth only half that of men's and a non-Muslim woman's testimony is worth less than that of a Muslim woman. US-IRFR 2006, 'Near East and North Africa: Saudi Arabia'. See <http://www.state.gov/g/drl/rls/irf/2006/71431.htm>.

22 US-IRFR 2008, 'Near East and North Africa: Saudi Arabia'. See <http://www.state.gov/g/drl/rls/irf/2008/108492.htm>.

23 Nasr goes on to note that the 'MWL has credibility in those places', in 'Global Islam: Unusual Guests, a Most Unusual Host', *The Economist*, 24 July 2008. The article continues: 'What people are not used to is the idea of Saudi Arabia and its monarch, King Abdullah, as a propagator of tolerance both within Islam, and between Islam and other faiths. Yet this month the king stepped up his effort to be a cultural and religious bridge-builder by convening a "World Conference on Dialogue" – as dreamily inclusive a title as anyone could ask for. Has the king – or even the whole kingdom – had a change of heart? Since taking the throne three years ago, the monarch has presented himself as an opponent of "extremism", which he often describes as "deviancy" from Islam at its best; and he has urged his compatriots (including the ultra-conservative clergy that still holds a lot of power) to be ready for dialogue with other faiths. Is this anything more than rhetoric?'

24 Ibid.

25 King Abdullah II bin Al-Hussein of Jordan called for tolerance and unity in the Muslim world, on 9 November 2004 on Ramadan, and subsequently convened 200 Islamic scholars from 50 countries to issue clarifying statements on three controversial points relating to extremism: 1) the validity of all eight Mathhabs of Sunni, Shi'a and Ibadhi Islam, of traditional Islamic Theology (*Ash'arism*), of Islamic Mysticism (Sufism), and of true Salafi thought; 2) given this definition, forbidding *takfir* (declarations of apostasy) between Muslims; and 3) the pre-conditions for issuing fatwas to expose ignorant and illegitimate edicts in the name of Islam. See <http://ammanmessage.com/>.

26 US Department of State, Bureau of Democracy, Human Rights and Labor, International Religious Freedom Report 2006, 'South and Central Asia: Uzbekistan'. See <http://www.state.gov/g/drl/rls/irf/2006/71417.htm>.

27 Hizb ut-Tahrir presents a three-stage campaign for creating a worldwide Islamic Caliphate by overthrowing secular governments, including in Central Asia, and justifies acts of armed jihad and terrorism, though it claims to be non-violent. Akromiya is an informal association that promotes business along the lines of Islamic religious principles, though the government claims it as a splinter group from HT that has joined with the terrorist group the Islamic Movement of Uzbekistan (IMU) to overthrow the state via armed rebellion in Andijon in May 2005. Tabligh Jamoat is an Islamic missionary group with origins in South Asia whose worship, dress and grooming practices are based on the time of the Prophet Muhammad. Other banned groups include alleged 'Wahhabists', strongly conservative Muslims whose roots derive from prominent ultraconservative imams in the early 1990s – i.e., Imams Nazarov, Parpiev and Mirzaev. US–IRFR 2006, 'South and Central Asia: Uzbekistan'. See http://www.state.gov/g/drl/rls/irf/2006/71417.htm>.

28 The Committee for Religious Affairs (CRA) routinely rejects groups' attempts to register: a Jehovah's Witnesses' Tashkent congregation was denied registration on the claim of an invalid address; local officials withheld approval to Christian churches with ethnic Uzbek members; the Ministry of Justice 'deregistered' groups, including the only Protestant church in Nukus; and the Cabinet of Ministers suddenly changed restrictions on NGO faith-based entities operating in the country.

29 Brian Robert Calfano and Emile Sahliyeh, 'Determining Democracy in the Organization of the Islamic Conference', in *Social Science Quarterly* 89 (3) (2008), pp. 751–764; see also Sohail Hashmi, 'Is There an Islamic Ethic of Humanitarian Intervention?', in *Ethics & International Affairs* 7 (1993), pp. 55–73.

30 Some 600,000 expatriates live in Oman, most of whom are guest workers from Pakistan, Bangladesh, Egypt, Jordan, India and the Philippines. US Department of State, Bureau of Democracy, Human Rights and Labor, International Religious Freedom Report 2008, 'Near East and North Africa: Oman'. See <http://www.state.gov/g/drl/rls/irf/2008/108490.htm>.

31 Giacomo Luciani in *The Arab State* (London: Taylor & Francis, 1990), p. 7, argues that the forgotten 'backwater' state of Oman that 'hardly ever figures in Arab nationalist literature' enjoys one of the 'longest continuous statehoods … rivaled only by Egypt'. See also Christopher M. Blanchard, *Islam: Sunnis and Shiites*, CRS Report for Congress, RS21745 (11 December 2006), p. 4: 'Ibadis believe strongly in the existence of a just Muslim society and argue that religious leaders should be chosen by community leaders for their knowledge and piety, without regard to race or lineage.'

32 They preferred to call themselves the Shurat, 'those who have sold their souls to God', just as the Ibadi also reject the term 'Kharijite' for *ahl al-'adl wal istiqama* or 'people of justice and uprightness'. 'Khariji', in *The Islamic World: Past and Present*, John L. Esposito (ed.), *Oxford Islamic Studies Online*. See <http://www.oxfordislamicstudies.com/article/opr/t243/e183>. Valerie J. Hoffman, 'The Articulation of Ibadi Identity in Modern Oman and Zanzibar', in *The Muslim World* 94 (April 2004), pp. 201–216: 'Although Ibadism emerged from Kharijism and shares with it … the desire to found a righteous Muslim society, and the belief that true Muslims are only to be found in their group, Ibadis see themselves as quite different … Whereas the Khawarij had labeled all Muslims

who committed grave sins without repentance *mushrikun* (unbelievers whose guilt is tantamount to idolatry and merits the capital punishment deserved by all apostates of the faith), Ibadis see such people as *kuffar ni'ma* (monotheists who are ungrateful for the blessings God has bestown upon them)' (p. 204).

33 Ussein Ghubash, *Oman: The Islamic Democratic Tradition,* tr. Mary Turton, (London and New York: Routledge, 2006).

34 For Eurocentric critiques of the Western modern state, see Dipesh Chakrabarty, *Provincializing Europe: Postcolonial Thought and Historical Difference* (Princeton University Press, 2000); Partha Chatterjee, 'Whose Imagined Community?', in Gopal Balakrishnan (ed.), *Mapping the Nation* (London, Verso: 1996), pp. 214–225; Bertrand Badie, *The Imported State: The Westernization of the Political Order* (Stanford University Press, 2000); James Scott, *Seeing Like a State: How Certain Schemes to Improve the Human Condition Have Failed* (New Haven: Yale University Press, 1998); Michael Hardt and Antonio Negri, *Labor of Dionysus: A Critique of the State-Form* (University of Minnesota Press, 1994); Anthony Giddens, *The Nation State and Violence: A Contemporary Critique of Historical Materialism, Vol. 2* (University of California Press, 1987). It is also worth noting, however, that when it comes to protecting the rights of minorities and genuinely instituting respect for diversity, the state has proved historically invaluable to such endeavours.

35 Robert Mackey, 'Saudis Debate Ban on Women Drivers', in *The Lede: The New York Times News Blog* (7 May 2009). See <http://thelede.blogs.nytimes.com/2009/05/07/saudis-debate-ban-on-women-drivers>; Laura Bashraheel, 'The Driving Force!' in *Arab News* (26 April 2009). See <http://www.arabnews.com/?page=1&section=0&article=121896&d=26&m=4&y=2009>. See also Khan's website, <http://www.n7nudrive.com/>.

36 Roger Hardy, 'Saudi Scholars Back Women Drivers', BBC News: Middle East, 21 February 2008. See <http://news.bbc.co.uk/2/hi/middle_east/7257295.stm>; Metib Al-Awwad, 'Shariah does Not Bar Women from Driving,' *Saudi Gazette*, 18 June 2009. See also Simon Henderson, 'Saudi Arabia's Debate on Women Driving Masks a Deeper Divide', *PolicyWatch* 1037, Washington Institute for Near East Policy (21 October 2005). See <http://www.washingtoninstitute.org/templateC05.php?CID=2383>.

37 Elise Labott, 'Officials: Social Networking Providing Crucial Info from Iran', CNN.com, 16 June 2009. See <http://www.cnn.com/2009/TECH/06/16/iran.twitter.facebook/index.html>.

38 Brian Shelter and Brad Stone, 'Stark Images, Uploaded to the World', in *The New York Times* (17 June 2009). See < http://www.nytimes.com/2009/06/18/world/middleeast/18press.html?ref=world>.

39 Ibid.

40 Ibid.

41 Doug Gross, 'Iranians Dodging Government's Internet Crackdown', CNN.com, 18 June 2009. See <http://www.cnn.com/2009/TECH/06/18/iran.dodging.crackdown/index.html>.

42 Ibid.

43 Gross (2009). See <http://www.torproject.org/>.

44 Less often considered in this context is the recent spate of public opinion polls that have begun to document, perhaps more than at any time before, what ordinary

Muslims are thinking from different parts of the world (including US and European diasporic populations). Gary R. Bunt, *iMuslims: Rewiring the House of Islam* (Chapel Hill, NC: University of North Carolina Press/London: Hurst & Co., 2009). Few would underestimate such macro-structural trends as globalization and foreign direct investment, for instance, in influencing how states relate to their own economies, *vis-à-vis* the global economy and the resulting integrated way in which the world conducts business. Likewise, the increased role of international organizations (IOs) and non-governmental groups (NGOs) as actors in states and on the international scene has changed the role of norms and the law internationally.

45 What is lost in separating out jurisprudential scholarship from political analysis is the constituting role that diverse methods of legal reasoning play, not only in designating insider groups in Islam, but in giving texture, authority and historical continuity to the worldwide *ummah*. Beyond the four dominant Sunni schools of *fiqh* – the oldest and largest Hanafi, Maliki (North and West Africa), the second largest Shafi'i, and Hanbali (Saudi Arabia) *madhhabs* – it is worth mentioning the Shi'a school of Ja'fari, as well as key minor traditions, including the Zaydi and Musta li Fatimid Isma iliyah (See Geographic Distribution of Four Sunni Madh'hab, for a very nice overlay of the Sunni *madhhabs* onto a US government map). Circulated by Wikipedia. Far before contemporary economic globalization, legal traditions functioned as key transnational forces that pressured and transformed the *ummah*, as well as offering vehicles for involving Muslims in cross-border conversations about the changing meaning and role of the *ummah*. See Abdullahi Ahmed An-Na'im, *Islam and the Secular State: Negotiating the Future of Shari'a* (Harvard University Press, 2008).

46 Armando Salvatore, 'The Exit from a Westphalian Framing of Political Space and the Emergence of a Transnational Islamic Public', in *Theory, Culture & Society* 24 (4) (2007), pp. 45–52.

47 John R. Bowen, 'Beyond Migration: Islam as a Transnational Public Space', in *Journal of Ethnic and Migration Studies* 30 (5) (September 2004), pp. 879–894: 880. The two examples presented above indicate that the transnational public space of Islam in France is firmly anchored in Islamic norms of justification. Debates within that sphere concern the proper ways to interpret Islamic knowledge and to apply it to conditions today, in this case in France. Muslims participating in these debates may take account of norms, laws and conditions prevailing in France, as elements that are normatively external but pragmatically internal to the debates. Thus, Muslim actors may not cite French social and legal norms of gender equality or religious freedom as independent norms that might counter norms derived from Scripture. Such an argument would immediately raise charges of seeking to reshape reality according to Islam rather than the proper action of using Islam to reshape reality. Not even the most 'liberal' Muslim public intellectuals in France make such arguments (see Bowen, forthcoming, p. 890).

48 Part of the transnational public sphere debate lies too strictly within a growing body of literature that documents discursive or cultural dimensions of globalization, which mistakenly ignore political, economic and other social factors that comprise the *ummah*. Invariably the signs and symbols that overflow the bounds of nations, the cultural region mapped by imaginative flows, and cultural

and identity hybrids born of globalization have international political economic referents beyond debates over cultural homogenization or heterogenization. Arjun Appadurai, *Modernity at Large: Cultural Dimensions of Globalization* (Minneapolis, University of Minnesota Press, 1996).

49 V. Kahani-Hopkins and N. Hopkins, '"Representing" British Muslims: The Strategic Dimension to Identity Construction', in *Ethnic and Racial Studies* 25 (2) (2002), pp. 288–309; D. F. Eickelman and J. Anderson (eds), *New Media in the Muslim World: The Emerging Public Sphere* (Bloomington: Indiana University Press, 1999); D. F. Eickelman and J. Piscatori (eds), *Muslim Travelers: Pilgrimage, Migration, and the Religious Imagination* (Berkeley: University of California Press, 1990).

50 In what is surely a point of disagreement, Hirschkind (2001) has argued that not only the standardization of the Qur'an, but the requirement to pray in Arabic, and the popular enjoyment of reciting and writing verses of the Qur'an, promote among ordinary Muslims the sense of participation in a universal message; Armando Salvatore, *Public Islam and the Common Good* (Brill, 2004) p. xii; Armando Salvatore, *Dilemmas of Religious Reform (Islâh): Reinstitutionalizing Shari'a*, pp. 81–98; <http://ema.revues.org/index1503.html>.

51 Nancy Fraser, 'On the Legitimacy and Efficacy of Public Opinion in a Post-Westphalian World', in Special Section: Transnational Public Sphere: Transnationalizing the Public Sphere, Theory, Culture & Society 24 (4) (2007), pp. 7–30: 7.

52 Fraser (2007: 16) also argues that, with post-Cold War geopolitical instabilities and globalization, it has become 'necessary to rethink public sphere theory in a transnational frame'. However, 'these same phenomena' make us face hard questions: is the concept of the public sphere so thoroughly Westphalian in its deep conceptual structure as to be unsalvageable as a critical tool for theorizing the present? Can the concept be reconstructed to suit a post-Westphalian frame? In the latter case, the task would not simply be to conceptualize transnational public spheres as actually existing institutions but to reformulate *the critical theory of the public sphere* in a way that can illuminate the emancipatory possibilities of the present constellation. With satisfactory answers to these questions absent, we lack a usable *critical* theory of the public sphere. At stake in these questions is a more genuine commitment to social change and the political mechanisms for that change.

7

Power Struggle in the Religious Field of Islam: Modernization, Globalization and the Rise of Salafism

Melanie Reddig

Islam is currently passing through a dramatic process of transformation (Abou El Fadl 2005: 5; Aslan 2006: 277). Part of this transformation process is a religious renaissance in which various religious movements are unfolding simultaneously (Roy 2004: 3; Hassan 2008: 2). These religious movements, ranging from the positions adopted by Muslim moderates to the Salafi call for strict implementation of the Shari'a, are competing to define the 'true Islamic faith'.

In this struggle, Islamist movements with a Salafist orientation have achieved a powerful position, strongly influencing the religious discourse surrounding the tenets of Islam and the religious consciousness of Muslim believers. This is a serious challenge for the Muslim world because Salafism, with its oversimplifications, intolerance and its all too frequent call for violence, endangers the theological and moral foundations of Islam. Understanding the conditions for the success of these movements is a crucial task. In the following I will therefore address the question: which processes have contributed to the rise of Islamist movements with a Salafist orientation?

The success of Islamist movements promoting Salafism did not occur suddenly, but has resulted from a complex theological, political and social struggle within Islam (Waardenburg 2002: 287). The religious field studies of the French sociologist Pierre Bourdieu (1991) contain an elaborate theoretical approach to examining the structure and dynamics of this struggle. Although Bourdieu studied solely the Judaeo–Christian religious field, his approach is also readily transferable to the religious field of Islam. From this perspective Islam is considered as a religious field consisting of power relationships between religious agents in a market for salvation goods and religious services. Religious specialists holding religious capital compete in a constant power struggle for religious authority by serving the religious interests of the laity and in return obtaining legitimacy. Changes in religious interest can lead to a power shift in the religious field. Since religion has the crucial social function of expressing and legitimizing the existing, or desired, social order, religious interest is therefore interwoven with the interest of the laity to affirm its identity and status. For this reason the attraction of religion derives to a great extent from its potential to express and legitimize this interest in identity and status.

Based on these theoretical considerations I will show that the rise of Islamist movements with a Salafist orientation can be traced back to a power struggle in the religious field of Islam. Colonialism and postcolonialism led with the ensuing processes of modernization and globalization to a power loss of traditional religious authority in Islam. This created space for the development of new religious movements. At the same time, modernization and globalization strongly affect the need of the laity for affirmation of identity and status, thus causing a change in the religious interest. Islamist movements with a Salafist orientation take advantage of the erosion of traditional religious authority by serving and moulding the new religious interests of the laity and thereby gaining substantially in power.

Islamist Movements and Salafism

Islamist movements are movements which perceive Islamic theology and law as an authoritative frame of reference in any social or political situation and therefore want to impose their interpretation of Islam on various areas of society (Abou El Fadl 2005: 18). This definition of Islamist movements is clearly very broad. However, it also needs to be broad to take in the wide range of these movements. Perceiving Islamic theology and law as an authoritative frame of reference can have different meanings and consequences: it can, for instance, mean striving to create a theocratic state with draconian laws, but it can also simply imply Islamic ethics and morals in matters of public concern. Thus, the particular interpretation of Islamic theology and law is the decisive criterion to classify Islamist movements more precisely (Diaa 2007: 15; Waardenburg 2002: 288).

Salafism is just such a theological orientation that distinguishes different Islamic movements. Originating at the end of the nineteenth century, Salafism emerged out of the attempt to reform Islamic and Muslim sovereignty in the face of colonialism. The term '*salaf*' means predecessors and refers to the period of the Prophet and his companions. Salafism idealizes the lifetime of the Prophet and his companions as the 'Golden Age' of Islam and demands that all Muslims should return to what Salafis perceive as the pristine and uncorrupted Islam. Salafism is based on the conviction that the Qur'an and Sunna are self-explanatory, which implies the repudiation of the various interpretive communities of Islam.[1] However, in the early days of Salafism the simplistic rejection of the traditional interpretation was first and foremost directed against the perceived backwardness and powerlessness of the religious establishment at that time (Roy 2004: 233). It was not yet a call for the authoritarian implementation of the Shari'a, but aimed at the liberation of Muslim societies.

This liberal phase of Salafism ended in the mid-twentieth century, and from that time onwards Salafism evolved irrevocably into a strict authoritarian and supremacist creed. A decisive factor in this development was the influence of Wahhabism. The creed of Wahhabism was founded in the eighteenth century by Abd al-Wahhab and, like Salafism, it was based on the conviction that Muslims had abandoned the 'straight path to God' and urgently needed to return to the pure and pristine faith of the 'Golden Age' (Waardenburg 2002: 229). The theological orientation of the founders of Salafism and Wahhabism were almost identical, except that Wahhabism was far more intolerant and authoritarian. Wahhabism claimed that the return to the 'true Islamic faith' was achievable solely by implementing the commands of the Prophet literally and by adhering strictly to the correct ritual practice. This conviction resulted in extreme hostility towards the traditional interpretative communities and towards all forms of rationalism, intellectualism and mysticism in Islam.

The similarities between Salafism and Wahhabism led to a merging of the two creeds: 'The bonding of the theologies of Wahhabism and Salafism produced a contemporary orientation that is anchored in profound feelings of defeatism, alienation, and frustration' (Abou El Fadl 2005: 57). The new theological orientation is a purist and intolerant view which considers the rich tradition of plurality in Islam merely as a contamination of the 'true Islamic faith'. The resulting belief is that God is manifest in the divine law in the form of indisputable legal commands covering nearly all aspects of life and that the sole task of Muslims is to obey these commands. The Shari'a is seen as a collection of technical laws defining the straight 'path to God' and, as a consequence, all moral considerations outside these laws are perceived as misguided on principle. Embedded in the security of indisputable legal commands, this view fosters a supremacist polarization between the 'rightly guided' and the 'misguided' who must be fought and punished. The 'rightly guided' are inherently superior to all 'others'– these latter comprising the majority of Muslims, who are perceived as heretics, as well as all non-Muslims.

For Salafists, the West is waging 'war against Islam and Muslims' and threatening the Muslim identity (Esposito and Mogahed 2007: 87). The Muslim identity must be restored and protected by reinforcing the Shari'a. Striving for a strict and mechanical implementation of the legal commands is thus an integral part of identity politics: 'A key function of these mindsets is to repair and assert Muslim identity' (Hassan 2008: 2). This includes the eradication of all forms of ambiguity. Islam is constructed in opposition to the West and therefore Muslims are commanded to strengthen their Muslim identity by distinguishing themselves from non-Muslims. This orientation, which Hermansen defines as 'internationalist identity Islam', is most concerned with Western domination and the feeling of powerlessness (Hermansen 2003: 306). The central aim is to gain recognition and status through the use of power and its symbols.

The confluence of Salafism and Wahhabism resulted in a theological orientation with a wide range of ideological variations and tendencies. Until now no consistent terminology for this new creed is in use. Abou El Fadl (2005: 18; 2003: 57) uses the term 'Salafabism' or 'Puritanism' due to the absolutist and intolerant nature of this theological orientation. Gellner (1981: 110), on the other hand, chooses the term 'Neo-puritanism' for this rigorous creed in order to distinguish it from puritanism in the sense of scripturalism and pietism, which was historically at the heart of urban elite Islam. In addition, Aslan (2007: 264) uses the term 'Fundamentalism', whereas Roy (2004: 233) considers the term 'Neo-fundamentalism' more accurate to distinguish the historical Salafi movement from its current successors. These various attempts to find the most accurate term for the blend of Salafism and Wahhabism lead, as can be expected, to considerable terminological confusion. However, all these different terms label the same creed. The adherents of this creed mostly call themselves Salafis and therefore 'Salafism' is still the most commonly used term, which I will use in the following.

Although Salafism is certainly not one of the dominant theological orientations in Islam, it is nevertheless on the rise and is challenging mainstream Islam. Hassan's (2008: 54) empirical survey indicates that this creed has gained considerable influence on the religious consciousness of Muslims.[2] It is especially strong in Egypt, Indonesia, Malaysia and Pakistan, but in all countries included in the survey the approval rating for the statement 'The Qur'an and Sunna are completely self-sufficient to meet the needs of present and future societies' is high or even very high. However, it must be stressed that what Muslims mean when they say that they support the Shari'a can vary drastically (Esposito and Mogahed 2007: 54). The Shari'a as the 'path to God' represents the moral compass for Muslims' personal and public life and is therefore of major importance for Muslim identity. Accordingly, the Gallup's World Poll survey reveals that the majority of Muslims support the Shari'a as *one* source of legislation.[3] Nevertheless, just a minority supports the Shari'a as the *only* source of legislation. This minority is mainly composed of political radicals.[4] The main concern of these radicals is to enhance the status, recognition and power of Muslims. The Gallup survey furthermore indicates that the political radicals are not generally the poor and uneducated. On the contrary, the average political radical is better educated and with a higher income than the moderate Muslim.[5] Hassan (2008: 100), who comes to a similar result, concludes that the modern or modernizing Muslims in particular tend to transfer their allegiance to Salafism.

For a better understanding of this development it is important to consider the power configurations within Islam. The religious field studies of Pierre Bourdieu provide a suitable tool to examine the structure and the dynamics contributing to the rise of Islamist movements promoting Salafism.

The Religious Field of Islam

The work of the French sociologist Pierre Bourdieu is at present considered to be one of the most innovative and influential approaches in sociology. Bourdieu studies the forces and conflicts between individual and collective agents, whereby his theory of the field is of eminent importance for his work. Bourdieu defines a social field as a configuration of power relationships between positions occupied by agents possessing various forms of capital (Bourdieu 1985: 724; Wacquant 1989: 38). The relative position of the agents in the field depends on the distribution of capital which provides decisive power over the rules of the field and thus over the profit at stake (Bourdieu 1986: 241; Harker *et al.* 1990: 8). The agents strive to maintain or improve their position in the field: 'To put it simply, each field can be seen as a "game", in which "players" fight according to specific rules for a specific "stake", which appears to them "worth" the time and energy that have to be invested in the competition' (Schultheis 2008: 35).

The field is characterized by a constant power struggle aimed at either preserving or transforming the power configuration in the field. The agents compete for positions of legitimate authority and use their strategies to impose a hierarchical structure on the field which is most favourable to themselves and their own products. The extent to which the 'consumers' request these products is crucial for the position of the agents in the field. Bourdieu regards the field as a 'market place' in which the agents are producers of symbolic goods and services destined for the 'consumers'. In exchange for their products the agents receive legitimation which gives them authority within the field. To reduce competition, the agents seek to establish a monopoly for their products in the market by excluding other agents. Therefore, the question of inclusion and exclusion is constantly embattled in all social fields.

For Bourdieu, the social cosmos of modern societies is differentiated into various social fields which all follow their own 'rules of the game' and are relatively independent of each other (Wacquant 1989: 39; Calhoun 1993: 77). One of these fields is the religious field. Max Weber's work on ancient Judaism and the emergence of Christianity inspired Bourdieu to study the power relationships and dynamics in the Judaeo–Christian religious field (Bourdieu 1987: 119; Diantiell 2003: 535). Weber stresses in his religious sociology the material basis of the interaction between various religious specialists and the laity: priests, prophets and magicians offer their religious goods to the laity – the latter comprising various social groups, each having different salvation needs according to their social position in society (Weber 1980: 259). Bourdieu takes up this notion of religious interaction and develops it into the concept of the religious field, thereby focusing on the structural relationships between the agents and the influence of symbolic power (Bourdieu 2000: 118). For Bourdieu, the religious discourse within societies is deeply interwoven with the social structure. However, the religious discourse should not be perceived as a mere reflection of the social structure. Bourdieu emphasizes the role of religious specialists who produce religious ideologies. These religious ideologies respond indeed to the religious needs of various social groups, but at the same time these ideologies are also an autonomous power symbolically structuring the social world (Swartz 1996: 73; Robbins 1991: 93). In the following, the concept which Bourdieu developed in his religious studies will be adapted to the religious field of Islam.

Similar to his general definition of the social field, Bourdieu defines the religious field as a configuration of power relationships between positions occupied by religious agents. These agents, possessing religious capital accumulated by their religious labour, claim the right to produce religious beliefs and practices which they offer to the laity to meet their religious needs (Bourdieu 1991: 23). The religious field of Islam is therefore regarded as a power configuration between religious agents competing to establish their various concepts of Islamic beliefs, norms and practices. These concepts of Islam are offered to and adopted by the *ummah*, the community of all Muslim believers. Islam is by no means a single entity, and in the course of Islamic history distinct variations have developed (Waardenburg 2002: 211). Hassan distinguishes between at least five different cultural and religious centres in contemporary Islam, each of which could be separately studied as a religious field (Hassan 2008: 230).[6] However, the rise of Islamic movements with a Salafist orientation can be regarded as an overall trend and therefore, in order to examine the general structures and dynamics behind this development, the power configuration within Islam will be studied from a broad perspective.

The emergence of a religious field is linked with the distinction between those agents included in the field and those who are excluded. As long as there is no monopoly on the production and administration of religious beliefs and practices, any individual can create his or her own religious beliefs, symbols or rituals (Schultheis 2008: 36). This situation changes when certain groups raise and enforce the claim that they are the religious specialists and are therefore socially recognized as the exclusive holders of religious competence (Bourdieu 1991: 8). A religious field emerges when religious goods and services are monopolized by these religious specialists. In the course of this process the religious beliefs and practices are systematized and developed into a general moral system. This results in the dichotomy between the included religious experts and the excluded laity, who are negatively defined as the religiously untalented. The laity is deprived of religious capital in the form of the 'knowledgeable mastery' of religious norms and ideologies and is left only with a certain 'practical mastery' of religion.

In Islam, the generation and administration of beliefs, norms and practices is not as centralized as in Christianity, because there is no church with a hierarchically structured institution of priesthood: 'The community of the faithful is not, in theory, internally differentiated into a lay society and the body of extraspecially faithful' (Gellner 1981: 48). Without such a single authoritative institutional centre the *ummah* becomes of crucial theological importance in Islam (Aslan 2005: 146). For Islamic scholars, the *ummah* is the nucleus of the Muslim faith because it unites the bearers of Islam, sharing their faith and implementing Islamic law. The *ummah* is perceived as a divinely inspired community through which salvation is achieved. Since Islam has no concept of priesthood through which God's word must be transmitted to the unenlightened laity, these latter are not excluded and dispossessed of religious capital to the same extent as in Christianity.

Nevertheless, the religious field of Islam emerged like all other religious fields from the monopolization of religious knowledge by a body of religious experts. In Islam these religious experts are called the *ulama*, the 'learned men of God'. The *ulama* claims the legitimate religious authority to lead the *ummah* on 'the straight path to God' and thus determines the authoritative concepts of orthodoxy (the correct interpretation of faith) and orthopraxy (the correct interpretation of rituals). In Islam the power configuration of the field is characterized by multiple centres of religious authority. The religious clerics of the *ulama* represent the four legitimate law schools of Islam, with all of these schools having an equal claim to religious authority. However, since Islam is perceived as a religion of law based on religious science, the religious knowledge is largely monopolized by the four law schools.

The religious authority of the *ulama* derives from its knowledgeable mastery of the Shari'a gained through the discipline of *figh*, the Islamic jurisprudence deducing religious rules from the Qur'an, Sunna and other religious sources (Waardenburg 2002: 387). An indispensable requirement for a religious expert is a profound qualification in one of the four law schools. The accumulation of this kind of religious capital is extremely costly in terms of time and for the laity it is therefore virtually impossible to achieve. Furthermore, the *ulama* ensures its monopoly over religious authority in the form of its knowledgeable mastery by upholding the 'closing of the gates of *ijtihad*'.[7]

Starting from informal gatherings of like-minded religious experts, the *ulama* developed at the end of the tenth century into the four institutionalized law schools. At this point in time *ijtihad* was rejected as legal practise of Islamic law. This was also a means to constrain the theological plurality and to inhibit the emergence of new centres of religious authority within the field of Islam. The *ulama* formulated the Shari'a as a comprehensive body of rules guiding the life of all Muslims. Since the Qur'an itself is not a book of laws comprehensively regulating Islamic belief and practice, the Shari'a results from the interpretation of the Qur'an and the Sunna according to complex methodologies and rules (Abou El Fadl 2005: 31; Aslan 2005: 162). With the formulation of the Shari'a, the *ulama* systematized Islamic belief and practice and consolidated its position as a religious establishment.

However, the power struggle within the religious field is not terminated with the consolidation of a religious establishment. The religious agents remain involved in a constant 'competition for the monopoly over the administration of the goods of salvation and over the legitimate exercise of religious power' (Bourdieu 1991: 22). The competitors struggle for the religious authority to impose their scholarly doctrine on the laity. The religious establishment strives to legitimate the distinction between themselves and those other religious agents who are excluded. Thus the power struggle in the religious field is necessarily centred on the conflict between orthodoxy and heresy. The religious establishment is only able to uphold its religious monopoly if the excluded accept their status as legitimate. For this reason heretics are a major threat to the religious establishment. They challenge the authority of the establishment by questioning its religious competence and institutional prestige. If the heretics become influential, the competition between orthodoxy and heresy can alter the power relationships in the religious field.

The power configuration in Islam has constantly changed in the course of history (Gellner 1981: 9; Waardenburg 2002: 289). Even from its inception there were religious movements which questioned the *ulama* regarding its interpretation of the sources as well as its abolition of *ijtihad*. However, religious movements directed against the *ulama* became eminently influential in the eras of colonialism and postcolonialism. At this time the religious authority of the *ulama* started to crumble under the influence of modernization and Western power (Abou El Fadl 2005: 35). Religious institutions were replaced by civil institutions and the *ulama* lost its privileged position in Muslim societies. The weakened position of the *ulama* led to the emergence of a power gap in the religious field of Islam.

From its beginnings Islamic movements promoting Salafism took advantage of this power gap and challenged the religious authority of the *ulama* (Musallam 2005: 7; Aslan 2005: 232). Salafism is directed against orthodox Islam and denies the theological relevance of the *ulama*. The religious authority is restricted to the Scripture, with *ijtihad* only being allowed within certain limits (Abou El Fadl 2001: 171). Salafism perceives the interpretation of the Scripture by the *ulama* as a deviation from the 'straight path to God', caused by the incompetence and corruptness of the *ulama*. This is a serious attack on the religious authority of the *ulama*. By rejecting the long tradition of scholarship in the Islamic sciences of religion, Salafism devalues the religious labour of the *ulama* and deconstructs the traditional notions of established authority within Islam. As a result, the power relations in the religious field have been shifting. Indeed, Abou El Fadl speaks of a severe crisis of authority in contemporary Islam (2005: 26). In the course of the erosion of traditional religious authority, those Islamist movements promoting Salafism gained influence.

To understand this power shift in the religious field of Islam the concept of religious interest is revealing. Bourdieu defines religious interest as the interest taken by social groups or classes in the production and consumption of specific religious beliefs and practices (1991: 15). The various groups within the laity require different religious beliefs and practices according to their position in society. For Bourdieu the correlation between the social position of the layperson and his or her religious interest results from the social function of religion (Rey 2007: 57). Religion not only comforts humans in the face of contingency, misery and death by providing orientation and salvation, but it also legitimates the good fortune of the dominant classes, as well as promising the dominated classes a compensation for injustice and suffering. Moreover, religion is a means to stress the distinction between 'us' and the 'others'. The production and consumption of religious goods and services is therefore an important part of the 'symbolic struggle over the power to produce and to impose the legitimate vision of the world' (Bourdieu 1989: 20). In this struggle the agents compete to enhance their self-image as well as the image of their social position in society, striving to impose the classifications of perception and evaluation most favourable on themselves. The religious interest of the laity derives, to a considerable extent, from the role of religion in this symbolic struggle within society.

Starting from this conception of religion, the religious interest of various groups within the laity can be deduced, in my opinion, more precisely: religious interest is linked to the potential of religion to symbolize and legitimate the identity and status of various groups in society. Firstly, religion is a means to affirm personal and collective identity because the identification with religious beliefs and practices has a strong impact on the self-image and self-esteem of the believers and, moreover, religious beliefs and practices stress the similarities between believers, while at the same time distinguishing the one religious group from other groups within society. Secondly, religion is a means to assure social status, because the divine order mirrors the social order. Certain religious beliefs and practices consolidate the status of dominant groups in society. However, religious beliefs and practices can also express the rejection of the social order and thus legitimate the desire of dominated groups to escape from their inferior status. For such groups, religious beliefs and practices also provide credibility for the perception of their own superiority since through religion the social order can be redefined.

For Bourdieu, the dynamic development of the religious field depends on the ability of the agents in the field to serve the various religious interests of the laity. Those agents who offer religious beliefs and practices most desired by the laity, whether orthodox or heretical, gain power over the field: 'The exchange relations established between specialists and laypersons on the basis of different interest, and the relations of competition, which oppose various specialists to each other in the religious field, constitute the principle of the dynamic of the religious field and therefore of the transformation of religious ideology' (Bourdieu 1991: 17). Heretics can transform the theological orientation and inculcate in parts of the laity an altered religious habitus if they are able to mobilize concurrent 'heretical religious interests' (Bourdieu 1991: 24).[8]

Islamic movements promoting Salafism are such heretical movements which successfully mobilize adherents, thereby shifting the power configuration within Islam (Abou El Fadl 2005: 7; Hassan 2008: 48). To understand the attraction of these movements it is necessary to examine the religious interest of their adherents. Since the theological orientation of Salafism gained influence especially in the era of modernization and globalization it is furthermore crucial to consider how these transformation processes influence the religious interest of certain groups within the *ulama* in a manner that makes Salafism attractive for them.

The Impact of Modernization

The process of modernization led to the erosion of traditional institutions, values and social ties, and fundamentally changed Muslim societies (Roy 2004: 139). The radical social changes, caused by the differentiation of society and the crossing of social frontiers, almost inevitably evoked resentments and fears (Meyer 1989: 17). The emerging plurality of lifestyles and values causes insecurity and overstrains certain groups of society which are unable to meet the new demands for the affirmation of their personal and collective identity. In the case of Muslim societies, modernization is to a large extent linked to colonialism, which accelerated the process of social change since colonial rulers often purposely dismantled the traditional structures of Muslim societies (Aslan 2005: 222). Muslims were forced to abandon their traditional social order and to adopt instead Western institutions and values, thereby devaluing Muslim culture and identity. Most rulers of Muslim societies, remaining dependent upon Western powers, promoted the process of Westernization further on in the era of postcolonialism. This resulted in a widespread fear of modernization and 'Westoxification', dispossessing Muslims of their identity, unity and strength. But, at the same time, the West has still a strong appeal for Muslims (Esposito and Mogahed 2007: 42; Abou El Fadl 2003: 41). This ambivalent attitude regarding modernization and Westernization can cause severe identity crises.[9]

Appealing to Islam is a means of protesting against the sensed identity crisis because Islam is, like all other religions, an essential source for the affirmation of personal and collective identity (Waardenburg 2002: 364). The recourse to Islam has, throughout history, been interwoven with protest whenever Muslim identity was thought to be endangered. However, Islamic movements with a Salafist orientation take advantage of this religious potential for protest by promoting an 'identity Islam' exclusively focused on the defence and assertion of Muslim identity (Hermannsen 2003: 310).

Accordingly, Salafism is most notably successful in attracting Muslims who experience an identity crisis in the face of modernization (Waardenburg 2002: 310; Stern 2003: 69) Salafism meets the rejection of modernization by demonizing modern culture as being sinful and decadent to the core (Marty and Appleby 1991: 822; Lawrence 1989: 2). All social changes and problems arising during modernization are interpreted in religious terms as a departure from the 'straight path to God'. With this religious interpretation of social change Salafism seems to reveal the cause of the identity crisis and thus offers simplistic explanations to those who sense insecurity and inequity in the modern world. The purist interpretation of the Scripture and the strict rules provide firm guidelines for mindset and conduct regarding nearly all spheres of life.

Rejecting the plurality of interpretations and beliefs and strictly discriminating between good and evil, Salafism masks the ambiguities of life and thus facilitates the affirmation of identity (Abou El Fadl 2001: 7). The regulation of rituals and personal appearance in apparent distinction from all 'others' is a means of creating a distinct and authentic self-image of the believer. Facing a devaluation of Muslim identity by the West, Salafism reduces Islam to the expression and defence of Muslim identity, thereby drawing a strict distinction from the hostile West. Hence, the main concern is the affirmation of Muslim identity: 'What is reconstructed here is not only religion: it is the self itself, in some sort of permanent representation and staging of the self' (Roy 2004: 267).

However, this also implies that Salafism expresses more than just an apparent opposition to modernization. Indeed, Salafism also meets the changed demands regarding the affirmation of personal and collective identity (Roy 2004: 5). Released from the traditional social bonds in the process of individualization, the modern individual has to abandon the tradition and accept the sole responsibility for his or her life, thereby stressing independence and uniqueness (Beck 1986: 115; Bauman 2004:

29). Since the human need for social affiliation does not simply disappear in an individualized society, individuals also strive for the affirmation of their collective identity. These modern requirements for the affirmation of personal and collective identity can have a decisive impact on the religious interest of Muslims.

Salafism meets the demands of this religious interest because it delinks religion from tradition and creates a 'deculturated Islam', rejecting the various Islamic customs of, for example, specific rituals or music as being a deviation from 'true Islam' (Roy 2004: 22; Hermannsen 2003: 310). Islam stands above the traditional social communities, which means that the believer is released from an ascribed religious affiliation and perceived as making his or her own decision regarding faith. The highest authority in questions of faith is not the traditional religious institution, but the sovereign self (Beck 2008: 47). The allowance of *ijtihad* in certain limits corresponds to the individualized religiosity: it is not the task of traditional religious institutions to conclusively define the interpretation of the Scripture. Instead, it is the individual Muslim who is, at least principally, considered able to understand the meaning of faith autonomously. Accordingly, individual spiritual needs, the religious commitment of the believer and his or her individual relationship to God take centre stage (Roy 2004: 268). Hence, Salafism is not traditional, but modern in the sense that it creates an individualized concept of Muslim religiosity.

Although religiosity is individualized, Salafism also offers its adherents a strong feeling of social belonging (Beck 2008: 107). The religious community is created as an 'identity group' encapsulated in a threatening environment (Roy 2004: 35). The differentiation between the moral adherents and the immoral, dangerous outsiders affirms the collective identity of the adherents by fixing the social borderlines and uniting the adherents in their defence against the enemy. Moreover, Salafism creates the individualized religious community in the form of an abstract community that unites all 'true believers' in an 'imagined *ummah*' cut off from all real cultural interaction. This virtuality of the religious community reconciles both individualism and collectivism since it facilitates a strong sense of belonging and yet allows a high degree of individuality.

A further aspect of Salafism is that it also affirms the social status of its adherents in modern society. The process of modernization confronts the individual with changed demands for achieving and securing his or her status in society, because the traditional social structure erodes and social mobility increases. The resulting uncertainty about the individual's social status can be lessened by the adoption of Salafism, confirming to its adherents that they are the 'rightly guided' and have therefore an inherently high status (Abou El Fadl 2005: 78). The modern concepts of equality and meritocracy have an important impact on the individual claim for status too, since these concepts entail the demand for justice and thus emancipation from the dominance of the traditional ruling classes.

Salafism regards all members of the religious community as equal (Waardenburg 2002: 292). The rejection of the ruling elite is expressed with recourse to the Shari'a as the embodiment of justice and defence against oppression from the ruling elite (Esposito and Mogahed 2007: 36). The polarization between the superior believer on the one hand, strong enough to implement the strict rules on the 'straight path to God', and the weak sinner on the other hand, meets the norm of meritocracy. The main concern is the individual effort to achieve a position of moral supremacy, especially in contradiction to the sinful West (Abou El Fadl 2005: 95).

Moreover, the modern concept of meritocracy also leads to the demand for wealth and influence as a reward for achieved merit. But since social status based on merit entails the comparison with the merit of others, individuals cannot be certain about their attainable social status. This uncertainty is further increased by social change during the course of modernization. This can lead to the feeling of relative deprivation, meaning the frustration of individuals resulting from a perceived discrepancy between their expected and their actual status (Gurr 1972: 33; Walker and Smith 2002: 2). Individuals feel frustrated when they compare their social status with that of others and conclude that their own status is lower than they deserve. Often it is among the middle classes in particular that this feeling of relative deprivation develops, because the process of modernization raises their expectations regarding social status, but at the same time frequently disappoints these expectations. This possibly explains why the adherents of Salafism are often better educated and have a higher income than Muslims with a moderate religious orientation.

Salafism can express the feeling of relative deprivation, thereby interpreting relative deprivation in a religious framework. Juergensmeyer speaks of a 'religionized' political conflict (2004: 3). Social change and conflict resulting in frustration are ascribed to a cosmic struggle between the good forces and the evil forces which are bringing injustice into the world and leading society to the brink of the precipice. The interpretation of the Scripture mirrors the social experience: 'In fact, despite their claims of objectivity, the puritan orientation forces religious texts to validate the social and political frustrations and insecurities of its adherents' (Abou El Fadl 2005: 96). Moreover, the 'rightly guided' Salafis are legitimized, in fact are obliged to fight their opponents and change the social order of society.[10] Striving for a renewed social order is also a means to change the 'rules of the game'. Salafis demand a social order in which their assumed moral superiority is acknowledged and accordingly they are entitled to a high social status in society.

In addition, Salafism interprets the Scripture in a way that secures male domination (Hassan 2008: 183). Women are regarded as subservient to the power of men and as a source of civil disorder if they are not controlled. The attraction of this attitude can also possibly be explained in relation to the concept of relative deprivation. Hassan's empirical survey indicates that the approval of patriarchal and misogynous attitudes is especially high in countries in which government policies have strengthened women's rights and therefore men, relative to women, have forfeited their status: 'In Muslim societies where men have experienced greater status loss than women, they have compensated for that loss by developing more conservative attitudes towards women, including support for veiling, seclusion and patriarchy' (Hassan 2008: 213).[11]

The Impact of Globalization

The process of globalization which accelerates the crossing of national boundaries has an important impact on the religious consciousness of Muslims (Hassan 2008: 227). Since globalization opens new opportunities to learn about fellow Muslims around the world and to exchange experience and knowledge, it fosters the emergence of a global Muslim identity. The increasing awareness that Muslims have similar convictions and interests in all parts of the world calls for the creation of a transnational solidarity between Muslims (Beck 2008: 62).

In addition, globalization also leads to increased migration. Muslims who have migrated to the West have to cope with a lack of traditional affiliations and guidelines and also often with the experience of discrimination. For this reason they strive for the affirmation of their Muslim identity (Roy 2004: 122). Identity affirmation is achieved by defining the meaning of being a Muslim and identifying with the global Muslim community. Migrants who have lost their social and cultural connection to their country of origin tend to favour a concept of Muslim identity which defines Islam independently of a particular cultural setting. This is especially the case for second- and third-generation Muslims in the West, who are trapped in a marginal position, disconnected from the cultural background of their parents and at the same time only partly integrated into Western society and culture. These young Muslims often experience a serious identity crisis, which they resolve by turning to Islam (Clarke 1990: 198).

Globalization, moreover, not only reveals the similarities, but also the dissimilarities between the various Islamic cultures around the world, because religious norms and practices differ considerably between Muslim countries. The cultural variety within Islam can cause uncertainty about religious identity, thus adding to the general uncertainty resulting from the erosion of pristine culture in the course of globalization (Appadurai 2006: 22). Nothing seems to be worse than a unified global culture, especially if this is associated with the spread of Western culture: 'Given the power of the West and Western-dominated globalization (political, economic, and cultural), many may fear being overwhelmed by Western culture and losing their Muslim identity, independence, and values' (Esposito and Mogahed 2007: 141). This fear of identity loss and Western domination fuels the desire to establish a clear distinction between Muslims on one side and Westerners on the other. For these reasons, globalization can have a considerable influence on the religious interests of Muslims.

A special characteristic of Salafism is, moreover, that it adapts to the process of globalization by meeting the changed religious interests of Muslims (Roy 2004: 258). It disseminates the vision of a 'globalized Islam' delinked from territory. Indeed, Salafism promotes globalization because it rids Islam of all cultural traditions: 'Born-again Muslims are more prone to launch a halal McDonald's than a restaurant that serves couscous or traditional "Indian' food"' (Roy 2004: 145). Salafism can be practiced in any society, whereby the adherents, scattered around the world, are encouraged to unite in a global 'imagined community'.

Salafism therefore appeals in particular to migrants striving for the affirmation of their Muslim identity independent of cultural and territorial affiliations. The strict differentiation between Muslims and Westerners facilitates the development of a Muslim identity as distinct from Western society, which is often experienced as being hostile to Muslims. For young Muslim migrants the strict rules and the deculturated content of Salafism affirm their identity when remaining in a marginal position. In addition, the appeal to the 'sophisticated' scripturalism of Salafism is a means to distance themselves from the 'unsophisticated' traditional attitudes of their parents.

The Salafistic purification of Muslim identity furthermore reduces the uncertainty about the cultural plurality within Islam, because it acknowledges only one 'pure' form of Islamic faith. Salafism professes to defend Muslim identity against the corrosive influence of the West, thereby setting Muslims strongly apart from Westerners. With this kind of identity affirmation Salafism provides orientation and security in the face of globalization – but at the cost of an impoverishment of the Islamic faith and the fuelling of distrust between Muslims and Westerners. For Hassan, the struggle between 'hybridity' and 'authenticity', resulting from the process of globalization, is probably one of the most serious challenges for the *ummah* and an important factor behind the rise of Islamic fundamentalist movements (Hassan 2008: 228).

Finally, the development of an interconnected world society has changed the demand of Muslims regarding their status in the world. The new communication technologies disseminate information about Western wealth, influence and lifestyle around the world. The dynamic of the global economy affects all parts of the world, thereby tightly linking the winners and losers of economic globalization and increasing the competition for power in the world (Appadurai 2006: 102; Hassan 2008: 231). This interconnectedness of the world encourages Muslims to compare themselves with the wealth and influence of Westerners. In the face of the apparent dominance of the West and the assumed 'Western war against Islam and Muslims', this comparison with Westerners often leads to frustration. This kind of frustration can be described as a global relative deprivation: as a result of globalization the reference point for individuals who compare their own status with the status of others shifts (Reddig 2007: 298). Individuals compare themselves not only with groups within their own country, but also with groups in other parts of the world. If this comparison leads to the perception that their own status in the world is lower than deserved, this causes frustration. As the centre of power, the West is the most prominent point of reference for the comparison of wealth and status. The frustration resulting from this comparison leads to the claim for recognition by the West as well as to the rejection of the West.

This tension between attraction and rejection of the West can cause 'intellectual dissonance' which makes the affirmation of Muslim identity and status especially difficult (Abou El Fadl 2003, 41). Most notably, professionals and elites in Muslim countries sense this ambivalence in their relationship to the West: since the Western standards for professionalism and well-being are disseminated around the world, these groups are strongly attracted to the West, but at the same time they often experience discrimination and denial of immigration to Western countries. 'So, sadly, the dreamers and the haters are not two groups. They are often one and the same persons' (Appadurai 2006: 124). This ambivalence in relation to the West possibly increases the feeling of global relative deprivation because it intensifies the comparison with the West as well as the feeling of injustice.

The increasing number of Muslim migrants living in the West often experience a similar frustration. Migrants normally make their decision to migrate to the West because they are attracted by the expectation of higher income and status. When these expectations cannot be realized, disappointment and frustration follow. Comparing their own status in Western society with that of Westerners, the migrants perceive an unjust discrepancy. Second- and third-generation migrants sense this injustice most notably, since they were born in the countries to which their parents migrated and thus demand equal rights and treatment.

Salafism is a means to express the frustration resulting from these social conditions. It condemns the West and its corruptness and sinfulness in an emotionally charged manner. It asserts the moral superiority of its adherents and thus compensates for feelings of discrimination and powerlessness (Abou El Fadl 2005: 95; Hassan 2008: 46). Furthermore, it legitimizes the ambitions of status improvement as well as the attempts to change the world order, frequently leading to a call for violence. Striving to restore Muslim influence and pride, Salafism reduces Islam to a sheer symbol of power. The rise of Islamist movements promoting

Salafism is therefore indeed a severe threat to the theological and moral foundation of Islam.

Conclusion

Islamic movements promoting Salafism gained power in the religious field of Islam by adapting to the changed religious interest of particular groups within the *ummah*. Modernization and globalization set new guidelines for the affirmation of identity and status and expanded the individuals' possibilities to adopt these guidelines. Released from the traditional social bonds, the individual is required to take over the sole responsibility for his or her life. This raises expectations but can also lead to insecurity and frustration. In Muslim countries the processes of modernization and globalization are associated with the power and dominance of the West. This means that the West is an appealing point of reference, but also causes the fear of identity loss and the devaluation of Muslims' status in the world. The ambitions and fears resulting from modernization and globalization influence the religious interest of Muslims, since religion is a means of expressing and legitimizing the social order and the corresponding attitudes towards it.

Salafism meets these changed religious interests because it enables its adherents to express their sensed identity crisis and their rejection of modernization and globalization in simplistic religious terms. Salafism blames the corrupt elites of Muslim societies as well as the ruthless West for the perceived crisis and is thus attractive for those who experience insecurity and frustration in the face of modernization and globalization. The adoption of Salafism simplifies the affirmation of personal and collective identity and legitimates ambitions for status improvement, which also includes the claim for changing the 'rules of the game' in society.

However, Salafism attracts adherents not only with its apparent opposition to modernization and globalization but also because it likewise meets the social and cultural conditions resulting from these processes of social change. Salafism is an individualized and deculturated creed that coincides with the modernized and globalized life of its adherents. The main concern is the modern individual and his or her place in the globalized world. The vision of an abstract community that unites all 'true believers' in the global *ummah* is disseminated. The virtuality of the religious community reconciles individualism and collectivism since it encourages both a strong social affiliation and a strong individuality. Salafism thus appeals to individuals who experience alienation and frustration but at the same time have internalized the modern demands for the affirmation of identity and status.

The rise of Islamist movements promoting Salafism contributes to the decline of traditional religious authority and endangers the theological and moral foundation of Islam. It is thus one of the most serious challenges for the Muslim world (Hassan 2008: 39). Indeed, the power relations in the religious field of Islam have undoubtedly shifted, leading to considerable confusion about religious authority (Abou El Fadl 2005: 26). At the present time, however, it is by no means clear who will win the power struggle in the religious field of Islam. In order to prevent Salafism from seizing the religious authority in the field, the changed religious interests within the *ulama* need to be taken seriously. A transformation of the religious field in the course of modernization and globalization is surely unavoidable, but the various agents in the religious field should be aware that they have the chance to influence the direction of this transformation.

NOTES

1 Abou El Fadl defines interpretive communities as 'groups of people who share common hermeneutical methodologies, linguistic skills, and epistemological values and coalesce around a particular set of texts and determine the meaning and import of these texts.' (Abou El Fadl 2003: 39)

2 In the survey over 6,300 Muslims were interviewed in the six major Muslim countries of Indonesia, Pakistan, Malaysia, Iran, Kazakhstan, Egypt and Turkey (Hassan 2008).

3 The Gallup's World Poll survey was carried out between 2001 and 2007, conducting tens of thousands of interviews with residents of more than thirty-five nations that are predominantly Muslim or have a substantial Muslim population (Esposito and Mogahed 2007).

4 The Gallup survey detects significant differences in the sample between the group of moderates and the group of political radicals, which amount to 7 per cent. These 7 per cent think that the 9/11 attacks were completely justified and view the United States unfavourably. Within the group of political radicals, 59 per cent support the Shari'a as the only source of legislation, whereas only 32 per cent of the moderates support this (Esposito and Mogahed 2007: 93).

5 Sixty-seven per cent of the political radicals have secondary or higher education (versus 53 per cent of the moderates) and 65 per cent of the political radicals say that they have average or above average income (versus 55 per cent of the moderates) (Esposito and Mogahed 2007: 71).
6 For Hassan, these centres are Arabic Middle Eastern Islam, African Islam, Central Asian Islam, Southeast Asian Islam and the Islam of Muslim minorities in the West.
7 *Ijtihad* describes the practice of qualified Islamic scholars deciding independently on legal issues if the Qur'an and Sunna do not provide clarity on these issues.
8 This concurrence results for Bourdieu from 'the homology between the positions of the producers in the structure of the field and the positions of the consumers of their products in the structure of class relations' (Bourdieu 1991: 22).
9 Shayegan describes this ambivalence caused by modernization and Westernization as 'cultural schizophrenia' (Shayegan 1989: 4).
10 Sageman considers the role of relative deprivation in the context of rising expectations for members of the global Salafi jihad (2004: 95)
11 Among the studied countries the approval for veiling, seclusion and patriarchy is especially strong in Egypt and Indonesia (Hassan 2008: 213).

BIBLIOGRAPHY

Abou El Fadl, Khaled, *Speaking in God's Name: Islamic Law, Authority and Women* (Oxford: Oneworld, 2001).

Abou El Fadl, Khaled, 'The Ugly Modern and the Modern Ugly: Reclaiming the Beautiful in Islam', in O. Safi (ed.), *Progressive Muslims: On Justice, Gender and Pluralism* (Oxford: Oneworld Publications, 2003), pp. 33–77.

Abou El Fadl, Khaled, *The Great Theft: Wrestling Islam from the Extremists* (New York: HarperCollins, 2005).

Appadurai, Arjun, *Fear of Small Numbers: An Essay on the Geography of Anger* (Durham: Duke University Press, 2006).

Aslan, Reza, *No God But God: The Origins, Evolution, and Future of Islam* (New York, Random House, 2005).

Bauman, Zygmunt, *Identity: Conversations with Benedetto Vecchi* (Cambridge: Polity Press, 2004).

Beck, Ulrich, *Risikogesellschaft: Auf dem Weg in eine andere Moderne* (Frankfurt a. M.: Suhrkamp, 1986).

—*Der eigene Gott: Friedensfähigkeit und Gewaltpotential der Religionen* (Frankfurt a. M., Leipzig: VDR, 2008).

Bourdieu, Pierre, 'The Social Space and the Genesis of Groups', in *Theory and Society* 14 (1998), pp. 723–744.

—'The Forms of Capital', in John G. Richardson (ed.), *Handbook of Theory and Research for the Sociology of Education* (New York, Greenwood Press, 1986), pp. 241–258.

—'Legitimation and Structured Interest in Weber's Sociology of Religion', in S. Whimster and S. Lash (eds), *Max Weber, Rationality and Modernity* (London: Allen & Unwin, 1987), pp. 119–136.

—'Genesis and Structure of the Religious Field', in *Comparative Social Research* 13 (1991), pp. 1–44.

—*Das Religiöse Feld: Texte zur Ökonomie des Heilsgeschehens* (Konstanz: UVK, 2000).

Calhoun, Craig, 'Habitus, Field, and Capital: The Question of Historical Specifity', in C. Calhoun, E. LiPuma and M. Postone (eds), *Bourdieu: Critical Perspectives* (Cambridge: Polity Press, 1993), pp. 61–88.

Clarke, Peter, *The World's Religions: Islam* (London: Routledge, 1990).

Diaa, Rashwan, *The Spectrum of Islamist Movements* (Berlin: Verlag Hans Schiler, 2007).

Dianteill, Erwan, 'Pierre Bourdieu and the Sociology of Religion: A Central and Peripheral Concern', in *Theory and Society* 32 (2003), pp. 529–549.

Esposito, John L. and Mogahed, Dalia, *Who Speaks for Islam? What a Billion Muslims Really Think* (New York: Gallup Press, 2007).

Gellner, Ernest, *Muslim Society* (Cambridge: Cambridge University Press, 1981).

Gurr, Ted, *Why Men Rebel* (Princeton, NJ: Princeton University Press, 1970).

Harker, Richard, *et al.*, *An Introduction to the Work of Pierre Bourdieu: The Practice of Theory* (Houndsmills: Macmillan Press, 1990).

Hassan, Riaz, *Inside Muslim Minds* (Melbourne: Melbourne University Press, 2008).

Hermansen, Marcia, 'How to Put the Genie Back in the Bottle? "Identity" Islam and Muslim Youth Cultures in America', in O. Safi (ed.), *Progressive Muslims: On Justice, Gender and Pluralism* (Oxford: Oneworld Publications, 2003), pp. 306–319.

Juergensmeyer, Mark, 'From Bhindranwale to Bin Laden: The Rise of Religious Violence', *in Global and International Studies Program: eScholarship Repository University of California* (Paper 20, 2004), pp. 1–9.

Lawrence, Bruce B., *Defenders of God: The Fundamentalist Revolt Against the Modern Age* (San Francisco: Harper & Row, 1989).

Marty, Martin E. and Appleby, Scott R., *Fundamentalism Observed* (Chicago; London: The University of Chicago Press, 1991).

Meyer, Thomas, 'Fundamentalismus. Die andere Dialektik der Aufklärung', in T. Meyer (ed.), *Fundamentalismus in der modernen Welt* (Frankfurt a. M.: Suhrkamp, 1989), pp. 13–22.

Musallam, Adnan A., *From Secularism to Jihad: Sayyid Qutb and the Foundations of Radical Islamism* (Westport and London: Praeger, 2005).

Reddig, Melanie, 'Deprivation, Globalisierung und Globaler Dschihad', in T. Kron and M. Reddig (eds), *Analysen des Transnationalen Terrorismus: Soziologische Perspektiven* (Wiesbaden: VS Verlag, 2007), pp. 280–309.

Rey, Terry, *Bourdieu on Religion: Imposing Faith and Legitimacy* (London and Oakville: Equinox, 2007).

Robbins, Derek, *The Work of Pierre Bourdieu: Recognizing Society* (Buckingham: Open University Press, 1991).

Roy, Olivier, *Globalized Islam: The Search for a New Ummah* (New York: Columbia University Press, 2004).

Sageman, Marc, *Understanding Terror Networks* (Philadelphia: University of Pennsylvania Press, 2004).

Schultheis, Franz, 'Salvation Goods and Domination: Pierre Bourdieu's Sociology of the Religious Field', in J. Stolz (ed.), *Salvation Goods and Religious Market: Theory and Applications* (Bern: Peter Lang, 2008), pp. 31–49.

Shayegan, Daryush, *Cultural Schizophrenia: Islamic Societies Confronting the West* (London: Saqi Books, 1989).

Stern, Jessica, *Terror in the Name of God: Why Religious Militants Kill* (New York: HarperCollins, 2004).

Waardenburg, Jacques, *Islam: Historical, Social and Political Perspectives* (Berlin and New York: Walter de Gruyter, 2002).

Wacquant, Loic, 'Towards a Reflexive Sociology: A Workshop with Pierre Bourdieu', in *Sociological Theory* 7 (1989), pp. 26–63.

Walker, Ian and Smith, Heather, 'Introduction', in I. Walker and H. Smith (eds), *Relative Deprivation: Specification, Development and Integration* (Cambridge: Cambridge University Press, 2002), pp. 1–9.

Weber, Max, *Wirtschaft und Gesellschaft: Grundriss der Verstehenden Soziologie* (Tübingen: J. C. B. Mohr, 1980).

8

Yusuf al-Qaradawi and Chandra Muzaffar: How Theology Impacts Reformist Views on Islam and Secularism.

David L. Johnston

Since at least the nineteenth century, 'cultural constructions of Islam have taken place against the presence of a powerful enemy, colonialism and colonialist culture. Islam, as universality, extended meaning to the anti-colonial struggle in the Muslim world' (Abu-Rabi' 2004: 128). No doubt, hegemonic capitalist modernity in the nineteenth century radically disrupted traditional sociopolitical and religious institutions throughout the Muslim world, and most notably through its secularization of education and law – creating a number of responses among its people. The first intellectual current to provide an explanation for the developmental lag and increasing powerlessness of the Muslim peoples was the Islamic reform movement spearheaded by Jamal al-Din al-Afghani (d. 1897) and Muhammad Abduh (d. 1905). With the Muslim world in crisis, a theological reconfiguration of the Islamic tradition was required. But whereas the activist al-Afghani focused his energies on bringing all Arabs back under a united tent with an enlightened, modern Islam as their covering (pan-Islamism), his disciple Abduh was more inclined to reshape Islamic theology and law so as to revitalize and reinvigorate his native Egypt, of which he eventually became the Grand Mufti.

This reform movement, alternatively labelled *islah* (closest Arabic word for 'reform'), or Salafism (for its desire to faithfully emulate Islam's righteous forebears, the *salaf*), is also ancestor to the wide phenomenon of Islamic resurgence that we have been witnessing since the 1980s from Morocco to Indonesia, which can be seen as both religious revivalism (sociologically) and a religious-based ideology with political ambitions. One reason for this is that Muhammad Abduh's collaborator on the popular journal *Al-Manar* ('The Lighthouse'), Rashid Rida (d. 1935), took Abduh's thinking in a more politically defensive posture, particularly after Atatürk's abolition of the caliphate in 1924. In fact, that date marks the parting of the ways between those reformists who wanted to see the caliphate re-established (Islam is both religion and state, *din wa-dawla,* asserted Rida in a 1923 book) and those in favour of a 'secular' Islam playing the role of Christianity in Europe, and thus circumscribed to the faith and practice of individual believers. This group was best represented by the Al-Ahzar scholar, Ali Abd Al-Raziq, whose 1925 book seeking to refute Rida ('Islam and the Principles of Government') cost him his career, both as teacher and judge.

More importantly, this conservative side of the reform movement, or Islamism (the conviction that Islamic law must impact upon the sociopolitical realm in some way or another), was given a great boost in the 1920s through the founding of the first modern Islamic mass movement, the Egyptian Muslim Brotherhood (1928). Hasan al-Banna, its charismatic founder, gifted communicator, organizer and indefatigable promoter (he never married), had planted more than one hundred branches all over Egypt by 1936, with offshoots soon to take root in neighbouring countries. Besides its dense network of preaching, teaching, training, publications and charitable societies, the Muslim Brotherhood was already becoming an influential player on the Egyptian political scene. Though al-Banna was assassinated by government agents in 1949 and the organization underwent its great *mihna* (persecution) in 1954, the Brotherhood continued to grow – first, mostly in the prisons (where we would find al-Qaradawi in the 1950s), and then, as an underground movement semi-tolerated by the state. Today it remains a powerful political force on the Egyptian scene, though still not officially recognized.

Though the Muslim Brotherhood has officially renounced violence since the 1950s, terrorist splinter groups have regularly emerged, aiming to overthrow regimes deemed 'un-Islamic'. But more importantly, there has also been the explosion of a grassroots Islamic fervour spilling into all sectors of society across the Muslim world, with noticeable repercussions in Europe and North America. In B. A. Roberson's words:

> the current reformation of Islam has been a result, in the wake of the First World War, of an ongoing steady Islamization and return to a personal piety and, concurrent with these developments, Islamic

> groups have not only sought the reform of Middle East governments, but also resisted the infliction of unwanted external influences and impositions on their society. (2003: 10)

This statement conveniently sets the stage for this chapter: Yusuf al-Qaradawi and Chandra Muzaffar, however differently they approach the task of Islamic reform, both share the burden of reshaping the way the Islamic tradition has been co-opted both by authoritarian regimes and by extreme 'puritanical' movements such as the Taliban and al-Qa'ida (Abou El Fadl 2005). Both scholars have an international following and believe that global civil society should resist the hegemonic pretensions of the current neo-liberal, Western-led globalization project; and both staunchly resist Islamic 'fanatics' who would bar women and non-Muslims from being elected to parliament. Yet their reformist impulses come from diametrically opposed methodologies. I argue here that their methodologies are largely dictated by their respective theologies. But first, what do I mean by theology?

Theology as Discourse

By 'theology' I mean here an ongoing reflection based on the sacred texts about how God intends his followers to live out their allegiance to him in their particular setting. But this reflection never starts with a *tabula rasa*; rather, it participates in a tradition of religious thought passed down over the centuries, modified here and there by the intervention of hierarchies, and a process further influenced by crisis moments in history or the shifting political and social alliances of politicians, knowledge-elites (the *ulama*, in this case) and the institutional politics of competing schools of law and Sufi orders. That is as far as the received tradition is concerned, or 'upstream'. 'Downstream', that is, the theological reworking of the tradition to fit new contexts, cultural perspectives and circumstances – one can look at how the emerging theological discourse actually functions. How does it read the sacred texts – is it a literalistic hermeneutic, or does it focus on ethical values while sidelining specific commands? Who produces it? What is the sociological context, both of the producer and of the targeted audience? What does it seek to accomplish and what might its unintended consequences be? In the case of the two scholars examined here, both seek to impact the political arena, in specific national contexts, but also internationally. So, more specifically, how is this theological discourse meant to shape today's globalized world politically, socially and economically?

By complexifying and problematizing traditional notions of theology, I am following the methodology of scholars like Mohammed Arkoun (2006),[1] Armando Salvatore (1997 and 2007), and others.[2] Arkoun, following Jacques Derrida, intentionally engages in 'historical epistemology', seeking to uncover the assumptions about how one comes to know, which can be discerned under the surface of various theological discourses. What is more telling than what is actually said, he argues, is what is left out – the consistent thread running through all his writings about the 'unthought' and the 'unthinkable'. Further, these discourses are manipulated by 'powers', those who have the authority and power to decree what is 'orthodoxy' and thus to proscribe those considered 'heterodox' – for him the constant interplay between 'powers and remainders' (*puissances et résidus*). This sociopolitical dynamic will become evident in our discussion of al-Qaradawi.

Here, especially for the concept of secularism, I turn to Salvatore (2007), a sociologist of religion who freely borrows his methods from philosophy, history, political science and anthropology, arguing that the conventional dichotomy of tradition–modernity is over-simplistic and misleading. In his view, notwithstanding the usefulness of Habermas' 'communicative action', one cannot truly understand the emergence of the modern public sphere without tracing the genealogy of concepts like 'practical reason' and religious tradition in the sense defined by the philosopher Alasdair MacIntyre. Secularism, therefore, as a guiding principle of the modern nation state, not only can reaccommodate itself to the contributions of various religious discourses, but by allowing those voices to thrive alongside all the others, it would bolster the democratic legitimacy of the state and enrich conversations in today's pluralistic public sphere, whether local or global.[3]

With these theoretical concerns in mind, I propose to examine the work of Yusuf al-Qaradawi and Chandra Muzaffar along the following lines of inquiry: a) textualism versus values; b) the sociological dimension of their theological discourse; and c) its political dimension.

Yusuf al-Qaradawi: The Mainstream Islamist *'Alim*

By any measure, Shaykh Yusuf al-Qaradawi is a towering figure for Muslims around the world today. Ibrahim Abu-Rabi' calls him '[t]he foremost living authority in contemporary Islamism' (2004: 137). Noah Feldman begins his essay on him with these words:

> As one glance at his official website, www.Qaradawi.net, will reveal, Yusuf al-Qaradawi is a phenomenon. On the site one can listen to Friday sermons (*khutba*), purchase a dozen of his books (far from his entire literary output), and retrieve transcripts of numerous interviews on a wide range of subjects. The site offers a useful guide to the number of visitors (75,000 in May 2002 alone) and to the costs of site maintenance ($5,000 a year by latest count). Via satellite, al-Jazeera beams Arabic-language programs featuring al-Qaradawi into millions of homes. (2007: 104)

The best English biographical information for now comes from Ana Belén Soage's essay, which she begins with his institutional achievements: 'the co-founder and president of the International Association of Muslim Scholars and the European Council for Fatwa and Research' (2008: 51).[4] This was deliberate on her part, since al-Qaradawi was both trained as a legal scholar (*alim*, plural: *ulama*) at the al-Azhar University in Cairo, still the most prestigious centre of Islamic learning, and has managed to keep good relations with his Alma Mater, where he obtained his doctorate in 1973, despite his past membership of the Muslim Brotherhood (he was jailed three times for this: in 1949, 1954–1956 and 1962).[5] As I will try to show, putting forward his authority as a jurist is central to the task to which he has devoted his life.

Despite this self-identification as a jurist *(alim, faqih* or mufti) who will give legal responses (fatwas) to those who come asking, whether on his website or through the two councils of *ulama* he co-founded (one international and the other European), al-Qaradawi, as Feldman puts it, 'somehow manages to fit into multiple niches that in the cases of others might well seem mutually exclusive' (2007: 106). He is not just a classically trained *alim* – a category of people systematically derided as the puppets of the state by the young Islamist leaders, who themselves have little or no formal training in the Islamic sciences, but al-Qaradawi is also the most influential mouthpiece of the Islamic resurgence movement – Salafism or Islamism, as noted above – which traces its origins to al-Afghani's and Abduh's Islamic reform movement in the nineteenth century. After the 1967 military defeat, which signalled the death of the secular and socialist pan-Arabist movement, Salafism was re-energized and metamorphosed into a new, more conservative movement, also known as the *sahwa al-Islamiyya*, the 'Islamic Awakening', the term that al-Qaradawi has consistently used for it. Salvatore wisely adds to this the adjective 'solutionist', referring to the Islamist slogan in vogue since the 1970s, 'Islam is the solution'.[6]

That 'Awakening' is a global wave al-Qaradawi is still very skilfully surfing – and it helps that he has mastered both television and Internet communication. But originally, his move to Doha, Qatar, had nothing to do with escaping President Gamal Abd al-Nasir's systematic clampdown on Islamists. He was sent there by al-Azhar University to establish an affiliated branch there; hence, 'he established the department of Islamic Studies and the Faculty of Islamic Law and Islamic Studies at the Teacher Training College' (Soage 2008: 53). As his leading position in the weekly al-Jazeera 'Shari'a and Life' programme attests, he has managed to judiciously juggle those two positions: both the traditional *alim* and the Islamist leader – assuring him a global following.

Yet there is also a third 'niche' al-Qaradawi has managed to fill – or a 'hat' he seems to wear with great legitimacy, rightly mentioned by both Feldman and Soage: '[he] can plausibly be presented as a follower of the modernist Islam of Muhammad Rashid Rida.' Yet this comes with a caveat, a theme we explore in this chapter:

> As we shall see, it is not unreasonable to associate al-Qaradawi with the modernist Islamic tradition, but neither does he squarely fit within the broad category of liberal Islamic reformism that calls for a fairly radical rereading of the Qur'an in pursuit of values associated with Western liberalism (Feldman 2007: 106).

In effect, this neatly states the difference between al-Qaradawi, who will never budge from a literal reading of the 'fixed' (*qat'i*) texts of the Qur'an and Sunna, and Chandra Muzaffar, whose emphasis is precisely on those liberal 'values' he sees coming out of the texts. To this dimension we now turn.

Al-Qaradawi: Textualism Versus Values

Several of al-Qaradawi's books in the 1980s and 1990s were directed to the youth – both leaders and followers of the more radical branch of Islamism, with the purpose of admonishing them to become more moderate and even lenient, because that is what the Qur'an calls for: 'And in the same way you are a middle nation that you might be witnesses to the people' (Q. 5, 143). His way of rendering 'middle nation' is 'the moderate position' or the theme of 'moderate Islam' (*al-Islam al-wasatiyya*) overarching the whole span of his writings since the 1970s. Though this is the focus of the next section, it is telling that in one of these books, *Islamic Awakening Between Rejection and Extremism*, al-Qaradawi upbraids those Muslims who call 'extremists' people who 'consider adherence to clear-cut Islamic teachings concerning eating, drinking, beautification, or the call for application of Shari'a and the establishment of an Islamic state' (1995: 30). They even consider a young man who grows a beard or a young woman who wears a hijab, or even groups who call for the power to 'command the good and forbid evil' (an injunction found several times in the Qur'an), to be 'extremists'. Further, a 'moderate' Islam will never water down its basic tenets:

> Although a basis of faith in Islam is to believe that our religion is right and that those who do not believe in it are wrong, there are Muslims who object to considering those who take a religion other than Islam as *kuffar*, considering this as extremism and bigotry. This is an issue upon which we must never compromise. (1995: 30)

All the above examples lead us to believe that for al-Qaradawi the literal reading of the text is the meaning God expects all believers to hold and apply to their lives, wherever they live or age they inhabit. At the same time, his position is not quite that simple. In a more recent book (2001), al-Qaradawi reworks some of his tried and proven themes: the destructive nature of secularist thought, especially for Muslim societies; the comprehensive nature of the Islamic faith, which encompasses every area of life; and his moderate reading of the sacred texts which confers upon the 'Islamic solution' 'scientific' rationalism, pragmatism, flexibility and a future-oriented perspective.[7] In the tenth chapter (out of sixteen altogether) entitled 'The Static Nature of Religion and the Changes of Life', al-Qaradawi answers the arguments of the 'Muslim secularists', and in this case that put forward by the Atatürk regime, the first to choose secularism as its cornerstone: since religion is based on unchanging sacred texts, it acts 'as an impediment in the way of progress, development and socioeconomic uplift' (2001: 61).

Our sheikh's rebuttal is framed around the idea that 'about ninety-nine percent' of the Shari'a is composed of 'debatable' texts (*zanniyya*) which cover only a small part of human activity, that is, all of the religious rituals (*'ibadat*) and just a few areas of 'human interactions' (*mu'amalat*), which include everything from economics to politics. What is pertinent here is the contrast between the 'fixed' and the 'changing'. The fixed, or non-negotiable elements of religion (*thawabit al-din*) include three areas: a) the creeds (*'aqa'id*) 'concerning faith in God, his angels, his books, his apostles, and the Last Day' (2001: 61); b) the 'categorical' rulings (*al-ahkam al-qat'iyya*) in the texts; c) ethical values – which he describes as follows:

> And along with that [the creeds], other fixed points are: the foundations of ethical values, like truthfulness and trust, justice and goodness, righteousness and mercy, shame and self-control, sacrifice and generosity, humility and gentleness, and other similar virtues and noble moral traits (*makarim al-akhlaq*). All the divine messages called its hearers to live out these values and generation after generation of humans inherited them. (2001: 62)

As can be seen from this quote, al-Qaradawi has placed 'values' before the immovable fixtures of the texts. This is significant, as I see it, because the ethical values relate to the 'purposes of the Shari'a', a strategy followed by many authors today.[8] But before we look at this in more detail, it is important to see exactly what he is saying with regard to the 'categorical rulings', those based on unambiguous texts, and therefore leaving no room for new rulings by qualified jurists (*ijtihad*). Unlike the allowed 'legal wiggle room' in the case of 'debatable texts', 'that which is fixed in categorical (*qat'iyya*) texts is very little indeed, though very important at the same time, as it represents the fixed points for the *umma*, thereby embodying its contractual, intellectual, emotional and practical unity, rendering her an *umma* both mighty and impregnable, invulnerable to penetration or division' (p. 62).

The assertion seems to be that the 'Muslim nation' (the international body of Muslim believers, or the *umma*) is united in its unique identity through its strict adherence to the sacred texts, and in particular, to its 'categorical injunctions'. Controversially, these would include a husband's discretionary right to marry up to four wives, and for brothers to inherit twice as much as their sisters; it would require that anyone leaving their Islamic faith be punished in this life, the maximum fine being the death penalty (the classical juridical consensus on apostasy);[9] the witness of a male in court is worth that of two females; finally, it would entail the enforcement of all the prescribed punishments (*hudud*), like cutting off the hand of thieves. Clearly, here and elsewhere in his writings, these all form part of the 'immutable' dimension of God's law – though here and there he states that mercy in all cases should prevail.

Further, al-Qaradawi's textualism on women from the Islamic perspective is somewhat mitigated by some unconventional positions. On the one hand, though the Qur'anic ruling on women inheriting half of their brothers' inheritance cannot be bypassed or explained away, he encourages them to pursue careers that are on a par with men. As Soage puts it:

> he rejects that Islam sanctions their reclusion and forced marriage, practices which he identifies as a factor in their estrangement from religion. He encourages female education and is proud to mention that three of his daughters hold doctorates in science from British universities. (2008: 59)

What is more, he advocates full political participation on the part of women, including the possibility to run for office. But as elsewhere in his writings or lectures, the subtext is always a positioning or posturing relative to the 'extremists' – who for him actually oppress women in the name of Islam. Just as we began this section by mentioning his books addressed to the youth, we will now delve more in depth into this sociological dimension.

The Sociological Backdrop of Theological Discourse

In light of the above, though we might be tempted to conclude that al-Qaradawi is a textualist who cares mostly about literal interpretations of the sacred texts, we have already seen that this literalism is at times tempered by a concern for the ethical values the Shari'a seeks to achieve. Sociologically, Sheikh Yusuf al-Qaradawi has positioned himself as an *alim* who can guide the *umma*, not only away from the hostile shoals of secularism, but also away from the treacherous shoals of extremism.

In *Islamic Awakening* he dons the mantle of the religious leader who shepherds his flock – on the one hand, advocating the fiery youth who, in their idealism, have espoused positions considered extreme by the mainstream, yet sanctioned by some jurists. 'We should not try to force him [the extremist youth] to act against his conscience', he pleads with the older generation. Rather, 'Our duty is to appeal to him with wisdom, argue with him patiently and nicely, and try to convince him by citing evidence in the hope that he may change his mind and accept what we believe to be the truth' (1995: 32). On the other hand, he gently rebukes those who are tempted by 'extremism', which he defines as 'a person obstinately devoted to his own opinions and prejudices, as well as rigidity, which deprives him of clarity of vision regarding the interests of other human beings, the purposes of Shari'a, or the circumstances of the age' (p. 33). Among the symptoms of extremism are the following: a) bigotry, intolerance and rigidity; b) going beyond what is required and pressuring others to do the same; c) an over-emphasis on minor points of doctrine or practice and thus being divisive; d) treating others harshly; e) slandering even some of the great Muslim leaders of the past (pp. 33–43).

Throughout his writings al-Qaradawi characterizes the extremists as the Zahiriyya – the juridical school attributed to the Andalusian scholar Ibn Hazm (d. 1064), which in its extreme literalism rejected the use of analogical reasoning. His rebuttal to this narrow hermeneutic is that they demonstrate 'a lack of knowledge of – and insight into – the purposes, spirit, and essence of *din*' (1995: 50). Theirs is a 'semi-knowledge' which leads people to focus on trivial, peripheral issues rather than the core issues (*furu'* instead of *usul*); this, coupled with vanity and pride. Thus he differentiates the 'genuine *ulama*' from the 'semi-*ulama*'; and one easy way to tell them apart is that 'a genuine *alim* never innovates, but a semi-*alim* does' (p. 51). Failing to understand the ethical values behind the text's injunctions inevitably leads one to commit injustices, to harm younger or especially new converts, and to create divisions in the *umma*. All this is a result of these 'pseudo-scholars', most of whom have only limited knowledge of the rich Islamic tradition, including the sciences of jurisprudence, of Qur'anic commentary, of historiography, philosophy or of *Hadith* criticism.

In a later book parallel to this one (1992),[10] al-Qaradawi characterizes the Islamic Movement as imbued with the following traits: scientific, realistic, traditionalist, revivalist, balanced, futuristic. He argues that his philosophy of gradualism and his wealth of knowledge as an *alim* qualify him as an ideal guide who can channel the idealism and energy of the youth and provide the balance and the wisdom of his experience and legal expertise. For instance, the Movement is 'traditionalist' in the best sense – providing 'an intellectual methodology based on an application of an understanding of the provisions of the Qur'an and the guidelines of Sunna by the best generations of the Umma; the Prophet's Companions and those who followed correctly on their path' (1992: 129). In practice, this methodology includes: 'understanding secondary concepts and subsidiary judgments in the light of the principles and generalities'; 'advocating *ijtihad* (the *alim*'s personal reasoning) and renewal, and denouncing rigidity and imitation' (p. 129); 'advocating facilitation, not complication, in the field of jurisprudence' (p. 130). These are subtleties lost on these self-proclaimed scholars fresh out of engineering schools or with expertise in contemporary science.[11] His final words to the young hot heads: 'respect specialization!'

The Political Dimension of Theological Discourse

Clearly, al-Qaradawi celebrates the great resurgence of Islamic fervour, particularly among the youth since the 1970s, and he sees himself as a key leader able to guide both the young, who are often attracted to extremist views, and the older believers, who have also, in large numbers, thrown their lot in with 'the Islamic Awakening'.[12] But his textualism has also led him to take some political stances viewed as subversive by the regimes in place, and in his native Egypt in particular. What exactly is 'secularism' for al-Qaradawi, and why should it be combated?

In *Secular Extremism*, in a chapter entitled 'Secularism and the Shari'a', al-Qaradawi blasts the secularist policies of Turkey since the 1920s, which not only dismissed the clear text of the Shari'a in a cavalier manner, but ignored the crucial role of legislation:

> Islam – by its very nature – refuses to be just a prop of life, when in fact it is life's guide and shaping force. It refuses to simply be secularism's guest, when in fact it is the owner of the house! From

> this we can see why Islam and secularism are on a collision course, and in most instances why they must collide with regard to each one of Islam's four chief dimensions: dogmas, worship rituals, ethics and legislation. (2001: 26–7)

This thesis is more fully developed in a recent book (2007) commissioned by the General Trust of the European Fatwa and Research Council.[13] The book's central thesis, and a refrain running through all his writings, is that the secularists wrongly deny Islam its comprehensiveness – a code word for the duty to implement the Shari'a in tangible political, social and economic ways.

Since the purpose of the Shari'a, continues al-Qaradawi, is to 'apply the laws [*ahkam*], teach the *umma* and protect her from evil and corruption', then this task will have to include holding the reigns of the state. Uthman, Companion of the Prophet and the third caliph, is reported to have said, 'God has restrained through the Sultan what was not restrained by the Qur'an.' And this is all the more necessary in a day and age when the state piles up authority in all areas of life, 'from education to the court system, to culture, to the media, to the mosques, to the economy and society' (2007: 76). So the reformer cannot possibly carry out a policy of reform except by means of the state. Al-Qaradawi then quotes from a book written by a recent Sheikh al-Azhar, Muhammad al-Khidr Hussayn, 'Messages of Reform' (*Rasa'il al-islah*). Here is textualism at its best:

> The Shaykh goes on to explain that 'many of the Qur'an's *aùkäm* are not about the unity of God (*tawhid*) or rites of worship (*'ibadat*), but about buying and selling, about usury, mortgage, and bearing witness in court; about marriage, divorce, and the oath of condemnation [allegation of spouse's adultery]; about loyalty and oaths of repudiation, and the prohibition relative to orphans; about wills and inheritance; about rules of reprisal, blood money, cutting off of thieves' hands, the flogging of the adulterer and the accuser of chaste women, and the punishment of those who bring about corruption in the land'. (2007: 86)

Later on, he sets out to refute the 1925 book of Ali Abd al-Raziq, the first modern voice within the *ulama* establishment to call for a secularized state as the most congenial to the practice of Islam. First, the texts are clear: 'Obey God, obey the Prophet and your political leaders' (Q. 4, 58–59).

Ibn Taymiyya had built his argument on those two verses in his famous work, *The Politics of Shari'a* (*al-Siyasa al-shar'iyya*). Then this *Hadith*: 'He who dies without the oath of allegiance around his neck (*al-bay'a*) dies a *Jahiliyya* death.'[14] He concludes that both in the texts and in all the theological and legal writings a state is always understood to be necessary.

Further, the nature of Islam itself bespeaks the necessity of a political infrastructure to enable Muslims to live out their faith. The modern state is based on ideology (like communism) and its political apparatus not only secures its borders and maintains the peace within them, but also shapes the values of its citizens at will. The Islamic state is different; its purpose is deeper and greater than that: 'its function is to teach the *umma* and train it according to the guidance and principles of Islam, creating a positive atmosphere and a favorable climate to the transforming of Islam's creeds, ideas and teachings into a concrete reality that would become an example to all who seek divine guidance and a sign for those on the path of evil' (2007: 147). So it is a 'creedal state' (*dawla 'aqa'idiyya*). Furthermore, 'this is not a local state, but an international one, because God has entrusted the *umma* with a call addressed to humanity to receive the guidance and light in its midst'. The *umma* exists not for its own sake, but for the purpose of witnessing God's message. Hence, he concludes, right after the Treaty of Hudaybiyya, the Prophet addressed letters to the surrounding kings, summoning them to receive the message of Islam (p. 147).

Yet again, as with the issue of women, Qaradawi is considerably more flexible than this rhetoric might sound. In summary, here are some of the points he makes (here and elsewhere):

1 The Islamic state is a civil state, meaning it is not a theocracy, or the rule of clerics. The *ulama* can act as a consulting body but the state is run by qualified people, both in the executive and legislative branches.[15]

2 'The Islamic state is a consultative state in agreement with the essence of democracy' (2007: 171), meaning that the Islamic terms *shura* (consultation) and *bay'a* (oath of allegiance) operate within the structures of a modern democratic state in which all leaders are elected by and accountable to the people; hence, they can also be removed by them.[16]

3 Though the ideal is an international Muslim political entity, the first step is to build more and better Islamic states within existing national boundaries. The motto again is 'gradualism'.[17]

4 Regarding pluralism: non-Muslims are citizens of the Islamic state (he only mentions Jews and Christians, however), with the full freedom to practice their faith, and though they have the right to their own personal status laws, Shari'a rules are closer to the essence of their revelation.[18]

Chandra Muzaffar: A Muslim Global Justice Activist

With a focus on Malaysian political scientist and human rights activist Chandra Muzaffar (b. 1947), we literally move to the other end of the reformist spectrum. While al-Qaradawi is primarily concerned with the sacred texts, Muzaffar is mainly concerned with the ethical values emanating from the text. While al-Qaradawi's 'moderate' or 'middle way' (*al-islam al-wasatiyya*) Islam includes values as one of its four indispensable components, Muzaffar castigates all religious elites in all religious traditions who continue to use their monopoly of textual interpretation as a means of maintaining hegemonic power over their respective communities (2005: 125–126). In fact, while al-Qaradawi's audience is exclusively Muslim, Muzaffar's is mostly broader. Though maybe a third of his nearly twenty books and scores of articles are directed to Muslims in Malaysia and beyond, the rest is perhaps best described as a clarion call for the integration of religious values (from all religions) into the work of global civil society on behalf of a more peaceful and just world.

Another difference is that Muzaffar has managed to remain active simultaneously in the academic and NGO worlds throughout his career. Starting in 1970, he taught for many years at Universiti Sains Malaysia (USM) in Penang; then he was named Professor and Director of the Centre for Civilizational Dialogue at the University of Malaya in Kuala Lumpur. He has now come back to USM as the Noordin Sopiee Professor of Global Studies. From the beginning too he has poured his energy into non-governmental efforts to promote human rights, founding in 1977 the multi-ethnic National Consciousness Movement (ALIRAN), which aimed to rebuild Malaysia, both ethnically and religiously, into a more democratic and politically participative society. Then in 1992 he became the president of the International Movement for a Just World (JUST), an agency seeking to promote human dignity and social justice in the global arena.

At this time, Muzaffar combines his work at USM with his leadership of JUST, teaching, researching and writing, while also lecturing abroad and organizing for the establishment of a more just and compassionate human civilization on the basis of shared spiritual and moral values.[19] The first event he organized that received international attention was a conference in Kuala Lumpur in December 1994 on the theme of 'Rethinking Human Rights', with the participation of human rights activists and academics from over sixty countries. Two years later Muzaffar edited and published the conference proceedings in *Human Wrongs: Reflections on Western Global Dominance and its Impact Upon Human Rights* (1996).[20]

Though the theme of Western hegemony, and that of the USA in particular, has remained a constant in his writings, Muzaffar has increasingly turned his attention to interfaith dialogue and the role of religion in solving the seemingly intractable problems faced by the international community. In July 2008, for instance, USM and JUST co-sponsored an international conference in Kuala Lumpur on the theme, 'Religion in the Quest for Global Justice and Peace'.[21] The first of fourteen points in the Plan of Action agreed upon by the delegates was a request that:

> the Noordin Sopiee Chair in Global Studies and the Centre for Policy Research and International Studies (CenPris), Universiti Sains Malaysia, to establish a global network of scholars and activists who are committed to harnessing the values and principles embodied in their own religion and in other religions to promote global justice and peace.[22]

With this brief introduction in mind, I now proceed to the outline followed in our examination of al-Qaradawi's reformist theology: theology versus values, sociological implications of his theological discourse, and finally, its political implications.

Chandra Muzaffar: Theology and Values

As even a cursory glance at the above quote will show, 'values and principles' as contained in various religions represent for Muzaffar the necessary motivation and tools that will enable global civil society to move the world in a more just and peaceful direction. In his first book, focusing mostly on religious values (2002), he offers this list of theological points he feels are common to most religious traditions:

- *Where do I come from?* I am from God, a product of God's eternal power of creation.
- *Who am I?* I am God's vicegerent, God's steward, the bearer of God's trust.
- *Why am I here?* I am here to fulfil God's trust, to carry out God's will.
- *How am I to fulfil God's trust?* By adhering to all the values and principles which God has conveyed to the prophets and sages through time. These eternal, universal values and principles constitute God's guidance to humankind.
- *Where do I go from here?* I return to God to be judged on the basis of my deeds in this life. (2002: 115)

To what extent this common theologizing can effectively connect with non-theistic traditions like Hinduism and Buddhism is not our concern here. What is important is his theology of humanity that seeks to build on the 1993 *Declaration of the Parliament of the World's Religions.*[23] The Hebrew prophets, for instance, spoke out for the 'liberation and emancipation' from the oppression of tyrants. Jesus Christ's 'central message of love and forgiveness' stood in contrast to 'the rigid dogmatism of rabbinical authority in Palestine'. Some theologians teach that his crucifixion represented 'selfless sacrifice in the struggle against all forms of tyranny' (2005: 124). Islam, in parallel fashion, empowers the human as God's trustee (*khalifa*) on earth and thus swears allegiance to God, forswearing all entanglement with wealth and hegemonic power:

> In the process he commits himself to eternal, universal values such as justice, respect, compassion and dignity since loyalty to God is, in the ultimate analysis, fidelity to the better side of human nature as embodied in noble spiritual and moral principles. It is by ensuring the triumph of these values at the individual and collective level that the human being as *khalifah* fulfils God's trust (*amanah*). (2005: 125)

Clearly, Muzaffar, concerned as he is to enlist the support of all people of faith, is not a textualist in the least. In a reworked version of a paper Muzaffar presented at a conference sponsored by a Muslim reformist network he had helped to found (Asian Muslim Action Network, AMAN) entitled 'The "Values" Approach to Islam', Muzaffar argues that *tawhid* (the oneness of God) implies the unity of humankind and the unity of moral values across the religious spectrum: 'justice, freedom, love, compassion and equality'. He then explains that in this light these values 'rather than forms and symbols, rituals and practices would be the bedrock of our faith' (2002: 41). This view of Islam 'where the primacy of God means the primacy of eternal, universal spiritual and moral values would distinguish us from those who adhere to the *fiqh* oriented approach to Islam' (p. 42). The *fiqh* approach, by its prioritizing of rules, regulations (read: law), forms, rituals and practices, lays emphasis on particularism and not universalism.[24]

Here is where Muzaffar most blatantly clashes with al-Qaradawi. For Muzaffar, the recent resurgence of Islam has sadly been accompanied by 'the growth of a certain kind of obscurantism in the Muslim mind' (2002: 44). The problem with Islamic law, he writes, is that it includes much 'that is different from the universal, humane spirit of the Qur'an' (p. 45). He singles out the consensus in the medieval Sunni schools of law regarding *dhimmis* (non-Muslims), women and apostasy. In the same collection, another essay on religion in Asia bemoans the fact that 'the majority of revivalists are not prepared to unshackle themselves from the fetters of the past' and this is why 'they adopt positions which are inimical to the dignity of women and the well-being of religious minorities' (2002: 55).

The Sociological Subtext of Muzaffar's Theological Discourse

Chandra Muzaffar's evident distaste for literalism and textualism sets him on a collision course with al-Qaradawi, whom he would see as one of the 'religious elites' who use their influence to pressure ordinary believers into following their dictates – not just in how to read the sacred texts, but also in their agenda for radical political change. In this section I highlight the central role 'global civil society' plays in Muzaffar's thought and action.

In an essay devoted to this theme, he defines his particular focus as being on those groups of civil society worldwide that seek to promote various causes: '[a]nti-globalization organizations, environmental groups, human rights outfits, women's caucuses, indigenous rights clusters' (2005: 147). These groups naturally represent a great variety of ethnic, religious, cultural and linguistic backgrounds, and they certainly do not speak with one voice on any of the issues. Yet their active campaigning achieved some notable accomplishments. The Anti-Landmines Treaty and the Kyoto Accord of 1997, and the Rome Statute of 1998, which launched the International Criminal Court (ICC), would not have passed without vociferous and sustained civil society pressure. Equally, the massive protests in Seattle (1999), which peaked in Florence (2002), forced the political and economic powers behind the globalization juggernaut to take notice and incorporate greater concern for issues of employment, fair trade and environmental protection (149).

Yet the zenith of 'people power' – the greatest concerted protest in human history, notes Muzaffar – came with the 15 February 2003 demonstrations against the proposed US invasion of Iraq. Civil society, though unsuccessful in stopping the war, nevertheless scored three important victories: a) several governments opposed the war; b) 'people power forced Washington and its staunch ally, London, to delay the war'; c) the UN refrained from endorsing the war (2005: 148).

Taking note of all these achievements in the age of instant global news through satellite TV and the Internet, Muzaffar nevertheless sees one main obstacle in achieving the goal of a more just world: this global civil society lacks a coherent and unified philosophy. One dominant current has come from the NGOs grouped together under the umbrella of the World Social Forum (WSF, yearly gatherings in Porto Alegre, Brazil and most recently in Mumbai, India). Here Muzaffar is critical, but not primarily because of their leftist ideology. The WSF has a fundamental flaw:

> Socialism's prescription for the transformation of the social order is based upon a skewed, distorted understanding of the human being. By denying the human being's perennial quest for the transcendent and the sacred, socialism has shut out one of the most powerful impulses for human and social transformation …
>
> This is why they should absorb, in a creative manner, the spiritual and moral worldview that lies at the heart of all the world's religions. For it is a worldview which offers a more holistic understanding of

> the human being – his magnanimity and his meanness; his generosity and his greed; his selflessness and his selfishness – than any secular philosophy is capable of. It is therefore in a better position to furnish us with the wherewithal necessary for fundamental human and social transformation. (2005: 152)

The Political Subtext of Muzaffar's Theological Discourse

Muzaffar's promotion of civil society as the key to implementing social justice on a global scale is of course also political in nature. Both he and al-Qaradawi would assert that faithfulness to the call of the Qur'an and Sunna has political implications. Yet whereas 'the Islamic state' is central for al-Qaradawi, it is problematic for Muzaffar.[25] Further, the 'secularism' so consistently and pugnaciously opposed by al-Qaradawi is not even an issue for Muzaffar, except perhaps in its most militant and anti-religious version, French *laïcité*. What counts are principles of good governance and policies that practically ensure the best delivery of justice and social harmony, locally and internationally.

But the political, the sociological and the theological all come together for both scholars. Along with al-Qaradawi, Muzaffar notes the significance of the resurgence of religious faith in the last three decades. Yet Muzaffar's interest is in all religions, not just Islam. That is why he keeps coming back to the issue of a global ethic, which can only be adopted and implemented as people worldwide see this as flowing out of their religious convictions. Its four directives as ratified by the Parliament of World Religions are:

1. Commitment to a culture of non-violence and respect for life.
2. Commitment to a culture of solidarity and a just economic order.
3. Commitment to a culture of tolerance and a life of truthfulness.
4. Commitment to a culture of equal rights and partnership between men and women. (2005: 13, 28)[26]

Muzaffar shows, point by point, how these directives are consonant with the values emanating from the Qur'an and Sunna (2005: 28–33). Yet formidable obstacles remain in the way of its actual implementation. One is that we live in a world in which 'global power is concentrated in the hands of a few' and the gap between rich and poor continues to widen with no end in sight. 'It is this more than anything else – the glaring iniquities in the military, political, economic, cultural and information spheres – that negates the evolution of a shared global ethic for the whole of humankind' (p. 34). Muslims, more strongly than any other groups, are keenly aware of these injustices, seeing themselves as the prime victims. Besides Afghanistan and Iraq, 'for Muslims everywhere, the expulsion of Palestinians from their homeland and their subsequent subjugation and oppression remains the most tragic and traumatic representation of global injustice' (p. 34). Many other injustices can be listed as well, including 'the not infrequent outbursts of Islamophobia encountered by Muslims living in the West' (p. 35).

What is needed, then, is for Christians and Jews from the centres of power to stand alongside Muslims, in the name of these pivotal values stemming from their faith, and to stand against all the oppressive structures entrenched in our world. Then they can join forces with other branches of global civil society, religious or not, to seek structural changes, if only small ones to begin with. This is already happening, he writes, in Christian, Jewish and in Muslim circles.[27] For Muzaffar, the solution to the grave perils faced by humanity today can only come from a united front all across the globe that promotes tolerance and mutual respect, and refuses the blight of exclusivism and narrow identity politics.

Muzaffar and al-Qaradawi in Theological Perspective

In practical terms, however, one cannot help but be struck by the many areas of political agreement between al-Qaradawi and Muzaffar. They agree on the diagnosis of the global economic inequalities, the unjust power structures, the corrosive effect of Western-dominated globalization and the spiritually deadening effect of advertising and consumerism. Even in terms of solutions, they might meet halfway in discussing what good governance means for Muslim nations, with both emphasizing the values of justice, compassion, equity and modesty. The power of the people to elect their leaders and to hold them to account would also serve as common ground.

Having said this, the discussion would break down in the area of theology. In the end, al-Qaradawi remains a textualist. For him, the unequivocal texts of the Qur'an and Sunna are meant to apply to all times and places. They may be very few, as he never ceases to proclaim, but in practice they loom very large on the horizon of any serious project of Islamic reform. Sociologically and politically too, his theological discourse assumes the necessity of strong *ulama* input in the fulfilling of the long-term dream of a new kind of global Islamic community.

Muzaffar, for his part, lives out his calling as a Muslim scholar–activist in the secular public sphere. Only there can he hope to draw in people of faith concerned about how to change the world in more equitable and nonviolent ways. But whereas this might be a means to an end for al-Qaradawi, this is an end in itself for Muzaffar. For true and authentic religion must live up to the wellspring of eternal values bubbling up from its core. Thus for him a chasm separates 'revivalist Islam', or '*fiqh* Islam' – religion of the forms, rituals and practices – and the Islam of values which he sees as the necessary engine, along with similar emphases in other faiths, for global civil society to carry out its transformative mission in the present context.

Admittedly, these authors only represent two points along a contemporary spectrum of reformist thought in the Islamic community. Al-Qaradawi works within the broad Salafist tradition initiated by Abduh and made more political by Rida in the 1920s. Muzaffar, on the other hand, represents the more 'secularized' version of *islah*, as articulated by Abd al-Raziq in that same period.

Yet both positions are also 'cultural constructions of Islam' against the backdrop of a postcolonial reality of Western political and economic hegemony. And in a sense, both confirm Salvatore's insight that religious discourse is on the rise within the global public sphere. No doubt, the de facto secularism of this sphere is what permits the multiplicity of voices and the maximization of democratic participation. But as these two case studies show, the way one reworks a received faith tradition is both impacted by and impacts in return on the sociopolitical forces one seeks to mobilize and change. Put otherwise, theology is not a dispassionate reflection on creeds and texts. It is also – inevitably – a discourse of power inserted in a particular context.

NOTES

1 Algerian–French Sorbonne scholar, who, for decades, has been calling for all the tools of contemporary philosophy and the social sciences to be applied to Islamic Studies. In essence, he has been doing what Edward Said did for the Western discourse on the Middle East and Islam ('Orientalism') with the Islamic tradition itself – a challenge Said never tackled himself.

2 This is also one of the threads running through my book, *Earth, Empire and Sacred Text: Muslims and Christians as Trustees of Creation* (London: Equinox, 2009).

3 As does Olivier Roy (2007), it is helpful to distinguish secularization (a natural process by which religion progressively looses its grip on society) and secularism (various state-initiated and enforced policies by which the role of religion is regulated in public life, of which France's *laïcité* is an extreme example). I agree with Noah Feldman (2003) when he argues that the common gauge of secularism as the separation of church and state is beside the point. Religion plays a much greater role, for instance, in US politics than it does in European politics. But all these countries are considered democracies to the extent that basic religious freedom is guaranteed for all.

4 I deliberately wrote 'for now', as the first full-length book on al-Qaradawi is about to be published: Bettina Graf and Jakob Skovgaard-Petersen (eds), *Global Mufti: The Phenomenon of Yusuf al-Qaradawi* (New York: Columbia University Press, 2009).

5 Though he claims to have left the Muslim Brotherhood (MB), Soage tells us that he has always remained close to it. He publicly sided with the younger leaders who decided to leave the ranks of the MB in 1996 and form the Party of the Centre (*Hizb al-Wasat*), and then in 2002 he was offered the top MB executive post, the Supreme Guide, which he turned down (2008: 55).

6 I would argue that Salvatore's 1997 *Islam and the Political Discourse of Modernity* has been sadly underestimated in the subsequent literature on Islamism. For instance, he argues that 'Islam in movement' (or the 'Islamic Awakening') has as it lowest common denominator 'Political Islam' – that is, the contention that Shari'a must be implemented in the sociopolitical realm in order to bring about the necessary solutions to the debacle of the postcolonial Arab states. Yet this is far from a monolithic discourse; rather, it is best understood as the 'hermeneutic field of political Islam', or, put differently, 'the terrain of interpretive contentions on the relationship between Islam and politics' (1997: xv). These positions range from Islamic fundamentalism and Islamic revivalism to radical Islam. Abu-Rabi' aptly calls this 'political Islam' the 'Shari'a movements' in which al-Qaradawi plays a leading role (2004: 135–140).

7 Al-Qaradawi's leading role in burgeoning Islamic revival following the 1967 defeat was sealed by a trilogy of books which sought to analyse the failure of the postcolonial Arab regimes, especially in Egypt, Syria and Iraq, and outline the 'Islamic solution' – all published in Beirut: *Al-Hullul almustawrada wa kayfa janat 'ala ummatina* ('The Imported Solutions and How They Harmed Our Umma', 1971); *Al-Hall al-Islami farida wa darura* ('The Islamic Solution: A Duty and a Necessity', 1974); *Bayinat al-hall al-Islami wa shubuhat al-'ilmaniyyin*

wa-l-mutagharribin ('The Clear Proofs of the Islamic Solution and the Doubts of the Secularists and Westernizers', 1987).

8 See David L. Johnston, '*Maqasid al-Shari'a*: Epistemology and Hermeneutics of Muslims Theologies of Human Rights', *Die Welt des Islams* 47 (2007), pp. 149–187.

9 Soage reports from an al-Jazeera programme from 2005 on the issue of religious freedom that al-Qaradawi thought apostates should be socially ostracized, not killed – though he did express the opinion in another context that the journalist Faraj Fawda, assassinated by Islamist extremists in 1992, received his just desserts, considering that he was not just an apostate, but promoting apostasy (2008: 59). Al-Qaradawi later wrote that someone calling others to leave the faith is dangerously sowing the seeds of division (*fitna*) in the *ummah* and that this is tantamount to the crime of treason that even Westerners see as worthy of capital punishment. But Islam is lenient, he continues, and such a person should be imprisoned and with the help of dialogue be led to repentance (2007: 196).

10 It only appears to be earlier, because it is the first edition, while I was quoting from the third edition of *Islamic Awakening*.

11 In this century, he writes, the best advocate for this traditionalism was Rashid Rida and his *Al-Manar* journal. He 'was the originator of the golden rule which was adopted by Imam Hassan Al-Banna, namely, "We should cooperate in what we agree upon, and find excuses for each other in what we differ on"' (1992: 135).

12 Another sociological insight comes from Olivier Roy's two recent books (2004; 2007): al-Qaradawi as an expatriate (an Egyptian living in Qatar since 1962) is an apt leader for a global movement that through the Internet, satellite television and massive emigration to the West, is 'neofundamentalist': uprooted from cultures of origin, it singles out religious norms of purity and selects a few doctrines that allow its adherents to then move to a higher level of commitment than the masses. It is a religion of the 'born-again', a phenomenon that is parallel to the growth of Pentecostalism in many regions or of a variety of new religious cults.

13 He was also asked to give the opening address at its sixteenth annual meeting in early July 2006 on the theme, 'Political *Fiqh* of Muslim Minorities in Europe'. This book grew out of that occasion.

14 *Jahiliyya*, or 'the age of ignorance', is the term by which Muslims have remembered pre-Islamic seventh-century Arabian society.

15 He hints at a 'repugnancy clause', as that stipulated by the recent Afghan and Iraqi constitutions (Feldman 2008).

16 The main argument in favour of democracy (remember, God is still the ultimate ruler, but through his divine sovereignty and the revelation of his laws, or the Shari'a) is that the alternative is tyranny, a greater evil by far.

17 I have no room here to comment on a fascinating book in which Egyptian journalist Sayyid al-Yasin (1999) gathered articles he had publicly exchanged with al-Qaradawi and secular Muslim philosopher Kamal Abu-al-Majd. Accused by al-Yasin of wanting to bring back the caliphate, al-Qaradawi retorts that though he does agree with those who call for pan-Arabism and pan-Islamism, he understands that times have changed and that a return to the caliphate of the past is neither desirable nor possible (1999: 90).

18 But they are free not to follow Shari'a rules they find objectionable, like the ban on alcohol.

19 Muzaffar sits on the board of at least a dozen other international NGOs.

20 I have dealt with Muzaffar's writings on globalization in detail in 'Chandra Muzaffar's Islamic Critique of Globalization: Malaysian Contribution to a Global Ethic', in *Centre for Dialogue's Working Papers Series* 2006, No. 3 (La Trobe University), pp. 1–19.

21 In the interest of full disclosure, I participated as one of three respondents to Muzaffar's keynote speech ('Towards a Universal Spiritual and Moral Vision of Global Justice and Peace'). I was the Christian theologian, while the other two were Muslim and Hindu scholars respectively.

22 This is in a document sent to the delegates in September 2008.

23 See Hans Küng and Karl-Josef Kushel (eds), *A Global Ethic: The Declaration of the Parliament of the World's Religions* (New York: Continuum, 1993).

24 He writes, 'It is interesting that leading Islamic reformers throughout Islamic history also emphasized values' (2002: 43). Ironically, he lists all the reformers mentioned by al-Qaradawi, but then adds Muhammad Iqbal, Malik Bennabi and Fazlur Rahman, who 'often lamented the failure of Muslim intellectuals to develop a clear hierarchy of values rooted in the Qur'an which could serve as signposts for humankind'. He then brings up Sufis like Jalal al-Din Rumi and Ibn Arabi who 'could empathize with the underlying bond that unified the human family (p. 44). Finally, the list of value-oriented Muslims includes the philosophers like Ibn Sina, al-Razi, Ibn Rushd and Ibn Khaldun – 'all those distinguished Muslim minds which came into conflict with religious elites who derived their authority from perpetuating an Islam built around rituals, symbols and practices' (p. 44).

25 Secularism does crop up in one place. In a chapter on the media, he falls at times into an 'essentialist' mode, which colours his description of the clash between 'Islamic Thought' and Western Enlightenment civilization. Secularism, as the separation of 'Church' and 'State' has a particular history in Western Europe. This may not apply to other societies, he notes. On the Muslim side, however, those advocates of an 'Islamic State' based on Shari'a 'are not prepared to admit that their model does not in any way guarantee that good values and practices will prevail in politics and government' (2005: 107). Both sides should avoid 'being trapped in ideological postures' and be ready to examine the realities on the ground, he advises.

26 Muzaffar is quoting from Küng and Kuschel (2003: 24).

27 He cites the two Indonesian movements, 'the Nahdatul Ulama (NU) and the Muhammadiyah, with 40 and 35 million members respectively' (2005: 38).

9

Civil Islam, Means and End of Liberal Piety: Ethnographic Notes from among Turkey's Charitable Foundations

Jeremy Walton

Introduction: Aspirations to Pious Publicness and a Civil Dispensation

> Just look around when you're walking in the streets here in Istanbul. Nobody stops, everyone is on their way somewhere. The public sphere is just somewhere people *pass through*, from their private homes to their jobs. It wasn't like this during Ottoman times. In the Ottoman era, the public sphere was a place that people *dwelled in*. It wasn't just a point of transit (*geçiş*). But it's not so anymore. Of course, we would like it to be this way, to live as Muslims in the public sphere.[1]

I sipped casually at my tulip-shaped glass of Black Sea *çay* as Cemal Bey,[2] the vice-president of the Journalists and Writers Foundation (*Gazeteciler ve Yazarlar Vakfı*), expanded upon the gentle prompt that I had offered him. My interviews with Cemal Bey were reliably fascinating – he was one of my more effusive interlocutors and is a prominent voice in general within the Gülen community in Turkey.[3] In addition to his professional role in the foundation itself, Cemal Bey is a journalist in his own right, and publishes frequent editorials in the newspaper *Zaman*, a liberal Islamic daily considered to be one of the Gülen group's most important media soapboxes (Turam 2007; Yavuz and Esposito 2003).[4] As he paused to collect his thoughts, I encouraged him to expand upon the foundation's valorization of Ottoman times. He continued: 'You see, the Ottoman state wasn't really engaged in anything other than military affairs. All of the services people needed were provided by the foundations (*vakıflar*). And, in this way, services were also separate from politics.'[5]

In this brief exchange, Cemal Bey precisely summarized many of the themes that emerged throughout my research on Turkey's contemporary Islamic civil society organizations. His idealistic vision of the public sphere as a sort of pedestrian, streetside sociality, a context of recumbent being rather than urgent passage, articulates an ideal of pious publicness rooted in a nostalgia for the Ottoman era and the unalienated, unproblematic mode of religiosity that supposedly characterized it. Under this view, an ineluctable aspect of the Ottoman dispensation was the unobtrusive, limited role of the state in matters of both publicness and piety. Ottoman foundations (*vakıflar*) – the very forebears of contemporary civil society organizations such as the Journalists and Writers Foundation – were a central means to civil piety outside of the purview of the state.

Over the course of two years of fieldwork among a congeries of different pious civil society organizations in Turkey, I consistently encountered ideals, aspirations and anxieties similar to those expressed by Cemal Bey. All told, my ethnography shuttled among institutions affiliated with Turkish Alevism[6] (*Alevilik*), Turkey's Nur community[7] (*Nur Cemaati, Nurcular*) and a variety of different Sunni groups, as well as the aforementioned Gülen community. In each of these different contexts, I encountered a common commitment to a liberal, pluralist mode of piety and to a civil dispensation towards religion that functions as both a means to and an end of this liberal piety. In the self-understanding of my informants, this civil, liberal piety is definitively non-political, at least in any traditional sense of politics as statecraft. Nonetheless, as I hope to suggest over the remainder of this chapter, liberal piety and civil Islam challenge the very horizons of the political in contemporary Turkey by interrogating the fundamental presuppositions of Kemalism, the laicist form of Turkish secularism.

Islamic Civil Society in the Heartland of Kemalism?

When I first began to think critically about a project on Turkish Islam and Turkish secularism, I imagined that I would conduct fieldwork by ensconcing myself within a state ministry – the Bureau of Religious Affairs (*Diyanet Şleri Bakanlığı*) or perhaps the General Directorate of Foundations (*Vakıf Genel Müdürlüğü*). I had never been to Turkey at that point, and had no idea of the practical, bureaucratic hurdles that such a project would inevitably involve; because my knowledge of the

Turkish political and historical landscape was formed primarily by classic political science texts, such as those by Niyazi Berkes (1964) and Metin Heper (Heper and Landau 1991), I assumed that a study of Turkish secularism would be coextensive with a study of the Turkish state. When I arrived in Istanbul for my first ethnographic foray in July of 2004, I was quickly disabused of this faulty presupposition on both pragmatic and conceptual grounds. Not only were my calls to the Bureau of Religious Affairs and other state ministries entirely futile, but, more importantly, I realized that the most fascinating negotiations with, challenges to, and rearticulations of Kemalist secularism were not occurring within the explicit domain of the state at all. Contrary to my expectations, my attention was drawn to the vibrant, heterogeneous domain of Turkish civil society – the space of non-governmental organizations and the 'third sector' – as a crucial site of contemporary debates surrounding secularism and Islam.

The enigmas surrounding Turkish secularism are coeval with the foundation of Republican Turkey itself. From the remnants of the Ottoman Empire, rent asunder by the First World War and the subsequent occupation, Mustafa Kemal Atatürk and his cohorts fashioned a state premised upon an ethno-linguistic nationalism that was, paradoxically, both religious and anti-religious at once (Lewis 1961: 262; Berkes 1965: 461; Mango 2002). In the transition from a multi-ethnic and multi-religious empire to the homogeneous Turkish state, Islam – in particular, Sunni Islam of the Hanafi School – was taken to be definitive of Turkishness itself (Lewis 1961: 255). Almost immediately, however, Atatürk's strong central government in Ankara began to enact a series of stringent curtailments on practices and expressions of Islam. Most significant in the context of this chapter, the authority to define the legitimacy of all Islamic precepts and practices was invested exclusively in the state itself, and, in particular, in the Directorate of Religious Affairs (Diyanet Şleri Bakanlığı), heir to the Ottoman *Sheik-ül-Islam* (Shankland 1999: 29; Yılmaz 2005: 100; Davison 1998: 139). In a schematic sense, the history of Islam and secularism in Republican Turkey can be understood as the interplay between these two divergent imperatives: privatization and minimization, on the one hand, and monopolization and homogenization on the other. These two contrastive principles are reconciled and united in the political ideology of Kemalism. In essence, Kemalism is the doctrine of étatism applied to matters of religion. As a laicist ideology, Kemalism implies that questions of the traditional legitimacy and the publicness or privacy of religious practices and discourses are subordinate to the legitimizing (and delegitimizing) control of the state.

Undoubtedly, the schematic, abstract hegemony of Kemalism as an étatist ideology of secularism has always been hypothetical rather than actual in Turkey, at least to a degree. As Şerif Mardin (1989) and Michael Meeker (2002) have detailed in different ways, the modern Turkish state's aspirations to monopolize and enforce the privatization of Islam did not entirely deny continuities and accommodations on the part of practices, discourses and institutions with longer historicities and more complex sociologies. Nonetheless, the fates and trajectories of both Kemalism and Turkish Islam have changed radically over the past quarter of a century. Since the early 1980s, Turkey has experienced an efflorescence of civil society in tandem with a neo-liberal turn in both domestic economic policies and electoral politics (Heper 1991; Öniş 2004). While the initial interventions of the neo-liberal reforms of the Eighties were economic in nature – a large number of state industries were rapidly privatized and protectionist, import-substitution policies were overturned – reverberations in Turkey's sociocultural and political spheres followed closely on their heels. One particularly striking outcome of Turkey's neo-liberal turn has been the proliferation of religious non-governmental organizations – divided into the two legal categories of foundations and associations (*vakıflar* and *dernekler*) – devoted to a congeries of causes, both pious and mundane. Whereas the state had carefully regulated and often curtailed religiously oriented civil society organizations earlier in the history of the Republic (Çızakçı 2000: 86), the novel economic and political terrain of the Eighties proved to be a salubrious context for the rapid expansion of charitable foundations and associations. On the basis of this institutional efflorescence outside of the full purview of the state, a new, civil Islamic pluralism has arisen to challenge the hegemony of both the Kemalist imperative of the privatization of religious practice and the state-based definition of legitimate Sunni–Hanafi Islam.

Academic interrogation of Kemalism in relation to the neo-liberal Turkish present has become a burgeoning cottage industry for scholars of Turkey in recent years. Anthropologists such as Esra Özyürek (2006), Yael Navaro-Yashin (2002a, 2002b) and Jenny White (1999, 2002) have made insightful observations concerning the effects of privatization and commodification on both Kemalism and Turkish Islam (see also Hart 1999 and Çınar 2005). More broadly, social scientists such as Martin Stokes (1992, 1999), Nilüfer Göle (1996), Ayşe Öncü (1997), Sam Kaplan (2006) and Çağlar Keyder (1999) have assessed the recent fate of the project of Turkish modernity in relation to diverse questions of popular music, gender, bourgeois domestic intimacy, primary school education and urban space (see also Keyman 2007).

My own study builds upon this focus on the neo-liberal Turkish present by arguing that the institutions of Turkish civil society provide the matrix for an emergent liberal piety that challenges the presuppositions of Kemalism. More specifically, two key tenets of Kemalist secularism – the reduction of religious practice to the private realm and the subordination of questions of religious doctrine and education to the authority of the state – no longer maintain the hegemonic status that they did during the earlier history of the Republic. While Islamically oriented parties such as the Justice and Development Party (AKP), the Felicity Party (Saadet Partisi) and their predecessors, the Welfare Party (Refah Partisi) and the Virtue Pary (Fazilet Partisi), have certainly been influential in this process (White 2002), an equally important, and less recognized, role has been played by a wide spectrum of foundations and associations dedicated to a multitude of pious causes. Over the course of this chapter, I discuss a number of the foundations that played an important role in my research. I will make a variety of specific arguments and expositions concerning the orientation and activities of these foundations; on a broader level, I hope to demonstrate that together, the foundations that I have studied adumbrate a broader field of Islamic civil society existing in Turkey today. Finally, I will argue that my research points to the general manner in which the methodological tools of anthropology can contribute to the theorization of secularism across national, political and cultural divides and contexts.

The Istanbul Science and Culture Foundation: *Nurculuk* and the Creation of Islamic Civility

The offices of the Istanbul Science and Culture Foundation (İstanbul İlim ve Kültür Vakfı) are located in a resplendently restored sixteenth-century *medrese*, designed by the Ottoman Empire's pre-eminent architect, Mimar Sinan, himself, and noted for its unique octagonal plan, tucked away among the more prominent tourist attractions and municipal government offices in Sultanahmet, the so-called historical peninsula that is the crown jewel of both Istanbul's and Turkey's historical pride, not to mention the object of endless advertising campaigns. Each Thursday night, a group of approximately twenty men, young and old, gather in the 'Ottoman-style' conference room of the *medrese* to read from the *Risale-i Nur,* the collected works of Bediuzzaman Said Nursi, quite possibly the most famous Turkish Muslim philosopher of the last century. The members of the class are university students, professors, physicians, lawyers, businessmen and more than a few successful merchants from the nearby Kapalıçarşı – in short, a swathe of the burgeoning new Muslim bourgeoisie which has fascinated the Turkish media in the fifteen years or so since the beginning of the renaissance of political Islam in Turkey (Soydemir 2003).

Typically, the class – known as a *ders* in Turkish – lasts for approximately two hours, including a break for evening prayers. Passages from one of the thirty-three 'Words' (Sözler) of the *Risale-i Nur* are read aloud by the *hoca,* or teacher – usually the senior member of the class, who has had formal training in Qur'anic studies, Islamic law, Islamic philosophy and the traditions of the *Hadith.* Much of the discussion during these weekly gatherings focuses on interpretation and translation of Said Nursi's language, as his dense, literary Ottoman, heavily peppered with Persian and Arabic vocabulary, is not immediately accessible to speakers of contemporary Turkish. Common topics of conversation include formal questions of Islamic law (*fiqh*) and *içtihad* (exegesis based upon the Sunna and *Hadith* traditions), the role of Islam in post-Ottoman Turkey, the challenges of secularism and the triumphs and limitations of 'Western' science in relation to Islam. Enveloped within these more abstract concerns are debates over the trivia and trials that constitute quotidian life as a devout Muslim man in present-day Istanbul. Above all, questions of political and economic practice are opened to spirited debate within the context of both the *Risale-i Nur* and the ritualized intimacy that the class promotes.

During my fieldwork in Istanbul, I attended the weekly *Risale-i Nur* class at the Science and Culture Foundation for approximately a year and a half; throughout my attendance, I was consistently impressed by the level of sophistication that characterizes the theological and jurisprudential debates that arise from the discussion of Nursi's *Sözler.* After one particularly abstract session, a younger volunteer at the foundation suggested that I attend another weekly *ders*, located across the Bosporus in Üsküdar, for the sake of comparison. When I arrived at the *dershane*, I was immediately struck by the contrast between the two class environments. Although the format of the class was the same – a *hoca* reading from the *Risale-i Nur*, and providing interpretations based upon the students' questions – the composition of the class and the content of the discussion differed significantly from that of the Sultanahmet class. Here, at least three generations of participants were present: elderly and middle-aged men, younger men (usually university students or recent returnees from military service), and preadolescent boys, typically the sons of the older men and brothers of the younger men. Both because of the wider age range among the students of the class and because of the generally lower educational level among the participants on the whole, the conversation tended towards more practical, concrete concerns. The *hoca* chose passages of a more allegorical, rather than philosophical, nature for the discussion, and then related these allegories to the everyday concerns of the class members. For example, one parable considered related the story of two brothers who fall down a well, only to meet opposite fates on the basis of their polar religious–ethical constitutions, the first selfish and the second devout. The *hoca* put this parable in context by discussing the two opposite faces that Istanbul presents to the visitor: the morally corrupt seat of vice, a Babylon on the Bosporus with its seedy centre in the fleshpots and beer halls of Taksim, and the post-imperial jewel in the crown of Islamic glory, embodied in the masterworks of Sinan, the pilgrims congregated at the Tomb of Eyüp Sultan, and, needless to say, the *Risale* study circles of Üsküdar. A discussion of the competing vices and virtues of daily life in the metropolis, which clearly frustrated and fascinated each of the students, immediately followed from this hermeneutical specification.

From the perspectives of class, level of education and generational diversity, the two *Risale-i Nur* classes that I have attended differ significantly, yet a similar process of construction of subjectivity occurs in both of them. Briefly, through the interpretive reading of Nursi's works, coordinated primarily by the *hoca*, the *Risale* classes inculcate a civic Muslim subjectivity which achieves a hesitant reconciliation with the strictures of Kemalist Turkish national identity. I employ the term 'civic' here in the same spirit as Max Weber, *eminence gris* of the social scientific inquiry into religion, used the term 'capitalist' to describe the practices of world-weary New England Puritans in his groundbreaking work, *The Protestant Ethic and the Spirit of Capitalism*. Weber argues that a 'capitalist' ethic or habitus – to appropriate Pierre Bourdieu's famous category – emerges as an inevitable effect of the religiosity of Calvinist merchants, who adopt an orientation towards worldly economic activity on the basis of their fatalistic, binary theodicy (Weber 1958). In the same vein, I would argue, the recitation and conversation that constitute the *Risale-i Nur* classes inculcate a liberal, civic-minded piety that is commensurate with, but not identical to, officially authorized Turkish national–secular identity. The egalitarian setting of the class, which exists both as a model of and a model for Said Nursi's interpretation of the Qur'an and the *Hadith*, interpellates an intimate, distinctly Islamic counterpublic. In particular, the face-to-face conversation and debate that characterizes the *ders* echoes back to the coffee house democracy of the eighteenth century, which was the inspiration of Jurgen Habermas' theory of the public sphere (Habermas 1991).

On the whole, the *Risale-i Nur* classes and Turkey's Nur community raise two crucial questions about Kemalist secularism: the relationship between Kemalism and liberalism, and the legitimacy of the Kemalist definition of secularism itself. In a schematic sense, the Nur community, with its emphasis on the ethic of positive action (*müspet*)[8] and the impossibility of compulsion in matters of religion (*dinde zorlama yok*), advocates an interpretation and practice of Islam that is fully commensurate with the imperatives of political liberalism (as members of the community are quick to note themselves). However, they refrain from any identification with secularism (*laiklik*), at least in its Kemalist mode, which implies the pre-eminence of the state in defining the domain of religion itself. This decoupling of liberalism and Kemalist secularism creates a space for the interrogation of the Kemalist definition of secularism itself. In general, members of the Nur community advocate a notion of secularism as toleration towards all religious practices and the non-interference of the state in matters of religious affairs; interestingly, as I will discuss later, this critical reinterpretation of secularism (the so-called American model, or *Amerikan örnegi*) shares much in common with the aspirations of Turkey's Alevi minority community. For the moment, however, I want to punctuate the liberal, civic ethic that the *Risale-i Nur* classes espouse, which is definitively nonsecular, at least in the Kemalist understanding of the term.

The fostering of liberal piety that characterizes the *Risale-i Nur* classes is possible precisely because they exist institutionally within the domain of Turkish civil society. The members of the classes are adamant in their emphasis on personal virtue – rather than organized political mobilization – as the proper organizing feature of an Islamic public at large. While there is certainly a tacit identification in general between the Nur community and the parties of the new Islamic political establishment, the Justice and Development Party and the Felicity Party (Adalet ve Kalkınma Partisi or AKP; Saadet Partisi), to the extent of my knowledge, the political affiliation of the class members is never discussed in the classes themselves. Indeed, one of the senior members of the New Asia Foundation (Yeni Asya Vakfı), another organization dedicated to the propagation of Said Nursi's writings and philosophy, told me in no uncertain terms that he has had more difficulty dealing with the AKP government than he had during the earlier tenure of a Kemalist governing coalition. More generally, the discussions of the Nur classes underscore Said Nursi's own commitment to a non-political rejuvenation of faith, in which politics is regarded as a mistaken entanglement in worldly affairs (Vahide 2005: 172–173).

It is precisely because the *Risale-i Nur* classes occur under the auspices of a civil society organization, the foundation, that they are capable of reconciling an Islamic civic ethic with Turkish secular national identity. As the 28 February 1997 military coup, which removed the Islamically oriented Welfare Party (Refah Partisi) and its PM, Necmettin Erbakan, from power, demonstrated, the political mobilization of Islam and the state establishment in Turkey still exist in tension with each other. In an opposite manner, the gradual 'secularization' of the AKP has also demonstrated this contradiction. By achieving institutional status as civil society organizations, however, organizations such as the Istanbul Science and Culture Foundation are able to foster an Islamic civic (rather than political) identity that does not immediately or necessarily contradict the political prerequisites of Turkish state secularism. This civic Islamic identity is based upon the subjectivity that comes into being within the institutional context of the *ders*, and, indeed, is a definitive feature of the Nur community as a whole. In fact, the institutionalization of the Nur community within a panoply of foundations and associations – largely a phenomenon of the last twenty years – can be interpreted as an answer to the dilemma of politics which Said Nursi himself never fully reconciled during his own lifetime. As Şerif Mardin (1989) has masterfully demonstrated, the Nur movement first emerged as a grassroots response to the marginalization of Islam that occurred during the early Republican period in Turkey – the *Risale-i Nur*, through its re-establishment of Islam as the essential principle of social being, resonated with a large segment of the Turkish population that had not yet recovered from the shock administered by the end of the Ottoman Empire and the subsequent displacement of the institutional authority of Islam. However, during the nascence of the Republic, and even up through the multi-party period of Democrat Party rule during the 1950s, the institutionalized paranoia of the secular military state establishment denied any official recognition of the *Risale-i Nur* or the Nur community. Nothing is more demonstrative of this paranoia than the removal of Said Nursi's body from his tomb in Şanlı Urfa and its subsequent reinterment in an unmarked grave somewhere in western Turkey, conducted by the military several months after his death (Vahide 2005: 345). In this light, the fact that the *Risale-i Nur* and the Nur community have achieved efflorescence within the institutional framework of civil society, less than a half a century later, is nothing short of remarkable. The next section of my presentation will examine how the Gülen community, an offshoot of the Nur movement, has achieved a further level of commensuration between national and Islamic imperatives and discourses through activity within the sphere of civil society.

The Turkish Journalists and Writers Foundation: Liberal Islam and Ottoman Nostalgia

The Turkish Journalists and Writers Foundation (Türkiye Gazeteciler ve Yazarlar Vakfı) is located in an affluent business district of European Istanbul, Harbiye, near to both the thriving centre of the Istanbul financial world and the most overt military facilities within Istanbul's urban domain. Their offices are of a decidedly luxurious character, occupying several floors of a high-rise office building, and include a large publishing house and elegant conference room, designed and decorated again in high Ottoman style. The overarching goal of the foundation is to provide both domestic and international support for the educational and ethico-religious projects of Fethullah Gülen, an ideological heir of Said Nursi and major sponsor of the Turkish Schools, an international network of private primary and secondary educational institutions that combine moral and intellectual pedagogy in a single setting. In addition to providing bureaucratic and financial support for the Turkish Schools, the Journalists and Writers Foundation has also organized a series of conferences known as the Abant Platform, dedicated to promoting 'dialogue, accord, tolerance, love, and acceptance of all people in and of themselves' (Gündem 1998: 7). During the final year of my fieldwork alone, the foundation sponsored two Abant Platform meetings, one in Paris and one in the town of Abant itself, located in the Turkish province of Bolu (the platform was first held in Abant, and was therefore named after it). Furthermore, the foundation sponsored a related seminar, the 'Conference on Global Hunger and Poverty', which took place in Istanbul in February 2006.

At an initial glance, the ideals of the Abant Platform might appear to be a rather tepid reiteration of principles of cultural pluralism and tolerance, as practised in the liberal democracies of Western Europe and North America. However, the Journalists and Writers Foundation consistently emphasizes that its liberalism derives from an entirely separate historical tradition, that of Ottoman Islam. Over the course of several interviews, one of the organizers of the Abant Platform outlined for me the Ottoman heritage of cultural tolerance from which both Fethullah Gülen's philosophy and the activities of the foundation derive inspiration. This nostalgic version of Ottoman liberalism relies on two separate foundations: the Ottoman *millet*[9] system and the Ottoman foundation system (*vakıf sistemi*). The millet system, for its part, provides a wholly Islamic precedent for a liberal politics of tolerance, pluralism and coexistence among minority religious and ethnic communities. According to the rather rose-tinted view that my informant espoused, the Ottoman *millet* system ensured both political autonomy and political equality for the minorities of the Empire – Jews, and a variety of ethnically and doctrinally different Christian communities. Each community was allowed self-governance under the overarching authority of the Divine Porte; this guarantee of self-governance was itself the principle of equality among communities. This spirit of equality and autonomy of communities serves as an ideological inspiration for the contemporary liberal activism of the foundation itself. Crucially, for my interlocutors at the Writers and Journalists Foundation, the source of this communitarian liberalism is understood to be Ottoman Islam, rather than the philosophical tradition of liberalism dating back to the Western European Enlightenment. I had the opportunity to witness a demonstration of the rekindling of the *millet* ideal at the Conference on Global Hunger and Poverty, which was sponsored by the foundation. The conference brought together representatives from Turkey's different religious populations, the Armenian, Greek and Syriac Orthodox Churches, as well as Jewish and Sunni Muslim communities – in short, the contemporary heirs to the Ottoman *millet*s.

While the Ottoman *millet* system informs the Islamic liberalism promoted by the Abant Platform and Journalists and Writers Foundation, the institutional form best suited to a tolerant, liberal Islamic society is provided by the category of the foundation itself, as understood in its Ottoman form, rather than its later, contemporary, post-Republican incarnation. As Cemal Bey of the Writers and Journalists Foundation emphasized, foundations, rather than the Sultanic state, were the crucial providers of community services – ranging from soup kitchens to religious schools – during the Ottoman era. Furthermore, all of my informants explicitly advocated this civil dispensation of service in favour of a state-based model. One need not read too much between the lines to detect a tacit criticism of the strong welfare state, a model that was hegemonic during the early years of the Republic, and therefore complicit in the social and political marginalization of Islam in Turkey.

Of course, the fact that this criticism of Turkey's statist dispensation remains implicit in the activities and discourse of the Journalists and Writers Foundation is not to be discounted. Without a doubt, both the activities sponsored by the foundation and the opinions expressed by members of the foundation themselves advocate a model of social welfare based upon a combination of liberal Islamic piety and a vibrant civil society that supports this liberal piety through the provision of services, both material and spiritual. However, the critique of the Turkish statist dispensation, and, in turn, Kemalist secularism, that this advocacy implies remains inexplicit and, therefore, arguably apolitical. Like the *Risale-i Nur* classes that the Istanbul Science and Culture Foundation sponsors, the conferences and seminars that the Journalists' Foundation and the Abant Platform host perform a strategic decoupling of liberalism and secularism, which, in turn, implies the necessity of a redefinition of secularism itself. This redefinition is achieved by means of intervention within the realm of Turkish civil society through the promotion of a renovated, public yet non-political programme of Islamic virtue. The process of this intervention is reciprocal. As the institutional and discursive space of Turkish civil society broadens in scope and achieves a greater degree of independence from explicit state interference, the opportunities for new institutional forms of Islam increase. Simultaneously, as these opportunities increase, civil society itself begins to take on an Islamic character, at least in some of its realizations. As I hope to argue later, this efflorescence of an Islamic civil society ultimately has horizons that extend beyond the national borders of Turkey itself.

Civil Society, a Terrain of Political and Ideological Conjugation: Alevi Foundations and Associations

While the Journalists and Writers Foundation is a pre-eminent example of a contemporary Turkish non-governmental institution devoted to an Islamically based pluralism, the foundations and associations dedicated to Turkish Alevism, or *Alevilik*, demonstrate the potential plurality of the institutional forms of civil society themselves. In other words, the Turkish Alevi community – partially by virtue of the persistent refusal of the Turkish state to recognize it as a legitimate 'religious' minority – has achieved expression in a fractal array of foundations and associations, which, together, represent the diversity of political ideologies, devotional beliefs and practices that potentially 'count as' Alevi. In what follows, I will briefly discuss three of the Alevi organizations that have figured prominently in my research.

The offices of the Cem Foundation (Cem Vakfı), one of Turkey's largest and most vocal Alevi organizations, are located in the far-flung neighbourhood of Kocasinan, in the region of Yenibosna, one of European Istanbul's thriving suburbs, where rows of anonymous prefab apartment blocks and massive billboards advertising insurance, automotive parts and high fashion line the freeway that leads west towards Atatürk Airport and the exurban expanses of Büyükçekmece and beyond. Although the Cem Foundation was initially located in şişli, near the commercial centre of European Istanbul, as the scope of its activities increased, so too did its need for a more spacious headquarters. Its new home – a multi-storey office building dedicated entirely to the foundation – includes myriad offices, a large cafeteria, several conference rooms, and a *cem* house (*cem evi,* the definitive Alevi space of worship), as well as the studio and broadcast facilities of Cem Radio (see also Erdemir 2005). As this short description suggests, the Cem Foundation fulfils manifold functions. In addition to its publishing and broadcasting activities, it hosts weekly *cem* ceremonies,[10] frequent conferences, and private education classes focused on preparing Alevi students for Turkey's infamous standardized tests, such as the O.S.S. and L.G.S.

Ideologically, the Cem Foundation dedicates itself to lobbying the state, as embodied by the Office of Religious Affairs, for recognition of Alevism as a legitimate religious minority. In doing so, it necessarily initiates a process of defining the constituitive beliefs and practices of Alevism itself. This process is undertaken by a cadre of researchers who are affiliated with the foundation and receive support from it. Over the course of a series of interviews that I conducted with several of these researchers, I was presented with a remarkably consistent definition of Alevism. A summary of this definition would include the following clauses: Alevism is a uniquely Anatolian synthesis of Shi'a Islam and Turkic–Central Asian shamanism, which has the *cem* house as its unique site of worship and is dedicated politically to secular principles of pluralism, embodied by freedom of worship, equality among religions and gender equality.

From an institutional perspective, the efforts towards a definition of Alevism that the Cem Foundation promotes are rather peculiar, even potentially contradictory. On the one hand, the demands of political representation require an abstraction from and denigration of the particularities of Alevi practice. This process of abstraction and codification is a textbook instance of the general imperatives that liberal secular democracy places upon religion (Chatterjee 1998). On the other hand, because the state has remained obdurate in its refusal to recognize Alevis – though there are signs that this may be changing – the aspirations of consensus and definition articulated by the Cem Foundation have not yet been achieved. In the absence of state recognition, a plethora of other Alevi foundations and associations continue to voice heterogeneous political and historical claims concerning Alevism, in spite of the Cem Foundation's attempts to occupy an authoritative, definitive role for the community.

The Hacı Bektaş Veli Anatolian Culture Foundation, (Hacı Bektaş Veli Anadolu Kültür Vakfı), another Alevi foundation with which I conducted research, presents a stark political contrast to the Cem Vakfı, despite the fact that many of the activities and perspectives of the two organizations are quite similar. The Hacı Bektaş Foundation, which consists of twenty-six regional outposts in addition to the foundation headquarters in Ankara, is a key member the Union of Alevi-Bektaşi Organizations Federation (Alevi Bektaşi Kuruluşları Birliği Federasyonu) and provides a significant foil to the considerable influence that the Cem Foundation wields in the debate over Alevi identity. Interestingly, the Hacı Bektaş Foundation's interpretation of Alevism does not differ significantly from that of the Cem Foundation, though its members tend to place more emphasis on the Central Asian, rather than Shi'a, sources of Alevilik. The Hacı Bektaş Foundation's political activism, on the other hand, presents a stark contrast to the efforts of the Cem Foundation. As one member of the foundation put it:

> The basic difference between us and them [the Cem Foundation] is this: They claim that the state should support both Sunnis and Alevis. In our opinion, the state should support neither Sunnis nor Alevis. Each community should attend to its own needs, separate from the state. This is the meaning of secularism.[11]

Although the Hacı Bektaş Foundation and the Cem Foundation largely agree on the general tenets of Alevism itself, the political mobilization that they summon on behalf of these tenets differs radically. For instance, the Cem Foundation devotes itself to lobbying for funding from the Turkish state, while the Hacı Bektaş-i Foundation focuses on suits against required religion classes in schools, which encompass Sunni Islam without discussing Alevism at all.

The political activities of the Cem Foundation and the Hacı Bektaş Foundation express fundamentally different understandings of secularism as a relationship between state authority and religious tradition – the Cem Foundation advocates a plurality of religious communities which receive equal financial and ideological support from the state, while the Hacı Bektaş Foundation prefers a more stringent separation between state authority and religious practice and belief. Nonetheless, the two organizations adhere to the same substantive definition of Alevism. The same cannot be said for a third Alevi organization that I interviewed for my research, the Ehl-i Beyt Foundation (Ehl-i Beyt Vakfı). The members of the Ehl-i Beyt Foundation whom I spoke with enunciated an interpretation of Alevism that is entirely devoid of Central Asian or shamanistic roots – under the Ehl-i Beyt definition, Alevism is essentially identical to Twelver Shi'a Islam, as practised among the Shi'a of Iran,

Iraq and Lebanon. Indeed, the name Ehl-i Beyt itself indicates allegiance to the sacred familial circle of the Prophet Muhammad – Muhammad himself, his daughter Fatima, his son-in-law Ali, and his grandsons Hasan and Hüseyin (Ali's sons). For the Ehl-i Beyt Foundation, key aspects of Alevi practice, such as the *cem* ceremony, are ritual innovations that are inappropriate to 'true' Alevism.

Undoubtedly, the Ehl-i Beyt Foundation represents a marginal, radical current within Turkish Alevism as a whole. Most Alevis whom I have spoken to dismiss the Ehl-i Beyt group as a cynical departure from Alevi tradition that panders shamelessly to Sunni political elites, both within the AKP government and within civil society at large. And, indeed, I was initially referred to the Ehl-i Beyt Foundation by one of Turkey's pre-eminent Sunni foundations, the Turkish Charitable Organizations Foundation.[12] In general, when I have queried members of various Sunni-oriented foundations about Alevism, they have tended to distinguish between the Ehl-i Beyt Foundation, for which they reserve respect, and the vast majority of Alevi groups, which they view as aberrations of 'true' Islam. From an organizational and institutional perspective, however, the ties between the Ehl-i Beyt Foundation and the Charitable Organizations Foundation, like those among various Alevi foundations and associations that form the Alevi-Bektaşi Federation, demonstrate yet another crucial aspect of the relationship between Turkish Islam and Turkish civil society – the formation of a pan-Islamic civil society, which glorifies doctrinal uniformity over diversity of practice. I will discuss this phenomenon more thoroughly in the following section.

As a conclusion to this discussion of Alevism and Turkish civil society, I would like to highlight, in general terms, the ineluctable relationship between the interpretation of tradition and the politics of representation that Alevi organizations negotiate. Because Alevi foundations and associations have come to function as the institutional means of political representation for Turkey's Alevi community as a whole, they necessarily engage with the terms of religious and cultural legitimacy defined by the state itself. For a number of reasons that I cannot explore fully in this context – chief among them, the Bureau of Religious Affair's role in defining Sunni tradition as the sole legitimate interpretation of Islam in Turkey – Alevi organizations such as the Cem Foundation and the Hacı Bektaş Foundation are compelled to define Alevi tradition as a means to political legitimacy. As anthropologist

Aykan Erdemir has pointed out, these negotiations and rearticulations of Alevi tradition are evident in the ritual contexts of *cem* ceremonies themselves (Erdemir 2005). From the perspective of my own research, this relationship between the interpretation of tradition and political representation is fascinating precisely because it occurs within the fraught terrain of civil society. Rather paradoxically, the plethora of Alevi foundations and associations is both a testament to the discursive and institutional vibrance of civil society and an index of Alevism's continued illegitimacy from the perspective of the state. In this brief context, I have merely suggested some of the strategies and forms that have characterized Alevi organizations' negotiation of this dilemma of politics and tradition.

The Union of NGOs of the Islamic World and the Turkish Charitable Organizations Foundation: The Global Horizons of Turkish–Islamic Civil Society

The conference room at the luxurious Ramada Kaya Hotel, located deep in the vast western expanses of European Istanbul, was abuzz with anticipation following the intermission for the evening call to prayer. Those of us in the audience had already listened to several hours of welcoming speeches by clerics and representatives from Indonesia, Mauritania, Qatar, Palestine, China, Indonesia, and even a Muslim convert from Germany, as well as the requisite host of Turkish luminaries. They had each regaled us with the importance of the location of the meeting, Istanbul, former and, as some suggested, potential future nexus of the Islamic world. But the main event, the keynote speaker, the immeasurably famous Egyptian-Qatari theologian and legal scholar Yusuf al-Qaradawi, was yet to come.

All told, the content of the speeches at the Second General Assembly Meeting for the International Union of Muslim Scholars, including al-Qaradawi's, was rather predictable and repetitive: exhortations for Muslim unity, appeals for collective action in support of Palestinians, Iraqis, Pakistanis left homeless by the earthquake of November 2005 and Indonesians affected by the Boxing Day tsunami of 2004 and the more recent Jogjakarta quake of May 2006, and condemnations of aggressive 'Western' secularism, as expressed both by the war in Iraq and the cartoon controversy that began in the Danish newspaper, the *Jyllands Posten*. The dense institutional context in which the meeting occurred, however, was fascinating. The two groups responsible for organizing the cosmopolitan assembly were the Turkish Charitable Organizations Foundation (Türkiye Gönüllü Teşekküller Vakfı) and its sister organization, the Union of NGOs of the Islamic World. In particular, the latter organization, the Union of NGOs of the Islamic World, represents a new phase in the development of Islamic civil society in Turkey. The union was devised as a method for maintaining stronger contacts among Islamic NGOs after Islamic civil society organizations from 139 different countries gathered together for a conference in Istanbul on 1 May 2005 (Union of NGOs 2006: 7). The union consists of a council of twenty members from as many different nations, and was officially established at the end of 2005 through a special legal process which required the signed approval of the head of every government ministry in Turkey (ibid.: 8). Indeed, one of the most striking features of the union is that it belongs to a unique category of Turkish civil society organizations, 'Organizations with International Character', as outlined in Turkish law No. 3355. In contrast, the vast majority of Turkish non-governmental organizations are either legally classified as foundations (*vakıflar*) or associations (*dernekler*).

From the perspective of my research, the Turkish Charitable Organizations Foundation and the Union of NGOs of the Islamic World demarcate both the institutional and conceptual horizons of Islamic civil society in contemporary Turkey. Just as the Union of NGOs of the Islamic World seeks to coordinate activity among Islamic civil society organizations globally, the Turkish Charitable Organizations Foundation aims to foster ties among the ever-increasing number of Islamic foundations and associations within Turkey itself. Tellingly, I was first referred to the Charitable Organizations Foundation by my contacts at the Journalists and Writers Foundation. Even more so than the Journalists and Writers Foundation or the Istanbul Science and Culture Foundation, the Union of NGOs of the Islamic World and the Charitable Organizations Foundation have capitalized on the expansion of Turkish civil society in order to coordinate a self-professedly apolitical, deeply cosmopolitan project of Islamic renaissance. It is almost needless to say that the international relationships that the union has fostered would be unthinkable for a politicized Islamic movement in Turkey – the vanguard of the Turkish secular military state apparatus simply would not accept the influence of cosmopolitan Islam upon their domain of institutional and ideological hegemony. For this reason, new Islamic cosmopolitanism in Turkey necessarily articulates itself within the relatively autonomous space of civil society. At the same time, however, this new Islamic cosmopolitanism has not abandoned concerns of nation and locality entirely. As I mentioned briefly above, Ottoman nostalgia was a prominent theme for all of the speakers of the International Union of Muslim Scholars, Turkish and non-Turkish alike. Istanbul maintains pride of place in the imaginary geography of civil Islamic cosmopolitanism. And fittingly, perhaps, both the Turkish Charitable Organizations Foundation and the Union of NGOs of the Islamic World are run out of an antique Ottoman building, just outside the city gates of old Istanbul, which once functioned as a *tekke*, or Sufi shrine.

By Way of a Conclusion, a Contrast: Bureaucratic State Islam, Politicized Islam and the Possibility of Post-Politics

With this discussion of the Turkish Charitable Organizations Foundation and Islamic cosmopolitanism, the primary ethnographic exposition of my chapter draws to a close. Although I have made a variety of specific arguments based upon my research with the Istanbul Science and Culture Foundation, the Journalists and Writers Foundation, the various Alevi organizations and the Turkish Charitable Organizations Foundation, my panoramic goal has been to outline, however partially, the parameters of Turkish civil Islam and its characteristic, liberal mode of piety. Most importantly, I have argued that this civil Islam articulates both challenges to and reconciliations with traditional Kemalist secularism. This process of challenge and reconciliation between civil Islam and étatist secularism is, in my estimation, a relatively recent historical development in Turkey – although its roots extend back to the beginning of multi-party politics in the late 1940s and the overhaul of Turkey's foundation law in the late 1960s, the efflorescence of Islamic civil society in Turkey essentially began with the more general 'opening' of civil society following the neo-liberal reforms of the Özal government in the 1980s.

While I have categorized each of the foundations that I have discussed here as avatars of Turkish–Islamic civil society, I certainly do not want to obscure the differences between them. On the contrary, the very fact that each of the organizations I have discussed has been able to advocate an interpretation of Islam on the basis of institutional articulation within the field of civil society ensures the existence of a diversity of civil Islamic beliefs and practices. As a point of contrast to the multifarious field of Islamic civil society in contemporary Turkey, one might point to the relatively homogeneous interpretation of Sunni, Hanafi Islam propagated by Turkey's Bureau of Religious Affairs. The Bureau of Religious Affairs, as my Alevi informants consistently complained, is the site of production for official, statist Islam in Turkey: the bureau is responsible for training all imams, approving and funding all mosques, and preparing the texts and material for the mandatory religion classes taught in public schools. In a different vein, one might compare the plural field of Islamic civil society that I have sketched with the current incarnations of politicized Islam in Turkey, the AKP and, in particular, the Felicity Party (Saadet Partisi).

In November 2006, I attended a demonstration at Çağlayan Square in Istanbul, organized by the Felicity Party in protest against the imminent arrival of Pope Benedict XVI to Turkey. At Çağlayan, I was immediately struck by the contrasting context and theatricality of politicized Islam in comparison to the modes of civil Islam and liberal piety that I have adumbrated in this chapter. The unified indignation of the crowd – from my perspective, a postmodern performance of the stereotyped mob mentality analysed in the nineteenth century by Gustave Le Bon (Le Bon 1896) – the vicious placards pillorying Benedict, and the evident cult of personality surrounding the head of the Felicity Party, Necmettin Erbakan – in short, the mobilization of Islamic identity in the cause of political protest that I witnessed was a far cry from the 'rationalized', civil Islam articulated by the foundations or, for that matter, the bureaucratic, statist Islam of the Bureau of Religious Affairs. Of course, this 'crowd' was in no manner spontaneous or undirected, in the manner of Le Bon's famous collective subject. Rather, the participants of the rally in protest against Benedict XVI's Turkish honeymoon engaged in an astute, self-reflexive performance of 'crowdedness', a display of rancorous, uniform nativism that clearly played to the assembly of media elites on hand. I was most immediately struck by the fact that this pageant of crowded, politicized indignation is precisely the representation of Islamic sentiment that the civic dispensation of the foundations and associations which I have studied downplay and even criticize.

By way of a conclusion, I would like to make a few tentative remarks on the broader lessons that an ethnographic inquiry into religious practice within civil society have for an anthropological investigation of secularism – the ultimate theoretical and methodological aspiration of my research. As I noted at the outset, I had initially planned to construct the site of my ethnography as the state itself. While there were manifold practical reasons why I ultimately did not do this, there were also more abstract reasons. In general, the state has been a notoriously difficult concept for anthropologists to interrogate, both because of the discipline's traditional focus on non-state societies and because of the state's own resistance to competing regimes of knowledge (Abrams 2006). However, as I hope my presentation has suggested, an anthropological inquiry into the mechanisms and effects of state practice does not necessarily have the state as its ethnographical site per se. This is where the concept of secularism becomes crucial. I would argue that secularism cannot be understood separately from the demands that modern and postmodern state practice place upon the traditions and practices of religion. While Turkey, as a national context, is rather unique in that it possesses an explicit ideology of secularism, propagated by both the state itself and within civil society and the public sphere – here I am thinking of such organizations as the Ataturkist Thought Association (Atatürkçü Düşünce Dernekler) – the *secularizing logic* which demands and recognizes a certain type of religion as legitimate is not unique to Turkey alone.[13] Therefore, the study of both Turkish secularism and religious practice in Turkey must expand beyond the narrow horizons of a history of the state itself. By focusing on the commodification of both secular and Islamic symbols, anthropologists such as Yael Navaro-Yashin (2002) and Esra Özyürek (2006) have already demonstrated that a study of Turkish secularism must incorporate an understanding of the socio-economic and cultural processes through which the tangible iconography of both secularism and religion are produced, circulated and consumed. My own research, on the other hand, emphasizes the manner in which the beliefs and practices of Muslim communities respond to and accommodate the pressures of the state within the realm of civil society. In this vein, I have attempted to understand secularism not as a tool of the state, but, rather, as a process by which religion is configured in relationship to the institutions and ideologies of both state and civil society. It is my firm belief that this conception of secularism has the potential to be applied across national contexts, wherever religion confronts and adjusts to the disciplinary logics of the modern–postmodern state.

Finally, the various aspirations, activities and horizons of possibility articulated by the foundations and associations that constitute the domain of Turkish–Islamic civil society demand a reassessment of categories such as 'civilization' and 'politics', both within Turkey and more generally. Organizations such as the Journalists and Writers Foundation and the Union of Islamic NGOs of the Islamic World often invoke the concept of 'Islamic civilization' in order to advocate a 'reconciliation' or 'union' among civilizations (*medeniyetlerin uzlaşması, medeniyetlerin ittifakı*) as an explicit critique of the ideology of the clash of civilizations (Huntington 1993). Furthermore, the very institutional category of the *vakıf*, with its roots in both the Ottoman foundation system and modern legal and bureaucratic non-governmental structures, begs the very exclusivity of civilizations that the clash of civilizations hypothesis presupposes. With regard to the question of politics, I strongly believe that the frequent insistence on the part of key members of Turkey's Islamic foundations that they avoid politics altogether should be taken seriously. This is not to say that the foundations and associations I have discussed are apolitical; on the contrary, the manner in which they question and critique the presuppositions of Kemalist secularism is highly politicized. However, they nonetheless eschew traditional politics as a legitimate means to virtue or religious legitimacy. Even Alevi foundations consider their lobbying of the Turkish state as an incrimination of, rather than participation in, politics as usual. For this reason, I have chosen to describe the goals and activities of the foundations and associations discussed in this chapter as 'post-political', in the specific sense that the means they employ are explicitly apolitical, regardless of the politicized nature of their effects (see also Bayat 2007). Indubitably, this space of post-political organization is crucial to civil society itself. The degree to which it is characteristic of NGOs broadly, both within Turkey and globally, is a question of provocative comparative potential.

NOTES

1 *İstanbul'da gezerken gözlerinizi açın. Hiç kimse durmaz, herkes tıkır tıkır bir yere gider. Ne yazik ki kamusal alan sadece bir geçiş yeridir, insanların evlerinden iş yerlerine gittikleri bir yer. Osmanlı döneminde hiç böyle değildi. O zamanlarda insanların yaşadıkları, hayatlarını sürdükleri bir yerdi kamusal alan. Yalnız bir*

geçiş değildi. Artık öyle değil ... tabii ki eski tarzını tercih ederiz, Müslümanlar olarak kamusal alan yaşamak isterdik ...

2 *Hanım* and *Bey* are common feminine and masculine honorifics in Turkish, similar to 'Miss' and 'Mister' in English. I use them throughout the chapter in reference to various informants.

3 The Gülen Community (or movement) is a vast network of charities, schools, businesses and media outlets that serves as the institutional bedrock for the theological, pedagogical and cultural projects of Fethullah Gülen, arguably the most important religious figure in Turkey today. I expand further on the Gülen Community below.

4 Since January 2007, *Zaman* has also been issued as a daily English language newspaper, both in print and online, and entitled *Today's Zaman*.

5 *Bakın, savaş yapmaktan başka Osmanlı devlet pek bir iş yürütmedi. Bütün insani ihtiyaçlar vakıflarca karşılandı. Ki hizmetler siyasetten ayrı tutuldu.*

6 Alevis are a minority religious community in Turkey, with practices and beliefs deriving both from Shi'a Islam and Central Asian shamanistic traditions. See Shankland 2003, Stokes 1996 and Erdemir 2005.

7 The Nur Community, like the Gülen Community, is a prominent modernist Sunni group in contemporary Turkey, organized in a nexus of civil society organizations and semi-formal reading circles (*dersler*). The inspiration and inheritance of Said Nursi (1877–1960) and his opus, the *Risale-i Nur*, is the prolonged work of *tafsir* (Turkish *tefsir*) or Qur'anic interpretation. See Yavuz 2003 and Vahide 2005.

8 For a detailed discussion of the role of positive action, or *müspet*, in the writings of Said Nursi, see Aladdin Basar (2007), 'A Lifelong Principle: Positive Action', on Nur webpages, <http://www.nur.org/index.php?WS=9&ItemID=169&Page=ItemPrint>.

9 '*Millet*' is one of the Turkish terms for 'nation', as in '*milletçilik*' (nationalism). In this context, however, it is better translated as 'community' or, perhaps, 'nation' or 'tribe' in the sense of a religiously, linguistically and ethnically defined collectivity.

10 The *Cem* is a definitive ritual practice of Alevism. There are a variety of different types of *Cem*, often coordinating a re-enactment of the Prophet Muhammad's ascent into heaven (Arabic *mi'raj*, Turkish *miraç*) and glorifying Ali, Muhammad's son-in-law and the first of the Shi'a imams. In general, a *Cem* features circumambulatory *semah* performances by both men and women, accompanied by bards (*ozanlar*) playing lutes such as the *bağlama* and *saz*. For more detailed descriptions of *Cems*, see Shankland (1993: 140) and Stokes (1996).

11 *Diyanet'le işimiz yok. Bizce Diyanet olmasın, oylece daha iyi olurdu. Cem Vakfi'yla aramızda en önemli fark budur, onlara göre devlet hem Sunnileri hem de Alevileri desteklesin, bizce ise ne Sunnileri ne de Alevileri desteklemesin. Bütün cemaatler, topluluklar kendi ihtiyaçlar baksın, karşılaşsın. İşte laikliğin gerçek anlamı budur zaten.*

12 Furthermore, I frequently encountered the chairman of the Ehl-i Beyt Foundation at functions organized by the Turkish Charitable Organizations Foundation (TGTV), where he was present as the sole Alevi 'representative' of the Turkish non-governmental sphere dedicated to pious charity. For instance, I ran into him unexpectedly at the yearly Ramadan fast-breaking meal (*iftar*) sponsored by the TGTV in both 2006 and 2007.

13 This approach owes allegiance to Talal Asad's (2003) crucial distinction between 'secularism' as a political doctrine and 'the secular' (or 'secularity') as an epistemological and ontological formation.

BIBLIOGRAPHY

Abrams, Philip, 'Notes on the Difficulty of Studying the State', in Aradhana Sharma and Akhil Gupta (eds), *The Anthropology of the State: A Reader* (Malden, MA: Blackwell Publishers, 2006).

Asad, Talal, *Formations of the Secular: Christianity, Islam, Modernity* (Stanford: Stanford University Press, 2003).

Bayat, Asef, *Making Islam Democratic: Social Movements and the Post-Islamist Turn* (Stanford: Stanford University Press, 2007).

Basar, Aladdin, 'A Lifelong Principle: Positive Action', on Nur webpages (2007), <http://www.nur.org/index.php?WS=9&ItemID=169&Page=ItemPrint>.

Berkes, Niyazi, *The Development of Secularism in Turkey* (Montreal: McGill University Press, 1964).

Chatterjee, Partha, 'Secularism and Tolerance', in Rajeev Bhargava (ed.), *Secularism and Its Critics* (Dehli: OUP, 1998), pp. 345–379.

Çınar, Alev, *Modernity, Islam, and Secularism in Turkey: Bodies, Places, and Time* (Minneapolis and London: University of Minnesota Press, 2005).

Davison, Andrew, *Secularism and Revivalism in Turkey: A Hermeneutic Reconsideration* (New Haven: Yale University Press, 1998).

Erdemir, Aykan, 'Tradition and Modernity in Turkey: Alevis' Ambiguous Terms and Turkey's Ambivalent Subjects', in *Middle Eastern Studies,* Vol. 41, No. 6: November 2005, pp. 937–951.

Göle, Nilüfer, *Forbidden Modern* (Ann Arbor: University of Michigan Press, 1996).

Gündem, Mehmet (ed.), *İslam ve Laiklık* (İstanbul: Gazeteciler ve Yazarlar Vakfı Yayınları, 1998), p. 7. My own translation.

Habermas, Jurgen, *The Structural Formation of the Public Sphere,* tr. Thomas Berger (Cambridge, MA: MIT, 1991).

Hart, Kimberly, 'Images and Aftermaths: The Use and Contextualization of Atatürk Imagery in Political Debates in Turkey', in *Political Anthropology* 22 (I) (1999), pp. 66–84.

Heper, Metin (ed.), *Strong State and Economic Interest Groups: The Post-1980 Turkish Experience* (Berlin and New York: Walter de Gruyter, 1991).

Heper, Metin and Landau, Jacob (eds), *Political Parties and Democracy in Turkey* (London and New York: I.B. Tauris and Co., 1991).

Huntington, Samuel, 'The Clash of Civilizations?', in *Foreign Affairs,* Vol. 72, No. 3 (Summer 1993), pp. 22–49.

Kaplan, Sam, *The Pedagogical State: Education and the Politics of National Culture in Post-1980 Turkey* (Stanford: Stanford University Press, 2006).

Keyder, Çağlar, 'The Housing Market from Informal to Global', in Çağlar Keyder (ed.), *Istanbul: Between the Global and the Local* (Lanham: Roman & Littlefield Publishers, 1999).

Keyman, Emin Fuat (ed.), *Remaking Turkey: Globalization, Alternative Modernities and Democracy* (Plymouth: Lexington Books, 2007).

Le Bon, Gustave, *The Crowd: A Study of the Popular Mind* (Kitchener: Batoche Books, 1896; 2001).
Lewis, Bernard, *The Emergence of Modern Turkey* (London, Oxford and New York: OUP, 1961).
Mango, Andrew, *Atatürk* (New York: Overlook Press, 2002).
Mardin, Şerif, *Religion and Social Change in Modern Turkey: The Case of Bediuzzaman Said Nursi* (Albany: SUNY Press, 1989).
Meeker, Michael, *A Nation of Empire: The Ottoman Legacy of Turkish Modernity* (Berkeley, LA and London: University of California Press, 2002).
Navaro-Yashin, Yael, *Faces of the State: Secularism and Public Life in Turkey* (Princeton: Princeton University Press, 2002).
—'The Market for Identities: Secularism, Islamism, Commodities', in Deniz Kandiyoti and Ayşe Saktanber (eds), *Fragments of Culture: The Everyday of Modern Turkey* (New Brunswick: Rutgers University Press, 2002b), pp. 221–253.
Öncü, Ayşe, 'The Myth of the "Ideal Home" Travels across Cultural Borders to Istanbul', in Ayşe Öncü and Petra Weyland (eds), *Space, Culture and Power: New Identities in Globalizing Cities* (London and New Jersey: Zed Books, 1997), pp. 56–72.
Öniş, Ziya, 'Turgut Özal and His Economic Legacy: Turkish Neoliberalism in Critical Perspective', in *Journal of Middle Eastern Studies* 40 (4) (July 2004).
Özyürek, Esra, *Nostalgia for the Modern: State Secularism and Everyday Politics in Turkey* (Durham and London: Duke University Press, 2006).
Shankland, David, *Alevi and Sunni in Rural Turkey: Diverse Paths of Change* (Dissertation thesis, Cambridge, UK: Cambridge University, Darwin College, 1993).
—*Islam and Society in Turkey* (Huntingdon: Eothen, 1999).
—*The Alevis in Turkey: The Emergence of a Secular Islamic Tradition* (London and New York: Routledge and Curzon, 2003).
Soydemir, Ç. Begum, 'İslami Burjuvazi Nerelere Gidiyor?', in *Istanbul Life,* October 2003, pp. 26–30.
Stokes, Martin, *The Arabesk Debate: Music and Musicians in Modern Turkey* (Oxford: Clarendon Press; New York: OUP, 1992).
—'Ritual, Identity and the State: An Alevi (Shi'a) Cem Ceremony', in Kirsten Schulze, Martin Stokes, and Colm Campbell (eds), *Nationalism, Minorities and Diasporas: Identities and Rights in the Middle East* (London and New York: Tauris Academic Studies, 1996).
—'Sounding Out: The Culture Industries and the Globalization of Istanbul', in Çağlar Keyder (ed.), *Istanbul: Between the Global and the Local* (Lanham: Roman & Littlefield Publishers, 1999).
Turam, Berna, *Between Islam and the State: The Politics of Engagement* (Stanford: Stanford University Press, 2007).
Union of NGOs of the Islamic World, Handbook 2006.
Vahide, Şükran, *Islam in Modern Turkey: An Intellectual Biography of Bediuzzaman Said Nursi*. Edited and with an Introduction by Ibrahim M. Abu-Rabi (Albany: SUNY Press, 2005).

Weber, Max, *The Protestant Ethic and the Spirit of Capitalism,* tr. Talcott Parsons (New York: Charles Scribner's Sons, 1958).
White, Jenny, 'Islamic Chic', in Çağlar Keyder (ed.), *Istanbul: Between the Global and the Local* (Lanham: Roman & Littlefield Publishers, 1999).
—*Islamist Mobilization in Turkey: A Study in Vernacular Politics* (Seattle: University of Washington Press, 2002).
Yavuz, Hakan, *Islamic Political Identity in Turkey* (Oxford and New York: OUP, 2003).
Yavuz, Hakan and Esposito, John (eds), *Turkish Islam and the Secular State: The Gülen Movement* (New York: Syracuse University Press, 2003).
Yılmaz, Ihsan, *Muslim Laws, Politics and Society in Modern Nation States: Dynamic Legal Pluralisms in England, Turkey and Pakistan* (Aldershot, UK and Burlington, VT: Ashgate, 2005).

Muslim Society in the West

10

Indigenous and Immigrant Faces of Islam in Poland

Katarzyna Górak-Sosnowska

Discussions about Islam and Muslims in the West usually limit the geographical scope to Western Europe and the United States (see e.g., Kepel 1997; Hunter 2002; Nielsen 2005; Pędziwiatr 2005). Some of the authors focus their attention on these regions intentionally and point to it accordingly in the title, while others tend to overlook the fact that Europe can be politically understood far beyond the Oder River and up to the Ural Mountains. The few broader-reaching studies on Muslims in Europe that include the southeastern and eastern parts of the continent (e.g., Nonneman *et al.* 1997, Parzymies 2005) often have editors or co-editors originating from that area. Certainly there are good reasons to perceive Islam and Muslims in the West through the lens of West European reality, with the relatively recent history of immigration, similar concerns and positioning in social structures of the host societies, as well as big numbers of Muslim inhabitants. An additional, rather pragmatic point, is the lack of relevant literature on Muslims in Eastern Europe, with limited sources available in local libraries, either in Germanic or Romance languages. Still, this way a significant part of the European adventure with Islam is missed out. One such story, barely told, is the one of Muslim communities in Poland.

Statistically speaking, Poland is one of the dozen European countries in which Muslims comprise less than 1 per cent of the population.[1] The number of Muslims varies between 25,000–45,000, in a country of 38 million people. There are hardly any mosques (just three in the whole country, two of them being small buildings in villages in eastern Poland, Bohoniki and Kruszyniany) or an Islamic infrastructure, and hardly any veiled women or Muslim children in the schools. On the other hand, Poland has a very long tradition of encounters with the Islamic world.

The first description of Poland originates from a Hispano–Arabic traveller called Ibrahim Ibn Yacoub, around 960 AD – around the time Poland's first historical ruler, Duke Mieszko I, was baptized (966 AD), which signified the state's adoption of Christianity. Muslim settlements on Polish land began four centuries later and was related to the Mongol invasion. Their descendants, the Tatars, still inhabit eastern Poland. The late twentieth century brought another category of Muslims to Poland – immigrants – who, even though far less numerous than in most Western countries, easily outnumbered the Tatars.

Despite the common denominator – Islam – both social categories do not share much in common, and even their religiousness and religious practices differ. What is more, they have to negotiate their roles, influences and positions within the Muslim minority. Tatars have been dominating historically, the newcomers quantitatively. Both have to act in a homogeneous Polish society, of which 97 per cent declare to be of Polish (ethnic) nationality and 90–95 per cent adhere to the Catholic religion. All these factors make the Polish Muslim community very complex and diverse and worth investigating.

Tatars: The Indigenous Face

Tatars have been present in Poland for over 600 years, since the time of Mongol invasions which reached as far as Eastern Europe. Most of them came to the Great Duchy of Lithuania from the Golden Horde and Crimea.

During these few centuries of Tatar presence in Poland they became integrated fully into mainstream society and in some respects even assimilated. First, they changed their way of living, from the traditional nomadic to the settled way of life. This was facilitated by land endowments granted by the Grand Duke Vytautas in return for military duty, which was for a long time the basic occupation of the Polish Tatars. Their separate units within the army supported Polish rulers in many crucial battles, from the Battle of Grunwald (1410 AD) to the Second World War (Dziekan 2003: 203–204). Throughout that time, the Tatars were loyal to the Commonwealth and never revealed any desires to establish a separate country. The only exception was the time of Ottoman invasion, which posed a great challenge for Tatar soldiers. They had to choose between fighting against other Muslims or fellow Poles. Some of them called Lipka joined the Turks, revolting against their maltreatment at the hands of the Poles, fuelled by the Catholic Church. But apart from this, Polish–Tatar and Christian–Tatar relations have been peaceful.

The change of lifestyle was followed by linguistic assimilation; thus the Tatars forgot their mother tongues in the eighteenth century and started to use Polish (or the Polish–Belarusian dialect). This assimilation progressed quickly. The Tatars, despite their common name, never constituted a homogeneous ethnic group, as they came from Turkish, Mongolian, as well as Tungusian peoples, and thus did not share a common language or culture. Polish thus was not only a key to get in touch with Polish society, but also to some extent a tool with which to communicate with each other. Moreover, they became involved in mixed marriages, and added the Slavic sufix *–icz* (e.g., Józefowicz from Yusuf, or Abrahamowicz from Ibrahim, etc.) to their family names (Dziekan 2000: 41). An interesting and unique exception to this rule is the religious literature of Tatars (*khamail*), which was written in Polish, but with the Arabic alphabet adjusted to Slavic languages (including Polish ą, ę, ś, ć, dź, dż, ź and ż). In order to read a *khamail* one had to know not only Polish and Arabic script, but also the 'coding'. This might be explained by the notion of *ijaz al-Quran* (the inimitability of the Qur'an). Writing religious scriptures with Arabic letters (even in the Polish language) was a way of showing respect to the Arab script and strengthened its religious character (Dziekan 2002: 185–191).

Interestingly, the admiration for the Arabic language took another form in the times of socialism, as any contact with the Middle East was limited due to political reasons. Some of the Tatars used to collect labels in Arabic cut from imported products. Sometimes they were used as religious ornaments – as it was not easy to get oneself a *muhir*.[2] Now and again these *muhirs* were hung upside down, which indicates both a lack of any knowledge of written Arabic and at the same time a deep admiration for it (Górak-Sosnowska and Łyszczarz 2009). In fact, the Arabic language is used for *salat* only, and, if so – often with a peculiar Slavic pronunciation.

Assimilation with the mainstream society and very limited – if any – contact with 'oriental' Islam is reflected in Tatar religious practice. *Salat* is performed mostly during the Friday afternoon prayer, as it would be hardly possible in a non-Muslim society to perform five prayers daily. This is also the reason for selective fasting during *Ramazan*[3] – by abstaining from consuming coffee, alcohol or cigarettes, and having a healthier lifestyle. *Zakat* is not institutionalized; there is, however, *sadoga* – facultative alms distributed during *Kurban Bajram* (*'Id al-Adha* in Arabic). *Hajj* is a privilege of a few – due to the financial burden (Łyszczar and Marek 2007: 632–634). Most of Tatar religious practice is limited to the private sphere. Only the most important religious holidays (such as Kurban Bajram, Ramazan Bajram and practices related to the life cycle) are celebrated in public by the community.

In some cases the assimilation process went even further, as often against the Sunni notion of Islam (to which Tatars adhere),[4] Tatar rituals overlap with local and Christian traditions. Polish Tatars celebrate Christmas and Easter, as well as All Saints' Day; following their Christian neighbours, they prefer to get married in mosques, but they perform various Christian wedding rites (e.g., showering the newlyweds with grains; Kamocki 2000: 140; Dziekan 1999: 11). There are wreaths in Tatar funeral ceremonies and women are allowed to participate in the procession. Tatar gravestones might be distinguished from the Christian ones only by the symbol of the crescent and *basmala* or *shahada* inscriptions (Drozd 2003: 49–50). Furthermore, one may find portraits of the deceased, which clearly contradicts the Muslim iconoclasm.

For many centuries the Tatars did not have any religious organization. The Muslim Religious Union (Muzułmański Związek Religijny, named hereafter as MZR) was only founded in 1925. After over a decade, Islam became an officially recognized religion by the state of Poland, which ranks this country among the European pioneers in this regard. The legal basis for this recognition is the Law of 21 April 1936 with regard to the relation of the State to the Muslim Religious Union in Poland. The law regulates, among others things, ways of appointing a mufti, the Highest Muslim Council and imams, representing members of the MZR before the state and local authorities, as well as Polish Muslims – in case of international relations. MZR was clearly Tatar-oriented, especially as one has to have Polish citizenship or a Permanent Resident Card in order to become a MZR member. The head of the MZR and mufti of Poland is Tomasz Ali Miśkiewicz – a Tatar who received his religious education in Saudi Arabia. There are eight regional communities – two in the only Tatar villages (Bohoniki and Kruszyniany) and the rest in the biggest Polish cities with a significant Tatar population (Białystok,

Bydgoszcz, Gdańsk, Gorzów Wielkopolski, Poznań and Warsaw). MZR has rougly 5,000 members – the entire Tatar population.

Nowadays the number of Tatars in Poland is estimated at between 3,000–5,000. They are fully integrated into Polish society, with religion (and to some extent appearance) being the sole difference. Even though they are often considered as an ethnic rather than a religious community, it was religion that kept them from complete assimilation. Until recently they were the only Muslims in Poland. Being Muslim in Poland meant that one was Tatar, while these two categories, religious – Muslim and ethnic – Tatar, were used interchangeably.[5] The influx of immigrant Muslims brought for the Tatars two challenges: maintaining their dominant role in the Polish Muslim community and redefining their religion.

Others: The Immigrant Face

The last decade brought considerable changes to the ethnic and social structure of the Muslim population in Poland. Starting from the early 1970s, students from socialist Arab countries (Algeria, Egypt, Iraq, Libya and Syria) came to Polish universities in pursuit of education. This was enabled by cooperation agreements between Poland and other socialist countries. At the same time, the Polish skilled labour force (engineers, doctors, etc.) went to these countries to work. Many of the Arab students decided to stay in Poland after graduating. Currently this first generation of Arab immigrants, often Polish citizens, belong to middle- or even upper-middle-class families. Several factors made it possible, including the provision of an obligatory, intensive Polish language course that all foreign students had to get through before they could start studying. This way they were able to study and get a good education (Masters degrees, sometimes more). As the majority of immigrants were male, many married Polish wives – and put down roots in Polish culture even more. They had no other choice but to socialize with Polish people, as there was simply no one else around. All this made the first generation socially and to a great extent culturally integrated into mainstream society.

The early 1990s and the collapse of the Soviet bloc, followed by economic and political transformation, introduced to Poland new Muslim migration, which additionally increased after it joined the EU. Some of these new immigrants (mostly Turks, Arabs and Bosnians) decided to try their luck in the emerging Polish capitalist economy (Nalborczyk 2003: 229). Some of them were really successful, but most – especially the newcomers – made their living working in small shops or kebab bars as hired labour. They often could not find another job either due to lack of proper education or the language barrier. An interesting new category are matrimonial immigrants – men from tourist resorts, mostly in Tunisia and Egypt, who met their Polish girlfriends during their holidays (Kubicki and Mansour-Ismail 2007). Many of their relationships did not survive the test of time, but still the immigrants managed to get to Europe. There are also refugees, mostly from Chechnya[6] – their number (estimated at 5,000)[7] is fluctuating, as they try to get beyond the western border.

The immigrant Muslim population is not homogeneous. It consists of various national groups of a few hundred people, predominantly males. According to the 2002 census, most immigrants with residence permits come from the Middle East (Algeria, Iraq, Libya, Syria and Turkey), Central Asia (Azerbaijan, Uzbekistan) and Nigeria (GUS 2003: 330–333). In big agglomerations they usually know each other and keep in touch at least with some, but in smaller cities and villages it is hardly possible. Moreover, a generational divide exists, as the new immigrants acquire their language skills in an informal way, by working or picking up some words from their Polish wives or girlfriends. Lack of language skills translates into limited work opportunities, as only the highest-skilled professionals in TNCs can enjoy the privilege of not knowing Polish and working in Poland. The same applies to low-skill jobs, which new immigrants often perform. Immigrants differ also in terms of their religion – not only their denomination, but also their religiousness. Similar to other European states, it was not the first Muslim immigrants who cared about the religious infrastructure. The 'oriental' type of Islam that challenges the legacy of the traditional Tatar is a very recent phenomenon (Kubicki 2007).

Since the estimated number of Muslims in Poland ranges between 25,000–45,000, of which Tatars and refugees constitute around 5,000 respectively, around 15,000–35,000 Muslims in Poland are immigrants.[8]

The first immigrant Muslim organizations were established in the early Nineties – the Association of Muslim Students (Stowarzyszenie Studentów Muzułmańskich, founded in 1989) and the Muslim Association of Cultural Upbringing (Muzułmańskie Stowarzyszenie Kształtowania

Kulturalnego, founded in 1990). Both organizations had rather limited representation and aimed both at promotion of Islam in Polish society as well as at cultivation of its tradition and dogmas (Dziekan 2003: 225). They did not interfere with the Tatar MZR, nor did they challenge its legacy, as they were legally not religious unions but associations. It was in 2004 that the first significant immigrant Muslim religious union was officially registered – the Muslim League in Poland (Liga Muzułmańska w RP, named hereafter as LM).[9] It was clear that LM was established in order to represent the interests of immigrants – as one could become a member even if one had a temporary resident permit. Moreover, the Tatar-dominated MZR seemed to be too far in cultural terms. The statute of LM comprises many similar points to that of MZR, such as: building mosques, running a parish register, promotion of knowledge about the religion and culture of Islam, as well as observing Muslim rites (Górak-Sosnowska 2009). LM has 120 members, but the number of its supporters is much bigger and estimated at several thousand (Kubicki 2006). It has eight national branches (Lower-Silesia, Lublin, Łódź, Małopolska, Mazovia, Podlasie, Silesia and Great Poland). The head of the union is Samir Isma'il. Since 2008 LM also has a mufti – Nidal Abu Tabaq.

The Social Context

Despite the long tradition of Muslim settlement in Poland and their place in Polish history and tradition, quantitatively their presence is very limited.[10] Most Poles have never had a chance to meet a Muslim in person, as there are hardly any Muslim neighbours, students or co-workers. Therefore, many Poles learn about Islam and Muslims indirectly from the mass media. The image of Islam provided by world media has been a subject of wide-ranging criticism and discussion, regardless of the country or region they are covering (Hafez 2002; Said 1997; Marek and Nalborczyk 2005). In the case of Polish Muslims, the image of their religion is built almost solely on information from external sources, reporting news and cases that they themselves have nothing to do with. Unlike many other EU states, Poland has not (yet?) experienced any problems related to the socio-economic integration of Muslims: there are no Muslim ghettos, most Polish Muslims speak Polish and are well educated, and the Islamic identity is hardly visible in the public sphere. There is no 'Islamic challenge' – neither economically, nor socially or culturally. It is not the peculiar case of Muslim, but the general case of any ethnic, national or religious minority, as Poland is not, and will not soon become, the destination country for immigration – compared to older EU member states.

But lack of challenges, and even actual lack of Muslims, does not translate into positive attitudes towards them. According to a CBOS (research agency) survey from 2007, every one in two Poles would be against having his daughter or son marry a Muslim, but the other 45 per cent would not mind. In the case of Jews, 47 per cent would be against the idea of their offspring marrying a Jew, 38 per cent against marriage to an atheist or someone of the Orthodox faith, and 31 per cent against marriage with an Evangelical (CBOS 2007: 5). This relatively unfavourable attitude towards Muslims (and Jews) also illustrates the results of a Pew Research Centre survey done two years earlier. Every third Pole (30 per cent) declared a negative attitude towards Muslims – not dissimilar to France or Spain (34 per cent and 37 per cent respectively), and less than in Germany or the Netherlands (47 per cent and 51 per cent), but far more than in the UK (14 per cent). Less than every second Pole expresses a positive attitude towards Muslims (46 per cent) – similar to the Dutch, Spanish and Germans, but less than the French (64 per cent) and the British (72 per cent). Moreover, compared to other EU states, the Polish have the least positive (54 per cent) and most negative (27 per cent) attitude towards Jewish people (PRC 2005: 4). One can therefore attribute the negative attitude towards Muslims to two factors: a negative stereotype of Muslims, and greater social distance towards non-Christian religions.[11]

Of Muslim nations, it is the Arabs who usually 'represent' this religious category in most sociological research. It might be a result of the so-called 'Arabization of Islam' – combining Muslim and Arab. That leads not only to a belief that all Arabs are Muslim, but also to a tendency to perceive events, customs and beliefs in Arab countries as typical of the whole Islamic world (Górak-Sosnowska 2007: 150). Probably a German citizen, if asked about Muslims, would mention Turks, and Frenchmen – a Maghrebian, as both communities are present in the society and public discourse. The Tatar community in Poland is too small and insignificant, and so is the Polish Muslim community in general. At the same time, most news and information about Muslims refers to international politics. That is why Polish public opinion tends to Arabize, and not, for example, 'Tatarize' Islam – even though the latter would be probably far more positive for the whole Muslim community.

According to a TNS OBOP (research agency) survey, a typical Arab is perceived as religious, but also lazy and a terrorist (TNS OBOP 2008). Since 2002, as CBOS has included Arabs in its annual survey on attitudes towards nations, Arabs have been ranked in the last and second-last position (alternately with Roma) on the favourability scale. In December 2008 Arabs were liked by 21 per cent of Poles and disliked by 49 per cent. Compared to previous years, their standing has improved in absolute terms (e.g., in 2005 it was 6 per cent and 70 per cent respectively). However, as they still occupy the last position, one can assume the improvement has more to do with Polish people becoming more tolerant towards other nations (including Arabs; CBOS 2008). Since 2005 there are other Muslim representatives in the research – Turks, who scored slightly more positive answers (+7 points on favourability and -12 on unfavourability in 2008) – similarly to other non-European nations included in the research. The difference might be explained by the Arabization of Islam, rather than any peculiar feature of Turks living in Poland which could significantly influence their score.

Taking into account both factors – no problems related to the Muslim presence in Poland, and information flows built from external sources rather than personal experience – one might call the strong negative attitude towards Muslims 'platonic Islamophobia'[12] – meaning feelings of anxiety towards non-existent Muslims (or Arabs). One can suspect that, paradoxically, the Tatars are excluded from this 'phobia', even though they are also Muslim, as they are perceived rather as an ethnic group and a part of Polish traditional folklore. This division is just another block in the dispute about Polish Islam.

The Clash of 'Islams'

Despite the fact that international events and Muslims in Europe occupy most of the media coverage, there are also articles and news items on Polish Muslims occasionally. In such cases, these two categories are juxtaposed by presenting the 'good old Polish' Muslims (meaning the Tatars and the MZR) and the 'bad, dangerous, alien' Muslim immigrants (and the Muslim League).[13] The tension diffused even to academic discourse – as one of the authors describes Polish Muslims in the following way (Sobczak 2004: 208–209):

> theres a hidden fight between Muslims originating from the Polish or Lithuanian Tatar environment, usually quite strongly laicized and a group of neophytes and Muslims settled in Poland in recent years, zealously religious and remaining under the strong influence of Arab 'missioners'.

Laicization – or rather assimilation – of Polish Tatars can be a fact, provided one does not forget about the first generation of Muslim immigrants and a number of new immigrants, who are also not religious. Adding that the mufti of MZR did his religious studies in Saudi Arabia blurs the black-and-white picture presented above even more.

Polish Muslims, even though not numerous, belong to a social category that is very hard to investigate – due to its diversity. Studies on Tatars fit into ethnology or sociology; in order to carry out research on the converts one has to have a background in theology; for refugees – social studies would be needed; and for other immigrants – knowledge of their languages, or at least the countries they are originally from. The only field that is relatively well researched and documented is Tatar history and tradition. However, even studies on contemporary Tatars, especially on their life, rather than folklore, hardly exist; the case of other Muslims in Poland is even worse. This is partly due to their reluctance to take part in research (probably due to distrust, but also due to the multitude of BA and MA theses on Islam whose authors try to win the same dozen or so Muslim respondents), but also to an interdisciplinary approach that such research would need. Moreover, as the number of Muslims in Poland is small, they also fall outside most national reports, e.g., on national minorities, or immigrants (as these categories are dominated by people originating from Poland's neighbouring countries).

Bearing in mind all the shades of grey, one can still point to a clash of 'Islams' between the Tatars and the newcomers. It is visible on the Tatar side, as they used to be the sole representatives of Muslims in Poland. Now their legacy is challenged twofold – by Muslim immigrants and by the image of Islam worldwide. The clash of traditions is illustrated by the quotations of Tatar respondents in research on attitudes to Muslim consumer culture (Górak-Sosnowska and Łyszczarz 2009).

Many respondents felt a need to relate their own tradition to Arab culture and show their incompatibility, despite a common religion. One way to do this is to differentiate between religion and culture:

> For me, religion is tradition and inner experience. Arabs have a completely different attitude. For them, religion is their whole life, regardless of what they're doing at the moment. For me this is zealotry.
>
> For me, Islam and not Arab culture is important. Arab culture had an impact on Islam, that is clear. But Arabs themselves can't differentiate between their own culture and the tradition of the Prophet Muhammad. What is important is what Muhammad did, not that he was an Arab.

Differences between Tatar and 'immigrant' practice related even to the very basics such as the concept of halal food or the hijab. As Muslims, the Tatars do not eat pork, and this is all they understand by *haram* in terms of food. Ritual slaughtering is practised occasionally during religious holidays. Details and regulations related to pork-related ingredients in food, or extending ritual slaughtering to any meat consumed, was unknown to them, before the newcomers arrived:

> I don't eat halal as we don't have any. Religion prohibits eating pork and carrion and I abide by that … In fact we never had any halal, even this word is rather new. Arabs came in the early nineties and then people started to talk about it.
>
> More than once I've heard from different people coming here that eating non-halal food is a sin. I kept answering that we have been living here for 600 years and survived without halal, and still are Muslim. Besides, the Arabs who started families here and live here for a dozen years or so start to see it themselves. The old eagerness goes, and they notice that in the long run life here is completely different to that in Arab countries or in the West, where many Muslims are.

Interestingly, the latter respondent points to the fact that it is the Tatars who are right, as even some Arabs understand that this is the way to live in Poland as a Muslim. Tatars often tend to defend their way of life in two ways: by referring to the tradition (this is the way we have been living for centuries) and Polish reality (even if one would like to adhere to these principles, it is hardly possible in Poland). Similarly the hijab is treated as something that does not fit the Tatar daily life, as women use it occasionally for religious holidays.

> The case of the hijab is an interesting one. The older accept it, as it's a traditional element of religious life, they pray in the hijab in the mosque or in the cemetery. That it is often tied wrongly, so that it doesn't cover all the hair, is in this case a detail that Tatars overlook. Younger people have a different attitude. Most of them reject the hijab completely. For them the hijab is an example of the village bigotry of Sokółka Tatars, or Arab immigrant zeal.

Sometimes the negative feelings are expressed even more directly:

> I am not fond of Arab–Islamic culture, because I associate it with religion classes led by Arabs. That wasn't a nice experience, that's why I often didn't take part. Arabs imposed on us their interpretation of religion, they told us what is allowed and what's not. Instead of teaching us prayers, we crammed the Arabic alphabet, but we will never use it … The Arabs didn't understand at all that we live in Poland, that we're in the twenty-first century. They are from another world. I am Muslim, my ancestors were Muslim, but I keep away from Arabs, because they don't understand us.

This case reflects another important point of the clash. As most of the Tatars hardly know any Arabic, their access to religious sources (including the Qur'an) is very limited. Some of the Arab immigrants were keen on providing them with proper religious knowledge – often by organizing religious classes. For some Tatars, it provided a window for a better understanding of their religion, but many others reacted in a way presented above – as the experience did not fit their religious needs and tradition. There were also few positive opinions on Arabs, but still their culture was perceived as exotic:

> Sometimes I smoke one [shisha] with Arab friends. However, it happens rarely, because I don't have much free time. Smoking with Arabs is remarkable, they can sit and talk for several hours. I envy them, as it must be quite a stress reliever.

The quotations present just one side of the story, but one can easily imagine the other part of the 'clash' – religious immigrants from the Middle East encountering in Poland people, who in a way 'forgot' the religion in terms of now knowing Arabic,[14] and who have rather a 'skimpy' religious practice.

A Way Up to the Future?

As the Muslim community in Poland is very diverse, its situation is influenced predominantly by factors related to the legal and socio-economic status of its members rather than a common religion. Still, many problems that they face are similar to those encountered by Muslim communities in other EU states – or, more broadly speaking, ethnic or national or religious minorities in general. From the refugee point of view, one of the most important issues is the regulation of their legal status in Poland by obtaining refugee status – which is not an easy task. The first generation of Muslim immigrants, especially those from the Middle East, might have to cope with the negative image of Islam promoted by the media – however, no information regarding discrimination against them is provided so far. New immigrants will have to face the challenge of adaptation in legal and social structures of their host country. Their descendants – often from mixed marriages – will have to build their identity from all the cultural pieces.

Some of the issues are typically Polish though. One of them is the generation gap in the Tatar community. Tatars with proper religious knowledge are already advanced in age, while the next generation is less than thirty. Also, Tatar folklore is in danger of being lost, since the community is small and young people might not be so interested in cultivating their tradition. One has to remember that in the case of some of its elements one can rather speak of 'invented traditions', in the Hobsbawm sense. In fact, a lot of the effort which has been made by Tatars recently to promote and develop their tradition has to be perceived as a reaction to the growing immigrant presence.

Muslims in Poland will also have to face the challenge of platonic Islamophobia, especially as their presence becomes more visible. This issue is a concern primarily for immigrants, who try to show that 'Muslims who live in Poland are most often simply ordinary Poles rather than some "alien element" one should be afraid of'.[15] Social context should in fact bring both groups together in order to overcome this image. Only in June 2006, on the eightieth anniversary of the MZR, did both organizations declare themselves willing to collaborate.[16]

Until that point, hardly any signs of cooperation had been visible to the public.

As the issue of Muslims in the West emerged, fuelled by the 11th September attacks, the case of peaceful coexistence between Christians and Muslims (Tatars) in Poland that has been working for so many centuries seemed to be a promising solution one could use in other EU countries as a model. Regardless of the historical and quantitative differences, this reality from the early 2000s seems not to exist any more. Despite their efforts and the support of the Polish state, the Tatar culture is being eradicated so that is is more and more to be found in ethnological books than in real life. It is the immigrants that will most probably take the helm in the long term, despite the historical legacy of MZR. As the Muslim community in Poland is experiencing a transition period it is hard to predict the consequences and the end result. Still, despite being barely a few thousand people, it is very dynamic and diverse – providing a window for a new narrative that is usually untold in the whole discourse on Islam in the West.

NOTES

1 Others include the Czech Republic, Estonia, Finland, Hungary, Latvia, Lithuania, Malta, Portugal, Romania, Slovakia and Slovenia.

2 *Muhir* is a word of Turkish origin (*mühür* is a seal) meaning a framed fabric with Qur'anic inscriptions, a sort of Islamic devotional item.

3 Polish Tatars use turkized names of the rites, often with Slavic elements, e.g. ablution before *salat* is *gusiel* (read: *goushyel*), from the Arab *ghusl;* while the small ablution (Arabic *wudu*) is called *abdeś* (read: *abdesh*) from Turkish *aptes* (Dziekan 2003: 206).

4 Hanafi *madhab*, to be exact.

5 An anectode points to confusions that arose from treating these two categories as equal. In a conversation with a Polish scholar in Arabic studies, a Tatar mentioned that he met a Sudanese Tatar. The scholar was surprised, as there have not been any recordings of Tatar migration to this part of the world. Having asked for some details, he found that the Tatar in question was acually referring to a Muslim person from Sudan. It was the two categories (religious and ethnic) that were overlapping.

6 According to UNHCR data, refugees constituted over 90 per cent of applicants in 2005 – *Uchodźcy w Polsce 2005*, <http://www.unhcr.pl/aktualnosci.php?news=323&wid=618&current_section=statystyki>.

7 A. Siejka, *Uchodźcy odsyłani do Polski*, Refugee.pl, 16 June 2007, <http://www.refugee.pl/?mod=knowbase&path=1352&PHPSESSIE=60208acf0c8e84e40b919181a81d069>.

8 Another category, which does not fit either and is far less numerous, is converts. Most of them are the Polish wives of Muslim immigrants who decided to convert to Islam for the sake of bringing up their children in one religion or for other personal reasons. There are also a few artists, scientists and students of Arab and Islamic faculties who found in Islam their way of living.

9 Some authors suggest that it was incompatible with the law of 21 April 1936, regarding bilateral relations between the Polish State and the MZR, which clearly states that the sole representative of Muslims in Poland in their relations with the Polish state is the MZR (see e.g., Nalborczyk 2003: 230–231). On the other hand, it is not the only Muslim religious community registered by the state of Poland. Others include the Association of Islamic Unity (Stowarzyszenie Jedności Muzułmańskiej) – a Shi'a community; the Muslim Association of Ahmadiyya (Stowarzyszenie Muzułmańskie Ahmadiyya) – related to the Ahmadiyya movement; and the Islamic Assembly Ahl ul-Bayt (Islamskie Zgromadzenie Ahl ul-Bayt) – another Shi'a organization. Moreover, two other religious unions can be related to Islam by their name (the Western Sufi Order in Poland, Zachodni Zakon Sufi w Polsce) or tradition (the Religious Union of Baha'i Faith in Poland, Związek wyznaniowy Wiara Baha'i w Polsce). See *Kościoły i związki wyznaniowe wpisane do rejestru kościołów I innych związków wyznaniowych,* Ministry of Interior and Administration, <http://www/mswia.gov.pl/index_wai.php?dzial=92&id=223>.

10 One of the side-effects is the so-called 'Invented Orient' – emerging oriental-style cafés and bars offering *shishas,* or belly-dancing classes, which became very trendy among urban youth. The peculiarity of this sort of entertainment is that their main performers and consumers are Polish natives. These places are not designed for and by immigrants so that they feel 'like home', but to resemble an 'oriental place' for a Polish layman. Sometimes it might result in rather odd combinations – especially in smaller cities – such as oriental disco with religious calligraphy as flashing visualization, or a pub called Mecca. Not to be considered intentional, but rather as badly informed.

11 One should also stress the positive impact of Polish religiousness, as this dimension provides a tool for mutual understanding. Despite the marginal number of Muslims, there were several interfaith initiatives which resulted, among others things, in establishing, in 1997, a Common Council of Catholics and Muslims, and in setting 26 January as 'The Day of Islam' in the Catholic Church (Nalborczyk 2003: 237). Both initiatives began before 9/11, which proves that they were not a consequence of it.

12 This wording is derived from Jerrold Post, who used it first while analysing the revival of anti-Semitism in Eastern Europe. 'Platonic anti-Semitism' refers to anti-Semitism without Jews, just as platonic love means love without sex.

13 See for instance A. Pakulska, *Polskie dzieci Allaha,* Nowe Państwo 3 (357), March 2005 or D. Koźlenko, *Dokąd zmierza polski islam?,* Ozon, 16/05, 4 August 2005.

14 One of the Muslim Students Association's representatives claimed that Tatars forgot Arabic due to assimilation. In fact they never knew Arabic as their mother tongues belonged to a different language family, and anyway they were

never exposed to Arab Islam. See M. Łyszczarz, *Polscy Tatarzy, polscy muzułmanie,* ARABIA. pl, 26 May 2004, <http://www.arabia.pl/content/view/274040/55/>.

15 Iwona Alkhalayla – the former leader of LM – at a press conference announcing the 'Muslim Declaration', 15 September 2005.

16 During these celebrations the mufti of Poland, Tomasz Miśkiewicz, stated that one of the most important aims of MZR is to cooperate more closely with the other Muslim religious associations in Poland (the Muslim League) as well as with other Muslim organisations (see M. Kubicki, *Plany MZR-u na najbliższe lata*, <http:/www.arabia.pl/content/view/283747/2/>). At the same time, the Muslim League issued an official congratulatory letter to the MZR in which common goals and activities were emphasized (see *List do uczestników obchodów 80-lecia Muzułmańskiego Związku Religijnego*, <http://www.islam.info.pl/images/stories/islaminfo/list_do_mzr.pdf>).

BIBLIOGRAPHY

CBOS, *Stosunek do innych narodów*, BS/193/2008 (Warsaw, 2008).

CBOS, *Przejawy dystansu społecznego wobec innych narodów i religii*, BS/3/2007 (Warsaw, 2007).

Drozd, A., *Współczesne oblicze kultury Tatarów Rzeczypospolitej*, in A. Abbas (ed.), *Zagadnienia współczesnego islamu* (Poznań: Uniwersytet im. Adama Mickiewicza, 2003).

Dziekan, M., 'Religia Tatarów polsko-litewskich', in A. Drozd, M. Dziekan and T. Majda, *Meczety i cmentarze Tatarów polsko-litewskich* (Warsaw: Res Publica Multiétnica, 1999).

—*Tatarzy – polscy muzułmanie*, 'Jednota', No. 8–9 (2000).

—'Einige Bemerkungen über die islamische Literatur der polnisch-litauischen Tataren', in S. Leder (ed.), *Studies in Arabic and Islam: Proceedings of the 19th Congress, Union Europeennee der Arabisants et Islamisants, Halle 1998* (Paris, 2002).

'*Historia i tradycje polskiego islam*', in A. Parzymies (ed.), *Muzułmanie w Europie* (Warsaw: Wydawnictwo Akademickie Dialog, 2003).

Górak-Sosnowska, K., 'Wizerunek islamu i muzułmanów w Polsce w świetle badań socjologicznych', in M. Malinowski and R. Ożarowski (eds), *Współczesne problemy świata* islamu (Gdańsk: Wydawnictwo Uniwersytetu Gdańskiego, 2007).

Górak-Sosnowska, K., 'Organizacje muzułmańskie w Polsce', in E. Firlit (ed.), *Instytucje religijne i religijność w Europie* (Warsaw: Szkoła Główna Handlowa, 2009).

Górak-Sosnowska, K. and Łyszczarz, M., '(Un)Islamic Consumers: The Case of Polish Tatars', in J. Pink (ed.), *Muslim Societies in the Age of Mass Consumption* (Cambridge: Cambridge Scholars Publishing, 2009).

GUS, *Migracje zarobkowe ludności 2002* (Warsaw, 2003).

Hafez, K., *Die politische Dimension der Auslandsberichterstattung. Das Nahost- und Islambild der deutschen überregionalen Presse* (Baden-Baden: Nomos Verlagsgesellschaft, 2002).

Hunter, S., *Islam, Europe's Second Religion: The New Social, Cultural, and Political Landscape,* (Westport: Center for Strategic and International Studies, 2002).

Kepel, G., *Allah in the West: Islamic Movements in America and Europe* (Stanford: Stanford University Press, 1997).

Kamocki, J., 'Zderzenie obyczajów i zwyczajów muzułmańskich Tatarów ze zwyczajami ludowymi chrześcijańskiej ludności polskiej', in *Orient w kulturze polskiej. Materiały z sesji jubileuszowej z okazji 25-lecia Muzeum Azji i Pacyfiku w Warszawie. 15–16 October 1998* (Warsaw: Wydawnictwo Akademickie Dialog, 2000).

Kubicki, M., *Nieoczekiwana zamiana miejsc. Polscy muzułmanie w cieniu islamu wahabickiego*, Tygodnik Powszechny', No. 41, 8 October 2006.

Kubicki, P., 'Muzułmanie w Polsce', in K. Górak-Sosnowska, K. Pędziwiatr and P. Kubicki (eds), *Islam i obywatelskość w Europie* (Warsaw: Elipsa, 2007).

Kubicki, P. and Mansour-Ismail, K., *Arabowie i muzułmanie żyjący w związkach mieszanych z Polkami – szansy i bariery dla integracji społecznej,* paper presented on XIII Ogólnopolski Zjazd Socjologiczny in Zielona Góra, 13–15 September 2007.

Marek A. and Nalborczyk, A., *Nie bój się islamu. Leksykon dla dziennikarzy* (Warsaw: Więź, 2005).

Nalborczyk, A., 'Status prawny muzułmanów w Polsce i jego wpływ na organizację ich życia religijnego', in A. Parzymies (ed.), *Muzułmanie w Europie* (Warsaw: Wydawnictwo Akademickie Dialog, 2003).

Nielsen, J., *Muslims in Western Europe* (Edinburgh: Edinburgh University Press, 2005).

Nonneman, G., Niblock, T. and Szajkowski, B., *Muslim Communities in the New Europe* (London: Ithaca Press, 1997).

Pędziwiatr, K., *Od islamu imigrantów do islamu obywateli. Muzułmanie w krajach Europy Zachodniej* (Cracow: Nomos, 2005).

Pew Research Center, *Islamic Extremism: Common Concern for Muslim and Western Publics: 17-Nation Pew Global Attitudes Survey* (2005).

Said, E., *Covering Islam: How the Media and the Experts Determine How We See the Rest of the World* (London: Vintage Books).

Sobczak, J., 'Położenie prawne polskich wyznawców islamu', in R. Bäcker and S. Kitab (eds), *Islam a świat* (Toruń: Mado, 2004).

TNS OBOP, *Postawy Polaków wobec imigrantów i pomocy udzielanej imigrantom* (Warsaw, 2008).

11

Muslim Converts and Islamophobia in Britain[1]

Leon Moosavi

The most potent weapon in the hands of the oppressor
is the mind of the oppressed.
Steve Biko

Introduction

Tahir Abbas, the founding director of Birmingham University's Centre for the Study of Ethnicity and Culture, has written: 'Since the genesis of Islam, awareness of Muslims in Europe has been negatively tinged' (Abbas 2005: 11). This perfectly summarizes the notion that Islamophobia is a remarkably old prejudice deep-seated in the European psyche. However, it took The Runnymede Trust's release of a groundbreaking report entitled *Islamophobia: A Challenge for Us All* (1997) for the idea that there is a specific prejudice that circulates in Britain about Islam and Muslims to become widely accepted. Since then, Islamophobia has been condemned in all spheres of society, and several interest groups who seek to monitor Islamophobia in Britain and beyond have been established, including The Islamic Human Rights Commission (IHRC), The Forum against Islamophobia and Racism (FAIR), Islamophobia-Watch.com, and, more recently, The Association for European Muslim Rights. Additionally, mainstream campaigns such as Let's Kick Racism out of Football (also known as Kick It Out) have focused on combating Islamophobia in football with prominent Muslim Premiership footballers like Mido and Nicolas Anelka. A once-unrecognized prejudice has been identified and branded unacceptable in mainstream society.

In academia, commentators have debated what Islamophobia is, where it comes from and why it exists. However, this body of literature is still surprisingly under-theorized. It has been argued by Chris Allen

(2007) – and rightly so, in my opinion – that the definition and explanation of Islamophobia provided by The Runnymede Trust in 1997 has been over-relied upon by most academics, who have failed to critically engage in exploring the complexities of Islamophobia. For instance, at a basic level, even though the concept of 'Islamophobia' has several shortcomings, it has rarely been critiqued. There are even fewer accounts that convey the way in which Islamophobia impacts on the everyday lives of Muslims or that acknowledge the different forms that Islamophobia can take in different circumstances. In particular, the encounters that Muslim converts have with Islamophobia have barely been touched upon. Therefore, in this chapter – in order to rectify some of these significant gaps – I will examine some of the Muslim converts' perceptions and experiences of Islamophobia. This will lead me to rethink some key theoretical issues relating to Islamophobia. By the end of the chapter, I hope that I will have offered some original and useful insights into the way in which Islamophobia operates.

'I feel more of a target now'

It is overwhelmingly considered to be the case in the literature about Islamophobia that this form of prejudice is one of the most virulent in British society (Abu Sway 2005; Kundnani 2007). This understanding of Islamophobia as being widespread is inevitably highest among Muslims who are said to feel that they are living in a time when they are being specifically singled out as the 'folk devil' to be blamed for all social problems. Commentators have often argued that the 'War on Terror' era that began after 11th September 2001 specifically constructed Muslims as the enemy (Abbas 2005; Kundnani 2007). This discourse that construes Muslims as victims, living in an era where Islamophobia is widespread, was definitely present in the minds of the Muslim converts I interviewed. Many of them believed Islamophobia was rife and a part of life that they had come to expect. They suggested that Islam was perceived with considerable contempt by non-Muslims and that discrimination was something that Muslims constantly had to overcome. The Muslim converts' belief in the widespread nature of Islamophobia was unquestionable. In fact, some of the Muslim converts were so troubled by Islamophobia that it had serious implications on how they lived their lives. For example, some were so worried about Islamophobia that it caused them to conceal their Muslim identity (Kose 1996: 138). Verity, a twenty-one-year-old medical student, was one of the interviewees who spoke about her reluctance to wear the headscarf because she knew it would automatically disclose her conversion to Islam, which may lead to Islamophobic encounters: 'I think that's why I'm hesitating to wear it though because I feel like I would face discrimination wearing it … So I might wear it, I might not. I'm planning on wearing it but I don't know if I actually will step out of the door and arrive at hospital wearing it because I feel like … I don't know …' Those who had 'come out' as Muslims were still anxious and troubled by their belief that Islamophobia was virulent. For instance, some of the interviewees were so worried about it that it even caused them to curtail their mobility, avoiding going out at certain times and to certain places where they thought they may attract unwanted Islamophobic attention. For instance, Laura, a thirty-five-year-old mental health nurse, explained the following: 'I must admit, it's affected how … wearing hijab has affected the times of day I'll go out … coz I wouldn't feel safe … like, during the day, I'm okay. I mean, I go to the car, I drive. But there's no way in this world I would go and walk down the street after a certain time on my own, I couldn't do it … I would have but I feel more of a target now.'

What is remarkable about this perception of Islamophobia as being widespread is that it had very little relationship to the Muslim converts' actual experiences. Despite the Muslim converts' belief that Islamophobia was pervasive, when asked if they had experienced Islamophobia they reported experiencing very few incidents. For example, there were next to no reports of experiencing Islamophobia in the form of physical attacks. Furthermore, there were no clear-cut reports of discrimination in services or employment for being a Muslim. There were some reports involving verbal insults, although they were not particularly aggressive but more in a teasing manner such as being called 'Bin Laden', 'Taliban', 'Terrorist' or even 'Paki'. While these slurs can be used in an aggressive or threatening tone, the Muslim converts gave the impression that they were only exposed to them occasionally from either teenagers who thought it was funny to shout them out or from people who were intoxicated. Thomas provided a typical example:

> I've encountered things like that, whispers and … I can remember some lad driving past and shouting 'OSAMA BIN LADEN!' at us

> and shaking his fist. And I quite liked that! I shouted 'TAKBIR'! They were louts, white kids in a battered car in York. This was after 9/11. It was great fun! They weren't threatening, they were having a laugh. But no, *alhamdulillah*, I've never been threatened or subject to violence or anything like that.

Thomas dismissed the incident as rather mundane and even 'fun'. He also pointed out that he has never felt threatened, even after this incident. Other interviewees typically conveyed their experiences of such Islamophobic slurs in a similar manner, construing them as a nuisance that arose every now and then rather than a persistent problem. This suggests that although the Muslim converts' perception of Islamophobia was that it was widespread, it was not something that confronted them in their everyday lives. Zach's and Alison's responses when I asked them how much of a problem Islamophobia was in their life demonstrates the way in which the Muslim converts were typically untroubled by Islamophobia:

> None. No. I can't think of … I don't find myself in a world full of prejudice particularly. Prejudice against Muslims is clearly something which, you know, I would feel strongly about. But on an individual level I don't find it, you know, when meeting people or whatever. When seeing interactions between people, I don't see it. Not in my … not when I walk through in my own life. (Zach)
>
> Not a problem at all because it hasn't got to a physical or extreme level so I don't notice it and it doesn't bother me. There's the things you'd expect, and you understand where they're coming from, and that's about it. There's nothing to be upset about or anything like that or to be overly concerned about for me. (Alison)

What must be remembered while suggesting that Islamophobia did not appear frequently in the lives of the Muslim converts, though, is that Muslim converts are often not visible as Muslims, meaning that it is perhaps less likely that they would encounter Islamophobia. Suzanne, a thirty-two-year-old PhD student, and Thomas, a thirty-eight-year-old university lecturer, both understood this well:

> For a lot of converts, they're not visible as Muslims so they're less likely to experience anything. (Suzanne)
>
> No [I haven't experienced Islamophobia] … because I'm not obviously Muslim. I think if I were, I might have … the fact that I haven't suffered any discrimination doesn't mean that Muslims

> don't normally suffer discrimination. The fact [is] that you're interviewing a section of the Muslim community who can hide their identity very well and who do hide their identity all the time either consciously or unconsciously, and even if your subjects tell you they don't hide it, they're lying, they do hide it ... (Thomas)

That Muslim converts may experience less Islamophobia due to their non-visibility is supported by my observation that it was those Muslim converts who were visible as Muslims that reported the few Islamophobic experiences that were spoken of. Therefore, perhaps lifelong Muslims who may be more visible as Muslims experience more Islamophobia than Muslim converts, as the former are more likely to be recognizable as Muslims. But just because some Muslim converts are not visible as Muslims, it does not mean that all Muslim converts are non-visible or even that the ones that are non-visible to strangers are non-visible to acquaintances. By this, I am highlighting that some Muslim converts appear Muslim (typically through wearing particular items of clothing such as the headscarf) and that some are known as Muslims to people they interact with even if they do not wear such symbols. Significantly, even the Muslim converts who were visible and/or known as Muslims still did not report very many Islamophobic experiences. I therefore believe the divergence between the perception of Islamophobia and the experiences of Islamophobia are not to be explained solely by the fact that those who I interviewed were Muslim converts. In other words, due to the aforementioned reasons and also as a result of my own personal observations and discussions with lifelong Muslims, I expect the mismatch between the perception of the severity of Islamophobia and the minimal experiences of it to be a trend found among Muslims in general. Alison, a twenty-year-old university student, was one of the few Muslim converts who recognized that Islamophobia is less of a problem than many think, as she said: 'I think people are making it out to be bigger than it is, especially like the media. I think non-Muslims are quite friendly towards Muslims in the sense that ... as long as they don't feel threatened and don't feel that Islam is being forced on them, they're very happy to allow Muslims and any religious group to practice their belief.' These accounts that show that Islamophobia is not so severe that it constantly appears in the Muslim converts' lives are partially refreshing, as much of the literature on Islamophobia would have readers believe that any time Muslims go out in public they are exposed to all sorts of violent aggression and hostile treatment. While this surely does happen far too often and such incidents should not be overlooked, the experiences of the Muslim converts I spoke to suggest that it is indeed rare and that generally, they do not directly experience Islamophobia on a regular basis. It appears to me that such blatant forms of Islamophobia only arise on a minimal number of occasions.

Phobia of Islamophobia

Generally then, we can see that despite the Muslim converts' lack of Islamophobic experiences, they often had a fear that an experience of Islamophobia is 'waiting around every corner'. Perhaps I can say then that there is a 'phobia of Islamophobia' or an irrational fear of Islamophobia. The Muslim convert may be fearful that he or she is going to encounter Islamophobia, even though it may not be that likely, and so the phobia of Islamophobia actually becomes more detrimental to the life of the Muslim convert than the actual Islamophobia. Muslim converts may come to torment themselves about the severity of Islamophobia when they need not, thus assembling Islamophobia in their own mind through their fear of it. Returning to Laura, she demonstrated how her own perception reified the world she lives in:

> I tend to notice [Islamophobia] when I'm feeling a bit ... because I have good days and I have bad days. I suppose everybody's the same. You have days when your faiths stronger, days when it's weaker ... I suppose I have days when I'm more self-conscious and ... you know, the lovely whispers about how I'm looking one day [she is being sarcastic here as she said earlier she sometimes feels 'ugly' when she wears the headscarf, which she attributed to the devil's whispers]. So some days I'm more self-conscious and [on one of these days] I was walking down the street, I could see these people coming towards me – like a young couple – and they were talking and then the girl looked at me and I saw it out of the corner of my eye and they just burst out laughing as they were walking past and I think I heard them say something like 'Look at the state of that'.

It seems to me that Laura's comments resonate with this notion of a phobia of Islamophobia. She explains that she was anticipating Islamophobia when she felt she was the target of Islamophobia. Although it is impossible to know for sure, Laura's experience here may be explained by her expectation that Islamophobia was imminent or because she was being 'self-conscious', as she describes it. From this example, it is evident that the Muslim converts' phobia of Islamophobia can inflict a lot of upset and distress on the Muslim convert. Alison also provide a fascinating account of how this can happen, as she explained that at her part-time job in a grocer's she constantly worries she is being perceived negatively by customers because she is Muslim even though they are typically pleasant towards her. She said the following:

> I'm really paranoid but I don't know what non-Muslims think and they probably don't think those [Islamophobic] things because everyone's generally really friendly. But if I do get a bad customer, I'll tend to think it's because I'm Muslim that they're treating me like that ... But I think being Muslim, you are a lot more paranoid about what people are thinking, even if you get the slightest look.

She went on to explain that she was too 'intimidated' to search for a job because she was fearful that Islamophobic prejudice would prevent employers from seriously considering her for the position. Even though Alison is aware that she may be 'paranoid', she is unable to contain it and her perception of Islamophobia as widespread affects the way she experiences her life. It can be seen to cause her distress, anxiety, make her suspicious of people around her and even convince her to abolish her aspirations. Many other examples from the interviewees can be drawn upon to demonstrate the Muslim converts' phobia of Islamophobia, as there were several incidents narrated by the Muslim converts in response to me asking them to tell me about any Islamophobic experiences they had had which they considered Islamophobic, even though no motive was made clear. In other words, they were seeing Islamophobia in incidents where Islamophobia was not apparent. For example, Verity thought she was the victim of Islamophobia when a white man pushed his tray into her hands in a food queue, Zach thought he was the victim of Islamophobia when some Asian youths made some strange remarks as he walked past, and Amber thought she was the victim of Islamophobia when a Turkish employee of a pizza shop was rude to her. What is most interesting to me is that such experiences were confidently identified as Islamophobic even though no Islamophobic motive was made clear. I do not want to undermine the seriousness and even prevalence of Islamophobia, but rather I want to explain that the Muslim converts had a fear that Islamophobia surrounded them to a very large extent even though they had very little substantial experiences to support such a view.

The notion of a phobia of Islamophobia can be better understood with reference to the ideas of Frantz Fanon (1961, 1967) and particularly his focus on what we now term 'internalized racism' (Lipsky 1987). Although Fanon wrote in a time when European colonialism was operating extensively across the globe, I believe his insights are still applicable, as we live in a postcolonial world where the legacy of colonialism continues to shape the relations between different peoples. In focusing on the psychological aspects of colonialism, Fanon recognized that one of the most profound mechanisms by which the colonizer subjugates, dominates and controls the colonized is by perpetuating ideas that the latter are inherently inferior to the former and that they should be grateful for having been enlightened by the colonizer, ideas which the colonized come to internalize and accept. This is extremely important when we think about the Muslim converts' phobia of Islamophobia because I believe that part of the reason why they believe Islamophobia is so widespread is because upon converting to Islam they adopt a mentality that Muslims, a once-colonized people (and arguably, a still colonized people), are socialized into internalizing which is that they should think of themselves as inferior to non-Muslim Europeans. Adopting such a mentality involves accepting that, in general, non-Muslims look down on Muslims and see them as inferior and as an 'other' to be suspicious of and even to hate, hence a self-deprecation and phobia of Islamophobia ensues. This process can be related to the idea of minorities adopting a 'double conciousness', as W. E. B. Du Bois argued, whereby the minority learns to understand how the majority imagines them in racist terms (Essed 1991: 1–2). Alternatively, it can be compared to a Foucauldian understanding of the *panopticon* whereby the individual disciplines oneself into routine ways of being. Fanon has explained how the colonized can be constructed in such a way and how this can impact on their self-perception:

> The Negro is an animal, the Negro is bad, the Negro is mean, the Negro is ugly; look, a nigger, it's cold, the nigger [page] is shivering, the nigger is shivering because he is cold, the little boy is trembling because he is afraid of the nigger, the nigger is shivering with cold, that cold that goes through your bones, the handsome little boy is

> trembling because he thinks that the nigger is quivering with rage, the little white boy throws himself into his mother's arms: Mama, the nigger's going to eat me up … I sit down at the fire and I become aware of my uniform. I had not seen it. It is indeed ugly, (Fanon 1967: 113–114)

So when a Muslim convert embraces a Muslim identity, due to the historical efforts that have gone into debasing Islam/Muslims and that arguably continue today, Muslim converts may accept themselves to be, or at the very least comprehend that others see them as, the 'quintessence of evil' (Fanon 1961: 32). To me, this offers an illuminating explanation for comments such as the following: 'It's kind of like that paranoid thing which happens. Like if anything goes wrong dealing with non-Muslims, you will immediately think it's because you're a Muslim' (Alison). Here, I believe Alison is showing that she has internalized an Islamophobic discourse that has convinced her that others naturally dislike her because she is Muslim. So it seems to me that the Muslim converts' phobia of Islamophobia is related to their understanding of how they perceive others to perceive them, which can be quite independent of their own experiences, and so this goes some way in explaining why the Muslim converts had a perception of Islamophobia that did not seem to match with their experiences of it.

To me, one of Fanon's main objectives was to inspire those who had been colonized to acquire self-confidence and belief in their own worth, without feeling they had to emulate others, suppress their identity or fear how they were perceived by those who constructed them as 'other'. Indeed, Fanon wrote: 'I propose nothing short of the liberation of the man of color from himself' (Fanon 1967: 8); and elsewhere: 'What I want to do is help the black man to free himself of the arsenal of complexes that has been developed by the colonial environment' (Fanon 1967: 30). With this in mind, it would make sense for the response to the phobia of Islamophobia to focus on empowering the Muslim converts so that they realize that they should take pride in their identity and have a more positive image of how they can be received. Bluntly, we could say that Muslims should be taught to overcome their 'inferiority complex', as Fanon often put it. To some extent, I believe this is an appropriate response to the type of paranoia that can manifest itself in the minds of Muslims as a phobia of Islamophobia. I do believe that Muslims should be more optimistic in their outlook on how people perceive them and what they can achieve in British society. Yet, to me, this cannot be the only recommendation, because it suggests that Islamophobia is only a problem in the minds of Muslims. This limitation is what I will go on to discuss in the next section.

Are Muslims Just Paranoid?

If one is to agree with the idea that Muslims have a phobia of Islamophobia, one may come to the conclusion that Islamophobia is therefore not much of an issue and only a problem in the minds of Muslims. After all, a phobia is defined as an *irrational* fear, and hence one that should not exist because the object of fear is not really harmful. One could say that if this is the case, it is Muslims who need to rehabilitate themselves and stop feeling sorry for themselves rather than bemoaning Islamophobia and Islamophobes. Well, if you were to take this line of thinking, you would not be the first, since this is exactly what Kenan Malik has argued in an article entitled 'Islamophobia Myth' (2005). As the title of his article suggests, Malik argues that the severity of Islamophobia has been greatly exaggerated in order to silence the critics of Islam and stifle free speech. Malik asks: 'But does Islamophobia really exist? Or is the hatred and abuse of Muslims being exaggerated to suit politicians' needs and silence the critics of Islam?', to which he goes on to answer: 'The charge of "Islamophobia" is all too often used not to highlight racism but to stifle criticism. And in reality discrimination against Muslims is not as great as is often perceived – but criticism of Islam should be greater' (Malik 2005). Malik offers a provocative argument and I have to agree with some of what he says. For instance, I was relieved to witness Malik taking an original approach to Islamophobia, such as when he writes: 'So pervasive is the acceptance of Islamophobia, that no one even bothers to check if it is true' (Malik 2005). Yet, even though what I have written earlier in this chapter about Muslim converts having a phobia of Islamophobia may seem to run parallel to Malik's claims that Islamophobia is exaggerated, I cannot agree with Malik's analysis. For instance, Malik argues that Muslims regularly and consciously overstate Islamophobia in order to acquire sympathy and more influence in society. Perhaps some shrewd Muslims do this, but for the average Muslim, such as those Muslim converts I interviewed, I believe they genuinely believe Islamophobia to be a serious threat to them and their fellow believers. As I showed earlier, their perception of widespread Islamophobia truly did hinder their state of mind, their life choices and their aspirations.

More important than this though in preventing me from agreeing with Malik's claims, and something that is essential to bear in mind when noticing the low number of Islamophobic experiences the Muslim converts offered, is the question of how Islamophobia is being understood. For instance, Malik is confident in dismissing it because Muslims are not subjected to routine violence and because the majority of Muslims are not stopped and searched by the police. What Malik does not take note of is that such ways of understanding Islamophobia are only one crude dimension of how it can manifest itself. Yet it is understandable that Malik conceives of Islamophobia in this way since this is generally how racisms of all kinds are understood. Moreover, I believe this is also how the Muslim converts I interviewed understood Islamophobia. This is the crucial point that must be grasped, and the reason why we cannot dismiss Islamophobia as just a 'myth', as Malik does. Just because Muslims are not regularly subjected to overt forms of abuse does not mean that Islamophobia is redundant and benign. In fact, it only suggests to me that Islamophobia is more disturbing because it is operating on a level that is difficult to detect. It is present without being visible. What is required, in my opinion, is a reconsideration of how Islamophobia is typically conceived of and how it is thought to operate.

In order to justify this claim, I find the work of those who have focused on subtle forms of racism – what has also been termed 'microaggression' – to be highly relevant. For instance, Philomena Essed (1991) has argued that despite widespread beliefs in North America and Europe that racism is no longer a major issue ('the myth of tolerance', as Essed puts it (1991: 115)), racism has merely taken on a new guise in the form of 'everyday racism', a type of racism which frequently appears in mundane interactions and is not always so strikingly prejudiced. She explains it as follows: 'everyday racism has been defined as a process in which socialized racist notions are integrated into everyday practices and thereby actualize and reinforce underlying racial and ethnic relations. Furthermore, racist practices in themselves become familiar, repetitive, and part of the "normal" routine in everyday life' (Essed 1991: 145). In showing how 'everyday racism' operates, she discusses 'Rosa N.' as a case study, which she says pertinently reflects the experiences of other black people:

> Rosa N. has never been physically molested, her life has not been threatened. She hardly has to deal with blatant 'bigots'. She has not been fired. She has been called a Black 'whore' only once. She is gifted, she has a job, and she is pursuing a promising career. She is a 'successful Black'. So one might ask: what is the problem? The problem is exactly that which is at the heart of everyday racism: the invisibility of oppression and the imperceptibility of Rosa N.'s extraordinary perseverance, despite multiple forms of oppression. Rejection, exclusion, problematization, underestimation, and other inequities and impediments are regularly infused into 'normal' life, so that they appear unquestionable. This is a story of oppression in the fabric of everyday life. Some of her experiences are obvious indications of racism. Many others are concealed and subtle. (Essed 1991: 146)

I believe the story of 'Rosa N.' resonates with many of the Muslim converts I interviewed. Similarly to 'Rosa N.', the Muslim converts I spoke to had little blatant Islamophobic experiences but continued to feel affected by the extent of Islamophobia in Britain.

In case anyone thinks Essed's ideas are outdated, since she introduced 'everyday racism' almost twenty years ago, Barbara Trepagnier has recently argued in her book *Silent Racism* (2006) that we still live in an era when the majority of white people think they are anti-racist but are still involved in perpetuating it in discreet ways. Both Essed's and Trepagnier's accounts can be explained with the help of David Goldberg's in-depth account in *Racist Culture* (1993) in which he argues that Western culture has been imbued with racist ideas and assumptions ever since the Enlightenment philosophers positioned reasoned and rational European men as superior to barbaric 'black others'. He writes: 'By working itself into the threads of liberalism's cloth just as that cloth was being woven, race and the various exclusions it licensed became naturalized in the Eurocentered vision of itself and its self-defined others, in its sense of Reason and rational direction. Racial divisions and racist dominations came to be normalized in the Western sociophilosophical tradition' (Goldberg 1993: 10). In short, Goldberg rigorously demonstrates that there is a long history of Eurocentricism in the minds of white Europeans that remains intact, meaning that, in a nutshell, racism is bound up with Western societies. For Essed, Trepagnier and Goldberg, whether it is made visible or not, 'everyday racism', 'silent racism' or 'racist culture' is ever-present and will continue to manifest in subtle ways regardless of our hopes that race no longer matters. I believe that efforts to understand Islamophobia in a similar manner must also be made. Yes, thankfully it does not manifest overtly in many situations and therefore the Muslim converts had few clear-cut accounts to narrate, but no, unfortunately that does not mean that Islamophobia is just a 'myth', as Malik claims. Rather, Islamophobia is typically more subtle, covert and harder to detect. So, while I earlier suggested that the phobia of Islamophobia could be explained by reference to an 'internalized racism' in the minds of the Muslim converts, here I must go on to say that I do not think that the phobia of Islamophobia is always based on a paranoia but that it can also be based on a tacit knowledge of the presence of Islamophobia, even though one has little tangible evidence to support such a feeling. In fact, Essed pointed out that minorities are aware that they are often perceived as being too sensitive and paranoid about detecting racism and therefore it is often the case that a person who suspects racism may not mention it for fear of being seen as 'having a chip on their shoulder', seeking sympathy or encouraging 'political correctness' (Essed 1991: 82–87, 150). Therefore, it is quite possible that the Muslim converts had countless examples of suspected Islamophobia they could have offered but which they held back, for fear of being judged as too sensitive. I also believe this is compatible with Fanon's approach, as he was not simply arguing that the colonized are deluded in perceiving racism to be pervasive, but he was arguing that minorities internalize a very real and ever-present prejudice that they can detect whether it is or is not blatantly visible.

So if Islamophobia is often so subtle, then how can one be sure it is ever present? Essed answers this by arguing that the black women she interviewed were well positioned to identify subtle forms of racism because, over time, after generating an understanding of what behaviour is normal and what is abnormal in given situations, and then being informed about racist beliefs and practices, black women, and black people in general, acquire an ability to detect racism (Essed 1991: 73–75). She writes:

> Given the ubiquity of racism and the often covert nature of its contemporary manifestations, the women firstly classify actions in terms of acceptable or unacceptable behavior in a given situation. When actions have been interpreted as unacceptable, and the implications and effects of the actions are consistent with previously

> existing social representations of racial issues and of racism, and if there are no acceptable excuses, the hypothesis is formed that the actions may be manifestations of racism. Then a search for supporting (or disqualifying) information is bound to follow. Thus motivated to make correct assessments of the event, Black women seek more information to make plausible, to prove, or to reject the hypothesis of racism (Essed 1991: 126).

I would agree with this idea that minorities can become skilled at detecting when racism, or Islamophobia, is in operation but not in an absolute sense where we would construct them as having a 'sixth sense'. Rather, I believe that Muslims, for example, can draw upon their own experiences, other peoples' experiences and their own tacit knowledge of social customs and discourses, which enables them to make a reasonably good assessment of whether a person they are dealing with is making negative judgements about them based on an Islamophobic attitude. But how Essed could have answered the above question need not rely on the tautological logic of 'we know subtle racism exists because we know it exists'. However, sometimes subtle racism becomes less subtle and surfaces to the brink of being overt. This is a much more reliable way of demonstrating how subtle racism or subtle Islamophobia operates. In the next section, I provide an example of an instance where 'subtle Islamophobia' emerges into being almost apparent.

Intimate Islamophobia

Acts of Islamophobia directed towards oneself – and even racism more generally – are often thought of as originating from strangers, not those who one is 'close to' and interacts with regularly. Furthermore, if one is unfortunate enough to experience such prejudice, it is commonly thought that one would be well aware that it happened. This makes sense, as it is unlikely that one would surround oneself with people who are Islamophobic. Furthermore, it may seem like a contradiction for one to consider someone who is Islamophobic towards oneself as 'someone close'. However, here I would like to argue that this ignores a very important dimension of Islamophobia, that which can be called 'intimate Islamophobia', as it derives from those who one is 'close to', or those we call friends and family. I suggest that it is quite possible – and even common – for Islamophobia to originate among one's friends and family without them being seen as adversaries by the victim. Indeed, I would argue that these forms of Islamophobia can be highly damaging, as they derive from those people whom one may value and they manifest in the subtlest of ways. Muslim converts are specifically susceptible to this form of Islamophobia because they will have many non-Muslim relatives and most likely numerous non-Muslim friends from their 'previous life'. They will therefore be more likely to encounter those they consider as 'close' holding Islamophobic prejudices. To me, intimate Islamophobia is a prime example of how Islamophobia can operate subtly in the everyday lives of Muslim converts.

Perhaps the clearest way that this intimate Islamophobia materialized in the experiences of the Muslim converts I interviewed was in the reactions of the Muslim converts' families when they found out their relative had become a Muslim. Overall, the Muslim converts reported that their families had overwhelmingly been opposed to them converting to Islam. Those who had managed to announce to their families that they had converted to Islam spoke of feeling they had to avoid raising their Muslim identity with their family because it was such a sensitive issue. Such was the case for Verity, who had told most of her family but still said: 'I like to keep it as a personal thing when I'm with my family because I know it's a bit of a touchy subject so I keep it to myself then.' In some cases, it is said that families are so disappointed by their relatives' decision to convert to Islam that they even disown them, and perhaps this was the fear Verity had (Anway 1996: 57-61; Lang 1994: 60-61). One of the interviewees whose family reacted particularly negatively was Zach, a twenty-five-year-old trainee teacher, who explained his family's reaction as follows: 'They were aggrieved … they burst into tears – my mum and my sister – when I told them.' He continued with a more descriptive account:

> I was like, 'Look, I've got something to tell you …' Yeah, my sister, my mother, my father, round the table for dinner and erm … it went very quiet when I told them … I was just like 'Look, I've got something to tell you … you know, I've been thinking about religion …' I expect this is what I said. I can't remember that clearly to be honest. What I do remember saying is 'I've got something to tell you … I've become Muslim.' And then there was … everyone was quiet. You know, and I got looked at. So I tried to explain myself a bit and erm … I went on defending myself for maybe ten

> minutes or so. I remember looking up and my mum was just balling, you know, tears running down her cheeks and everything and my dad was just ... he was just err ... very angry ... I hadn't expected it to be so severe a reaction ... I thought it would be negative but I didn't think it would be like this scale man. They were just utterly, like, shocked ... So it was like: 'What's happening!? What's happened to our son!?'

Reactions such as this are not uncommon for Muslim converts. So why were the families' reactions to their relative converting to Islam consistently negative? These reactions may be partly explained by the idea that all religious belief is somewhat out of fashion and often considered as superstition. However, I also believe that the negative reaction is not just about becoming religious, but specifically about becoming Muslim, and this is why I feel these negative reactions can be explained by an underlying Islamophobic prejudice. Anthony Johns and Abdullah Saeed have observed this in Australia, although I would suggest it also applies to Britain:

> There is a pecking order in the popular assessment of religions in Australia. Buddhism is intellectually chic, and there is a broad appreciation in educated circles of the sacred sites and spirits and reverence for land and nature of Aboriginal spirituality. Islam, on the other hand, is widely viewed through stereotypical lenses, and conversion to Islam (as opposed to Buddhism, for example) is regarded as an aberration. (Johns and Saeed 2002: 209)

The families often have such negative views about Islam that for their relative to become Muslim, it appeared as a great tragedy to them. While in the Muslim convert's eyes, converting to Islam may be about becoming a 'better person', for the family of the Muslim convert, it is rarely seen like this. A useful account that provides a parent's perspective on finding out their child has converted to Islam has been provided by Carol Anway, whose daughter converted to Islam:

> When Jodi came home to visit us that Thanksgiving day and shared the news with us of her conversion to Islam, it was like she had stabbed us with a knife. How could our sweet daughter do anything as bizarre as this? Both my husband, Joe, and myself were deeply hurt ... We were numb, but we were also angry and not sure we wanted our daughter as a part of our family. Should we just consider

> she was no longer welcome in our home and treat her as if she were dead? (Anway 1996: 173)

This type of reaction, which is similar to the accounts the Muslim converts provided me with, shows that for the relatives of the Muslim convert, choosing to become a Muslim is something incomprehensible that forever changes who the person is in a detrimental sense. I believe this extremely negative reaction signifies an Islamophobic understanding of what converting to Islam entails. The relatives of the Muslim convert were unable to accept that their relative had found something in Islam that was valuable. This is a clear example of when the Muslim converts have been subjected to Islamophobia but which is not typically identified as such since it does not fit with a commonsense understanding of how it works and where it comes from. Even though the Muslim converts did not categorize such reactions as Islamophobic, they repeatedly reported that people they knew had tried to dismiss their conversion to Islam. It was not enough for the Muslim convert to say that they had intellectually evaluated the tenets of Islam and that it appeared as sound to them. A common way of understanding the older Muslim convert's choice to become a Muslim was by suggesting it was related to them going through a 'mid-life crisis' or experiencing the menopause. The younger Muslim converts' conversions were dismissed by claiming they were 'going through a phase' or participating in the latest fad. For example, Verity, who was twenty-one and had only been a Muslim for six months, said: '[I]n her mind, [my mother thinks] that it's just a phase I'm going through or something. And I think my aunties think that as well …' In other situations, the relatives of the Muslim convert tried to link the conversion to depression or going through a difficult time. For others, their conversion to Islam was credited to them having been 'brainwashed' by Muslims. Laura summarized these ideas that relatives of the Muslim convert may employ to explain their relatives conversion to Islam when she said: 'My dad … truthfully, still does think I've done it for my husband. He thinks it's a fad. The word brainwashing came up …' The Muslim converts' families found it necessary then to try and make sense of why their relative had converted to Islam. Perhaps this was a coping strategy for some of the relatives as it gave them some hope that their relative would not remain a Muslim permanently. More importantly though, I think it demonstrates some Islamophobic assumptions about Islam having nothing of value to offer, meaning that a reason for conversion needs to be found because it seems counterintuitive that people would choose to convert to Islam based solely on the teachings of Islam. This is a clear-cut case of subtle Islamophobia in operation.

'Nothing too serious'

Another way in which subtle Islamophobia revealed itself in the experiences of the Muslim converts, which again can be considered as 'intimate Islamophobia', was through the Muslim converts' encounters with Islamophobic jokes. Several of the Muslim converts discussed the way in which jokes were told to them, especially by their friends and family, about them being Muslim. I argue that even though these jokes were typically dismissed by the Muslim converts as trivial and harmless, they are still based on an Islamophobic undertone. Kalpana Seshadri-Crooks (2000: 82–84) takes a similar position as she argues – in a psychoanalytic fashion – that racist jokes represent ideas from the subconscious that cannot be easily articulated. Following Sigmund Freud's assertions, she sees jokes as similar to dreams in this respect, operating as an outlet for one's innermost thoughts and feelings. Essed also considers racist jokes as 'the ventilation of racism' (Essed 1991: 257). Borrowing such an approach, I do believe the jokes that the Muslim converts spoke of could actually say more about the presence of subtle Islamophobia than about good humour. For example, Peter, a thirty-five-year-old warehouse operator, provides two useful examples, followed by a similar example from Alison:

> I've had friends who've said – mainly joking – 'Oh, you're gonna become like a radical terrorist', you know, like extremist. And I said, 'No. I think I got my wires crossed too much.' I think they're just making light fun of it. Nothing too serious. (Peter)
>
> I think it was just joking like: 'You're gonna go extreme and go to Pakistan and join a training camp.' You know what I mean? ...[I wasn't offended because] it was just a joke. I mean, it came from a good friend, so we always debate on the issues of Christianity and Islam and what's going on in the world. We have open dialogue. A comment like that coming from the wrong person, from a stranger, could be very insulting. (Peter)
>
> There's been jokes with regards to me being Muslim ... Well, Bermuda's really hot so there's been jokes like: 'Oh, take that thing

> off your head, it's hot outside, go put on some shorts, I know you're hot.' Erm ... I've been called 'Taliban' by relatives, which they thought was a joke ... Because I know it's family and I know it's a joke, I'm not bothered by them or their comments. I don't get offended. I'll laugh if I think it's funny as well. But that's because it's family. I mean if someone else was to do it, if a stranger was to do it I wouldn't feel comfortable, if a friend was to make a joke like that then I'd be okay because I have a sense of humour and I'm able to laugh. (Alison)

The association of Islam with extremism, terrorism and the suggestion that the headscarf is in some way oppressive are all Islamophobic discourses that surface in these jokes. Interestingly, in all three of these examples, Peter and Alison dismiss and defend the Islamophobic tone of the jokes they have been exposed to. When the Muslim converts' came close to acknowledging the Islamophobic nature of such jokes here and elsewhere, they were quick to pardon their relatives by saying they did not mean it in a terribly nasty way or that it was not their fault. I think that what is going on here is a reluctance to acknowledge the Islamophobia that is present, mainly because it is originating so 'close to home', which is the last place one would expect it to stem from. The Muslim converts could be said to be in denial that their relatives or friends could be Islamophobic. It was much more likely that they would worry about the type of aggressive Islamophobia that comes from strangers.

I believe that Muslim converts are right to be concerned about Islamophobia but wrong to be primarily concerned about the aggressive type that comes from strangers, as this form is rare, and that they should be more concerned about the intimate Islamophobia that is much more common and less comfortable to recognize. This is a useful example of how a rigid understanding of Islamophobia prevents the Muslim converts identifying other forms of Islamophobia that can be just as harmful as the overt instances that come from strangers. To me, this demonstrates how urgent it is to reconceptualize how Islamophobia can manifest in such covert ways. In particular, jokes such as these need to be challenged, because they are not just harmless pieces of humour but can actually reify Islamophobic prejudice by perpetuating the misconceptions and stereotypes about Islam/Muslims in a similar way that other racist jokes naturalize ideas about race and racism (Goldberg 1993: 226; Seshadri-Crooks 2000: 92). The Muslim converts' encounters with jokes are an example of how subtle Islamophobia can become not so subtle. This is a typical way that Islamophobia can be expressed when overt forms are deemed unacceptable by mainstream society; as Seshadri-Crooks has written: 'hostile jokes substitute for the violence that is forbidden expression in a homogeneous, civil society, just as obscene jokes substitute for the spontaneous touching that is also forbidden by moral law' (Seshadri-Crooks 2000: 91). In other words, Islamophobic jokes are a symptom of 'the myth of tolerance', whereby on the surface Islamophobia is denounced but deep down is still persistent.

Conclusion

In this chapter I have sought to contribute a more complex understanding of what Islamophobia is, how it operates and how it impacts on the lives of Muslim converts by referring to Muslim converts' everyday perceptions and experiences that relate to Islamophobia. Despite the Muslim converts' general lack of direct Islamophobic experiences, they still hold the perception that Islamophobia is widespread. I made sense of this by suggesting that Muslim converts have a 'phobia of Islamophobia', which has repercussions on how they live their lives. Thus, the phobia of Islamophobia negatively restricts and causes distress to many Muslims before they have even encountered Islamophobia. I also went on to argue that just because it *appears* that direct Islamophobic experiences are few and far between does not mean that Islamophobia is non-existent in British society but that it is operating on a more subtle level. For instance, the way that many families respond to a relative converting to Islam and the way that they make jokes about Islam suggests to me that Islamophobia does indeed inform many peoples' perceptions of Islam/Muslims, even if the Muslim converts are reluctant to acknowledge this 'intimate Islamophobia' as Islamophobia. There are several other examples that could be taken from the Muslim converts' lives which may seem mundane at first glance, but can reveal the presence of Islamophobia on closer inspection. Islamophobia, then, often takes on a more subtle character and is often unspoken, not made explicit. It can also originate much closer to home than people think. Therefore, rather than just understanding it through clichés about Muslim women having their headscarves torn from their heads by racist thugs, it appears to me that we need to also highlight the more common and everyday forms it takes, as it is this type of Islamophobia that affects Muslims' lives more than the rare instances of physical violence or verbal abuse. Overall, I believe I have shown that a re-examination of Islamophobia is extremely important in order for it to be recognized in all forms. More investigation into how Islamophobia manifests is required, as the few examples I have given in this chapter only highlight some of the diverse ways in which it can penetrate the lives of a certain type of Muslim. For instance, in this chapter I have not discussed the way in which Islamophobia can be perpetuated through the representation of Islam and Muslims in the domains of politics, entertainment and news media. Islamophobia will continue to be an ever-present prejudice until we recognize the many guises it takes.

NOTE

1 This chapter is based on thirty-seven interviews I conducted with a variety of Muslim converts in Britain between 2008 and 2009 as part of my doctoral research.

BIBLIOGRAPHY

Abbas, T., 'British South Asian Muslims: Before and After September 11', in *Muslim Britain: Communities under Pressure* (London: Zed Books, 2005), pp. 3–17.

Abu Sway, M., 'Islamophobia: Meaning, Manifestations, Causes', in *Palestine–Israel Journal of Politics, Economics & Culture* 12 (2/3) (2005), pp. 15–23.

Allen, C., 'The "First" Decade of Islamophobia: 10 Years of the Runnymede Trust Report "Islamophobia: A Challenge for Us All"'. Accessed on 12 November 2007 at <http://chris-allen.moonfruit.com/>.

Anway, C. L., *Daughters of Another Path: Experiences of American Women Choosing Islam* (Lee's Summit, MO: Yawna Publications, 1996).

Essed, P., *Understanding Everyday Racism: An Interdisciplinary Theory* (California and London: Sage, 1991).

Fanon, F., *The Wretched of the Earth* (Hammondsworth: Penguin Books, 1961).

—*Black Skin White Masks* (New York: Grove Press, 1967).

Goldberg, D. T., *Racist Culture: Philosophy and the Politics of Meaning* (Oxford: Blackwell Publishers, 1993).

Johns, A. H. and Saeed, A., 'Muslims in Australia: The Building of a Community', in Y. Y. Haddad and J. I. Smith, *Muslim Minorities in the West: Visible and Invisible* (Walnut Creek, CA and Oxford: AltaMira, 2002), pp. 195–216.

Kose, A., *Conversion to Islam: A Study of Native British Converts* (London: Kegan Paul International, 1996).

Kundnani, A., 'Integrationism: The Politics of Anti-Muslim Racism', in *Race & Class* 48 (4) (2007), pp. 24–44.

Lang, J., *Struggling to Surrender: Some Impressions of an American Convert to Islam* (Beltsville: Amana Publications, 1994).

Lipsky, S., *Internalized Racism* (Seattle: Rational Island, 1987).

Malik, K., 'Islamophobia Myth' (2005). Accessed on 12 January 2010 at <http://www.prospectmagazine.co.uk/2005/02/islamophobiamyth/>.

Runnymede Trust, *Islamophobia: A Challenge for Us All* (Runnymede Trust, 1997).

Seshadri-Crooks, K., *Desiring Whiteness: A Lacanian Analysis of Race* (London: Routledge, 2000).

Trepagnier, B., *Silent Racism: How Well-Meaning White People Perpetuate the Racial Divide* (London: Paradigm Publishers, 2006).

12

Islam in Brazil: Reflections on Economic Life and Religiosity in a Minority Context

Cristina Maria de Castro

Introduction

This chapter focuses on the impact of economic life on the bonding and religiosity of Muslim groups in Brazil, host country to the largest Muslim community in Latin America. According to the theorists in the Ethnic Economy area, economic self-defence strategies may help immigrants overcome cultural, social and economic disadvantages, besides contributing to the preservation of cultural aspects in a situation where they represent a minority (Light 2005). The Muslims in Brazil, a religious minority originating mainly from Lebanon, have achieved truly successful economic self-defence strategies (Castro 2007a). Through a shared Islamic identity, the former immigrants were encouraged to help newcomers to overcome linguistic, cultural and social obstacles. However, the minority status of Muslims imposes the need to negotiate with the Brazilian host society, which is characterized by the strong presence of Catholicism, the growth of Protestantism, a secular state, a basically Western culture, dependence on the US and the pressures from a traditional Brazilian way of life that strongly absorbs immigrants in a process of assimilation (Castro 2007b).

Through a comparative study of two Muslim immigrant groups in the state of São Paulo,[1] one deeply marked by the ethnic economy and the other one with members working independently within the economic scope, this chapter analyses to what point a common economic activity can bond an immigrant group, rendering it more resistant to the assimilation pressures in Brazil. The construction of Muslim identities in the Brazilian religious field is used as an example to measure the resistance to assimilation in both communities.

Disseminating Islam throughout the country or simply making it a socially accepted immigrant religion are the different goals presented by both groups. Signs of a Muslim religiosity experienced within the public sphere, such as the use of a beard and veil, are more widely observed in the first group, which is marked by the ethnic economy. According to its members, Islam has arisen to correct Christianity, and Brazil is a Catholic country only on account of tolerance by Arabs, who offered freedom of worship to the Iberian countries during their rule. The second group, on the other hand, presents a more modest discourse towards the Brazilian religious field, concentrating its efforts on showing how Islam is accepted and appreciated by Catholicism, the predominant religion in Brazil.

The research method used in the present work was participant observation, and the research period was from 2004 to 2006. Friday sermons, Arabic and religion classes held on Saturdays, lectures, religious celebrations, marches and events organized by leaders and members of both mosques were visited frequently in order to gain a deeper insight into Muslim life in São Paulo.

This chapter is divided into four sections, plus a conclusion. First, a brief overview of the Brazilian religious field is presented. The second section provides fundamental information about the Muslim presence in Brazil. Then some details are given about the ethnic, occupational and spatial distribution profiles of the two aforementioned communities. Finally, the fourth section compares the different constructions of identities realized by each Muslim community towards the Brazilian religious field.

A Brief Overview of the Brazilian Religious Field

From the official religion in the country up to the Proclamation of the Republic, Catholicism is currently the religion declared by 74 per cent[2] of Brazilians, although this number does not correspond to doctrinaire adhesions (ecclesiastical practices), institutional loyalties or regular practices. This is due to the fact that 'to declare oneself as a Catholic in Brazil, more so as a Christian, is often equivalent to acknowledging oneself as a part of the human species' (Carneiro and Soares 1992: 13). At the end of the 1980s, Brandão went even further, saying that the idea that 'everyone has a religion' or at least 'respects religion' is a consensus in the country, as well as 'to be Brazilian is to be Catholic' (Brandão 1988: 33).

However, with the expansion of Pentecostalism and the increasing number of people who declare having no religion in recent years, this statement needs to be refined. Brazil remains the 'largest Catholic nation in the world', with 125 million Catholics attested, out of 170 million inhabitants. However, if we compare the census held in 1980 with that in 2000, we see that the Pentecostals have increased from 6.6 per cent to 15 per cent of the population, while the number of people who stated having no religion increased from 1.6 per cent to about 7 per cent of the Brazilian population.

Pierucci (1997) supports the idea that there is a 'transition from a monopoly or hegemony of a single religion to a diverse scenario of religious pluralism fully accepted and clearly installed', which is distinctly consistent with the secularization process undergone by societies in the process of modernization and by the societies of advanced capitalism (p. 116). Synchronously to the pluralization process of religious offers in Brazil, the quota of 'disengaged individuals from any religion' increases, affecting mainly the Catholic Church, according to Pierucci (2004).

Despite changes observed in recent years in the configuration of the Brazilian religious field, the highest symbolic capital within the field still belongs to Catholicism. The very intonation of the answer to the simple question 'What are you?' already suggests a direction to understanding the relations of symbolic power in the Brazilian religious field: 'a Catholic responds with the naturalness of the obvious; an Evangelical with a militant faith confession; and a Kardecist spiritualist halfway between an opaque confession by a Catholic and the motivated affirmation of a Protestant, depending on the quality of his adherence to spiritualism. The *exclusive* followers or those *also* participants in some form of African–Brazilian worship will respond with an aura of mystery' (Brandão 1988: 33).

However, for the Afro-religion adepts, it is assumed they are 'multisocial and multi religious' people. The main element of these cults is that they have mostly visiting groups rather than a regular flock of believers. Many followers of Candomblé and Umbanda classify themselves as Catholics, assuming a complementary relationship between both faiths.

Islam fits into the role of religious minorities of immigrants as, for instance, Judaism and Orthodox Christianity, the latter introduced by the Russians. It is known that it was brought to Brazil by African slaves, but was practically abolished from the national scene after the Malês Revolt (a slave rebellion in Brazil) in 1835, only returning to the Brazilian religious field with the arrival of Arab immigrants. The next topic provides more details about the history of the Islamic presence in Brazil.

The Muslim Presence in Brazil: A Short Introduction

Several local Muslim religious leaders claim that the Islamic presence in Brazil dates back to the Age of Discovery.[3] This may be a strategy to create a place in the 'founding' history of this country and to legitimate the claim that Muslim presence is as old as Christianity in Brazil. However, it was only with the beginning of slave traffic to Brazil that a substantial number of Muslims arrived in the country. *Malês*, Muslims of Yoruban[4] descent, are the most well known of these immigrants. In 1835, they organized an uprising, based on the Islamic right to self-defence, which they took to the streets of a very important northeastern city (Salvador) for many hours, leading to repercussions that were felt as far away as Europe. Some of the participants of this uprising were deported; others were arrested, beaten or even condemned to death (Reis 2003).

As a consequence of this uprising, Islam was seen as something to be feared and controlled, and it all but disappeared from Brazil's religious scene, returning only with the arrival of new Syrian and Lebanese immigrants, especially from the 1940s onwards. These immigrants represent the majority of Muslims in Brazil today. However, it should be noted there were several phases in the Syrian–Lebanese immigration to Brazil, the first of which was marked by the almost exclusive arrival of Christians (Truzzi 1993). This immigratory movement began in 1880, when the 'Great Syria'[5] was dominated by the Ottoman Empire. At the root of the emigrational movement were demographic, political, economic and cultural factors. The successful experiences in 'America', described in letters sent to relatives and friends in Lebanon (along with substantial sums of money), encouraged many people to come to the New World, even if they did not know exactly where that was. Many believed that the US, Argentina and Brazil were the same country. Others came to Argentina or Brazil because somebody had told them that those lands were America too. Finally, some went to the US but were refused entry due to poor health or because of stricter immigration laws. To avoid a complete waste of time and money spent on travelling, they were persuaded to come to South America instead. The decadence of the Ottoman Empire and the subsequent French dominion prompted the emigration of increasing numbers of Muslims who felt belittled by the preferential treatment of Christians in Lebanon (Gattaz 2001).

Unlike Italian, Portuguese, Spanish and other European groups, Syrians and Lebanese did not receive financial support to immigrate to Brazil. An immigration system was set up by the Brazilian government to recruit workers for rural labour and, starting in the early twentieth century, for the industrial sector. However, Syrians and Lebanese were excluded because they did not satisfy the criteria of Brazil's immigration policies, aimed primarily at 'whitening' the country's population. Although they did not pose a threat to the ideal of 'whitening', as did Africans and Asians, they were not the ideal immigrants the government was looking for. Therefore, they did not receive support from the Brazilian government, but neither did they encounter obstacles to entering the country.

Since the Lebanese immigrants arrived without contracts to work either on farms or in industry, they became merchants. Most of them had no capital to invest, but street peddling presented a possible path to rapid riches (Osman 1998). This soon became their main activity in the host country. After saving a little money, they started opening small shops and inviting friends and relatives to work for them, selling their goods through consignment. Successful shopkeepers invested their savings in wholesale businesses and later in industry. The process came full circle as older immigrants who had become wholesale merchants or manufacturers then supplied goods to the more recent immigrants working as street peddlers or shopkeepers.

The arrival of Lebanese immigrants in Brazil coincided with the beginning of the country's urbanization process. This contributed to the immigrants' commercial success, which was much greater here than it was, for example, in the United States (Truzzi 1993). Lebanese immigrants attempted to do the same thing, in the United States, but the context was different, since the urbanization process was already well advanced and other immigrant groups already occupied those commercial activities. According to Muslim leaders like Mohamed Habib from the Islamic Center of Campinas, the majority, or 90 per cent, of Muslims in

Brazil are of Lebanese descent. Syrians make up the second largest group, followed by Palestinians. The latter came to Brazil mostly after the creation of the state of Israel. Egyptians, Moroccans, Sudanese, Nigerians, South Africans and Mozambicans represent other nationalities of Muslim immigrants who settled in Brazil, albeit in fewer numbers.

There are no reliable statistics about the number of Muslims in Brazil, for they are classified under a generic category called 'others' in censuses. Islamic organizations claim they are almost a million; however, according to the geographers Waniez and Brustlein (2001), the real number may be as few as 200,000 individuals, including the category 'others'. Muslims in Brazil are concentrated mainly in the states of São Paulo, Paraná and Rio Grande do Sul. São Paulo is Brazil's wealthiest and most industrialized state, and its capital is home to the country's largest Muslim community. On the other hand, most of the Muslim immigrants in Paraná and Rio Grande do Sul live in cities other than the capitals of those states. Their main host cities are Foz do Iguaçú in Paraná and Uruguaiana in Rio Grande do Sul, because these locations are geographically favourable for commerce. Both cities lie on the border with Argentina, and Foz do Iguaçú also borders on Paraguay. Almost 60 per cent of the Muslims in Brazil engage in commercial activities. Wealthier and better educated than the average population, many own their business, and about 40 per cent are employers in Brazil (Waniez and Brustlein 2001).

The next section describes in greater detail the ethnic and occupational profiles of the two communities of this study. The first, the Islamic Youth League, has a more typical profile, considering the majority of Muslims in Brazil, i.e., a Lebanese background and dedication to commerce. The Islamic Center of Campinas, on the other hand, is a very interesting case for comparison, since it comprises heterogeneous ethnic backgrounds and members concentrated on educational activities.

The Islamic Youth League

The Islamic Youth League Mosque is located on the border between the neighbourhoods of Brás and Pari in São Paulo, the main host city for Muslims in Brazil. Like other blue-collar neighbourhoods in São Paulo, Brás and Pari display a strong ethnic and cultural diversity. Italians, Portuguese, Spanish and Lebanese were already numerous there in the early 1930s (Silva 2005). Starting in the mid-1940s, large numbers of migrants from northeastern Brazil started arriving in São Paulo's Brás neighbourhood, fleeing a water crisis of major proportions in their native states (Moura 1980). The 1970s saw the arrival of Korean immigrants, followed soon thereafter by Bolivian, Paraguayan and Peruvian immigrants to work in the Korean immigrants' garment factories (Silva 2005).

A Sunni mosque was built in that neighbourhood in 1995,[6] to provide a place of prayer for recently settled Lebanese immigrant businessmen. Arab countries such as Egypt, Saudi Arabia, the United Arab Emirates and Kuwait contributed to institutionalizing Islam in that community, not only financially but also by offering its leaders religious training and education. The main source of funding, however, was provided by the community's own successful members residing in Brazil. The community consists of about 200 families, most of them from Tripoli, Lebanon. These Muslim families followed the example of the first Lebanese immigrants in Brazil: the entry into commercial activities, based on a system of mutual cooperation, whereby the earlier immigrants help recent ones to learn the language, obtain goods to sell through consignment or get a job. Their region of origin has directed Muslims to specific neighbourhoods and cities in Brazil, and the socialization offered to newcomers has led them to concentrate their activities in the same type of business. Muslim immigrants who settled in the city of São Bernado do Campo, for example, sell furniture. Recent immigrants who are members of the Islamic Youth League specialize in the blue jeans business, in a region currently dominated by the clothing industry and commerce.

Mohammed Chedid, one of the League's founders, states in an interview that the support successful Muslim immigrants offer to newcomers is a religious duty (Castro 2007b). The region of origin played an important role in directing immigrants to certain cities and neighbourhoods, and Islam has completed the link, encouraging solidarity and mutual cooperation. However, it should be noted that the immigrants' network of solidarity has expanded to help individuals with no ethnic or national connection to that group apart from the same religious affiliation. During my fieldwork, I saw a considerable number of converted women, migrants from Brazil's northeastern states, being absorbed into the immigrants' network of solidarity. After facing disadvantages in the work market due to their lack of social capital in

São Paulo, and religious discrimination because of their use of the veil, these girls are usually hired by immigrant Muslim businessmen. Brazil's northeast is the poorest region of the country and a typical region of emigration. The Brás and Pari neighbourhoods, on the other hand, are traditional hosts of migrants from Brazil and abroad and are commonly marked by inter-ethnic and religious frictions.

The Islamic Center of Campinas

The Islamic Center of Campinas was founded in 1977 on the initiative of its current president, Mr Ismail Hatia, a South African immigrant of Indian descent. In the 1970s, Mr Hatia decided to travel to South Africa to raise funds to institutionalize Islam in Campinas. A donation of $25,000 from the Indian Muslim community was used to buy land and start the construction of the mosque. Subsequently, continuing support of the project was provided by Muslims residing in Campinas and the surrounding region, comprising immigrants of Lebanese, South African, Palestinian and Egyptian descent.

The Muslim community of Campinas is an exception for various reasons, one of which is the greater ethnic and national heterogeneity of its members compared to other Islamic centers in the state of São Paulo. According to Mohamed Habib, the leader of this community, this heterogeneity is explained by the presence of the State University of Campinas (Unicamp[7]). Many Egyptians fled their country due to the political persecution of Nasser's regime and some of them became professors at Unicamp. One of these professors is the community leader and current pro-rector for extension and community affairs, Professor Mohamed Habib. Libyans moved to Campinas to join graduate programmes as research fellows or members of the teaching staff in the same university. Other groups, like the South Africans of Indian Gujarati background, make up the community. These fled apartheid and settled in Campinas, many as English teachers. Some of them have set up their own English language schools. Immigrants from Malaysia and the Guianas also settled in Campinas and the surrounding region, albeit in fewer numbers.

At one point, Mozambicans of Indian Gujarati background were the majority Muslim group in Campinas. According to informants from the Islamic Center of Campinas, however, disenchanted with Brazil's economic crises, most of the Mozambican immigrants gave up their 'American dream' and left the country between 1985 and 1990, during the administration of President Sarney. This abandonment may be explained by the lack of a supportive ethnic economy and the fact that their cultural capital[8] fell short of that of other Muslims associated with Unicamp, preventing them from being assimilated into the university as members of the teaching and graduate research staff. Unlike the Gujarati Indians from South Africa, they did not speak fluent English, which goes far in explaining why they were unable to follow the example of their fellow South African Muslims. In addition, the economic recession of the times was unfavourable for the development of a new ethnic economy.

The poor mobilization of internal social capital for developing an ethnic economy in the aforementioned Muslim immigrant community was not the result of ethnic heterogeneity, but was in fact due to its members' particular cultural capital. Even more so than in other Islamic centres of the country, the common religious identity in Campinas' Muslim community suffices to justify marriage between immigrants of different ethnic backgrounds. Since their religious identity is enough to encourage this type of connection, there is no reason to believe it would not also suffice to articulate those individuals around the same economic activity. The main reason for the poor use of internal social capital for economic purposes by that group is the differentiated cultural capital of its members, which enabled them to become part of the teaching and graduate research staff of Unicamp and to embark on the English-language teaching business.

The ethnic heterogeneity in Campinas emphasizes the ideal of *ummah*, since it appears to be practically the sole reason for the construction of a collective identity for the members of that group. As for the presence of Brazilian converts, this is quite rare in Campinas, where there are only about six converts, according to one informant of the Islamic Center and eighteen, according to another one, in a group of 300 people. The Islamic Center of Campinas has not offered religious classes or any other event to attract new followers from outside the borders of the immigrant community. Its members are scattered around the city of Campinas and in smaller towns nearby. Moreover, they work independently, mainly in educational and research activities.

There is no ethnic economy based on interdependent commerce, nor is there a concentration of immigrants in any particular neighbourhood.

The use of the veil is exceptional in Campinas, and only four women wore it during the time of this research. The hijab has become the 'prayer clothes' in Campinas. Taken together, these factors render Muslims in Campinas almost invisible. Hence, no verbal attacks from Pentecostalists were reported in that city during my fieldwork. Between January 2004 and January 2005 one group of six evangelical women visited the Islamic Center once, but they did not return. Islam in Campinas remains an immigrant religion and this situation is not expected to change, at least not in the foreseeable future.

The Impact of the Ethnic Economy on Religiosity: The Construction of Muslim Identities in the Brazilian Religious Field

I concur with the idea that successful ethnic economies bond immigrant groups and strengthen them against the pressures of assimilation, since permanency brings more benefits than abandonment. The example of Brás enables us to go further, not only displaying a portrayal of increased resistance to assimilation but also a more daring and combative stance regarding the Brazilian religious field, compared to what happens in Campinas, SP, Brazil.

I will initially introduce examples of discourses that clarify the type of position that prevails in each group concerning the Brazilian religious field and its participants. During my field research, I was able to observe the relationship of Islam with Catholicism, which is the predominant religion, and with Pentecostalism, a religious segment that most emphasizes the relationship of opposition and competition in Brazil (Brandão 1988).

The following excerpt from a Friday sermon held at the Islamic Center of Campinas on divine unity reveals the concern in showing that Islam and Muslims are positively viewed by the Catholic Church:

> The Declaration 'Nostra Aetate', the declaration of the relation of the Church with Non-Christian religions – The Vatican, 1966, approved by 2,221 votes, more than 96 per cent, defines the Islamic religion: regarding Muslims, the Church holds them in high regard and love, because they love a single and subsistent God, merciful and almighty, creator of heaven and earth, who spoke to men. Regarding their similar precepts, they seek to subject themselves wholeheartedly, as Abraham gave himself onto God, who the Muslim belief refers to

> with satisfaction. They do not recognize Jesus as God; but revere him as a prophet. They honour Mary, his virgin mother and sometimes even invoke her with devotion. Moreover, they anticipate Judgment Day, when God will reward all those who are resurrected. Consequently, they value a moral life and worship God in the highest degree by prayer, fasting and alms.

In turn, Islamic tolerance, not only of Catholicism but also Christianity and Judaism in general, in other words the religions of the so-called 'Peoples of the Book', are also emphasized in a sermon given in Campinas:

> Analyzing the kinship resulting from the marriage of a Muslim with a Jewish or Christian woman, we realize that by human nature this creates the support and cooperation between both sides. It is a wonderful feeling produced among the children and their paternal and maternal uncles. This is tolerance, the prerequisite for peace.

In a TV interview given to TV Bandeirantes in April 2004, Nasser Mussa, a civil engineer immigrant of Palestinian origin responsible for leading prayers in that mosque, stressed:

> There is an excerpt in the Qur'an that states that a Muslim does not sleep well if he has a neighbour who has problems, and if this neighbour is a Muslim is not exactly specified in the text. That is, a Muslim should strive for the well-being of his neighbours, Muslims or otherwise, he must ensure the good of humanity, without distinction of religion.

In the end he stated that 'we all pray to the same God'.

Mohamed Habib, a leader of the Campinas community, said in one of the dominical meetings that 'to be a Muslim is to believe in all religions' (Abrahamic).[9]

As Edward Said points out (1981), the Islamic doctrine can be viewed as justifying religious tolerance as well as exclusivism. Thus, it is interesting to see that between both options, the official discourse of the Islamic Center of Campinas falls within the first view, an attitude that is compatible with the community's outlook: small, scattered, with members working in a relatively independent manner of each other and with a high rate of exogamous marriages. For example, the very person responsible for the Friday lectures is married to a Brazilian Catholic and 'only quite a while' after their marriage converted to Islam.

As might be expected, there were times I witnessed moments when members of the community sought to emphasize the differences between Christianity and Islam, playing the point considered crucial: the divinity of Jesus. At the start of the study, a South African man of Indian origin asked me if I knew the apocryphal Gospel of Barnabas, saying he would send me a copy of this for me to *understand* the truth about Jesus, demonstrating that Jesus was a prophet of God and not his son. Finally, at a dinner in the house of a family of a Palestinian immigrant with his converted Brazilian wife and son, the issue was once again broached. The couple's son, a forty-year-old Brazilian engineer, tried to delicately show me that 'both are monotheistic (Christianity and Islam) and the message of Christ must be respected and followed, but to view him as the son of God is a mistake, possibly a misinterpretation of the Scriptures'. On that occasion the patriarch said that, 'that story of God the Father and God the Son' did not make sense to him. 'How can that be?' he asked himself.

As for evangelical Christianity, it was mentioned only once by a young South African university student of Indian origin. In our first meeting at the mosque she defined Islam as a rather tolerant and flexible religion, referring to evangelicals as 'the other': 'no one is forced to stay without cutting your hair or things like that ... If it is not possible to perform the five daily prayers, it's okay. It is a very flexible religion', she concluded. When I asked her about using the veil, she said she didn't use it because it wasn't common in Brazil and she would be embarrassed with the way others looked at her.

Finally, the only case of 'discrimination' experienced by Muslims in that community, by other religious groups, and reported to me, was by the son of the couple mentioned earlier, who were invited to baptize the child of a Brazilian friend, but were prevented by the priest due to the fact they are Muslims and do not follow Christianity.

Religious tolerance is also found in the official discourse of the Muslim Youth League in Brás, but there the role of Christianity holds a much larger diacritic aspect concerning the immigrant community's identity construction process.

The concept that it is a Muslim's duty to believe in the previously revealed religions (Christianity and Judaism) and in their Prophets, is part of the official discourse of the Brás Muslim Youth League, demonstrated in the Friday sermons, in the religion lessons taught on Saturdays and on the website of the League: 'Islam acknowledges all previous religions; Christianity, Judaism and (Muslim) must recognize the entire chain of Prophets. They are brothers of a single source, with a single message.'[10]

Respect not only for the 'Prophet Jesus' but also for the Virgin Mary (the most often cited woman in the Qur'an, according to the sheikh) is quite often stressed. But here, unlike Campinas, the differences between religions are much more delineated, starting with the 'reliability' of the sacred books of both religions. In a sermon, it was stated that the Bible was written 300 years after the death of Christ, unlike the Qur'an, which states it was written while the Prophet Muhammad and his friends were still alive. This argument is used to justify the presence of errors in the Christian doctrine. The veracity of Christ's message is not denied, nor the divine origin of his teachings, but it puts into question the official *record* of his message, which would have been responsible for many misunderstandings in the transmission of Jesus' doctrine.

On the League's website we can see the following explanation:

> The essence of Islam, which is the voluntary submission to the will of God, was revealed to Adam (peace be with him), who transmitted to his children all the revelations following Noah, Abraham, Moses, Jesus and Muhammad (may the Peace and Blessing of Allah be upon them), they were in accordance with that message ... any contradiction between the revealed religions is viewed by Islam as a component made by man, introduced in these religions.[11]

In April 2006, I witnessed the conversation of a converted woman with a reporter from Rede Record Television, who was visiting the mosque with the alleged intention of raising information for a future article about Lebanon and its customs. On that occasion, the Brazilian woman converted to Islam defined the other religions in a way which summarizes the leaders' argument at the League. Coming from a Catholic family and a former member of the Universal Church of the Kingdom of God, this thirty-five-year-old woman said she felt proud of her religious training: 'All religions are true, and Islam recognizes that. The priests and pastors do their best, but express what they have access to, the Bible, which is incomplete and has flaws because it was written 300 years after the death of Christ.' The Christian religions have made mistakes by not having 'full' access to information, 'for example, they say that Jesus is the son of God, but he was just a prophet'. In addition, there is the idea that the Qur'an, unlike the Bible and the Torah, is the very word of God, while the others constitute a kind of narrative, a transfer of the *meaning* of the word of God and not the word itself. In the Qur'an the word comes from God, that is why there is the Qur'an and the *Hadith*, the latter containing the words of the Prophet Muhammad.

The Muslims in the League define themselves as tolerant for acknowledging other religions, as opposed to the Jews, 'who do not recognize Christ' and the Christians, 'who do not recognize the Prophet Muhammad', according to the words of the teacher of the beginner's class at that institution.

In short, in the Islamic Youth League, religious tolerance is part of the local ideology, but *highlighting* that Christianity is marked by a series of misunderstandings generated by the original message having been inefficiently transmitted: 'Islam did not arrive to repeal the other religions, it came to fix them', said the religion professor of the beginner's class.

The Islamic religion is explained in class to those converted from Christianity or those just interested in it, not only because it is based on the Judaic–Christian religious heritage, but because the majority of the population follow this faith. And the 'other' Christian that both the Campinas leaders as well as the League refer to, in most cases, means *Catholic.* This is not only because of the obvious use of the word 'Catholicism', but also due to the reference to the pope.

Books, brochures and conferences about Jesus as a prophet of Islam have been produced by institutions such as CEDIAL (Center for Dissemination of Islam in Latin America) and WAMY (World Assembly of Muslim Youth), both located in São Bernardo do Campo.[12] This city is the largest producer and distributor of Islamic information not just in Brazil but in the whole of Latin America. Their religion communication material can be easily found at both the mosques surveyed, and also in some Muslim shops in the Brás district. In this material there is a very similar message to the current discourse of the League: the need to respect the Abrahamic religions and all their Prophets, together with the *clarification* of some misunderstandings by these religions, the most substantial of these being the attribution of divinity to Jesus. This type of information coexists with scenes such as a Muslim businessman offering his employees Easter eggs in April 2006, generating much satisfaction not only from Christians, but also by the converted employees working there. 'But we don't commemorate Easter, the boss gave out chocolate eggs out of respect for the employees', said one young woman in the same establishment where the Cedial brochures were within reach of the customers.

The two centres I studied indicated that the leaders directed their discourse primarily at Catholic Christianity, to whom the highest symbolic capital belongs within the Brazilian religious field. Furthermore, a strong presence of Pentecostals was observed (mainly from the Assembly of God) in classes for those interested and the converted members in the League on Saturdays. Some women were not just from the aforementioned church but also from the Universal Church and later on they converted to Islam. However, some of these people, namely young males, were not there with the intention of converting to Islam. They came as Christians interested in a dialogue between religions and the opportunity to learn the Arabic language for free. They brought forth polemic issues in the religion classes, asking questions in line with the media coverage about Islam and Muslims, as for example: 'Is it true that a suicide bomb man goes to heaven and gets seventy-two virgin brides? And the women, what do they earn?'

Embarrassing questions such as these were always raised by such young people. The teacher never lost his patience and always tried to answer them. However, some of the converted members knew what they were up to and what was at stake in those classes and did not like the presence of such people. When I mentioned the large presence of 'evangelicals' interested in the Saturday classes one converted member immediately rebuked: 'But they are not interested in learning the religion at all, that's not the reason they come …' Some Evangelicals may be attending classes not because they are interested in converting to Islam, but, rather, to try to prevent further conversions to Islam, or even to take advantage of the classes as a training opportunity for their evangelizing missions in Muslim countries. The Arabs do not seem to understand the hidden reasons of such individuals, but those who were converted do in fact perceive there is something wrong, perhaps because they are more accustomed to the evangelization strategies, especially from previous experiences with Pentecostal religions.

One day, after religion class, I walked with one of those guys to the subway station and, on this occasion, we started to talk about the role of women in Christian and Islamic religions. I argued that the submission of women to their husbands is part of both doctrines. He agreed, but emphasized that Muslim women are different because they are 'enslaved': 'they cannot drive cars, cannot go out alone in the street without the presence of a man from the family'. He mentioned that he read this on a leaflet that the Assembly of God Church distributes about Muslims. It is interesting to note that the church has been devoting time to producing and distributing pamphlets about the Muslim religion, with criticism about how they treat their women, one of the favourite points used to assail Islam.

A consistent fact with the profile of Pentecostalism outlined according to Brandão is 'the manner of being religious that most activates and highly differentiates the Brazilian religious field, as well as most stresses this, in an increasing diversity of religious life forms, the most intense relationships of opposition and competition' (Brandão 1988: 40).

It should also be noted that the young man in question justified his view of Muslim women not from what he witnessed in the mosque, but from the information provided in the leaflet distributed by his church. He was not influenced by the ideology of the group, according to which Islam is the religion that most respects and protects women, nor was he influenced by certain scenes witnessed at the mosque, as for instance the Arabic teacher, of Lebanese descent and married, who always went to the mosque alone, driving her own car, as did some other converted women, single or married, with Arabs who did the same ...

In her study on converted women to Islam in São Paulo, Vera Marques (2000) points to the discrimination cases and verbal attacks made by evangelicals against Muslim women:

> The Evangelical believers assail. One believer said 'that Muslims worship another God'. In a country where there is so much bloodshed (referring to the countries with a Muslim majority), how can they worship God? She spoke about a part of the Bible (which I did not understand), I said nothing and turned to talk to another client. The Protestant believers do not accept this' (Woman, twenty-one years old, converted three years ago). (Marques 2000: 136–137)

I asked the converted women of the League about this, who promptly confirmed the tension between them. According to one of them, a twenty-one-year-old woman, converted two years ago, the Muslims are criticized for 'not believing in Jesus'. 'But this is a mistake', she said, 'because we believe in Jesus! As a prophet, not as the son of God.' 'They conclude that we are against Jesus', said another woman, approximately thirty-five years of age, converted eight years ago.

Nothing of the sort was observed at the Islamic Center of Campinas during the period I attended the mosque, which was from January 2004 to January 2005. The absence of Pentecostals at that religious institution may be explained by the low manifestation of the Muslim community in Campinas, a community with a small number of people scattered throughout the city, established in a neighbourhood away from the main centre, with a very low number of converted individuals, almost no women using the veil in public and a lack of infrastructure to attract many new members; for instance dissemination strategies, religious teachings or large events. The Islamic Center of Campinas has continued to be a meeting point for prayer and socializing, where practically everyone has known each other for many years.

Only once did I witness a direct reference by the Arab leaders to the evangelicals, and it was in reference to the case that involved 'kicking the saint', a controversial gesture by Bishop Von Helder of the Universal Church of the Kingdom of God. This episode took place on 12 December 1995, the official day of Our Lady Aparecida, the patron saint of Brazil, when Von Helder kicked a statue representing Our Lady Aparecida. The Bishop's intention was to criticize the devotion to images such as this one, made of clay, that could not 'see, hear or react'. This event was originally broadcast at dawn, in a programme transmitted by the Record Television Network, owned by Edir Macedo, founder of IURD. The event caused much shock and anger across the country, generating several attempts at retaliation against that church, through complaints at police stations or in court, and even attacks on their temples. The Globo Television Network, the main station in Brazil, contributed greatly to highlighting the fact and criticizing the IURD for religious intolerance and for disrespecting the patron saint of Brazil.

In the inaugural religion class for beginners, held at the League on 11 February 2006, the president of the Muslim Center of Brazil and a founding member of the Muslim Youth League made reference to the case:

> Isn't it wrong to take the Prophet of more than a billion people and caricature it? Is this freedom of expression? The 'priest' who kicked

> the holy statue hurriedly left Brazil because the police could not protect him. I do not pray for an image, but I believe what they did to the holy image is despicable. Stomping on the Brazilian flag is an insult to all Brazilians; it is not freedom of expression.

He used the attack on the Catholic symbol by a member of another religion to address the seriousness of the offence against Islam caused by the Danish cartoonists, hence justifying the indignation felt by Muslims. Mostly, it was interesting how he acknowledged the Catholic patron saint image as a symbol of the country, acknowledging the strength of Catholicism in Brazil. That same day, however, he stressed:

> When Islam ruled the world, it did not steal from anyone. England and France robbed Africa and the Middle East. Not because the Arabs are noble, but because Islam forbids one to do that. Brazil is a Catholic country due to the tolerance of Islam, because when they (the Arabs) ruled Portugal, they allowed freedom of belief to Christians.

With this sentence one can observe a very different view of the relationship between religions from what is seen in Campinas. While the Islamic Center of Campinas is concerned with showing that Islam and Muslims are appreciated by the Catholic Church, at the League they mention that Catholicism prevails in Brazil only on account of Muslim tolerance, which provided freedom of religion to the Iberian countries during their rule.

Besides the aforementioned differences regarding the size and spatial distribution of both communities, set in a specific manner by the presence or absence of the ethnic economy (a small, scattered, low-profile group with a low percentage of converted individuals in Campinas; a large group, concentrated in the same neighbourhood, highly visible and with a considerable number of converted individuals in Brás), there are two relevant points explaining the differences in attitudes of both communities concerning the Brazilian religious field: the greater economic capital of the Muslims in Brás and the generation difference. While in Campinas the majority of immigrants are about sixty or seventy years old and their descendants, the League is comprised of recent immigrants and only young individuals are on its directorship. The vitality of the young individuals in the League, in addition to more substantial resources, is employed with the explicit objective of spreading the word of God in the host country:

> The Arabs were able to bring *esfihas* (baked crust and filling) to every bar on every corner, but what about the word of God? It didn't go further than the first corner. We failed at this and it should be our contribution to Brazilians, taking the word of God to them.

There is talk in Campinas about spreading the divine word beyond the borders of the immigrant community, but what prevails is a greater concern about a broader acceptance and approval by the broader society as shown in the following comment on the formation of effective leadership, referring to the dissemination of knowledge and understanding in the country:

> [the] educator needs to know the teachings and the Islamic pedagogical content, based on the Sacred Scripture (Qur'an), in line with the guidance by the Prophet Mohammad (*saawas*) and the expressions and opinions of the Muslim scholars and theologians. Furthermore, such an educator needs to know the society in which the Muslim community lives, their culture, their habits, and other aspects, to make the lives of Muslims viable, without losing their identity, and at the same time to be respected and admired by non-Muslims.

This part of a sermon in Campinas is also illustrative: 'In a non-Muslim society, as is the case in Brazil, we must seek to create conditions so we can go to the mosque without losing our harmony with the community and without harming our social and professional commitment.'

Lastly, I quote the words of a sermon that explains more clearly the positioning of the Islamic Center of Campinas with respect to conversion to Islam, a speech in which the good behaviour and training (not only religious but also professional) of the Muslims must come before the spreading of the divine word to others:

> Many believe that the spread of Islam is confined to convincing non-Muslim people to leave their religion behind and convert to our spiritual code. They are wrong. Disseminating it does not mean simply taking the word of the creator to those who do not know it fully or partially. The success of propagating it is not and cannot be

> determined by the number of those converted to Islam. Faith is quality and not quantity. Building the divine religion the way that God revealed it to the Prophet Muhammad (*saawas*) as a code based on the principles of social justice, ethics, cooperation, of brotherhood and peace is the responsibility of every good Muslim. However, every Muslim should, first of all, set an example through their behaviour and their conduct. He should pursue becoming well informed, in order to become such an example of a serviceable citizen, thus respected by society. He should become qualified to be able to communicate and defend his point of view and therefore be convincing with his arguments … We have to meet the minimum standards in all areas of knowledge and professional practice. We cannot all be theologians, physicians or engineers. We must diversify our participation in society, ever pursuing to help the general commonwealth of society. That is how the first generations of Muslims were. And in that manner they formed a great civilization that lasted over 700 years.

Conclusion

The ethnic economy developed by Muslim immigrants in the district of Brás in São Paulo, as a strategy to combat cultural, social and economical disadvantages, generated not only an economically successful group, but also religiousness at least apparently more robust and resistant to pressures of assimilation. In Campinas, the kind of cultural capital displayed by its members enabled them to focus on the sector of higher education and the business of teaching English, reducing the need to mobilize the religious capital for the creation of an ethnic economy. Working essentially independently and living in different regions of the city, the Muslims of Campinas have a religious discourse that is more moderate and modest, much more concerned about acceptance than with a possible expansion, and an almost invisible practice of their religion in the public sphere.

NOTES

1 Main host of Muslim immigrants in Brazil.
2 According to the census held in 2000.
3 <http://www.mubar.org/jerrahi/Artigos_Palestras/Historia_da_presenca_Islamica_/historia_da_presenca_Islamica_.html>.
4 An ethnic group from West Africa.
5 'Great Syria' corresponded to the current territories of Syria, Lebanon, Jordan and part of Iraq.
6 <http://www.ligaIslamica.org.br/quem_somos_.htm>.
7 In 2007, UNICAMP joined the ranks of the world's 200 top universities, according to *The Times' Higher Education Supplement*. UNICAMP ranks in 177th place, while the University of São Paulo (USP) ranks as the 175th best university. UNICAMP was founded in 1967 and is considered new compared to USP, the alma mater of the Brazilian State University, and therefore more open, while USP was established in 1934. European universities are centuries old, while Brazil's oldest universities were established in the 1920s. Before that, the country had only a few independent institutions of superior education founded after 1808, upon the arrival of the Portuguese Court. See <http://www.unicamp.br/unicamp/divulgacao/2007/11/25/reitor-comenta-inclusao-de-unicamp-e-usp-entre-as-melhores-do-mundo>.
8 Cultural capital corresponds to the set of intellectual qualifications produced by the educational system or transmitted by the family (Bourdieu 1975).
9 Islam is presented as the last and definitive revelation of God's word, initiated by Abraham, and Christianity and Judaism as the religious bearers of the first revelations of the divine word.
10 Class given in May 2006.
11 See <http://www.ligaislamica.org.br/jesus_no_islam.htm>.
12 Peres and Mariz (2006) report that in São Bernardo do Campo some of those converted to Islam are later hired as spreaders of the religion and have to study not only Islam but other religions too, in order to make their work easier when presenting and explaining the Islamic religion to people from other religious backgrounds.

BIBLIOGRAPHY

Bourdieu, Pierre, *A reprodução: elementos para uma teoria do sistema de ensino* (Rio de Janeiro: Francisco Alves, 1982).

Brandão, Carlos Rodrigues, 'Ser católico: dimensões brasileiras um estudo sobre a atribuição através da religião', in Sachs, Viola (ed.), *Brasil e EUA: Religião e Identidade Nacional* (Rio de Janeiro: Graal, 1988).

Carneiro, Leandro Piquet and Soares, Luiz Eduardo, 'Religiosidade, Estrutura Social e Comportamento Político', in Bingemer, Maria Clara Lucchetti, *O impacto da modernidade sobre a religião* (São Paulo: Edições Loyola, 1992).

Castro, Cristina Maria de, 'Anotações sobre economia étnica e resistência à assimilação entre muçulmanos em São Paulo'. Paper presented at the First Thematic Seminar Centrality and Frontiers of Enterprises in the 21st Century (UFSCar 2007a).

—*A construção de identidades muçulmanas no Brasil: um estudo das comunidades sunitas da cidade de Campinas e do bairro paulistano do Brás*. PhD thesis defended at the Postgraduate Programme of Social Sciences, Federal University of São Carlos (2007b).

Gattaz, André Castanheira, *História Oral da Imigração Libanesa para o Brasil – 1880 a 2000*. Tese de doutorado defendida no departamento de História Social da USP, em 2001.

Jacob, Cesar Romero *et al.*, *Atlas da Filiação Religiosa e Indicadores Sociais no Brasil* (Rio de Janeiro: ed. PUC-Rio; São Paulo: Loyola, 2003).

Light, Ivan, 'The Ethnic Economy', in Neil, J. and Swedberg, Richard (eds), *The Handbook of Economic Sociology* (New York: second edition, Russel Sage Foundation, 2005).

Moura, Paulo Cursino de, *São Paulo de outrora: evocações da metrópole* (São Paulo: Editora da Universidade de São Paulo, 1980).

Osman, Samira, *Caminhos da Imigração Árabe em São Paulo: história oral da vida familiar*. Dissertação de mestrado, Departamento de História da USP, São Paulo, 1998.

Pierucci, Antônio Flavio, 'Secularização e declínio do catolicismo', in *Sociologia da Religião e Mudança Social* (São Paulo: Paulus, 2004), pp. 13–21.

Ramos, Vlademir Lúcio, *Conversão ao Islam: uma análise sociológica da assimilação do ethos religioso na sociedade muçulmana sunita em São Bernardo do Campo na região do Grande ABC*. Dissertação de Mestrado apresentada ao Programa de Pós-Graduação em Ciências da Religião da Universidade Metodista de São Paulo, São Bernardo do Campo, 2003.

Said, Edward W., *Orientalismo: o Oriente como invenção do Ocidente* (Editora Companhia das Letras, 1990).

Truzzi, Oswaldo, *Patrícios – Sírios e Libaneses em São Paulo* (São Paulo: Hucitec, 1997).

Wuthnow, Robert, 'New Directions in the Study of Religion and Economic Life', in Smelser, Neil J. and Swedberg, Richard (eds), *The Handbook of Economic Sociology* (New York: second edition, Russel Sage Foundation, 2005).

13

Italian Secularism Revisited? Muslims' Claims in the Public Sphere and the Long Struggle Towards Religious Equality

Enzo Pace and Annalisa Frisina

Introduction

New and unexpected religious pluralism, reshaping the European landscape, is the outcome of the long-term cycle of migration over the past forty years. Some European countries have only recently experienced the arrival of the migrants and the socio-religious change. A new religious public sphere is arising where not only the traditional religious actors (churches and the historical religious minorities), but also new ones interact and compete for recognition.

Those societies which are more flexible in coping with the new religious pluralism, with an open market of salvation (Stolz 2006) and the transformation of the public sphere, have been growing slowly but seriously, in spite of the emergence of the right-wing and xenophobic political movements that are identifiable by their anti-Islam rhetoric. Such movements exist in Flemish Belgium and in the Netherlands. And where the religious market is ruled by a monopolistic actor (like Catholicism in Ireland, Italy, Spain and Poland), access to the public sphere has been restricted to the participation by the representatives of the new religious realities, created by the migrants (Muslim, Sikh, Hindu, Buddhist, and Neo-Pentecostals from Africa, Asia and Latin America). In those countries where, until now, Catholicism has influenced the social and political life, like Italy, the Catholic Church paradoxically plays a double function: a) to act as a unique authorized speaker in the public sphere and b) to act as social and religious *broker* of the conflicts between the local communities or the state, on the one hand, and the various religious communities on the other.

Our aim is to expose the Italian paradox, focusing on the presence of Islam in Italian society (approximately 1 million people coming from very different geographic regions: Maghreb and Mashreq, Egypt, Nigeria, Pakistan, Bangladesh, Senegal, Somalia, Jordan, Syria, Iraq, Iran, Lebanon, Palestine, Bosnia, Albania and Kosovo). As the second religion in Italy (Allievi 2003), Islam has not been able to play a coherent role in the public sphere and thus reduce the influence of the Catholic Church. In contrast, it has reinforced the monopolistic function played by the Catholic Church in the media and in society as whole, particularly for those Italians who are orphans of Oriana Fallaci. However, this role has been experienced positively by the Muslim communities which, in many cases – at the local level, and coping with hostilities and discrimination by the political leaders at the municipal level – were advocated by Catholic priests or bishops.

The explanation is to be found in the historical compromise between the state and the Catholic Church, in spite of the constitutional separation between the two. Up to now it has been impossible to have another religious actor as well as the Catholic Church. Therefore we are looking at the Italo-Muslim second generation as the new actors able to enlarge the boundaries of the religious public sphere and to represent the new voice in the public communication process.

Italian Secularism: The Historical Compromise

The basic hypothesis that we intend to set forth in the pages that follow is based on the idea that ordinary Italians consider themselves Catholic but have a variety of different ways of interpreting their practical involvement with the Catholic Church. Also, set against this background of shifting boundaries in terms of affiliation with the birth religion, we find both such phenomena as forms of postmodern syncretism, which elude straightforward measurement with quantitative instruments, and the forceful entry into the broader social and religious panorama of other religions, some of which are decidedly alien to Italy's cultural history, such as, for instance, the Sikh religion (Denti, Ferrari, Perocco 2005).

One particularly illustrative example of shifting boundaries within the Catholic belief system can be found in the general Italian attitude towards the sacramental practice of confession. Half of all parish priests now state that this practice has been in decline for some time, even among practising Catholics, while 80 per cent of all parish priests believe that changes of some sort must be undertaken in order to restore meaning and value to the ritual of confession (Garelli 2003; Osservatorio Socio-Religioso del Triveneto 2006).

The first indication that emerges from the major studies is that Italian society continues to portray itself as a relatively homogeneous society in religious terms. The social and linguistic commonplaces that mark the horizons of significance of the universe of Italian life continue to serve as a mirror offering a reflection to collective self-awareness. Catholicism is the matrix that engenders those appearances. The vast majority of Italians, to state this matter differently, continue to define themselves as Catholics, and in keeping with that view, they are relatively faithful to the ritual forms of behaviour prescribed by the Catholic Church (especially Sunday Mass). On average, in comparison with other European countries (except for Ireland), Italy has the highest level of religious observance, and religious socialization still remains at high levels, while trust in the Church as an institution remains equally high (above 60 per cent). From this point of view, initially, it would appear difficult, if not impossible, to speak of moral and religious pluralism.

All the same (and this is the second important finding of the study) the unanimous Catholicism of the Italians conceals (and has done for some time) a plurality of ways of conceiving the meaning of belonging to the Catholic Church, varying forms of religious practice, and the relative independence of a number of areas of social and individual life with respect to a system of belief in which, apparently, people identify themselves. From the earliest studies by Burgalassi, in the Sixties and Seventies, to more recent investigations, we find a general trend line in the analysis of the social and religious phenomenon and the moral attitudes of the Italians that we can summarize as *unity in diversity*. The Italians continue to believe that the Catholic religion makes it possible to perceive unity in a situation that, in point of fact, has become increasingly differentiated, both in religious and ethical and moral terms. The presence of the *other*, identified as the *Muslim*, and in more general terms, immigrants, bringers of a different culture, has contributed – at least in part of the Italian population – to a reinforced sense of the existence of shared cultural roots in the form of Catholicism. We are faced with a collective belief that is nourished by the long-term historical trend and that is solidified, even today, though to a lesser degree than in the recent past, in an array of concrete social bonds that individuals establish within various institutional contexts (parish churches, Catholic associations, volunteer groups and the like), which exist at a grassroots level as manifestations of the Catholic Church throughout the Italian territory (especially in the form of the parish churches, and particularly in central-northern Italy and sanctuaries in the south).

For that matter, for a long period of the history of the Italian state the Italians have encountered numerous and substantial stumbling blocks in their attempts to feel fully integrated in a shared national identity. They have been divided, over the years, into a number of ideological families: liberals, socialists, Catholics, both intransigent and modernist; and then Fascists, Communists, Christian Democrats, as well as League members, post-Fascists, post-Christian Democrats, post-Communists, and so on. So many macro-identities that, nonetheless, have done nothing to hinder the recognition of a patrimony of shared values, above and beyond the ideological divisions that are physiological in an open society capable of bottom-up self-government, such as is the case in Italy. Catholicism has performed this difficult role and will continue to do so, a role that has not been served by Italy's national history (Pace 1998).

We cannot ignore all the tensions to which the ethnic and cultural identity of the Italians, if such an identity has ever existed in this land of a thousand 'bell towers' (an idiomatic reference to fragmented local identities – *translator*), has been subjected. If we were to overlook this tension, we would be unable to comprehend why a majority of Italians turn today to the resource of collective feeling constituted by Catholicism. From this point of view, the Catholicism of and for the Italians (believers or non-believers, and with differing ideological viewpoints) is a generalized symbolic code that makes it possible to reduce the degree of contingency and differentiation that actually exists in society.

The Italians no longer subscribe en masse to the institutional objectives and the religious observance of their 'mother church', but they do continue to think that their national identity finds a strong point of reference in a generic sense of affiliation with the 'religion' represented by the Catholic Church, working with interest and love to ensure that there are no traumatic rendings of that collective memory. If we adjust, for historical context, the Catholicism of the Italians (much like the Catholicism of the Poles, the Irish and, in part, the Spanish) is a way of believing in one's collective identity. The fact that the Italian Catholic

Church has invested greatly in this diffuse moral sentiment among the Italians should not lead us to think that this sentiment has been or continues to be an automatic reflection of the sense of affiliation with the Church itself. The status of belonging is in fact uncertain and has shifting boundaries, as shown by various recent studies. In conclusion, we may say that outside of Catholicism there is no way of imagining a collective sense of identity, even if the quest for salvation is no longer a monopoly held by the Catholic Church.

While a significant portion of the Italian population – a portion that is somewhat higher than that found in other European counties – continues to maintain both *religious faith and practice*, acting on and believing in their creed, there is another, smaller, but all the same significant sector (roughly a third of the national population) for whom religious belief seems to exist independently of any specific subject of belief. The specific subject of belief acquired movable and indeterminate boundaries; a monad with doors and windows that does not necessarily need to avail itself of an authoritative source to certify the existence of boundaries for the belief itself. If, therefore, the Italians show a level of trust in the Catholic Church (above 60 per cent) that is higher than in other European societies, it is also true that this level of trust does not necessarily correspond to similar percentages both in the realm of religious practice and belief and in the realm of ethical choices. The ethics of the situation prevails over that of consistent belief, anchored to a belief system that finds its meaning and ultimate foundation in a principle of religious truth.

In the everyday practice of the majority of Italians we find a sort of relative autonomy of the system of belief from the moral sphere. The moral sphere appears to be characterized by a twofold contingency. On the one hand, the social and religious players who attempt to define the key for access to the moral code find themselves competing among themselves in a differentiated environment, in an attempt to impose their respective points of view (concerning this or that ethical or moral issue, such as artificial insemination, gay marriage, abortion, and so on), and, on the other hand, individuals tend to regulate their behaviour independently, often paying greater attention to a search for meaning than to an obedience to the rules. I choose not so much because I have been guided by the rules, but rather because I believe that the choice that I am making, in a given situation, satisfies my conscience. My conscience and not something other than me, serves as a criterion of validity for the choices that I must make. Partial or total adherence to a system of (religious) belief is not sufficient to reassemble this fracture that is so typical of religious modernity.

Even the sphere of economics, in its relationship with ethics, may appear to be characterized by a relative autonomy from the realm of religion. Within the context of observant Catholics, in fact, the ethics of universal brotherhood is broken down and reassembled on the basis of moral and political orientations, often diverse and contrasting. To put it lightly, at Sunday Mass, when the congregation is urged to exchange a 'gesture of peace', the phrase can take on a radically different meaning if one belongs to a social group oriented more towards neo-liberalist, or free trade, views (whereby every individual is the entrepreneur of his or her own destiny and must therefore pursue 'a career in competition with the others' without excessive concern over whether others are left behind on the social ladder), or, on the other hand, if one identifies with a set of beliefs that we can generically describe as oriented towards solidarity, and which, therefore, entail a model of regulation of social justice which relies upon the political community and the state to play a role in the redistribution of national wealth and equity. In the first case, the group of Catholics in question is probably more homogeneous, in ideological terms, with those who identify themselves as non-believers or non-practising Catholics, but who share the same point of view. Likewise, in the second case, there is an objective ideological and moral closeness of those Catholics with a sector of the secular, non-believing world that guides its own actions in accordance with the principles of social solidarity. From this point of view, it is as if we were verifying, statistics at hand, the point to which the differentiation external to a system of religious belief had established itself in a modernized society like that in Italy, and the degree to which this differentiation had been transferred into the interior of the system of beliefs, rendering more complicated the task facing those who, *professionally*, are meant to act as religious and moral guides. The acknowledgment by the majority of the Italian population of the public role of the Catholic Church should not mislead us. It may also be interpreted as a recognition of the specialization of the social function of the Church. In certain contexts it should be seen as an authoritative interlocutor that has the right and the duty to state 'its own view', even though everyone is now free to do as they believe.

Italian society, unequal in comparison with the times and ways of Catholic civilization (divided by territorial areas, profound ideological fissures, and accelerated processes of economic and social change), in the final analysis seems to emerge, photographed by all the studies, with all its ancient wrinkles and, at the same time, with a *nova facies*, precisely in moral and religious terms. What emerges is the affirmation of autonomy in terms of freedom of worship, even in a society like that of Italy, still influenced in many ways by the Catholic belief system. It is in terms of religious individualism or, perhaps, the belief in *relative* forms that render possible moderate forms of pluralism, dissonant models of belief, both religious and moral, within the context of a shared nominal symbolic reference.

To sum up, all the elements we have evoked explain:

a) in spite of the decrease in religious practices, the Catholic Church has been able to defend and reaffirm its role as Master of Public Ethics, safeguarding the national values and supervising of the collective memory;
b) the process of transformation of the Catholic traditional power into a power of communication, able to mobilize public opinion on ethical issues, with the Church acting as a religious lobby to the political leaders or deputies in the Italian Parliament;
c) instead of using the power of dogma, the representatives of the Catholic Church act as the opinion-makers, trying to confirm its centrality in the public sphere;
d) after the fall of the internal Berlin Wall (i.e., the collapse of the ideological cleavage between Catholics and Communists), the Catholic Church played an important role in coping with the attempt made by a new political party – Lega Nord – which claimed the secession of the northern from the southern part of Italy, defending the integrity of the national identity, rooted in Catholicism. In this sense the majority of Italian people feel that Catholicism represents till now shared values, a common feeling of belonging to a nation, despite the secularization process in many fields of everyday life. Catholicism represents the historical compromise that rescues the weak national consciousness and allows Italians to think a nation that shares common moral values in spite of the social differentiation, the economic and cultural cleft

between north and south and the decline of the political ideologies which the people favoured (the Christian Democratic Party, Socialism, Communism, Liberalism, and so on). How should one put it? *Extra ecclesiam nulla nation* and ... every man for himself (do-it-yourself religion).

Managing Islam in the Religious Public Sphere (RPS)

To frame the infrastructure of the RPS in Italy and the function allotted to Italian Islam, it is important to be reminded briefly of the constitutional rules, comparing four histories' movements. In the table opposite we sum up the evolution of the relation between the state and the Catholic Church.

The table shows that, in spite of the crucial turning points in Italian history (from Liberal to Fascist state, from the Resistance to the Republican Constitution, from the *internal cold war* (between Whites and Reds) to the collapse in 1992 of the political system (in which the major political parties like the Christian Democrats, Socialists and Communists, and Post-Fascist vanished), from the sharp differentiation between the majority of Italian people from the Church's orientation with regard to issues like divorce, abortion and contraception, to the re-establishment of the hegemonic moral role of the Catholic Church in the public and political spheres (i.e., bishops are able to press the government to approve a rule on the end-of-life testament coherent with the Catholic doctrine that considers the force-feeding of those who are in a vegetative condition as a therapy and therefore a duty for the doctors to continue, despite wills written).

This is clear, particularly, under the rule of the right-wing government and the role played in the alliance by the political party, Lega Nord, that marks its ideological identity by anti-Islam rhetoric (Guolo 2003). Up to now the Italian Parliament has not been able to pass a law on the freedom of religion, which currently is non-existent in spite of the liberal sentences in the 1948 Constitution. The discussion began ten year ago, and has not made any real progress. The reason for this impasse is relatively simple to explain. On the one hand, the new law introduces the idea of equality of various religious institutions and communities before the state, while, on the other, it implies the end of the cult regime, because there will be a common rule both for the religion of the majority and for that of the minorities.

TABLE 1
State–Catholic Church Relations

1848 Carlo Alberto of Savoia Statute (pre-Italian state)	The 1929 Concordat between (Fascist) state and church	The Concordat in the Republican Constitution	The 1984 revisal of the Concordat (centre-left government)	2001 political change
Catholicism religion of the state	Catholicism religion of the state	On the one hand, the principle of separation between state and church, on the other the Constitution recognizes the 1929 agreement (Article 7). It means it recognizes Catholicism as the state religion	Abolishing the formula 'Catholicism is the religion of the state', it reaffirms the centrality of Catholicism in the national identity	Since 9/11 the politicians (more from the right-wing, less from the left) encouraged the Catholic Church to play *de facto* the role of the religion of the state
The other religious minorities (Waldensians and Jews an so on) are recognized by the state	The other religious minorities are recognized *as admitted cults* on the basis of the government's decision	The regime of the admitted cults continues	Revisal of the previous regime, introducing the new one: the agreement (*intese*) between the state and those religious minorities which intend to rule the relation according to the general principles that frame the Catholic church–state relations.	Meanwhile the public sphere has been completely occupied by the Catholic Church and re-establishes the admitted cults regime (i.e., no agreement with the Jehovah's Witnesses, Buddhist Federation and Muslim communities)

Indeed, there is an objective convergence between the Catholic Church (at least the Italian Bishops Conference or CEI) and the right-wing political parties (and also some factions within the left-wing parties) to maintain the Concordat regime because it warrants:

a) a set of privileges to the Catholic Church (from financial support from the state to the centrality of Catholic teaching in public schools;
b) the recognition of the public guardian of the collective memory and the national identity, reducing the incumbent effect of the religious pluralism that is shaping the Italian landscape;

c) the reaffirmation of the historical compromise and division of moral 'labour' between the state and the church, actually integrating religion and politics (according to the *entente cordiale* model) for maintaining social order.

The Catholic Church firmly opposed the text of the new rule on the freedom of religion, precisely because of that affirmation of the equality of all religions before the state. In other words, the following graphic reflects the mutual interest of the Church and the political establishment in conserving the hierarchic structure of the relation with the state, a privileged axis that relegates the other religious minorities to second position in a sort of scale of relevance of religions in Italy. In this sense you could understand the irrelevance of the other confessions in the public sphere: as a rule they are relegated to the backstage and in the media their points of view on various topics (euthanasia, abortion, gay unions and so on) do not appear. Among them, in this ideal scale, Islam represents the tolerated religion that the 'wicat' (White Italian Catholic) has to regard with suspicion, limiting its influence and presence in society (e.g., the idea launched by the Lega Nord to submit the opening of a mosque to a popular referendum).

GRAPHIC 1
Islam in the public sphere according to the hierarchic structure of the religious field in Italy

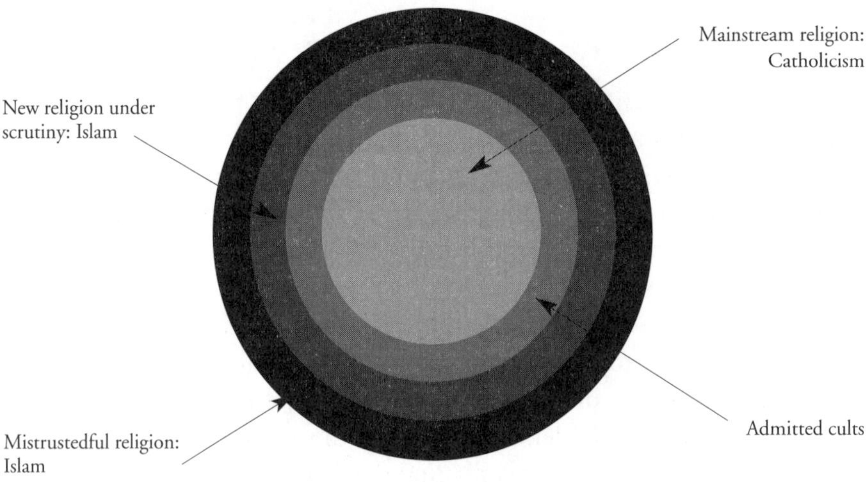

Islam is not recognized as a public player because, it is assumed, of a fear of the supposed shared values preserved by Catholicism, in spite of the social action on the part of the Catholic base communities to help immigrants integrate into the community, independently of their religious affiliation. Therefore, so-called Islam – more correctly those who belong to Islam in various ways – is not the subject of public communication, but the object, a passive reference to be manipulated by others, functionally ordered to show its incompatibility with the democratic and religious traditions of the Italian people.

The puzzle of the recognition of the second religion in Italy, Islam, continues to this day, in spite of the efforts inaugurated by two ministries in 2005 and 2006 (one right-wing and the other left-wing) to establish a Council of Islam in Italy. The body has been conceived as a preliminary step to sign an agreement between the state and the Muslim communities, indeed, with different orientations. But since the new government came into office in 2007, the open-door policies seem to have been discarded by the Ministry of Internal Affairs, run by the representative of the Lega Nord, which partially attracts votes because of its clear anti-Islam ideological pattern of political action.

Islam is now a silent religion in Italy. In two senses: it has been reduced to silence and Muslims are feeling so intimidated that they prefer to keep silent (the one exception was during the Gaza war in January 2009 when there was a public protest by migrants from Arab countries, with a prayer by Muslims before the Milan Dome or Bologna Cathedral at the end of the demonstration). This attitude is changing slowly because a new generation of Italo-Muslims is emerging which is capable of speaking sometimes in the public sphere: a new timid voice.

Challenging Italy, Challenging Islam: Generation and Gender in Muslim Claims

Among the social religious players present in Italy, the Young Muslims of Italy Association (Giovani Musulmani d'Italia or GMI) is the first organized expression of a growing population: immigrants' sons and daughters, who were born and grew up in Italy. It was founded soon after 9/11, and in a few years it has gained a remarkable *public visibility* (Frisina 2006 and 2007), challenging openly the dominant collective representation of Italy as a monolithically Catholic country.

The founders of the GMI association have grown up with the reality of the Islamic association, and in 2001 they felt the need to have more autonomy from the UCOII, the main associative reality of the immigrant Muslim, culturally connected to the Society of the Muslim Brothers (Allievi e Dassetto 1993; Pace and Perocco 2000, Frisina forthcoming). The GMI have founded the association[1] in a growing climate of insecurity and suspicion towards Islam.

The eyes of 'others' have urged their process of individualization: feeling constantly under scrutiny and living daily with the burden of stigmatization, they entered the public space introducing themselves as *Italian citizens of Islamic faith*, in order to 'reinvent' a more inclusive national identity and promote claims of social inclusion.

This has created a distance from the adults' associative realities, in order to build an 'Italian Islam', somehow different from the one transmitted from the immigrant parents, i.e., more independent and autochthonous.

Concerning the *external side*, the GMI have tried to pass from object to subject of the speech and to have access to the mass media, the main vehicle of stereotypes and prejudices towards Islam (Said 1997; Bruno 2003) that continues to represent Italy as a monolithically Catholic country and Islam as the threatening Alterity. It acts as a pressure group and has sent hundreds of emails and written many protest press releases directed against those television programmes that feed a climate of fear and suspicion towards Muslims in Italy. In the past few years GMI representatives have appeared on talk shows, variety shows and, on some occasions, on the news. They have also managed to draw the interest of the press, releasing many interviews with the main national newspapers and showing a peaceful face of an 'Italian Islam'. In the second place, GMI members have committed themselves to a *civic formation*; for example, participating at the National Youth Forum (www.forumnazionaledeigiovani.it), attending a course on Human Rights Education (in December 2004 in Spain) and a course on Active Citizenship Education (in August 2005 in Estonia). However, the best road to becoming a citizen seems to remain *participation on a local level.* In the towns where they live, GMI members have become protagonists of many cultural activities, especially in the schools. They have found themselves as experts of Islam and started to work as mediators, becoming more professional day by day. The local level has also been strategic in tying up relations with the civil society and creating volunteering experiences, often in Catholic-oriented associations. In the third place, the GMI has been very active in *interreligious dialogue*, taking part in many meetings.

The more frequent meetings happened with various youth groups of the Catholic associations, especially with ACLI, but meetings also took place with Waldensian groups, Buddhist groups and also with the Young Italian Jews Union (UGEI).

During the first meetings of young Muslims and Jews, only the leaders met, because of the wariness of the two associations, but later on the commitment was extended to the less active members. The target with the passing of time has slightly changed: it is not only to have a deeper understanding of the religion of the other and to introduce one's own, but also to *openly confront each other with matters that both sides find difficult, in particular with the limits of Italian secularism*, without hiding the existing conflict. The challenges are twofold: learn together, talking to each other about religious pluralism and values; promote more equality among religions, bringing the discussion of the hegemony of Catholicism to the fore and contesting those who use it in the political arena in an ethnic and discriminatory way.

On the internal side, the GMI aims at creating a sense of European belonging among the young members and at harmonizing Islamic religiosity with the life of the Italian society in which they were born or have grown up. Through meetings and work groups it fosters the reflectivity of the participants so that they can avoid falling into the trap of responding to discrimination by withdrawing, and can defend their rights as citizens of Islamic faith. It is a work of empowerment, of strengthening self-esteem and encouragement to be an active part of society. Concerning religious formation, the youth showed intolerance towards the trainers of the association linked to UCOII and progressively looked for alternatives. One of the strategies was to increase the workshops as opposed to lessons; another was to invite scholars (some not Muslims) who could offer conceptual tools useful to pick up the changes in progress among European Muslims; yet another was to look for international exchanges to meet young Muslims from other countries and to be trained accordingly.

The dissent with the adults' association had at its core the rejection of symbolic violence intrinsic in the dichotomous logics that counter-pointed *us*-Muslims (positive polarity) against *them*-Italians (negative polarity). The GMI's effort from the inside was, above all a tiring struggle for cultural influence, summarized in the linguistic dilemma: Italian or Arabic during the training meetings? For the youth born or bred in Italy, the answer was simple: Italian, because this is the language they know better. They also had a particular slang: for example, during the participant observation among the GMI I, they discovered that the Muslim Brothers were named 'the iguana', transliterating creatively the Arabic word for 'brothers', *ikhwan*.

The adults' associations, as many are responsible for the mosques, have continued to invite trainers from their countries of origin, mainly Arabic-speaking. The language is certainly also metaphoric: it refers to a problem of interpretative traditions of Islam that to many youths appear obsolete, too rigid and conservative.

> If I think about the four law schools of Islam, it seems to me they are founded in a traditional way. We were born here. We have understood, we were taught that it is not like this and that's all, one behaves like that and it is right and that's it. There is more than a choice, different interpretations, because one can interpret in a way, while another one could interpret the same things in a different way. (Amr, twenty-one years old, grew up in Italy, of Tunisian origin)

For this reason many of them hardly go to the mosque, not yet having a clear alternative for their religious training.

Some of them are discovering the *new voices of Islam* (Noor 2002; Zu Furstemberg 2004), often persecuted in their countries of origin, who find space in European and American universities and live in exile in order to foster a cultural framework without borders:

> Studying the history of Islam at university, I was forced to question all I had learned before. For example, I was taught that the *kalifs* were enlightened, but studying more objectively I learned about power struggles, violence ... The study of thinkers such as Abu Zayd helped me as well ... I considered him impious, but now I consider him one who chose freedom. (Anouar, twenty-one years old, grew up in Italy of Moroccan origin)

These new voices are very precious in a global contest where the delegitimization of the religious authorities brought us the phenomenon of learning on the Internet and of self-proclamation of leaders through the mass media that very often lead to dogmatic and neo-fundamentalist versions of Islam (Roy 2003: 69–80). Despite its democratic potentialities, the Internet nowadays seems to transmit a legalist version of Islam centred in the definition of what is admissable (halal) and what is inadmissable (haram) for a good Muslim. Also, when I visited the site of GMI, I had the impression that while meeting in flesh and bone the members of GMI, the religious discourse that emerged was more elaborate and complex. The public image presented is often distant from the private experience: from one side there are strict rules to respect and from the other there is a personal ethic with doubts and possible negotiations.

The basic problem is that these young Muslims who were born or grew up in Italy, members or not, do daily *ijtihad* (interpretative efforts) that hardly find public recognition. In my empirical investigation *the girls* are on the frontline in these tiring changes and cultural negotiations, both internally and externally.

Internally, they seek more space for autonomy[2] and at the same time they want to build a common memory with their parents. What is often criticized is the tightening of the normative version of religion: many young girls maintain that orthopraxis without intention has no sense.

> A girl might be in a long dress, wear the veil but have an evil heart. It is very subjective, 'the gown does not make the friar'! Wearing the hijab is not enough, to me it makes no difference ... What matters is how one behaves. (Rachida, twenty years old, born in Italy, of Moroccan origin)

The majority of the young Muslim girls I met think that the value given to the *spirit* is more important than that given to the word, to *the purity of heart* than to the ritualistic practice.

This interiorized religiosity has always been present in Islam, not only in the mystical tradition but also among the 'common Muslims '(Babès 2000: 180). For the young girls I met, it is a direct relation with God told in words such as abandonment and happiness. Being Muslim also means going through these states of well-being, of peace. Those who pass through these experiences of holiness feel they can live their faith with more freedom. Religion is experienced as a choice, a heritage to regain in order to make sense, and there are also those who go beyond and imagine another education for their sons, allowing more space for confrontation with other faiths.

> A thing I want to teach to my sons is something important I learned about religions. I wish they could come in contact with all religions … My parents at school did not allow me to learn the Christian religion, the Catholic one, but I have always learned it. I think it is right to confront each other. In the end there's not much difference between the three monotheistic religions.
>
> The same theme appears … Maybe one dresses differently … one wears the veil! But in the end the theme is the same, love each other. (Leila, nineteen years old, grew up in Italy, of Moroccan origin)

This way of thinking is stigmatized by the parents (more generally by the adults), and the mosques and associations, and remains in a weak position because it stems from young people who have few theological tools to legitimate it. Through daily conflicts and negotiations, those who believe 'differently' continue to also feel Muslim and point out the significance of *respect*,[3] in his or her experience, as the most authentic message of Islam.

On the external side, also in Italy, there are new Muslim female subjects emerging. They are claiming public pluri-belongings and are capable of multiple loyalties and criticisms.

Far from being passive victims of orientalist discourses of colonial origin (Said 1991) and of their side-effects towards women (Ahmed 1995), such subjects resist daily the inferior representations with their cultural creativity, and they denounce 'the hypocrisy of the assumed neutrality and equality of the individuals in the public sphere or the artificiality of the border line between the public and private sphere, casting light on the classic opposition of secularism and religiosity' (Salih 2008: 144).

I take as examples two voices of young Italian Muslims that have became popular in the Italian public sphere, Randa Ghazy and Sumaya Abdel Qader, starting with their books, recently published. 'Today Maybe I Do Not Kill Anybody' (Ghazy: 2007) tells the story of Jasmine, a young Muslim of Egyptian origin who 'strangely is not a terrorist'. Jasmine feels 'like a djinn', good and often angry because she is misunderstood. She rebels against the autochthonous admirer who perpetuates stereotypes about Arabians and Muslims. Her main weapon is irony:

> Veal is like depilatory wax: do it whenever you want, ignore what others expect from you. You feel you can do it, when it is not too

> extreme a sacrifice. Men would like us always perfectly depilated. Forget it. I'M NOT FEMINIST, BUT ... Muslim men should spend more time examining themselves instead of spending it watching what a woman says, what she wears, how she laughs, how many times a month she plucks out her eyelids, maybe things would turn out better. (p. 16)

> Anything a Muslim woman says, beware, beware, she draws scandal. As if she has a note on her forehead: WORK IN PROGRESS, EMANCIPATION PROCESS RUNNING and as if any trying to break with certain tradition would cause a spreading uneasiness. (p. 147)

'I Wear the Veil, I Love the Queen' (Abdel Qader 2008) tells the story of Sulinda, a young Muslim girl of Palestinian/Jordanian origin who feels she is part of a new generation of Italians and refuses the categorizations based on the origins of her immigrant parents. Sulinda goes regularly to the mosque and she wishes to have the tools and places to grow her faith and transmit it to her daughters, but in Italy today it is not that easy:

> Victimism persecuted me up to high school. Until rage and pride burst inside me and I decided to turn to an attack position. Stop suffering in silence! Without mentioning that a new element made me an easy target: the veil ... The change arrived with the professor of religion, when one day she asked me to join her in the classes to talk about Islam and Arabians. It's easy, I thought, I can skip the hours of maths and Italian. The illusion disappeared soon. I realised I was completely ignorant about Arabian history and culture. Before many religious questions I had no answers. And where was I supposed to find them? The mosque was just a hole where nobody was prepared to teach the youth. My mother taught us what she could. My poor dad was always at work. (pp. 136 and 144–145)

> [Her daughter Shadia, six years old] has a lively inquiring mind and as soon as she enters the mosque she asks, 'Why is it so disgusting here and the church is so beautiful?' That's true. It is impossible not to wonder why, when we are in an industrial shed turned into a mosque that's freezing in winter and too hot in summer, humid, dark, without a garden, without grass, with nothing attractive. What can I answer her? That the local council or the municipality won't allow a real mosque be built? Or that somebody has fed people with

> so much fear that as soon as we think to build a place of Islamic worship or a gathering place a general psychosis and panic spreads everywhere so that nobody has the courage to give any permit? She wouldn't understand. And I would risk transmitting to her a sort of rage and hatred against the institutions that they would deserve but it's not right and not constructive. I just tell her, 'We are looking for a new place that will be beautiful.' I hope I won't have to lie forever. (pp. 120–121)

The Long Struggle Towards Religious Equality

The Italian constitution grants equal social dignity to all citizens, and equality 'without distinctions of sex, race, language, religion, political opinions, personal and social conditions' (Art. 3); moreover it also protects all the religious confessions to be 'equally free' and to have the right to organize themselves (Art. 8). In the daily experience and the life of many Muslims of Italy this is not applied, especially for those who live in local contests where Lega Nord rules and has politicized the mosque matter so that freedom to worship is no longer a right but a concession that non-Muslims can or cannot grant through a citizens' referendum. The rhetoric used is dichotomous between 'us' (Catholic–Christian–liberal–modern citizens/landlords) and 'them' (Muslim–authoritarian–traditionalist strangers/guests). Following the debate in the Italian media it is clear that the cultural and religious diversity of Italy has been built as a problem (Saint Blancat and Schmidt of Friedberg 2005; Triandafyllidou 2006; AlBahari 2007); what they use is a nationalist rhetoric that ethnicizes Catholicism, making it converge with the 'culture and values of the Italians'.

The case of Meryem is a model because it shows how difficult the struggle for religious freedom in Italy is nowadays, at the same time casting light on how the new generations are decisively contributing to democratic change.

Meryem[4] is a young Muslim girl of Treviso, a stronghold town of Lega Nord and of Lord Mayor Gentilini, whose xenophobia is well known internationally. In December 2007, on Aid Al Kabyr Day, she protested against the irruption of police during a prayer in a hall in the province of Treviso, and she promised to commit herself to 'the dignity of the Muslim community'.

> It wasn't the first time we were offended ... it won't be the last either. But inside me, looking at the policemen that once more stepped in to check us during the prayer and walked on carpets, I said that's enough, it's not possible that an old man (Gentilini) can keep all these people under control. So I decided to react, to change the way the Treviso people see us, and I showed the old man that we do not have to feel like guests, we have rights ...

Meryem managed to concretize this effort in April 2008 when, against another refusal for the concession of a gathering and prayer place for the Muslims, she rallied other young Muslims like herself and for three months they organized a protest each Friday for half an hour (from 12 to 12.30).

> With the elections it is clear that things are getting worse ... the racism and fascism of the local politicians vexing the Muslims increases. After trying to work together with the Islamic associations, I realized they wanted to subordinate the youth and therefore we continued in our own way. They said 'Good Luck' ... I remember the discouragement and the perseverance. I took the Civil Code and had a revelation: the public spaces! Spaces for all citizens. Also ours! Of course without disturbing.
>
> Then I looked for a parking place near the stadium, huge and always empty. I called other young people and we put on blue t-shirts and had the Italian flags ... We prayed together. We were twenty, thirty, up to fifty or sixty boys and girls. It depended on the weather! Day after day the police came to check us and they became friends ... In the end they seemed embarrassed to do their job ... One policeman in particular, who spends his holidays in Morocco, told us 'It is an order, I execute it, but you are right ...'

In July 2008 she received a letter containing death threats. It contained her photo cut from local newspapers surrounded by crosses. It was written that she had to die, together with her family and the left-wing politicians who favoured opening mosques in Italy.

At first she did not want to denounce the threats because of fear of not being believed, but then her parents convinced her to go to the police headquarters. She chose not to inform the media, since she did not trust them. Anyway, she did not give up, and in the summer, while other youths were on holidays, she founded the offices for the association of which she would become president: 'Second Generation'. The owner of the premises is from Treviso and lived a long time in Libya, where he learned to know and respect Muslims. He was immediately threatened by Gentilini with jail. In front of the association there are Italian flags and one morning they found blasphemous words offending Allah and comparing the Prophet Muhammad to Satan. The provocations did not stop here. One evening a car arrived in the blind alley of the association and a man spat and then shouted 'Immigrants, go back home'. Meryem's parents were present and decided to call the police but while the father stopped the car the mother was hit by the car door.

'The day after, we realised he was a Lega Nord city councilman. In the version given to the media the aggressor becomes victim.'

Meryem decided to approach some serious journalists, but she thought that there was no real pluralism in Italy ('They want to sell more than tell the true facts') so then she chose Al Jazeera, as she thought it would be objective and also able to draw the solidarity of other Muslims in the world. She shot amateur videos to explain the situation in Treviso and sent the tapes by mail, reaching her target. A troupe of Al Jazeera arrived in her town and, together with her, prepared a report on the Muslims in Italy. A short documentary was shot called 'Italy's Other Religion' that was broadcast in the programme 'People and Power' on 14 February 2009.[5] Among the protagonists we can see Meryem, who is the face of young Italian Muslims fighting for their civil rights.

Meryem was not looking for individual promotion. After a year of intense public scrutiny she was tired and the presidency passed to another girl.

Meryem wants to concentrate on university (she is in the second year of International Economy) and earns her living working as a shop assistant in a big store in Treviso. She claims it should not be a personal struggle, but collective and with a long-term perspective.

> The base problem is that when the people of Treviso say 'the Muslims must respect our rules', they do not think about the constitution … or the payment of the taxes! They repeat what the politicians say on the television, ending up thinking their rules are … Christianity! Yes, never directly, but if addressing you with 'you have to compromise' and not giving us the chance to open a mosque, in the end what are they saying? We should become Christians? I met good Christians, a Catholic priest who gave the parish to Muslims so they could pray, and he doesn't think in that

> way ... The ones holding the power are pushing ... and influence our lives ...

The priest mentioned by Meryem stopped giving the place in his parish after the local media reported the fact in a sensationalist way, 'the church became a mosque', and then the prohibition of the ecclesiastic hierarchies arrived.

Meryem remembers that when she was a child in Casablanca, her mother worked as a housekeeper in a Jewish family. In her class, besides Jews there were Christians, and when it was time for the religious lesson each pupil went to learn with the teacher about his or her correspondent faith but during the religious festivities everybody had the chance to know each other and stay together. In her latest holiday in Morocco Meryem says that besides cathedrals and synagogues now there are also Buddhist temples, for the Chinese and Indian workers who immigrated recently.

Meryem is disappointed, since she thought Italy, being in Europe, was democratic; instead today she realizes there is no real pluralism. She does not stop hoping for change. She wishes to have not only Catholic teaching (Pace 2005) in Italian schools, but an education oriented towards pluralism.

> All the students should be able to participate and confront big topics ... the discriminations concerning women, for example. And not just to discuss religious topics ... Since violence towards women is not only a religious matter. And also topics such as peace, justice ... Everybody can learn something more by living together ...

In my research I have met other youth who desire more pluralism, starting from the public schools (Frisina 2006b). The most critical ones are not the Muslims, but young Jews and Waldesians. The former lived with a strong uneasiness in the presence of Christian symbols in the public sphere (the crosses), while the latter paid attention to more material questions, such as the economic privileges that the Catholic Church accumulates with the inland revenue declaration (8 x 1000). In their discourses about secularism these youth point often to the word 'equality'.

The distance these days between political discourse and media discourse is enormous, and some youth imagine themselves as Europeans to envision possible solutions. However, none of them think still to pass from claiming their rights to legal struggles to make them effective. In other European countries this is happening, and religious discrimination turns out to be a more significant category (Amiraux 2005).

The deputy mayor, Gentilini, is today backed up by the Berlusconi government, but his declarations have spread all over Europe and can incite 'hate crimes' (he offended not only Muslim citizens but also Roma citizens, and he even invoked the 'ethnic cleansing' of gays. Would it be opportune for the European Commission to extend to the Muslims the protection levels from discrimination that are applied to other social groups (Modood 2006: 53) and prompt with incisive measures countries such as Italy to respect the democratic standards?

In any case, it seems the Italian match has to be played on the premise of the revision of the Italian secularism model and on a new law on religious freedom.

Conclusions: Italian Secularism Revisited?

Everywhere in Europe the public claims of Muslim citizens, as mentioned, first of all those of young women, 'cast a new light on the contradictions intrinsic in the liberal democracies, starting from secularism as clear separation between the public and private sphere, where the religious identity is linked to the first. Moreover, it is the universalistic promise to be called to attention and the complex relation on universalism and diversity' (Salih 2008: 143).

In Italy as well it became necessary to acknowledge the limits of the Italian secularism model; despite its flexibility compared to others (for example the French one), it cannot get rid of the weight of a past when Catholicism was the state religion.

From the institutional and political side the resistances to change are still strong; it is enough to mention the impact of the law on religious freedom and conscience that – defined ten years ago by the Prodi government – has found and still finds obstacles not only in the Italian Episcopal Conference but even more in those parties that become 'defenders of the Italian Catholic identity' in an anti-Islamic key (Lega Nord, but also Alleanza Nazionale).

Yet the law appears more than necessary in a climate of growing racism and institutional drifts to the most stringent and conservative versions of Catholicism (as emerged lately for the biological testament debate).

However, a legislative change, even if necessary, would not be enough to guarantee more pluralism in Italy, if there is no social base on which to build daily.

Despite the institutional hindrances at a national level, important news is emerging in many local contests (Clementi 2008: 135–167): for example, there are public schools experimenting with intercultural paths in a religious contest and encouraging the knowledge of different faiths, starting from the ones present in the classes, involving the students of immigrant origin and their families. It is from below that the signs of pluralism are coming, to gather, to enhance, to formalize good practices and to transfer them into new contests.

Besides, recent research (Frisina 2009: 120–121) shows that an 'ordinary cosmopolitanism' exists, practised by both Italian and immigrant origin citizens, allowing them to 'relativize Islam exceptionality and the security emergency after 9/11'. Among these social players, experts of multi-relational discourses (Baumann 2003) able to build a new more inclusive 'us' spring up new Muslim generations that slowly extend their borders in the Italian public sphere. An important challenge therefore appears, i.e., to foster strong and determined side alliances among citizens, Muslims or otherwise, interested in more religious pluralism in Italy.

In a time determined by a troubled Italian democracy (in relation to the limits of press freedom and to a government composed influential xenophobic forces) only civil society can lead to a change towards a more inclusive secularist model.

NOTES

1 Concerning the composition of the association: from 2001 to today there are about 350 subscribers a year; the majority are between sixteen and eighteen years old, while the leaders are between nineteen and thirty years old; there are more girls than boys in the association, and they are more active locally, but all five elected presidents are male: they are, in the majority, sons of Moroccan immigrants, but in the leadership there is a significant Near East component (the current president is of Egyptian origin); the majority attends the high school, while the leaders study at university (both science and humanities faculties); their fathers are mainly workers and small dealers; the mothers are mainly housewives and domestic assistants. In the end, the more numerous and active local sections are those of Lombardia, Emilia Romagna and Piemonte, while they are absent in southern Italy.

2 The most common conflicts concern: dress, free time, how and when to continue to study, if and when one should marry, and (above all) to whom one should get married.

3 The narratives about respect are distinctly different: *self-respect*, to avoid demeaning acts, to face difficult situations with dignity; *respect for parents* who delivered them into the world and made sacrifices to emigrate; and then *respect for others*, since if one steals someone's health one steals ones own because 'we are all human beings'.

4 The text of the interview and the information here reported are based on my interview conducted in Padova on 20 March 2009.

5 It is possible to watch it on the net at <http://english.aljazeera.net/programmes/peopleandpower/2009/02/2009214114451424970.html>. Accessed 15 March 2009.

BIBLIOGRAPHY

Abdel Qader, S., *Porto il velo, adoro i Queen: Nuove italiane crescono* (Milano: Sonzogno, 2008).

Allievi, S., *L'islam italiano* (Turin: Einaudi, 2003).

Amiraux, V., 'Discrimination and Claims for Equal Rights Amongst Muslims in Europe', in J. Cesari and Sean MacLoughlin (eds), *European Muslims and the Secular State* (Aldershot: Ashgate, 2006) pp. 25–38.

Cesareo, V., Cipriani, R., Garelli, F., Lanzetti C. and Rovati, G., *La religiosità in Italia* (Milan: Mondadori, 1995).

Denti, D., Ferrari, M. and Perocco, F. (eds), *I sikh, storia e immigrazione* (Milan: Angeli, 2005).

Frisina, A., *The Invention of Citizenship Among Young Muslims in Italy*, in G. Jonker and V. Amiraux (eds) (2006).

—'La diversità religiosa come critica sociale? Un processo di convergenza tra giovani ebrei e musulmani, italiani ed europei', in E. Colombo and G. Semi (eds), *Il multiculturalismo quotidiano: pratiche della differenza* (Milano: Franco Angeli, 2007), pp. 77–98.

—*Giovani Musulmani d'Italia* (Carocci: Roma, 2007).

—'Luoghi e attori di trasformazione sociale', in S. Allievi (ed.), *I musulmani e la società italiana: Percezioni reciproche, conflitti culturali, trasformazioni sociali* (Milano: Franco Angeli), pp. 94–121.

Garelli, F., Guizzardi, G. and Pace, E. (eds), *Un singolare pluralismo* (Bologna: Il Mulino, 2003).

Garelli, F. (ed.), *Sfide per la Chiesa del nuovo secolo* (Bologna: Il Mulino, 2003).

Ghazy, R., *Oggi forse non ammazzo nessuno: Storie minime di una giovane musulmana stranamente non terrorista* (Milano: Fabbri, 2007).

Guolo, R., *Xenofobi e xenofili* (Roma-Bari: Laterza, 2003).

Jonker, G. and Amiraux, V. (eds), *Politics of Visibility: Young Muslims in European Public Spaces* (Bielefeld: Transcript-Verlag, 2006).

Modood, T., Triandafyllidou, A. and Zapata-Barrero, R., *Multiculturalism, Muslims and Citizenship: A European Approach* (London and New York: Routledge).

—'Osservatorio Socio-religioso del Triveneto', in *La religione in stanby* (Venezia: Marciana, 2006).

Pace, E., *La nation italienne en crise* (Paris: Bayard, 1998).

—*L'islam in Europa: modelli di integrazione* (Roma: Carocci, 2004).

Saint-Blancat, C. and Schmidt di Friedberg, O., 'Why are Mosques a Problem? Local Politics and Fear of Islam in Northern Italy', in *Journal of Ethnic and Migration Studies*, Vol. 31, No. 6, November 2005, pp. 1083–1104.

Salih, R., *Musulmane Rivelate: Donne, islam, modernità* (Roma: Carocci, 2008).

Stolz, J. (ed.), *Salvation Goods* (Bern: Peter Lang, 2006).

Islam and Muslim Societies

14

Tradition and Response: Islam and Muslim Societies in a Nigerian City

David O. Ogungbile

Introduction

Nigeria, the most populous African country, with over 150 million people, has about 45 per cent of a Muslim population. A significant number of this population is concentrated in the northern part, being the region through which Islam made inroads as early as the ninth century. By the sixteenth century, Islam had penetrated the major cities of northern Nigeria; and through the Uthman dan Fodio's jihad of 1800 it expanded to the entire region. This gave birth to the establishment of the Fulani Empire, with its capital in Sokoto. The jihadists made frantic efforts to spread Islam to all parts of Nigeria. With the southward advancement of this jihadist movement and earlier peaceful contact of Islam by a few communities in the southwest, Islam has succeeded in making some impression on the entire country.

Through whatever means, peaceful or militant, jihad or mendicant preachers, Islam has contributed to the plurality of Nigerian structure in terms of ethnicity, culture and religion, competing with Christianity and decisively eroding the indigenous religion. Other modes of plurality are defined by the more than 250 ethnic groups with diverse cultures. It needs be remarked however, that though Islam and Christianity are two dominant religions in Nigeria, with a population almost evenly divided, the division is not evenly spread in terms of geography. While the Muslim population dominates the northern part of Nigeria, the Christians dominate the south. It also needs to be stated that Muslims in Nigerian are predominantly Sunni, of the Maliki school, which interprets and governs the Shari'a law. However, there is a significant Shi'a minority, primarily in Sokoto State. Furthermore, the Sufi brotherhoods, the

Qadiriyah and Tijaniyah being the most prominent, are widespread in the major cities of northern Nigeria. They played a major role in the spread of Islam in the northern and middle belt areas.

Since the emergence and development of Islam in Nigeria, there have also emerged diverse Muslim societies in the different regions, responding to the tradition with different levels of intensity and in unique ways. This study therefore examines Islam and selected Muslim societies in Òsogbo,[1] the capital city of Osun State, Nigeria. Adopting a combination of cultural-hermeneutical and historical-sociological approaches, it identifies, analyses and interprets the social, cultural and religious factors that inspire the various responses to and by Islam and Muslim societies through their historical emergence and development, and their practices against the monolithic stereotypes of Nigerian Islam. It discusses those responses that have shaped and continue to shape Islamic tradition in Òsogbo and the larger Nigerian community. It assesses the impact of Islam and Muslim societies on the social life of the community. The issues addressed include indigenous culture, Western education and literacy, youth and gender, health and healing, and a new wave of Islamic propagation and evangelization.

Historical Development of Islam in Òsogbo

Islam had its first contact with Òsogbo in the 1820s through the activities of some Muslim traders and mendicant preachers from Oyo[2] in the present Oyo State of Nigeria. This move was smooth and peaceful, Òsogbo being one of the earliest commercial centres in the region (Johnson 1921). The Fulani Jihadists' invasion of the 1830s marked another historical epoch in Islamic activities in Yorùbáland (Atanda 1973; Law 1977). These jihadists, after overrunning the northern part of the country, marched towards the south, displacing some Oyo communities from the present Oyo, Kwara and Kogi states of Nigeria.

Having been sacked by these Fulani jihadists in 1835, the displaced people, who were predominantly Muslims from places like Ibadan, Ogbomoso, Ikoyi, Igboho, Offa, Erin and Iganna, migrated to those towns which they had frequented for their trade during the period of peace (Johnson 1921). As Òsogbo was one of the towns that these settlers had frequented, it became the best option for relocation. The belligerent jihadists were bitter that the reigning Àtáója of Òsogbo (the paramount ruler of the town) accommodated the refugees. They therefore attacked the town itself about 1838. The Oyo-dominated Ibadan army, however, responded by sending a rescue army, which helped to defeat the jihadists finally in 1840. It is reported that the militant move of the jihadists was halted at Òsogbo.[3] With Àtáója's disposition towards the refugees and the assistance rendered by the Ibadan army, the migrants were fully integrated into the Òsogbo community, stabilizing Islamic faith and giving impetus to Islamic presence in Òsogbo.

Both spiritual and human agencies played decisive roles in the planting and development of Islam in Òsogbo. Specifically, the socio-cultural model of accommodationism embedded in Yoruba indigenous tradition, indigenous cultural values and perceived functions of the newly introduced faith formed the foundation for its planting and development. From the socio-cultural paradigm, Yoruba indigenous religion is not a conversion-driven or a competing faith; it is a religion that accommodates and incorporates the practices of other religious traditions. Thus, the prediction of Ifa – the diagnostic medium which is central to indigenous religiosity – that the paramount ruler would assent to the coming of a 'strange' faith into the land was consistent with the nature of indigenous traditions. The king, regarded as semi-divine, is the paramount ruler of his people, and the custodian of all the religions that exist in his domain is expected to direct the affairs of his domain through the prediction and control by Ifa divination. This level of spiritual–human ordering assisted in the entire affairs of a community. Secondly, it is affirmed for the Yoruba community that the religion of the ruler most times influences the subject in a variety of ways.

The second proposition is the functionalist model. That the faith-carriers were able to resolve the problem of barrenness for the paramount ruler provided the basis for the acceptance of Islam, the provider of 'superior power'. Barrenness is considered a misfortune and curse among the Africans. Though, by tradition, the Ataoja had several wives out of which one was barren, the barrenness of one was still regarded as misfortune and this often caused envy and bitter rivalry among the co-wives, a thing of concern for the husband. Possession of several children is held as part of the wealth and affluence of the king.

The above theoretical implications provide explanations for the strong Muslim presence in Òsogbo. This has consequences for the religious mapping as well as the place and prominence of Islam on the traditional political institution of the community. Oral traditions claim that the visitation of a group of three Muslim clerics had been predicted by one Babaláwo Kújenyò during an Ifa festival in Òsogbo which usually preceded the Òsun Òsogbo festival.[4] This was during the reign of Àtáója Oládéjobí Oládélé, Mátànmí I (1854–1864). As predicted, the visitors who wore turbans and carried loads on their shoulders[5] came through Ìdí Bàbá, a boundary of Òsogbo. It was also predicted that Òsogbo would witness prosperity, progress and development if the visitors were accommodated.

Nineteen days later, the visitors, Muslim scholars who had migrated from Bornu in the northern state of Nigeria, arrived in Òsogbo. The visitors were taken to the Àtáója, who offered them rousing hospitality. But they decided to leave on the second day. The Àtáója persuaded them to stay for a while longer. He further requested that they should recite some Qur'anic verses to pray for the progress and development of the town, and also for one of his wives who was barren. The clerics were persuaded by the Àtáója to settle in the town, but agreed to leave without Sheikh Ibrahim Uthman, the oldest among them.

Uthman settled at Ìdí Àkó near the Òkòòko River. It was here that Uthman built the first mosque in Òsogbo. Coincidentally or in answer to the cleric's prayer, Àtáója's barren wife became pregnant through Uthman's recitation of some prescribed *tírà*.[6] This amazed the king and, as a result, he converted to Islam. The new baby was named Harun, a Muslim name, and was trained in fundamental Qur'anic doctrines and Islamic practices under Uthman. Harun later became a renowned Muslim scholar and the Chief Imam of Ìbàdàn in 1922.[7] It was reported that the Àtáója Oba Mátànmí I had earlier given his daughter in marriage to Uthman, through which Ashir, who later succeeded Uthman as the Chief Imam in Òsogbo, was born.

The influence of Sheikh Uthman on the Muslim presence in Òsogbo was remarkable. He established Qur'anic schools, where he trained many pupils who later built mosques and other Qur'anic schools attached to these mosques. There were other Islamic teachers from other towns, including Ilorin, who paid regular visits to Òsogbo during this period. This contributed to the strong foothold of Islam in Òsogbo. For example, Alfa Sanusi Olúgún, being skilled in proper translation of Arabic Qur'an, pioneered and established *tafsîr al-Qur'ân*, which dealt with pure Islamic education. Through this effort, Islam became a popular religion in Òsogbo and drew a large following. Numbers are uncertain, but clearly Islam had a considerable following as attested during a courtesy visit by indigene Muslims. On seeing these adherents, the Àtáója Olúkáyé Olúgbèjà, Mátànmí II (1903–1917) exclaimed, '*Ogede àwon omo ìlú niyii*?' ('Are all these Òsogbo people?').[8]

The consent of Ifá to accommodate Islam in Òsogbo, as well as the support of the royal throne through the Àtáója, contributed significantly to the development and growth of Islam. There were other factors that gave high impetus to the huge success of Islam in Òsogbo. First, certain practices in Islam are similar to those of indigenous religions, in contrast with Christianity, which was competing with Islam. A new religious movement would gain a ready appeal if its practices accorded with existing customs. Examples of these similar practices are polygyny, and the burial of the dead in the residences of the deceased, which contrasted with the Christian practices of monogamy and burial of the dead in a church cemetery (Awe and Albert 1995).

The formation of socio-religious Muslim societies and associations was another significant factor that helped in the growth of Islam. The earliest of these movements were Egbe Bínúkonú, which existed as far back as 1864, and Egbe Alásàláátù, a society established in the early 1870s, which consisted largely of prominent Muslim social elite; these being complemented by the introduction of Islamic societies for the youth, one of which was the Ansar-Ud-Deen movement founded in 1923. These societies won the heart and admiration of most reigning Àtáója. As a result, some members of these societies served in the traditional political administration of Òsogbo, as certain prominent Muslims were honoured with traditional chieftaincy titles. This paved the way for various Muslim ceremonies to take place in the Àtáója's courtyard at which the Àtáója himself was in attendance.[9]

The entrance and acceptance of Islam in the palace inspired its further development in the town. It is worth noting that many of the past Àtáója were Muslims. The incumbent Àtáója, Oba Iyìolá Oyèwálé Mátànmí III, is a devout Muslim and an Alhaji.[10] The influence of the royal throne on the beginning and subsequent expansion of Islam probably explains the existence of numerous mosques and architectural Muslim designs surrounding the premises of the palace complex of the Àtáója. The three major streets of Sábó Road, Gbáèmú Street and Ìsàlè-Òsun Street are cases in point. Thus, the presence of Islam in Òsogbo has a strong effect on the indigenous culture of the people. Besides the structural designs, Muslim names and naming have become a strong identification mark in Òsogbo.

Typology of Muslim Societies

Since its introduction and development, there have emerged several Muslim societies and movements in Nigerian communities, and particularly in Òsogbo. While a few of these are global[11] in name and expression, some are national;[12] others are local, reflecting the social needs of the different local communities, groups and sexes. These movements could be classified into four categories, namely a) conservative, b) liberationist, c) liberal and d) mystical. These classifications are based not strictly on 'orthodox' beliefs, tenets and pillars of Islamic faith, but primarily on the historical emergence and distinct and divergent practices of these movements. The other factor is their pragmatic approaches and reactions to contemporary social realities, situations and issues. This factor may include attitudes to socialites, the cultural milieu in which Islam finds itself, gender biases, age groupings, educational interests, theological emphases and rediscoveries, and religious revivalism.

Among the conservative movements are the Lánasè and Bámidélé based in Yorùbáland. The Isabat-Ul-Deen movement is an example of a liberation group that emphasizes the renewal of Islam. The Ahmadiyyah, Nawair-Ud-Deen and the Ansar-Ud-Deen movements are in the liberal group, while the 'mystic' movements may run across those movements or include individual devotion to spiritual experiences. The activities of liberation movements produce a lot of intolerance, which often leads to inter- and intra-religious violence and communal crisis and unrest. It should be mentioned that the most prominent group in Òsogbo falls within the 'liberal' movement. This liberality is attributable to the Yorùbá worldview, which underlines human communality and blood relationship rather than religious differentiation, this often instigating intolerance, narrow-mindedness, disunity and dissension in other communities. Liberal movements also include those groups interested not in the renewal but in the revival and revitalization of Islam.

We shall discuss some of these movements, showing their unique characteristics and the impact of their activities on the Òsogbo community.

Muslim Societies, Western Education and Cultural Issues

The Ansar-Ud-Deen Society

The Ansar-Ud-Deen Society emerged as the first distinct Muslim society in Òsogbo. Formed by a group of Muslim elite in Lagos in 1923,[13] it was not until 1947 that its branch was established in Òsogbo through one Alhaji Ibraheem Amusat, an indigene of the town. The memorandum of the decision to create the Òsogbo council of the movement had been passed on 19 September 1946 and forwarded to the national headquarters in Lagos.

It should be remarked, however, that Amusat initially faced some hostility from the indigenes, who were deeply involved in the traditional practices associated with the worship of the goddess Òsun. Amusat's initial effort was to enforce a movement that would bring a renewal of Islam. He came to terms with the people through persuasion and later made some converts from the Muslims. He was later given a portion of land to build a mosque.

The main focus of the Ansar-Ud-Deen Society was on education. The decision of the members to focus on education is captioned thus: 'this society's constitution laid down that Muslims were to be given a full and complete training in the Islamic sciences and that the society was to enter into a broader field of education on the model of the Christian missions'.[14] The purpose, according to them, arose from their intention to acquire Western education and simultaneously instil and imbibe 'unpolluted' and 'undiluted' Islamic religion and Arabic education. The movement therefore encourages Muslims to embrace Western-style education. The society thus has the reputation of being the first movement to have established Muslim-initiated, named and directed primary and secondary schools in Òsogbo; recently, it established a nursery school. This was in response to the fact that Christianity's strong influence on the Western education curriculum design and pupils' enrolment in public schools was seen as posing a threat to Islamic religion. For it was alleged that pupils who enrolled in the public schools were forced to drop their Muslim names and convert to Christianity, the initial evidence being an adoption of Christian names.

Several explanations that could be given for this phenomenon range from religious, cultural, psychological and political. Certain aspects of the allegations might be true in the sense that early schools were established by Christian missions, which designed the curricula from their denominational biases.[15] On the other hand, the allegation has been proved not to be totally true. It has been affirmed that a good number of practising Muslims today, including the present Àtáója, who had early education in such Christian missionary-oriented public schools, remain strong Muslims and even commended the efforts of the missionaries who introduced a Western type of education.

The Ansar-Ud-Deen Society thus combines Western and Arabic–Islamic forms of education to create a new expression of a dynamic Islam. This has contributed to the growth of Islamic influence in the town. In its support for educational growth, the society gives bursary awards to distinguished students in higher institutions of learning. Moreover, the society organizes social programmes through conferences and seminars which have educational advantages. The society, through such forums, encourages integration of socialites into such events as marriage, naming and burial. The society teaches through persuasion that Muslims should not be involved in those practices that are not in consonance with Islamic practices, such as Òsun, Egúngún, Ògún and Sàngó festivals and ritual.

One other thing that distinguishes the Ansar-Ud-Deen from some other Muslim societies is the creation of a cemetery. The movement has a large expanse of land in the Sábò area of Òsogbo where they bury their dead. The Muslims generally bury their dead inside their houses or within their compound premises. The interpretation of the Ansar-Ud-Deen is that since that expanse of land is fenced and enclosed, it is regarded as a building, and not outside a building.

There are some other Muslim societies in Òsogbo that are committed to integrating Western education into Islamic religious practices to allow the religion to fit into the contemporary social situation. Islaudeen Missionary Association and Kamar-Ud-Deen are good examples. Islaudeen Missionary Association is a movement that claims to commit itself to bringing life into Islam through educational programmes and intensive evangelization. Also, the Nawair-Ud-Deen society, though known for its emphasis on strict Islamic ways of life, contributes to the educational development of young Muslims by establishing schools.

Muslim Societies and Revivalism

Young Muslim Propagation in Islam (YUMPI)

The founding of some Muslim societies in contemporary times could be interpreted from two important but decisive points. First, the 1990s marked a heightened period in Christianity and female evangelization sporadically swept across Nigeria. Secondly, the impact of Pentecostal youth in such evangelization has been unsurpassed in Nigerian Christian history. It is suggested that the activities of Pentecostal-driven Christian youth were allegedly intimidating the youths of other Christian denominations and religions, leading to their conversion to Pentecostal movements. As earlier studies suggest, these Christian youth go on to full-time ministerial work, establishing what they call independent Christian fellowships, centres, chapels and missions. In our universities, colleges of education and polytechnics, they hold daily meetings in the evening and convert most of the lecture rooms into chapels of worship. They employ their creativity, dissipate their energies, and exploit every situation and circumstance for evangelical activities, including organizing seminars, workshops, etc.[16]

Young Muslim Propagation in Islam (YUMPI) was founded in Òsogbo as a revivalist movement on 15 February 1990 through the efforts of Alhaji Abdul Fatah Kólá Mákindé, the chairman, and Shuaib David Adéwùmí, the secretary, both indigenes of Òsogbo. Fatah is from Òkè-Baálè Compound and Shuaib is from Lakarin Compound in Òsogbo. These two founders had been, at one time or another, members of the Ansar-Ud-Deen movement.

As its name suggests, the group is a movement of young energetic Muslim scholars and believers who aim at propagating Islam across Nigeria. The society has its headquarters in the Tannísí area of Gbónmi quarters in Òsogbo and has expanded; it currently has branches in Ìwó and Ede in Osun State, and Ìbàdàn in Oyo State. The movement establishes scholarship awards to assist less privileged Muslims to pursue various courses of interest up to university level. It organizes Muslim gatherings, especially during the Id'el Fitri, where symposia and seminars are held to create some awareness of the importance of being Muslim.

It should be remarked that there was an allegation made by some Muslim scholars when the society began that the movement might cause a schism of young Muslims from the main fold. Thus, the movement encountered stiff opposition and strong attacks, leading to an early setback. After several months of persistence, the young leaders were able to convince their antagonists of the 'genuineness' of their intention.

Diyaul-Deen Movement (DDM)

The Diyaul-Deen Movement (DDM) is the second of our case studies on the evangelization model but its own area of intended coverage is Yorùbáland in the southwestern part of Nigeria. The society was inaugurated as a brainchild of a conference held at Ìbàdàn, the capital of Oyo State, on 27 April 1991, as an association of young and old Muslims of both sexes. It aims at extending the movement to the people at the grassroots and encourages more commitment to the worship of Allah and the practice of Islam. Further to this conference, Alhaji Hamzat Afolábí, a native of Òsogbo from Eesa Abinuyo Compound, was sent to establish a branch of DDM in Òsogbo. Thus, Afolábí founded the Diyaul-Deen Movement on 3 June 1991. He was supported by Alhaji Mumini, Alfa Jamiu, Alfa Kazeem Bello and Wasiu Kólápò. Alhaji Mumini was the chairman, while Alfa Jamiu was the secretary. The permanent site of the movement is presently at Òkè-Baálè in Òsogbo.

As a vehicle for propelling their activities, the Diyaul-Deen Movement emphasizes education. The movement claims to offer scholarships to Muslims who show some promise in the world of Islam and those students who display brilliance in their academic careers. The post-Ramadan visitations to motherless homes and hospitals where *zakat* is paid are incorporated into their programmes. Furthermore, the movement organizes social programmes and symposia.

Another group whose aim is slightly similar to YUMPI and DDM is the Kamar-Ud-Deen Society, an Arabic school founded to train scholars of Islam. Claiming to be committed to the aggressive propagation of Islam, the society was formed by a group of Muslims as an organized institution to promote Islamic religion. The graduates of this school engage in open-air preaching under the name of their school. A particular achievement that attests to their commitment was the fundraising that generated a huge sum of money used to build the large mosque where they currently hold their daily worship.

A New Wave of Islamic Evangelism and Resurgence

The Nasiru-Laahi-Fathi Society (NASFAT)

The Nasiru-Laahi-Fathi Society (NASFAT) is a new phenomenon in Nigerian Islam. The phenomenon, according to Alhaji Fatai Araòkanmí, a member of NASFAT, is comparable to the Redeemed Christian Church of God (RCCG),[17] which arguably is the fastest growing Pentecostal church in Nigeria. Its tentacles continue to spread across the globe.[18] In an interview conducted with Alhaji Fatai Araòkanmí, Araòkanmí notes the current activities of the RCCG, particularly the Holy Ghost service usually held on the last Friday or Saturday of every month at The Redemption Camp along the Ìbàdàn-Lagos Expressway. This camp ground is noted to have turned the RCCG into a household phenomenon in Nigerian Christian religious experience.[19] The monthly prayer meeting of the RCCG is patronized by people of different denominations and religions, as it claims to offer participants healing and miracles. The emergence of NASFAT is a response to the perceived threat from evangelical and Aládurá brands of Christianity, whose mainstay of activities is prayer through which many have converted to Christianity.[20] These Christians hold several kinds of prayer and fasting meetings, including all-night vigils, weekly, bi-monthly, monthly, 7-day, 21-day, 40-day, etc.

NASFAT emerged after the meeting of 'some Muslim elite' who claimed they 'were inspired (and) had met individually on the need for Muslims to have enough opportunity to rub minds with Islamic scholars with a view to learning about their religion'.[21] The meeting came in the form of a prayer meeting, held on Sunday 5 March 1995 at the residence of Alhaji Abdul-Lateef Wale Olásùpò in Lagos. Alhaji Olásùpò was made the first Muqadam. The aim of the society is stated as 'to maximise favourably the leisure time that exists amongst Muslims who laze away Sunday mornings'.[22] That the movement arose not only as a prayer group but also in the selection of 'Sunday mornings' for prayer services has an implication on the nature of contestation and competition among Muslims and Christians in Nigeria.

Furthermore, the movement emerged in the southwestern part of Nigeria where Christianity seems to have a dominant presence. It is intended that it will cover the whole of Nigeria with each of the states to have a branch that oversees its organization and a spiritual head who serves as the missionary. Thus as a matter of principle and practice, it is stated in the movement's general programme that 'all strata of the membership of the society attend' the following programmes in order of priority: 1) *Asalatu* session, every Sunday morning, from 8.30 a.m.–12.30 p.m.; 2) *Tahajud* session, the night of every first and third Fridays of the month (12.00 a.m. till *Subhi*); 3) Ramadan programme (throughout the holy month); and 4) *Lai-latul Quadri* (night of majesty),[23] etc.

Just as most religious groups would legitimize their existence by claiming certain spiritual experiences or drawing their authenticity from their most revered sacred text, NASFAT draws its inspiration from the holy Qur'an, of which the two most important verses are:

> Let there arise out of you a band of people inviting to all that is good, enjoining what is right, and forbidding what is wrong: they are the ones who attain felicity. (Q. 3:104)

The second verse focuses on the movement's main activity which, according to the Òsun State chairman of NASFAT, Alhaji Abd Ganiyu Oyèládùn, is in accordance with the commandment of the Almighty Allah:

> And your Lord said, call on me and I will respond to your call, verily those who scorn my worship and do not invoke me will surely enter Hell in humiliation. (Q. 40:60)

Competing with and contesting the Christian evangelistic mission of the late twentieth and twenty-first centuries, the society uses government building spaces, though it proposes that each of the 36 states of Nigeria as well as Abuja, the federal capital territory, will acquire its own land to build prayer venues that can accommodate a great number of devotees. It is suggested that this strategy attempts to impose the state's recognition of the society. As a counter-force against the RCCG and other similar groups, NASFAT now acquires and uses a very large expanse of land along the Ìbàdàn-Lagos Expressway, very close to the site of the RCCG Camp ground. It should be noted that the RCCG has been using this place for over a decade. Since NASFAT arrived here, it has added to the traffic confusion and agony of motorists and travellers along this road, as the population becomes uncontrollable. It is further suggested that the contestation and competition theory is attested by the stated goal of the movement voiced by a prominent member, Alhaji Oyèládùn:

> Between now and 2010, the whole country should become Muslim. God be with us, the whole of Nigeria, even the remotest villages must have accepted Islam. Islam is the only acceptable religion by God. It is our duty to make all Nigerians become Muslims by 2010. We will continue to preach good things and forbid bad things. We will intensify our membership development programmes.[24]

Thus, NASFAT emerged in Nigeria as a revolutionary evangelical movement within Islam. Its intention is to create awareness in order to inspire and encourage the Muslim elite and youths to appreciate the beauty of and take pride in Islam. As a relatively high-class Muslim society, it claims to try to attract lukewarm or nominal Muslims, and to empower members to realize their potential spirituality. The movement, it is asserted, 'assists them [members] to develop their whole being so that they can achieve all their desires. If any member finds himself in any problem, he has to pray and his prayer will be answered without delay *Insha'Allah*.'[25] It further claims to be interested in reinforcing the uniformity of global Islam. It defines itself as a prayer movement rather than a secessionist or distinct movement. This is the main activity of this society.

As a response to sociopolitical and economic issues, NASFAT focuses on its goal by designing a threefold programme – namely spiritual development, economic empowerment and social interaction. In the bid for spiritual development, the leaders teach members 'to learn how to pray to (your) God and obtain instant answers to your requests. [They] train people how to seek help only from God.'[26] The development of social interaction where members link up with prominent members in all walks of life and around the world is crucial to the members. Leaders claim to assist members to further their aspirations. In recent times, events have proved that leaders lobby at all costs to secure political appointment and employment for members from government institutions at local, state and federal levels. The common slogan has been that 'the Muslims need a voice'. Furthermore, though the leaders maintain that the society is not a political movement and is not interested in presenting candidates on the platform of the society, they emphasize that they can render spiritual support for their members who go into partisan politics.

It is also important to note that the society proposes certain developmental programmes that compete with those of their Christian counterpart. These include the establishment of a Women's Specialist Hospital that caters for women and children, to be run by Muslim medical specialists, secondary schools, and NASFAT University. This point becomes germane to our discussion of the 'response' paradigm. In Nigeria, besides the public medical institutions that are alleged to have Western orientation in practice, there are Christian-oriented hospitals and clinics, like Wesley Guild, and several Christian-owned ones; there are also more than ten Christian-established universities, and a few Muslim-owned. We suggest that the NASFAT agenda presents a parallel to its Christian counterpart.

The establishment of the Òsogbo chapter of NASFAT on Sunday 17 June 2001[27] illustrated a heightened evangelical and charismatic expression of modern Nigerian Christianity. For instance, the advertising strategy throughout Òsun State involved the production of vehicle stickers which bear the inscription 'NASFAT'. These were stuck on cars and commercial vehicles. The formation of special NASFAT guilds with special uniforms who served as ushers at the various programmes of the society is noteworthy. Alhaji Oyelade boastfully reflected on the success of the movement: within a year of its emergence, the movement, which had begun with forty members, now recorded about ten thousand. Though it is impossible to verify this figure, one important point to make is that the influence of NASFAT is visibly strong in the quality of the membership and the significant achievements already made. The society has acquired its own ten acres of land situated on Òsogbo-Ìlobu Road, costing one and a half million Naira (N1.5 million). According to Alhaji Araòkanmí, some of the prominent members of the societies are the incumbent Àtáója of Òsogbo, Oba Oyèwálé Mátànmí III, the former governor of Òsun State, Chief Adébísí Àkàndé, and the former State Commissioner of Police. The movement now has a common prayer book which contains various matters of human concern. This is a strange phenomenon in Nigerian Islam. Members meet every Sunday between the hours of eight in the morning and twelve noon for prayer sessions; they hold their *Tahjud* night on the first and last Friday of every month.[28]

Woman Founder and Healing Practices in Muslim Societies: Fadilullah Muslim Mission of Nigeria (FMMN)

The Fadilullah Muslim Mission of Nigeria (FMMN) presents to us another unique response in the Muslim tradition. An assessment of this movement requires an insight into the religious and cultural milieu from which it emerged. A comparative analysis of the practices of indigenous religious tradition, Christianity and Islam in Nigeria in general and Òsogbo in particular, offers us a number of points to reflect upon. The two focal points of our analysis include women and leadership in religion, and the subject and practice of healing. Our research confirms that the founding of Muslim societies by women is not a commonplace practice. Secondly, there are a great number of women priestesses of Orisa in indigenous religions of Òsogbo. Notably, the goddess Òsun, the principal deity of Òsogbo, has full-time devotees where priestesses serve as diviners, healers and medicine-women. Thirdly, African Initiated Churches, known as the Aládurá (owner or custodian of prayers) and evangelical missions in Nigeria have women founders of churches and healers. Hydrotherapy is a commonplace phenomenon employed by indigenous female devotees as well as Aládurá prophetesses and prophets.

It is in the above regard that we can understand the uniqueness of the Fadilullah Muslim Mission. There are two distinct qualities in the new expression. Firstly, the Fadilullah Mission was founded by a woman. Secondly, it was founded as a distinct prayer movement within Islam. These two, combined, present a somewhat strange expression in Nigerian Islam. However, it has become a point of attraction to the yawning population who are faced with existential physical and metaphysical problems which include barrenness, misfortunes, lunacy, and other things. The Mission is committed to problem-solving, not only for Muslims but also for people of different religious traditions.

The FMMN was founded by Alhaja Sheidat Mujidat Adéoyè from Mogbà Compound, Òsogbo. The spiritual experience which led to the emergence of the movement began on 23 August 1997. Mujidat claimed to have been seized by a spirit while she was in her rice and beans store, being a wholesaler in those foodstuffs at Oluode Market in Òsogbo. Caught in a frenzy, she instructed co-wholesalers, multitudes of hawkers and customers who surrounded her, to cover their heads. Her initial experience, which involved shouting, was interpreted by observers as mental derangement. However, she started to recite '*Lai lah, illah 'llah*',

'There is no god but Allah.' In this state of spirit-possession, she started to prophesy. When she regained consciousness, her colleagues narrated how she behaved in her state of unconsciousness. She was stupefied, as she was neither a committed Muslim nor educated in the Qur'an.

She narrated her experience to her husband, Alhaji Abdul-Lateef Adéoyè. Abdul-Lateef was astonished, as this experience was strange to him even as a staunch Muslim and founder of the Sherif-Deen Muslim Movement. Notwithstanding, Mujidat engaged in seven days of fasting and praying. However, both Mujidat and Abdul-Lateef would not show any enthusiasm for or recognition of this strange phenomenon. Rather, they discarded it and continued along as normal, in their social and business lives. Mujidat began to experience some mysterious disappearances of her food items and monies realized from the sales. Also, she could not seem to sell anything, no matter how long she stayed in her store, to the extent that most times she would return home in anger. Furthermore, each time she travelled to buy goods from the north, she would lose money and foodstuff. Her business began to run into debt. On the other hand, she started to get visits from clients requesting prayers, claiming they had been led to her by some mysterious and strange influences.

Two issues began to engage her mind. The first was financial. Would this mean that she would have to leave her trading? If she did, and accepted this call, what would she live on? The second was the question of the practice of the praying. How would she begin to administer the prayers, being a new kind of experience, on the clients? She had never seen people practice it, and she had not received any specific divine step-by-step 'how to' guide. However, she reluctantly started performing this divine task and her clients would testify to the efficacy of her prayers. Also, while staying at home performing the divine mission, her trading colleagues would sell some items for her, and would bring the money to her at home. With this realization, she decided to yield to the divine call. This 'reluctance' was reminiscent of biblical figures such as Moses and Jeremiah, except that in this case it was a woman, of course.

Thus, it became clear to her and her husband that she could not resist this divine assignment, and subsequently clients began to multiply. However, there were challenges, in particular discouragement and persecution from some Muslim bigwigs and movements. They challenged the authenticity of this strange practice. Mujidat and her husband were accused of using 'talismanic' power. But after careful observation of their practices, some among the persecutors began to search for Qur'anic support and precedents from the *Hadith* and other sources of Islamic theological thought, which they were to discover. According to Mujidat and Abdul-Lateef, there was also some pressure from Christian groups trying to entice Mujidat, the divine possessor, with money and materials. They suggested that such a gift could be used among them since the practice was strange among Muslim *ummah* but would be appreciated in the Aládurà group of churches. She quickly declined.

It is remarkable to note that what started at Ìsàlè Aro has grown into a large congregation such that they have now erected a mosque and a house on the plot they bought to build their personal residence before this strange experience. This is on fairly developed land in the Òkè Ayépé area of Òsogbo. The prominence of this movement is so strong that the street leading to the place has been named after the movement, Fadilullah Muslim Mission. The mosque, which can accommodate about two thousand people, also has a tent constructed on an eight-acre piece of land surrounding it.

As the movement took shape and clients multiplied, it was given the name Fadilullah Muslim Mission, derived from *Ash-ah-min-Fadil-ul-llah, Ash-ah-dul-Fadil-ul-rubi-l,* meaning 'this is a sign from God', an expression from the Surat of *An'am* or *The Cattle*, in the Qur'an (6:124–125). The husband, Abdul-Lateef, interpreted this Qur'anic verse to mean that Allah sometimes worked in mysterious ways, as was the case with Mujidat's spiritual experience. Thus, Fadilullah, *Àmì Olórun*,[29] indicates the sign from Allah which evinces in the miraculous works and efficacious prayers of Alhaja Sheidat Mujidat Adéoyè, and validates her spiritual experience.

The Fadilullah Muslim Mission is spiritually headed and directed by Sheidat Mujidat, who dresses in a white gown with flowing scarf signifying the purity of God and her desire to be simple. Her decision to choose white as her uniform was, according to her, to place on herself a restriction against worldly fashion, as she claimed that she used to be a lady of fashion and loved dressing in various kinds of apparel and jewellery. But Allah, she claimed, told her to jettison all worldly fashions, and prescribed white for her. She engages herself in constant prolonged personal and private prayers and fasting, for seven days at a time, or twenty-one, or sometimes forty-one days. The forty-one-day prayer is done once a year. This starts from July and runs through the celebration of the founding of the movement, which is 23 August.

Prayer and fasting meetings are organized for members. The founder has a band of assistants called '*afàdúràjagun*' (prayer band), who attend to clients on her behalf for not-too-difficult cases. All their activities are done in and around her mosque premises. The Mission has a river very close to the mosque for clients who receive prescription to bathe in the stream. Clients might also decide to go to streams of their choice.[30] It is noteworthy that people come with various problems such as barrenness, blindness and deafness, and chronic illnesses. Though the mosque receives both male and female clients, the females outnumber the males; they include people from various religious traditions. Sheidat Mujidat attends to clients from nine in the morning until all have been attended to every day of the week except on Friday, which she chooses for her rest and for the *Jumat* service. Congregational prayers are held every Thursday from three to six in the afternoon and every Sunday from eleven in the morning to three in the afternoon. The Sunday prayer is called *Àdúrà Ìségun* or Victory Prayer. There is also a fortnightly prayer meeting from Friday evening through Saturday morning. Pregnant women have their prayer meetings on Tuesdays. There is also an annual seven-day prayer, which usually occurs from 10–17 May. It is done with prayer and fasting through morning and evening. Prayer services are extemporaneous and hilariously interspersed with choruses in the Yorùbá language, which express the importance and potency of prayer, beyond the influence of destiny. The interpretation of their common song[31] goes like this:

> Destiny may not favour me, Let prayer avail for me, Lord
> Destiny may not favour me, Let prayer avail for me, Lord;
> It has been long since the vulture has suffered from the falling of the rain (x2)
> The wicked ones of the world always drive one to meet his/her fortune (x2)
> So, destiny may not favour me, Let prayer avail for me.

The praying practice of this society involves the use of olive oil, water, sponges and toilet soap. Clients bring these items that have been prescribed for them to be prayed upon. They use the items as directed by Sheidat

Mujidat. Clients bring toilet soap and water fetched inside the keg, olive oil and such items that may be prescribed relevant to the client's problems. Clients may be told to rub the ailing part of her of his body with consecrated olive oil. Members are restricted from going to traditionalists to seek any help. For the daily 9 o'clock 'clinic', clients queue up on benches arranged outside the mosque. They enter one after the other for spiritual consultation. Sheidat Mujidat prays extemporaneously. She then explains any revelations she may have received during her prayer, after which she prescribes appropriate remedies for the clients.

Sheidat Mujidat claims she does not charge consultation fees; rather she accepts gifts and freewill offerings from clients.

It is important to mention that the Fadilullah Muslim Mission asserts its claim to Islam by following certain practices in the mosque. For instance, it has an imam who conducts the Friday *Jumat* service in its mosque.

Conclusion

This chapter argues that Islam should not be seen as a monolithic tradition. Like most religious traditions, Islam – as well as the founding of Muslim societies in Nigeria – has been discovered to create some responses to social, cultural, religious and political milieus and situations that Islam encounters and interacts with. This has been demonstrated among the people of Òsogbo, a typical African community where Islam flourishes. It is noted that Islam succeeded in Òsogbo not through militancy but through peaceful means, and it was able to contribute meaningfully to the social life of the people as an agent of change. Not only this, it responds in a decisive way to the discussion of gender dynamics in a patrifocal African community. The study of Islam and Muslim societies in the Òsogbo community of Nigeria suggests the need for a more ethnographic and historical approach to such movements in African communities where there are varied expressions of the same tradition. It tries to provide a model for analysing and interpreting religious phenomena in a contemporary religiously plural, sensitive and diverse global community.

NOTES

1 Òsogbo is a nodal town that links the six other major Yorùbá towns of Ilorin, Ilesa, Ede, Ilobu, Ife and Ibokun, all in Òsun State. It is on latitude 7.7°N and longitude 4.5°E. See *History of Òsogbo* (Òsogbo: Òsogbo Cultural Heritage Council, 1994). The Federal Ministry of Housing and Environment had estimated the population at 1,574,352. For further reading on some details on the population growth of Òsogbo see Layi Egunjobi (1995).

2 Oyo is a major sub-ethnic group of the Yorùbá kingdom. The Ibadan army was a local regional army that defended the kingdom during the civil strife of the period.

3 T. G. O. Gbadamosi, *The Growth of Islam Among the Yorùbá 1841–1908* (London: Longman, 1978), p. 10.

4 Osun Osogb, hegemonic festival of the community, is the celebration of the cultural birthday of the settlement. The other festival in which the paramount ruler and the entire community participate is Ifa (Ogungbile 2003).

5 This describes the pattern of dressing and appearance typical of Muslim clerics and missioners during the early period.

6 *Tírà* is sometimes prepared by a Muslim cleric who inscribes verses of the Qur'an, wrapped and tied with black or red threads. It is believed that the use of such *Tírà* has a therapeutic effect. The client whispers his or her requests or intended results to it. He or she keeps it inside the pocket; it could sometimes be put under the pillow while sleeping.

7 Harun was addressed by the people as Aafaa Òkè Gégé, Muslim priest (imam) of Òkè Gégé. Òkè Gégé is a compound in Ibadan.

8 T. G. O. Gbadamosi, p. 55.

9 Ibid.

10 Alhaji (male) or Alhaja (female) signifies a status attributable to a rite of passage of a Muslim who has gone on pilgrimage to Mecca/Medina. It is viewed highly in Nigerian social and religious settings.

11 Ahmadiyyah and Tijaniyyah are good examples.

12 Examples are Nawair-Ud-Deen and Ansar-Ud-Deen.

13 Peter B. Clarke, *West Africa and Islam*, *op. cit.*, p. 225.

14 P. B. Clarke (1982).

15 This view is buttressed by the documentary from Chief Ifagbenusola Atanda, the Asiwaju Awo Agbaye and Aare Alasa Osogbo; the World President of Healing, Teaching & Tourism Temple African Faith International (HATTAF), <www.hattaf.org>.

16 David O. Ogungbile, 'Ìjèsà Cultural Factors and the Growth of Christianity in Nigeria since the 20th Century', in *Dialogue and Alliance: A Journal of the Inter-Religious Federation for World Peace (The Influence of Interfaith Consciousness)*, Vol. 19, No. 2 (2006), pp. 47–78; 'Religion and National Policy in Nigeria: A Case Study of the Impact of Christian Youth Movement on NYSC Programme in a Nigerian Community', in *The Living Word: Journal of Philosophy and Theology*, Alwaye, India, Vol. 105, No. 2 (1999), pp. 115–131.

17 Personal interview, Araòkanmí.

18 Asonzeh F. K. Ukah, *A New Paradigm of Pentecostal Power: A Study of the Redeemed Christian Church of God in Nigeria* (Africa World Press, 2008); Ogbu

U. Kalu and Alaine M. Low (eds), *Interpreting Contemporary Christianity: Global Processes and Local Identities* (Wm. B. Eerdmans Publishing Company, 2008). Read further the activities of RCCG at <http://www.rccg.org>.

19 David O. Ogungbile, 'Ìjèṣà Cultural Factors and the Growth of Christianity in Nigeria since the 20th Century', in *Dialogue and Alliance: A Journal of the Inter-Religious Federation for World Peace (The Influence of Interfaith Consciousness)*, Vol. 19, No. 2 (2006), pp. 47–78.

20 *Saturday Tribune*, 15 June 2002, p. 15.

21 Ibid.

22 <http://nasfat.org/about.php>.

23 <http://nasfat.org/programmes.php>.

24 'NASFAT is Not a Cult', *op. cit.*, *Saturday Tribune*, 15 June 2002, p. 15.

25 Ibid.

26 Ibid.

27 Its inauguration was on Sunday 16 June 2002.

28 *Saturday Tribune*, 15 June 2002, p. 15.

29 *Ash-ah-min-Fadil-ul-llah, Ash-ah-dul-Fadil-ul-rubi-l*: 'this is a sign from God'. This expression comes from the sign God showed to the generation of the Prophet Sahliu. The generation of Sahliu requested him to show them a sign that Allah had truly sent a message to them. Allah descended cattle to the Prophet to show to the people. The people asked him what this strange appearance was. He then told them that it was a sign from Allah. But the people still rejected it. But they began to exercise the fear that this cow would not allow them to have sufficient water to drink since it was such a big cow that it would consume all the water that was meant for them. They rejected this sign. Allah then told them that if they rejected it, they would be punished (Q. 6:125).

30 *Àfọ̀se* and *Olúgbohùn* are magical voices of imprecations which are used to cause things to happen. They are commonly used by traditional medicine men, while *hàùntúrú* and *Tírà* are commonly found among Muslim herbal men. It is claimed that some groups of the Aládurà movement use *Olúgbohùn*. For *'hàùntúrú'*, it is the practice of inscribing on slate ink (usually black) some Arabic letters or statements, which is washed with water or any liquid and drunk by the client to effect a curse, most probably on one's enemies, while *'Tírà'* contains Arabic causative inscriptions wrapped and tied with cloth strings. Such is kept as a protection against any unforeseen incidence or accident.

31 *Bi kadara ko ba mi gbe/Kadura o gbe mi/Bi kadara ko bag be mi/Kadura ko gbe mi/Ojo ti n pa'gun bo, se'b'ojo ti pe (x2)/Bi karada ko bag be mi/Kadura o gbe mi.*

BIBLIOGRAPHY

Atanda, J. A., *The New Oyo Empire: Indirect Rule and Change in Western Yorubaland* (London: Longman, 1973).

Awe, Bolanle and Olawale, Albert, 'Historical Development of Òsogbo', in C. O. Adepegba (ed.), *Òsogbo: Model of Growing African Towns* (Ibadan: Institute of African Studies, University of Ibadan, 1995), pp. 1–12.

Clarke, Peter B., *West Africa and Islam* (London: Edward Arnold, 1982).

Durkheim, Emile, *The Elementary Forms of the Religious Life* (New York: Free Press; London: Allen & Unwin, 1965).

Egunjobi, Layi, 'Òsogbo: Aspects of Urbanization, Physical Planning and Development', in C. O. Adepegba (ed.), *Òsogbo: Model of Growing African Towns* (Ibadan: Institute of Cultural Studies, University of Ibadan, 1995), pp. 13–24.

Gbadamosi, T. G. O., *The Growth of Islam Among the Yoruba 1841–1908* (London: Longman, 1978).

Hick, John, *An Interpretation of Religion: Human Responses to the Transcendence* (New Haven: Yale University Press, 1989).

Johnson, Samuel, *History of the Yorubas* (London: C.M.S., 1921).

Kalberg, Stephen, *Max Weber's Comparative-Historical Sociology* (Chicago: The University of Chicago Press, 1994).

Law, R. C., *The Oyo Empire, 1600–1836* (London: OUP, 1977).

Ogbu, U. Kalu and Alaine, M. Low (eds), *Interpreting Contemporary Christianity: Global Processes and Local Identities* (Wm. B. Eerdmans Publishing Company, 2008).

Ogungbile, David O., 'Ìjèsà Cultural Factors and the Growth of Christianity in Nigeria since the 20th Century', in *Dialogue and Alliance: A Journal of the Inter-Religious Federation for World Peace (The Influence of Interfaith Consciousness)*, Vol. 19, No. 2 (2006), pp. 47–78.

—'Religious Experience and Women Leadership in Nigerian Islam: Alhaja Sheidat Mujidat Adeoye, Founder and Leader of the Fadillulah Muslim Mission, Òsogbo, Nigeria', in *Journal of Interdisciplinary Gender Studies*, Vol. 9, No. 1 (2004), pp. 17–40.

—'Myth, Ritual and Identity in the Religious Traditions of the Osogbo People of Western Nigeria', Doctoral Dissertation submitted to the Obafemi Awolowo University, Ile-Ife, Nigeria (2003).

—'Religion and National Policy in Nigeria: A Case Study of the Impact of Christian Youth Movement on NYSC Programme in a Nigerian Community', in *The Living Word: Journal of Philosophy and Theology*, Alwaye, India, Vol. 105, No. 2 (1999), pp. 115–131.

—'Islam and Cultural Identity in Nigeria: The Osogbo-Yoruba Experience', in *Orita: Ibadan Journal of Religious Studies*, Vol. XXX/1–2 (1998), pp. 123–137.

Òsogbo Cultural Heritage Council, *History of Òsogbo* (a publication of the Òsogbo Cultural Heritage Council, 1994).

Personal interviews with:

- Adéoyè, Alhaja Sheidat Mujidat (thirty-two years old), founder of the Fadilullah Muslim Mission, Oke Ayepe, Òsogbo, June 2002.
- Adéoyè, Alhaji Abdul-Lateef (forty-seven years old), husband of Sheidat Mujidat Adéoyè, Fadilullah Street, Òkè Ayépé, Òsogbo, June 2002. A member of the Sherif-Deen Muslim movement.
- Araòkanmí, Fatai (forty-seven years old), Fadilullah Street, Òkè Ayépé, Òsogbo, June 2002.

Saturday Tribune, 15 June 2002.

Smart, Ninian, *Worldviews: Crosscultural Explorations of Human Beliefs* (New Jersey: Prentice-Hall, 2000).

Smith, Jonathan, *Map is Not the Territory: Studies in History of Religions* (Chicago and London: The University of Chicago Press, 1993).

Smith, Wilfred Cantwell, *Patterns of Faith around the World* (Oxford: Oneworld Publications, 1998).

Ukah, Asonzeh F. K., *A New Paradigm of Pentecostal Power: A Study of the Redeemed Christian Church of God in Nigeria* (Africa World Press, 2008).

Weber, Max, *The Protestant Ethic and the Spirit of Capitalism*, tr. Talcott Parsons (New York: Charles Scribner's and Sons; New York: The Free Press, 1978).

<http://www.hattaf.org>

<http://nasfat.org/about.php> (Accessed 5 August 2008).

<http://www.rccg.org>

15

Religion–State Relations in Malaysia

Joseph B. Tamney

Malaysia is a relatively modern, religiously diverse society with a Muslim-majority population. There is no institutional separation of religion and the state in Malaysia. However, the Malaysian situation is in flux, allowing observers to note the prevailing reasons for both integration and separation of religion and the state. To develop this point, I discuss three contemporary, contested issues: apostasy, proselytization and moral policing (the state enforcement of religious norms *because* they are religious norms). At the present time, apostasy by Muslims is a punishable offence, the state curtails the proselytizing of Muslims, and moral policing of Muslims is widespread. To begin with, however, I consider the meaning of religion–state separation and explanations for its occurrence.

Religion and State Separation

In early human societies the institutional distinctions we make routinely never entered human consciousness. For instance: 'In these earlier societies, religion was "everywhere", was interwoven with everything else, and in no sense constituted a separate "sphere" of its own' (Taylor 2007: 2). Subsequently distinct institutions were created, which, however, were not independent. For instance, the political organization was 'in some way connected to, based on, guaranteed by some faith in, or adherence to, God, or some notion of ultimate reality' (p. 1).

Modernization supposedly entails structural differentiation, that is, increasingly, each institution comes to operate according to its own laws and principles. For instance, a secular state is concerned with achieving goals unique to itself such as to provide national economic development and security, protect the public health and enhance national power (Smith

1970: 116). A secular state does not prescribe, proscribe, support, or criticize any religious belief or practice. Moreover it does not interfere in the workings of religious groups or favour any one religion or all religions with monetary aid or other forms of assistance. Individuals enjoy religious freedom, and religious groups are not restricted or favoured by government (Kosmin 2007: 12). Of course, complete separation of institutions is impossible. In every society, institutions influence each other. The critical question is whether such influence results in one institution, such as the state, serving the needs of another institution, such as religion.

Causes of Religion–State Separation

Based on the Western experience, it is suggested that the separation of the religious and political institutions results from these conditions: the creation of religious specialists, a scepticism about religious truths that weakens religious authorities, an emphasis by religious people on ethics and sincerity rather than theology, and the appearance of a general intellectual movement based on valuing human freedom.

Why does structural differentiation occur? One argument is that an agricultural revolution produces a surplus that allows the appearance of specialists not tied to the production of goods, such as clerics and politicians. Then, according to this Weberian model, these specialists rationalize the social institutions, that is, each institution becomes more clearly and solely devoted to its own purposes; each becomes more differentiated from the others.

An example of the Weberian process is the argument of Roger Williams for the creation of the American state, Rhode Island. Williams believed separation from the state was necessary to preserve the authenticity of religious practice. Even at their best, governments compromise on moral principles, and thus churches become polluted by engaging in politics. Moreover, when churches get involved in politics, Williams wrote, they run the risk of being manipulated by politicians for their own purposes (Fishman 2007).

However, religious specialists may not favour differentiation but theocracy, as was the case when Calvin controlled Geneva. The presence of religious specialists is a necessary but not sufficient reason for institutional separation.

In American history, religious diversity was said to be a reason, if not *the* reason, for the first amendment to the constitution, which established the separation of church and state. A major supporter of the Bill of Rights, James Madison, said that the defence of religious freedom resulted from the 'multiplicity of sects which pervade America' (Levy 1999: 6). However, pluralism does not necessarily cause the establishment of a secular state. Pluralism may also result either in the legal protection and, to some extent, empowerment of minority religions such as under the Millet system of the Ottoman Empire, or in the official establishment of multiple religions, as in some American states at the time of independence. Religious pluralism seems to be neither necessary nor sufficient to cause the separation of religion and the state.[1]

In European history, church–state separation was supposedly rooted in the fact that religious conflict made it impossible to base public order on religion. Religious conflict following the Protestant Reformation exhausted politicians and people. During the sixteenth century: 'Doctrinal differences fuelled political ambitions and vice versa, in a deadly vicious cycle that lasted a century and a half' (Lilla 2007: 52). Tolerance was supposedly a result of a political stalemate. But the political settlements of European religious conflicts during the sixteenth and seventeenth centuries often broke down. Thus Perez Zagorin concluded that political expediency by itself was not sufficient to make religious freedom a morally and politically desirable goal (2003: 9–12).

The separation of religion and the state in the West was furthered by a growing scepticism about religious claims. Scepticism may arise from the awareness of theological disputes in a pluralist society, because observers see that well-meaning people are equally convinced of differing religious opinions (Zagorin 2003: 107–108). In other cases, scepticism results from a growing understanding of human psychology. For example, Thomas Hobbes (1588–1679) argued that all 'truths' are biased by the motivations of those proclaiming them and thus justified his totalitarian model for a state, in part, by calling into question the validity of religious doctrines. For Hobbes, the first step towards getting people to accept a secular state would occur if people became sceptical of claims of revelation; if they learned to distrust priests and ministers; if they questioned political interpretations of scripture; if they linked religious fervour with political violence – in short, if they began to think of religion as a human phenomenon rather than a divine one (Lilla 2007: 218).

During the seventeenth century, the appearance of scepticism, as well as of science, had the 'effect of modifying and liberalizing religious beliefs, weakening clerical authority, and undermining theological orthodoxy' (Zagorin 2003: 9).

Roger Williams was influenced by the seemingly, at least to him, unsettleable disputes among Christians.[2] If churches themselves gain power, Williams argued, the risk is that they will then try to force their beliefs on others, which is unchristian; in his opinion, the Puritans of the time committed the sin of pride by feeling certain that they alone knew the will of God and that they therefore had a mandate to enforce their views on others (Fishman 2007).

In addition, Perez Zagorin has argued that new Christian perspectives in modernizing Europe required religious freedom (2003: 289). This belief was encouraged by the appearance of Christian humanism and by a new appreciation of the importance of a person's inner disposition for salvation.

Christian humanism, part of the Renaissance, preceded the acceptance of religious freedom. Christian humanists put less stress on theology and more on ethics. For instance, Erasmus 'placed the human figure of Christ of the Gospels at the heart of religion as an emblem of love, kindness, tenderness, humility, and simplicity' (Zagorin 2003: 53; see also 84–86, 101, 154–155 and 294). As a result, these humanists tended to see religious persecution as morally wrong.[3]

In the Christian West, the use of force in religious matters had been widely accepted. Saint Augustine had said the freedom to choose what to believe about God was the 'freedom to go to hell' (Noonan 2005: 156). He believed that the fear of punishment could encourage people to reconsider their opinions and thus influence them to accept the truth of Catholicism. Other Christians argued that heretics could be forced to read or not read certain works, or to engage in external practices that might help to change their minds. Others argued for the use of force to save the good people. Throughout the Middle Ages and into the seventeenth century, it was widely believed that salvation came only through the believer's own church and that heresy was a defilement and an infection that had to be eliminated to preserve the health of the political body and thus save countless souls. In contrast, some Christians, such as Voltaire, argued that force breeds hypocrisy or rebellion. They believed that religious conviction must be held voluntarily, that salvation requires sincerity (Zagorin 2003: 27–31, 43–44, 64, 223, 243, 263, 297 and 358).

Finally, in the West, favouring the separation of religion and the state was an aspect of a broad intellectual movement centring on individual freedom. The radical enlightenment fully embraced the values of 'toleration, personal freedom, democracy, equality racial and sexual, freedom of expression, sexual emancipation, and the universal right to knowledge' (Israel 2006: 11; see also 866). The radicals wanted to protect freedom of conscience and to bring about the separation of church and state.

The architects of the American Bill of Rights were influenced by the European enlightenment. They were concerned about the primacy of freedom. Thomas Jefferson held a very limited view of the role of government. As he wrote in *Notes on the State of Virginia*: 'The legitimate powers of government extend to such acts only as are injurious to others. But it does me no injury for my neighbor to say there are twenty gods or no god. It neither picks my pocket nor breaks my leg' (Fishman 2007: 39).

Judging by the experience of Western countries, the differentiation of religion and the state is a long-term process. For instance, the acceptance of the US Constitution did not end moral policing. Throughout American history, moral reform movements have appeared that sought to use government to criminalize sins for fear that divine judgement would punish the whole community for failing to do so (Young 2006: 77). Again: when the American Constitution was written, half the states accepted the establishment of religion, in the sense that governments aided financially the prevalent Christian churches within a particular state. All such state practices ended by 1833, yet in 1985, then-Chief Justice William H. Rehnquist wrote that the First Amendment 'did not require governmental neutrality between religion and irreligion, nor did it prohibit the federal government from providing non-discriminatory aid to religion' (Levy 1999: 80).

The timing of changes in religious freedom is, no doubt, affected by political considerations. As Anthony Gill has emphasized, politicians are more likely to grant more religious freedom when such actions might increase their chances of political survival, for instance, by increasing government revenue, promoting economic growth, minimizing social unrest or lessening the cost of ruling (2008: 47). For example, all else being equal, government officials will favour religious groups that justify the regime's power (Gill 2008: 95).

In sum, it is suggested that the separation of the religious and political institutions results from these conditions: the creation of religious specialists, a scepticism about religious truths that weakens religious authorities, an emphasis by religious people on ethics and sincerity rather than theology, and the appearance of a general intellectual movement based on valuing human freedom. However, the timing of the separation depends on purely political factors.

In this chapter, three current issues in Malaysia relevant to the separation of mosque and state are discussed: Islamic apostasy, political control of proselytizing and moral policing.

Malaysia has a population of about 23 million people. The ethnic composition of the citizenry in 2000 was as follows: Malay – 53.4 per cent, other indigenous peoples – 11.7 per cent, Chinese – 26 per cent, Indian – 7.7 per cent, others – 1.2 per cent.[4] In 2000, 60.4 per cent of Malaysians were Muslims, 19.2 per cent were Buddhists, 9.1 per cent were Christians, 6.3 per cent were Hindus, and 4.6 per cent belonged to other religions or claimed no religious identity. Almost all Malays are Sunni Muslims. Slightly over half of the Christians are among the indigenous peoples of East Malaysia, that is, of Sabah and Sarawak. Most Christians on peninsula Malaysia are Chinese, although only about 10 per cent of the Malaysian Chinese population is Christian.

Malaysia modernized significantly during the second half of the last century. Between 1970 and 2000, the percentage of the total Malaysian population living in urban areas – defined as a place with 10,000 or more people – grew from 27 to 62 per cent (Saw 2006: 6). During that same time span, the percentage of twenty-to-twenty-four-year-olds who finished eleven years of education almost doubled from about 20 per cent in 1980 to nearly 40 per cent in 2000. The enrolment rate for tertiary education 'has increased from 3.7 per cent in 1970 to 21.5 per cent in 2000' (Lee 2006: 235). Between 1970 and 2002, the percentage of people living in poverty declined from 52.4 to 5.1 (Hew 2006: 270).

Malaysia is a constitutional monarchy modelled on the British form of government. It is neither a truly secular state nor is it a theocracy. Unlike a theocracy, the Malaysian system makes the constitution, which guarantees freedom of religion, the supreme law of the land (Faruqi

2005). Unlike in a truly secular society, a specific religion, Islam, is, according to the constitution, the religion of the federation. It is lawful for both the federal and state governments to assist Islamic institutions (Hassan 2005: 41). Malaysia may be said to have a hybrid form of government (Faruqi 2005).

Islamic laws govern 'matters relating to Islam'. These are state laws and are enforced by state bodies. If a Malaysian is a Muslim, she or he cannot opt out of Islamic law. During the 1990s, and since, what is an Islamic matter has been widened from 'jurisdiction over personal status law on marriage, divorce, custody, and maintenance, to matters related to the individual's personal piety, practices, and preferences' (Othman, Anwar and Kasim 2005: 79). Islamic Criminal Offences Enactments, which have been adopted in most states, allow 'for the criminal punishment of Muslims found guilty of consuming alcoholic beverages in public places, eating in public during the month of Ramadan, and committing the "sexual offence" of *khalwat* ("close proximity between a male or female who are not *muhrim* [a relative or kin whom one cannot marry] and not legally married")' (Othman, Anwar Kasim 2005: 93). These Islamic laws are examples of moral policing.

In 2009, an Islamic court sentenced a Muslim woman and a Muslim man to six strokes of the cane and fines of RM5,000 (about $1,362) each for drinking alcohol in separate places. The presiding judge said he had spared them a jail sentence but had given the maximum fine and caning in order to deter other Muslims from drinking. Although Muslims are rarely punished for drinking, the leader of the youth wing of the Islamist party, PAS, agreed with the ruling.[5] As he said: 'It is to remind Muslims not to drink' (Agence France-Presse 2009).

Apostasy

Background

There are three theological views about apostasy within Islam. 'First is the orthodox view of death to all apostates. The second view prescribes the death penalty only if apostasy is accompanied by rebellion against the community and its legitimate leadership. The third view holds that even though apostasy is a great sin, it is not a capital offence in Islam. Therefore a personal change of faith merits no punishment' (Anwar 2005: 129). However, most Islamic legal schools call for converts to be executed. This judgment is not based on Qur'anic statements but on two *Hadith* (stories supposedly quoting Muhammad). The authenticity of the *Hadith* has been questioned because they seem inconsistent with the Qur'an, which affirms that people cannot be forced to be religious, and with the actions of Muhammad, who pardoned apostates. Laws allowing the execution of Islamic apostates exist in Afghanistan, Iran, Pakistan, Saudi Arabia, Sudan and Syria (Morarjee and Murphy 2006; BARAZA editors 2007).

The Malaysian Case

Lina Joy was the centre of a court case that concerned whether a Muslim has the constitutional right to convert. The Federal Constitution guarantees freedom of religion. Article 11 reads: 'Every person has the right to profess and practice his religion ...' The constitution places no limits on this right. However, in 1988, Article 121 of the constitution was amended to read that the civil courts 'shall have no jurisdiction in respect of any matter within the jurisdiction of the Islamic courts' (clause 1A). The implication is that apostasy cases might fall under the jurisdiction of the Islamic courts and their legal traditions.

Born a Muslim (Azlina Jailani), in 1998, at the age of twenty-eight, Joy was baptized a Catholic. In 1999 the National Registration Department allowed her to change the name on her identity card but not her religious affiliation. As long as her official identity was Muslim, she could not legally marry the man she had chosen because he was not a Muslim. In 2001, she started proceedings in a civil court to change her religious identity so that she could marry her Catholic fiancé. She argued that since she is no longer a Muslim, her case should not be heard in an Islamic court. After lower civil courts had ruled against her, her case went to Malaysia's highest court.

In May 2007 the chief justice of this court gave the majority opinion that Joy had to use the Islamic courts, where her request to leave Islam would be considered. Chief Justice Ahmad Fairuz Abdul Halim wrote that since Islamic courts have jurisdiction over those embracing Islam, then 'by implication' the courts deal with issues regarding leaving Islam. The judge wrote: 'In short, she cannot, at her own whim, simply enter or leave her religion ... She must follow rules.' The chief justice wrote that Article 11 of the Federal Constitution does not give 'unrestricted freedom'. 'The right to profess and practice a religion should always be subjected to the principles and practices determined by that religion.' Once a person professes Islam, she must follow Islamic rules for renouncing the religion. The justice wrote that this requirement would prevent Muslims converting just to avoid punishments under Islamic law. 'In my view relating to Islam, Article 11 cannot be interpreted so widely as to cancel out all laws that a Muslim is required to execute and abide by. This is because Islam has a special position in the Federal Constitution which is different from other religions. Therefore, Article 11 should not be interpreted as a supreme right; and the right to profess and practice a religion is subjected to the religion that governs the individual' (Soon 2007a; see also Hong 2007, English 2007). The chief justice wrote that no one is stopping Lina Joy from marrying a Christian. 'She is merely required to fulfill certain obligations, for the Islamic authorities to confirm her apostasy, before she embraces Christianity' (Hodgson 2007).

The dissenting judge, a Kadazan Christian from Sabah, wrote that in matters of fundamental rights, there must be express authorization in the constitution for any curtailment of those rights, but there is no such authorization relating to Joy's case. He added that the requirement to have the matter decided by an Islamic court was unconstitutional; it was unreasonable, he said, to ask a person to go before a court and 'self-incriminate' herself, given that if she sought a certificate of apostasy from an Islamic court, she would be considered an apostate, and if she did not return to Islam, she would probably be sent to an Islamic centre for rehabilitation (Perlez 2006). The Federal Territory, where Joy lives, has no specific law concerning apostasy, but this court could be guided by Islamic traditions.[6]

The president of the Bar Council issued a statement that supported the supremacy of the Federal Constitution. The president agreed with the minority opinion that it was unreasonable to require Joy to apply for a certificate of apostasy, when doing so would likely expose her to some form of punishment. 'Little comfort is drawn from cases of those who wish to leave or change religion,' especially given the very recent 'case of Revathi in Malacca who was deprived of her liberty and access to her husband and minor child' (Bar Council 2008: 34).

To consider the meaning of being sent to a detention centre, I review the experience of Revathi Masoosai. Revathi was born into a Muslim family. She married a Hindu man in a Hindu ritual and became a practising Hindu. The marriage was not registered because Revathi's identity card said she was a Muslim, although when picked up by the authorities she claimed that she had been raised as a Hindu by her grandmother. After she tried to register the marriage and to declare herself a Hindu, Revathi was charged with apostasy, her fifteen-month-old daughter was given over to her Muslim mother, and Revathi was sent to Ulu Yam Baru, 32 kilometres outside the capital in Selangor. It 'is ringed like a prison by barbed wire with dormitories protected by a second ring of barbed wire. Outside a sign says, "House of Faith," and inside the inmates spend much of their time studying Islam' (Perlez 2006). At the Ulu Yam Center she was told that she could not renounce Islam (Farish 2007). After spending a hundred days in the centre, the Islamic court ordered her to stay there another eighty days. Subsequently the court ordered her to stay with her Muslim parents. Revathi insisted that she was not a Muslim. She and her baby visited her husband during the day. A Muslim councillor at the rehabilitation centre said that Revathi knew little about Hinduism; he said: 'In short, it's not Hinduism that she has converted to, it is "husbandism"' (Fauwaz 2007a; see also Malaysiakini 2007a, 2007b).[7]

Support for Court Decision

The President of the Islamist political party (PAS) said apostasy cases such as Joy's should not be interpreted in terms of freedom of religion but in terms of 'controlling Muslims' (Beh 2007). According to the director of PAS's research centre, given that apostasy is an internal Muslim matter, any attempt by others to negotiate the matter would be an unwelcome intrusion and perceived as arrogant. In his opinion, 'if one chooses Islam and becomes a Muslim willingly and consciously, he or she ceases to have the freedom to opt out of Islam. This would be tantamount to renouncing and declaring war against the Almighty Allah ...' As justification, he cited the authentic tradition of the Prophet (Dzulkifli 2007).[8]

The mufti of a Malaysian state, Negri Sembilan, called for stiffer preventive and punitive measures against apostates. He said: 'Apostasy can affect the collapse of the institution of family and Islamic society. Our failure to defend these two institutions will lead to the collapse of Islam and the Muslim community' (Fauwaz 2006b). The mufti of another state, Perak, supported serious action against apostates. As he said: 'The

Muslim community is like a body. For example, if a leg has become gangrenous, it should be cut off, otherwise it would be dangerous for the rest of the body. Apostates can influence the rest of the community' (Anis 2006).

These Islamic scholars think in terms of the Muslim community, not in terms of human rights. Their reasons for punishing apostates show the influence of group-thinking: kill individuals for the well-being of the community.

Moreover, relations among religious groups in Malaysia are inseparable from race relations. Any loss of Islamic power is perceived as a threat to the Malay community. An Islamic NGO (ABIM)[9] publicly asked a court to dismiss an apostasy case because 'Allowing Malays to leave Islam automatically will erode the status, the rights, and the privileges of Malays' (Hamid and Liau 2006).

The close association of religious and racial feelings was apparent at a public forum organized by the Malaysian Bar Council, which was entitled 'Conversion to Islam'. The forum was held on 9 August 2008 to address issues arising when people were caught between the separate jurisdictions of the civil and Islamic courts. The forum was to include discussions of topics related to conversion, such as converts not informing their spouses about the change, and the conversion of children without the consent of both parents. The forum began at 9 a.m. and was scheduled to end at 1:30 p.m. However, about three hundred people began a protest outside the council's office prior to the start of the forum. During the protest, individuals shouted such slogans as 'Crush the Bar Council', 'Long Live Islam', 'Don't Challenge Islam', as well as 'Go Back to China' (Ong 2008). The responses to the forum demonstrated the intertwining of religious and racial feelings.

The president of PAS emailed a statement to the council vehemently opposing the forum. He wrote that any discussions about Islam should involve those who are authorities on the subject. The president of the Muslim Lawyers Association told a reporter that discussions of Islamic matters should not be in a public forum but should involve the appropriate groups (Chan 2008). The education minister, Hisammuddin Hussein, said Malaysians should 'not think that openness is an absolute right' (Associated Press 2008a).The deputy prime minister told reporters that such sensitive matters as the conversion of Muslims should not be discussed openly but behind closed doors (Bernama

2008). A Bar Council official, in contrast, told a reporter: 'We believe that the continued suppression of open and respectful discourse, not public forums, will cause tension and jeopardize national unity' (Fauwaz 2008b).

Several years earlier, the National Conference of Ulamas had called for less public discussion of sensitive issues involving Islam – such as religious conversions of Muslims and the jurisdiction of Islamic courts. The scholars feared that such discussions might cause confusion among Muslims and heighten tensions between religious communities. In place of public discussions, the *ulama* suggested creating a forum in which Islamic experts would discuss sensitive matters in private and reach a consensus which would be enforced by the religious authorities (Associated Press 2006).

Defenders of Islam (Pembela Islam) was formed initially by a hundred Muslim lawyers who wanted to counter liberal positions regarding apostasy taken by other lawyers. Their spokesperson said: 'Some quarters have questioned and challenged the position and status of Islam in this country by using the argument that the human rights of individuals is higher than Islam' (Fauwaz 2006a). He went on to say that allowing Muslims to apostatize would imply that individuals could interpret for themselves the meaning of Islamic sacred texts and practise the religion in whatever way they chose. The preservation of group homogeneity, and thereby of group unity, was perceived as requiring the punishment of apostates.

The issue is whether people think in terms of groups or in terms of individuals. The arguments against Lina Joy are based on a worldview in which the group, in this case the Islamic and racial communities, is more important than the individual, a worldview in which the human rights of individuals cannot be more important than keeping the body of the community healthy. Consistent with this worldview, important decisions are to be made by leaders who are considered representative of the group and not by the people in open public discussions. Decisions made behind closed doors prevent 'confusion' (read: scepticism) from developing among the members of the group. In contrast, open discussion would encourage people to believe that individuals should decide religious matters for themselves.

Such thinking is not surprising. 'In the late Middle Ages, the belief seems to have been universal that heresy was a defilement and an infection that must be removed, and that it was right to punish and kill impenitent heretics' (Zagorin 2003: 43). Throughout the Middle Ages and into the seventeenth century, it was widely believed that heresy was a contagious evil that would lead to the damnation of countless souls (p. 44). Heretics, including apostates, were a disease that had to be eliminated to preserve the health of the body.

Undoubtedly group-thinking has deep cultural roots in Malaysia. But such thinking is reinforced by the actions of Western countries. Muslim societies are dominated by the sense of being immersed in a hostile world order controlled by the West, and especially the United States. As chairman of the Organization of the Islamic Conference, Malaysia's prime minister, Abdullah Badawi, discussed the strained relationship between the two great civilizations, the Christian West and the Muslim world. The latter, he said, 'sees the suppression of Palestine, the invasion of Afghanistan, the conquest of Iraq, and the destruction of Lebanon as a complicity to humiliate Muslim countries' (Agence France-Presse 2006).

The president of an Islamic NGO (ABIM) said that Islam is under scrutiny; it stands 'accused'. Muslims, he said, are 'becoming more frustrated, desperate, pressured, and cornered because of others' ongoing action of putting Islam in the dock, in the accused's corner … There is a strong feeling of being victimized' (Husna Yusop 2006: 16).

The global environment strengthens identification of individual Muslims with the Islamic community. The oppression of Muslims 'has created a situation where Muslims are convinced that they are under siege. Consequently a significant segment of the Muslim community … has chosen to defend itself by reasserting its religious identity. Malaysian Muslims, who are already acutely conscious of their identity, are part of that trend' (Chandra 2007).

Opposition to Decision: Individual Rights

The existence of a variety of religions in the same social context inevitably creates boundary issues, such as the case of Lina Joy. While the result may simply be the assertion of the primacy of the dominant religion, such cases will also fuel calls for equality of religions and, in the current global environment, for the religious freedom of individuals.

The Council of Churches of Malaysia said that the Lina Joy decision had denied her, and others like her, fundamental rights, most notably the freedom to follow one's conscience in choosing a religion, as guaranteed in the Malaysian Constitution (Council of Churches of Malaysia 2008). The secretary general of the National Evangelical Christian Fellowship Malaysia said: 'If they rule against Lina Joy, the whole question of religious liberty – the freedom of conscience, choice, expression, and thought of an individual – will be greatly affected' (Hamid and Liau 2006). The Hindu Sangam issued a statement calling on parliament to enact laws that would ensure that persons who do not profess Islam are not subject to the Islamic court. As the statement read: 'The fundamental liberty of all Malaysians to profess and practice their faith in peace and harmony must be respected, both in fact and in law' (2008: 27).

A feminist Islamic NGO, Sisters in Islam (SIS), in conjunction with other women's groups, called on the government to uphold fundamental liberties such as the freedom of personal faith. Their public letter about the Joy case also criticized the court's decision on the basis that it denied women various basic rights, such as the right to marry a partner of their choice and to choose their country of domicile, as Muslims would have to leave Malaysia should they wish to marry non-Muslims (AWAM, SIS, WAO and WDC 2008).[10] In recent years, SIS has added to its agenda advocacy for democracy and human rights because these are preconditions for the effective advocacy for women's equality (Othman, Anwar and Kasim 2005: 100).

As the Malaysian political scientist Chandra Muzaffar noted, secularism is often championed by religious minorities, such as Muslims in India and Christians in Malaysia (Chandra 2005: 70).[11] That is, religious pluralism increases interest in human rights. But it is not only religious pluralism that has this consequence. As SIS demonstrates, all minorities find it useful to use arguments based on individual rights.

Moreover, some Muslim scholars, who would probably be identified as 'liberals', are committed to religious freedom for Islamic reasons. Dr Azzam Tamimi, who is Director of the Institute of Islamic Political Thought in London, came to Malaysia at the invitation of the Muslim Professionals Forum (MPF). While in the country, he gave a talk about freedom in Islam at the University of Malaya. Tamimi said freedom of choice is a cornerstone of Islam. He explained that there is no punishment for apostates stipulated in the Qur'an; the relevant *Hadith* had to be understood in the context in which they were uttered, to wit, in a situation when apostasy was viewed as treason, as undermining the Islamic community. As he said: 'If submission to Allah involves free choice, then the same principle must apply if one wants to leave the faith.' Again: 'But if one leaves the religion out of free choice, let them become what they want.' Muslims need more self-confidence. 'Nothing will happen to Islam if people leave the religion' (Surin 2006). The newspaper story was posted on the MPF website.

However, mixed opinions existed among members of the Muslim Professionals Forum. Dr Musa bin Mohd Nordin posted an opinion on the MPH website in which he emphasized 'the fact there is overwhelming evidence in the Qur'an of freedom of conscience, belief, and worship' (Musa 2007). In contrast, another member criticized liberal Muslims such as Dr Tamimi for 'making Islam subservient to prevailing notions of rights, freedoms, and gender equality' (Mazeni 2006).

The role of coercion in Islam is controversial. PAS's spiritual leader, Nik Abdul Aziz Nik Mat, launched a month-long missionary campaign by saying that Islam must be accepted voluntarily. 'We cannot force people to enter heaven. They must do it of their own free will' (Associated Press 2007). However, like many Muslim scholars, the mufti of Negri Sembilan, a Malaysian state, argued that: 'The Qur'anic verse "There is no compulsion in religion" does not mean that a Muslim can leave Islam as he wishes; it means that non-Muslims cannot be forced to enter Islam. The verse has been misquoted by so many. Once someone is a Muslim, he is bound by its rules, just as those professing other faiths are bound by theirs' (Anis 2006; see also Faruqi 2005: 261).

However, because agreement on this matter is lacking among Muslims, some Islamic scholars were free to separate the issue of requiring the use of the Islamic court and the matter of punishing apostates. Anwar Ibrahim, an important leader of the political opposition to the government, said that it was appropriate for the matter of apostasy to be considered by the Islamic court, but that there should be no recrimination, as freedom of conscience was an Islamic value (Anwar 2008). An Islamic legal scholar suggested that apostasy needs regulation because apostasy may lead to divorce, the loss of the custody of children and the loss of the special privileges given to Malays. Thus: 'Procedural hurdles in the way of apostasy are justified. But criminalization is not' (Faruqi 2007: 8). The Director-General of the Institute of Islamic Understanding of Malaysia disagreed with the use of detention centres, but said about the

Lina Joy case: 'the community of Muslims has a right to consult with her and ask her why she wants to leave Islam'. They have 'a responsibility to the *ummah* to ask this question. If you deny them this right, obviously the Muslims will get upset' (Damis 2007).[12] These suggestions would retain a traditional procedure, but they also accept the importance of religious freedom.

After the court's decision, the de facto law minister told people to have more faith in the fairness of the Islamic court. As he said: 'What is the point of keeping a person if they no longer believed in the faith and made that publicly known?' (Bernama 2007). Of course this is an argument for killing apostates. The fact that the minister apparently could not conceive of this punishment suggests that the rationale for the apostate process is being undermined. That is, the process of coming to value individual freedom is well under way.

The fate of apostates is tied to the relative appeal of group-thinking and thinking in terms of human rights. The traditional view is that society is composed of groups, and that it is the role of government to protect privileged groups. In the case of Muslims, this perspective is strengthened by the American-dominated global order. In defence of group preservation, some leaders want to avoid the public discussion of contentious religious issues because public awareness of religious controversies may evoke scepticism and thus weaken religious authorities and communal unity. But signs of change exist. The execution of apostates seems out of bounds, and proponents of compromise want to separate the use of Islamic courts in apostasy cases from the right of such courts to punish apostates. In addition, minorities are taking advantage of human rights discourse to further their interests; while such tactics indirectly reinforce group-thinking, they also raise awareness about human rights issues. Finally, the presence of liberal Islam suggests a possible shift in the meaning of Islamic piety away from conformity to group rules and toward ethics and personal sincerity.

Proselytizing

The Federal Constitution allows Malaysian states to control the propagation of any religious doctrine other than Islam among Malays. For instance, the government restricts the distribution in peninsula Malaysia of the Malay-language Bible (US Department of State 2006).[13]

Bibles in Malay must be labelled 'Not for Muslims' (Fauwaz 2008a). In 2006, in the midst of a controversy concerning the state's protection of Islam, the prime minister urged both that state governments enforce their laws that bar preaching other faiths to Muslims and that states without such laws adopt them. These laws, he said, preserve religious harmony (Reuters 2006).[14]

In 2007, the Catholic weekly *Herald* was told that its printing licence might not be renewed because it was using the word 'Allah' in the Malay-language version of the weekly. Allah is the word for God in the Arabic Bible, in the Malaysian Malay-language Bible and in the Indonesian Bible (Soon 2007c).[15] Allah has been used by Malay-speaking Christians since the nineteenth century. However, a Muslim cleric told a reporter that Muslims feared that the use of Arabic words would make proselytizing easier. 'Muslims have long feared Christian proselytizing and the fear surfaced strongly after the Lina Joy case' (Kuppusasmy 2008). The president of ABIM told a reporter: 'We have to question Christians' motives for wanting to use this obviously Muslim word. It appears to be for conversions. All Muslim Malays in Malaysia are against this' (Koswanage 2009).[16]

A government minister said about the matter: 'Don't play with fire and challenge the Muslims. We are willing to do anything to protect our religion' (*Straits Times* 2009a).[17] The editor of the *Herald* said: 'We are a scapegoat, a means for the Malay-Muslims to rally together' (Reuters 2008). However, the Catholic Church argues that the ban is a violation of religious freedom and is seeking a court order that would allow the use of Allah in its publications. Moreover, as a reporter noted, the ban symbolizes to non-Malays the erosion of their religious freedom, 'while for many Muslims, a lifting of the ban would be seen as a blow to Malay supremacy in the country' (Associated Press 2009). The government's protection of Islam is both a defence of the political power of Malays and a defensive reaction against proselytizing by Christians.

In part, restrictions on proselytizing are a legacy of colonialism. The protection of Islam is one of the pre-independence compromises between the Malays and the non-Malays that was made 'in order to insulate Malays against internationally-funded and powerful proselytizing forces that had become entrenched in the country because of official support from the colonial government' (Faruqi 2007: 6). This is an ongoing issue in Malaysia. During the mid-Eighties, accusations were made 'that Christians are offering jobs and women to Muslim youths in order to convert them' (Lee 1988: 404). Today 'There is a legend going around in Malay circles that Christian churches give out "holy water" and if a Malay drinks it, he/she will be possessed and become a Christian' (Noor Yahaya Hamzah 2008: 207). While these charges may not be true, they portray the state of mind of Malaysian Muslims. The president of an Islamic NGO (ABIM) told a general assembly that the Islamic community is being attacked by Christian evangelists who are trying to convert Muslims to Christianity (Yusri 2006: 36).

As one Muslim scholar wrote:

> It is respectfully submitted that the primary purpose of this provision [controlling proselytizing] is to insulate Muslims against a clearly unequal and disadvantageous situation. During the colonial period, many non-indigenous religions were vigorously promoted by merchants, the military, and the missionaries of the colonial countries. Even today, the proselytizing activities of many Western-dominated religious movements that are internationally organized and funded have aroused resentment in many Asian and African societies. (Faruqi 2005: 158)

Because of aggressive Christian tactics, a Malaysian legal professor has advocated the need for ground rules for proselytizing. 'It is insulting and narrow-minded to tell the believer of another faith that his/her God is not the true God and that he/she needs to "see the light".' Some activities, he wrote, are just unacceptable:

> 'Ambulance chasing' by some proselytizers who roam hospital corridors to try to secure conversion of the dying, the critically injured, or their relatives is despicable … Attempted conversions of minors through direct or indirect 'social activities' must be strictly controlled.
>
> 'Check-book conversions' by resorting to financial benefit for the proselytizer as well as the proselytized must be condemned. (Faruqi 2007: 8)

It is not just Muslims who criticize aggressive proselytizing by Christians. In 2007, a doctor in Singapore wrote a letter to the *Straits Times* newspaper about this issue. The previous year, he sent one of his patients to a Christian-supported community hospital. After being discharged, the patient told Dr Tan about her experience. During her hospital stay, she was repeatedly visited by young people bearing gifts, who asked her to become a Christian. She had been a devotee of Kuan Yin, the Buddhist Goddess of Mercy. The doctor advised his confused patient that whatever religion gave her peace of mind was the right religion for her. Subsequently the patient had a life-threatening experience and was readmitted to the same hospital. A staff member told her that God had saved her from death, so the woman decided to convert to Christianity – although she thought that she would try to postpone the baptism. Dr Tan objected to the attempt to convert patients in hospitals. He believes that pastoral care workers 'must be trained to empower a patient to draw on his religious affiliation to deal with the physical suffering'. Further, he urged the Ministry of Health to establish 'guidelines on pastoral care for all the community hospitals so that the religious affiliation of patients is respected and protected' (Tan 2007). Dr Tan based his recommendation on respect for the individual.

In 2004 The National Heritage Party of Sri Lanka, which is led by Buddhist monks, tried to get a law passed that would outlaw religious conversions. The monks supported the proposed law because they believed that United States-funded evangelical groups were trying to convert Buddhists by offering cash payments to converts (Reuters 2004).[18]

Buddhist monks in the Jogye Order, the largest order in South Korea, have become involved in anti-government protests. A spokesperson for the order said: 'Religious peace in our country is being threatened by those who dream of turning it into a medieval Christian kingdom through a church-elder president' (Choe 2008). President Lee Myung Bak is an elder in a Presbyterian church. He is supported by the Korean conservative Christian churches, which are criticized for their supposedly assertive proselytizing and disrespect for other religions. Families have become divided as some Protestants refuse to take part in traditional ancestor ceremonies. Video clips have circulated depicting Protestant preachers saying disparaging things about Buddhism. The secretary-general of the Christian Ethics Movement of Korea, a Protestant civic group, commented: 'Buddhists' sense of crisis over their declining influence in South Korea, and society's, not just Buddhist, unease with Protestants' aggressive proselytizing, have exploded under Lee's government' (Choe 2008).

In 2008 Kyrgyzstan's government passed a law increasing control of proselytizm. Among other things, handing out religious literature in public places is prohibited, and private religious teaching is banned. Religious education will take place in the public schools. The new law is said to be an attempt to limit the influence both of Islamist organizations and of Christian evangelical groups. Supporters of the law argued that it will lessen religious tension and preserve the peace (Associated Press 2008c).[19]

Religious conflict in the world order is used to justify the political protection of religions, including Islam. As Olivier Roy wrote: 'A common complaint among [Islamic] fundamentalists is that Christian missionaries are pursuing an aggressive campaign of conversion (which is true, incidentally ...) (2004: 156). Aggressive proselytizing by Christians evokes and is used to justify group-based responses such as Malaysia's laws that protect Muslims.

Moral Policing[20]

By the early 1980s most state religious councils had introduced strict penalties for people caught in 'close proximity' (close proximity between men and women in secluded areas). Zealous individuals sought '*khalwat* couples' in dormitories, cars and corners of public buildings (Nagata 1984: 255, note 13). In 2006 the director of the Perak (state) Islamic religious department justified spying on couples in hotels on the basis that the state is responsible for preventing sinful acts (Bernama 2006).[21]

In 2008 a judge in an Islamic Court of Appeal recommended that *non-Muslims* who committed *khalwat* should be punished in the civil courts. The Islamic Lawyers Association of Malaysia (PGSM) supported the suggestion. The president of PGSM said that all laws have their origin in moral rules, which in turn have roots in religion-based norms. 'What would happen if laws governing moral behavior were to be abolished?' (Malaysiakini 2008b).The director-general of the Malaysian Institute of Islamic Understanding (IKIM) criticized the suggestion, because it jeopardizes Muslim friendship with non-Muslims. 'In Islam it says to you yours to us ours in terms of religion.' Islamic law, he said, does not apply to non-Muslims (Malaysiakini 2008a). A politician from the opposition party, Democratic Action Party, called the recommendation 'arrogant and insensitive to the non-Muslims' and an example of 'creeping Islamization' (Hassan 2008). None of these participants in the debate argued against moral policing itself.

The enforcement of laws against 'close proximity' has received much attention in the media. The mufti of Perlis at the time, Dr Mohamad Asri Zainul Abidin, said that the police should be concerned about sinful acts that harm society such as theft and robbery (Nadzri 2006). The information minister said: 'There are other pressing issues [than sexual sins] such as robberies, muggings, illegal racing, and drug abuse committed by our youths which need more urgent attention' (Nadzri 2006). The problems mentioned by Asri and the government minister would be acknowledged as legitimate state concerns even for a secular state. The enforcement of relevant laws would not constitute moral policing.

In his address to an Islamic NGO (ABIM), the president said that some liberal Muslims argue that a state 'has no right to set laws which dictate what an individual can or cannot do in his moral life. The existence of such laws supposedly is against the right of individual freedom and is not appropriate in modern times.' In Malaysia, such laws ban, among other things, drinking alcohol, gambling, adultery and *khalwat*. In contrast, the president quoted with approval an Indonesian scholar's response to those who criticize moral policing: 'Isn't it better to be forced to go into heaven than willingly go into hell!' (Yusri 2006: 13).

The issue is what the appropriate activities by religious groups in a secular state are. Casanova (1994) claimed that it is appropriate for such groups to enter the public sphere to raise moral questions about public policy. Religious political involvement is acceptable, he argued, to encourage collective self-reflection on ethical matters. As an example, Casanova mentioned the Catholic public stand on abortion in support of 'the right to life' (1994: 38). However, the key is whether a religious group is trying to use the state to serve strictly religious purposes. Is abortion a crime because it is the murder of a human being or because it is the sinful violation of a supposed natural law? If the latter, such criminalization would be moral policing and thus inappropriate for a secular state.

In 2005 Sisters in Islam (SIS) condemned moral policing. In a public letter, the organization asked: 'Is it the duty of the state, in order to create a moral society, to turn what it considers "sins" into "crimes against the state"?' (Hong 2005). In their bulletin, SIS published an essay by a Muslim scholar, Abdullahi Ahmed An-Na'im. He argued that to be an ideal Muslim requires living in a secular society. A secular state, that is, 'one that is neutral regarding religious doctrine', is necessary to facilitate 'genuine piety' – that is, freely chosen piety. Abdullahi also emphasized the importance of Islamic values. 'When observed voluntarily, Shari'a-based values can shape laws and public policy through the democratic process.' However, religious compliance motivated by force or fear is not genuine religiosity. That is, salvation cannot be attained by acting out of fear, such as fear of the police (Abdullahi 2007).

Criticism of moral policing is part of a religious mindset that focuses on the individual. Regrettably, from SIS's point of view, policies regarding Islam are considered the exclusive preserve of religious scholars. SIS argues that 'the only authentic [religious] source is the text of the Quran' (Chong 2006: 42), and that the revealed word of God must be distinguished from the human understanding of that revelation, which is fallible and changeable (Othman, Anwar and Kasim 2005: 99). SIS believes that practices that imply the inferiority of women are the result of men having had control of the process of interpreting the Qur'an. Thus it is imperative that women participate in this process. In 2006, SIS's newsletter contained an interview with an Islamic scholar who called for the 'democratization of interpretation' (Editorial 2006). In liberal Islam, all Muslims must take responsibility for the meaning of their religion.

Not surprisingly, ABIM perceives liberal Islam as a tool of the West. According to an article in their newsletter, because the West has failed directly to undermine Islam, it encourages liberal Islam as a means of achieving this goal (Azizuddin 2005). Similarly the chairman of MPF (the Muslim Professionals Forum) wrote: 'The neocons' "war on terror" is using liberal Islam to do its bidding in the Muslim world. They are natural allies as both have a healthy dose of disdain for people who prefer to live their lives as Muslims rather than succumb to western culture …' (Mazeni 2005: 9).

If politicians believe that they could keep people from eternal damnation by criminalizing sins, they would feel it necessary to do so. Ending moral policing, that is, ceasing to make sins into crimes, depends on religious changes taking place among Muslims. They must come to believe that salvation depends on pure intentions, and not the outward behaviour of individuals. They must accept that individuals are responsible for deciding what Islam requires of them. Ending moral policing, therefore, is related to the acceptance of liberal Islam, which emphasizes values more than norms, the importance of religious sincerity, and the need for the religious freedom of individuals. But the appeal of this form of Islam is undermined by its association with the West.

The Political Context

The United Malays National Organization (UMNO) was formed in 1946 'to fight for the rights of the Malays' (Abdullah 2006: 18). In the constitution, a Malay is defined, in part, as a 'person who professes the Muslim religion'. Thus defending the rights of Malays includes defending their religion, Islam. Since independence in 1957, party coalitions led by UMNO have ruled Malaysia.

The espousal of group-thinking is part of the political ideology of the UMNO ruling party. For example, the long-serving prime minister, Mahathir, said in an important speech made in 1991 that the political goal is to create 'a social system in which society will come before self' (Ooi 2006: 68–69). He espoused the Asian-values rhetoric that prioritizes 'harmony, consensus, community and the family'. Such discourse by political leaders has been used 'to justify their authoritarianism as *the* Asian brand of democracy' (Ng, Maznah and Tan 2006: 140). The emphasis on the need for the desires of individuals to be subordinated to achieving the needs of the state undermines the effectiveness of messages about the value of the individual, human rights and freedom of religion.

The emphasis on harmony serves the interests of those in power and slows down social change. For instance, in January 2006, nine non-Muslim cabinet ministers called for a review of Article 121 (1A) of the federal constitution, as amended in 1988, which now states that the civil courts 'shall have no jurisdiction in respect of any matter within the jurisdiction of Islamic courts' (Ooi 2006). Within two days, the prime minister announced that the legislation in question required no changes, although he also promised to review Article 121. The ministers withdrew their request. On 22 August 2006 the minister in the prime minister's department announced that the division of power between the civil and Islamic courts is quite clear. Thus, he said, the government believed 'that there is no necessity for any body to be formed to discuss religious matters, such as the Interfaith Council or Article 11 [an NGO coalition to defend religious freedom]' (Ram 2006). The government warned that such discussions could create religious tensions and thus should not continue.

The focus on religious harmony is justified as Asian, but it also implies the value of the status quo and, in Malaysia, the preferential policies towards Islam. In the name of religious harmony, the UMNO government protects Malay Muslim interests in order to retain their support. Thus UMNO is likely to slow or possibly halt the process of increasing religious freedom in the country.

Conclusion

The separation of mosque and state in Muslim countries can be firmly established only when Muslims accept such separation on religious grounds. As an Islamic scholar argued, the need for a religious justification for secularism is not sufficiently appreciated. While the material conditions of coexistence may force a level of religious tolerance and diversity, this is likely to be seen as temporary political expediency by believers unless they are also able to accept it [secularism] as at least consistent with their religious doctrine (Abdullahi 2007: 3)

Regarding the separation of religious and political institutions, I suggest that this proposition means that Muslim acceptance of mosque–state separation depends on these changes:

- changing from thinking in terms of the welfare of groups to thinking in terms of the welfare of individuals;
- coming to think that the essence of Islam is the ethical ideals found in the Qur'an;
- and coming to believe that salvation depends first and foremost on a freely chosen religiosity.

Continuing modernization will undermine group-thinking generally. In addition, the promulgation of liberal Islam favours the acceptance of the separation of religion and the state on religious grounds. The prospects for liberal Islam are enhanced both by the public discussion of religious issues that might weaken religious authorities and by the affirmation of religious freedom that is fuelled, in part, by the global human rights movement.

The appearance of a Malaysian secular state is related to the struggle within Islam between traditionalist and liberal forms of the religion. Clive Kessler is an anthropologist who has long studied Malaysian matters. Reacting to recent controversies, he wrote a short essay about 'the long march towards desecularization' (2006). Led by Islamic NGOs,

Kessler believes that there is a movement to isolate liberal Muslims, to stigmatize their suggestions as heretical, and to portray them as dupes of Islam's enemies. Marzuki Mohamad, a research scholar at Australian National University and a member of the Central Executive Committee of ABIM, responded to Kessler's comments. Campaigns to allow apostasy and to increase the power of civil courts for disputes involving Muslims and non-Muslims are meant, he wrote, to achieve the complete 'Secularization of Islamic Society' (Marzuki 2006: 5). Secularization means accepting the 'primacy of individuals over the family, the community, and the state when it comes to matters of personal faith' (2006: 4–5). On the one hand, Kessler perceives an internal struggle between traditionalist and liberal forms of Islam. On the other hand, Marzuki sees a contest between Islamic values and Western individualism. To the extent the internal struggle is transformed into a civilizational one, religious change is slowed because of the current hostile global world order.

Once religious conflict exists among Muslims in an Islamic society, religious pluralism favours liberal Islam. The awareness of theological disputes in a pluralist society such as those discussed in this chapter may cause scepticism, because observers see that well-meaning people are equally convinced of differing religious opinions (Zagorin 2003: 107–108). Scepticism, in turn, favours the democratization of the interpretation of religious texts.

Moreover, non-Islamic leaders are more likely to be able to work with liberal Muslims. Leaders in two Malaysian NGOs suggested it would be appropriate for the government to base itself on shared values, broadly conceived. The president of the Human Rights Society of Malaysia, Malik Imtiaz Sarwar, said: 'When we say there's no role for religion in governance, we are not rejecting the value base as long as that value base is a universal value base. In making a decision in the public sphere, when we decide what's good for the country as a whole, we have [our basis] in law, the constitution, in particular, in human rights, and with a universal basis' (Fauwaz 2007b). A member of an interfaith organization shunned by Islamic groups said that the government can 'draw positive points' found in all the religions in Malaysia, such as creating a just society, helping the poor, protecting human rights, and standing up against exploitation and corruption (Fauwaz 2007). Of course, the emphasis on shared values might turn off religious people who fear the loss of a distinct religious identity and thus indirectly contribute to support for Islamism. But the liberal emphasis on ethical values as the essence of Islam allows for broad cooperation among religious groups in a pluralistic setting.

In the present global environment, the threat implied by liberal Islam to Islamists is that Islam will be interpreted through the lens of Western values. But Islamists cannot ignore values such as human rights. A PAS deputy president, when explaining that the party wants to appeal to non-Muslims, said: 'We still want an Islamic state. But we want to discuss it in the context of universal values and rights, good governance, and justice issues' (Tisdall 2006: 2). According to PAS's statement concerning the nature of an Islamic state, the state guarantees the freedom and rights of the individual – such as freedom of speech and assembly, freedom of religion, the right to private property. All the rights contained in the Universal Declaration of Human Rights are also protected by the Islamic state. However, their enforcement must not be contrary to the provisions of Shari'a law (PAS 2008) – of course a severe limitation. Charles Taylor (2007) noted that the Enlightenment succeeded in the West because the Christian influence on governments declined. What is happening in Malaysia seems to be a more interactive process of change: religious groups somewhat accommodate human rights, allowing these rights to gain more political significance, thereby making state policies more consistent with religious freedom, and thus increasing the pressure on religious groups to accommodate human rights.

At the same time, some conditions favour the continuation of the entanglement of religion and politics in Malaysia. Traditionalist group-thinking remains widely prevalent. Such thinking is encouraged by the near identity of Malayness and Islam, by the antagonistic political and religious world order, and by UMNO, whose political ideology favours authoritarianism and whose political appeal is based on the protection of Malay interests.

NOTES

1 Moreover religious authorities were weakened in the United States by the dispersed settlement pattern, which made surveillance of the population by religious leaders difficult, and by the possibility for religious dissidents to move to parts of the country in which they were difficult to control (Zagorin 2003: 302).
2 Roger Williams argued that individuals should be free to follow their consciences because no authority existed that could determine the truth of conflicting theological doctrines (Zagorin 2003: 204–205).
3 Spiritualists and mystical Christians had a similar perspective.
4 In 2000, 5.9 per cent of the population were not citizens. The figures in this paragraph are from the 2000 census (Saw 2006).
5 PAS is the Parti Islam SeMalaysia.
6 In Malaysia, the punishment of convicted offenders in Islamic courts is limited by law to three years in jail, a RM5,000 fine, or six strokes of the cane. 'Caning in Islam is humane – it is akin to caning in school – quite unlike the cane punishment imposed in Malaysian criminal courts – the latter is regarded by human rights advocates as torture' (*Malaysia Today* 2006).
7 Muslim women cannot marry non-Muslims.
8 The director referred to Sahih Al-Bukhari, Vol. 9, No. 57.
9 Angkatan Belia Islam Malaysia (Malaysian Islamic Youth Movement).
10 Besides Sisters in Islam, the groups were All Women's Action Society, Woman's Aid Organization, Women's Centre for Change and Women's Development Collective.
11 Anthony Gill provides historical evidence for the proposition: 'Hegemonic religions will prefer high levels of government regulation (i.e., restrictions on religious liberty) over religious minorities. Religious minorities will prefer laws favouring greater religious liberty' (2008: 45).
12 The legal adviser to Malaysia's Council of Buddhism, Christianity, Hinduism and Sikhism gave his personal view that a compromise could be worked out whereby the Islamic court would be authorized to make sure that the convert from Islam was not coerced into making this decision (Soon 2007b).
13 Restrictions are slightly less severe in East Malaysia, where Christians form a larger part of the population. Forty-two per cent of the people in Sarawak are Christians, as are 28 per cent of those in Sabah (Saw 2006).
14 Proselytizing Malays is illegal except in Penang, Sabah, Sarawak and the Federal Territories.
15 Probably most Malay Muslims are unaware that 'Allah' is the word for god in Arabic and know only that the word is used to designate the Muslim God.
16 To allay this fear, Christians emphasize that Arabic words are used only in Christian publications intended for non-Muslims.
17 However, Muslim leaders are not all in agreement on the matter. Significantly, the spiritual adviser to PAS believes it is not against the Qur'an for non-Muslims to use the word 'Allah' (*Straits Times* 2009b).
18 However, the Supreme Court said that, as worded, the law was unconstitutional.
19 Hindu nationalist groups charge Christians in India with bribing and pressuring especially low-caste Indians and indigenous peoples to convert. An official in the VHP said: 'Hindu culture is under attack' (Associated Press 2008b). The Hindu

nationalist groups have themselves been accused of indulging in the politics of hate for political reasons. But Catholics in the city of Mangalore joined Hindus in accusing a Pentecostal group, New Life Fellowship Trust, of forcible conversions. The group denied the charges and said people are converting for reasons such as the experience of healing through participation in their rituals (Jayaram 2008).

20 Legislation empowering Islamic courts to enforce compliance with Islamic rules concerning such matters as irregular mosque attendance, not fasting during Ramadan, and deviant teachings date back to colonial days, when similar laws existed also in Europe (Peletz 2002: 55–57).

21 The mufti of Perlis criticized state religious police for raiding private homes and hotel rooms looking for unmarried couples in 'close proximity' as an invasion of privacy and, therefore, unIslamic (Nadzri 2006). In the PAS-controlled state of Kelantan, the Islamic enforcement agency must first get an order from an Islamic court before raiding homes or rented rooms of couples suspected of 'close proximity'. Muslims, the Kelantan Religious Affairs Committee chairman said, are not supposed to spy on each other (*The Star* 2006).

BIBLIOGRAPHY

Abdullah, Ahmad Badawi, *Islam Hadhari* (Petaling Jaya, Malaysia: MPH Publishing, 2006).

Abdullahi, Ahmed An-Na'im, 'Negotiating Authenticity and Justice', in *BARAZA!* 1 (3) (2007), pp. 3–4.

Agence France-Presse, 'Abdullah warns of Christian-Muslim rift' (2006), on <http://straitstimes.asiaone.com/vgn-ext-templating/v/index.jsp?vgnextoid=06a21008ce59/> Accessed on 29 November 2006.

—'Malaysian waitress ordered to be caned for drinking' (2009), on <www.straitstimes.com/print/Prime%2BNews/Story/STIStory/>. Accessed on 14 January 2009.

Anis, Ibrahim, '30/11: Use ISA on those who leave Islam, says lecturer', on <www.Malaysia-today.net/blog2006/newsncom/php?itemid=1072/>. Accessed on 30 November 2006.

Anwar, Ibrahhim, 'Preserving the Spirit of the Constitution', in Nathaniel Tan and John Lee (eds), *Religion Under Siege?* (Kuala Lumpur: Kinibooks, 2008), pp. 15–16.

Anwar, Zainah, Law-making in the Name of Islam: Implications for Democratic Governance', in K. S. Nathan and Mohammad Hashim Kamali (eds), *Islam in Southeast Asia* (Singapore: Institute of Southeast Asian Studies, 2005), pp. 121–134.

Associated Press, 'Scholars want forum for Islamic debate', on <http://straitstimes.asia1.com.sg/vgn-ext-templating/v/index.jsp?vgnextoid=06a21008ce599/>. Accessed on 11 July 2006.

—'PAS chief blasts extremist Islamic teachers', on www.straitstimes.com/vgn-ext-templating/v/index.jsp?vgnextoid=06a21008ce59901/>. Accessed on 15 May 2007.

—'Too risky for debate?', on <www.todayonline.com/articles/270056print.asp/>. Accessed on 11 August 2008a.

—'Hindu attacks on Christians up', on <www.straitstimes.com/print/Breaking%2BNews/Asia/Story/STIStory_285133.html/>. Accessed on 2 October 2008b.

—'Kyrgyzstan passes restrictive religious law', on <www.iht.com/bin/printfriendly.php?id=17581518/>. Accessed on 6 November 2008c.

—'Non-Muslims can use "Allah"', on <www.straitstimes.com/print/Breaking%2BNews/SE%2BAsia/S/>. Accessed on 2 March 2009d.

AWAM, SIS, WAO, WCC and WDC, 'Constitutional Right to Freedom of Belief is Made Illusory', in Nathaniel Tan and John Lee (eds), *Religion Under Siege?* (Kuala Lumpur: Kinibooks, 2008), pp. 28–31.

Azizuddin, Ahmad, 'New challenges and preparations in the Islamic movement', in *Demi Masa* (Malaysia), 15 June 2005, pp. 10–11.

Bar Council, 'Federal Constitution Must Remain Supreme', in Nathaniel Tan and John Lee (eds), *Religion Under Siege?* (Kuala Lumpur: Kinibooks, 2008), pp. 33–35.

BARAZA editors, 'Apostasy in the Muslim World', in *BARAZA!* 1 (3) (2007), pp. 10–13.

Beh Lih, Yi, 'Abdullah a "weak" premier', on <www.malaysiakini.com/news/70658/>. Accessed on 1 August 2007.

Bernama, 'Perak religious department to continue raids on hotels', on <http://malaysia-today.net/blog2006/newsncom.php?itemid=1420/>. Accessed on 20 December 2006.

—'Western media "bashing Islam"', on <www.straitstimes.com/print/Asia/Malaysia/Story/STIStory_125034.html/>. Accessed on 2 June 2007.

—'Not proper to hold open forum on "Conversion to Islam", says Najib', on <www.bernama.com/bernama/v3/news_php?id=351242/>. Accessed on 7 August 2008.

Casanova, Jose, *Public Religions in the Modern World* (Chicago and London: University of Chicago Press, 1994).

Chan, Kok Leong, 'PAS opposes Bar's Islam forum', on <www.malaysiakini.com/print?c=news&id=87433/>. Accessed on 7 August 2008.

Chandra, Muzaffer, *Islamic Resurgence in Malaysia* (Petaling Jaya, Malaysia: Penerbit Fajar Bakti Sdn., 1987).

—'Public Education on Religion and Interfaith Initiatives', in Lai Ah Eng (ed.), *Facing Faiths, Crossing Cultures* (Singapore: Institute of Policy Studies, 2005), pp. 53–84.

Choe, Sang-Hun, 'Religious peace threatened in South Korea', on <www.iht.com/bin/printfriendly.php?id=16935374/>. Accessed on 20 October 2008.

Chong, Terence, 'The Emerging Politics of *Islam Hadhari*', in Saw Swee-Hock and K. Kesavapany (eds), *Malaysia* (Singapore: Institute of Southeast Asian Studies), pp. 26–46.

Council of Churches, 'Freedom of Religion has been Severely Diminished', in Nathaniel Tan and John Lee (eds), *Religion Under Siege?* (Kuala Lumpur: Kinibooks, 2008), pp. 26–27.

Damis, Aniza, 'Ikim D-G sheds light on Subashini case: "This has nothing to do with religion"', on <www.nst.com.my/Current_News/Monday/Frontpage/2120906/Article/index_html/>. Accessed on 15 January 2008.

Dzulkifli, Ahmad, 'Dark alley of self-destruction', on <www.malaysiakini.com/print.php?id=69369/>. Accessed on 3 July 2007.

Editorial, 'Diversity of opinions: An Islamic legacy', in *Baraza* (Malaysia) 1 (2) (2006), pp. 1–2.

English, Thomas, 'Joy decision a violation of constitution', in <www.malaysiakini.com/print.php?id=69383/>. Accessed on 2 July 2007.

Farish, Noor, 'Malaysia's shame', on <www.othermalaysia.org/index2.php?option=com_content&>. Accessed on 13 July 2007.

Faruqi, Shad Saleem, 'The Malaysian Constitution, the Islamic State, and Hudud Laws', in K. S. Nathan and Mohammad Hashim Kamali (eds), *Islam in Southeast Asia* (Singapore: Institute of Southeast Asian Studies, 2007), pp. 256–278.

—'Constitutional Perspectives on Freedom of Religion', in *BARAZA!* 1 (3) (2007), pp. 5–8.

Fauwaz, Abdul Aziz, 'Lawyers set up group to defend Islam', on <www.geocities.com/membela_islam/lawyers_set_up_group_to_defend_islam.htlm/>. Accessed on 17 August 2006a.

—'Apostasy: Tighten law, says Negri Sembilan mufti', on <www.malaysiakini.com/print.php?id=60289/>. Accessed on 29 November 2006b.

—'Revathi's Mother: I pray this ends soon', on <www.malaysiakini.com/print.php?id=69783/>. Accessed on 11 July 2007a.

—'Secular M'sia does not mean anti-religion', on <www.malaysiakini.com/print.php?id=70421/>. Accessed on 27 July 2007b.

—'Bibles confiscated by Customs Dept.', on <www.malaysiakini.com/print.php?c=news&id=77782/>. Accessed on 4 February 2008a.

—'"Conversion" forum goes ahead', on <www.malaysiakini.com/print.php?c=news&id=87467/>. Accessed on 8 August 2008b.

Fishman, Ethan, 'Unto Caesar', in *The American Scholar* 76 (4) (2007), pp. 36–44.

Gill, Anthony, *The Political Origins of Religious Liberty* (Cambridge: Cambridge University Press, 2008).

Hamid, Jalil and Liau Y-Sing, 'Malaysia braces for ruling on Islam conversion', on <http://news.yahoo.com/s/nm/20060813/wl_nm/religion_malaysia_dc&printer=1/>. Accessed on 17 August 2006.

Hassan, Hazlin, 'Non-Muslims in khalwat cases "should be charged"', on <www.straitstimes.com/print/Asia/Malaysia/StorySTIStory_2/>. Accessed on 3 April 2008.

Hassan, M. Kamal, 'Islam', in M. Kamal Hassan and Ghazali bin Basri (eds), *The Encyclopedia of Malaysia: Volume 10: Religions and Beliefs* (Singapore: Archipelago Press, 2005), pp. 10–59.

Hew, Denis, 'Globalization and the Challenges Facing Malaysia's Economy', in Saw Swee-Hock and K. Kesavapany (eds), *Malaysia: Recent Trends and Challenges* (Singapore: Institute of Southeast Asian Studies, 2006), pp. 260–274.

Hindu, Sangam, 'Hindus gravely concerned', in Nathaniel Tan and John Lee (eds), *Religion Under Siege?* (Kuala Lumpur: Kinibooks, 2008), pp. 27–28.

Hodgson, David, 'Malaysia's shackles on religious freedom', on <www.brisbanetimes.com.au/news/opinion/malaysias-shackles-on-religious-freedom/>. Accessed on 22 June 2007.

Hong, Bede, 'Article 11 launches video documentaries', on <www.malaysiakini.com/print.php?id=64867/>. Accessed on 21 March 2007.

Hong, Carolyn, 'Muslim group calls for religious law review', on <http://straitstimes.asia1.com.sg/sub/storyprint friendly/0,5578,299290,00.html/>. Accessed on 4 February 2005.

Husna, Yusop, 'Giving voice to Islam', in *The Sun Weekend,* 18–19 February 2006, pp. 13–16.

Israel, Jonathan I., *Enlightenment Contested* (Oxford: OUP, 2006).

Jayaram, P., 'Hellish times for India's Christians', on <www.straitstimes.com/print/Asia/Asia/Story/STIStory_279676.html/>. Accessed on 18 September 2008.

Kessler, Clive S., 'Malaysia: The long march towards desecularization', in *Asian Analysis* (October 2006), <www.aseanfocus.com/asiananalysis/latest.cfm?/>. Accessed on 6 November 2006.

Kosmin, Barry A., 'Contemporary secularity and secularism', in Barry A. Kosmin and Ariela Ketsar (eds), *Secularism and Secularity* (Hartford, CT: Institute for the Study of Secularism in Society and Culture, 2007), pp. 1–13.

Koswanage, Niluksi, 'Christians battle with Muslims over Allah', on <www.tiscali.co.uk/news/newswire.php/news/reuters/2009/03/11/world/>. Accessed on 13 March 2009.

Kuppasasmy, Baradan, 'Holy row over Arabic words', on <www.malaysiakini.com/print.php?c=opinions&id=76931/>. Accessed on 11 January 2008.

Lee, Hock Guan, 'Globalization and Ethnic Integration in Malaysian Education', in Saw Swee-Hock and K. Kesavapany (eds), *Malaysia: Recent Trends and Challenges* (Singapore: Institute of Southeast Asian Studies, 2006), pp. 230–259.

Lee, Raymond, 'Patterns of Religious Tension in Malaysia', in *Asian Survey* 28 (1998), pp. 400–418.

Levy, Leonard W., *Origins of the Bill of Rights* (New Haven and London: Yale University Press, 1999).

Lilla, Mark, *The Stillborn God* (New York: Alfred A. Knopf, 2007).

Malaysia Today, 'Lina Joy, the decision (Council's explanation)', on <http://malaysia-today.net/blog2006/letters.php?itemid=5177/>. Accessed on 5 June 2007.

Malaysiakini, 'Legal action to free Muslim woman, children', on <www.malaysiakini.com/print.php?id=66064/>. Accessed on 17 April 2007a.

—'Hindraf: Revathi's rights violated', on <www.malaysiakini.com/print.php?id=69804/>. Accessed on 11 July 2007b.

—'Religious scholar dismisses khalwat proposal for Non-Muslims', on <www.malaysiakini.com/print.php?c=news&id=80940/>. Accessed on 5 April 2008a.

—'Syariah lawyers back action on khalwat against Non-Muslims', on <www.malaysiakini.com/print.php?c=news&id=81010/>. Accessed on 7 April 2008b.

Marzuki, Mohamad, 'Zainah Anwar's hate ideology: Desecularization or deIslamization, or both?', on <http://malaysia-today.net/blog2006/guests.php?itemid=322/>. Accessed on 30 October 2006.

Mazeni, Alwi, 'Islam and a Tale of Two Reformations', in *MPF News* (Malaysia) 2 (2) (2005), pp. 8–10.

Morarjee, Rachel, and Murphy, Dan, 'Conversion a thorny issue in Muslim world', on <www.csmonitor.com/2006/0327/p01s04-wosc.htm/>. Accessed on 4 April 2006.

'MPF statement regarding PM Datuk Seri Abdullah Ahmad Badawi's directive that issues of religious sensitivity should not be openly debated in the public arena', on <http://mpf.org.my/articles/20060809badawidebate.html/>. Accessed on 16 August 2006.

Musa bin Mohd, Nordin, 'Apostasy revisited', on <www.mpf.org.my/articles/20070514%20-%20apostasy.html/>. Accessed on 30 May 2007.

Nadzri, Syed, '19/12: Of sex, snooping, and open minds', on <http://malaysia-today.net/blog2006/newsncom.php?itemid=1402/>. Accessed on 20 December 2006.

Nagata, Judith, *The Reflowering of Malaysian Islam* (Vancouver: University of British Columbia Press, 2004).

Ng, Cecilia, Maznah, Mohamad, and Beng Hui, Tan, *Feminism and the Women's Movement in Malaysia* (London and New York: Routledge, 2006).

Noonan Jr, John T., *A Church that Can and Cannot Change* (Notre Dame, IN: University of Notre Dame Press, 2005).

Noor, Tahya Hamzah, 'Lina Joy: Anything to Do with Islam, Hands Off Please', in Nathaniel Tan and John Lee (eds), *Religion Under Siege*? (Kuala Lumpur: Kinibooks, 2008), pp. 207–209.

Ong, Andrew, 'Protesters stop Bar's "conversion" forum', on <www.malaysiakini.com/print?c=news&id=87519/>. Accessed on 9 August 2008.

Ooi Kee Beng, 'Malaysia's thin line between state and faith', on <http://straitstimes.asia1.com.sg/sub/storyprintfriendly/0,5578,367043,00.html/>. Accessed on 24 January 2006.

Othman, Norani, Anwar, Zainah, and Kasim, Zaitun Mohamed, 'Malaysia: Islamization, Muslim Politics, and State Authoritarianism', in Norani Othman (ed.), *Muslim Women and the Challenge of Islamic Extremism* (Petaling Jaya, Malaysia: Sisters in Islam, 2005).

PAS, 'The Islamic State Document', in Nathaniel Tan and John Lee (eds), *Religion Under Siege?* (Kuala Lumpur: Kinibooks, 2008), pp. 130–147.

Peletz, Michael G., *Islamic Modern: Religious Courts and Cultural Politics in Malaysia* (Princeton and Oxford: Princeton University Press, 2002).

Perlez, Jane, 'Once Muslim, now mired in Malaysia's courts', on <www.malaysia-today.net/Blog-n?2006/08/once-muslim-now-mired-in-malaysias/>. Accessed on 25 August 2006.

Ram, B. Suresh, 'Nazri: Article 11 stays as it is', on <www.malaysia-today.net/Blog-n/ 2006/08/nazri-article-11-stays-as-it-is.htm/>. Accessed on 22 August 2006.

Reuters, 'Sri Lanka: Court blocks anticonversion bill', in *New York Times*, 19 August 2006, A11.

—'Malaysia PM calls for halt to proselytizing of Malays', on <www.malaysia-today.net/Blog-n/2006/08/malaysia-pm-calls-for-halt-to.htm/>.

—'Paper may close in "Allah" row', on <www.straitstimes.com/print/Breaking%2BNews?SE%2BAsia/S/>. Accessed on 17 December 2008.

Roy, Olivier, *Globalized Islam* (New York: Columbia University Press, 2004).

Saw Swee-Hock, 'Population Trends and Patterns in Multiracial Malaysia', in Saw Swee-Hock (ed.), *Malaysia* (Singapore: Institute of Southeast Asian Studies, 2006), pp. 1–25.

Smith, Donald Eugene, *Religion and Political Development* (Boston, MA: Little, Brown, 1970).

Soon Li Tsin, 'Lina Joy judgment at a glance', on <www.malaysiakini.com/print.php?id=67952/>. Accessed on 30 May 2007.

—'A secular constitution protects all religions', on <www.malaysiakini.com/print.php?id=68387/>. Accessed on 8 June 2007b.

—'Sabah church sues PM over book ban', on <www.malaysiakini.com/print.php?c=news&id=76371/>. Accessed on 24 December 2007c.

The Star, 'Court order required for khalwat raids in Kelantan', on <http://Malaysia-today.net/blog2006/newsncom.php?itemid=1433/>. Accessed on 20 December 2006.

Straits Times, 'Clash over use of "Allah"', on <www.straitstimes.com/print/Breaking%2BNews/SE%2BAsia/S/>. Accessed on 2 February 2009a.

—'Non-Muslims can use "Allah"', on <www.straitstimes.com/print/Breaking%2BNews/SE%2BAsia/S/>. Accessed on 2 March 2009b.

Surin, Jacqueline, 'Choice a cornerstone of Islam', on <www.mpf.org.my/20061211%20-%choice.html/>. Accessed on 11 December 2006.

Tan Chek Wee, 'Community hospitals must not aid conversions', on <www.straitstimes.com/print/ST%2BForum/Story/STIStory_179213.html/>. Accessed on 22 November 2007.

Taylor, Charles, *A Secular Age* (Cambridge: Belknap Press of Harvard University Press, 2007).

Ting, Helen, 'Gender Discourse in Malay Politics: Old Wine in New Bottle?', in Edmund Terence Gomez (ed.), *Politics in Malaysia*, (London and New York: Routledge, 2007), pp. 75–106.

Tisdall, Simon, 'Malaysia's Islamists learn lessons', in *Guardian Weekly*, 27 January–2 February 2006, p. 2.

US Department of State, *International Religious Freedom Report 2006*, at <www.state.gov/g/drl/rls/irf/2006/71347.htm/>. Accessed on 17 September 2007.

Young, Michael P., *Bearing Witness Against Sin* (Chicago and London: University of Chicago Press, 2006).

Yusri, Mohamad, *Kemurnian Risalah Paksi Kejayaan Misi Dakwah*, tr. Fadli Fawzi (Kuala Lumpur: Ankatan Belia Islam Malaysia, 2006).

Zagorin, Perez, *How the Idea of Religious Toleration Came to the West* (Princeton and Oxford: Princeton University Press, 2003).

16

The Islamist Movement in Syria: Historical, Political and Social Struggle

Radwan Ziadeh

The Role of Religion in Syrian State Politics

The relationship between the Syrian state and Islam, as represented in its governmental or non-governmental establishments or through the discourses of the people who believe in the role of religion in people's lives, goes back to a period prior to Syrian political independence in 1946.[1] Since then, the religious institutions in Syria have developed and been affected by the nature of their relations with the different government establishments according to the political party in power.

Since it came to rule in 1963, the Ba'ath Party has adopted a secular stance, though not necessarily opposed to religion, and when President Hafiz al Assad came to power in 1970, he aimed to incorporate the religious movement to a greater extent, because he believed that by doing so he could gain the trust of the Sunni population, who make up the majority in Syria. Thus, he extended his hand to the religious scholars, and took every opportunity to show his respect for them and his concern for their causes, giving several high-ranking Islamic figures seats in the People's Assembly appointed in 1971, including the Mufti of the Republic, Sheikh Ahmad Kuftaro, and the Mufti of Aleppo, Sheikh Mohammed al Hakim.[2] Assad was generally striving for widening the ground for his rule, so he restructured the political framework on new foundations, which differed from the original structure when the Ba'ath Party had come to power in 1963. In 1971 he established the People's Assembly, and in 1972 founded the 'National Progressive Front', which was considered a form of legitimizing political pluralism. It joined all of the political parties allied with the Ba'ath Party and acknowledged the manifesto of the 'Front', which agreed to the Ba'ath Party's permanent leadership of it. A new constitution was then announced in 1973, amending the temporary constitution of 1969 which gave legislative powers to the ministry. The amendments now transformed the country into a presidency. Assad tried, through his restructurings, to widen the political and popular support base for his leadership and increase its legitimacy by secularizing his establishments.[3]

Following his coming to power in November 1970, he went on a tour of most of the Syrian governates, and tried to meet with a number of well-wishers. He knew from experience the importance of winning over the religious movements, as this would decrease people's reservations about his legitimacy as president of the country, being a member of the Alawite minority. He, therefore, tried, within the boundaries of his secular nationalist discourse, to get closer to the religious scholars. In order to achieve this, he made huge personal donations in 1973 to the religious schools in the province of Hama, and to Islamic charitable societies in the province of Homs, and then, in 1974, increased the salaries of employees in religious institutions. This increase included 1,138 imams, 252 religion teachers, 610 preachers and 280 Qur'an reciters. In 1976, and then once again in 1980, he increased their financial benefits; and in 1976, under his sponsorship, 5.4 million Syrian pounds was designated to the building of new mosques.[4] Every year until his death in 2000, he would hand out the Iftar on a certain day of Ramadan with the highest rank of Islamic scholars.

The Ba'ath Party had strongly supported Ahmad Kuftaro gaining the position of Mufti of the Republic against the candidacy of Sheikh Hassan Habnaka al Miladi in 1965.[5] Kuftaro belonged to a Kurdish family who had lived in Damascus for a long time, and his father held an important religious position. He had also become well known since the 1940s for his efforts at 'building harmonious relations between Muslims and Christians'. The Ba'ath Party succeeded, through pressure on the High Council of Fatwas, in ensuring that Kuftaro won the position.[6]

Assad appointed Kuftaro as a member of the first People's Assembly in 1971, and won over other Islamic scholars, most of whom were graduates of religious schools and institutes, led by the Islamic charitable association al Gharra, which gradually began to cooperate with the authority to ensure that their small religious establishments could continue, while at the same time giving Assad complete backing and support. Sheikh Kuftaro considered that the re-election of Assad during the periods of leadership referendums should be seen as 'religious duty and national obligation'.[7]

When Bashar al Assad came to power in 2000, he continued in the path of his father in approaching the religious movement by winning over influential religious scholars and bringing them closer.

However, the presence of religious establishments is limited to the area of education and propaganda. For example, there are no religious universities, as is the case in some other Arab countries, and the Friday sermon is not transmitted on television. Nor does the president begin his speeches in the name of God, and very rarely does he cite Qur'anic verses. The Ministry of Religious Endowments (al-Awqaf) has the job of supervising and also of guiding and organizing the religious sector.

Because the ministry is responsible for mosques and religious schools, the Minister of Religious Endowments is chosen with precision and care. After the death of Abdul Majeed al Trabulsi, who was formerly an active member of the Muslim Brotherhood, and one of their radical leaders, and who had been chosen by Assad Senior as a political message to the Muslim Brotherhood, new types of ministers were appointed. Rather than having influential religious or jurisprudent authority in Syrian society, these people could be considered 'technocrats'. Mohammed Ziada and Mohammed Ziad al Ayoubi, the current Minister of Religious Endowments, who were both appointed under the rule of Bashar al Assad, had both worked previously in administrative positions in the ministry with no authority of any influential religious or political presence.

The Ministry of Awqaf supervises all of the mosques in Syria, even though most – if not all – of them have been built with charitable and civic donations. The ministry chooses the Friday sermon and the imam, which are also subjected to the order of the provincial Director of Religious Endowments, who administratively follows the Ministry of Religious Endowments. At the same time there is also supervision of the mosques and Friday sermons by the political security department, which produces constant reports about the sermons and the attending worshippers and their reactions.

On official and national occasions, the Ministry of Religious Endowments sends instructions to the orators of the Friday sermons to order them to speak about a specific subject, for example, the presidential referendum or the American threats against Syria. The orators are obliged to speak about these subjects, otherwise they will be subjected to questioning by security, and, in the case of continual ignoring of instructions, may be punished, as has happened to mosque preachers on more than one occasion.

The authority also retains control over the position of the Mufti of the Republic. After the death of Sheikh Ahmad Kuftaro in 2005,[8] who had been able to construct a personal establishment carrying his name, concerned with preaching and missionary activities, a presidential decree appointed Ahmad Hassoun (born in Aleppo in 1949) as Mufti of the Republic, thereby breaking the tradition requiring the mufti to be chosen from one of the influential traditional families of Damascus.

He holds a certificate in Arabic Literature and a Doctorate in Islamic 'shafi'i' jurisprudence from al-Azhar University, and had been appointed Mufti of the province of Aleppo in 2002, having been a Member of the People's Assembly since 1999.

The selection of the Mufti of the Republic usually happens by mutual statement on the part of the High Council of Iftaa, which is made up of twenty-five members, who are the muftis of the fourteen different provinces of Syria, and the directors of the Awqaf of Damascus and Aleppo, and others appointed by the council itself. Among themselves, they agree on the choice of the Mufti of the Republic, and then publish a decree confirming the new mufti. However, this operation was completely ignored this time, and Hassoun was appointed as a mufti under the provisions of a presidential decree. The mufti maintains strong relations with the political authorities whose side he always takes, and his strongly biased political statements have played a role in the large-scale loss of his credibility in big sections of Syrian society. The last of these statements, for example, was when he described the election of President Bashar al Assad for a second presidential reign, in May 2007, as a 'Bai'a similar to that of the Prophet'.[9] Despite that, he is given credit for his courageous and reformative position in defending women's issues, including their right in granting their children nationality, and for his position towards what are known as 'honour crimes'.[10]

Boundaries of Official Religious Discourse

The influence of religious establishments can be measured by observing the juristic educational institutions spread throughout the country. The Islamic Law (Shari'a) secondary schools follow administratively the

Ministry of Awqaf, which funds them and stipulates their religious curriculum. They have been established since 1971 and have become increasingly widespread in all areas of Syria, with the numbers of students rising continuously,[11] creating a need for the foundation of middle and high institutes. One of the most prominent of these institutes is the Abu Noor Islamic Centre, managed by Mufti Ahmad Kuftaro, which contains a college for teaching Arabic as a foreign language to non-Arabs studying Shari'a and Islamic studies, and is a partner organization to the Islamic University in Um Durman in Sudan.[12] Another is the al Fateh al Islami Institute, which forms a branch of the al Azhar Mosque in Damascus and is directed by the Mufti of Damascus, Abd al Fatah al Bizem. It contains three stages: the first is primary and secondary studies of Shari'a, the second is the Islamic university stage, and the third is the stage of higher studies. The centre also contains a preparatory institute for the teaching of Arabic language for a period of two years in order to give non-Arabic speakers a firm foundation in Shari'a studies. In 1998 the number of students in the institute had reached almost 218, from 34 different nationalities.[13]

Syrian universities do not recognize most of the higher certificates distributed by these Shari'a institutes, and when the Syrian government tried, in 2007, to organize the religious education system by making the completion of the basic phase of schooling obligatory for those who wish to then enter a Shari'a school, this caused resentment by many influential and prominent religious men. Thirty-nine of them consequently signed a letter to the Syrian president accusing the Ministry of Education of forming a 'conspiratorial', 'designed to dry up and destroy the streams of the Shari'a Secondary Schools', and also criticizing 'mixed schools', as well as implying that 'the Shi'ite Hawza [schools] are continuously ignoring instructions and are determined not to respond to them, and the Shweifat private schools and the foreign [French, American and Pakistani] missionary schools are continuing in their own special curriculum and teaching styles without any opposition'.[14]

The letter had a huge effect, particularly as the signatories were the most active and influential scholars in Syria. Among them were, for example: Mohammed Saeed Ramadan al Bouti, who was close to President Hafiz al Assad, Salah Kuftaro, son of the deceased Mufti Ahmad Kuftaro and director of the Abu Noor Centre after his father, the previous Minister of Awqaf, Mohammed al Khatib, the Sheikhs

Sadiq Habanake and Abdul Razzaq al Halabi, Mohammed Abdul Kareem Rajeh (nicknamed Sheikh al Qora'), Wahba al Zahili, a teacher in the Shari'a College in the University of Damascus and Osama Rifa'ee, a preacher in the Rifa'ee Mosque in the area of Kafr Susi who holds wide influence in Damascus society.

After the announcement of the signed letter, President Bashar al Assad held a meeting with a delegation of them, including Sheikh Rafa'ee, Dr al Bouti and the Mufti of the Republic, Ahmad Hassoun, and he immediately promised to solve the problem by returning to the unified curriculum under government supervision.[15]

This event showed the extent of the influence that religious scholars had come to have within Syrian society and the extent of the Syrian government's sensitivity to conflict with this religious current, so the government attempted to contain and enclose it as much as possible. For this reason, several procedures were put into place, such as the foundation of a Shari'a College in Aleppo, and the establishment of Islamic banks, including Bank al Sham, the Syrian State Islamic Bank and Bank al Barake. The capital of each of these banks reaches around $100 million, which is three times the legal limit for non-Islamic banks.[16] In addition to this, there are the institutes for memorizing the Qur'an, which are found in most Syrian mosques and are called 'Assad Institutes for memorization of the Qur'an'.

The number of students in the Shari'a faculty in the University of Damascus is gradually increasing. This faculty contains 7,603 students (of which 3,337 are female) compared to the original figure of 48,000. Every year 650 students graduate from the college. In addition to this, the number of mosques in Syria has reached more than 9,000, and around 30 per cent of Syrians participate in Friday prayers.[17] As for women, the al Qobeysiat Movement is working under a semi-official shadow at forming a network with large religious influence.[18] However, this growing enthusiasm for religious practices cannot be explained in fundamental or political terms, but rather as an expression of spiritual need in a region considered as a source of religions, the influence of which is always dominant. Given the political, social and cultural isolation in which we live, we should expect more and more people to adhere to religious practices.

After the American invasion of Iraq in March 2003, Syria witnessed a number of violent actions targeting official quarters and foreign embassy buildings. The most famous targets were the radio and television building in June 2006 and the site of the American embassy in Damascus.[19] The Syrian security services accused a number of Islamic extremists belonging to the al-Qa'ida network of carrying out these attacks, and took some careful steps towards putting visible pressure and constant control on religion. On 28 February 2006 the Ministry of Religious Endowments issued an order to all mosques, containing ten points including:

> Mosques must not be opened between prayer times, and the sound of the dawn and afternoon calls to prayer should not be too loud in order to keep the neighbourhood rest. Religious lessons are prohibited, and Quran lessons must be cut from being held daily to once or twice a week. Also, any financial or material donations may not be accepted unless they are accompanied with the necessary statement from the Directorate of Religious Endowments (Awqaf).[20]

Preachers of Friday sermons were all instructed to speak about 'moderate Islam, and encouraging fathers to protect their sons from the expiatories' in order to increase young people's awareness and prevent them from slipping into extremist ideological movements'.[21]

A change could even be noticed in the political speeches of the Ba'ath Party itself, which was founded as a secular party, towards becoming closer to the Islamic movements. In addition to its political alliances with Hamas, the Palestinian Islamic party, and Hezbollah in Lebanon, it still has special relations with the Turkish Justice and Development Party in Jordan, and other Islamic parties. Some, like Hamas and the Jordanian Islamic Labour Front, are regional branches of the international Muslim Brotherhood organization. However, the Ba'ath Party forbids any involvement with the Muslim Brotherhood in Syria.

The party itself also began to celebrate Muslim festivals, such as the anniversary of the birth of the Prophet,[22] and started frequently reiterating the necessity of a Nationalist–Islamist alliance 'to face external pressure'.[23]

These policies are just part of the inclusion strategy which the Syrian government practised decades ago, and through which it aims to gain legitimacy by becoming closer to the most popular movements and taking advantage of this closeness to ensure that the Muslim Brotherhood cannot return to the way they were. It is a strategy for survival by building useful alliances to avoiding the effects of harmful alliances.

Syria and Policies for Religious Minorities

It is well known that Syria contains a plurality of religious sects, denominations and ethnicities, and it is this that has affected to a great extent the nature and balance of the ruling power, which has continuously tried to earn the friendship of the different minorities or, at least, to avoid entering into direct conflict with them. For this reason, Syria has not witnessed furious sectarian conflicts like those seen by its close neighbour, Lebanon, during the periods of civil war, and so the relation between the different sects in Syria, especially the Muslim and Christian ones, has remained good, characterized by respect and mutual friendship, and the political authority continues to support the policy of Muslim–Christian dialogue by organizing many conferences and discussion groups under the remit of 'national unity'.

The political authority has no policies that directly discriminate, legally or politically, against any of the sects presented in Syria, although the court system retains a form of division which bears in mind the interests of the different sects.

The Syrian court system is divided into civil courts and religious courts. The civil courts give rulings in civil and criminal cases, while the legal, sectarian and religious courts have special authority to give ruling in Personal Status Law and family cases, and in cases of inheritance for Syrian Muslims and Muslims from other countries that apply Islamic laws in these situations. There are three Shari'a (legal) courts in Damascus and Aleppo, and one in each other province. The sectarian courts are made up of a Muslim Druze judge who has the authority to ensure the commitment of the Druze in the field of Personal Status Law of their denomination. Meanwhile, the spiritual courts take responsibility for the settling of cases of Personal Status Law for Christians, Jews and other non-Muslim groups. The sentences of all religious courts can be appealed against before courts representing them following the Court of Cassation.

The Muslim Brotherhood and the Struggle for Power

The first political conflict within the political establishments, especially in the parliament, came with the negotiations about the form of the constitution of 1950, in the texts of which are discussed the relation between religion and the state.[24] The Muslim Brotherhood demanded that the constitution include a direct statement saying that 'the state religion is Islam', which would discriminate against the Christian and Jewish minorities and other vulnerable denominations, like the Druze, Alawite and Ismaelite minorities present in Syria. This period saw violent disputes between all political movements over the ideal form[25] the constitution should take, and the position of the minorities resulting from the suggested form.[26]

The Muslim Brotherhood entered a completely new phase with the Ba'ath Party's arrival in power in 1963, and this was demonstrated very clearly by what is known as the Hama Rebellion in April 1964, lasting twenty-nine days, which was led by Hama leaders of the Muslim Brotherhood, headed by Marwan Hadeed and Saeed Hawa, who were influenced by the latest writings of Sayyid Qutb[27] who took a very strong line, calling Muslim societies 'pre-Islamic times' and accusing their leaders of infidelity because they did not follow 'the Rule of Allah'. From this came the famous term 'al Hakimia' (Governorship)[28] which began to be used continuously by Islamic extremist movements as justification for breaking laws.[29]

The Hama Rebellion was an early indicator of the rise of a 'Jihadi movement' within the Brotherhood, inconsistent with their political, peaceful and democratic theses. This movement, carrying the name 'Battalion (Kata'b) of Mohammed', is the same group later known as 'Militant Vanguard' which embarked upon the tragic events in Hama in 1982. The transformation can only be explained by looking at the transformation of the opposing side, represented by the hegemony of the political authority, the declaration of a state of emergency and the ending of political plurality and independent newspapers, as the beginning of the creation of a 'third republic' in Syria, built on 'revolutionary legitimacy' rather than 'constitutional legitimacy'.[30] These types of processes make political contest pointless, and motivate many political movements to resort to violence as a means to solve disputes. Islamic movements may be the most susceptible to this, due to the fertile religious and Shari'a ideas that allow radical movements to interpret enough texts in such a way as to justify its armed procedures. Also at this time, the political struggle was breaking out in its worst form between competing regional and national Ba'ath movements. Behind this was concealed a conflict between the countryside and the city, and a sectarian and class clash, demonstrated clearly by many disasters, especially in 1966 when the 23rd of February Movement succeeded in holding off their rivals, punishing them cruelly and violently, and gaining control of the party and the rule. They adopted a strong left-wing stance, which terrified the conservative society in Syria into supporting en masse President Hafiz al Assad in his movement against Salah Jdeed, and into hoping to get rid of the childish left-wing rhetoric prevailing within the Ba'ath Party leadership at the time.

The first clash between the Syrian Authority and the religious movement came when the new Syrian constitution was published on 31 January 1973. Protests broke out, especially in Hama, because the conditions which stated that the president of the republic should be Muslim had been dropped from the draft proposal of the constitution. This condition had been present in the constitution of 1950 and was maintained again in later constitutions.[31]

Complaints increased in Hama and Homs, and the influential Sheikh Hassan Habanake led a campaign in the al Midan area of Damascus. So Assad ordered the People's Assembly of that time to add an item stating as a condition that 'the religion of the President of the Republic is Islam',[32] but he declared at the same time that true Islam should be 'far from the narrow-mindedness and awful extremism, as Islam is a religion of love, progression, social justice and equality'.[33]

Assad realized that the influence and effect of the Muslim Brotherhood differed from one province to another, and that its influence in the capital, Damascus, was the weakest, due to the different political, cultural and economic influences on its inhabitants. For this reason Assad tried to attract Damascus' religious scholars by winning over the moderates and building a network of economic interests between those scholars and the Damascus tradesmen who were considered the principal providers of charitable and religious donations, and who took care of the scholars. The tradesmen began supporting Assad, especially as he pursued more liberal economic policies than those in the previous periods of Ba'ath rule, which suited their interests and those of the large property owners in the capital.

Assad was thereby able to neutralize a large section of the religious movement whose only real interest was their personal safety and the maintaining of their interests and their ability to fulfil their religious duties freely. At the same time he worked to take advantage of the many deep divisions which began to appear in the ranks of the Brotherhood. The clash between the Syrian security services and the Muslim Brotherhood reached its climax in the 'Artillery Incident' in 1979, led by Captain Ibrahim al Yousef. The reaction of the Syrian authorities was strong and violent, especially after the discovery of an attempt to assassinate the president, Hafiz al Assad, in June 1980, whereupon the Military Defence Units, led by Rifa'at al Assad, fired at Muslim Brotherhood prisoners in their cells in Tadmor (Palmyra) Prison and over 700 prisoners were killed.[34]

At the same time a campaign of random arrests, covering the whole country, was taking place. Thousands of activists, opposition members and even supporters of the movement (or indeed those 'suspected' of being so) were arrested. Prisons became overcrowded with these people, who were sentenced to very long periods in prison – the average period being over ten years. All of this had very negative effects on Syrian society, which was unable to forget this 'national catastrophe'[35] that was described very well by a Syrian writer as being 'a victory to the authority over its society in its war against it'.[36] No government inflicts war against its own citizens? The methods of elimination that the government used, especially in dealing with the Islamists, left scars that cannot be healed in this wide movement whose members remained cut off from the outside world for many years. The news spread about the physical and mental torture that they were subjected to, causing retaliatory action, the effects of which can still be seen today, and for that reason the young generation, which came after the 'disaster of the Eighties' as it became known, and especially those with religious leanings or who were committed Muslims, were naturally concerned for their personal safety and avoided not only involvement in politics, but also even discussion of it or listening to news of it. This avoidance goes as far as becoming a 'phobia',[37] preventing participation in politics or anything that could lead to it.

This can be regarded as one of the most important political and social results of the violent conflict between the Muslim Brotherhood and the Syrian security services, which also caused deep cracks between different factions of the Muslim Brotherhood, each blaming the other for entering into an 'unequal confrontation' with the authority. President Hafiz al Assad was intelligent enough to benefit from these quarrels and use them to his advantage. He distinguished, on 22 December 1979, between those 'who caused affront to religion in the name of religion, of whom there are "misguided" members, unaware of the harm that their actions carry to their religion and their world, and "misguiding" members, aware of what they are doing, whose suspicious movements have a connection to the aims of Camp David'.[38]

He also distinguished between the Muslim Brotherhood and the conservative Muslims 'who form a large and important part of our country and deserve the greatest care'[39] in an attempt to draw public support which could be won by the Muslim Brotherhood from their religious and conservative base.

However, after the dramatic rise of bloody confrontations, Assad directed his efforts towards reaching a legal settlement through the publication of Law No. 49 and a security settlement by following a policy of pursuit and surveillance, and random and group arrests, which ended in a complete crushing[40] by the military in Hama.

None of the negotiations that were held between al Bayanouni, the new head of the Muslim Brotherhood in Syria, and a number of the Syrian security service leaders, to solve the issue of the Muslim Brotherhood as a political party and the regaining of its important role,[41] were successful. The Syrian political authorities followed a policy of giving individual pardons and negotiating the return of several members as individuals, not as leaders of the Muslim Brotherhood, as happened in the case of the return of the ex-leader Sheikh Abdul Fatah Abu Ghida at the end of 1995, a year in which all the mediations aiming to settle the case of the Muslim Brotherhood as a political Islamic movement in Syria failed.

The severity that the regime used to oppose the return of the Brotherhood and their reconciliation since the end of the Eighties, and even now, can be seen in reality with the continued use of Law 49, passed on 7 July 1980, which sentenced all members of the Muslim Brotherhood[42] to death by hanging. However, the implementation of the sentence to hanging was replaced by a sentence of ten to sixteen years in jail, as happened with several people who had been accused by the government of belonging to the forbidden Muslim Brotherhood.[43]

After the death of President Hafiz al Assad in June 2000, his son Bashar al Assad came to power and continued to follow the same path as his father in dealing with this case. Discussion of it was closed completely, despite the accumulation of social, humanitarian and familial issues contained within it, and it was administrated from the point of view of security only, which is what caused the extreme sensitivity, mentioned previously, of the new – and even old – generations of people emerging from prison recently, towards having any role in politics.

After that, the Islamic scene in Syria was limited to a number of religious scholars who maintained good relations with the government and had regional influence on society, which began to witness a clear return to a traditional type of religion, shown by the number of mosques and the number of people attending them. However, all of this is not necessarily linked to the politicization of religion so much as it can be considered a filling of spiritual gaps rising from long years of political repression and closure towards attempts to change and open up the society. This had built a state of, so to speak, 'domesticated Islam', for the government had succeeded in containing, to a large extent, the prominent characters in it as they emerged, through a series of carefully elaborated steps.

The Muslim Brotherhood had ended up as a leadership outside the country which was ineffective on the inside, where it became a number of individuals scared to say, or even to hint, that they belonged to this 'forbidden group'. After President Bashar al Assad came to power in June 2000, the Brotherhood published what was called the 'Gentleman's Statement for Political Action', in which they announced their renunciation of all forms of violence and their support for the principle of a 'civil state',[44] and then published their political programme, which can be seen as a 'huge leap' in the movement's speech and actions. But despite these political steps, there was no change in the authority's dealing with them.

The statement talks about what it calls 'the modern state', which is 'a contractual one, whose contract springs from a free and conscious desire between the ruler and the ruled, and the contractual form of the state is one of the things offered by Islamic Shari'a to human civilisation'. Also,

> the modern state is a state of establishments, built on a foundation from the base of the pyramid to its peak, and on the division of powers and the ensuring of its independence, for there is no place in the modern state for the supremacy of any individual or power or party over state utilities. In the modern state, the rule of law claims the highest position, and the social security is more important than the security of the authority, and a state of emergency never takes the place of the natural state of the rule of law.

The statement adds that

> the modern state is a democratic one, where free and fair ballots build the basis for the rotation of power between all citizens. It is a pluralist state in which different and varied visions, opinions and standpoints exist, and the strength of the political opposition and civil society establishments help to monitor and guide so that the state doesn't become repressive or corrupt.

The Muslim Brotherhood committed in their statement to 'the mechanisms and means of democratic political action, and ensuring equal rights for all in benefiting from the state's capabilities in improving their positions, proposing their programmes and seeing their visions come real', and to 'the renunciation of violence from its means and recognizing that the security solutions to the problems of the state and the society, and the violence of the executive authority, is an example of the presence of corruption'.

Here there is a clear transformation in the political thinking mechanism of the most prominent Syrian Islamic movement, especially in terms of its acceptance of a democratic principle and peaceful rotation of power, and moving to work as a civic political party with an Islamic background or authority, as is the case with democratic Christian groups in Europe.

Conclusions for the Future

It is clear that religion has become a part of the strategy of the ruling Ba'ath Party in Syria in order to ensure its survival in power. In spite of the fact that there is no parallel political discourse trying to invest religion openly, clearly, as has happened in more than one Arab country like Egypt, Algeria and Iraq during the period in which Saddam Hussein was in power, the attitudes and political statements of the Syrian president and officials are taking an explicit ideological position towards investing in religious feelings, the thing that has clearly emerged during, for example, the crisis of the Danish cartoons.

We can say that this discourse is somehow falling behind the return of religious appearances strongly within Syrian society: as it applies to both the older and younger generations who did not find an open road to political life in which to exercise political activity. They were therefore affected significantly by different degrees of religious speech.

Taken that these phenomena, as we have said, did not necessarily mean an overwhelming presence of political Islam in Syria, especially of the Muslim Brotherhood, the severe repression they suffered prevents younger generations from thinking of joining this movement. For the Syrian political system it is not soon expected to allow an internal arrangement for the movement or its return, especially with the heightened external pressures on Syria, which makes the regime interpret any step towards reconciliation as a political concession. Therefore, the internal situation for political Islam will witness a state of relative stability, as was the case during the three previous decades, without precluding the emergence of some fundamentalist groups and extremist Salafi that may initiate some armed operations at intervals, but without having any political or social impact.

As for the religious minorities, which are considered as a part of the religious investment strategy, the regime tries to intimidate them with the tide of religious fundamentalism, and thus convince them that the status quo is better and safer for them, and that loyalty to the regime ensures their protection. It is a very sensitive game, but it seems successful so far.

NOTES

1 David Dean Commins, *Islamic Reform: Politics and Social Change in Late Ottoman Syria* (New York: OUP, 1990, and this book has been translated into Arabic.

2 Hanna Batatu, *Syria's Peasantry, the Descendants of Its lesser Rural Notables and Their Politics* (Princeton, NJ: Princeton University Press, 1999), pp. 260–261.

3 Voker Perthes, *The Political Economy of Syria Under Asad* (London and New York: I.B. Tauris, 1995), pp. 135–140.

4 Hanna Batatu, *Syria's Peasantry*, p. 261.

5 For more on Sheikh Hassan Habnaka al Medanee see: *Joranaes Reissner, Ideologie und Politick der Muslimbrruder Syriens* (Freiburg: Klaus Schwarz Verlag, 1980).

6 Hanna Batatu, *Syria's Peasantry*, p. 263.

7 Ibid., p. 264.

8 *Al Ba'ath* (Damascus), July 17 2005.

9 Sheikh Abdul Salam Rajeh, teacher of Religion Principles in the al Fateh al Islami Institute and member of the Syrian People's Assembly, considered that 'Participation in the referendum is a "religious individual duty".'

10 *Al Hayat* (London), March 1 2007.

11 According to statistics of the Syrian Ministry of Religious Endowments, the number of students in Shari'a schools doubled in six years from 5,574 students in 1991 to 9,647 in 1998, and from 38 institutes and schools to 50.
12 National Report on Human Development in Syria 2005, *Education and Human Development: Towards Better Efficiency* (Leadership of the Council of Ministers, UN Development Programme 2005), pp. 82–83.
13 Sha'aban Aboud, 'Religious Education in Syria', *al Hayat* (London), 23 July 2000.
14 *Al Hayat*, 6 July 2006 , and *al Nahar* (Beirut), 6 July 2007.
15 *Al Hayat*, 6 July 2006.
16 Ibid., 10 April 2006 .
17 *Al Nahar*, 30 January 2006.
18 Refer to a long report on 'al Qobeysiat', their traditions and their influence and role in Syrian society in *Al Hayat*, 3 May 2006.
19 *Al Hayat*, 10 April 2006.
20 *Assafir* (Beirut), 19 June 2006.
21 *Assafir* (Beirut), 19 June 2006.
22 *Al Hayat*, 10 April 2006.
23 See *al Hayat*, 12 April 2006 and Sha'aban Aboud, *The Coming Dangers from the Islamists* (Beirut: Annahar, 17 September 2006).
24 Joranaes Reissner, *Ideologie und Politick der Muslimbrruder Syriens* (Freiburg: Klaus Schwarz Verlag, 1980), also published in Arabic.
25 Joranaes Reissner, *Ideologue and Policy for the Muslim Brotherhood in Syria*, pp. 379–391; also Abdula Hanna, *The Civil Society in the Arabic Modern State* (Damascus: Dar Almada, 2002), pp. 349–363.
26 Mohammad Jamal Barout, 'Islamic Brotherhood in Syria', in Mohammad Jamal Barout and Fisal Darraj (eds), *The Encyclopedia of Islamic Movements and Parties* (Damascus: The Arabic Center for Strategic Studies, 2000), p. 258; also Abdul Rahman Alhaj, 'The Political Islam in Syria', in Radwan Ziadeh (ed.), *The Reform in Syria Between Domestic and International Politics* (Arraya Centre for Research, 2004), pp. 132–133.
27 For more about the writings of Sayyid Qutb and its influence, see Radwan Ziadeh, *The Question of Renewal in Contemporary Islamic Discourse* (Beirut: Dar al-Madar al Islmee, 2004), pp. 93–114, and refer to his book *Sayyid Qutb: Signs on the Road* (1968).
28 For more about the 'al Hakimia' concept, see Hisham Jafar, *The Political Dimensions for the Concept of 'Hakimia'* (USA: The International Institute for Islamic Thought, 1995).
29 On this subject see Mohammad Jamal Barout, *Islamic Brotherhood in Syria*, pp. 266–269; and also Said Hawaa, *This My Experience and My Proof* (Algeria: Dar Alwafa, 1991), pp. 72–75.
30 For more on this subject see Radwan Ziadeh, *Decision-making and Foreign Policy in Syria* (Cairo: al-Ahram Center for Political and Strategic Studies (ACPSS), 2007); Raymond Hinnebuch, *Syria: Revolution from Above* (London and New York: Routledge, 2001); Steven Heydeman, *Authoritarianism in Syria: Intuitions and Social Conflict 1946–1970* (Ithaca and London: Cornell University Press, 1999); Raymond A. Hinnebusch, *Authoritarian Power and State Formation in Ba'athist Syria: Army, Party and Peasant* (Boulder, CO: Westview Press, 1998).
31 Patrick Seale, *Asad of Syria: The Struggle for the Middle East* (London: I.B, Tauris, 1988).

32 Article 3 from the Syrian constitution of 1973.
33 Hanna Batatu, *Syria's Peasantry*, p. 261.
34 Patrick Seal, *Asad and the Struggle for the Middle East*, pp. 532–533. See also the report prepared by the Syrian Committee for Human Rights in London on 26 June 2001 at <www.shrc.org>.
35 Radwan Ziadeh, 'Limits of Syrian Reform: Mechanisms of Power Transfer and Change Stakes', in Radwan Ziadeh (ed.), *The Reform in Syria Between Domestic and International Politics* (Arraya Centre for Research, 2004).
36 This phrase comes from the writer, Abd al Razzaq Aeedin, in one of his articles in the Lebanese newspaper *al Nahar*.
37 Husam Jazmattie, 'Youth and Islam in Syria', in *Lecture* magazine, issue 11–12, November–December 2005.
38 Hanna Batatu, *Syria's Peasantry*, p. 270.
39 Ibid., p. 271; and Eyal Zisser, 'Hafiz al Asad Discovers Islam', in *The Middle East Quarterly*, Vol Vi, No. 1, March 1999.
40 Nikolaos Van Dam, *The Struggle for Power is Syria: Sectarianism, Regionalism and Tribalism in Politics: 1961–1978* (London, 1979); Fred H. Lawson, 'Social Bases for the Hama Revaluation', in *Middle East Research and Information Project Reports* (November–December 1982), pp. 24–28; and Robert Fisk, *The Times*, 19 February 1982; and for the account of the government see *Islamic Brotherhood in Syria: Black History* (Damascus: Ba'ath Party Office, 1985).
41 Ibid., pp. 313–318; and Ibraheem Hamedie, 'History of the Secret Relations Between Damascus and Islamic Brotherhood', in *al Hayat*, 23 February 1997.
42 See *The Unfair Laws in Syria – The Law 49* (London: The Syrian Committee for Human Rights).
43 Razan Zeitouneh and Abdul Haï al-Sayyed, *Can Extraordinary Courts Ensure Justice: Supreme State Security Court* (Damascus Center for Human Rights Studies (DCHRS), May 2007).
44 *Al Hayat*, 4 May 2001.

17

Many Hijabs: Interpretative Approaches to the Questions of Islamic Female Dress

Rachel Woodlock

Islamic female dress, referred to colloquially as hijab,[1] is overloaded with contradictory symbols and meanings that reveal as much about the commentator as the object of comment (Werbner 2007). As such, there is not one hijab that is universally liberating or oppressive, but there are many hijabs that declare a range of symbols and meanings. As Franks (2000: 918) argues, 'the power relations with which it is associated are situated not only in the meaning with which it is invested but also in the circumstances under which it is worn'. In addition, women wearing Islamic female dress (however interpreted) are performing a religious act, even if it has other cultural, sociological and political implications. Thus, the question of who has the right and authority to interpret religious dress is part of a wider debate over religious authority generally, where women's bodies have become the contested battleground for Islamic authenticity and identity (Mir-Hosseini 2007; Werbner 2007; Yeğenoğlu 1998).

Saeed (2007) has provided a preliminary taxonomy of various trends and orientations current among Muslims in the context of responding to modernity and globalization. These are legalist traditionalists; theological puritans; militant extremists; political Islamists; secular liberals; cultural nominalists; classical modernists; and progressive *ijtihadi*s. In more detail: legalist traditionalists are 'primarily concerned with maintenance of the law as conceptualized in the classical schools' (Saeed 2007: 397). They reject reform and reinterpretation of Islamic law, and attempt to revivify pre-modern interpretations and apply them without contextualization. Theological puritans, who are *Wahhabi-Salafi*s,[2] emphasize a strict monotheistic theology, and reject what they consider to be un-Islamic innovation, particularly what has developed in Shi'i and Sufi Islam as well as in the traditional schools of jurisprudence. Militant extremists focus on and react to what they perceive as the subjugation of Muslims at the hands of Western neo-colonialists, most specifically the United States of America. They reinterpret jihad and permit the use of terror, particularly given the power and resource differential between themselves and the states and coalitions they fight. Political Islamists believe the establishment of an Islamic state (and the primacy of Islamic law within the state), through gradual conversion and change, will counter the decline of Muslim societies that has occurred, particularly since colonization of much of the Muslim world. They are contrasted by secular liberals who eschew the politicization of religion and call for the separation of mosque and state. Cultural nominalists are those Muslims whose link with Islam is purely through cultural heritage and not through the meaningful practice of Islam as a religion. Classical modernists seek reform of Islamic law, through a revival of the tool of *ijtihad*[3] and with an emphasis on harmonizing rationality and religious faith. This group has spawned the birth of progressive *ijtihadis*, who call for a major overhaul of the methodologies of interpreting Islam and Islamic law. They focus particularly on the arena of human rights, justice and pluralism. Accordingly, representatives of these orientations possess varied opinions on the role, meaning and interpretation of hijab.

Saeed shifts focus from historical boundaries of political, legal and theological difference and instead asks how Muslims are responding to questions of modernity, secularism, globalization and the conceptualization of law, justice and human rights. However, the classification is preliminary and there is a group missing from Saeed's taxonomy: Sufis, whose understanding of Islam is expressed through various forms of Islamic mysticism. This group includes Muslims raised in the faith as well as Western converts who may or may not incorporate other aspects of Islamic practice into their experience.

For this chapter I have collapsed Saeed's categories into four general orientations: traditionalists, secularists, fundamentalists and contextualists. Traditionalists are Saeed's legalist traditionalists as well as those Sufi practitioners whose source of authority lies in pre-modern interpretations of the religion. They look to the past with a sense of melancholy, and wish to re-establish the link that modernity ruptured between themselves and their societies, and the generations of pre-modern

Islamic scholars who developed the normative, orthodox interpretations of Islam and its sacred law. Secularists are Muslims who argue for the separation of religion and state, and the privatization of religion. They see no role for religious institutions in the structures of society, particularly as they pertain to governance and legislation. Because of their lack of interest in religion as a political and sociological force, we can include within this group the cultural nominalists, whose affiliation with Islam is primarily through cultural connection to Muslim ancestors, families and friends rather than active religious belief and practice. Fundamentalists,[4] incorporating theological puritans, militant extremists and political Islamists, feel that the present pitiable state of Muslims is caused partly by stagnation of traditional pre-modern Islamic institutions; the incorporation of inauthentic innovations (both historical and modern) into the interpretations of Islam; and the consequent inability of Muslims to withstand the onslaught of Westernization. Although they are fully rooted in the modern world, their solution is to seek a return to the fundamentals of Islam, what they believe are the Prophet's original teachings carried on by the first generations of Muslims. Fundamentalists, being modern, assert there is an objective historical truth to possess: a pure Islam that is untainted, and of which they are the only guardians. Contextualists, evolving out of classical modernists, are Saeed's progressive *ijtihadis*. They are those Muslims who accept the postmodern premise of bracketed truth-claims, and whose approach to interpreting Islam takes into consideration that Muslims are characterized by diversity through time and space. Thus, Muslims living in different periods, cultures and climes are required to assess and reassess whether particular interpretations of religion live up to the underlying Qur'anic *Weltanschauung* and the Prophet Muhammad's paradigmatic example, with a particular focus on human rights, justice and pluralism.

These groups, along with interested non-Muslim politicians, policy-makers, academics, media representatives and other social commentators, are engaged in a contest of authority, to speak for Islam and Muslims. The purpose of this chapter is to examine the different interpretative approaches to the sources and claims of authority asserted in the context of discourse about the hijab, which has become so emblematic of Islamic identity. As such, it can be placed among the literature that looks at the authoritative interpretation of Islamic beliefs and practices – particularly with regard to women and female dress – and the underlying political and sociological trends that propel questions of authoritative interpretation (Abou El Fadl 2001a, 2001b, 2005; Abu Zayd, Amirpur and Setiawan 2006; Donnan 2002; Esack 2001; Marty and Appleby 1991a; Mir-Hosseini 1999; Saeed 2006b; Wadud 1999). The rest of the chapter will survey the main positions on Islamic female dress offered in the four orientations, looking at their interpretative approaches to claims of authority.

Sources for Interpreting Islamic Dress

A comprehensive survey of pre-modern Islamic dress is outside the present chapter's scope, and has been addressed elsewhere (for example, El Guindi 1999; Stillman 2003). However, briefly, there are a number of passages in the Qur'an that deal with male and female dress:

> O Children of Adam! We have bestowed upon you raiment (*libasan*) to cover your nakedness and as adornment. And the raiment of God-consciousness – that is the best. That is from the signs of God; that they may remember. (Q7:26)

> O Children of Adam! Procure your beautiful apparel (*zinatakum*) for each place of worship, and eat and drink, but do not waste for verily He does not love the wasters. (Q7:31)

> O you who believe! Do not enter the houses of the Prophet except when permission is given to you ... And if you ask them [the Prophet's wives] for things, ask them from behind a curtain (*hijabin*). That is purer for your hearts and for their hearts. (Q33:53)

> O Prophet! Tell your wives and your daughters and the women of the believers to lower over themselves their outer gowns (*jalabibihinna*); thus it is more likely they will be known and not annoyed. God is forgiving, merciful. (Q33:59)

> And tell the believing women to lower their gaze, to guard their private parts (*furujahunna*), and to not display their adornments (*zinatahunna*) except that which is outwardly visible of them, and to cast their headcovers (*khumurihinna*) over their breasts (*juyubihinna*), and to not display their adornments except to their husbands or their fathers, or their husbands' fathers, or their sons, or their husbands' sons, or their brothers, or their brothers' sons, or

> their sisters' sons, or their women, or their slaves, or those male servants who lack sexual desire [for women], or children who are not cognizant of women's nudity; and to not stamp their feet in order to make known the adornments they hide. And turn to God in repentance all of you, O believers, that you may succeed. (Q24:31)
>
> And the post-menopausal from among the women that are not hoping for marriage, carry no blame if they discard their garments (*thiyabahunna*) provided they do not become flaunters with their adornments. And their being modest is best for them, and God is hearing, knowing. (Q24:60)

Face-veiling itself is not specifically mentioned, although references exist to specific items of clothing commonly worn by Arab women of the time, namely the *khimar* (headcover), the *jilbab* (long, loose gown) and the *thawb* (clothes, garments, or more specifically a gown with sleeves) (El Guindi 1999; Roald 2001; Stillman 2003).

The *Hadith* dealing with dress are too numerous to mention in any great detail, but cover matters of permissibility, prohibition and general comment on what the Prophet and his companions wore. I have provided a selection below, each demonstrating particular sartorial practices that have been invoked in the various interpretations of appropriate female dress:

> It is related that Umm 'Atiyya said, 'We were ordered to bring out the … veiled women on the days of the two festivals … A woman said, "Messenger of Allah, what if one of us does not have a veil?" He said, "Her friend should share her veil with her."' (Al-Bukhari, 9/344)
>
> It is related that Ibn 'Umar said, 'A man stood up and said, "Messenger of Allah, what clothes do you command us to wear in *ihram*?"[5] The Prophet, may Allah bless him and grant him peace, replied … "The woman in *ihram* should not wear a veil on her face nor gloves."' (Al-Bukhari, 33/1741)
>
> It is related that 'A'isha said, when this *ayat* was revealed, 'That they should draw their head-coverings across their breasts' (24:31), they [the female *émigrés* from Makkah] took their wrappers and tore them at the edges and veiled themselves with them.' (Al-Bukhari, 68/4481)

> Az-Zuhri said that Anas ibn Malik had told him that he saw Umm Kulthum, peace be upon her, the daughter of the Messenger of Allah, may Allah bless him and grant him peace, wearing a striped silk mantle. (Al-Bukhari, 80/5504)

> Narrated Abu Hurayrah: 'The Apostle of Allah (peace be upon him) cursed the man who dressed like a woman and the woman who dressed like a man.' (Abu Dawud, 32/4087)

> Narrated Umm Salamah, [the Mother of the Believers]: 'When the verse "That they should cast their outer garments over their persons" was revealed, the women of Ansar came out as if they had crows over their heads by wearing outer garments."' (Abu Dawud, 32/4090)

> Narrated Aisha, [the Mother of the Believers]: 'Asma', daughter of Abu Bakr, entered upon the Apostle of Allah (peace be upon him) wearing thin clothes. The Apostle of Allah (peace be upon him) turned his attention from her. He said: "O Asma, when a woman reaches the age of menstruation, it does not suit her that she displays her parts of body except this and this," and he pointed to her face and hands.' (Abu Dawud, 32/4092)

> Narrated Dihyah ibn Khalifah al-Kalbi: 'The Apostle of Allah (peace be upon him) was brought some pieces of fine Egyptian linen and he gave me one and said: 'Divide it into two; cut one of the pieces into a shirt and give the other to your wife for a veil.' Then when he turned away, he said: 'And order your wife to wear a garment below it and not show her figure.' (Abu Dawud, 32/4104)

According to Stillman (2003), male and female clothing worn in the Prophetic period consisted of largely similar items, but differed in the style of wrapping, choice of fabric textures and colours, and accoutrements. Both men and women wore at least a wrap or mantle when moving about in public, and for free men and women usually some form of headcovering. Over time, the male headcovering become synonymous with Muslim identity, so much so that it was called a 'badge of Islam' and 'divider between unbelief and belief' (Stillman 2003: 16).[6] As in the pre-Islamic period, noble women also covered their faces, as men occasionally did as well (El Guindi 1999; Stillman 2003).

Traditionalists on Hijab

It is undoubtedly true that pre-modern religious law, which evolved from around the second and third centuries onwards,[7] rested firmly on a patriarchal reading of the religion that differentiated between the male and the female, divinely endowing the former with rights and prerogatives on the basis of this essentialized biological difference (Al-Hibri 1982; Barlas 2002; Wadud 1999).[8] Nevertheless, interpretations of rulings could be extremely flexible, a natural feature of *ijtihad* and the diversity of opinions that flourished in Islamic civilizations over the centuries (Hallaq 1984; Sonbol 2003).

Unlike in the modern period, classical jurists were mostly concerned with female dress pertaining to that necessary for the two categories of free and slave women to cover during ritual prayer. A majority opinion on appropriate female dress in public did emerge in each of the various schools of religious law, with distinctions made for different social classes and in different environments and contexts.[9] Areas of disagreement occurred over whether slave women were required to cover their breasts and back; and whether free women were expected to veil their faces, and if so to what extent (Abou El Fadl 2001b; Mir-Hosseini 2007; Roald 2001).[10] Important jurists who gave opinions permitting the face, hands and/or feet to remain exposed include Abu Hanifah, Malik ibn Anas and al-Tabari.

However, the experience of modernity intertwined with colonialism had a rupturing effect on many Muslim societies. Many classical structures of pre-modern Shari'a-based societies were eliminated in the name of progress, and what was once a relatively flexible and organic Shari'a system became a mutilated, codified and increasingly fossilized set of rulings restricted to the realm of piety and family law (Hatem 1986; Kandiyoti 1991b). As Sonbol (2003: 232–233) writes, the new Shari'a courts crystallized 'particular laws suitable to nineteenth-century Nation-State patriarchal hegemony'. Because traditionalists argue that Muslims need to emulate and implement pre-modern religious law, despite and against the cultural and sociological differences that modernity has brought, there is little questioning of the perceived immutability of patriarchy, or taking into consideration the diversity and adaptive nature of pre-modern Shari'a.

An example of this is an online fatwa[11] given by Ebrahim Desai (2006), a Deobandi mufti based in South Africa, to a question on veiling submitted from Pakistan.[12] Desai's reply, based on his reading of both classical and Deobandi texts,[13] provides an interpretation of veiling and seclusion that effectively and permanently removes women from the public sphere:

> Veil is legitimately defined as the dress that covers the whole body of the woman including her head, face, hands and feet. It should be long, loose and plain, not defining her shape … As Allah states, 'And stay in your houses, and do not display yourselves like that of the former times of ignorance' … Veiling is the tradition of Muslim women. Since its prescription, the Prophet's wives, daughters and other believing Muslim women have strictly observed it. Today also, the Muslim ladies must keep it up.

Traditionalists are thus required to explain the discrepancy between the historical freedom of movement of early Muslim women, as well as the differences of opinion held by pre-modern jurists on the extent of women's covering in public,[14] in comparison with their advocating the effective removal of women from the public realm. They do this by explaining that women's entrance in the public sphere is only permitted where there is not a fear of *fitnah*, a word the Qur'an uses for the tests suffered by believers and the trials of civil war, but which in the language of religious scholars took on overtones of sexual immorality when applied to the movement of women. They then freeze the state of potential *fitnah*, rendering women's freedom of movement relegated to the past. In *Ma'ariful-qur'an* (Shafi' and 'Usmani 2005), the Deobandi Qur'an commentary which Desai references, Muhammad Shafi' writes:

> According to those who have called it permissible [for a woman to leave her face and hands uncovered in public], the permissibility is subject to the condition that there should be no apprehension of *fitnah* (situation resulting in some evil consequence). Since the face of a woman is at the center of her beauty and embellishment, therefore, the absence of any apprehension of *fitnah* is a rare likelihood. Ultimately, for this reason, under normal conditions, opening the face etc. is not permissible. (Vol. 7: 223)

As Abou El Fadl (2001b) points out, these rationales become nonsensical when acknowledging the classical position of slave women and female servants (whether Muslim or not) appearing bare-breasted and bare-headed in public. Nevertheless, the arguments chosen by these traditionalists demonstrate a tension between patriarchal gender norms, class distinction and modern sensibilities, particularly those advocated by the next group to be discussed in this chapter: the secularists.

Secularists on Hijab

In the twentieth century, many social commentators predicted that secularism would spell the death of religion, both in the Western world and in the Muslim-majority world where it was prophesied that secularism would bring the Arabs and Muslims into the modern world and bestow on them progress and enlightenment. Women and their bodies became emblematic of the struggle between the opposing forces of secularism and religious revivalism in the construction of the modern nation state (Kandiyoti 1991a). This was the philosophy behind the changes wrought by Mustafa Kemal Atatürk in Turkey and Mohammad Reza Pahlavi, the last Shah of Iran, both of whom banned traditional forms of cultural dress, including male turbans and female veils. As Nasr (1999: 560) writes: 'Controlling popular culture as a prerequisite for socioeconomic change has been the avowed policy of secular nationalist states.'

Secular positions have animated much Western feminist writing on Muslim female dress, usually with virulently anti-Islam passion, for which reason secular feminism has found little acceptance among Muslims except, perhaps, with the Western-educated elite (Hamid 2006). For secularists, female veiling practices are associated with backwardness, misogyny, and the undesirable imposition of patriarchal religion intruding in public life. With contradictory arguments, secularists have asserted the hijab represents *both* the passive oppression of women as victims and the aggressive assertion of religion in the public sphere (Scott 2005; Werbner 2007), while denying any other symbols or meanings for Muslim female dress.

This was the case with French arguments surrounding the ban on religious symbols in public schools that particularly targeted Muslim girls wearing headcovers (Werbner 2007). In a telephone interview for *Voice of America*, French sociologist Juliette Minces (Felten 2004) superimposes a monolithic veiling semiotic, thereby muzzling the voices of those Muslim women who might object to her categorization of Islamic dress:

> The veil has a real meaning in religion and in the society. And the meaning of the veil is the fact that women are inferior to men. They are not equal to men. They have to obey men. They have to be defined. They have to be nice. And they have to hide from other men. So, it means that every other man who doesn't belong to the family is a potential rapist and is superior to a woman. So, as a feminist, for example, we cannot accept these differences.

She continues by describing wearing the veil as 'a political challenge' implying the visibility of the headscarf is a threat to notions of French identity. Minces belongs to the orientalist category of Western observer, which Said famously criticized as a way of 'dominating, restructuring, and having authority over the Orient' (Said 1995: 2–3). She speaks about Muslim women, for Muslim women, denying any alternative readings those women themselves might give to Islamic female dress.

The secularist voices decrying the influence of Islam in public life generally, and Islamic dress specifically, are found not only among Western observers like Minces, but also from Muslims and former Muslims such as Parvin Darabi, Taslima Nasrin, Ayaan Hirsi Ali, Irshad Manji and Maryam Namazie. Mirroring the French secularist arguments, central committee member of the Worker-Communist Party of Iran and spokesperson for the Council of Ex-Muslims of Britain, Namazie has called for Islamic dress to be banned (Namazie 2007): 'A ban on the burqa, chador, neqab and its likes is important but it is nowhere enough. The hijab or any conspicuous religious symbol must be banned from the state and education and relegated to the private sphere.' She describes such dress as sexual apartheid, and on a par with straitjackets, body bags, chastity belts, female genital cutting and *sati*,[15] hence she rejects women's right to choose the veil as a religious freedom. In protesting forced veiling, she calls for forced *un*veiling. She infantilizes veiled Muslim women by denying they are able to choose Islamic dress, and paternalistically says: 'It is about protecting human beings sometimes even from themselves.'

Secularism imposed on, or adopted by, Muslims, references modern Western ideas and ideals, without acknowledging the passionate internal debate that is animating the question of what it means to be Western. Roy (2007) points out that the particular 'problem' of Muslim migrants and their religion is a mirror focusing a crisis of identity for Europe. That crisis has been occasioned by the permanent settlement of non-European minorities; the rise of religious revivalism; and the reassertion of conservative religious voices (Christian, Muslim, Jewish, etc.) rejecting the secular, liberal values that dominated European intellectual and political consciousness, particularly since the second half of the twentieth century. Islamic female dress is thus seen as tangible evidence that secularism in Europe and elsewhere in the Western world is under threat, most specifically from the third orientation discussed in this chapter: fundamentalism.

Fundamentalists on Hijab

The third category of claimant to authority in the discourse about Islamic female dress is fundamentalism, a modern phenomenon that developed in reaction to colonialism married with secularism and Westernization. Fundamentalists are critical of what they see as the excesses and innovations of classical interpretations of Islam; the harrowing pace of modernization affecting Muslim-majority countries; and the threat of identity-loss for Muslims living in diasporas. They are characterized by feelings of threat, of being part of a cosmic war between good and evil, and of needing to preserve their distinct identity (Marty and Appleby 1991b).

Fundamentalists claim to resurrect the original teachings of Islam that have been neglected or masked by incorporation of un-Islamic innovations. They do this through a pragmatic, selective retrieval of past doctrines, where 'the retrieved and updated fundamentals are meant to regain the same charismatic intensity today by which they originally forged communal identity from the formative revelatory religious experiences long ago. In this sense contemporary fundamentalism is at once both derivative and vitally original' (Marty and Appleby 1993: 3).

Because fundamentalists seek a purified Islam they do not accept the notion of culturally mediated forms of Islam, where the manifestation of the religion takes on different particular cultural forms depending on time and space. Roy (2004: 25) writes:

> Fundamentalism is both a product and an agent of globalisation, because it acknowledges without nostalgia the loss of pristine cultures, and sees as positive the opportunity to build a universally religious identity, delinked from any specific culture, including the Western one perceived as corrupt and decadent.

However, a reverse movement also occurs with the ethnicization of religion, where Muslims become a minority ethnic group within the Western world, whatever the state of religiosity of individual Muslims, and despite their ancestral diversity (Bloul 2008; Humphrey 2001; Roy 2004).

The discourse about Islamic female dress is one of the most important symbols and boundary markers of Muslim identity. The hijab in fundamentalist discourse is removed from any notion of cultural traditional Islamic dress, and fundamentalists have sought to elucidate an objective singular truth on what hijab means for all Muslim women, everywhere. That veiling practices in the pre-modern era varied (as mentioned previously) is of little consequence to fundamentalists, who seek a definitive teaching of the Prophet on the topic that is eternally prescriptive. Mir-Hosseini (2007) argues that by doing this, they effectively move the question of Islamic female dress from the realm of *mu'amalat* to *'ibadat.*[16]

Although proposing a definitive interpretation, in practice fundamentalists differ on what they define as proper hijab. Some (mostly those of the *Wahhabi-Salafi* persuasion) require that for the woman, the entire body be covered with an opaque, loose, flowing outer cloak or wrap that starts from the head. The face must be covered, either with this garment, or with a separate piece of affixed material, often referred to colloquially as *niqab, or* 'mask, face-veil'. Eyes may be uncovered depending on need. For example, from *fatawá* given on the *Islam Q&A* website (Al-Munajjid 1997–2008): 'The difference between hijaab and niqaab is that the hijaab is that which covers all the body, whilst niqaab is that which covers a woman's face only.' Thus women are to cover 'the entire body from head to toe', including the face, although an opening 'only as big as the left eye' is permitted.

Other fundamentalists (such as the Muslim Brotherhood and Jama'at-e-Islami) give permission, even encourage, Muslim women to leave the face and hands uncovered, but require loose, opaque clothing that covers the body, usually some sort of coat or dress, coupled with a headscarf pinned or tied so that it covers the ears and neck, draping down onto the shoulders and/or chest. This is a new type of Islamic dress, referred to by fundamentalists as *al-ziyy al-Islami* (Islamic attire) or *al-ziyy al-shar'i* (Shari'a attire) (El Guindi 1999: 134; Stillman 2003: 158). It is not taken from any one particular traditional culture, but has quickly become globalized, in much the same way that men from many different non-Western cultures around the world now wear the Western-style business suit. As Douglass (2007: 11) wryly notes:

> The [Western] business suit confers modesty by conforming almost exactly to the requirements for Muslim women's public appearance: it covers all but the head and the hands, and does so in a way that is sober, often with dark, uniform color, and a shape that conceals more than it reveals ... The best way to think of the difference between Muslim and Western norms of dress is as follows: in Western culture, the norm of understated dress that completely covers the body is applied to the male, whereas in Islam, it is applied to the female.

Fundamentalists, with a very modern rationality, attempt to provide sociological and political arguments for why women should dress and cover in the manner they prescribe, often relying on an essentialist interpretation of biological difference between men and women and holding women responsible for preserving moral decency in society. The most common themes in fundamentalist arguments are: hijab (as interpreted by the fundamentalists) is commanded by God; it promotes dignity, respect, modesty and chastity for Muslim women, and prevents men from falling into temptation; it protects women from the untoward advances of predator males; it is in concert with the true feminine nature that is modest, shy and virginal; it negates the objectification of women's bodies; it allows women to move freely in public; and it preserves a woman's beauty for her husband's consumption only.

These are all themes put forward in a *Wahhabi-Salafi* article ('Why Should I Wear the Hijaab?' Anon 2007) where the anonymous author concludes with a sentence packed with binary oppositions: 'So a Muslim woman in hijab is dignified, not dishonoured, noble, not degraded, liberated, not subjugated, purified, not sullied, independent, not a slave, protected, not exposed, respected, not laughed at, confident, not insecure, obedient, not a sinner, a guarded pearl, not a prostitute', and asks how any Muslim woman could thus fail to see the beneficial nature of hijab.

One important distinction is that in the fundamentalist conception of Islamic female dress, the purpose of hijab is to provide women access to the public realm, not to seclude them from it. In many pre-modern cultures, upper-class women's seclusion was a badge of wealth and distinction. In fundamentalist discourse, the hijab provides a portable privacy that allows women to participate in public life (El Guindi 1999). It is not insignificant that this new form of veiling was adopted when women in emerging middle classes needed to participate in the workforce due to economic necessity (Ahmed 1992).

However, although fundamentalists are modern in their methodology of interpreting Islam, as An-Na'im (1995: 55) points out, they are 'backward-looking in content'. Fundamentalists do not question the underlying patriarchal premise of their interpretations, and often quote the same Qur'anic *ayat* and *Hadith* as traditionalists, although as Mir-Hosseini (2007) points out, they are sensitive to criticisms of patriarchal bias, hence the apologetic tone of their arguments. Where they differ is in the search for one definitive ruling in a question of Islamic law that applies for all Muslims across time and space, and in their desire to 'return' to the original source texts for interpretation, dismissing unquestioned allegiance to received wisdom of the traditional schools of law. In their search for the definitive, monosemous reading on Islamic dress, fundamentalists cement patriarchy as a universal Islamic prescription. It is precisely this notion that is challenged by the last group to be covered in this chapter, the contextualists.

Contextualists on Hijab

Contextualists are Muslims who argue that Islam – and in particular religious law – must be understood contextually (Esack 2005). That is, Muslims have always interpreted religion through paradigmatic lenses of particular time periods, places, cultures, language groups and classes. Because of this, Muslims developed rich and varied interpretations of Islamic belief and practice, unified around the core doctrines of monotheism and the prophethood of Muhammad. Contextualists argue that Muslims must continue this interpretative project for Muslims living in the modern world, both in Muslim-majority contexts and as minorities in the West. They argue that classical exegetes and jurists were fallible human beings who approached the texts with their own particular biases (Mir-Hosseini 2007). Therefore, today's Muslims have the right to question the classical interpretations and rulings, where they no longer make sense or appear to contradict the Qur'anic *Weltanschauung* (Barlas

2002). Thus, they assert the right to perform *ijtihad.* Contextualists come from the modernist school of thought that arose in the late nineteenth and twentieth centuries (for example see Fazlur Rahman's methodology for interpreting Islam in Rahman 1982; Saeed 2006a; Sonn 1991).

Among the contextualists are Muslim feminists who question the traditionalist, secularist and fundamentalist assumption that Islam prescribes patriarchy. Their argument goes as follows: the Qur'an recognizes that patriarchy has been the normal state of affairs for most societies, and provides rulings to limit its more extreme manifestations (Wadud 1999). Nevertheless, it does not prescribe patriarchy as a desired state, but instead promotes an underlying ethic of egalitarianism towards which Muslim societies should strive to move (Afkhami 1997). The few Qur'anic *ayat* that appear to limit women's rights are always context specific. Where the societal context changes, and gender equality and women's autonomy may be pursued, then the application of these limiting rulings no longer applies (Barlas 2002; Hassan 1996; Wadud 1999). Furthermore, Muslim feminists seek to establish precedents from the lives of the women surrounding the Prophet, and the earliest generations of Muslim women, many of whom acted in ways that contradict the stereotype of the passive, secluded, subordinate female (Stowasser 1994).

In the context of Islamic female dress, many contextualists have taken the view that the underlying thrust of the Qur'an and Prophetic tradition is one of modesty, while different cultures may interpret the specifics of modest dress differently (Barlas 2002; Shaaban 1995; Shahroor 2000; Zuhur 1992). This was a theme that arose in a 1990 meeting organized by Women Living Under Muslim Laws (WLUML), where participants discussed a variety of different gender-related issues in Qur'anic interpretation, including dress, modesty and sexuality. Participants drew a distinction between the philosophy of modesty and the elaboration of what constitutes modest dress in diverse situations (WLUML 1997). As one participant argued: 'The law of modesty in the Qur'an applies to men and women both and applies to them equally ... You have to interpret the Islamic law of modesty, a) according to your own conscience and b) according to your cultural context. What is modest in one society is not modest in another society and so on' (p. 215).

Various participants also challenged and disagreed with some of the traditionalist, secularist and fundamentalist rationales for the purposes behind Islamic dress and covering practices. These included that hijab itself does not protect against molestation; that emphasizing hijab may have the counter-effect of permitting or encouraging the sexualization and objectification of women's bodies and even sometimes violence against women; that segregation and the reserving of public space for men is not an Islamic ideal; that there is not a single interpretation of what Islamic modesty or immodesty means; that precedents from Islamic history show women acted assertively and publicly; that veiling carries signals including pre- and non-Islamic meanings, and alternatively that hijab has long been a part of Islamic practice; that there has been evolution in the meaning of hijab and even the meaning of words describing specific items of clothing, over time; that dress can be liberating as well as oppressive; that women should not have to bear the weight of symbolizing national identity; that Western standards of modesty and liberation are not necessarily normative for all women across the globe; that there are class dimensions to veiling practices; that change in challenging segregation or veiling practices should be slow and organic, not imposed quickly; and that equality for women does not mean sameness as men.

For contextualists (including Muslim feminists), there is an acceptance of postmodern claims of bracketed truths. As such, there is not one single answer to the question of what is appropriate Islamic female dress. There is a strong emphasis on rationality and the right of individuals to interpret Islamic injunctions regarding modesty and dress, within the societal norms of their particular environments.

Conclusion

Ismail (2004) questions the notion of a trans-historical, pure Islam against which Muslims are measured as moving closer to, or further away. Muslims construct and reconstruct their conceptions of Islam from a multiplicity of sources and referents including local context, the interplay of power relations, as well as the influence of transnationalism and globalization. All of the four orientations discussed in this chapter represent four competing and overlapping narratives of claims to authenticity and authority. First, traditionalists, who acknowledge as their source of authority the received interpretations and rulings of religious law that developed over many centuries; however, in the process of reacting to modernity and postmodernity, they have codified and crystallized pre-modern patriarchal notions of gender norms. Second, secularists, who, in seeking Western-style models of the separation of religion and state and the privatization of religion, impose on Muslim women the archetype of the passive, oppressed, secluded and veiled creature in order to reject her. Their source of authority is the orientalist narrative that was developed in Western academia. Third, fundamentalists, whose source of authority lies with charismatic preachers arguing for a singular, definitive interpretation of God's will that decontextualizes and globalizes the Muslim identity, and promotes an essentialized view of biological sex difference, affirming patriarchy. Lastly, contextualists, who accept the postmodern notion of bracketed truth claims, and who assert the right of individuals (including women) to interpret religion and develop varying sartorial practices depending on time, place and culture. Their source of authority is the modernist trend of the twentieth century, which called for a revival of the use of *ijtihad*.

The four orientations discussed in this chapter represent broad trends, and I have not emphasized the diversity of voices that also exists within these trends. There are milder forms of secularism, for example, that do not seek to eradicate religious influences in society, but merely to inhibit particular religious authorities from accessing and wielding state power in God's name. Not all contextualists are feminists, and even among those whose field of interest is gender issues, not all claim the feminist label, given its sometimes pejorative connotations as being a Western imposition.[17] There are traditionalists who recognize the usefulness of the tool of *ijtihad* appropriately wielded, and who have attempted to offer more gender-inclusive rulings. Also, those who nevertheless reject the patriarchal premise of male rule over women have adopted a number of fundamentalist arguments about the usefulness of hijab. These include some Western converts, for whom wearing Islamic dress is a matter of asserting Muslim identity, and feminists who use the veil to challenge the panopticon of the male gaze (Bullock 2002).

So, what is the future of the debate about religious authority, particularly in the context of women and Islamic dress? It seems likely the question of the hijab's symbolism will not disappear any time soon. Periodically, debates about Islamic female dress flare up in the Muslim world (such as in Iran with the annual crackdowns on 'bad hijab') as well as in the Western world, where an underlying theme regularly appearing in political and social comment is of Islamic dress marking wilful separation and avoidance of assimilation into Western society. The most recent example of the latter is French president Nicolas Sarkozy's 2009 speech against Islamic body and face-veiling as being anti-French. All of the various meanings attributed to hijab are symptomatic of the much deeper debate about who may speak for Islam and Muslims, and so long as that question is contested, Islamic female dress will continue to be a hotly contested issue.

NOTES

1 There are many words associated with Islamic female dress, however the word hijab (which literally means veil or curtain) increasingly is being used to represent both the practice of covering the head and body (and sometimes face) in public with loose, opaque clothing, as well as the Muslim female headscarf specifically.
2 Belonging to the sect founded by eighteenth-century reformer Muḥammad ibn 'Abd al-Wahhab (d. 1792), currently predominant in Saudi Arabia.
3 The application of mental exertion in independent systematic reasoning to derive an answer to a unique question of religious law.
4 I use the label 'fundamentalist' with some caution, as it is a hotly contested term.
5 Sacred state a pilgrim enters to perform the rites of pilgrimage. Some things that are ordinarily permissible are prohibited in the state of *iḥram*, including wearing perfume, having sexual intercourse with one's spouse, and trimming the hair and nails.
6 It is ironic that in the modern period, interest in male dress has now given way to obsession with female coverings: it is now the hijab and not the turban that has become the boundary-marker of Muslim identity.
7 With the emergence and coalescence of the schools of religious law, the five largest and most well known of which are the (Sunni) *Ḥanafi, Maliki, Shafi'i, Ḥanbali* and (Shi'i) *Ja'fari* schools.
8 It is worth noting that there exists a history of early female scholarly activity that is largely unacknowledged in the English-language literature about Islam. The possible exception to this is the wife of the Prophet 'A'ishah's role in the transmission of Sunni *Hadith* and religious interpretations, which is all but impossible to ignore.
9 That is, rules on veiling during pilgrimage and negotiating marriage differed than when generally in public.
10 For example, the following classical texts narrate the opinion preferring body- and face-veiling: (Keller 1999; Ibn Rushd 1994; Thanwi 2004).
11 A fatwa (pl. *fatawá*) is an answer given by a mufti (a person qualified to issue a fatwa) on a question of religious law.
12 The international and technological character of Desai's fatwa demonstrates the globalized and postmodern context of this traditionalism.

13 He references *Ma'ariful-qur'an* by Muḥammad Shafi 'Usmani; *Fat'ḥ al-bari* by Ibn Hajar al-'Asqalani; *'Umdat al-qari* by Badr al-Din al-'Ayni; and *Fatawa rahimiyah* by 'Abd al-Rahim Lajpuri.

14 Abou El Fadl (2001b) notes that juristic discourse about free women's covering, which was discussed in the context of what is covered in prayer, arrived at the majority position of requiring the whole body with the exception of the face and hands to be covered. Minority opinions variously allowed feet, calves, forearms, upper-arms and/or hair to be uncovered, or alternatively required the whole body including face and hands to be covered. In contradistinction, most jurists held that female slaves and servants are not required to cover their hair, forearms or calves, with some permitting the breasts to remain uncovered, and others requiring headcovers during prayer, but not in public generally (El Guindi 1999). Thus, a mutually reinforcing spiral was generated between the sartorial customs of early Muslim cultures and the opinions of religious lawyers generating interpretations of sacred law.

15 A funeral ritual practised by some Hindus (but now outlawed in India) in which a recently widowed woman immolated herself on her husband's funeral pyre.

16 Traditional jurists divided the realms of law into matters of *'ibadat* (ritual worship) and *mu'amalat* (generally used to mean social affairs). The rulings for the former category were strictly defined based on the Prophetic prescription. The latter category was more loosely regulated, and therefore contained a great deal more diversity in interpretation and implementation.

17 Muslim feminists who accept the label disagree, however the mud has firmly stuck in many parts of the Muslim world.

BIBLIOGRAPHY

Abou El Fadl, Khaled, *And God Knows the Soldiers: The Authoritative and Authoritarian in Islamic Discourses* (Lanham, MD: University Press of America, 2001a).

—*Speaking in God's Name: Islamic Law, Authority and Women* (Oxford: Oneworld, 2001b).

—*The Great Theft: Wrestling Islam from the Extremists* (New York: HarperSanFrancisco, 2005).

Abu Dawud, '*Partial Translation of Sunan Abu-Dawud*', tr. Ahmad Hasan (Center for Muslim–Jewish Engagement, University of Southern California). Retrieved 7 May 2009 from <http://www.usc.edu/schools/college/crcc/engagement/resources/texts/muslim/hadith/abudawud/>.

Abu Zayd, Nasr, Amirpur, Katajun, and Nur Kholis Setiawan, Mohamad, *Reformation of Islamic Thought: A Critical Historical Analysis* (Amsterdam: Amsterdam University Press, 2006).

Afkhami, Mahnaz, 'Claiming our Rights: A Manual for Women's Human Rights Education in Muslim Societies', in Mahnaz Afkhami and Erika Friedl (eds), *Muslim Women and the Politics of Participation: Implementing the Beijing Platform* (Syracuse, NY: Syracuse University Press, 1997), pp. 109–122.

Ahmed, Leila, *Women and Gender in Islam: Historical Roots of a Modern Debate* (New Haven, CT: Yale University Press, 1992).

Al-Bukhari, Muhammad ibn Isma'il, '*The Sahih Collection of al-Bukhari*', tr. Aisha Bewley (Sunnipath). Retrieved 7 May 2009 from <http://www.sunnipath.com/library/Hadith/H0002P0000.aspx>.

Al-Hibri, Azizah, 'A Study of Islamic Herstory: Or How Did We Ever Get Into This Mess?', in *Women's Studies International Forum* 5 (2) (1982), pp. 207–219.

Al-Munajjid, Muhammad Saalih, *Islam Question and Answer*, 1997–2008 (2009). Retrieved 25 February 2009 from <http://www.islam-qa.com/>.

An-Na'im, Abdullahi, 'The Dichotomy Between Religious and Secular Discourse in the Twenty-First Century', in Mahnaz Afkhami (ed.), *Faith and Freedom: Women's Human Rights in the Muslim World* (Syracuse, NY: Syracuse University Press, 1995), pp. 51–60.

Anon, *For Ourselves: Women Reading the Qur'an* (Grabels, France: Women Living under Muslim Laws, 1997).

Anon., Why Should I Wear the Hijaab? (Troid Publications, 2007). Accessed 25 February 2009 at <http://www.troid.org/index2.php?option=com_content&task=view&id=155&pop=1&page=0&Itemid=429)>.

Barlas, Asma, *'Believing Women' in Islam: Unreading Patriarchal Interpretations of the Qur'an* (Austin, TX: University of Texas Press, 2002).

Bloul, Rachel A. D., 'Anti-Discrimination Laws, Islamophobia, and Ethnicization of Muslim Identities in Europe and Australia', in *Journal of Muslim Minority Affairs* 28 (2008), pp. 7–25.

Bullock, Katherine, *Rethinking Muslim Women and the Veil: Challenging Historical & Modern Stereotypes* (Herndon, VA: International Institute of Islamic Thought, 2002).

Desai, Ebrahim, '*Fatwa #13998 from Pakistan', in Ask the Imam: Islamic Q&A Online* (Darul Ifta, Madrasah In'aamiyyah 2006). Retrieved 5 March 2009 from <http://www.askimam.org/fatwa/fatwa.php?askid=0fa3005a27b626c083c2467d3ef35484>.

Donnan, Hastings, *Interpreting Islam* (London: SAGE, 2002).

Douglass, Susan L., 'The Fabric of Muslim Daily Life', in Virginia Gray Henry-Blakemore (ed.), *Voices of Life: Family, Home, and Society* (Westport, CT: Praeger Publishers, 2007), pp. 1–34.

El Guindi, Fadwa, *Veil: Modesty, Privacy and Resistance* (Oxford: Berg, 1999).

Esack, Farid, '*What Do Men Owe to Women? Islam & Gender Justice: Beyond Simple Apologia*' (2001). Retrieved 4 March 2009 from <http://uk.geocities.com/faridesack/fewhatdomenowe.html>.

—*The Qur'an, a User's Guide: A Guide to Its Key Themes, History and Interpretation* (Oxford: Oneworld, 2005).

Felten, Eric, '*On the Line: The Veil in France*' (2004). Retrieved 5 March 2009 from <http://www.voanews.com/uspolicy/archive/2004-09/a-2004-09-20-6-1.cfm>.

Franks, Myfanwy,. 'Crossing the Borders of Whiteness? White Muslim Women Who Wear the Hijab in Britain Today', in *Ethnic and Racial Studies* 23 (2000), pp. 917–929.

Hallaq, Wael B., 'Was the Gate of Ijtihad Closed?' in *International Journal of Middle East Studies* 16 (1984), pp. 3–41.

Hamid, Shadi, 'Between Orientalism and Postmodernism: The Changing Nature of Western Feminist Thought Towards the Middle East', in *HAWWA* 4 (2006), pp. 76–92.

Hassan, Riffat, 'Rights of Women within Islamic Communities', in John Witte, Jr and Johan D. Van der Vyer (eds), *Religious Human Rights in Global Perspective: Religious Perspectives* (The Hague: Martinus Nijhoff Publishers, 1996), pp. 361–386.

Hatem, Mervat, 'The Enduring Alliance of Nationalism and Patriarchy in Muslim Personal Status Laws: The Case of Modern Egypt', in *Gender Issues* 6 (1986), pp. 19–43.

Humphrey, Michael, 'An Australian Islam? Religion in the Multicultural City', in Abdullah Saeed and Shahram Akbarzadeh (eds), *Muslim Communities in Australia* Sydney: UNSW Press, 2001), pp. 33–52.

Ibn Rushd, *The Distinguished Jurist's Primer,* tr. Imran Ahsan Khan Nyazee (Reading, UK: Garnet, 1994).

Ismail, Salwa, 'Being Muslim: Islam, Islamism and Identity Politics', in *Government and Opposition* 39 (2004), pp. 614–631.

Kandiyoti, Deniz, 'Identity and Its Discontents: Women and the Nation', in *Millenium: Journal of International Studies* 20 (1991a), pp. 429–443.

—'Women, Islam and the State', in *Middle East Report* 173 (1991b), pp. 9–14.

Keller, Nuh Ha Mim (ed. and tr.), *Reliance of the Traveller: The Classic Manual of Islamic Sacred Law 'Umdat al-Salik* (rev. edn, Beltsville, MD: Amana Publications, 1999).

Marty, Martin E. and Appleby, R. Scott, *Fundamentalisms and the State: Remaking Polities, Economies, and Militance* (Chicago, IL: University of Chicago Press, 1993).

—(eds), *Fundamentalisms Observed, Fundamentalism Project* (Chicago, IL: University of Chicago Press, 1991a).
—(eds), *The Fundamentalism Project.* 5 vols (Chicago, IL: University of Chicago Press, 1991b).
Mir-Hosseini, Ziba, *Islam and Gender: The Religious Debate in Contemporary Iran, Princeton Studies in Muslim Politics* (Princeton, NJ: Princeton University Press, 1999).
—'Islam and Gender Justice', in Omid Safi (ed.), *Voices of Change* (Westport, CT: Praeger Publishers, 2007), pp. 85–114.
Namazie, Maryam, 'What's All the Fuss About the Veil?', in *Women's Rights, the Veil and Islamic and Religious Laws* (London: Seminar 2007). Retrieved 5 March 2009 from <http://maryamnamazie.blogspot.com/2007/03/whats-all-fuss-about-veil.html>.
Nasr, S. V. R., 'European Colonialism and the Emergence of Modern Muslim States', in John L. Esposito (ed.), *The Oxford History of Islam* (Oxford: OUP, 1999), pp. 549–600.
Rahman, Fazlur, *Islam & Modernity: Transformation of an Intellectual Tradition* (Chicago, IL: University of Chicago Press, 1982).
Roald, Anne Sofie, *Women in Islam: The Western Experience* (London: Routledge, 2001).
Roy, Olivier, *Globalised Islam: The Search for a New Ummah* (London: Hurst, 2004).
—'Islam in Europe', *in Stanford Abbasi Program in Islamic Studies* (Palo Alto, CA: Lecture at Stanford University, 2007).
Saeed, Abdullah, 'Fazlur Rahman: A Framework for Interpreting the Ethico-Legal Content of the Qur'an', in Suha Taji-Farouki (ed.), *Modern Muslim Intellectuals and the Qur'an* (London: Oxford University Press, 2006a), pp. 37–66.
—*Interpreting the Qur'an: Towards a Contemporary Approach* (Abingdon, UK: Routledge, 2006b).
—'Trends in Contemporary Islam: A Preliminary Attempt at a Classification', in *The Muslim World* 97 (2007), pp. 395–404.
Said, Edward W., *Orientalism* (reprint. with new afterword edn, London: Penguin Books, 1995).
Scott, Joan W., 'Symptomatic Politics: The Banning of Islamic Head Scarves in French Public Schools', in *French Politics, Culture & Society* 23 (3) (2005), pp. 106–127.
Shaaban, Bouthaina, 'The Muted Voices of Women Interpreters', in Mahnaz Afkhami (ed.), *Faith and Freedom: Women's Human Rights in the Muslim World* (Syracuse, NY: Syracuse University Press, 1995), pp. 61–77.
Shafi', Muhammad and Taqi 'Usmani, Muhammad, *Ma'ariful-qur'an,* tr. Muhammad Shamim (2nd edn, Karachi: Maktaba Darul-Uloom, 2005).
Shahroor, Mohammed, 'Applying the Concept of "Limits" to the Rights of Muslim Women', in *Islam and Human Rights* (School of Law, Emory). Retrieved 25 February 2009 from <http://www.islam21.net/pages/keyissues/key2-10.htm>.
Sonbol, Amira, 'Women in Shari'a Courts: A Historical and Methodological Discussion', in *Fordham International Law Journal* 27 (2003), pp. 225–253.

Sonn, Tamara, 'Fazlur Rahman's Islamic Methodology', in *The Muslim World* 81 (1991), pp. 212–230.

Stillman, Yedida Kalfon, *Arab Dress: A Short History from the Dawn of Islam to Modern Times* (rev. 2nd edn, Leiden: Brill, 2003).

Stowasser, Barbara Freyer, *Women in the Qur'an, Traditions, and Interpretation* (New York: OUP, 1994).

Thanwi, Ashraf Ali, *Heavenly Ornaments,* tr. M. Masroor Khan Saroha (New Delhi: Idara Ishaat-e-Diniyat, 2004).

Wadud, Amina, *Qur'an and Woman: Rereading the Sacred Text from a Woman's Perspective* (2nd edn, New York: OUP, 1999).

Werbner, Pnina, 'Veiled Interventions in Pure Space: Honour, Shame and Embodied Struggles among Muslims in Britain and France', in *Theory, Culture & Society* 24 (2) (2007), pp. 161–186.

Yeğenoğlu, Meyda, *Colonial Fantasies: Towards a Feminist Reading of Orientalism, Cambridge Cultural Social Studies* (Cambridge, UK: Cambridge University Press, 1998).

Zuhur, Sherifa, *Revealing Reveiling: Islamist Gender Ideology in Contemporary Egypt* (Albany, NY: State University of New York Press, 1992).

18

Pluralistic and Informal Welfare Regime: The Roles of Islamic Institutions in the Indonesian Welfare Regime

Siti Kusujiarti

Introduction

Research and critical analyses on social welfare policies in Indonesia is very limited. This is partly due to the misleading assumption of the virtual absence of welfare policies and programmes in Indonesia, and negative perceptions among Indonesians of universal welfare provision and the state welfare system. Contrary to general assumptions, social provision for state employees, military personnel and other formal sector employees has been in existence since Indonesian independence, and significant supports for basic education, health services and programmes to alleviate poverty are among the few significant social services spearheaded by the government. During the New Order era, the government also initiated community-based social welfare programmes designed to mobilize support for the government's domestic policies and agendas while minimizing the cost for the state. However, the government is not the only leading institution that creates and coordinates social services. Indonesia can be categorized as having an informal welfare regime, where limited formal welfare provisions exist in conjunction with multiple alternative and informal sources for survival.

The notion of a welfare regime is used here instead of a welfare system to include a more complex and broader range of policies and institutions. A welfare regime refers to a set of rules, institutions and structured interests that constrain individuals through compliance procedures (Krasner 1983: 1–3; North 1990: 200–202). It represents various institutions involved in creating welfare policies and supports, and in generating welfare outcomes and stratification effects in the society.

As suggested by Gough and Wood (2004), the Indonesian welfare system fits the characteristics of an informal welfare regime where the complex interconnection of main social institutions such as the state, market, communities and households simultaneously provides social supports and creates a distinctive mix of welfare institutions deviated from the welfare state regime commonly found in the West. In the informal welfare regime a wider range of institutions and actors are involved in modifying livelihood structures and their outcomes (Gough 2004: 30). This chapter provides analysis of how the Islamic welfare system plays its role across the institutional landscape, paying special attention to the role of the Islamic welfare system at the state and communal levels.

Even though Gough and Wood (2004) do not specifically address the roles of religious institutions, as with other faith-based institutions, Islamic-based non-governmental organizations, associations and communities have played pivotal roles in organizing and providing social services and creating community welfare in Indonesia. Using funds and resources from *zakat,*[1] *infaq,*[2] *sadaqah*[3] *and waqaf,*[4] various Islamic organizations design and implement social programmes to create welfare and empowerment for the disadvantaged groups.

This chapter suggests that after the economic crisis and the social and political reformation in 1998, the roles of Islamic welfare programmes were strengthened in Indonesia. More limited economic resources, growing Islamization of social, cultural and political spheres as well as political decentralization and regional autonomy opened up opportunities for non-state institutions, especially Islamic welfare institutions, to play greater roles in providing welfare services. The declining hegemony of the state paves the way for more pluralistic welfare institutions in Indonesia, where civil society such as that supported and created by Islamic organizations increasingly becomes an integral part of the welfare regime in Indonesia. In addition to this, in the past twenty-five years, Indonesia has witnessed an Islamic resurgence (Feener 2007; Hefner 2000) and growing pressures towards Islamizing the state and formally recognizing the Islamic welfare system as the main welfare institution within the state. Islamic welfare programmes in Indonesia stem from heterogeneous sources such as the *dakwah* (Islamic outreach or preaching) movement, the 'renewal' or 'neo-modernist' Islamic movement, and socially engaged Islam that facilitates more complex Islamic welfare programmes.

Despite some pressures to centralize the collection and distribution of funds and resources from *zakat, infaq, sadaqah and waqaf*[5] in the hand of governmental institutions, there is growing pressure to strengthen and empower more autonomous Islamic grassroot organizations so that these organizations are able to infuse their influence, resources and roles in the society more effectively. Since Islam is embedded in Indonesian culture and society, embedded Islamic organizations that weave into the fabric of civil society will provide a more effective and democratic vehicle for providing welfare support for many Indonesians.

A pluralistic rather than a centralized welfare system in which Islamic institutions play important roles is more favourable for Indonesia's diversified and multicultural societies. If strong coordination and a civil relationship among these institutions involved in the welfare regime can be developed, this system will support the development of democracy and civil society. However, political negotiations, social cohesion and cultural dialogues among various social and religious institutions need to take place. Fierce and unhealthy competition as well as overlapping programmes may hinder the benefit of various interventions in the diverse communities of Indonesia. Despite certain challenges these efforts have been initiated by some non-governmental organizations, Dompet Dhuafa Republika being one example. Health, educational, social empowerment and charity programmes funded with *zakat, infaq, sadaqah and waqaf* funds have been implemented in several regions. This chapter presents the social and political processes of the struggles and challenges for strengthening the roles of Islamic institutions within the Indonesian welfare regime.

This chapter is divided into five main sections. The first is this introduction. The second outlines the New Order government's policies on social welfare and political, economic and social reformation triggered by the economic crisis in Indonesia and the consequences of these on welfare policies. Using a theoretical concept developed by Wood (2004) on an informal security regime, the third section provides critical analysis of the Indonesian welfare regime and examines to what extent the concept of an informal security regime applies to the Indonesian context. This section also addresses the roles of an Islamic welfare system within the general context of the informal welfare regime in Indonesia. A case study based on the experience of Dompet Dhuafa Republika is presented in the fourth section, followed by concluding statements that include challenges and a prognosis for the future development of the roles of Islamic welfare programmes in Indonesia.

The New Order Government, Economic Crisis and Social Change

During the New Order era (1966–1998), Indonesia exhibited a form of productivist informal welfare regime (Gough 2004: 170). This welfare regime relied on market mechanism and economic growth to create resources and private social provision. Access to the labour market and inclusions in the wage labour were the main channels through which people maintained their livelihood. In this productivist welfare regime, creating productive citizens through economic growth was the main goal of the government. With this policy, the formal state spending on welfare provision was minimized and played a subsidiary role. Welfare and its cost were mainly perceived as individual, domestic and social responsibilities. Family and households performed significant roles as providers, savers and redistributors of resources (Gough 2004: 170). These family and household supports were especially important for many workers since the labour force involved in the agricultural sector and the informal sector could not rely on the formal welfare benefits from their employment. Most families with resources had to save and create a cushion for unfortunate circumstances, while the majority of elderly either received income from family members and/or lived with families. The roles of international institutions such as international lending agencies and multinational corporations were also notably important. Lending agencies such as the World Bank provided funding for various safety net programmes for emergencies, and international corporations provided job opportunities. Another international component was remittance from the citizens working abroad, with their wages helping to support their families and create saving (Gough 2004: 175–176).

Other ideologies and religious-based political parties and movements were considered a serious threat to Indonesian unity and the sustainability of the New Order regime. Suharto, the New Order president, created limitation and depoliticized the influence and roles of Islamic parties and organizations. Even though several Islamic organizations such as Nadhatul Ulama and Muhammadiyah remained active, their political and social programmes were significantly limited. Some of their social programmes, such as health and education, were allowed to exist but they were closely monitored and had to prescribe to the government ideology of Pancasila.[6] Suharto used Pancasila as a vehicle to unite all segments of society, irrespective of people's religious affiliations or ethnic backgrounds (Jahar 2006: 360). By 1985, with Law No. 3, the government established a rule to require political parties and social organizations to adopt Pancasila as their sole ideological basis (Abbas 2005: 56). Any failure to comply with this rule resulted in the dissolution of the party or organization by the government (Ismail 1986: 17). Within this political context, efforts by Muslim activists to instil an Islamic welfare system within the New Order government's welfare system faced considerable challenges and created only a limited impact. The extent and characteristics of accommodation of Islamic interests to implement elements of Islamic welfare during the New Order were contingent on several factors. First, they depended on the patterns of social and political relations and negotiation between Islamic interest groups and the state. Second, they were influenced by the degree of perceived threat against the regime and the extent to which the government saw the potential of Islam and Islamic groups to support its interests *vis à vis* other political power. The fact that the Muslim population is comprised of more than 85 per cent of the population may have served as a potential liability or support for the state, depending on the power negotiation and process between the two.

Three different patterns of the relationship between Islam and the New Order state can be identified.[7] The first is the 'honeymoon' phase, at the very beginning of the history of the regime (late 1966 to early 1970s), when the regime was trying to establish itself and needed the support of the Islamic groups. During this time, the regime demonstrated more inclination to negotiate and provided limited access for Islamic political interests. The second is the 'hegemonic era' (early 1970s to early 1990s), when tight control was placed upon Islamic organizations and during which the regime gained its political, social and economic hegemony. Islamic political parties were consolidated into a single party, the PPP or United Development Party, creating very limited opportunities for Islamic groups to organize overt political movements. Islamic social organizations were also required to use Pancasila as their philosophical foundation instead of Islam. The third is the 'declining era' (from the early 1990s until the economic crisis of 1997), when the New Order government started to approach and recruit certain Islamic groups as allies to gain stronger legitimacy amidst stronger opposition from the growing middle class and civil society due to rampant corruption, nepotism and the authoritarian nature of the regime. The negotiation for implementing an Islamic welfare system was influenced by these different stages of the relationship between Islamic groups and the state. The nature of the relationship affects not only the implementation of an Islamic welfare system but also the interpretation, roles and objective of collecting various Islamic welfare funds such as *zakat*, *infaq*, *sadaqah* and *waqaf*.

The main effort launched by Islamic interest groups to implement Islamic principles in the Indonesian welfare system during the tenure of the regime was the centralization of *zakat* administration within the governmental structure. One of the most important steps for this effort took place between 1967 and 1969, and these steps eventually influenced the basic structure of formal Islamic welfare organizations until 1991, when the New Order government changed its strategies. During the honeymoon era between 1967 and 1969, two religious affairs[8] ministers initiated the centralized administration of *zakat*. During this era, Islamic groups had relatively stronger bargaining positions within the regime, not only because of the fledgling stage of Suharto's administration (who came to power in 1966) but also because of the significant roles played by the Islamic faction in helping the regime to eradicate communism. On 5 July 1967, Saifudin Zuhri, the religious affairs minister in his letter number MA/095/1967 proposed a draft of *zakat* administration law to the parliament and argued that *zakat* serves as potential revenue to finance social welfare programmes. This draft was refused by the parliament and the government (Abbas 2005: 49). The government, through its minister of finance, suggested that *zakat* was a private undertaking for Muslims and the state should not deal with it (Abbas 2005: 50). This response represents the New Order government's reluctance to embrace the Islamic welfare initiative for fear that it would be used to create more pressures to initiate and implement other laws based on Islamic teaching that would bind the Muslim population. It was especially concerned that the Islamic faction would create pressure for the insertion of the statement in the Jakarta chapter requiring the Muslim population to practise Islamic principles and law.

Zuhri's successor, Ahmad Dahlan, who represented the Islamic faction, initiated a Ministry of Religious Affairs Decree (*Peraturan Menteri Agama,* PMA) No. 4 on 15 July 1968. In this decree, instead of proposing *zakat* law, he laid the legal foundation of *zakat* administration within the Ministry of Religious Affairs purview. With this decree he urged that all levels of government administrations, ranging from provincial and district to sub-district levels, establish a Zakat Administration Committee (*Badan Amil Zakat, BAZ*) as the government bodies responsible for collecting Islamic welfare funds. To strengthen this effort, on 22 October 1968, the minister augmented the previous decree with Decree No. 5, 1968, regarding the institutionalization of the House of Assets (*bait al-mal*) in all level of government bureaucracy. This house would be responsible for the distribution and utilization of the funds for various social welfare programmes (Abbas 2005: 50–51). If these two decrees were fully implemented, it would have signified the integration of Islamic welfare institutions in the Indonesian state welfare system. Along with this decree, informal Islamic groups continued to put pressure on the government to implement *zakat* law, eleven influential *ulama* urging Suharto that it was important for him as the head of state and government, and as an individual Muslim, to set an example for the rest of the nation by paying and organizing *zakat* for the improvement of social welfare for the people (Abbas 2005: 51; Abdullah 1991: 51; Jahar 2006: 365). In response to this mounting pressure, the president made a speech at the Prophet's ascension celebration (*Isra' Mi'raj*) on 26 October 1968, and urged Indonesian Muslims to fulfil their *zakat* religious obligation. He underscored the importance of the national *zakat* administration and as a 'Muslim private citizen', he would take the initiative in leading a massive national *zakat* collection and submitting an annual report on its collection and distribution (Abbas 2005: 51; Abdullah 1991: 51; Jahar 2006: 365). To demonstrate his apparent intention, he issued Presidential Instruction No. 07/PRIN/10/1968 and appointed high government officials to assist him with *zakat* administration (Jahar 2006: 365). Despite all these political negotiations and public images of government intention, formal administration and enforcement of *zakat* performed and coordinated by the central government never fully materialized. Suharto did not implement his personal initiative to lead the nationwide *zakat* administration effort until 1982, when he established the Foundation for the Dedication of Pancasila Muslims (Yayasan Amal Bakti Muslim Pancasila, YAMP). Suharto served as the chairman of YAMP. However, this foundation reasserted the regime's position on *zakat* and represented that Pancasila and not Islam was the main ideology. YAMP collected *zakat*, *infaq* and *sadaqah* mainly from Muslim civil servants, military officials and from Muslim-owned corporations (Abbas 2005: 54). This was another form of a 'voluntary involuntary' social welfare programme, with the donation automatically deducted from military and civil servants' salaries. Considering the enormous power of the regime, most people were not in a position to refuse to pay the funds. YAMP funds were mainly dedicated to building physical structures such as mosques. By July 1990 YAMP had built 400 mosques and collected 83 billion rupiahs in total (Sadjali 1990, as cited by Abbas 2006: 54). This emphasis on physical development is another example of the regime's efforts to limit the social, political and religious impact of the fund.

The different ideological positions of Ahmad Dahlan and Suharto were apparent (Abbas 2005: 51; Jahar 2006: 365). The Minister of Religious Affairs, with his decrees, represented the interests for formally implementing and integrating Islamic principles by coordinating *zakat* administration through state institutions. Suharto and the New Order government, on the other hand, perceived that the state should not be directly involved in the collection of *zakat* because it would defy its supposedly neutral position on religious matters. The regime also saw that the centralized administration of *zakat* by the state might become a stepping stone for enforcing Islamic law on the Muslim population in Indonesia and potentially create a threat to the sustainability of the regime and the unity and stability of the secular Indonesian state. The two contradictory initiatives from the Minister of Religious Affairs and the president represented political negotiations and a bargaining process between the two political camps. Suharto's agreement to serve as a *zakat* administrator in his capacity as a private, individual Muslim citizen suggested that he wanted to control and centralize *zakat* administration by his own means. By putting himself in this position, he was able to initiate, control and procure the *zakat* mechanism and funding on his own without any clear control mechanism and accountability and effectively alienated the unwanted Islamic faction and its challenges from the process. He not only controlled the mechanism, but also controlled public discourse, images, practice and interpretation of *zakat* and used these for his political interests. *Zakat* became a representation of his individual gratuity towards the Muslim population; he created a public perception that he was the primary giver of *zakat*. With this move, along with his other efforts at depoliticization, he institutionalized an interpretation that *zakat* obligation was a personal or private undertaking, not a public or state responsibility. This prevented 'politicization' (ironically he was also politicizing *zakat* by depolicizing it) of *zakat* and curtailed the efforts to integrate *zakat* within the existing state institution. Despite the temporary insistence of the minister, the Department of Religious Affairs 'postponed' its regulation on *zakat* administration by issuing the Letter of Instruction No. 1/1969 (Jahar 2006: 365). The word 'postpone' was used instead of 'cancel' to save the minister's face and prevent protest from Muslim groups; it also implied that it could be reintroduced when the political situation was more conducive. This development left *zakat* in an unclear position within the Indonesian political structure. As a consolation and compromise, the Zakat Administration Committee, or Badan Amil Zakat or BAZ, a semi-governmental organization for coordinating *zakat* collection and distribution, was established at the end of the 1960s in some provinces (Abbas 2005: 52; Jahar 2006: 365). In 1973 BAZ changed into BAZIS (Zakat, Infaq and Sadaqah Committee) to include *infaq* and *sadaqah*. Structurally BAZIS was attached to governmental bureaucracy, but it was not totally managed by government bureaucracy, involving private citizens in its management instead, and its establishment was not mandatory for every region, depending on the governor's decision and interpretation on the political process of negotiation on *zakat* issues. Jakarta's Special Province Governor, Ali Sadikin, was the first to establish BAZIS in his province. In 1968, with the governor's decision number Cb. 14/8/18/68 BAZIS, Jakarta was established (Abbas 2005: 52). Interestingly, the governor mentioned that the reason for his decision to establish BAZIS was based on The Ministry of Religious Affairs Decree No. 4, 1968 (which was postponed by this time) and the president's suggestion to support the administration of *zakat*. This position represented an attempt to reconcile the ideological differences between the minister and the president. This initiative to establish BAZ/BAZIS was followed by several other provinces. However, until 1991, BAZIS virtually existed without a clear legal foundation because of the postponement of the ministerial decree that contained the instruction of the foundation of BAZIS.

Some scholars argued that the legal basis for the establishment of BAZIS was provided in 1991 when the Minister of Religious Affairs

(No. 41, 1991) and the Minister of Home Affairs (No. 29, 1991) issued a joint decree (Surat Keputusan Bersama, SKB) on the supervision and guidance of BAZIS (Abbas 2001: 54; Alfitri 2006: 4). The decree did not mention the previous Ministry of Religious Affairs Decree Nos 4 and 6, 1968, and it actually reinforced the ambivalent position of BAZIS. Despite the stipulation in the decree that BAZIS was a 'voluntary private organization', the governor and civil servants played important roles in its organization and activities, and its executive management, which was responsible for overseeing the daily programme, mainly consisted of civil servants appointed by local government authorities (Abbas 2005: 55). This stipulation reinforced the ambiguous positions of BAZIS and the government.

By the end of the 1980s and early 1990s, with a growing Muslim middle class, there were various initiatives to establish non-governmental Islamic welfare committees or organizations (Lembaga Amil Zakat, Infaq dan Sadaqah, LAZIS). LAZIS represents community participation in managing Islamic welfare funds by establishing a community foundation or *yayasan* (Tulus 2003, as cited by Abbas 2005: 53). LAZIS is different from BAZIS in that LAZIS is managed by full-time private citizen staff. Instead of developing programmes in line with government welfare programmes, LAZIS develop their own programmes according to the needs of the communities they serve. LAZIS also differs in its collection and distribution of *zakat*. Local religious leaders usually collect *zakat* funds incidentally and informally, and these funds are used mainly for the physical construction of religious facilities. LAZIS on the other hand has more formal organizations, some of which are managed quite professionally, and the funds are also used for promoting the welfare of the community, scholarship for the children of the poor and other more constructive programmes. Interestingly, the New Order government did not disband LAZIS, but the joint decree issued in 1991 did not mention LAZIS or cover the status of LAZIS. Even though the government obviously realized the existence of LAZIS, it refused to formally recognize it and yet it did not formally oppose it either. Some observers viewed that the joint decree signified changes in the New Order's attitude towards Islam (Effendy 1993; Anwar 1994). They argued that the joint decree demonstrated that the regime was more accommodating of Islamic aspirations. However, others suggested that the joint decree was made possible in part by the success of the regime in overcoming its political and ideological challenges by enforcing Pancasila as the state's main ideology (Abbas 2005: 55). Both of the explanations might be true. By this time, the regime felt more confident, so it tolerated and acknowledged BAZIS. LAZIS created more of a threat to the regime but it probably was not considered a serious threat, so the regime tolerated it but at the same time was not formally willing to acknowledge its existence. LAZIS was mostly spearheaded by the new middle-class Muslims who increasingly had strong economic and political positions in the government. Towards the end of the New Order, the regime tried to be more 'accommodating' to some Islamic groups to bolster its political legitimacy and to avert the growing criticism of its corrupt and nepotistic practices. At the same time, the new middle-class Muslim groups initiated strategies to voice Islamic public discourse and Islamization of the society by carefully orchestrating the foundation of various social groups, including LAZIS and ICMI or the Association of Indonesian Muslim Intellectuals.

The disenfranchisement of Islamic political parties led to the emergence of a new Islamic social movement. Instead of focusing on formal political parties, many Muslim activists began to engage in socially and culturally oriented Islam. Discourse on 'actualization' or implementation of Islam in daily lives and the creation of Islam as the driving force for social equality started to gain popularity (Feener 2007: 118–181). These movements were initiated by various Muslim groups, including the new middle-class Muslim intellectuals and the 'new' *ulama*. By the 1990's, these new middle-class Muslim groups and *ulama* actively tried to infuse Islamization without covertly being political. Their activities in LAZIS comprised one of their strategies to do this, as LAZIS was perceived as a social organization, but it also carried Islamic values and enabled the dissemination of Islamic principles and teaching. This development represented a precarious and intricate relationship between Islamic groups and the New Order, and there was constant bargaining of power and positions.

A Pluralistic and Informal Welfare Regime in Indonesia

Since the end of the New Order and after the economic crisis, Indonesia has experienced tremendous institutional and social change. One of the most important changes is the implementation of a new policy on regional autonomy that became effective on 1 January 2001. Law No. 22, 1999, on 'Local Government', and Law No. 25, 1999, on 'The Fiscal Balance Between the Central Government and the Regions', outline new policies on decentralization and regional autonomy. Law No. 22, 1999, was finally replaced by Law No. 32, 2004, to adjust to the new development and address the problems inherent in the previous law. The new policies mandate the central government to devolve authority to local governments in all administrative sectors, except for security and defence, foreign policy, monetary and fiscal matters, justice and religious affairs (Syaukani *et al.* 2002). However, some exceptions apply and the degrees of autonomy vary by region; for example, Aceh has more autonomy in various matters, including religious affairs.

Along with this development, decentralization of social policy and the growing roles of non-governmental organizations (NGOs) were in order. This opened opportunities for Islamic non-governmental organizations to play more significant roles in infusing and implementing Islamic welfare programmes; however, as religious-related institutions these NGOs continue to be monitored by the central government. With the growing roles of Islamic organizations in providing welfare support and programmes, the legal basis for the implementation of Islamic welfare activities was eventually achieved in 1999, with Law No. 38/1999 on *zakat* administration (Abbas 2005: 57; Alfitri 2006: 4).[9] This law was enacted by B. J. Habibie, who replaced Suharto as president. There were several factors that made this law possible.

The downfall of the New Order regime partially contributed to the emergence of this law. Habibie, as a civilian president, did not enjoy strong support from the military, and to compensate for this he needed support from the Muslim population and its interest groups. This need was augmented by the fact that his presidency was perceived as a transitional period so that he had to win the election in 1999 to maintain his position. Fortunately, Habibie had close affiliations with several Muslim groups, including ICMI, the Association of Indonesian Muslim Intellectuals. This connection dated back to the end of the New Order government when Habibie served as the ICMI's chairperson from 1990–1998. This relationship was perceived as mutually and politically beneficial. The new Muslim middle-class intellectuals, whose number started to increase in the 1980s, pursued a different strategy from the previous Muslim political activists. They did not focus their energy on pushing towards the creation of an Islamic state and the enforcement of Muslims to implement Islamic principles. Instead many of them chose to get involved in the existing regime (they started doing this towards the end of the New Order government) and tried to insert their Islamic values and change the regime by working from within. By doing this they participated in governing the country and at the same time were also active in non-governmental organizations (NGOs) and businesses (Abbas 2005: 58). Some scholars suggested that the increasing middle-class Muslim intellectuals and their roles in various spheres indicated a Muslim resurgence that gave Muslims political bargaining power against the New Order regime (Heffner 1998; Anwar 1995) and after the 'reformation'. One of the few implications of the closer connection between the state and Islamic groups was the recognition of Islamic banking and financial systems, which paved the way for the establishment of several Shari'a Banks and Baitul Mal wat Tamwil (BMT), or Islamic cooperatives or financial institutions across Indonesia. Because of this, since 1992 Indonesia has had a dual conventional and Islamic banking system. And it is common for BAZIS and LAZIS to cooperate with the Shari'a Bank in collecting their funds.

Supporters of ICMI, along with other new middle-class Muslims, established numbers of LAZIS or the non-governmental *zakat* and other Islamic welfare funds collectors, one of the most notable being Dompet Dhuafa (DD), which will be analysed in the next section. This type of LAZIS provides new direction for other *zakat* collector institutions. This new group of activists also played strategic roles in pushing the legislation of the *zakat* law. To coordinate and create a channel for communication among LAZISs and/or BAZISs, leaders of LAZISs established the Zakat Forum (FOZ or Forum Zakat) on 19 September 1997 (Abbas 2005: 59). One of the most important steps taken by FOZ in its first year of existence (early 1997) was the resubmitting of the draft of *zakat* law previously submitted by the Minister of Religious Affairs. Members of FOZ were active in lobbying members of the House of Representatives and other members of ICMI, and they convinced these members of the urgency needed in creating a legal basis for the inclusion of Islamic welfare initiatives within the Indonesian state system. The new *zakat* law proposal was quickly supported by the Minister of Religious Affairs (who was one of the leading organizers of ICMI and Muhammadiyah, a modernist associated Muslim group) and eventually endorsed by the

House of Representatives and signed by the president one month after it was proposed (Abbas 2005: 60).

The relatively smooth process of the legislation of *zakat* law and the government's enthusiastic support of it was possibly partly because of the government's underlying political interest in regulating *zakat* and other Islamic welfare funds. With the growing number and influence of the new and more progressive *zakat* institutions, the government saw the need for regulating or to some extent exercising control over them. The new 'reform' regime under Habibie demonstrated more tolerance of these organizations, but the regime might also have perceived that regulation was required to prevent the 'uncontrollable' development of *zakat* institutions that might cost politically. This intention was apparent in the stipulation of the hierarchical nature of the semi-governmental *zakat* institutions (BAZIS) and their attachment to the government's bureaucratic institutions and personnel, which essentially did not deviate from the practice of the New Order regime. Chapter III, Article 6 of the law indicates that only the government has authority to develop BAZIS. The establishment of the central BAZIS (BAZNAS or National BAZIS) is authorized by the president; BAZIS province should be established based on the proposal of the Provincial Religious Affairs Office and endorsed by the governor. A similar procedure applies to the lower levels of BAZIS, with district head and sub-district heads as the authorized agents for endorsing BAZIS in their respective regions (Article 6 of Zakat Law). This hierarchical structure signifies that, to a certain degree, the state establishes a political vehicle for controlling the financial flow of *zakat* income and the practices of BAZIS and LAZIS. The main significant change from the New Order regulation is the recognition of LAZIS. However, the new law requires LAZIS to be registered and approved by the Department of Religious Affairs. This law stipulates that religious affairs are under the purview of the central government, not local government, despite the decentralization process. Religious affairs are perceived as a very significant factor in influencing either the unity or disintegration of the nation, therefore the central government has to maintain its power to regulate, control and monitor this institution.

The Habibie government also faced economic pressure to increase Islamic-based welfare resources because of its limited economic resources to fund its much needed social safety or welfare programmes after the economic crisis. With the majority of its population Muslims, Indonesia's potential for *zakat* collection is substantial. In a 2000 survey, it was found that the average *zakat* per person was Rp. 124.200 per year or around $12 (PIRAC 2005: 3), which is quite substantial considering that the average annual salary was less than $500 per person at the time. The former Minister of Religious Affairs, Said Agiel Munawar, estimated that *zakat* potential in Indonesia could be worth as much as $7.5 billion. This estimate is based on the Central Bureau of Statistics data that there are 40 million heads of household in Indonesia, 32 million of which are considered 'prosperous', and that 90 per cent of them are Muslims and therefore are '*zakat* liable'. The data assumes that these families earn around $1,000 to $10,000 per year per head of household. With an assumption that these households pay 2.5 per cent of their salary, the total fund collected would be $7.5 billion. However, data shows that actual total funding collected from *zakat* funds is only $400 million (PIRAC 2005: 17–18). More vigorous efforts to collect *zakat* funds and other potential Islamic funding, as well as more attractive and convincing ways of doing so, need to be employed to tap this potential. A new assertion and reinterpretation of *zakat* was introduced to enable and assert the importance of *zakat* and other Islamic-based social funds for productive purposes and for creating social welfare and justice. Part II, article 5 of the law stipulates that *zakat* as a religious institution should function to create social welfare and justice. And article 16 mentions that *zakat* collection and other Islamic welfare funds should mainly be used for 'productive' efforts. It is interesting that the word 'productive' was used several times in the law, which may indicate the sustenance of the 'productivist' welfare regime. These stipulations are further clarified by the Ministry of Religious Affairs' Decree Number 8/2001. This decree suggests that Islamic welfare funds could be utilized for social or community development and poverty alleviation programmes, and to provide basic needs for the poor. To implement this regulation, the Ministry of Religious Affairs and Ministry of Social Affairs issued a joint decree Number 293/2002 ad 40/PEGHUK/2002 concerning empowerment of the poor and the needy with *zakat* funds (Abbas 2005: 61). This decree facilitates joint efforts between BAZIS/LAZIS and the Ministry of Social Affairs to develop and implement productive social development programmes. This also signifies a formal recognition and inclusion of *zakat* and other Islamic welfare initiatives as well as Islamic welfare organizations as part of the national welfare regime. This new interpretation deviates from the common practice during the New Order government, when Islamic welfare initiative were usually disbursed for building physical facilities and had very limited social implications.

The government's economic interest was not the only impetus for the introduction of the new interpretation of the usage of Islamic welfare funding. The new Muslim middle-class intellectuals and *ulama* have similar perceptions, and they are actively pushing for the need to use Islamic welfare funds for creating more constructive social programmes rather than following a more strict religious interpretation dominated by older *ulama*. They started to implement this within their newly established LAZIS and were actively lobbying the government to insert this stipulation into the *zakat* law.

To bolster the collection of *zakat*, the government issued law Number 38/1999, stipulating that *zakat* was an item deductible from income tax. The government then passed law Number 17/2000, recognizing that *zakat* has a similar function to tax as a means of wealth distribution. Article 9 of this law states that tax can only be withdrawn from the total wealth subject to tax after it is deducted by the amount paid for *zakat*. However, the law only covers income tax, it does not include property tax or profits from corporate economic activities. Furthermore, article 4 of the law mentions that funds collected by BAZIS/LAZIS from *zakat* and other Islamic welfare funds are exempted from tax.

Despite the support and facilities provided for *zakat* administration and payment, various factions who want to see stronger Islamization of the state suggest that there are several problems affecting *zakat* regulations and practices. First, the law only stipulates the state's role as regulator and facilitator of the *zakat* system, and the state's involvement is limited; it is not heavily involved in *zakat* administration. Second, the law does not require Muslim citizens to pay *zakat*, it leaves individuals to decide whether and how much they pay, thus in effect making *zakat* a private matter. Third, the law, to some degree, serves the government's interests more than Muslim's political and social interests. The law may pave the way for the politicization of religion by state officials since BAZIS structural organizations are attached to the government's bureaucratic system. In addition to these, there are several internal problems with the implementation of the law, such as a lack of coordination and communication among various institutions that collect and disburse *zakat* and other Islamic welfare funds. This creates overlapping and competing programmes that curtail the effectiveness and impact of the Islamic welfare programmes. One of the goals of the establishment of the Zakat Forum or FOZ was to create a medium for various *zakat* organizations to communicate and coordinate their programmes to minimize overlapping and competition. Since *zakat* organizations have to attract as many *zakat* payers (*muzakki*) as possible to finance their programmes, there is stiff competition among these organizations, they have to 'market' or advertise their programmes well and, as a consequence, *zakat* and Islamic welfare programmes become 'religious market commodities' (Jahar 2006: 371). Even though this may create better programmes and make more resources available, over-zealous marketing may distort religious intention. The new methods of interpretation, usage and marketing of these Islamic welfare programmes create a new leadership in *zakat* institutions that is mainly dominated by young professional *Muslim* intellectuals. This creates some strained relations between the new leaders and older *ulama*, who tend to subscribe to the more 'traditional' way of collecting and using Islamic welfare funds. Some *zakat* institutions, however, appointed *ulama* on their advisory boards to provide guidance on religious aspects and to minimize the conflict.

One of the biggest hurdles that creates ambiguity concerning the state's involvement in *zakat* administration is the stipulation in the Indonesian constitution (article 29) that gives Indonesian citizens freedom to practise (or not) their religions. Because of this, the state (in this case, central government) tries (even though it is not always successful) to stay clear of any intervention in people's observance of religious duties. One of the reasons for the establishment of the Department of Religious Affairs is to facilitate people to be able to practise their religions. Its main role, therefore, is as regulator and facilitator. Based on this argument, in the case of *zakat* law, the state maintains minimal direct involvement in the actual operation and implementation of *zakat*. Even though the law stipulates that *zakat* is the obligation of every Muslim, the law does not stipulate any consequence for failing to fulfil this. The law mainly provides guidelines for *zakat* administration and implementation without enforcing the obligation. Limited intervention from the state creates more freedom and prevents state coercion. However, this does not fully satisfy many Muslim activists, who have tried to push for the enforcement of *zakat* by the state. From the welfare policy perspective, the law and its subsequent regulations and practices create a more pluralistic and nuanced social welfare system. This signifies that the Indonesian welfare regime formally embraces Islamic welfare programmes into the statutory social welfare policy and provisions in Indonesia, while at the same time leaving room for individuals to have freedom of choice. And the ambiguity of the state's roles in *zakat* may also create a more positive impact in sustaining informal ways of collecting *zakat* and other Islamic welfare practices that maintain the pluralistic and informal nature of the welfare regime. This prevents the monopoly of the state and middle-class elite in *zakat* application and in Islamic welfare practices, and maintains the ability of the regime to reach all members of the Indonesian population.

With the new law and regulations, as well as the continued existence of older Islamic welfare institutions, several layers of Islamic welfare institutions and practices are in existence in Indonesia. According to Wood (2004: 30) there is an institutional matrix that depicts the complexity of the informal welfare regime. Applying this concept to the Islamic welfare system in Indonesia, four layers of institutions are identified. These are state, market, community and household. They all play significant roles in initiating, collecting and disbursing Islamic welfare funds. Table 1 describes these institutions and their Islamic welfare manifestations.

TABLE 1
Institutional Matrix of Islamic Welfare Regime in Indonesia

1	State	→	(central, province, district and sub-district levels)
2	Market	→	Shari'a Banks and other Islamic financial institutions, such as Baitul Mal wat Tamwil (Islamic cooperatives and micro credit institutions).
3	Community	→	LAZIS, Islamic educational institutions, neighbourhood or local mosques
4	Families	→	Individual direct beneficiaries

All four of these main institutions are interconnected or have a high degree of either positive or negative permeability. An understanding of these institutions and their interconnections is instrumental in creating more effective Islamic welfare institutions. Many analyses (i.e. Abbas 2005; Jahar 2006) of the Islamic welfare system in Indonesia tend to focus more on formal Islamic welfare institutions such as BAZIS and LAZIS. These institutions tend to be managed more professionally and are perceived to be able to bring about social welfare and justice more significantly. However, informal Islamic institutions such as neighbourhood mosques, informal associations and families have been heavily involved in collecting and distributing Islamic welfare funds. Interestingly, the *zakat* law does not have any clear stipulation on these informal institutions. It can be argued that the law assumes that these informal institutions are part of LAZIS or non-governmental *zakat* institutions; however, the law stipulates that these non-governmental institutions have to be registered and follow the government's rules. In practice, most *zakat* collection and initiatives led by neighbourhood mosques and informal associations are not registered and do not receive similar treatments as more formal, professionally run LAZIS. This is partially because many informal *zakat* institutions only exist temporarily; they commonly and specifically collect only *zakat al fitr* during the fasting month (Ramadan) and are dissolved after that. The more personal *zakat* distribution is even more obscure, with some people giving their *zakat* or other donations directly either to their friends, neighbour or relatives. They do this based on the belief that they need to help those who are closest to them first, and the funding or resources need to stay in the local communities. There is also a suggestion that this practice ensures that the funding or resources is given to the 'deserving' and is used for positive goals because of the close monitoring of the usage of this funding. Yet this more personal connection may reinforce existing social stratification and the status quo as well as personal clientelism and dependency (Wood 2004: 33). Even though religious teaching prohibits this direct power relation between the giver and the recipient, it is very apparent that personal connection may reinforce or strengthen patron–client relationships. Despite this adverse impact, many people rely on this more informal connection within the informal welfare regime.

Research conducted by PIRAC or the Public Interests Research and Advocacy Center in 2000, focusing on eleven cities, followed by more updated research in 2004, covering ten cities in Indonesia, demonstrates that most people (66 per cent in 2000 and 64 per cent in 2004) distribute their *zakat* to a *zakat* committee in their neighbourhood, including local mosques. The second highest category is giving *zakat* directly to the recipient (28 per cent in 2000 and 20.5 per cent in 2004). Even though the numbers of those giving their *zakat* to BAZIS and LAZIS are slightly increasing, these numbers are miniscule. Four per cent gave to BAZIS in 2000 and 9 per cent in 2004, while an insignificant percentage gave their *zakat* to LAZIS in 2000, and 1.5 per cent in 2004 (PIRAC 2005: 22). These results show that there are significant challenges facing BAZIS and LAZIS to collect more *zakat* and resources to be able to more effectively create social change. One of the challenges is the limited trust among the people of the more formal *zakat* organizations. Since these more formal organizations are usually located further away and use more impersonal approaches such as media or Internet to advertise their programmes, they can only reach limited numbers of potential *zakat* payers (*muzakkis*). Most LAZIS and even BAZIS are relatively new institutions; they have not totally embedded in the communities and not many people are aware of their existence. More information through local media and channels, as well as local representatives who offer a more personal approach, is required for BAZIS and LAZIS to perform better. LAZIS or Islamic non-governmental *zakat* organizations that are more rooted in local communities are needed.

Conventional usage of the funding from *zakat* persists in various communities. According to the Islamic principles, the rightful recipients of *zakat* are the eight *asnaf* (categories) of the poor, *zakat* collectors, converts, slaves, *gharimin* (debtors), those in *fisabililah* or on the ways or cause of Allah and *ibnu sabil* (travellers). This stipulation is quite general and can be interpreted in various ways. Those who supported the *zakat* law suggest that the funds and resources need to be used in productive ways so that they can help and support these *asnafs* in the longer term. Some respondents to the PIRAC 2004 survey seem to agree with this, with 33 per cent of the 1,936 respondents agreeing that the oppressed should receive support from *zakat* funds, and 30 per cent agreeing that the fund should be used for children's protection. However, programmes to support labour advocacy, environmental improvement, women's empowerment, human rights and law enforcement do not receive as much support from the respondents (PIRAC 2005: 24). These results suggest that changing perceptions on *zakat* implementation are underway but this potential needs to be strengthened and more widespread information needs to be delivered, especially to those who live in rural and isolated areas. More accountable and demonstrable results of various existing social reform programmes initiated by BAZIS and LAZIS need to be widely publicized to convince and recruit more public support. And more social reform-oriented programmes initiated by neighbourhood or local religious institutions need to be set up so that these organizations do not provide only a short-term impact.

An innovative programme designed by Dompet Dhuafa was used to create more localized programmes and to maintain its commitment to social reform and to the professionalism of LAZIS is Village Trust Fund or Village Baitul Mal (*Baitul Mal Desa* or BMD). Decentralization creates more public spaces for this type of institution to be established in various localities. Local resources and initiatives supported by professional and experienced LAZIS may create impetus for a more embedded and localized programme closer to the target groups. A description and analysis of Dompet Dhuafa and BMD is provided in the next section.

The Dompet Dhuafa Foundation (Dompet Dhuafa or DD) and the Village Trust Fund (Baitul Maal Desa or BMD)

The name Dompet Dhuafa literally means 'purse for the poor'. This represents its main mission as addressing poverty and empowering the poor. Dompet Dhuafa (DD) has been regarded as a pioneer and one of the most successful, inclusive and professional new types of non-governmental Islamic welfare organization (LAZIS). It provides programmes and donations across religions, ethnic groups, regions and gender (Helmanita 2006: 86). Its history is embedded in the emergence of the new middle-class Muslim intellectuals and its organization (ICMI) and the newspaper considered as the mouthpiece of ICMI, *Republika*. The political changes early in the 1990s, and the 'reformation' as well as decentralization process, are among the significant elements behind the establishment and speedy development of DD. DD was established on 2 July 1993 by a group of *Republika* journalists who were concerned about poverty and social problems (Saidi *et al.* 2006: 10; Helmanita 2006: 87). It was initially and formally recognized in 1994 as Yayasan Dompet Dhuafa Republika or Dompet Dhuafa Republika Foundation when it was registered with the Department of Social Affairs as a non-profit social organization. It was not until October 2001, after the *zakat* law was in effect, that the foundation became a formal *zakat* collector institution. The initial funding was collected from the *Republika* journalists, who received 'backhanders' from particular institutions or people for publishing their news, in some cases a type of bribery aimed at preventing negative or damaging publicity (interview with DD organizers). These journalists felt that they did not deserve this money. However, this practice was common during the New Order era and it was difficult for them to decline such a gesture. They were put in a difficult position since ICMI and *Republika* were considered to have close ties with the New Order regime at the time. They could not return the money, but felt that it was not 'honestly' earned, so they decided to donate it to a good cause to alleviate their guilt and to purify it. As a result, they received public empathy, since they publicly mentioned where the money had come from. Additional funding was also collected from salary deductions among the *Republika* staff. Their salary was automatically deducted by 2.5 per cent on the basis that a professional salary is a '*zakatable*' income. With this initial funding, inspired by social actions performed by university students conducting community development programmes in Gunung Kidul, Yogyakarta, these journalists then set up a similar programme in the region. Therefore, from the very beginning, even before the legislation of the *zakat* law, DD had implemented social development programmes from *zakat* and charity funds. It is also apparent that the founders of DD come from the urban middle classes and are mostly more secular-oriented Muslims, which represents a shift of the leadership composition of Islamic welfare institutions.

After successfully focusing on its internal fundraising, the foundation then launched efforts to raise funding from the *Republika*'s readers. The *Republika* newspaper allows DD to use new methods and approaches for advertising and utilization of Islamic welfare funds. It facilitates DD by giving use of a special column to publish *zakat* advertisements and to appeal to readers about the importance of *zakat* and giving, as well as its function for poverty alleviation and empowerment. This method enables DD to reach more diverse social and economic groups (Abbas 2005: 59). DD also publishes its programme reports, audited financial reports and the profiles of beneficiaries both in *Republika* and on its website (www.dompetdhuafa.org). This step represents a more transparent and public attempt at Islamic welfare practice, which had been largely performed informally and sporadically up until then. A strategic connection with private corporations, international agencies, banking institutions (Shari'a Banks) as well as various professional seminars and meetings are among other strategies employed by DD. DD has also played strategic roles in the development of LAZIS and BAZIS, and its leaders are among the initiators of the foundation of the Zakat Forum or FOZ. In its early history, during the end of the New Order, despite its apparent connection with the New Order regime, DD's founders played intricate strategy games to sustain their mission to establish a new paradigm in Islamic welfare and its infusion into the Indonesian social and political system. They changed not only perceptions of *zakat* and Islamic welfare but also the image of a more liberal and moderate Islam concerned with social justice and equality. They strategically used the more 'accommodative' approach of the regime and its growing dependence on the Islamic faction of the regime to achieve these goals.

Based on DD's activities and its social and political development, three different phases of its development can be identified (Helmanita 2006: 87–92). The first phase is the period between 1993–1998 during the New Order era when DD was closely connected with ICMI and *Republika* and was struggling to maintain its independence and identity. The second phase is the transitional phase between 1998 and 2000. With the new *zakat* law and the demise of the New Order, DD had to initiate new strategies because of the increasing number of LAZIS that created growing competition among them. Faced with this competitive field, there was an increasing debate within DD about whether it should keep its formal attachment to *Republika* or not. Many of the organizers suggested that DD needed to be independent to allow it to develop expanded programmes more flexibly and be more competitive. Furthermore, the changing political situation meant its political attachment to *Republika* was less appealing to the public. However, the debate ended with an agreement to keep *Republika* attached to DD's name, partially because many of the original founders from *Republika* kept on their influential roles. This transitional period, therefore, was mostly filled with internal reflection and expansion of programmes. The determining stage is the independent phase from 2001 until now.

By 2001, DD's management was separated from *Republika*. With increasing pressures towards strengthening civil society and more democratic and decentralized practices, DD strategically moved towards becoming a more independent institution. One of the main changes was the application of the Multicorridor Network (MCN) system, a spider-web-like organizational structure started in March 2003 (Helmanita 2006: 91). This MCN system was designed to promote professionalism, specialization and decentralization of its system. This system was composed of four main sub-networks. The first network operated and functioned as LAZIS (non-governmental organization for collection of *zakat* and other Islamic funding). The second network was the Reform Asset Network, focusing on efforts to reform and redistribute economic assets in society. The third was the Social Asset Network, concentrating on the creation and sustenance of social assets or social capital. And the fourth was the Commercial Network, focusing on establishing various businesses and creating networks with other business institutions. This system enabled each network or division to perform its programme in a more focused, independent and decentralized fashion, which put DD's central management in supporting and coordinating roles rather than involved in its daily activities. With this system DD aimed to achieve its missions. These missions were working as an 'engine' for social empowerment, developing a network for empowering societies, developing and utilizing local community resources, and advocating an economic justice paradigm (www.dompetdhuafa.org).

The second important change during the independent phase was the utilization of a marketing-based fundraising strategy (Helmanita 2006: 92). DD continued to employ innovative strategies in its fundraising that were markedly different from conventional *zakat* collection institutions, which tend to use unsystematic and incidental approaches. In addition to implementing better planned fundraising strategies, DD developed an internal manual to create a more professional work mechanism and introduced an incentive system to increase collection of its funding. It set a target of an average 20 per cent increase of funding collected annually. To reach this goal, it implemented several methods and approached certain social groups as its main target for receiving funding. Increasing funding from international sources and from the new middle class, such as business leaders, professionals and celebrities, was among the fundraising strategies. In addition to using *Republika*, it also advertised its missions, goals, programmes and ideas on TV, approached private companies through a Social Company Donations programme, Company Pengajian Events (or Islamic Religious Gathering events) and in-house *pengajian* or more informal Islamic gatherings. It also organized seminars, presentations, and had 'Zakat Pick Up' programmes whereby DD sends its staff to personally pick up *zakat* or donations of more than Rp. 1,000,000 or around $100.

With the increasing funds collected, DD continued to expand its programmes and outreach. DD's main existing programmes involve economic and social empowerment of *dhuafa* or the poor (this includes providing free or more affordable health services), education for the *dhuafa*, and charitable activities, especially programmes for those afflicted by disaster. Alongside the decentralization and growing roles of non-governmental organizations, one of DD's main goals is increasing the autonomy of its network system and applying devolution that involves decentralization and distribution of authority (www.dompetdhuafa.org). The development of the Village Trust Fund or Baitul Mal Desa (BMD) is one of the manifestations of DD's goals to empower the poor and local communities as well as support the recovery process for those suffering as a result of natural disasters.

BMDs were established in April 2007 as part of DD's efforts to decentralize its programmes and implement its economic and social asset reform. This programme focuses on creating asset reform in rural areas, since these areas have been suffering considerably from various economic and social disadvantages. Most programmes initiated by Islamic welfare organizations aim at supporting the urban poor while neglecting the rural poor, especially those who are involved in informal small-scale trading, home industries and agricultural sectors. One of the main goals of BMDs is to create communal assets and informal welfare institutions by and for rural communities. They prioritize the collection of *zakat, infaq*, *sadaqah* and *waqaf* from local communities and create institutions to redistribute the assets to empower local disadvantaged groups by organizing them into local community groups.

Twenty-five BMD were founded, fifteen in Bantul (Yogyakarta), three in the municipality of Yogyakarta City, three in the Jember District (East Java) and four in the Banyuwangi District (East Java). Most of the BMDs are in the province of Yogyakarta because the programme is designed to support the survivors of the earthquake in Yogyakarta in 2006. The earthquake created a more widespread poverty in the rural areas, especially in the Bantul District, which saw most of the casualties and destruction. The agricultural sector and micro enterprises such as small trade and home industries are the two most important sectors in the district affected by the earthquake. Destruction of rice fields, homes, traditional markets and equipment for small-scale industries created an increasing rate of unemployment and poverty in the district. The number of poor households almost doubled after the earthquake (from 45,577 households before the earthquake to 81,398 afterwards) and more than 30 per cent of all villages in Bantul are categorized as poor villages (BMD Report, August 2007). After collecting local data in various villages, DD staff and BMD organizers identified five main common problems faced by the poor: lack of educational funding, a high unemployment rate, lack of access to health services, especially for the elderly, a lack of capital for micro enterprises, and a lack of social welfare support. Based on this finding, BMD's programmes are designed to tackle these main problems. Fellowship programmes, employment opportunities, the foundation of local healthcare centres and free or affordable access to local healthcare services, micro credit programmes and saving associations have been established within various BMDs.

A BMD pilot project was initiated to create the foundation for establishing BMDs and fostering management skills and practices to create more accountable and professional Islamic welfare institutions in rural areas. The newly established BMD also managed a start-up fund from Dompet Dhuafa to initiate the pilot project for ten months (from April 2007 to January 2008), and after this initial period each BMD would be independent and self-sustaining. For the first ten months of its foundation, DD provided initial funding, preparing organizational and physical infrastructures, identifying local leaders and personnel to run the programmes, collecting data on poverty and potential donors, and disseminating the concept of BMD and its programmes among locals. Even though all BMDs have a similar mission, each BMD has its own unique focus and programme, depending on the main problems faced by the community and the decision made by the community as to which problems should be prioritized. The main goal of the programmes is collecting Islamic welfare funding for creating productive and sustainable activities based on local potentials to improve economic conditions of the poor and to empower them to create economic and social change. To achieve this goal, BMDs did not just focus on the poor but also approached those who had resources, including local business owner and leaders, so that they were willing to support the programmes and sustain the institutions. Creating closer connections and cooperation among different components in the local communities, and using local resources to create more productive Islamic welfare programmes, were the goals of BMD.

DD provided Rp. 12 million, or around $1,200, per BMD as a start-up funding, and each BMD had to use Rp. 5 million or $500 to pay a salary to two staff members to run and initiate the BMD. These two people came from local communities. One million rupiahs or $100 was allocated for infrastructure such as renting a place and buying office supplies or other needs to run the organization, while the rest (Rp 6 million or $600) was for creating and supporting the programme. In addition to this initial funding, each BMD needed to work towards collecting more funding from local donors, including local businesses.

Several of the BMDs create employment opportunities for local unemployed by investing part of the funding in local businesses such as small stores, animal husbandry, and arts and craft. Other BMDs created a pilot project for organic farming by renting a plot of land for the landless so that they were able to communally work on the land. This group was provided with subsidized seed and organic fertilizer and other farming needs. Proceeds from the harvest were divided among the workers. These participants were not perceived as farm labourers but became active shareholders. Therefore, this programme not only provided employment opportunities for the poor, but also created group solidarity and activities that made them more visible and gave them greater dignity in society. There are three models for the development of BMDs the first is creating its own independent productive unit such as the organic farm, the second is creating working relationships with existing local small businesses. In this case, funding from DD is invested in the existing businesses so that they can hire more labour from the pool of the unemployed in the local area, with proceeds from the investment being shared among these new workers. The third model is what they call 'syndication' between two or more BMDs to create new income opportunities. This step is taken if the BMDs need more funding and resources and perceive that pooling their resources will create a more productive and meaningful programme.

In addition to these productive activities, BMDs created a saving system for the participants. These participants are required to save part of their income earned from productive activities to create insurance when they need it. To sustain their programmes, BMDs have to be active in identifying and approaching local donors (*muzakkis*) and they also have to create a strong connection with local businesses and employers to initiate and maintain working relations and possible joint efforts.

At the time of the field research, BMD were in their initial stage (five months), and it was difficult to evaluate whether this programme would persist after the subsidy from DD was depleted and when they had to independently manage the programmes after the tenth month. Some members were positive and thought that the programmes would persist (interview with BMD Amanah organizers). However, there were several challenges facing BMD. Firstly, it was a new programme so it had not been widely recognized by the members of the communities. Organizers needed to keep introducing local communities to the concept of BMDs and convincing them of the significant benefits they were bringing. Secondly, recruiting capable, trustworthy and dedicated organizers was key to the sustenance of BMD, but it is a challenge to find individuals with these characteristics who are willing and have the time to get involved in BMD. Thirdly, there was potential for the organizers to be tempted to prioritize their own interests, so a strong mechanism was needed to ensure professionalism, transparency and accountability. Most of the organizers of BMD were relatively highly educated, and the gap in educational and economic levels between BMD organizers and their participants may have created hierarchical and less democratic relations between them so that the participants could not express their concerns and interests freely. In the long run, the participants needed to have the chance to organize and empower themselves, in order to enhance their opportunities for free space and to create social equality, in which Islamic welfare programmes could help facilitate its creation. Fourthly, most BMDs relied on local funding from *zakat*, *infaq*, *sodaqah* and *waqaf*, and in poor regions this may have created problems, since there were limited local resources that could be tapped, and efforts to find alternative sources were needed. Fifthly, BMDs could be perceived as competitors for the existing local *zakat*, *infaq*, *sadaqah* and *waqaf* institutions and their leaders. Local religious leaders who had important roles in these existing institutions may have seen BMD as a challenge to their status. Good working relations and communications with these existing programmes and their leaders were important to ensure the sustainability of BMDs, and concerted efforts and collaboration with these existing organizations would be required to enhance the efforts to address social inequalities and poverty in the community. Despite these challenges, BMD was able to serve as a model for developing localized Islamic welfare programmes and to establish a more significant contribution to the creation of welfare support in poor rural areas.

Conclusion

In the past twenty-five years, Islam has increasingly influenced Indonesian society. Multiple factors such as the New Order government policies and strategies in the 1980s and 90s, 'reformasi' or reform movements followed by growing pressures for democratization, the growth of the Indonesian Muslim middle class, the rapid development of local and international NGOs, the spread of liberalization accompanying globalization, and the influence of global Islamic movements create conducive environments for the greater involvement of Islamic welfare initiatives in Indonesia. However, the integration of the Islamic welfare system has been a turbulent process. Various political negotiations and bargaining processes make the position of the Islamic welfare system within the formal Indonesian welfare regulation unclear and uncertain at times. But this uncertainty does not negate the continuous roles of Islamic welfare programmes in providing welfare support for various segments of society throughout Indonesian history. Within an informal welfare regime, the state, the market, communities and families simultaneously provide welfare support, therefore even when Islamic welfare programmes were not recognized as part of the state-initiated welfare programmes, they persisted at community and family levels. However, political and social changes after the demise of the New Order opened up opportunities for Islamic welfare programmes to be embedded in various arenas, including the state, the market, communities and families, strengthening their position within the welfare regime. This enables Islamic welfare programmes to play more pivotal roles in the Indonesian welfare regime, which will affect stratification outcome and potentially create significant social changes to form a more equal and just society.

Within the context of Indonesia's pluralistic and informal welfare regime, growing numbers of Islamic welfare programmes have influence and provide broader outreach and coverage for the people. Programmes initiated by various Islamic NGOs do not only provide more coverage but also increase the Islamization of the society. However, this carries the caveat that if these NGOs focus more on their interests to gain power rather than to serve the communities, these programmes may create division rather than equality and justice.

The creation and maintenance of an autonomous, independent and democratic civil society in which Islamic welfare programmes emerge is pivotal for the sustenance of an informal yet democratic social welfare regime. In this context, the state should maintain its neutral position towards various Islamic factions and play a stronger role in coordinating and ensuring transparency and accountability, minimizing conflicting programmes rather than being directly involved in the implementation of the programmes and collection of the Islamic welfare resources. Direct involvement of the state creates the possibility for politicization of the Islamic welfare system and hegemony of the state, which may jeopardize the mission of creating social equality and justice. Fostering 'civil Islam' (Hefner 2000) creates a more positive impact than relying on the state's coercive mechanism. The development of a civilized and self-limiting state, as well as a civil society that ensures participation, tolerance and embraces pluralism, will create a welfare regime that minimizes inequality and injustices. The fledgling democratic process and social changes in Indonesia remain precarious, and we need to further understand and observe these developments. The jury is still out on what may happen in the future.

NOTES

1 There are two types of *zakat* in Islam, *zakat al-fitr* and *zakat al-mal. Zakat al-fitr* is a flat fee imposed on each person. According to Islamic principle, it is an obligation of every Muslim, except those who are suffering dire poverty, to contribute a certain amount of staple food or pay an equivalent monetary amount in the month of Ramadan before the Ied Al-Fitr, the Muslim festive season right after the fasting month. The amount of *zakat al-fitr* is a little more than two kilograms of wheat, barley, dates or rice, or the monetary equivalent of those. The proceeds are devoted to helping feed the poor during the celebration of Ied Al-Fitr. *Zakat al-mal* is levied only on Muslims whose wealth exceeds a threshold called *nisab*. Generally speaking, a Muslim should pay this *zakat* if their wealth exceeds the equivalent value of 85 grams of gold. Before *nisab* is calculated, the basic needs of the payer as well as the financial obligation and debt due are taken into account. Even though the amount of *zakat* for each category of property, such as land and agricultural products, varies, most Islamic scholars suggest that the amount of *zakat al-mal* is 2.5 per cent of the wealth (including a fixed salary). *Zakat* is the fourth of the five basic principles in Islam. The first principle is testifying that there is no deity but Allah and that Muhammad is the messenger of Allah, the second is an obligation to perform *shalah* or compulsory prayer, the third is fasting during the month of Ramadan and the fifth is performing *hajj* for those who can afford it.

The Qur'an contains a command for Muhammad as the head of the Islamic community in Medina to collect *zakat* (chapter IX: 103). In fact, the collection and distribution of *zakat al-mal* was managed by the state during Muhammad's era and his successors (the four guided caliphs) and it continued to be a function of Muslim governments until the fall of the Ottoman Empire (Alfitri 2006: 2). Because of this, many Muslims believe that the state is responsible for managing *zakat* (especially *zakat al-mal*).

2 *Infaq* or *infak* is a general term for giving or providing charity or voluntary donation. The amount may be more than *zakat*, depending on the donor's wishes.

3 *Sadaqah* refers to voluntary giving for the poor. It usually consists of a small donation given to the destitute, beggars and the like (Prihatna 2006: 8).

4 *Waqaf* or *waqf* can be categorized as a type of *infaq*; however some *ulama* suggest that *waqaf* is an endowment that has a relatively permanent nature (Prihatna 2006: 8) and is an inalienable religious endowment in Islam, typically devoting a building or plot of land for religious or charitable purposes. *Waqaf* plays an important role in supporting the establishment of Islamic institutions such as mosques, Islamic educational institutions and hospitals.

5 When *zakat* is mentioned in this chapter, it usually implies and includes *infaq, sadaqah and waqaf.*

6 Pancasila is the official ideological foundation of the Idonesian state. The New Order government argued that all social and political institutions, including religious organizations in Indonesia, were required to adopt Pancasila as their main ideological basis. Pancasila is comprised of five principles. The first principle is belief in the one and only God; the second: just and civilized humanity; the third: the unity of Indonesia; the fourth: democracy led by wise guidance

through consultation/representation; and the fifth: social justice for all Indonesian people.

7 Abdul Azis Thaha (1996) suggested three similar trends, yet his time frames are slightly different. According to him, the first phase (1967–1982) was the antagonistic period. The second, 1982–1985, was the reciprocal criticism when the regime imposed Pancasila as the sole ideological foundation for all political and social organizations. The third phase (1985–1994) was an active accommodation phase when the state started to build Muslim-based support (as cited in Salim: 2–3 and 181).

8 Even though the Indonesian state is not formally based on religion, the Ministry of Religious Affairs was formed in 1946 as part of a negotiation between Islamic factions and other parties in the new Republic of Indonesia proclaimed in 1945. Islamic factions wanted to form an Islamized state. These factions were successfully pressured to include in the Preamble of the Constitution (also known as the 'Jakarta Charter') a statement that the state is based on Pancasila, but the first principle is read as 'Belief in one God with the obligation of the Muslim population to practice Islamic Shari'a or Islamic law.' This controversial statement requiring the practice of Islamic law was eventually deleted from the preamble and the first principle only mentions 'the belief in one God'. This deletion was perceived as necessary to reach a compromise so that the predominantly Christian eastern region of Indonesia would agree to be part of Indonesia. However, this was perceived as a betrayal for many Islamic factions, and as a consolation, the Department of Religious Affairs was formed. One of the main purposes of the formation of this ministry is to support the needs of the Islamic community. This includes overseeing Islamic courts, administering marriage, divorce and inheritance issues, administering pilgrimage matters (*hajj*) and facilitating the collection of Islamic welfare funds and channelling funds to Islamic schools, colleges and tertiary institutions.

9 The acronyms for BAZIS is changed into BAZ, Badan Amil Zakat or Zakat Collecting Board and LAZIS becomes LAZ, Lembaga Amil Zakat or Non-governmental Zakat Organization. However, the law mentions that both of these institutions collect not only *zakat,* but also *infaq* and *sadaqah*; they also collect *kafarat* or fines for violating religious law.

BIBLIOGRAPHY

Abbas, S., 'The Struggle for Recognition: Embracing the Islamic Welfare Effort in the Indonesian Welfare System', in *Studia Islamika*, Vol. 12 (1) (2005), pp. 33–72.

Abdulah, T., 'Zakat Collection and Distribution in Indonesia', in Mohammed Ariff (ed.), *The Islamic Voluntary Sector in Southeast* Asia (Singapore: Institute of Southeast Asian Studies, 1991).

Alfitri, 'The Law of Zakat Management and Non-Governmental Zakat Collectors in Indonesia', in *The International Journal of Not-for-Profit Law*, Vol. 8 (2) (January 2006). Available at <http://www.icnl.org/knowledge/ijnl/vol8iss2/art_3.htm>.

Anwar, M. S., *Pemikiran dan Aksi Islam Indonesia: Sebuah Kajian Politik tentang Cendekiawan Muslim Orde Baru* (*Thoughts and Action of Indonesian Islam: A Political Study about Muslim Intellectuals in the New Order Era*) (Jakarta: Paramadina, 1995).

BAPPENAS (National Development Planning Agency) Report (Jakarta, Indonesia: BAPPENAS, 1999).

Baznas Dompet Duafa, *Programme Pengembangan Baitul Maal Desa: Laporan Perkembangan Pelaksanaan Bulan ke: 5* (*Programme for the Development of Village Trust Fund: Implementation and Development Report for the Fifth Month*) (Yogyakarta: Tim Pelaksana Programme Pengembangan BMD (Team for the Implementation of the Development of BMD, 20 July–20 August 2007).

Dompet Dhuafa at <www.dompetdhuafa.org>.

Feener, M., *Muslim Legal Thought in Modern Indonesia* (Cambridge: Cambridge University Press, 2007).

Gough., I., 'Welfare Regimes in Development Contexts: A Global and Regional Analysis', in Ian Gough and Geof Wood (eds), *Insecurity and Welfare Regimes in Asia, Africa and Latin America* (Cambridge: Cambridge University Press, 2004), pp. 15–48.

Hefner, R. W., *Civil Islam: Muslims and Democratization in Indonesia* (Oxford: Princeton University Press, 2000).

—'A Muslim Civil Society? Indonesian Reflections on the Conditions of Its Possibility', in R. W. Heffner (ed.), *Democratic Civility: The History and Cross Cultural Possibility of a Modern Political Ideal* (New Jersey and New Brunswick: Transaction Publishers, 1998), pp. 224–256.

Helmanita, K., 'Managing Islamic Philanthropy with Modern Management: The Experiences of Dompet Dhuafa', in Chaider S. Bamualim, Cheyne Scott, Dick van der Meij and Irfan Abubakar (eds), *Islamic Philanthropy and Social Development* (Jakarta: Center for the Study of Religion and Culture (CSRC), State Islamic University, Syarif Hidayatullah, 2006).

Ismail, F., 'Pancasila as the Sole Basis for all Political Parties and for all Mass Organizations: An Account of Muslims' Responses', in *Studia Islamika*, Vol. 3 (4) (1996), pp. 1–92.

Jahar, A. S., 'The Clash of Muslims and the State: Waqf and Zakat in Post Independence Indonesia', in *Studia Islamika*, Vol. 13 (3) (2006), pp. 353–396.

Krasner, S. D. (ed.), *International Regimes* (Ithaca: Cornell University Press, 1983).
North, D., *Institutions, Institutional Changes and Economic Performance* (Cambridge: Cambridge University Press, 1990).
PIRAC (Public Interests Research and Advocacy Center), *Muslim Philanthropy: Potential and Reality of Zakat in Indonesia – Survey Results in Ten Cities* (Jakarta: Piramedia, 2005).
Saidi, Z., Fuad. M. and Abidin, H., *Social Justice Philanthropy in Indonesia* (Jakarta: Piramedia, 2006).
Wood, G., 'Informal Security Regimes: The Strengths of Relationships', in Ian Gough and Geof Wood (eds), *Insecurity and Welfare Regimes in Asia, Africa and Latin America* (Cambridge: Cambridge University Press, 2004), pp. 49–87.

19

What They Say About the Treatment of Expatriate Workers in the United Arab Emirates[1]

Kathryn Schellenberg and Mohamed Daassa

More than 25 per cent of the world's migrant[2] workers are in six countries – Bahrain, Kuwait, Oman, Qatar, Saudi Arabia, and UAE – that comprise the Arab Gulf Cooperation Council (GCC) (Mellahi and Al-Hinai 2000). In the UAE per se, expatriates are estimated to make up 85 per cent to 90 per cent of all residents and 99 per cent of all private sector workers. A former UAE Labour Minister, Dr Ali Al Ka'abi, speculated that if current trends continued, citizens would account for a mere 4 per cent of the total population by 2020 (*Khaleej Times*, 4/22/2005).

A study sponsored by British banking group HSBC found that the 'UAE offers the most luxurious lifestyle for expatriates' and is one of the best places to live (*Gulf News*, 7/25/2008). However, the 'demographic imbalance' – or sheer numbers of foreigners relative to nationals – has raised serious concerns (*Gulf News*, 12/16/2008, 2/2/2009; *Khaleej Times*, 4/16/2009). In 2005, the federal government launched a new programme to, 'promote the national identity and practices of good citizenship within the UAE's diverse and multi-cultural society' (*Gulf News*, 6/27/2008). In this regard, the International Organization for Migration (IOM) has reportedly commended the UAE as a model in the 'humane' treatment of foreign workers (see *Al Ittihad*, 5/9/2007; *Khaleej Times*, 5/9/2007) but the 'practices of good citizenship' towards expatriate workers have been called into serious question by other international voices such as scholars (Keane and McGeehan 2008; Khalaf and Alkobaisi 1999), New York-based Human Rights Watch (2006; 2007; 2009a) and foreign journalists (e.g. Hari 2009).

In a 2006 report on the treatment of construction workers, Human Rights Watch (HRW) condemned the UAE for 'feeding off' poor migrants and treating them as 'less than human'. It also accused (especially federal) government of doing little to deter systematic abuses related, among other things, to non-payment of wages and called for reforms to bring UAE practices into line with international standards. Local media coverage of the report provoked Dr Mohammad Al Mutawa, a sociologist at the UAE National University to write a strongly worded response in the English-language *Gulf News* (11/28/2006). Al Mutawa asserted that humanitarian principles of Arab and Islamic culture prevail in the UAE and ensure that workers, who come of their 'own accord', receive full contractual rights to salaries, housing, and a decent life. He also criticized *English* newspapers for unflattering press coverage and blamed foreigners who fail to respect the local culture and abuse their privilege of access to English media to distort facts, 'promote lies about labor' and 'tarnish the image of the country'. Such accusations convey the implicit claim that Arabic-language coverage is free of bias or, at least, that it portrays expatriate labour issues in a more favourable light.

Regardless of language, press freedoms were seriously curtailed by a 1980 Printing and Publishing Law that made it a crime to publish news that was detrimental to the UAE currency or economy (*Gulf News*, 5/3/2005; *Khaleej Times*, 6/16/2005). In practice, restrictions eased over the years such that Reporters Without Borders ranked the UAE 69th of 173 countries on its 2008 Worldwide Press Freedom Index – down slightly from 2007 but a big advance over a 100th place rank in 2005 (also see *Khaleej Times*, 10/17/2007). A new media law will shield journalists from threats of imprisonment for doing their jobs (*Gulf News*, 6/29/2008). Critics, however, claim that although the new law is a major step forward in some respects, it still leaves journalists and publishers vulnerable to retaliation for negative reports about the country and its leaders (*Gulf News*, 1/20/2009, 4/13/2009; Human Rights Watch 2009b; *Khaleej Times*, 1/26/2009, 4/13/2009; Reporters Without Borders 2009).

Based on such critiques, the new law does not afford the measure of autonomy needed for the press to pursue a 'fourth estate' or 'watch-dog' function as investigators or adversaries of the power structure. Looking back over years that were under even tighter constraints, we would expect to find a far more submissive press with a predilection towards self-censorship and portraying the UAE in overly-glowing terms. This seems especially plausible in the case of Arabic papers which, by definition, cater to an Arabic-fluent, largely local audience with interests that are presumed to be closely aligned with those of the state. And what Al Mutawa asserts is a purposeful attempt to tarnish the UAE's image, may reflect an effort by the English press to play a delicately balanced 'guard dog' role of serving two masters – the official power structure as well as its largely expatriate readership. As Donohue, Tichenor and Olien (1995) explain, the guard dog metaphor:

> [D]oes not regard media as equal co-actors but as primarily dependent on the dominant powers. What may seem to be a tug-of-war is, from the guard dog perspective, primarily a result of reporting and reflecting the *conflicting views* among *divided political or economic bodies*. (Pp.121–122, emphases added)

In this chapter, we ask three questions: 1) what are the claims regarding the treatment of expatriate workers in the UAE, 2) how are those claims reflected in the English-language press, and 3) how are those claims reflected in the Arabic press? With respect to questions 2 and 3, we test Al Mutawa's implied hypothesis (*Gulf News*, 11/28/2006) that English coverage portrays the country in a more negative light than Arabic coverage. Finally, while external critics such as HRW focus attention on the most vulnerable workers, we draw on the analytical framework of organization (workplace) justice theory to consider broader concerns of expatriate workers in general.

Organizational (Workplace) Justice

Workplace justice scholarship examines issues related to distributive, procedural and interactional fairness, *perceptions* of fairness, and the notion of retribution (Bies and Tripp 2001; Byrne and Cropanzano 2001; Folger and Cropanzano 1998; Parks 1997). A sense of *injustice* can result from the feeling of being wrongfully harmed and/or the failure to receive help to which one feels entitled (Parks 1997).

Distributive justice focuses on *outcomes* (i.e. rewards, sanctions) and draws heavily on *equity theory* and a rational-utilitarian view that judges outcome fairness in light of inputs. It thus equates justice with *deservingness* and addresses such issues as whether workers' pay is fair in light of their efforts and contributions. A crucial element in assessing distributive justice, is the *referent* or comparison standard that serves as the basis for making judgements (Byrne and Cropanzano 2001).

Procedural justice focuses on *processes* and *criteria* that underlie outcome decisions. Justice scholars have found that people care as much for how decisions are reached as for the outcomes per se (Byrne and Cropanzano 2001). Here, the notion of *voice* – or opportunity to put forward one's position – is of paramount importance. Also, fair procedures reflect six attributes delineated by Leventhal (in Folger and Copranzano 1998: xxiii) as: '(a) consistent, (b) bias-free, (c) accurate, (d) correctable in case of error, (e) representative of all concerned (a feature related to voice), and (f) *based on prevailing ethical standards*' (emphasis added).

Interactional justice centres on whether the parties in relationships are treated with dignity and respect. Parks (1997) theorizes that those who experience interactional harm on top of other forms of abuse are more apt to seek *retributive justice* – depending on the consensus and intensity of feeling surrounding the norms in question. While victims vary in the resources they can marshal to seek redress, Parks stresses that scores can be balanced through multiple means. Some level of opportunity for 'retributive retaliation' (i.e. revenge) is available to all, but an aggrieved party can also seek 'retributive recompense' through withholding something the offender values, or by trying to diminish the individual's 'reputation'.

The justice criterion of deferring to 'prevailing ethical standards' raises questions about which standards are presumed to prevail in a country like the UAE. Thus far, workplace justice scholarship has largely focused on the United States, and 'the cultural baggage that goes with it' (McFarlin and Sweeney 2001: 68). However, cross-cultural studies have cast doubt on Western assumptions of fairness. Hofstede (1980; 2001), for example, has found that *cultural dimensions* that vary by nationality shape how justice is perceived (also see Folger and Cropanzano 1998; Hooker 2003; McFarlin and Sweeney 2001). As Collins (2002: 151) argues, workplace justice is produced through negotiations that are framed and shaped by 'local' norms:

> . . . labor markets are social and cultural constructions, deeply embedded in *local* institutions and practices. When workers and employers struggle over the terms and conditions of labor, these power-charged negotiations are never simply market transactions. They draw on rhetorical strategies, habits, and traditions . . . familiar to, if not endorsed by, both parties . . . involve provisional agreements about what constitutes justice, what is fair distribution of rewards

> and efforts, and how parties should behave toward one another. These "moral economies" of the workplace provide the grounds on which one group makes claims on another. (emphasis added)

Collins (2002) points out that globalization can lead to moral economies where workers and employers bring vastly disparate cultural perspectives to the meaning of justice. The UAE includes workers from 200 nations. The sub-continent contributes 87 per cent of the foreign labour force, with India, followed by Pakistan as the dominant sending nations with 13 per cent of migrants coming from other regions of Asia, the Middle East, North Africa, and the West (*Gulf News*, 12/16/2008). Country of origin diversity is further increased by the cultural and religious variation within national groups, such as Indians (*Gulf News*, 3/10/2006).

Despite this diversity, we presume that the tenets of Islam define the prevailing ethical standards of fairness against which at least some practices may be measured, and the UAE has invited prominent Islamic scholars to explicitly comment on the correct treatment of workers (*Al Bayan*, 10/10/2006). The authorities stressed that work is considered sacred in Islam and that God and the Prophet Muhammad love the hand of a worker that is 'rough' from labour (also see Abu-Saad regarding Islamic work beliefs). Further, the *Hadith* of the Prophet clearly delineates several obligations of employers towards workers, including: to show respect and kindness, to declare the terms of compensation before the work begins, to pay wages in full, and on time – or, in words oft-quoted by residents within the UAE per se – before the worker's 'sweat dries from his brow' (see Al-Sheha 2001: Section 6; Siddiqi 2009).

Data and Methods

Official Government Publications and Related References

In order to understand the legal framework of employer/employee relations, we have relied on the Federal Labour Law No. 8 (UAE 1980 [1999]), secondary sources that explain the law and other official dictates related to the labour market (Ahmed and Bowden 2008; Al-Tamimi 2003; Angell 2000). New labour legislation has been piecemeal and 'forthcoming' for several years but the 1980 law, which remains in effect, is loosely modelled on the International Labour Organization (ILO) conventions regarding hours of work, workplace conditions, vacation leave, and termination. It does not, however, allow for unions or collective bargaining and does not apply to domestic servants or workers in free zones. Also, the federal law does not apply to the public sector – where working conditions contrast sharply from, and provide a referent for, the private sector. However, Dubai (2006) has a human resources law that covers that specific public sector and similar standards are presumed to apply in other emirates and in federal agencies. Finally, we have utilized research reports published by Tanmia – an agency responsible for facilitating the employment of UAE nationals.

Interviews and Informal Observations

During four visits to the UAE (16 weeks total between February 2003 and June 2004) Schellenberg conducted open-ended interviews with a convenience sample of 48 individuals (29 men; 19 women). Half of the subjects are specialists in human resources (HR) or related fields. Other interviewees included: consuls general from three nations (in Asia, Africa, and the West), business owners/managers, academics, government officials, and (a few) front-line workers in a range of positions. Most interviews were conducted in English and in Dubai; however, a few interviews were conducted in the emirates of Sharjah and Fujairah and the Jebel Ali Free Zone. The national origins of interview subjects are as follows:

National Origin	**N**
West (Australia, Canada, Europe, UK, USA)	18
Sub-continent Asia (India, Pakistan)	10
UAE National	6
Other Arab	4
South Africa	4
Other Asia and Africa	6

In order to minimize feelings of potential vulnerability due to taking part in the study, Schellenberg took hand-written notes and did not ask subjects to sign a consent document. Rather, she began each meeting by explaining the study and gave each participant a letter stating that participation was voluntary and confidential, that she/he could refuse to answer questions, and could end the interview at any time. The letter also contained the following passage:

> I do not have a formal list of questions that I want to ask but I am generally interested in learning about the kinds of employment opportunities available to UAE nationals and foreign workers. I would like to know, for example, how employees are recruited, about compensation and benefits, and the kinds of difficulties that can arise for both workers and employers. I would also like to know how disputes are resolved.

The typical interview lasted 1–2 hours. Exceptions included: a PRO (public relations officer) who invited Schellenberg to shadow her for several days; a luxury hotel worker who provided a post-interview tour of the hotel's labour camp; a Dubai business owner who invited Schellenberg to accompany her to another emirate and watch her negotiate with a potential client.

In addition to formal interviews, Schellenberg has informally observed and interacted with many persons encountered in the course of seven visits to the UAE between 2000 and 2008. For instance, she has spoken with countless taxi drivers, hotel staff, and sales clerks about living and working in the UAE, consulted with faculty members from several colleges and universities, met with UAE national students, attended a career fair and participated in a wide range of social activities. She has also made special efforts to visit areas not usually frequented by outsiders – e.g. labour camps.

Daily Newspapers and Other Local Publications

We have collectively read more than 3,000 relevant articles published from fall 2002 onwards in online editions of two major English newspapers that target an expatriate readership – the *Gulf News* and *Khaleej Times.* (Examples of newspaper articles are selectively referenced throughout this chapter and itemized in Appendix 1.) We have gleaned additional information from other regional and local English publications (e.g. *Human Assets: Middle East,* a magazine for HR specialists).

In order to compare English versus Arabic press coverage of expatriate labour issues we qualitatively coded a sample of articles published in 2006, 2007 and 2008 in two leading Arabic daily newspapers – *Al Bayan* and *Al Ittihad* – as well as the *Gulf News* and *Khaleej Times.* We describe the method of sampling and coding criteria in the hypothesis test section below.

Analyses and Findings

We present our analyses and findings in four sections. First, we delineate broad labour market issues that interview subjects identified as expatriate concerns and incorporate citations of English articles that deal with those same issues. Second, we provide an overview of official responses to these concerns, and again cite examples of press coverage. Third, we offer a brief comparative summary of how expatriate labour issues are covered in Arabic papers. And fourth, we present the findings of our test of the implied hypothesis regarding the difference in coverage between the Arabic and English media.

What They Say in English: Interview and Newspaper Accounts

Interview and newspaper accounts highlight positive as well as negative views on living and working in the UAE. On the one hand, interviewees volunteered unfeigned appreciation and admiration for the country and its citizens. For instance, they extolled the nation as an oasis of stability, peace and safety in a troubled region and for its high tolerance of the cultural and religious diversity that foreigners bring – views that are widely shared according to a survey of 2,561 households in Dubai (see *Gulf News*, 1/25/2009). Overall, expatriates also praise the UAE for living up to its self-promotion as the 'land of opportunity' for millions of (but not all) migrants. The claim is supported by a report that 650,000 Bangladeshis in the UAE send home in excess of $1billion in remittances each year (*Gulf News*, 3/29/2009). This amounts to $1,538 per worker – more than four times the $360 per capita income in Bangladesh (World Bank 2004: 136). On the other hand, interview and press accounts also deem many aspects of expatriate experience onerous and unfair.

In considering work-related issues, an important contextual feature is that most UAE nationals are employed in the public sector while the majority of expatriates are employed in the private sector. This is an important distinction because private sector expatriates are *a priori* disadvantaged when compared to the referents of public sector UAE nationals. To cite just two examples, the typical government worksite adheres to a five-day week and seven-hour day that ends at 2:30 in the afternoon, while the typical private sector workplace operates on a six-day work week and eight-hour (split-shift) days.

Another contextual consideration is that the private sector is highly stratified along ethnic and national lines and overwhelmingly male. By law, men may sponsor wives and children only if they earn at least 4K dirhams[3] (Dhs) per month (or 3KDhs + housing). This is too little for most families to survive on and most jobs pay far less; thus a high percentage of expatriates (female as well as male) must live as 'bachelors'. Recently proposed changes would more than double the minimum income needed to sponsor a family (*Gulf News*, 12/17/2009) and if adopted, the prevalence of bachelors will increase.

Compensation

Justice entails more than legal imperatives, and workplace practices that are sanctioned by law may nevertheless be seen as unfair. Expatriate attitudes regarding compensation offer a strong case in point. A standard UAE compensation package for expats includes a base salary, health insurance, annual or bi-annual air-fare to the home country and end-of-service 'gratuity'. For higher-level positions, the employer also typically covers costs for vehicles, accommodation, and children's private school education. Apart from the nature of the position, the chief factor in the level of compensation is the worker's country of origin (Al-Awad and Elhiraika 2002). With few exceptions, equally qualified employees performing the same jobs, in the same organizations, are paid different wages. Contrary to ILO urging (*Khaleej Times*, 4/27/2005), there has been little inclination to equalize pay scales.

Table 1 shows average monthly base pay (US$) for selected professional/managerial positions. In most occupations, UAE nationals are at the top, with Arabs and Westerners close behind, while Asians receive far lower earnings and other benefits. Other gradations mean that New Zealanders generally earn less than Australians; Canadians less than American or British citizens; and Arabs from poor countries far less than GCC nationals or Westerners and so on. In some specialties, the pay gaps can be stunningly wide. As a case in point, a managing director interviewed by Schellenberg related that he would expect to pay a Western engineer about $12K a month. If possible, he avoids such hires, however, because he can get a very good engineer from Pakistan for $12K to $14K a year!

Apologists for this so-called *expatriate model* argue that it is fair on the grounds that the appropriate *referent* is what workers would be paid in their own countries – if they could get jobs at all. Since low-wage earners would make even less back home, UAE pay is deemed generous (especially if currency exchange rates favour the home country). Defenders seem to assume that expatriates also rely on country-of-origin wages as their own referent and thus agree about the fairness of their pay. As evidence, they cite the great competition for UAE jobs and argue that foreigners would not come if they saw the pay as unfair. This view was succinctly summarized by Schiphorst (2004: 8):

> . . . [Asian] migrants . . . are prepared to stay for years on end given the huge difference in opportunities in the UAE and at home . . . [they] have accepted to come for a certain job, at a certain level, and [are] not inclined to seek improvement.

TABLE 1
Average Monthly UAE Salaries (US$), 2008: Selected Occupations and Employee National Origins

Job Category	Asian Expatriate	Arab Expatriate	Western Expatriate	UAE National
CEO/MD/GM – $50M+	35,613	37,550	39,700	40,500
CEO/MD/GM – $10–25M	31,813	32,025	35,400	35,100
CEO/MD/GM – $1–10M	22,425	23,500	25,725	27,000
General Manager, MNC	16,425	19,725	19,110	13,500
General Manager, Local Firm	13,763	17,675	15,625	15,000
Head of Human Resources	12,750	14,400	14,900	18,900
Head of Information Technology	12,463	15,500	15,225	16,200
Head of Sales/Marketing, MNC	12,550	13,625	14,025	11,000
Head of Sales/Marketing, Local Firm	11,900	12,495	12,688	12,000
General Manager, Hotel	8,488	10,313	11,713	13,500
Accountant	4,950	8,325	9,600	6,000
Sales Manager	5,950	10,400	10,900	9,450
Business Development Manager	10,250	14,050	15,375	14,850
Real Estate Manager	9,175	11,900	12,400	12,150
Banking, Head of Operations	10,492	13,855	14,904	10,000
Banking, Branch Manager	11,500	10,475	17,250	7,000
Banking, Treasury Manger	12,892	12,700	17,967	13,000
Banking, Retail/Personal Manager	10,492	11,300	14,617	10,000
Media, Advertising/Creative Manager	8,675	9,750	11,975	10,800
Media, PR Director	7,813	8,600	11,975	10,800
Media, Publishing	7,163	8,525	11,375	11,000
Construction Project Engineer	10,388	14,050	17,925	15,000
Executive Secretary / PA	4,081	5,475	5,863	5,700

Source: 'Annual Salary Survey 2009: An Employer's Market', *Gulf Business*, Jan. 25 – Feb. 7, 2009, pp. 41–47.

Note: Figures represent tax-exempt base salaries and do not include value of other benefits that may be provided – e.g. medical insurance, company cars, bonuses, children's education, summer travel, and housing.

Individuals Schellenberg interviewed agreed with this line of argument partially at best (also see *Gulf News*, 5/29/2006, 6/8/2006, 2/13/2007). Interviewees suggested that migrants do use home country pay as a comparison standard when making a decision to migrate; but after they arrive, their referents shift to what others make in the UAE. At that point, passport-based pay fails the tests of distributive fairness based on 'equality' (everyone is rewarded the same) as well as 'equity' (merit-based inequality). Thus, it is not surprising that HR consultants, who conduct worker surveys in a broad range of firms, reported widespread dissatisfaction over pay differentials. As Harry (2003: 35) argues, 'even those [who are] grateful for a job cannot but help be resentful of those doing the same job for more money'.

An Asian HR manager with a Master's degree argued that the system is both fair and unfair. He initially saw his own compensation package (that included a two-bedroom apartment and small Toyota sedan) as a 'dream come true' but the euphoria waned when he realized that comparably qualified Westerners got much higher pay, a villa to live in, and an SUV to drive. He then reasoned that Westerners need more to woo them to the UAE but the gap ought to narrow over time because Asians face the same costs of living as Westerners (and often send money home as well). But for him and most workers in similar situations, the gap never closes.

Another rationale for pay disparity is a perceived superior value of a Western education. A survey of legal experts in the UAE found that '. . . the highest paid lawyers *qualified* in North America, followed closely by England and Wales . . . while lawyers who *qualified* in the Indian sub-continent remain the lowest paid on average' (*Khaleej Times*, 9/27/2008, emphasis added). Global Education Management Systems (GEMS), which runs private schools, also claimed that teachers with 'UK, Australian, South African or European teaching *qualifications, irrespective of nationality*, are paid on a higher scale' (in *Gulf News*, 2/13/2007, emphasis added). According to informants who spoke to *Gulf News*, Asians who teach for GEMS make 2200Dhs a month – less than a third of the 7,500Dhs paid to Westerners.

Schellenberg's interviewees disputed claims of Western educational superiority and also argued that Western credentials do not trump Asian passports. The point was underscored by a sub-continent national with a PhD from a prestigious US university and several years of related professional experience in the West. When asked if his compensation most reflected his elite Western credentials or Asian nationality, he stated that he made slightly more than if he had received his education in Asia but nowhere near what an American would make.

Reward differentials provoke angst and passionate discussion within, but not across, national and ethnic boundaries. All the same, Asians speculated that Westerners feel minimal discomfort due to their privileged position in the reward system. Previous research suggests that being 'overpaid' may engender some guilt feelings; but, 'people tend to get less upset when an inequity is in their favor' (in Folger and Cropanzano 1998: xxii). All but one of the 'advantaged' subjects that Schellenberg interviewed – namely 20+ American, Australian, British, Canadian, European and South African managers, business owners and HR specialists (plus three UAE citizen HR specialists) – agreed that the reward system is unfair to workers from poor countries. No one argued his or her own pay was excessive, but that others were paid too little.

Housing

The cost of housing is onerous for expatriates whose compensation does not include an (adequate) accommodation allowance. Despite legal limits on how much and/or how often rents could be raised, sudden, steep hikes were common prior to the economic downturn of 2008–2009 (*Gulf News*, 7/28/2007, 8/22/2007; *Khaleej Times*, 7/24/2008, 11/3/2008). A tiny studio apartment in Dubai that rented for 16K–20K Dhs a year in 2000, rented for 30K Dhs in 2006 (*Gulf News*, 1/24/2006). To circumvent controls when rents were spiralling, some landlords invented spurious charges in order to evict and replace tenants (*Khaleej Times*, 8/22/2007; 9/9/2007). Based on an index prepared by the Real Estate Regulatory Authority, Dubai rents had started to decline by spring of 2009 but only 7 out of 67 districts had studios for less than 40K Dhs per year (*Gulf News*, 5/11/2009) – far beyond the reach of the hundreds of thousands of workers whose incomes are less than 12K Dh ($3,270) per year.

Accommodation-sharing is illegal but widespread (*Khaleej Times*, 10/28/2008). Bachelors may not live in 'family' neighbourhoods or villas, and exorbitant rents often force 10 or more men to share a squalid room, raising health concerns as well as complaints from neighbours (*Khaleej Times*, 11/11/2008). For years, the English press has reported extensively on hazardous living conditions, illegal partitioning/subletting of units, government-ordered evictions, and crackdowns against landlords who rent villas to bachelors (e.g. *Gulf News*, 7/12/2005, 2/20/2006, 2/22/2006, 8/9/2007, 8/12/2007, 6/23/2008, 2/3/2009; *Khaleej Times* 5/6/2007, 9/9/2007, 11/8/2008).

To reduce the risk of exploitation, the ILO urges that governments require employers to provide housing and meals for low-wage migrants (Bohning 1996). While not mandatory in the UAE, some employers house low-level staff in labour camps of highly variable quality. One study found that 90 per cent of Abu Dhabi facilities satisfied government criteria (*Gulf News*, 10/15/2007) but a 2006 study in Dubai found, '75% of labor camps . . . were not fit for human habitation' (*Gulf News*, 2/19/2006). New initiatives are designed to spur the development of housing that meets global standards (*Gulf News*, 6/8/2009; *Khaleej Times*, 3/21/2009). However, anecdotal reports underscore the persistence of crowded, unhealthy, unsafe accommodations (*Gulf News*, 12/17/2008; 4/23/2009; *Khaleej Times*, 4/20/2009; Hari 2009).

Career Development

Employer-sponsored career development and training is not the norm. In the words of one expert interviewee, 'the history of HR . . . has been to recruit, import, utilize, and dispose'. Another explained that, the 'whole culture is "*plug and play*;" they hire fully-developed talent and replace [them] when their knowledge becomes outdated'. At that point, workers must 'struggle to find new jobs, especially back in their home countries where skills may have moved on and pay is lower' (Johnson 2003: 41). The practice of 'using up and pushing out' expats threatens professionals and managers in addition to rank-and-file staff. HR specialists, for example, take themselves out of the mainstream by going to the Gulf where their expertise is more narrowly utilized than in other areas of the world. The onus to stay abreast of professional developments in the field falls on the individual and failure to keep up can result in career stagnation for those who stay in the region too long. Over a period of several months in 2005–2006, the concerns of workers in HR (and some related fields) were heightened by a Labour Ministry initiative to replace expatriates with UAE citizens (*Gulf News*, 2/9/2006; *Khaleej Times*, 2/9/2006). However, a new labour minister was appointed before the plan could be implemented.

As with pay, training concerns are topics of hot discussion within ethnic communities. The feeling is that after 5–7 years, professional/middle-class people get 'trapped' in the UAE. They end up professionally depreciated while the labour market back home has gone on ahead. Even if they could go back, their families get used to the UAE lifestyle and would have a hard time with the return adjustment. The risk that one could get professionally 'knocked off . . . does things to peoples' mind sets [and they] engage in all kinds of compromises to keep [their] jobs'.

Judging Performance

Drawing on Hofstede (1980), McFarlin and Sweeney (2001) claim cultures that are high in collectivism (e.g. Indian and Arab) are cool towards the equity concepts of justice that prevail in the individualist West. Individualist views of performance, for instance, underscore distinctions between workers while collectivist cultures are concerned with preserving face and harmony; to merely discuss performance with a subordinate might result in 'an unacceptable loss of face' (p. 72). The face-saving ethos is so powerful in the UAE that it is very rare for newspapers to publish the names of individuals accused or convicted of serious crimes. In a similar vein, the *Gulf News Ethics Policy* (4/1/2007) stipulates that:

> People who will be shown in an adverse light . . . must be given a meaningful opportunity to defend themselves. This means making a good-faith effort to give the subject of allegations or criticism sufficient time and information to respond substantively.

In Islamic societies, there is also the assumption that 'everyone has total integrity or they would not be good Muslims . . . [making it problematic] to question or rate someone's integrity' (Johnson 2003: 42). HR specialists reported that the threat workers feel over being evaluated creates so much tension that some companies simply rate everyone as 'excellent'. However, sham praise elicits negative reactions if so-called excellent performance is not rewarded.

Abuse and Exploitation

Based on interviews and media accounts in the foreign as well as local press, countless practices exploit workers and assault their dignity. Recruitment by deceit is rampant. Recruiters within the UAE and in workers' home countries commonly demand large bribes in exchange for (sometimes bogus) job offers and many migrants arrive overwhelmingly debt-ridden (*Gulf News*, 7/11/2008). Numerous visa scams lead to non-existent jobs, while 'bait and switch' tactics lure workers into different or lower-paying jobs than promised (*Gulf News*, 6/28/2008; *Khaleej Times* 8/20/2007, 8/11/2008) or worse (e.g. forced prostitution). Poor migrants face the greatest risk of such abuses but interviewees in skilled positions reported similar experiences. After being hired, some workers are denied their full salaries and/or benefits (*Gulf News*, 3/6/2006, 6/17/2009; *Khaleej Times*, 5/22/2005, 7/10/2005) and low-wage labourers sometimes go without pay for months on end (*Gulf News*, 3/4/2006, 11/13/2007, 12/28/2008, 1/17/2009, 4/20/2009; *Khaleej Times* 2/2/2006, 2/13/2006). Many labourers in hazardous jobs lack adequate safety protection, including those who toil in the life-threatening summer heat (*Gulf News*, 6/30/2009, 7/7/2009; *Khaleej Times*, 7/8/2009). Although illegal, employers routinely keep workers' passports as a coercive means of limiting their mobility options – such as the option to abscond and leave the country (*Gulf News*, 1/17/2006, 8/16/2007, 5/17/2009; *Khaleej Times*, 1/15/2006, 7/30/2007). Calundruccio (2005) argues that seriously maltreated migrants are victims of outright human trafficking. They include maids who are not protected by the labour law and who live under virtual house arrest, subject to sexual, physical or mental abuse (*Gulf News*, 9/19/2005, 1/19/2006) as well as thousands of labourers in the construction industry. In 2009 the US State Department took a similar position, to the 'disappointment' of UAE authorities, who have made a concerted effort to place the UAE at the forefront of nations that combat trafficking (*Gulf News*, 6/20/2009; *Khaleej Times*, 6/23/2009).

Ostensibly, Ministry of Labour inspections should safeguard workers against the most egregious abuses. However, informants claimed that when workplace inspectors come, if they come, they focus almost exclusively on workers' legal status (or otherwise) rather than how they are treated (*Khaleej Times*, 10/19/2007). Also, the Ministry has been seriously understaffed; in 2006, a mere 80 inspectors had responsibility to oversee an average of 20,000+ workers each (*Gulf News*, 1/25/2006, 1/27/2006). By 2008, the inspection staff had grown to 400 and reportedly conducted over 231,000 inspections that year (*Khaleej Times*, 4/29/2009) – a level of coverage that is still small considering the estimated 240,000 businesses that employed migrant workers in 2006 (Human Rights Watch, 2006) – the number is presumed to have grown since then.

Few Options for Redress

Prohibitions against collective bargaining, unions and strikes create a severe 'voice deficit' (Prasad, Yang and Al Hashimi 2002) and leave workers who feel unjustly treated with few legal avenues of dissent. In general, the labour market is not *free* and they do not even have the right to quit. Since 2006, the law has been liberalized to allow expats to move more easily from one employer (sponsor) to another after a contract is fulfilled, but few workers can do so before contracts are completed (Mellahi and Al-Hinai 2000). Illegal forms of protest (e.g. demonstrations) put workers at risk of punitive sanctions (*Gulf News*, 3/13/2006, 5/4/2006, 8/2/2007, 8/21/2007, 2/14/2008). Those who wish to dispute with an employer can seek intervention from their national consulate, complain to the Labour Ministry (*Khaleej Times*, 2/4/2009) or seek a ruling from an adjudicator (*Khaleej Times*, 3/3/2006), and in some cases, if a dispute involves non-payment of wages, seek help through local agencies (*Gulf News*, 11/01/2005, 2/3/2006). Still, the threat of employer retaliation (*Gulf News*, 1/29/2009) is a strong disincentive to complain. Also, efforts to obtain legal remedies have often proven costly (*Gulf News*, 1/15/2006), time-consuming and futile (*Gulf News*, 12/23/2005, 1/18/2006). According to HRW (2006: 12):

> In theory, UAE labor law provides penalties for any violation of its provisions, including non-payment of wages, but Human Rights Watch has not been able to document a single instance where an employer was sanctioned, either by prison time or financial penalties, for failing to pay its workers. Even workers who have succeeded in obtaining judgments against their employers have been unable to enforce them to recover their wages, much less succeed in seeing the employer punished with fines or imprisonment.

Laying Blame

Although expatriates are highly critical of the alleged extent of abuse, interviewees were clearly reluctant to blame all their problems on nationals. To the contrary, they cited numerous examples of locals who embody Arab and Islamic ideals of hospitality and generosity and are circumspect in fulfilling the *Hadith* on the obligations of employers towards employees. If some nationals fall short of these ideals, the same is true of foreigners. Rather than 'knights in shining armor', expatriate employers and managers, although quick to lay blame at locals' doors, often exercise 'appalling treatment' themselves. HR experts claimed that many Western managers have been 'kicking around the Gulf too long', and resort to regressive, neo-colonialist, tactics. Further, expatriate job-seekers are commonly cheated by recruiters who are fellow-nationals (*Gulf News*, 7/28/2007b) and Vora's (2007) research found that Indian employers exploit fellow Indians. Finally, many expatriates, including Westerners, are prone to try and deflect their own vulnerabilities onto others.

In short, a chronic sense of injustice and threat is experienced *and perpetrated* at all levels by members of all nationalities. One result of these conditions is a management style where, in the view of one specialist, 'the mindset is to blame, victimize, and punish'. Another HR expert summed up predominant workplace relations as 'kiss up and kick down'.

The Government Response

As shown by the selected citations above, expatriates' claims of abuse and exploitation appear to be strongly supported by English press accounts – an observation that is 'consistent' with Al Mutawa's assertion (*Gulf News*, 11/28/2006) regarding the hostile stance of foreigners towards the UAE. However, the account thus far is incomplete.

While the English press exposes government and officials to criticism over labour issues, it is also a vehicle whereby the government disseminates its position. After the 2006 Human Rights Watch report, for example, the press reported the response from the (then) Labour Minister, Dr Ali Al Ka'abi. He *admitted* there were problems but also insisted, 'we are addressing any abuses within the framework of the supremacy of law and respect of human rights' (as quoted in *Gulf News*, 3/31/2006). And,

> We are not saying that infractions do not exist. There surely are some and we deal with them . . . . But to forget the positives and concentrate on infractions while ignoring the efforts made to fix them is unjust and arbitrary. (as quoted in *Khaleej Times*, 3/31/2006)

Media accounts prior to the HRW (2006) report highlighted labour abuse as a point of local and federal government attention. The Labour Ministry had issued stern warnings that it would accept no excuses for late salary payments and threatened to 'name, shame' and otherwise penalize recalcitrant employers (*Gulf News*, 10/5/2005, 2/13/2006; *Khaleej Times*, 11/17/2005). Officials also presented proposals to stem the manipulation of job contracts (*Gulf News*, 9/6/2004) and develop labour camps that meet global housing standards (*Gulf News*, 7/20/2005, 9/14/2005; *Khaleej Times*, 11/17/2005). In 2005, Dr Al Ka'abi issued a directive that required employers to give outside workers a midday break during the months of peak summer heat (*Gulf News*, 6/7/2005). Despite reports of non-compliance, the rule has been credited with dramatic declines in cases of sun-stroke and heat exhaustion (*Gulf News*, 6/29/2008; *Khaleej Times*, 7/1/2009). Between the 2006 and 2009 HRW reports, English papers further highlighted initiatives designed to improve wage payments, living standards, working conditions, and other human rights protections (*Gulf News*, 3/26/2007, 10/7/2007, 10/21/2008b, 3/09/2009; *Khaleej Times*, 10/22/2008). In 2007, a general amnesty (the third) allowed 'illegal' foreigners to either regularize their status or exit the country without penalty (*Gulf News*, 6/21/2007). For 2008, the Ministry of Labour reported settling 90 per cent of the '32,300 complaints from 46,800 workers' that year and referred 6,500 workers to the court (*Khaleej Times*, 4/15/2009). To counteract the threat of employer retaliation, the Ministry launched a hotline in 2009 that lets workers report complaints anonymously (*Gulf News*, 6/20/2009; *Khaleej Times*, 4/30/2009).

Officials have also called on labour-exporting nations to improve protections; for example by raising migrants' awareness of UAE laws and culture before they enter the country – and to reduce exploitation in recruiting. 'The protection of workers must start from the country of origin as those workers should not arrive in the UAE saddled with debts as a result of funds and commissions they paid to recruitment agencies' (in *Gulf News*, 3/9/2009).

As far back as 2002, officials even showed signs of softening categorical opposition to labour organizations (*Gulf News*, 12/2/2002). Following the 2006 HRW report, the labour minister announced 'plans' to present a draft amendment that would legalize peaceful assembly and allow workers to form trade unions (*Gulf News*, 3/31/2006; *Khaleej*

Times, 3/31/2006). The next year, the government published a comprehensive new draft labour law online and invited public comment. HRW (2007) quickly asserted that the law fell short because it continued to omit protection of domestic workers and still failed to give workers the right to form unions, protest and strike (*Gulf News*, 3/25/2007). In 2008, the Labour Ministry issued a new report 'highlighting respect for worker rights' which acknowledged that the UAE needs to do 'much more' to protect workers' rights and welcomed 'reasoned and rational . . . criticism as constructive and helpful' (in *Gulf News*, 4/26/2008). On the other hand, the report stressed challenges in dealing with rapid growth and a huge diverse expatriate labour force. It also cited the UAE's membership in international labour organizations as evidence of its commitment to protect the rights of workers while preserving national identity. Finally, it expressed confidence that revisions to the new labour law would meet with international standards and make the UAE a 'model for all countries, in the GCC region and beyond'.

In the ensuing months, English papers have continued to report on labour problems highlighted by local events and by foreign critics. As well, they have duly reported the official responses detailing the numerous measures taken to tackle those problems and decry critics for alleged failure to acknowledge the progress the country has made. On HRW's website, the online overview of its most recent (2009) UAE report notes: 'This 80-page report found that . . . the UAE government has moved to improve housing conditions and ensure the timely payment of wages in recent years [but] many labor abuses remain commonplace.'

What They Say in Arabic: Coverage of Expatriate Issues and Concerns

The Arabic newspapers under consideration shed light on expatriate issues that is highly 'consistent' with that of English newspapers. They give major coverage to preserving national identity (*Al Ittihad*, 11/7/2008) and challenges posed by the 'demographic imbalance' (*Al Bayan*, 12/9/2007, 23/5/2008; *Al Ittihad*, 4/1/2007, 10/9/2007, 12/9/2007). At the same time, there is broad recognition that the country needs a stable, expatriate workforce to keep the economy running. Documented workers should not be relegated to second-class status in terms of their labour rights because inadequate protection opens doors to exploitive practices that inevitably spill over and hurt all of the country (*Al Ittihad*, 9/23/2008). Moreover, the press promotes the message that the UAE is a welcoming place to live and extends full social and religious freedoms to all (*Al Bayan*, 4/24/2006; *Al Ittihad*, 5/18/2008, 9/22/2008).

Yet, exploitation and ill-treatment of foreigners is acknowledged. While illegal migrants are criticized (*Al Bayan*, 4/23/2006; *Al Ittihad* 1/17/2008, 7/2/2008), coverage is highly supportive of victims of human trafficking and places great emphasis on the UAE's determination to play a major international role in its eradication (*Al Bayan*, 5/20/2008; *Al Ittihad*, 1/14/2008, 2/25/2008, 4/11/2008, 12/18/2008). It is similarly sympathetic to desperate, poor, migrants who are cheated and duped by recruiting scams and UAE employers who exploit their vulnerability.

As in the English press, Arabic newspapers cover incidents where workers collectively 'gather' at consulates or government agencies to bring attention to grievances such as the non-payment of wages (*Al Bayan*, 1/31/2006, 3/13/2006; *Al Ittihad*, 12/16/2008). However, English papers often relate that workers 'march' to their destinations and use the terms 'demonstration' and 'protest' (as a noun and a verb) in describing such incidents. In Arabic reports, workers are never described as 'marchers' and accounts refrain from using the term *muthahara*, which translates most closely to the strident and defiant connotation associated with protest. Instead, they use the expression *tajammu*, which conveys a more muted image of gathering.

Parallel to the English press, a spate of articles appeared in response to the HRW (2006) report. While admitting that abuses are committed by UAE employers, accounts stress that many abuses are committed by expatriates against other expatriates (*Al Bayan*, 21/6/2007; *Al Ittihad*, 11/4/2008). Also, the Director General of the International Migration Organization was reported as criticizing 'loopholes' in the HRW report and defending the UAE. He offered the opinion that 'expatriate workers in the UAE are treated in a civilized and excellent manner [and where there are abuses] the UAE has tackled these in a realistic and humane way' (translated from *Al Ittihad*, 5/9/2007).

In this respect, a great number of articles portray government agencies and officials in a very favourable light. The Labour Ministry is frequently cast as a vigilant overseer and champion of workers' rights and interests; one that takes swift remedial action when any mistreatment of workers come to its attention. For example, it has issued many stern warnings to employers to not hire illegal workers, pay all monies due to employees, ensure safe working conditions, and provide decent accommodation (*Al Bayan,* 1/31/2006; *Al Ittihad*, 12/16/2008). And, it has shut down and/or sued businesses that defy its orders (*Al Ittihad*, 7/2/2008).

Our final observation here is that while the Arabic papers devote considerable space to addressing expatriate concerns, the vast majority of articles we surveyed appear to exclusively reflect an 'official' perspective on the issues in question. They rarely express expatriates' views – either as direct quotes or via reporters' paraphrased summations of interviews. In the section that follows, we systematically examine our sample of Arabic and English newspapers in this regard.

Hypothesis Test: Content Analysis of Sampled Newspaper Articles

In constructing our sample, we used a random start to select one full week from January 2006 and then selected every subsequent sixth week through December 2008 (26 weeks total). For each week, we selected articles that appeared in the online editions of *Al Bayan*, *Al Ittihad*, *Gulf News* and *Khaleej Times* from Sunday through Monday inclusive and that dealt with topics listed below. This sampling method was designed to yield a manageable data set that would nevertheless capture the most salient issues that arose over the three-year time frame. The focus in this analysis is on the five following topics/issues:

- Recruitment/hiring practices – e.g. exacting bribes for job offers; misrepresentation of job description or pay, fake job offers, etc.
- Compensation – e.g. complaints regarding low pay, lack of benefits, non-payment of wages, etc.
- Working conditions – e.g. hours, hazards (including heat), injuries, deaths, etc.
- Living conditions – e.g. cost/availability of food, cost of housing (and rent controls), quality of housing (crowding, sanitation), evictions, utility cutoffs, other harassment from officials, landlords, rental agents, etc.
- Legal status – e.g. issues related to visas (illegal entry, overstay), labour permits, representation of educational credentials, amnesty of 2007, etc.

It was relatively easy to identify target articles in the *Gulf News*, *Al Bayan* and *Al Ittihad* because the papers are organized by topics such as 'employment'. This is not the case for the *Khaleej Times* and we suspect that we missed some articles that we ought to have included – especially for 2007 where the number of articles is considerably lower than for other years. We were not able, however, to search the paper for past issues in order to locate missing articles.

In addition to coding[4] articles on the basis of the topic(s) addressed, we coded whether coverage gave 'voice' to workers, officials or 'other' parties (e.g. HRW or a foreign consulate). Voice could take the form of direct quotes or a *reporter's* first-hand summation of accounts from the sources involved. Absent a direct quote, a summary statement such as, 'The workers told *Gulf News* they were protesting at the Labor Ministry because their salaries are too low', would be attributed as giving voice to the workers themselves. However, an indirect or second-hand statement such as, 'The Ministry representative told *Khaleej Times* that the workers allege their salaries are too low', would be coded as representing an 'official' voice. Though the content of the statements is essentially the same, the different codes reflect their differential (workers vs. Ministry official) sources. We also coded each article on whether expat workers were (implicitly or explicitly) portrayed as victims, wrongdoers, or beneficiaries. With respect to the last point, we note that a few 'beneficial' codes reflect outcomes that are anticipated but which may or may not be realized. For instance, a 'beneficial' code was assigned to a *Gulf News* (7/28/2007) report that in light of proposed new regulations, 'unscrupulous agents swindling people . . . can be a thing of the past *in a couple of years*' (emphasis added).

On all three variables it was possible for a single article to be coded in more than one category. For example, an article might deal with the non-payment of wages (compensation) and workers' being forced to share a squalid room due to their inability to pay rent (living conditions), give direct voice to both workers and officials, and portray the workers as victims (of employer negligence) and beneficiaries (of mediation that led to a satisfactory resolution). Besides articles that offered multiple portrayals of expatriates, a few articles did not portray any particular image of expatriate workers. For both reasons, the summary values reported in Table 2 do not always total to 100 per cent.

TABLE 2
Coverage of Selected Expatriate Worker Concerns in Articles Sampled from English and Arabic Newspapers in the United Arab Emirates: 2006–2008

Selected Topics/Issues

	Recruitment		Compensation		Working Conditions		Living Conditions		Legal Status	
	English	**Arabic**	**English**	**Arabic**	**English**	**Arabic**	**English**	**Arabic**	**English**	**Arabic**
Voice granted to										
Workers	37.5%	8.3%	45.1%	10.8%	33.3%	0.0%	57.7%	0.0%	52.6%	1.1%
Officials	43.8%	83.3%	47.1%	97.3%	73.8%	95.0%	42.3%	93.4%	71.0%	94.7%
Other	37.5%	12.5%	9.8%	2.7%	7.1%	1.7%	6.4%	0.0%	10.5%	3.2%
Portrayal of expats										
Victims	93.8%	50.0%	83.4%	89.2%	66.7%	55.0%	91.0%	54.5%	42.1%	9.6%
Wrongdoers	6.3%	25.0%	15.7%	0.0%	45.2%	3.3%	12.8%	27.3%	39.5%	70.0%
Beneficiaries	6.3%	41.7%	25.5%	35.1%	45.2%	46.7%	21.8%	51.5%	39.5%	19.1%
Articles (N)	16	24	51	37	42	60	78	33	38	94

Source: English newspapers (*Gulf News* and *Khaleej Times*); Arabic newspapers (*Al Bayan* and *Al Ittihad*).

Table 2 reveals two broad findings. First, there is a wide difference between who is given 'voice' in the Arabic versus English press accounts of expatriate concerns. From 83 per cent to 97 per cent of Arabic articles gave voice to officials but directly represented workers' voices in 11 per cent of articles at best. With the exception of living conditions, English reports gave primacy to official voices as well. When comparing the two languages, however, English accounts gave voice to officials far less frequently than Arabic accounts (42 per cent versus 74 per cent of articles) and to workers far more often (68 per cent compared to 37 per cent of articles).

Besides the propensity to defer to 'official' perspectives, a higher percentage of Arabic than English accounts cast expats as 'beneficiaries' in labour-related issues. This could suggest that the Arabic press is dismissive of expatriate concerns but, with the exception of legal status, workers are also often portrayed as *victims* more often than as beneficiaries or wrongdoers. For recruitment and living conditions, the English values

(94 per cent and 91 per cent) are dramatically higher than the Arabic values (50 per cent and 55 per cent) but similar for working conditions (English – 67 per cent; Arabic – 55 per cent). In the case of compensation, the Arabic value (89 per cent) *exceeds* the English (83 per cent) value. What these findings suggest is that while official perspectives may focus a more positive light on official efforts to address expatriates' problems, they cannot do so without simultaneously giving credence to expatriate claims of victimization.

Discussion

Whatever national, religious and cultural sentiments divide expatriates, they converge on the view that the private sector workplace of the UAE is rife with injustice. Westerners and non-Westerners, Muslims and non-Muslims, Arabs and non-Arabs alike subscribe to an equity view of *distributive justice* and that unequal compensation for equal work fails the equity test of outcomes based on deservingness. The reliance on 'country of origin' wages as the referent for pay standards is viewed as invalid and therefore violates the sense of *procedural justice.* Also, the use of this referent fails to satisfy the procedural fairness attributes of being consistent, bias-free or representative of all concerned – especially in light of expatriates' lack of voice *vis-à-vis* employers. And, though employers who recruit by deceit or fail to pay wages in full or on time may be in the minority, these practices betray the prevailing ethical standards dictated by the tenets of Islam – the religion of many, if not most, expatriates as well as UAE citizens – a sentiment frequently echoed in both the Arabic and English press. Finally, the violation of *interactional justice* is strongly implied by descriptions of workplace relations based on a blame orientation and 'kissing up and kicking down'. In all these forms of injustice, the harm is disproportionately inflicted on migrants who are poor and thus least likely to be in positions of power.

Human Rights Watch argued that 'beyond the press . . . there are no private actors to fill the void of absent government protection and union championing of migrant workers' rights' (2006: 24). While the findings we have presented here are open to multiple interpretations, the variance in English and Arabic accounts of labour market issues suggests a marked divide in the degree to which newspapers overtly embrace this role. Whereas some might see evidence of a deliberate attempt to tarnish the image of the UAE, an alternative explanation is that the English press serves a 'guard dog' role and strives to offer a voice for migrants despite giving deference to official views. Also, while the Arabic press gives almost exclusive primacy to official accounts, they do so in a way that brings workers' grievances and the 'tarnish' of victim status to light.

Given the exploratory nature of this study, our findings are obviously preliminary and raise many questions that merit investigation in future research. To cite just a few, it would be valuable to learn whether the general patterns we have identified extend to other newspapers, magazines, television, radio, and websites and how coverage has changed across time. Also, variations in how prominently stories are displayed and accompanying visuals, etc., may have implications for how issues are perceived. Finally, it would be most important to learn how expatriate workers' themselves evaluate the accuracy and efficacy of how well the media represents their voices and whether the promises of justice extended by the government, and others, are fulfilled.

NOTES

1 Acknowledgements: Primary data collection for this study was funded through three Research Initiative Partnership Grants awarded to the first author through the Office of Research, University of Michigan-Flint. We thank the UM-Flint Research and Creative Active Committee for its support and the many interview subjects who shared their time and insights regarding the UAE labour market.
Direct correspondence to: Kathryn Schellenberg, University of Michigan-Flint, 303 E. Kearsley St (522 FH), Flint, MI 48502-1950 (email: kathsch@umflint.edu).

2 The UAE disputes the use of the term 'migrant' to denote expatriate workers in the country. Citing international law, however, Human Rights Watch (2006: 20) defines a migrant worker as any 'person who is engaged in remunerated activity in a State of which he or she is not a national'.

3 The UAE currency is the Dirham [Dh]. Its value is pegged to the US dollar at a constant exchange rate: $1.00 = 3.67Dhs.

4 English articles were compiled and coded by Kathryn Schellenberg; Arabic articles were compiled and coded (and where noted, translated) by Mohamed Daassa.

BIBLIOGRAPHY

Abu-Saad, I, 'Individualism and Islamic Work Beliefs', *Journal of Cross-Cultural Psychology* (2), 1998, pp. 377–383.

Ahmed, B. and Bowden, J., *Doing Business in the United Arab Emirates* (Dubai: Afridi & Angell, 2008).

Al-Awad, M. and Elhiraika, A. B., 'Skills, Gender, Nationality and Income Inequality in the United Arab Emirates, *Journal of Social Affairs* (19), 2002, pp. 37–51.

Al-Sheha, A. A., *Misconceptions on Human Rights in Islam* (Riyadh: Islamic Propagation Office, 2001) [translated from Arabic into English by Dr M. S. Dabas] online: retrieved 3/2/2006 from: http:www.muslimconverts.com/e-books/rights/rights/_aword.htm.

Al Tamimi, E., *Setting Up in Dubai: Business Investor's Guide* (Dubai: Cross Border Legal Publishing, 2003).

Angell, N. B., 'An Overview of Legal Structures in GCC Countries: Issues of Risk and Strength', paper delivered at the Gulf Oil and Gas Conference, Houston, TX, 3 April 2000, Dubai: Afridi & Angell, http://www.afridi-angell.com/publications/over_leg.pdf.

Bies, R. J. and Tripp, T., 'A Passion for Justice: The Rationality and Morality of Revenge, in Russell Cropanzano (ed.), *Justice in the Workplace: From Theory to Practice* (Mahwah, NJ: Lawrence Erlbaum, 2001), pp. 197–208.

Bohning, W. R., *Employing Foreign Workers* (Geneva: International Labour Office, 1996).

Byrne, Z. S. and Cropanzano, R., 'The History of Organizational Justice: The Founders Speak', in Russell Cropanzano (ed.), *Justice in the Workplace: From Theory to Practice* (Mahwah, NJ: Lawrence Erlbaum, 2001), pp. 3–26.

Calandruccio, G, 'A Review of Recent Research on Human Trafficking in the Middle East', *International Migration* 43 (1/2), 2005, pp. 267–299.

Collins, J. L., 'Deterritorialization and Workplace Culture', *American Ethnologist* 29, 2002, pp. 51–171.

Donohue, G. A., Tichenor, P. J. and Olien, C. N., 'A Guard Dog Perspective on the Role of Media', *Journal of Communication* 45, 1995, pp. 115–132.

Dubai, *Dubai Government Human Resources Management Law*, 2006 online: retrieved 11/14/2008 from: http://www.lexadin.nl/wlg/legis/nofr/oeur/lxweuae.htm.

Folger, R. and Cropanzano, R., *Organizational Justice and Human Resources Management* (Thousand Oaks, CA: Sage, 1998).

Hari, J., 'The Dark Side of Dubai', *The Independent* (London), online: retrieved 4/7/2009 from: http://www.independent.co.uk.

Harry, W., 'Localisation: Developing Host Country Nationals to Replace Expatriates – the GCC Experience', *Human Assets: Middle East* 2, 2003, pp. 24–27.

Hofstede, G., *Culture's Consequences: International Differences in Work-related Attitudes* (Thousand Oaks, CA: Sage, 1980).

—*Culture's Consequences: Comparing Values, Behaviors, Institutions, and Organizations across Cultures* (Thousand Oaks, CA: Sage, 2nd edn, 2001).

Hooker, J., *Working across Cultures* (Stanford, CA: University of California Press, 2003).

Human Rights Watch, *Building Towers, Cheating Workers: Exploitation of Migrant Construction Workers in the United Arab Emirates*, online: retrieved 2006 from: http://www.hrw.org/en/reports/2006/11/11/building-towers-cheating-workers.

—*The UAE's Draft Labor Law: Human Rights Watch's Comments and Recommendations*, online: retrieved 2007 from: http://www.hrw.org/en/reports/2007/03/25/uaes-draft-labor-law-human-rights-watch-s-comments-and-recommendations.

—*"The Island of Happiness": Exploitation of Migrant Workers on Saadiyat Island, Abu Dhabi*, online: retrieved 2009a from: http://www.hrw.org/en/news/2009/05/18/uae-exploited-workers-building-island-happiness.

—*Just the Good News, Please: New UAE Media Law Continues to Stifle Press*, online: retrieved 2009b from: http://www.hrw.org/en/news/2009/04/just-good-news-please.

Johnson, R, 'Easing out the Expats', *Human Assets: Middle East* 3, 2003, pp. 40–42.

Keane, D. and McGeehan, N., 'Enforcing Migrant Workers' Rights in the United Arab Emirates, *International Journal of Minority and Group Rights* 15, 2008, pp. 81–115.

Khalaf, S. and Alkobaisi, S., 'Migrants' Strategies of Coping and Patterns of Accommodation in the Oil-rich Gulf Societies: Evidence from the UAE', *British Journal of Middle Eastern Studies* 26, 1999, pp. 271–298.

McFarlin, D. B. and Sweeney, P. D., 'Cross-cultural Applications of Organizational Justice', in Russell Cropanzano (ed.), *Justice in the Workplace: From Theory to Practice* (Mahwah, NJ: Lawrence Erlbaum, 2001), pp. 67–95.

Mellahi, K. and Al-Hinai, S. M., 'Local Workers in Gulf Cooperation Countries: Assets or Liabilities?', *Middle Eastern Studies* 36, 2000, pp. 177–190.

Parks, J. M., 'The Fourth Arm of Justice: The Art and Science of Revenge', in R. J. Lewicki, B. H. Sheppard and M. H. Bazerman (eds), *Research in Negotiation in Organizations* (Greenwich, CT: JAI Press, 1997).

Prasad, S., Yang, G. and Al Hashimi, S., *Labour Relations in the United Arab Emirates: Recommendations for Further Development* (Policy Research Paper No. 8) (Dubai: National Human Resources and Employment Authority (Tanmia), Centre for Labour Market Research and Information, 2002).

Reporters Without Borders, *Worldwide Press Freedom Index 2005*, online: retrieved 10/17/2007 from: http://www.rsf.org.

—*Worldwide Press Freedom Index 2007*, online: retrieved 10/17/2007 from: http://www.rsf.org.

—*Worldwide Press Freedom Index 2008*, online: retrieved 7/15/2009 from: http://www.rsf.org.

—*World Report 2009*, online: retrieved 7/15/2009 from: http://www.rsf.org/en-rapport150-United_Arab_Emirates.html.

Saddiqi, M. H., 'Rights of Workers in Islam', 8/20/2006 [the response to a question posed on: Islamonline.net – Ask the Scholar] online: retrieved 7/11/2009 from: http://www.islamonline.net/servlet/Satellite?pagename=IslamOnline-English-Ask_Scholar/FatwaE/FatwaE&cid=1155193577227.

Schiphorst, F., *Voices from the Shop Floor: The Impact of the Multi-cultural Work Environment of UAE National Employees*, Paper No. 11 (Dubai: National Human Resources and Employment Authority (Tanmia), Centre for Labour Market Research and Information, 2004).

United Arab Emirates, *Federal Law No. 8: Regulation of Labour Relations and Its Amendments and Order Issued in Implementation Thereof* (1980; 7th edn, 1999).

Vora, N., 'Exceptions and the Exceptional: Transnational Indians and Globalization in Dubai', paper presented at the Annual Meetings of the Global Studies Association – North America, University of California-Irvine. Saturday 19 May 2007.

World Bank, *Doing Business in 2004: Understanding Regulation* (Washington, DC: World Bank and Oxford University Press, 2004).

APPENDIX 1

Cited References from English Newspapers

Gulf News

12/02/2002	Bigger role for workers under study
09/06/2004	All employment visas to include profession and salary details
05/03/2005	Self-censorship virus plagues media
05/03/2005	A free press is about the search for truth
06/07/2005	Workers 'must be given midday break'
07/12/2005	Bachelors hit hard by shortage of accommodation
09/14/2005	Dubai to build low-cost housing for expatriates
07/20/2005	Thousands 'will benefit from low-cost houses'
09/19/2005	Labour ministry powerless to prevent abuse of maids
10/05/2005	Companies late in paying wages to be named and shamed
11/01/2005	Hotline to deal with non-payment of salaries receives 10 calls on first day
12/23/2005	No salary despite three police complaints
01/15/2006	1500 workers march for unpaid salaries
01/18/2006a	Protesting workers allege they were beaten again
01/18/2006b	Labourers hold up work demanding unpaid wages
01/19/2006	Change in rule for sponsorship transfer of maids hailed
01/19/2006	Illegal trade in labour permits exposes workers to exploitation
01/24/2006	Tenants brace for big rent hikes
01/20/2006	Inspectors struggle to cope with workload
01/25/2006	More inspectors to monitor workers' rights
02/03/2006	Police help workers get Dh201m in unpaid wages
02/09/2006	Nationals to take over another job sector
02/13/2006	Companies delaying salaries will be penalized heavily
02/19/2006	Workers housed in villas deemed a security risk
02/20/2006	Civic bodies to scour more areas for workers in villas
02/22/2006	Labourers face eviction from residential areas
03/04/2006	Workers live in abject poverty as they fight for their rights
03/06/2006	Many employers 'illegally penalizing workers'
03/10/2006	Indian expats 'are equal to 29 nationalities'
03/13/2006	Cleaners protest after not being paid for 4 months
03/31/2006	New labour law may be 'enacted by December'
06/08/2006	Dubai Municipality to study income discrimination
11/28/2006	Malicious information tarnishes UAE's image
02/13/2007	Asian teachers say they are underpaid
03/26/2007	Al Ka'abi: UAE protects workers rights
03/26/2007	Watchdog report 'does not reflect ground realities'

05/09/2007	Abdullah holds talks with migration organization chief
06/21/2007	Hundreds apply for outpasses
07/28/2007	Toiling in the heat, serving with a smile
07/28/2007	Landlords find way to beat 7% annual rent cap
07/28/2007	Efforts on to curb agents swindling workers for visa
08/02/2007	Workers deported for demanding salary hike
08/09/2007	Realtors renting villas to bachelors to lose licence
08/12/2007	Drive against illegal housing intensifies
08/16/2007	Companies persuaded to return passports
08/22/2007	Dubai moves to calm soaring rental prices
10/07/2007	No more salaries in cash for workers from January
10/15/2007	90% of accommodations for labourers meet criteria
11/13/2007	Human rights watchdog seeks collective worker representation
11/13/2007	Firm 'has not paid wages for three months'
04/26/2008	UAE releases labour report highlighting respect for worker rights
06/23/2008	Man jailed for partitioning Abu Dhabi villa
06/27/2008	Educational system will be upgraded to promote UAE national identity
06/28/2008	Promised salary not always reality for Philippine workers in UAE
06/29/2008a.	Jail terms scrapped in draft media law
06/29/2008b.	UAE hospital to pass on heat-related workers cases to labour ministry
07/11/2008	Unserviceable debt drives more people to suicide
07/25/2008	UAE tops in providing luxury to expatriates
10/21/2008a	Yas Island site raises bar for labour accommodation
10/21/2008b	New body to monitor payments
12/16/2008	FNC calls for tightening of sponsorship rules
12/17/2008	70% of labour accommodations violate safety rules
12/28/2008	Workers seek redressal after sponsor fails to pay salaries for three months
01/17/2009	Scores of workers 'not paid for months'
01/20/2009a	Journalists 'not pleased with new media law'
01/25/2009	City of trust and tolerance
01/29/2009	Four women left homeless after labour dispute
02/02/2009	Uphold national identity, delegates say
02/03/2009	Expats welcome drive against overcrowded villas
03/29/2009	'UAE protects rights of workers'
04/20/2009	Company faces action over non-payment of salaries
04/23/2009	Lootah warns against overcrowding in rooms
05/11/2009	Rent calculator becomes official index
06/08/2009	Workers' accommodations to follow global standards
06/17/2009	Teachers protest over non-payment of salary
06/20/2009a.	It surely pays to complain
06/20/2009b.	US human trafficking report disappoints UAE officials

06/30/2009	Workers can report break violations anonymously
07/07/2009	RAK firms top list of companies violating summer midday break

Khaleej Times

04/22/2005	UAE 'is heading for a demographic collapse'
04/27/2005	ILO wants parity between local and expat workforce
05/22/2005	Workers 'forced in signing off' their legal dues
06/16/2005	'UAE publishing act is a breach of law'
07/10/2005	Firm forced us to sign papers, claim workers
11/17/2005	No excuse on salary delay to be accepted
01/15/2006	Govt stops dealing with firms that have non-Emirati PROs
02/02/2006	Irked Sri Lankan workers march to their consulate
02/09/2006	Human resources next on the emiratization agenda
03/13/2006	180 workers from two firms protest non-payment of wages
03/31/2006	UAE to allow workers unions by end of year
04/30/2006	UAE 'deported workers who protested seeking better conditions'
05/06/2007	Ajman to fine landlords for disconnecting power
	Watchmen make a killing out of bachelor tenants
07/30/2007	MOL issues warning to passport grabbers
08/22/2007	Abu Dhabi landlords go on eviction spree
	Grace period likely for departure of illegals
09/09/2007	Landlords play foul to force tenants out
10/17/2007	UN told UAE committed to human rights
	UAE fares well in World Press Freedom Index
10/19/2007	Over 50 firms found flouting labour laws
07/24/2008	Dubai rents jump 22pc
08/11/2008	Filipinas complain of contract substitution
09/27/2008a	'One villa, one family' make UAE residents jittery
09/27/2008b	Lawyers draw among the highest salaries in UAE
10/22/2008	Wage protection office set up to protect rights of workers
10/28/2008	Abu Dhabi takes tough stand on villa-sharing
11/03/2008	Housing rents rise up to 36 per cent in Abu Dhabi
11/08/2008	Villa-sharers left sweltering after DEWA power cut
11/11/2008	Labourers in crowded villas 'living like animals'
12/17/2008	Increase salary limit for family visa: FNC
01/26/2009a	Draft media law draws flak for 'shortcomings'
01/26/2009b	Need to explicitly ban imprisonment of journalists stressed
02/04/2009	Distressed workers lodge complaint with MOL
03/21/2009	Abu Dhabi civic body asks 503 firms to move staff to workers' cities
04/13/2009	Local press fears fines, jail in UAE draft law
04/152009	80 per cent of 32,300 labour complaints resolved
04/16/2009	Residency rules under review

04/20/2009	Labourers strike work in protest
04/29/2009	Ministry of labour strengthens inspections
04/30/2009	Decent housing for displaced workers
06/23/2009	US report on human rights lacks objectivity: Gargash
07/01/2009	Nearly two million workers to benefit from midday break
07/08/2009	Firms to face action if they fail to protect workers from heat

APPENDIX 2
Cited References from Arabic Newspapers

Al Bayan

01/31/2006	Al-Kaabi calls on all companies in the country to pay all monies due to their workers.
03/13/2006	Sharjah: 421 workers at AUPCO construction company demand unpaid wages
04/23/2006	MOL asks businesses not to employ workers on visitor visa during ban period
04/24/2006	Al-Kaabi: 27 housing compounds for workers in the country open to all sectors
04/24/2006	Leader of Coptic community in Abu Dhabi thanks UAE and in particular late Sheik Zayed and current UAE leader for the atmosphere of brotherhood, cooperation, and love they instituted in the Emirates
04/29/2006	Housing compounds for workers: the real beginning to organize and stabilize the job market
06/21/2007	Indians implicated in trafficking in maid who fled her employer
09/12/2007	Saif bin Zayed calls for dealing with demographic imbalance with spirit of responsibility
05/20/2008	Committee against Human Trafficking publishes its first annual report
05/23/2008	Committee on demographic imbalance discusses implementation of its strategy

Al Ittihad

01/3/2007	Foreign workers demand late wages
01/4/2007	Crime and demographic imbalance: most important drawbacks of expatriate workers
03/1/2007	Expatriate workers demand unpaid wages from employer
05/9/2007	Director of the International Organization of Labor: UAE treats its expatriate workers in civilized way
09/10/2007	At Zayed University: Academicians warn of impact of demographic balance on national identity
09/12/2007	Ministry of the Interior calls for dealing with the demographic imbalance with spirit of responsibility. National identity must be preserved

01/14/2008	Red Crescent opens shelter in Abu Dhabi for victims of human trafficking
01/17/2008	Authorities closed 179 businesses in Abu Dhabi last month and sued 39 for employing illegal workers
02/25/2008	Qaraqash: National strategy to combat human trafficking UN values UAE efforts
05/18/2008	UAE under Khalifa expanded human and civilization links
07/1/2008	Asians account for 80% of individuals who break immigration and residency laws
09/22/2008	U.S. values UAE's policy of religious tolerance
09/23/2008	MOL stresses the importance of employers paying workers in timely manner
09/25/2008	Immigration raids target beggars and illegals
11/4/2008	In Ras al-Khaima: Arab and Asians are arrested for human trafficking Victims include 5 maids who were 'sold' for 2500 Dhs to 5000 Dhs a person
11/7/2008	Abu Dhabi education council stresses the importance of national identity and warns of the risks posed by foreign influences
12/16/2008	MOL is preparing a health and work safety system based on international criteria
12/18/2008	Conference highlights UAE efforts in fighting human trafficking

Index

Page numbers in *italics* refer to figures and tables.